DATABASE SYSTEMS FOR NEXT-GENERATION APPLICATIONS

PRINCIPLES AND PRACTICE

Advanced Database Research and Development Series

Vol. 1 Database Systems for Next-Generation Applications - Principles and Practice

Vol. 2 Database Systems for Advanced Applications '91

Vol. 3 Future Databases '92

ADVANCED DATABASE RESEARCH AND DEVELOPMENT SERIES – VOL. 1

DATABASE SYSTEMS FOR NEXT-GENERATION APPLICATIONS

PRINCIPLES AND PRACTICE

Editors

Won Kim

UniSQL, Inc. U.S.A.

Yahiko Kambayashi

Kyoto University, Japan

In Sup Paik

Ajou University, Korea

World Scientific

Singapore • New Jersey • London • Hong Kong

Published by

World Scientific Publishing Co Pte Ltd
5 Toh Tuck Link, Singapore 596224
USA office: 27 Warren Street, Suite 401-402, Hackensack, NJ 07601
UK office: 57 Shelton Street, Covent Garden, London WC2H 9HE

British Library Cataloguing-in-Publication Data
A catalogue record for this book is available from the British Library.

DATABASE SYSTEMS FOR NEXT-GENERATION APPLICATIONS — PRINCIPLES AND PRACTICE

ISBN-13 978-981-02-1315-2
ISBN-10 981-02-1315-8

FOREWORD

This book is the first in the Advanced Database Research and Development Series. The series will include collections of refereed papers on advanced database systems research and development.

Codd's relational model of data provided impetus for research into databases during the 1970s, culminating in several commercial relational databases systems by the early 1980s. The relational model of data, and relational database systems, was designed largely to simplify the programming of traditional business applications. In the early 1980s researchers and users of database systems started recognizing the limitations of relational systems when they attempted to use relational systems to support non-traditional applications on both traditional and non-traditional machine organizations. The non-traditional applications include computer-aided design and engineering systems, programming systems, multimedia information systems, knowledge-based systems, real-time systems, and so forth. They typically require richer data models that capture more semantics than is possible with the relational model, spatial and temporal data management, friendlier user interfaces and application development tools, different notions of transactions, and so on. The non-traditional machine organizations include client-server architectures, multi-computer architectures, massively parallel computers, computers with optical storage devices, and so on.

The objective of this book series is to contribute to the wider dissemination of the results of research and development in database systems for non-traditional applications and non-traditional machine organizations. This first volume of the series contains papers prepared by the editorial committee members, as well as updated versions of selected papers from the Proceedings of the First International Symposium on Database Systems for Advanced Applications. The proceedings of the succeeding symposiums will be published in this series. The original proceedings can be obtained from

DASFAA'89 C/O Yoon. J. Lee
Department of Computer Science, KAIST
373-1, Kusong-dong, Yusong-ku, Taejon, Korea.

We would like to thank the authors of the papers included in this book, as well as the participants and organizers of the symposium series. Without the assistance of Miss Hitomi Yoshioka this book would not have been completed.

Won Kim
UniSQL, Inc. U.S.A.
Yahiko Kambayashi
Kyoto University, Japan
In Sup Paik
Ajou University, Korea

International Symposium on Database Systems for Advanced Applications (DASFAA'89) Organization

Honorary Symposium Co-Chairpersons:
Choul Hee Lee
Yutaka Ohno

Symposium Co-Chairpersons:
Hideko S. Kunii
Sukho Lee

Program Committee Chairperson:
Won Kim

Program Committee Co-Chairpersons:
Yahiko Kambayashi
In Sup Paik

Organizing Committee Co-Chairpersons:
Tsuneo Kurokawa
Yoon Joon Lee

Publicity:
Hae Chul Lim
Kenji Suzuki
Soon Chan Whang
Yoshihumi Masunaga

Tutorial:
Ki Joon Han

Local Arrangements:
Ky Hyum Um

Treasure:
Seog Park
Yoshioki Ishii

Secretary:
Katsumi Kanasaki
Mi Yeon Kim

International Coordinators:
Jogobrata Roy
J. C. Derniame
Ron Sacks-Davis
R. C. T. Lee
Shixuan Sa
Tiko Kameda
T. W. Ling

Program Comittee Members:
Song Chun Moon
Chee Hang Park
Jeon Young Lee
Leszak A. Maciaszek
Shojiro Nishio
Nobuo Ohbo
Hideto Ikeda
Shinya Fushimi
Hyun Chul Kang
Ji Hee Yoon
C. C. Chang
Young Hwan Lim
Hirofumi Katsuno
Jung Kook Hong
Akifumi Makinouchi

Organizing Comittee Members:
Myung Joon Kim
Yun Chul Choi
Woon Ho Song
Kazuhiro Satoh
Kyoji Kawagoe
Takaya Ishida
Doo Kwon Baik
Il Joo Chung
Bak Do Yoon
Yutaka Matsushita
Shunsuke Uemura

CONTENTS

KNOWLEDGE BASE SYSTEMS

OBJECT-ORIENTED AND ADVANCED DATABASE SYSTEMS

ENGINEERING DATABASES

DISTRIBUTED DATABASE AND REAL-TIME DATABASES

DATABASE APPLICATIONS

VISUAL DATABASE LANGUAGES

KNOWLEDGE BASE SYSTEMS

PATTERN-BASED KNOWLEDGE INDUCTION FROM DATABASES *

Qiming Chen, Wesley W. Chu and Rei-Chi Lee

Department of Computer Science
University of California, Los Angeles
Los Angeles, California

Abstract

A **pattern-based knowledge induction** approach is developed for discovering the inferential relationships and correlations between data objects from databases. This approach is characterized by providing quantitative measurement for approximate knowledge and supporting knowledge abstraction.

1. Learning From Databases

There exist two kinds of database intensional knowledge:

- *type based knowledge* such as schema, constraints and dependencies, and

- *instance based knowledge* that represents the collective characteristics of database instances, such as data inferential and correlation relationships.

The second kind of database knowledge is not explicitly expressed by the data schema and type descriptions. Instead, it is hidden in the database extensions, and very often is inaccurate. Discovering this kind of knowledge by inductive learning [5-7] can enrich the database intensional knowledge

A pattern-based knowledge induction approach is developed to systematically acquire the summary information about data correlation and inferential relationships from database instances. The induced knowledge is used for the following:

- Dealing with associated concepts through their inferential relationships and correlations.

- Providing intensional query answering in terms of the rules summarized from databases, rather than listing all the atomic data values [2].

- Enhancing the availability of distributed database systems by *inferring inaccessible data from correlated and accessible data* during network partitions [3].

At a given time, the database state can be viewed as a snapshot of an enterprise. Knowledge induction is used to reveal the inherent inferential relationships and correlations implicitly indicated by a database state. For example, from the table shown in Figure 1 with the following schema,

PEOPLE(NAME,ORIGIN,HAIR_COLOR,EYE_COLOR,HEIGHT).

NAME	ORIGIN	HAIR_COLOR	EYE_COLOR	HEIGHT
Smith	Sweden	blond	blue	1.75
Berdio	Holland	brown	olive	1.77
Chen	China	black	brown	1.80
John	Sweden	brown	olive	1.85
Kato	Japan	black	brown	1.69
Joe	Holland	blond	brown	1.85
Motro	Sweden	blond	blue	1.90
Zhang	China	black	brown	1.66
Wong	China	black	brown	1.65
Yokota	Japan	black	brown	1.65
Solbe	Holland	brown	olive	1.72
Kobe	Japan	black	brown	1.75
Worthy	Holland	brown	blue	1.75
Ape	Sweden	blond	blue	1.77
Rowley	Holland	brown	olive	1.72
Chin	China	black	brown	1.82
George	Sweden	blond	blue	1.85
Kim	Japan	black	brown	1.68
Date	Holland	brown	olive	1.70
Fox	Holland	brown	olive	1.71
Cristo	Sweden	blond	blue	1.85
Steven	Holland	brown	olive	1.79
Moore	Sweden	blond	blue	1.92
Zhou	China	black	brown	1.68
Lin	China	black	brown	1.67
Cox	Holland	brown	olive	1.72
Nagase	Japan	black	brown	1.67
Mentiz	Holland	brown	olive	1.74
Ben	Sweden	blond	blue	1.83
Nah	Japan	black	brown	1.75
Bertin	Holland	brown	blue	1.76
Kent	Sweden	blond	blue	1.81
Brad	Sweden	blond	blue	1.80
Mathew	Holland	brown	olive	1.79
Sam	Sweden	blond	blue	1.88
Page	Holland	brown	olive	1.73

Figure 1: A database instance

* This research is supported by DARPA contract N00174-91-C-0107.

the following knowledge may be summarized:

Most Swedish people have blond hair.
Most Dutch people have brown hair.

Decomposing a relation may not extract useful knowledge. For example, Figure 2 shows a projection of *PEOPLE*. The facts shown in that projection are not *deterministic*, and there is no *quantitative* measurement provided.

ORIGIN	HAIR_COLOR
Sweden	blond
Sweden	brown
Holland	brown
Holland	blond
China	black
Japan	black

Figure 2: A projection of *PEOPLE*

To extract *approximate knowledge* with a vagueness from databases, it is necessary to introduce a *quantitative measurement* for the data inferential relationships and correlations. In order to generate high-level knowledge, it is necessary to provide knowledge abstraction facilities.

In the following sections, we shall describe the pattern-based database knowledge induction model, introduce a bottom-up knowledge induction algorithm and discuss pattern-based knowledge abstraction.

2. Pattern-Based Knowledge Induction

In order to acquire generalized knowledge such as

Most Swedish people have blond hair,

rather than specific facts as

Smith has blond hair,

we introduce the notion of **pattern** as the abstract representation for a group of database instances with specified properties. We then view the relationships between data via the relationships *between patterns*.

Database objects may be divided into classes based on their shared properties. For instance, a relation can be viewed as a class of objects described by the same relation schema. A pattern is defined on a class of objects by a *query condition*. For example, a condition

ORIGIN = 'Sweden' or
HAIR_COLOR = 'black'

can be used to qualify a pattern defined on the class *PEOPLE*. The objects of that class satisfying the pattern condition *match the pattern*. To group the objects which match a pattern and offer an abstract view of the resulted group of objects, we introduce the notion of **abstract pattern class**.

Abstract Pattern Class

The set of identifiers of the objects matching a pattern form the Abstract Pattern Class (APC) of that pattern. The above Object identifiers (Oid's) are called the instances of the APC.

An APC can be denoted by $P(C)$ where P is its name and C is its pattern condition. For simplicity, $P(C)$ can be abbreviated as P_C.

From a knowledge acquisition point of view, when a pattern condition is taken as the premise of a rule, the size of its APC is sensitive to estimating the generality of the rule. For example, a pattern such as

P("*NAME*='Smith'")

has possibly only one instance, therefore a rule taking that pattern as premise has a very small coverage and thus less generality. To provide a measure of the size of an APC, we shall introduce the notion of population as defined below.

Population

The population of an APC named P is the number of distinguished Oid's involved in P and is denoted by $\rho(P)$.

APC's can be overlapped, providing an abstract view of the objects satisfying multiple pattern conditions. Further, one APC can subsume another in the following two situations:

- When a weaker pattern condition C_1 covers a stronger pattern condition C_2, the APC qualified by C_1 subsumes the APC qualified by C_2. For example, the APC qualified by "*HEIGHT*>1.80" subsumes the APC qualified by "*HEIGHT*>1.90" on the same class *PEOPLE*.

- When a super-class A subsumes a sub-class B, the APC defined on A subsumes the APC with the same pattern condition defined on B. For example, the APC qualified by "*HEIGHT*>1.80" on class *PEOPLE* subsumes the APC qualified by the same condition on a sub-class of *PEOPLE*.

Such relationships introduce the subsumption-based partial order and underlie the inferential relationships among APC's.

2.1 Inferential Relationship

An inferential relationship is represented by $A \rightarrow B$, where A and B are facts expressed in terms of predicates. A is the premise which can be conjunctive or disjunctive, such as "*ORIGIN*='Chinese' or *ORIGIN*='Japanese'"; B is the consequence such as "*HAIR_COLOR*='black'". Since the premise and the consequence can be considered pattern conditions, an inferential relationship is essentially between two patterns. Therefore, we relate the inferential relationship between facts A and B to the patterns taking A and B as conditions. Further, we measure it in terms of the inclusion relationship between APC's P_A and P_B.

Our measurement of inferential relationships ranges from strong to weak, covering both the deterministic and probabilistic situations. In the following discussion we assume the population of P_A is less than the population of P_B; that is, $\rho(P_A) \leq \rho(P_B)$. The dependencies between inferential relationship of A, B and the containment relationship of P_A, P_B are shown in Figure 3.

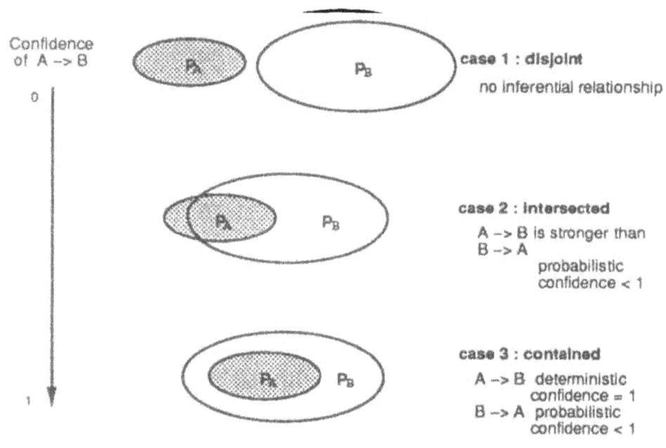

Figure 3: Inferential relationship measured by inclusion relationship between APC's

The strength of an inferential relationship is measured by the *inferential confidence* defined below.

Inferential Confidence
Let A→B be an inferential relationship extracted on the basis of APC's P_A and P_B, its inferential confidence, denoted by ξ(A→B), is defined as

$$\xi(A \rightarrow B) = \rho(P_A \cap P_B) \,/\, \rho(P_A)$$

and ranges from 0 to 1. If the confidence of an inferential relationship equals 1 then the inferential relationship is deterministic.

For example, in Figure 3, assuming $\rho(P_A) = 100$, $\rho(P_B) = 320$, and $\rho(P_A \cap P_B) = 80$, then $\xi(A \rightarrow B) = 80\%$, however, $\xi(B \rightarrow A) = 25\%$. Note that the confidences of inferential relationships for two opposite inference directions are neither symmetric nor complement.

When P_A and P_B have the same population, the confidences of inferential relationships for two opposite inference directions A → B and B → A are the same. An instance satisfying condition A also satisfies condition B and vice versa. If P_A and P_B are coincided, then the confidences of A → B and B → A are both 100%. This is the only situation to have a deterministic bi-directional inferential relationship.

2.2 Correlation

Correlation is defined from a *bi-direction inferential relationship* point of view. The correlation of the objects for the APC's P_A and P_B is measured by the inferential relationships A → B and B → A. If both A → B and B → A are deterministic, then the facts A and B are deterministically correlated.

Degree of Correlation
The degree of correlation between facts A and B, denoted by γ(A,B), is defined as

$$\gamma(A,B) = (\xi(A \rightarrow B) + \xi(B \rightarrow A))/2,$$

and ranges from 0 to 1. The correlation between A and B is deterministic if $\gamma(A,B) = 1$.

It is easy to see that $\gamma(A,B) = 1$ only takes place when $\xi(A \rightarrow B) = \xi(B \rightarrow A) = 1$, that is, when P_A and P_B have the same set of instances.

2.3 Combination of Inferential Relationships

While an inferential relationship A → B is extracted from the actual instances of a database, *its confidence is based on known facts rather than on data values obtained from random sampling.* More exactly, given inferential relationships A → B and B → C with certain confidences, the confidence of A → C may vary from case to case, depending on the instances of the APC's defined on these conditions. Below we shall discuss the basic combined forms.

composition

Given inferential relationships A → B and B → C, only when ξ(A→B) and ξ(B→C) are both 100%, then A → C is deterministic; that is,

$$\xi(A \rightarrow C) = 100\%.$$

Otherwise

$$\xi(A \rightarrow C) = \rho\,(P_A \cap P_C)/\rho(P_A).$$

disjunction

Since P_A and P_B may have various inclusion relationships from disjoint, intersection to containment, the confidence of (A ∨ B) → C does not depend on ξ(A→C) and ξ(B→C) directly. Instead, it should be computed based on the APC's as

$$\xi((A \vee B) \rightarrow C) = \rho(P_A \cap P_C \cup P_B \cap P_C) / \rho(P_A \cup P_B).$$

This expression is suitable for any case of the inclusion situations of P_A, P_B and P_C.

conjunction

The confidence of (A ∧ B) → C does not depend on ξ(A→C) and ξ(B→C) directly. Instead, the following basic formula can be used for any case of the inclusion situations of P_A, P_B and P_C.

$$\xi((A \wedge B) \rightarrow C) = \rho\,(P_A \cap P_B \cap P_C) / \rho\,(P_A \cap P_B).$$

Note that in certain situations ξ((A ∧ B) → C) may be much bigger than either ξ(A → C) or ξ(B → C). Therefore condition conjunction is a way to find stronger inferential relationships. For instance, the confidence of

HAIR_COLOR = 'blond' and *EYE_COLOR* = 'blue' -->
ORIGIN = 'Sweden'

is higher than both the confidences of

HAIR_COLOR = 'blond' --> *ORIGIN* = 'Sweden'"
EYE_COLOR = 'blue' --> *ORIGIN* = 'Sweden'".

The decision to combine certain inferential relationships is based on the database semantics and the heuristic trial for finding the inferential relationships with higher confidences.

Ranging is the extention of the inferential relationship with a disjunctive premise. It aims at gaining rules such as

IF 300 > a > 100 THEN b = 10.
IF a *within* $\{a_1, ..., a_n\}$ THEN b = B.

One way to construct such inferential relationships is to directly generate the APC in terms of the range condition. Since it is not easy to partition an attribute domain automatically, an alternative way is to combine a number of simple, individual inferential relationships, such as

$a = a_1 \rightarrow b = B$
:
$a = a_n \rightarrow b = B$

If all these inferential relationships are deterministic, then

a *within* $\{a_1, ..., a_n\} \rightarrow b = B$

is also deterministic; otherwise, its confidence is smaller than 100% and should be calculated as an inferential relationship with multiple disjunctive premises. The confidence of an inferential relationship with n-ary disjunctive premises

$a \in \{a_1, ..., a_n\} \rightarrow C$

can be measured by the following formula

$$\xi((A_1 \vee ... \vee A_n) \rightarrow C) = \rho(\bigcup_{i=1}^{n}(P_{A_i} \cap P_C) / \rho(\bigcup_{i=1}^{n}P_{A_i})$$

where $A_1, ..., A_n$ are patterns with conditions $a = a_1, ..., a = a_n$ respectively.

2.4 Popularity

Popularity is another important measure of an inferential relationship or a correlation for indicating "how common" it is, and therefore can be used for evaluating its practical value.

Consider the inferential relationship

NAME='Smith' $\rightarrow$ *HAIR_COLOR* = 'blond'

that has confidence of 100% but very little coverage relative to the total population of *PEOPLE*. Therefore it is not "popular" and is not worth "transferring" from a database to a knowledge base.

The coverage of an inferential relationship is measured by its *popularity*; that is, the percentage of its covered population in the total population of the given universe. Since a universe may include one or multiple classes, we shall introduce the following two types of popularities of an inferential relationship, where *unique name of attributes* is assumed.

- *local popularity* which is local to the class of objects where the inferential relationship is extracted from, and

- *referential popularity* which is measured by the coverage of the inferential relationship throughout the database via referential relationships.

An APC, P_A, defined on a class C_1 is *referred* in another class C_2 provided that the APC defined on the class C_2 by the same condition A is not empty. Local and referential popularities are defined as follows.

Local Popularity of An Inferential Relationship
Let C be the class on which APC's P_A and P_B are defined and the inferential relationship A→B is extracted. Let ρ(C) be the total population of C. The local popularity of the inferential relationship, denoted by $\eta_l(A \rightarrow B)$, is defined as

$$\eta_l(A \rightarrow B) = \rho(P_A) / \rho(C).$$

Referential Popularity of An Inferential Relationship
Let A→B be an inferential relationship extracted on the basis of APC's P_A and P_B. Let $C_1, C_2, ..., C_n$ be the classes where P_A is referred. and patterns $P_{A_1}, P_{A_2}, ..., P_{A_n}$ are defined by the condition A. The referential popularity of the inferential relationship, denoted by $\eta_r(A \rightarrow B)$, is defined as

$$\eta_r(A \rightarrow B) = \rho(\bigcup_{k=1}^{n} P_{A_k}) / \rho(\bigcup_{k=1}^{n} C_k).$$

2.5 Knowledge Induction via Atomic Patterning

The Oid's of a class of objects can be divided into a large number of APC's defined by various conditions. To reduce the amount of predefined APC's we can maintain the APC's defined on a single attribute and use them combinationally. The notion of *atomic patterning* is introduced to support the *bottom-up* approach for inducing inferential relationships from database instances.

We use atomic patterning to partition a relation into a set of APC's based on the distinguished values in each attribute domain [8] of the relation. Let R be an enterprise, A be an attribute and $a_1, ..., a_n$ be all the distinct attribute values of A, called the *interpretation* of A and denoted by I_A. An atomic patterning on A is denoted by Π_A and defined as

$$\Pi_A = \{P(\text{"A=a"}) \mid a \in I_A\}.$$

For example, the atomic patterning on the attribute "*ORIGIN*" of the relation *PEOPLE* contains patterns

P("*ORIGIN*='Sweden'"),
P("*ORIGIN*='Japanese'"),
:

the atomic patterning on the attribute "*HAIR_COLOR*" of that relation contains patterns

P("*HAIR_COLOR*='black'"),
P("*HAIR_COLOR*='blond'"),
P("*HAIR_COLOR*='brown'").

and so on.

The APC's resulting from atomic patternings on two attributes can be paired by the *cross product* operation. In general, the cross product of two atomic patternings on attribute A and B, denoted by Π_A and Π_B, is defined as

$$\Pi_A \times \Pi_B = \{(P, Q) \mid P \in \Pi_A \text{ and } Q \in \Pi_B\}.$$

For example, the cross product of the atomic patternings on attribute "*ORIGIN*" and "*HAIR_COLOR*" yields

```
{   (P("ORIGIN='Sweden'"), P("HAIR_COLOR='black'")),
    (P("ORIGIN='Sweden'"), P("HAIR_COLOR='blond'")),
    (P("ORIGIN='Sweden'"), P("HAIR_COLOR='brown'")),
    (P("ORIGIN='Japanese'"), P("HAIR_COLOR='black'")),
    (P("ORIGIN='Japanese'"), P("HAIR_COLOR='blond'")),
    (P("ORIGIN='Japanese'"), P("HAIR_COLOR='brown'"))
                    :
}
```

Knowledge induction from a relation via atomic patterning includes the following steps:

1. Applying atomic patterning on each attribute of the relation.
2. Applying the cross product operation to the resulted APC's to yield a set of pairs of APC's.
3. Inducing inferential relationships from each pair of APC's via two directions.
4. Ranging the obtained inferential relationships and combining them based on the database semantics and upgrade trial.
5. Based on a given threshold filtering out the resulted inferential relationships with low confidence, population coverage or popularity.
6. Generating rules from the meaningful inferential relationships.

Since a large number of inferential relationships may be extracted from database instances, it is important to reduce the results based on their accuracy, popularity, database semantics and domain knowledge. For example, by controlling the threshold of popularity, the inferential relationships already implied by database functional dependencies can be filtered out.

2.6 An Implementation Example

We shall use the table *PEOPLE* given in Figure 1 to demonstrate the proposed approach. In our implementation a pattern is represented by a pattern descriptor shown below

```
pattern_id   = 1
type         = ORIGIN
condition    = ORIGIN = 'Sweden'
population   = 11
APC          = 'Smith,John,Motro,Ape,George,Moore,Kent,
                Ben,Cristo,Sam,Brad'
consequence  = ''
```

In the descriptor of pattern *P*, "pattern_id" is its Pattern identifier (Pid); "type" is the attribute on which *P* is defined; "condition" is the query condition qualifying *P*; "APC" contains the Oid's of the objects matching *P*; population is the number of the Oid's. We are also interested in those inferential relationships which take *P* as premise and have confidences over a given threshold, and refer to the Pid's of their consequence patterns as the "consequence set" of *P*. This consequence set is recorded under attribute "consequence" of the pattern descriptor of *P*. Patterns with the same type and highly overlapping consequence sets may be considered similar and called neighborhood patterns.

By setting the confidence and popularity thresholds, the knowledge acquisition system extracts a number of inferential and correlation relationships from the table *PEOPLE*. A subset of these results with confidence c and popularity p are listed below

```
Inferential with confidence >= 0.75 & popularity >= 0.10

c = 0.91 : ORIGIN = 'Sweden' -> HAIR_COLOR = 'blond'
p = 0.31
c = 0.91 : ORIGIN = 'Sweden' -> EYE_COLOR = 'blue'
p = 0.31
c = 1.00 : ORIGIN = 'China' -> HAIR_COLOR = 'black'
p = 0.17
c = 1.00 : ORIGIN = 'China' -> EYE_COLOR = 'brown'
p = 0.17
c = 1.00 : ORIGIN = 'Japan' -> HAIR_COLOR = 'black'
p = 0.17
c = 1.00 : ORIGIN = 'Japan' -> EYE_COLOR = 'brown'
p = 0.17
c = 0.77 : ORIGIN = 'Holland' -> HAIR_COLOR = 'brown'
p = 0.36
c = 0.77 : ORIGIN = 'Holland' -> EYE_COLOR = 'olive'
p = 0.36
c = 0.91 : HAIR_COLOR = 'blond' -> EYE_COLOR = 'blue'
p = 0.31
c = 0.82 : HAIR_COLOR = 'brown' -> EYE_COLOR = 'olive'
p = 0.31
c = 1.00 : HAIR_COLOR = 'black' -> EYE_COLOR = 'brown'
p = 0.33
c = 0.83 : EYE_COLOR = 'blue' -> HAIR_COLOR = 'blond'
p = 0.33
c = 0.82 : EYE_COLOR = 'olive' -> HAIR_COLOR = 'brown'
p = 0.31
c = 0.92 : EYE_COLOR = 'brown' -> HAIR_COLOR = 'black'
p = 0.36

Correlation with degree >= 0.75 and popularity >= 0.10

c = 0.91 : ORIGIN = 'Sweden' <--> HAIR_COLOR = 'blond'
p = 0.31
c = 0.87 : ORIGIN = 'Sweden' <--> EYE_COLOR = 'blue'
p = 0.31
c = 0.75 : ORIGIN = 'China' <--> HAIR_COLOR = 'black'
p = 0.17
c = 0.75 : ORIGIN = 'Japan' <--> HAIR_COLOR = 'black'
p = 0.17
c = 0.84 : ORIGIN = 'Holland' <--> HAIR_COLOR = 'brown'
p = 0.31
c = 0.84 : ORIGIN = 'Holland' <--> EYE_COLOR = 'olive'
p = 0.31
c = 0.87 : HAIR_COLOR = 'blond' <--> EYE_COLOR = 'blue'
p = 0.31
c = 0.82 : HAIR_COLOR = 'brown' <--> EYE_COLOR = 'olive'
p = 0.31
c = 0.96 : HAIR_COLOR = 'black' <--> EYE_COLOR = 'brown'
p = 0.33
```

Patterns can also be defined on conjunctive and disjunctive conditions such as

HAIR_COLOR = 'blond' and *EYE_COLOR* = 'blue',
HAIR_COLOR = 'blond' or *HAIR_COLOR* = 'brown'.

Let us compare the confidences of the inferential relationships with premise patterns

P_A(*HAIR_COLOR* = 'blond')
P_B(*EYE_COLOR* = 'blue')
P_C(*HAIR_COLOR* = 'blond' and *EYE_COLOR* = 'blue')

and consequence pattern

P_D(*ORIGIN* = 'Sweden')

```
c = 0.91 : HAIR_COLOR = 'blond' -> ORIGIN = 'Sweden'
c = 0.83 : EYE_COLOR = 'blue' -> ORIGIN = 'Sweden'

c = 1.00 : HAIR_COLOR = 'blond' and
           EYE_COLOR = 'blue' -> ORIGIN = 'Sweden'
```

Assuming that A, B, C and D are conditions of P_A, P_B, P_C and P_D, the last inferential relationship with conjunctive premise can be determined by either

$$\xi(C \to D) = \rho(P_C \cap P_D) / \rho(P_C)$$

or

$$\xi((A \wedge B) \to D) = \rho(P_A \cap P_B \cap P_D) / \rho(P_A \cap P_B)$$

3. Knowledge Abstraction

Since the amount of inferential relationships extracted from database instances may be very large, it is necessary to generalize them for acquiring more abstract knowledge. We refer to extracting inferential relationships from database instances as the *first phase*, and generalizing abstract knowledge from the resulted inferential relationships as the *second phase* of database knowledge acquisition. Although both phases are pattern based, in the first phase, a pattern is concerned with its content (i.e., the database objects); while in the second phase a pattern is treated as an *atomic object* with a unique Pattern identifier (Pid). We shall show what can be abstracted in the second phase by the following simple examples.

Determining approximate functional dependencies

The first example is concerned with approximate functional dependencies which are further summarized from the induced inferential relationships. Considering the patterns defined on attributes *P* and *Q* by atomic patterning, if for any pattern defined on attribute *P* by condition p_i, there exists a unique pattern defined on attribute *Q* by condition q_j such that

$p_i \to q_j$ has high confidence,

then we say that there exists an approximate functional dependency relationship between attributes *P* and *Q*, and therefore can lift a collection of inferential relationships at the pattern level to a single abstract relationship at the attribute domain level. For example, based on the following inferential relationships extracted from the table *PEOPLE*,

```
c = 0.91 : ORIGIN = 'Sweden' -> EYE_COLOR = 'blue'
c = 1.00 : ORIGIN = 'China' -> EYE_COLOR = 'brown'
c = 1.00 : ORIGIN = 'Japan' -> EYE_COLOR = 'brown'
c = 0.77 : ORIGIN = 'Holland' -> EYE_COLOR = 'olive'
```

since each pattern defined on a value of attribute *ORIGIN* implies a unique pattern defined on a value of attribute *EYE_COLOR* with high confidence, the approximate functional dependency between attributes *ORIGIN* and *EYE_COLOR* can be summarized.

Grouping similar attribute values

The second example is concerned with grouping attribute values based on their similarity. We group together those inferential relationships which have the same premise and confidences over a given threshold such as

```
c = 1.00 : ORIGIN = 'China' -> HAIR_COLOR = 'black'
c = 1.00 : ORIGIN = 'China' -> EYE_COLOR = 'brown'

c = 1.00 : ORIGIN = 'Japan' -> HAIR_COLOR = 'black'
c = 1.00 : ORIGIN = 'Japan' -> EYE_COLOR = 'brown'
```

For each group, we record the consequence set (i.e. the Pid's of the consequence patterns) in the premise pattern descriptor under the attribute "consequence", such as

```
pattern_id   = 2
type         = ORIGIN
condition    = ORIGIN = 'China'
population   = 6
APC          = 'Chen,Zhang,Wong,Chin,Zhou,Lin'
consequence  = '7,10'

pattern_id   = 3
type         = ORIGIN
condition    = ORIGIN = 'Japan'
population   = 6
APC          = 'Kato,Yokota,Kobe,Kim,Nagase,Nah'
consequence  = '7,10'
```

where patterns defined by conditions *ORIGIN* = 'China', *ORIGIN* = 'Japan', *HAIR_COLOR* = 'black', *EYE_COLOR* = 'brown' have Pid's 2, 3, 7, 10 respectively. With the above information we can then classify values in an attribute domain based on the overlap of their highly confidenced consequence sets. For example, based on the above inferential relationships and corresponding pattern descriptors, it can be found that patterns defined on attribute *ORIGIN* by conditions

ORIGIN = "China"
ORIGIN = "Japan"

have the same consequence set containing Pid's 7 and 10, and therefore the values "China" and "Japan" on attribute *ORIGIN* are determined as similar ones from the racial point of view. A group of such similar values can be viewed as a "abstract concept" and given an abstract representation such as "Asian". Furthermore, knowledge acquisition based on abstract object representations can yield higher level rules and provide wider coverage.

Pattern-based knowledge abstraction

Our third example is concerned with representing abstract knowledge directly by patterns. Consider the pattern defined on the table *PEOPLE* by the following condition

"*ORIGIN* = 'Sweden' or *ORIGIN* = 'Holland' -> *HEIGHT* >= 1.75"

that can cover a set of people and be given a "name", say, *Europeans*. Such a name then becomes the abstract representation of the objects matching the above pattern. In this way, we can consider two-level spaces, one at *object-level* consisting of object domains; the other at *pattern-level* consisting of patterns as shown in Figure 4. This concept may be extended to multiple levels.

The database knowledge induction approach discussed in this paper essentially deals with the inferential relationships *between patterns*. Let us assume that patterns P_A, P_B, P_C, P_D are defined on *PEOPLE* by the following conditions:

A: *ORIGIN* = 'China' or *ORIGIN* = 'Japan'
B: *ORIGIN* = 'Sweden' or *ORIGIN* = 'Holland'
C: *HEIGHT* < 1.75
D: *HEIGHT* >= 1.75

and the following inferential relationships are extracted from database instances with confidences 0.70 and 0.67:

ORIGIN = 'China' or *ORIGIN* = 'Japan' $\rightarrow$ *HEIGHT* < 1.75
ORIGIN = 'Sweden' or *ORIGIN* = 'Holland' $\rightarrow$ *HEIGHT* >= 1.75

that is,

$A \rightarrow C$	with confidence = 0.70,
$B \rightarrow D$	with confidence = 0.67.

If we call patterns A, B, C and D by *Asians*, *Europeans*, *short* and *tall* respectively, then the above approximate inferential relationships can be expressed in a more abstract fashion as

Asians $\rightarrow$ *short*	with confidence = 0.70
Europeans $\rightarrow$ *tall*	with confidence = 0.67

Further, summary knowledge such as "In general Europeans are taller than Asians" can be derived.

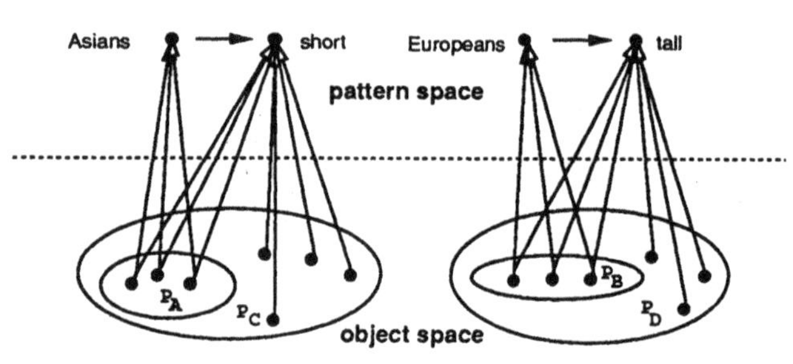

Figure 4: Patterns as abstract object representations

Thus the proposed pattern-based database knowledge induction approach supports different knowledge representations at different abstract levels, which is useful for providing generalized, neighborhood and associated query answering [1,4], and is useful for knowledge engineering in general.

Attribute value based knowledge abstraction

Our fourth example is concerned with another kind of abstraction that focuses on attribute values [1,2]. Based on known abstract attribute values, knowledge acquisition can be carried out at a higher level. For example, when values "blond" and "brown" on attribute *HAIR_COLOR* and values "Holland" and "Sweden" on attribute *ORIGIN* are abstracted to more generalized values "light" and "Europe" respectively, the pattern based knowledge acquisition approach can generate the following inferential relationships and correlations, which have simpler form and wider coverage as compared with those expressed in terms of low level object representations.

```
Inferential Relationship

c = 0.92 : ORIGIN = 'Europe' -> HAIR_COLOR = 'light'
c = 1.00 : HAIR_COLOR = 'light' -> ORIGIN = 'Europe'

Correlation

c = 0.96 : ORIGIN = 'Europe' <--> HAIR_COLOR = 'light'
```

The abstract representations of attribute values may be given by domain experts or learned by knowledge acquisition systems. Introducing abstract values by domain experts on some attributes may further help the system to group similar values on other attributes. In the above example, assuming that the abstract values are unknown, the knowledge acquisition results in the following inferential relationships and corresponding pattern descriptors

```
Inferential with confidence >= 0.75

c = 0.91 : ORIGIN = 'Sweden' -> HAIR_COLOR = 'blond'
c = 0.91 : ORIGIN = 'Sweden' -> EYE_COLOR = 'blue'
c = 0.82 : ORIGIN = 'Sweden' -> HEIGHT >= 1.80
c = 0.77 : ORIGIN = 'Holland' -> HAIR_COLOR = 'brown'
c = 0.77 : ORIGIN = 'Holland' -> EYE_COLOR = 'olive'
c = 0.85 : ORIGIN = 'Holland' -> HEIGHT >= 1.70 and
                                 HEIGHT < 1.8

pattern_id   = 1
type          = ORIGIN
condition     = ORIGIN = 'Sweden'
population    = 11
APC           = 'Smith,John,Motro,Ape,George,Moore,Kent,Ben,
                 Cristo,Sam,Brad'
consequence   = '5,8,13'

pattern_id   = 4
type          = ORIGIN
condition     = ORIGIN = 'Holland'
population    = 13
APC           = 'Joe,Solbe,Worthy,Steven,Mentiz,Bertin,
                 Rowley,Mathew,Page,Cox,Date,Fox,Berdio'
consequence   = '6,9,12'
```

Since 'blond', 'brown', 'blue' and 'olive' are treated as distinct values, patterns defined on *ORIGIN* values "Holland" and "Sweden" have different consequence sets {5, 8, 13} and {6, 9, 12}, and therefore they are not neighbors. However, by introducing *HAIR_COLOR* "light" as the abstract representation for "blond" and "brown", and *EYE_COLOR* "colored" for "blue" and "olive" the following inferential relationships can be acquired

```
Inferential with confidence >= 0.75

c = 0.82 : ORIGIN = 'Sweden' -> HEIGHT >= 1.80
c = 1.00 : ORIGIN = 'Sweden' -> HAIR_COLOR = 'light'
c = 1.00 : ORIGIN = 'Sweden' -> EYE_COLOR = 'colored'
c = 0.85 : ORIGIN = 'Holland' -> HEIGHT >= 1.70 and
                                 HEIGHT < 1.8
c = 0.85 : ORIGIN = 'Holland' -> HAIR_COLOR = 'light'
c = 0.92 : ORIGIN = 'Holland' -> EYE_COLOR = 'colored'
```

Based on these inferential relationships patterns defined on *ORIGIN* values "Sweden" and "Holland" are neighboring ones since they have relative highly overlapping consequence sets {5, 8, 13} and {5, 8, 12} as shown below:

```
pattern_id  = 1
type        = ORIGIN
condition   = ORIGIN = 'Sweden'
population  = 11
APC         = 'Smith,John,Motro,Ape,George,Moore,Kent,
               Ben,Cristo,Sam,Brad'
properties  = '5,8,13'

pattern_id  = 4
type        = ORIGIN
condition   = ORIGIN = 'Holland'
population  = 13
APC         = 'Joe,Solbe,Worthy,Steven,Mentiz,Bertin,
               Rowley,Mathew,Page,Cox,Date,Fox,Berdio'
properties  = '5,8,12'
```

Therefore, the values "Sweden" and "Holland" on attribute *ORIGIN* can be considered as similar and given an abstract representation such as "Europe".

Our experience indicates that knowledge abstraction is an iterative process. The acquired knowledge can enhance the system intelligence for further knowledge abstraction.

4. Summary

We have presented an approach for knowledge induction from database instances, which is characterized by accommodating approximation, providing quantitative measurement and supporting knowledge abstraction.

Learning from databases aims at acquiring the kind of knowledge which is not represented by human experts but by the *database instances*; that is, *content addressable*. Therefore we use *patterns* to match various parts of database content and study the inferential relationships between patterns. Our experience reveals that patterns provide a natural way to measure inferential relationships in terms of set manipulations and to develop abstract knowledge representations.

The rule selection and knowledge representation are application dependent. For certain applications, rules does not necessarily provide a more clear knowledge representation than relation tables. However, abstract knowledge always has higher level intensional semantics and wider coverage, and our approach supports iterative knowledge acquisition for obtaining abstract knowledge. The integration of the knowledge provided by domain experts and the knowledge acquired from database instances is currently under investigation.

References

1. Chu, W. and Q. Chen, "A Structured Approach for Cooperative Query Answering", to appear in IEEE Transactions on Knowledge and Data Engineering.

2. Chu, W., R. Lee and Q. Chen, "Using Type Inference and Induced Rules to Provide Intensional Query Answering", Proc. 7th International Conference on Data Engineering, Japan, 1991.

3. Chu, W., Q. Chen and A. Hwang, "On Open Data Inference and Its Applications", Proc. of Information Technology Conference, Canada Information Processing Society, Canada, 1990.

4. Motro, A., "FLEX: A Tolerant and Cooperative User Interface to Databases", IEEE Transactions on Knowledge and Data Engineering, Vol.2, No.2, 1990.

5. Boose, J. "Knowledge Acquisition Techniques and Tools: Current Research Strategies and Approaches", Proc. of International Conference on 5th Generation of Computer Systems, Japan, 1988.

6. Michalski, R. et al, (eds.) "Machine Learning: An Artificial Intelligence Approach", Tioga Press, Palo Alto, 1983.

7. Quinlan, J., "Induction Over Large Data Bases", STAN-CS-79-739, Stanford University, 1979.

8. Spyratos, N. "The Partition Model: A deductive Database Model", ACM TODS, Vol.12, No.1, 1987.

SOME PROPERTIES OF KNOWLEDGE INFORMATION INFERRED BY TWO INTERACTIVE DEFAULT REASONING SYSTEMS

Kenji MURAKAMI and Tsunehiro AIBARA

Faculty of Engineering, Ehime University, Matsuyama, 790, Japan

ABSTRACT

A new concept of beliefs called *interactive extension* which are derivable from two interconnected default reasoning systems is proposed, and its properties are discussed. Default reasoning proposed by R.Reiter is suitable for incomplete knowledge reasoning in artificial intelligence, logic programming and deductive database, because it can draw plausible conclusions from the incomplete axioms. Since the conclusions can be invalidated when the partial world description is supplemented by new information, the logic based on the reasoning is a nonmonotonic logic. When two default reasoning systems are interconnected and exchange their beliefs each other, each system has a set of beliefs finally by the default reasoning about the originally owned beliefs and the exchanged beliefs. A pair of acceptable sets of the beliefs for each system is called *interactive extension* of the systems. When a large scale default reasoning system (deductive database) is constructed by a consolidation of many small scale default reasoning systems, the beliefs of each system should be increased by the default reasoning and the interactions (communication) with other systems. In order to analyze the properties of the set of final beliefs acquired each system, the proposed interactive extension of the default systems is an indispensable concept.

I. INTRODUCTION

It has been known that artificial intelligence, logic programming and deductive database are interconnected in the area of logical reasoning.[1] The classical logical reasoning is always monotonic, i.e., the set of theorems increases monotonically with the set of axioms. The classical logic formalizing the reasoning, e.g., first order logic, is descriptively universal: Anything that can be expressed in any language can be expressed in the logic. The classical logic is, however, insufficient to solve effectively the sorts of problems in artificial intelligence, logic programming and deductive database. For example, such as the frame problem in artificial intelligence, a description using the classical logic may be extremely unwieldy. Moreover, since a good deal of what we know about a world is "almost always" true with a few exceptions, the natural first order representation explicitly lists the exceptions. Then, if we apply the rule, we have to know the information about the exceptions. An additional difficulty is that monotonic reasoning tends to be inflexible. In deductive database, only positive information about the world such as "Japan Air Line flight 123 connects Tokyo with Seoul", need be explicitly represented. Since in general the amount of negative information about the world such as "Japan Air Line flight 123 *does not* connect Moscow with New York" vastly exceeds the positive things known about it, we are forced to include in our database the results of applying the *closed world assumption* to every predicate in our world description. As soon as we do this, the world description becomes completely inflexible and incapable of incorporating new information.[1]

Recently there have been many proposals for augmenting classical logic to allow it to do nonmonotonic reasoning.[2)-6)] The logic can draw conclusions from incomplete axioms. Since such plausible conclusions can be invalidated when this partial world description is supplemented by new information, the logic is called *nonmonotonic logic*. The nonmonotonic logic is suitable for not only common sense reasoning or reasoning from incomplete knowledge in artificial intelligence, but also logic programming and deductive database. For example, the concepts such as some aspect of negation, null values and indefinite data, that could not be handled in conventional relational database, can be handled in nonmonotonic deductive database.

One of the most significant proposals for nonmonotonic reasoning is *default reasoning* proposed by R.Reiter.[7] In Reiter's default reasoning an indefinite data is represented by a *default*, and a set of defaults and first order formulae which represent definite data forms a default theory. A set of all beliefs (a set of first order formulae) derivable from the default theory (default reasoning system) is called *extension*.

In this paper we consider two interconnected default reasoning systems and their interactions. Each default reasoning system has different default theory. In this case a set of beliefs inferred in each system may interact among the systems, and consequently Reiter's default reasoning will not holds. Each interconnected default reasoning system acquires a set of beliefs finally from both the default reasoning by itself and those of other systems. The sets of beliefs are defined as the *interactive extension*.

When a large scale default reasoning system (deductive database) is constructed by a consolidation of many small scale default reasoning systems, the beliefs of each system should be increased by the default reasoning and the interactions with other systems. Each system deduces many beliefs from both the originally owned beliefs (definite knowledge and indefinite default knowledge) and the new beliefs (probably definite knowledge) obtained from other systems. Further, each system exchanges the deduced beliefs each other. After repeating the foregoing procedure, each system acquires a set of final beliefs. The situation is similar to the case that the beliefs of an agent who lives together with many other agents are increased by the deduction using the originally owned beliefs and the new beliefs obtained by the communication with other agents. In order to analyze the properties of the set of final beliefs of each system (agent), the proposed *interactive extension* of the systems is an indispensable concept.

II. DEFAULT REASONING AND INTERACTIVE EXTENSION

We shall be dealing with a first order language L consisting of the usual well formed formulae (wffs). A wff is said to be *closed* iff it contains no free variables.

A *default* d is any expression of the form

$$d = a : Mb / c$$

where a, b, c are wffs. A default d is *closed* iff none of a, b, c contains a free variable. We assume that the defaults discussed in this paper are always closed because a wff contains free variables can be dealt with a closed wff by substituting the instances for its free variables. We interpret the default d as "If a is true and it is consistent to assume that b is true, i.e., in the absence of any information contrary to b, infer that c is true". a and b are called *prerequisite* and *justification* of the default, respectively, and c is its *consequent*. Using the default, an incomplete assertion such as "Most birds can fly" can be expressed formally as the following default: $BIRD(x) : MFLY(x)/FLY(x)$. It is interpreted as "If x is a bird, then in the absence of any information to the contrary, infer that x can fly".

A *default theory* A is a pair (D,W) where D is a set of defaults and W a set of closed wffs. A default theory A=(D,W) is *closed* iff every default of D is closed. We assume that the default theories discussed in this paper are always closed.

A set of all beliefs (first order formulae) derivable from the default theory is called *extension*, and it is defined as follows:[7]

[Definition 2.1] Let $A=(D,W)$ be a closed default theory. For any set of closed wffs $S \subseteq L$ let $\Gamma(S)$ be the smallest set satisfying the following three properties:

D1. $W \subseteq \Gamma(S)$

D2. $Th(\Gamma(S)) = \Gamma(S)$

D3. If $a : Mb/c \in D$ and $a \in \Gamma(S)$, and $\neg b \notin S$ then $c \in \Gamma(S)$.

A set of closed wffs $E \subseteq L$ is an *extension* for A iff $\Gamma(E)=E$, i.e., iff E is a fixed point of the operator Γ. For any set of closed wffs $S \subseteq L$, define $Th(S) = \{w \mid w \in L,$ w is closed, and w is first order provable from premises $S\}$.

The extension obtained by the default reasoning is interpreted as a *reasonable* set of beliefs that one may hold about the incompletely specified world W.[8)-10)]

In this paper, two default theories (default reasoning systems), say $A_1=(D_1,W_1)$ and $A_2=(D_2,W_2)$, which are interconnected each other are considered. Two systems exchange their acceptable beliefs each other, and then they deduce sets of beliefs, E^1 and E^2. The concept is depicted in Fig.1.

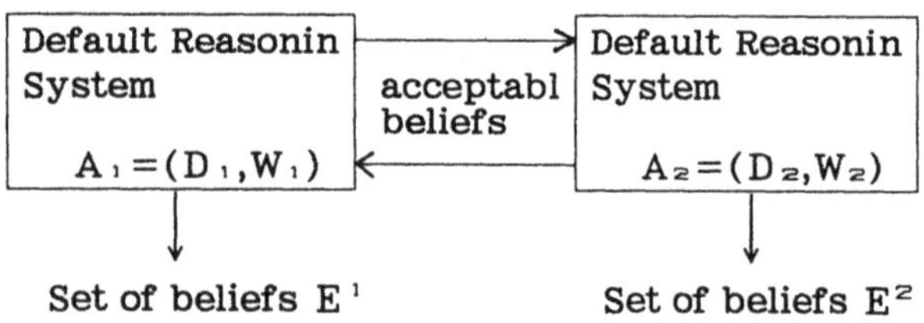

Fig.1. Interconnection of two default reasoning systems.

The pair of sets E^1 and E^2 is called *interactive extension*.[11)-13)] The interactive extension, E^1 and E^2, is interpreted as the *reasonable* sets of beliefs that one in E^1 may hold about the incompletely specified world W_1, and simultaneously, one in E^2 may hold about the incompletely specified worlds W_2. In this case the properties of the *reasonable* sets of beliefs (interactive extension) are influenced by the condition of the exchanged beliefs.[11)]

There are two properties which can reasonably be expected of the beliefs given from the system A_1 (A_2) to the system $A_2(A_1)$.

(1) The beliefs should be contained in E^1 (E^2).

(2) The beliefs should be consistent with E^2 (E^1).

We give the condition of the exchanged beliefs by defining the following interactive extension.

[Definition 2.2] Let $A_1=(D_1,W_1)$ and $A_2=(D_2,W_2)$ be closed default theories. For any pair of sets of closed wffs S^1, $S^2 \subseteq L$ let $\Gamma_1(S^1)$ and $\Gamma_2(S^2)$ be the smallest sets satisfying the following four properties:

D1. $W_1 \subseteq \Gamma_1(S^1)$
$W_2 \subseteq \Gamma_2(S^2)$

D2. $Th(\Gamma_1(S^1)) = \Gamma_1(S^1)$
$Th(\Gamma_2(S^2)) = \Gamma_2(S^2)$

D3. If $a : Mb/c \in D_1$, $a \in \Gamma_1(S^1)$ and $\neg b \notin S^1$ then $c \in \Gamma_1(S^1)$.
If $a : Mb/c \in D_2$, $a \in \Gamma_2(S^2)$ and $\neg b \notin S^2$ then $c \in \Gamma_2(S^2)$.

D4. If $g \in \Gamma_2(S^2)$ and $\neg g \notin S^1$ then $g \in \Gamma_1(S^1)$.
If $g \in \Gamma_1(S^1)$ and $\neg g \notin S^2$ then $g \in \Gamma_2(S^2)$.

A pair of sets of closed wffs E^1, $E^2 \subseteq L$ is an *interactive extension* for A_1 and A_2 iff the relations $\Gamma_1(E^1)=E^1$ and $\Gamma_2(E^2)=E^2$ hold simultaneously, i.e., iff E^1 and E^2 are fixed point of the operators Γ_1 and Γ_2, respectively.

The set of wffs $\{c\}$ in the condition D3 is the set of beliefs inferred by the default reasoning. The set of wffs $\{g\}$ in the condition D4 is the set of beliefs given from the other default theory. The set of wffs $\{g\}$ which did not exist in the foregoing definition of extension is interpreted as an acceptable set of beliefs belonging to the other default reasoning system.

We cannot expect this interactive extension to be unique. Unfortunately, there are sets of default theories with no interactive extension.

As an example, we show the interactive extensions for the following default theories, where the letters $p, q, r \ldots$ represent propositional logical formulae.

[Example 2.1] The following default theories A_1 and A_2 are considered.

$A_1=(D_1,W_1)$
$=(\{p : Mq/r, r : Ms/t, v : Mw/x\},\{p\})$

$A_2=(D_2,W_2)$
$=(\{u : M\neg t/\neg t, \neg t : Mu/v, t : My/z\},\{u\})$

They have two pairs of interactive extensions given by

$E^1=Th(\{p,r,t,u,v,x\})$
$E^2=Th(\{u,\neg t,v,p,r,x\})$

and

$E^1=E^2=Th(\{p,u,r,t,z\})$.

III. SOME PROPERTIES OF INTERACTIVE EXTENSION

A. Extension and Interactive Extension

Let $A_1=(D_1,W_1)$ and $A_2=(D_2,W_2)$ be default theories. In this section the relations between the extensions for A_1, A_2, $A_1 \cup A_2$ and the interactive extension for A_1 and A_2 are discussed. The extensions for A_1 and for A_2 represent the sets of beliefs acquired under the condition that two default reasoning systems A_1 and A_2 are independent, that is, two systems are disconnected and do not exchange their beliefs each other. The extension for $A_1 \cup A_2$, that is, for the default theory $(D_1 \cup D_2, W_1 \cup W_2)$, represents the set of beliefs acquired under the condition that two default reasoning systems A_1 and A_2 are completely combined. The interactive extension for A_1 and A_2 represents a pair of sets of beliefs acquired under the condition that two default reasoning systems A_1 and A_2 are connected interactively and their acceptable beliefs are exchanged each other.

(Property 1) The interactive extension for A_1 and A_2 is not identical with the extensions for A_1, A_2 and $A_1 \cup A_2$ in general.

[Example 3.1] For the default theories A_1 and A_2 discussed in Example 2.1, the extensions for A_1, A_2 and $A_1 \cup A_2$ are $Th(\{p, r, t\})$, $Th(\{u, \neg t, v\})$ and $Th(\{p, u, r, t, z\})$, respectively.

(Property 2) Even if both extensions for A_1 and for A_2 exist, The interactive extension for A_1 and A_2 does not necessarily always exist.

[Example 3.2] Two default theories $A_1 = (\{p : Mq / r\}, \phi)$, $A_2 = (\{: M\neg r / p\}, \phi)$ are considered, where ϕ represents an empty set. The extensions for A_1 and for A_2 are ϕ and $Th(\{p\})$, respectively. However, no interactive extension for A_1 and A_2 exists.

(Property 3) Even if both extensions for A_1 and for A_2 do not exist, the interactive extension for A_1 and A_2 exists in some cases.

[Example 3.3] Two default theories $A_1 = (\{: Mp / \neg p\}, \{\neg q\})$, $A_2 = (\{: Mq / \neg q\}, \{\neg p\})$ are considered. Both extensions for A_1 and for A_2 do not exist. However, the interactive extension for A_1 and A_2 is the pair $E^1 = E^2 = Th(\{\neg p, \neg q\})$.

(Property 4) Even if the extension for $A_1 \cup A_2$ exist, The interactive extension for A_1 and A_2 does not necessarily always exist.

[Example 3.4] Two default theories $A_1 = (\{: Mp / \neg p\}, \{r\})$, $A_2 = (\{: Mq / \neg q\}, \{\neg r\})$ are considered. The extension for $A_1 \cup A_2 = (\{: Mp / \neg p, : Mq / \neg q\}, \{r, \neg r\})$ is L (L is the first order language consisting of the usual wffs). However, no interactive extension for A_1 and A_2 exists.

(Property 5) Even if the extension for $A_1 \cup A_2$ does not exist, the interactive extension for A_1 and A_2 exists in some cases.

[Example 3.5] Two default theories $A_1 = (\{: Mp / q\}, \phi)$, $A_2 = (\{: Mp / \neg q\}, \phi)$ are considered. No extension for $A_1 \cup A_2 = (\{: Mp / q, : Mp / \neg q\}, \phi)$ exists. However, the interactive extension for A_1 and A_2 is the pair $E^1 = Th(\{q\})$ and $E^2 = Th(\{\neg q\})$.

The properties of the beliefs deduced from two interconnected default reasoning systems under the three conditions, i.e., two systems are independent, completely combined and conditional connected, have been discussed. From the discussions it is understood that the properties and the existence of the deduced beliefs are influenced considerably by the conditions of the connections. When a large scale default reasoning system is constructed by connecting small scale systems, for example, it is a useful result that even if each small scale system has no extension, the interconnected large scale system has some *reasonable* sets of beliefs (interactive extension) in some cases.

B. Some Properties of Interactive Extension

Some properties of the interactive extension concerning with those of the extension are given in this section.

[Theorem 3.1] Let $E^1, E^2 \subseteq L$ be sets of closed wffs, and let $A_1 = (D_1, W_1)$ and $A_2 = (D_2, W_2)$ be closed default theories. Define

$E^1_0 = W_1$

$E^2_0 = W_2$

and for $i \geq 0$

$E^1_{i+1} = Th(E^1_i) \cup \{c \mid a : Mb / c \in D_1,\ a \in E^1_i,\ \neg b \notin E^1\} \cup G^2_i$

$E^2_{i+1} = Th(E^2_i) \cup \{c \mid a : Mb / c \in D_2,\ a \in E^2_i,\ \neg b \notin E^2\} \cup G^1_i$

$G^1_i = \{g \mid g \in E^1_i, \neg g \notin E^2\}$

$G^2_i = \{g \mid g \in E^2_i, \neg g \notin E^1\}$.

Then the pair E^1 and E^2 is an interactive extension for A_1 and A_2 iff the following two relations hold simultaneously:

$E^1 = \cup_{i=0}^{\infty} E^1_i$

$E^2 = \cup_{i=0}^{\infty} E^2_i$.

Proof We begin by observing that $\cup_{i=0}^{\infty} E^1_i$ and $\cup_{i=0}^{\infty} E^2_i$ enjoy the following properties:

D1'. $W_1 \subseteq \bigcup_{i=0}^{\infty} E^1_i$

$W_2 \subseteq \bigcup_{i=0}^{\infty} E^2_i$

D2'. $Th(\bigcup_{i=0}^{\infty} E^1_i) = \bigcup_{i=0}^{\infty} E^1_i$

$Th(\bigcup_{i=0}^{\infty} E^2_i) = \bigcup_{i=0}^{\infty} E^2_i$

D3'. If $a : Mb/c \in D_1$, $a \in \bigcup_{i=0}^{\infty} E^1_i$, $\neg b \notin E^1$ then $c \in \bigcup_{i=0}^{\infty} E^1_i$.

If $a : Mb/c \in D_2$, $a \in \bigcup_{i=0}^{\infty} E^2_i$, $\neg b \notin E^2$ then $c \in \bigcup_{i=0}^{\infty} E^2_i$.

D4'. If $g \in \bigcup_{i=0}^{\infty} E^2_i$, $\neg g \notin E^1$ then $g \in \bigcup_{i=0}^{\infty} E^1_i$.

If $g \in \bigcup_{i=0}^{\infty} E^1_i$, $\neg g \notin E^2$ then $g \in \bigcup_{i=0}^{\infty} E^2_i$.

Hence, by the minimality of $\Gamma_1(E^1)$ and $\Gamma_2(E^2)$, we have

$$\Gamma_1(E^1) \subseteq \bigcup_{i=0}^{\infty} E^1_i \qquad (1)$$

$$\Gamma_2(E^2) \subseteq \bigcup_{i=0}^{\infty} E^2_i. \qquad (2)$$

(Necessity) When a pair of sets of closed wffs E^1 and E^2 is an interactive extension for the default theories A_1 and A_2, i.e., $\Gamma_1(E^1)=E^1$ and $\Gamma_2(E^2) = E^2$ hold, the relations $E^1 = \bigcup_{i=0}^{\infty} E^1_i$ and $E^2 = \bigcup_{i=0}^{\infty} E^2_i$ are proved. We inductively prove $E^1_i \subseteq E^1$ and $E^2_i \subseteq E^2$ for all $i \geq 0$, whence $\bigcup_{i=0}^{\infty} E^1_i \subseteq E^1$ and $\bigcup_{i=0}^{\infty} E^2_i \subseteq E^2$.

When $i = 0$, since $E^1_0 = W_1 \subseteq \Gamma_1(E^1)$ and $E^2_0 = W_2 \subseteq \Gamma_2(E^2)$ hold, and from the assumptions $\Gamma_1(E^1)=E^1$ and $\Gamma_2(E^2)=E^2$, then the relations $E^1_0 \subseteq E^1$ and $E^2_0 \subseteq E^2$ hold.

Next, assume $E^1_k \subseteq E^1$ and $E^2_k \subseteq E^2$, we prove $E^1_{k+1} \subseteq E^1$ and $E^2_{k+1} \subseteq E^2$.

1) Proof of $E^1_{k+1} \subseteq E^1$

Consider $p \in E^1_{k+1}$. At least one of the following three cases is caused: ① $p \in Th(E^1_k)$, ② there exists at least one default such that $a : Mb/p \in D_1$, $a \in E^1_k$, $\neg b \notin E^1$, ③ $p \in E^2_k$, $\neg p \notin E^1$.

When the case ① is caused, from the assumption $E^1_k \subseteq E^1$, the relation $p \in Th(E^1) = E^1$ holds.

When the case ② is caused, from the assumptions $E^1_k \subseteq E^1$ and $E^1 = \Gamma_1(E^1)$, the default $a : Mb/p \in D_1$ satisfying $a \in E^1_k$ and $\neg b \notin E^1$ is also satisfying $a \in E^1 = \Gamma_1(E^1)$. Then, from the condition D3, the relation $p \in \Gamma_1(E^1) = E^1$ holds.

When the case ③ is caused, from the assumptions $E^2_k \subseteq E^2$ and $E^2 = \Gamma_2(E^2)$, if $p \in E^2_k$ and $\neg p \notin E^1$ then $p \in E^2 = \Gamma_2(E^2)$ and $\neg p \notin E^1$. Then, from the condition D4, the relation $p \in \Gamma_1(E^1) = E^1$ holds.

From the results of ①, ② and ③, $E^1_{k+1} \subseteq E^1$ is proved.

2) $E^2_{k+1} \subseteq E^2$ is also proved by the same procedure.

Therefore, for all $i \geq 0$, $E^1_i \subseteq E^1$ and $E^2_i \subseteq E^2$ hold. Then $\bigcup_{i=0}^{\infty} E^1_i \subseteq E^1$ and $\bigcup_{i=0}^{\infty} E^2_i \subseteq E^2$ hold. From the equations (1) and (2) and the assumptions $\Gamma_1(E^1)=E^1$ and $\Gamma_2(E^2)=E^2$, the relations $E^1 = \bigcup_{i=0}^{\infty} E^1_i$ and $E^2 = \bigcup_{i=0}^{\infty} E^2_i$ hold.

(Sufficiency) When the relations $E^1 = \bigcup_{i=0}^{\infty} E^1_i$ and $E^2 = \bigcup_{i=0}^{\infty} E^2_i$ hold, it is proved that the pair E^1 and E^2 is an interactive extension for the default theories A_1 and A_2, i.e., $\Gamma_1(E^1)=E^1$ and $\Gamma_2(E^2)=E^2$ hold.

We inductively prove $E^1_i \subseteq \Gamma_1(E^1)$ and $E^2_i \subseteq \Gamma_2(E^2)$ for all $i \geq 0$, whence $E^1 = \bigcup_{i=0}^{\infty} E^1_i \subseteq \Gamma_1(E^1)$ and $E^2 = \bigcup_{i=0}^{\infty} E^2_i \subseteq \Gamma_2(E^2)$. By invoking the equations (1) and (2) we will then have $\Gamma_1(E^1) = E^1$ and $\Gamma_2(E^2) = E^2$ whence the pair E^1 and E^2 is an interactive extension for the default theories A_1 and A_2.

When $i = 0$, from the condition D1, $E^1_0 = W_1 \subseteq \Gamma_1(E^1)$ and $E^2_0 = W_2 \subseteq \Gamma_2(E^2)$ hold.

Next, assume $E^1_k \subseteq \Gamma_1(E^1)$ and $E^2_k \subseteq \Gamma_2(E^2)$, we prove $E^1_{k+1} \subseteq \Gamma_1(E^1)$ and $E^2_{k+1} \subseteq \Gamma_2(E^2)$.

1) Proof of $E^1_{k+1} \subseteq \Gamma_1(E^1)$

Consider $p \in E^1_{k+1}$. At least one of the following three cases is caused: ① $p \in Th(E^1_k)$, ② there exists at least one default such that $a : Mb/p \in D_1$, $a \in E^1_k$, $\neg b \notin E^1$, ③ $p \in E^2_k$, $\neg p \notin E^1$.

When the case ① is caused, from the assumption $E^1_k \subseteq \Gamma_1(E^1)$, $p \in Th(\Gamma_1(E^1)) = \Gamma_1(E^1)$ holds.

When the case ② is caused, from the assumption $E^1_k \subseteq \Gamma_1(E^1)$, the default $a : Mb/p \in D_1$ satisfying $a \in E^1_k$ and $\neg b \notin E^1$ is also satisfying $a \in \Gamma_1(E^1)$. Then, from the condition D3, the relation $p \in \Gamma_1(E^1)$ holds.

When the case ③ is caused, from the assumption $E^2_k \subseteq \Gamma_2(E^2)$, if $p \in E^2_k$ and $\neg p \notin E^1$ then $p \in \Gamma_2(E^2)$ and $\neg p \notin E^1$. Then, from the condition D4, the relation $p \in \Gamma_1(E^1)$ holds.

From the results of ①, ② and ③, $E^1_{k+1} \subseteq \Gamma_1(E^1)$ is proved.

2) $E^2_{k+1} \subseteq \Gamma_2(E^2)$ is also proved by the same procedure.

Therefore, for all $i \geq 0$, $E^1_i \subseteq \Gamma_1(E^1)$ and $E^2_i \subseteq \Gamma_2(E^2)$ hold. Then $\bigcup_{i=0}^{\infty} E^1_i \subseteq \Gamma_1(E^1)$ and $\bigcup_{i=0}^{\infty} E^2_i \subseteq \Gamma_2(E^2)$ hold. From the equations (1) and (2) and the assumptions $E^1 = \bigcup_{i=0}^{\infty} E^1_i$ and $E^2 = \bigcup_{i=0}^{\infty} E^2_i$, the relations $\Gamma_1(E^1) = E^1$ and $\Gamma_2(E^2) = E^2$ hold. ■

Using this theorem, we can ascertain whether or not a pair of sets E^1 and E^2 of closed wffs is an interactive extension for the default theories A_1 and A_2. We exemplify using Example 2.1.

[Example 3.6] For the default theories A_1 and A_2 discussed in Example 2.1, we show that the pair of sets $E^1=E^2=Th(\{p,u,r,t,z\})$ is an interactive extension. Let both E^1 and E^2 in Theorem 3.1 be $Th(\{p,u,r,t,z\})$, the sequences E^1_i and E^2_i are obtained as follows:

1) $E^1_0=W_1=\{p\}$
   $E^2_0=W_2=\{u\}$

2) $E^1_1=Th(\{p\})\cup\{r\}\cup\{u\}$
   $E^2_1=Th(\{u\})\cup\phi\cup\{p\}$
   (ϕ represents an empty set)

3) $E^1_2=Th(\{p,r,u\})\cup\{r,t\}\cup\{u\}$
   $E^2_2=Th(\{u,p\})\cup\phi\cup\{p,r\}$

4) $E^1_3=Th(\{p,r,u,t\})\cup\{r,t\}\cup\{u,p,r\}$
   $E^2_3=Th(\{u,p,r\})\cup\phi\cup\{p,r,u,t\}$

5) $E^1_4=Th(\{p,r,u,t\})\cup\{r,t\}\cup\{u,p,r,t\}$
   $E^2_4=Th(\{u,p,r,t\})\cup\{z\}\cup\{p,r,u,t\}$

6) $E^1_5=Th(\{p,r,u,t,z\})\cup\{r,t\}\cup\{u,p,r,t,z\}$
   $E^2_5=Th(\{u,p,r,t,z\})\cup\{z\}\cup\{p,r,u,t,z\}$

7) thereafter
   $E^1_5=E^1_6\cdots=Th(\{p,r,u,t,z\})$
   $E^2_5=E^2_6\cdots=Th(\{p,r,u,t,z\})$.

Therefore, since the relations

$E^1=\cup_{i=0}^{\infty}E^1_i$
$E^2=\cup_{i=0}^{\infty}E^2_i$

hold, the pair of sets $E^1=E^2=Th(\{p,u,r,t,z\})$ is an interactive extension for A_1 and A_2.

[Theorem 3.2] Suppose a pair of sets of closed wffs E^1 and E^2 is an interactive extension for the default theories $A_1=(D_1,W_1)$ and $A_2=(D_2,W_2)$. Then

$E^1=Th(W_1\cup CONSEQUENTS(GD(E^1,A_1)))\cup\{g\mid g\in E^2, \neg g\notin E^1\})$
$E^2=Th(W_2\cup CONSEQUENTS(GD(E^2,A_2)))\cup\{g\mid g\in E^1, \neg g\notin E^2\})$

where, for a default theory $A=(D,W)$ and a set E of wffs, $GD(E,A)$ and $CONSEQUENTS(D)$ are defined as follows:

$GD(E,A)=\{a:Mb/c\in D\mid a\in E, \neg b\notin E\}$
$CONSEQUENTS(D)=\{c\mid a:Mb/c\in D\}$.

$GD(E,A)$ is called set of generating defaults for E with respect to A, and $CONSEQUENTS(D)$ is called set of consequents of the defaults of D.

Since E^1 and E^2 are represented recursively in this theorem, the interactive extension for the default theories A_1 and A_2 can not be obtained form this theorem immediately.

[Theorem 3.3] Suppose a pair of sets of closed wffs E^1 and E^2 is an interactive extension for the default theories $A_1=(D_1,W_1)$ and $A_2=(D_2,W_2)$. Then

$E^1=Th(W_1\cup CONSEQUENTS(GD(E^1,A_1')))$
$E^2=Th(W_2\cup CONSEQUENTS(GD(E^2,A_2')))$

where

$A_1'=(D_1',W_1)$
$A_2'=(D_2',W_2)$
$D_1'=D_1\cup\{:Mg/g\mid g\in E^2\}$
$D_2'=D_2\cup\{:Mg/g\mid g\in E^1\}$.

From this theorem, E^1 and E^2 are the extensions for A_1' and A_2', respectively. But the reverse does not hold true, i.e., it is not always true that an arbitrary pair of extensions for A_1' and A_2' is the interactive extension for A_1 and A_2, because many extensions for A_1' or A_2' exist in general. We exemplify using Example 2.1.

[Example 3.7] For the default theories A_1 and A_2 discussed in Example 2.1, two interactive extensions exist. Concerning with one of the interactive extensions $E^1=Th(\{p,r,t,u,v,x\})$ and $E^2=Th(\{u,\neg t,v,p,r,x\})$, the default theories A_1' and A_2' defined in Theorem 3.3 are obtained as

$A_1'=(\{p:Mq/r,\ r:Ms/t,\ v:Mw/x,\ :Mu/u,\ :M\neg t/\neg t,\ :Mv/v,\ :Mp/p,\ :Mr/r,\ :Mx/x\},\{p\})$

$A_2'=(\{u:M\neg t/\neg t,\ \neg t:Mu/v,\ t:My/z,\ :Mp/p,\ :Mr/r,\ :Mt/t,\ :Mu/u,\ :Mv/v,\ :Mx/x\},\{u\})$,

respectively. $Th(\{p,r,t,u,v,x\})$ is the unique extension for A_1'. But, for A_2', both $Th(\{u,\neg t,v,p,r,x\})$ and $Th(\{u,t,z,p,r,v,x\})$ are the extensions. Therefore we understand that an arbitrary pair of extensions of A_1' and A_2' is not always the interactive extension for A_1 and A_2.

[Theorem 3.4] Suppose a pair of sets of closed wffs E^1 and E^2 is an interactive extension for $A_1=(D_1,W_1)$ and $A_2=(D_2,W_2)$. Then $E^1=L$ ($E^2=L$) iff W_1 (W_2) is inconsistent.

[Corollary 3.1] The pair $E^1=L$ and $E^2=L$ is an interactive extension for default theories $A_1=(D_1,W_1)$ and $A_2=(D_2,W_2)$ iff both W_1 and W_2 are inconsistent.

[Corollary 3.2] If two default theories $A_1=(D_1,W_1)$ and $A_2=(D_2,W_2)$ have an interactive extension $E^1=L$ and $E^2=L$ then this is only interactive extension.

[Corollary 3.3] If L and E, E is a set of closed wffs, are extensions for $A_1=(D_1,W_1)$ and $A_2=(D_2,W_2)$, respectively, then there exists at least one interactive extension for A_1 and A_2.

[Theorem 3.5] If two pairs of sets of closed wffs E^1, E^2 and $E^{1'}$, $E^{2'}$ are interactive extensions for $A_1 = (D_1, W_1)$ and $A_2 = (D_2, W_2)$, and $E^1 \subseteq E^{1'}$ and $E^2 \subseteq E^{2'}$, then $E^1 = E^{1'}$ and $E^2 = E^{2'}$.

Proof When $E^1 \subseteq E^{1'}$ and $E^2 \subseteq E^{2'}$, for $E^1{}_i$, $E^{1'}{}_i$, $E^2{}_i$ and $E^{2'}{}_i$ in Theorem 3.1, we inductively prove,

$E^{1'}{}_i \subseteq E^1{}_i$

$E^{2'}{}_i \subseteq E^2{}_i$

for all $i \geqq 0$.

When $i = 0$, since $E^1{}_0 = E^{1'}{}_0 = W_1$ and $E^2{}_0 = E^{2'}{}_0 = W_2$, $E^{1'}{}_0 \subseteq E^1{}_0$ and $E^{2'}{}_0 \subseteq E^2{}_0$ hold.

Next, assume $E^{1'}{}_K \subseteq E^1{}_K$ and $E^{2'}{}_K \subseteq E^2{}_K$, we prove $E^{1'}{}_{K+1} \subseteq E^1{}_{K+1}$ and $E^{2'}{}_{K+1} \subseteq E^2{}_{K+1}$.

1) Proof of $E^{1'}{}_{K+1} \subseteq E^1{}_{K+1}$

Consider $p \in E^{1'}{}_{K+1}$. At least one of the following three cases is caused: ① $p \in E^{1'}{}_K$, ② there exists at least one default such that $a : Mb / p \in D_1$, $a \in E^{1'}{}_K$, $\neg b \notin E^{1'}$, ③ $p \in E^{2'}{}_K$, $\neg p \notin E^{1'}$.

When the case ① is caused, from the assumption $E^{1'}{}_K \subseteq E^1{}_K$, the relation $p \in E^1{}_K \subseteq Th(E^1{}_K) \subseteq E^1{}_{K+1}$ holds.

When the case ② is caused, from the assumption $E^{1'}{}_K \subseteq E^1{}_K$ and $E^1 \subseteq E^{1'}$, the default $a : Mb / p \in D_1$ satisfying $a \in E^{1'}{}_K$ and $\neg b \notin E^{1'}$ is also satisfying $a \in E^1{}_K$, $\neg b \notin E^1$. Then the relation $p \in E^1{}_{K+1}$ holds.

When the case ③ is caused, from the assumption $E^{2'}{}_K \subseteq E^2{}_K$ and $E^1 \subseteq E^{1'}$, if $p \in E^{2'}{}_K$ and $\neg p \notin E^{1'}$ then $p \in E^2{}_K$ and $\neg p \notin E^1$. Therefore the relation $p \in E^1{}_{K+1}$ holds.

From the results of ①, ② and ③, $E^{1'}{}_{K+1} \subseteq E^1{}_{K+1}$ is proved.

2) $E^{2'}{}_{K+1} \subseteq E^2{}_{K+1}$ is also proved by the same procedure.

Therefore, when $E^1 \subseteq E^{1'}$ and $E^2 \subseteq E^{2'}$, the relations $E^{1'}{}_i \subseteq E^1{}_i$ and $E^{2'}{}_i \subseteq E^2{}_i$ hold for all $i \geqq 0$.

Since two pairs of sets of closed wffs E^1, E^2 and $E^{1'}$, $E^{2'}$ are interactive extensions for $A_1 = (D_1, W_1)$ and $A_2 = (D_2, W_2)$, the relations $E^1 = \bigcup_{i=0}^{\infty} E^1{}_i$, $E^2 = \bigcup_{i=0}^{\infty} E^2{}_i$, $E^{1'} = \bigcup_{i=0}^{\infty} E^{1'}{}_i$ and $E^{2'} = \bigcup_{i=0}^{\infty} E^{2'}{}_i$ hold. Then $E^{1'} \subseteq E^1$ and $E^{2'} \subseteq E^2$ hold. From the relations and the assumption of $E^1 \subseteq E^{1'}$ and $E^2 \subseteq E^{2'}$, the relations $E^1 = E^{1'}$ and $E^2 = E^{2'}$ are proved. ■

[Theorem 3.6] If a pair of sets of closed wffs E^1 and E^2 is an interactive extension for $A_1 = (D_1, W_1)$ and $A_2 = (D_2, W_2)$, and $E^1 \neq E^2$, then $E^1 \cup E^2$ is inconsistent.

Proof If $E^1 \neq E^2$, then there exists at least one wff p such as $p \in E^1$ and $p \notin E^2$ (or $p \in E^2$, $p \notin E^1$). If the pair E^1 and E^2 is an interactive extension for two default theories $A_1 = (D_1, W_1)$ and $A_2 = (D_2, W_2)$, then the relations $E^1 = \Gamma_1(E^1)$ and $E^2 = \Gamma_2(E^2)$ hold. Since, from the condition D 4 in Definition 2.2, the relation $g \in \Gamma_2(E^2)$ holds for all wffs g satisfying the relations $g \in \Gamma_1(E^1)$ and $\neg g \notin E^2$, the relation $g \in E^2$ must be held for all wffs g satisfying the relations $g \in E^1$ and $\neg g \notin E^2$. Therefore, for the p satisfying $p \in E^1$ and $p \notin E^2$, the relation $\neg p \in E^2$ must be held. From $p \in E^1$ and $\neg p \in E^2$, it is proved that $E^1 \cup E^2$ is inconsistent. In the case $p \in E^2$ and $p \notin E^1$, we can prove it by the same procedure. ■

From the foregoing discussions, the following results are obtained:

1) The properties of the interactive extension given by Theorem 3.1 and Theorem 3.2 are interpreted as some modifications of the extension. The points of the modifications are to describe the influence of the acceptable beliefs given from the other system, and to formulate the conditions (relations) for each beliefs as simultaneous equations.

2) Theorem 3.3 shows that the beliefs $\{g\}$ given from the other system can be written as the set of restricted defaults formed $: Mg / g$. The interactive extension is represented as a pair of extensions for the new default theories constructed by adding the restricted defaults to the original defaults, that is $D_1 \cup \{: Mg / g \mid g \in E^2\}$ and $D_2 \cup \{: Mg / g \mid g \in E^1\}$.

3) The properties of the interactive extension given by Theorem 3.4 and Theorem 3.5 are identical with those of the extension. Therefore, whether each default reasoning system exchanges its beliefs or not, the properties always hold .

4) The property given by Theorem 3.6 is a characteristic of the interactive extension, i.e., it is caused by the interactions of the systems. Therefore, if the default reasoning systems are independent, i.e., any belief is not exchanged, the property does not hold.

C. Interactive Extension for Normal Default Theories

A *normal default* is the one which has the form $a : Mb / b$ for wffs $a, b \in L$. Almost all naturally occurring default, e.g., the *closed world default* of the deductive database,[1),7)] can be represented in this form. A default theory $A = (D, W)$ is *normal* iff every default of D is normal. In this section properties of the interactive extension for closed normal default theories are discussed.

[Theorem 3.7] Every pair of closed normal default theories $A_1=(D_1,W_1)$ and $A_2=(D_2,W_2)$ has an interactive extension.

Proof Since A_1 and A_2 are normal default theories, each theory has a extension. If one of them is inconsistent, i.e., W_1 or W_2 is inconsistent, then there exists at least one interactive extension from Corollary 3.3. Hence assume both W_1 and W_2 are consistent.

The sets of wffs F^1_i and F^2_i are defined as follows:

$F^1_0=W_1$

$F^2_0=W_2$

for $i \geqq 0$,

$F^1_{i+1}=Th(F^1_i)\cup T^1_i$

$F^2_{i+1}=Th(F^2_i)\cup T^2_i$,

where T^1_i and T^2_i are the maximal set of closed wffs such that

(1) $F^1_i\cup T^1_i$ and $F^2_i\cup T^2_i$ are consistent, and

(2) If $p\in T^1_i$, then for some defaults $a:Mb/b\in D_1$, $b=p$ or $p\in F^2_i$, where $a\in F^1_i$. If $p\in T^2_i$, then for some defaults $a:Mb/b\in D_2$, $b=p$ or $p\in F^1_i$, where $a\in F^2_i$.

Using the F^1_i and F^2_i, define F^1 and F^2 as follows:

$F^1=\cup_{i=0}^{\infty}F^1_i$

$F^2=\cup_{i=0}^{\infty}F^2_i$.

We prove the pair F^1 and F^2 is an interactive extension for the normal default theories A_1 and A_2 by proving that

$T^1_i=\{b \mid a:Mb/b\in D_1,\ a\in F^1_i,\ \neg b\notin F^1\}\cup\{g \mid g\in F^2_i, \neg g\notin F^1\}$

$T^2_i=\{b \mid a:Mb/b\in D_2,\ a\in F^2_i,\ \neg b\notin F^2\}\cup\{g \mid g\in F^1_i, \neg g\notin F^2\}$

and invoking Theorem 3.1.

We abbreviate $\{b \mid a:Mb/b\in D_1, a\in F^1_i, \neg b\notin F^1\}\cup\{g \mid g\in F^2_i, \neg g\notin F^1\}$ and $\{b \mid a:Mb/b\in D_2, a\in F^2_i, \neg b\notin F^2\}\cup\{g \mid g\in F^1_i, \neg g\notin F^2\}$ to RHS^1 and RHS^2, respectively.

Clearly $T^1_i\subseteq RHS^1$ and $T^2_i\subseteq RHS^2$. By introducing the inconsistency of $T^1_i\neq RHS^1$ and $T^2_i\neq RHS^2$, the relation $T^1_i=RHS^1$ and $T^2_i=RHS^2$ are proved. Assume $T^1_i\neq RHS^1, T^2_i\neq RHS^2$.

1) Proof of the inconsistency of $T^1_i\neq RHS^1$

From the assumptions $T^1_i\subseteq RHS^1$ and $T^1_i\neq RHS^1$, there is a wff $p\in RHS^1-T^1_i$. By the maximality of T^1_i we must have that $F^1_i\cup T^1_i\cup\{p\}$ is inconsistent, i.e., from $F^1_i\subseteq Th(F^1_i)$, $Th(F^1_i)\cup T^1_i\cup\{p\}$ is inconsistent, i.e., $F^1_{i+1}\cup\{p\}$ is inconsistent, and, since $F^1_{i+1}\subseteq F^1$, $F^1\cup\{p\}$ is inconsistent. Therefore we must have $\neg p\in F^1$ which contradicts the fact that $p\in RHS^1$.

2) The inconsistency of $T^2_i\neq RHS^2$ is also proved by the same procedure.

From the facts $T^1_i\subseteq RHS^1$, $T^2_i\subseteq RHS^2$, $T^1_i\neq RHS^1$ and $T^2_i\neq RHS^2$, the relations $T^1_i=RHS^1$ and $T^2_i=RHS^2$ are proved. ■

The fact that some pairs of default theories have no interactive extension is not very encouraging for constructing a large scale default reasoning system. Theorem 3.3 gives the condition of default theories for which the interactive extension always exists.

For closed normal default theories $A_1=(D_1,W_1)$ and $A_2=(D_2,W_2)$, the following theorems hold. Proofs of theorems have not been included; they may be found in the reference 13).

[Theorem 3.8] Suppose D_1, D_1', D_2 and D_2' are sets of closed normal defaults with $D_1'\subseteq D_1$ and $D_2'\subseteq D_2$, and W_1 and W_2 are sets of consistent wffs. If the pair $E^{1\prime}$ and $E^{2\prime}$ is an interactive extension for $A_1'=(D_1',W_1)$, $A_2'=(D_2',W_2)$, then $A_1=(D_1,W_1)$ and $A_2=(D_2,W_2)$ have an interactive extension E^1 and E^2 such that $E^{1\prime}\subseteq E^1$ and $E^{2\prime}\subseteq E^2$.

What Theorem 3.8 tells us is that the beliefs of the interactive extension increases with increase of the normal defaults of the theories, i.e., the semi-monotonicity of the beliefs[7)] holds for the interactive extension.

[Theorem 3.9] If the closed normal default theories $A_1=(D_1,W_1)$ and $A_2=(D_2,W_2)$ have distinct interactive extension E^1, E^2 and $E^{1\prime}, E^{2\prime}$, then $E^1\cup E^{1\prime}$ or $E^2\cup E^{2\prime}$ is inconsistent.

This theorem shows that the orthogonality of the beliefs[7)] partly holds for the interactive extension.

From the foregoing discussions, the following results are obtained:

1) The property of the interactive extension given by Theorem 3.7 is identical with that of extension.

2) The properties of the interactive extension given by Theorem 3.8 and Theorem 3.9 are similar to those of extensions. But their conditions are slightly distinct, i.e., in Theorem 3.8 and Theorem 3.9 the conditions of the properties are given as " $E^{1\prime}\subseteq$

E^1 *and* $E^{2'} \subseteq E^2$ " and " $E^1 \cup E^{1'}$ *or* $E^2 \cup E^{2'}$ ", respectively. In order to discuss the relations between the interactive extension and each extension, we must take care the distinction of the conditions.

IV. CONCLUSIONS

A new concept of beliefs called *interactive extension* which are derivable from two interconnected default reasoning systems is proposed, and its properties are given. The properties of the interactive extension are influenced by the condition of the exchanged beliefs. Beside the condition discussed in this paper, various conditions can be considered. According to the conditions, various interactive extensions can be obtained.[11] Some properties of the interactive extension obtained in this paper are identical to those of extensions given by R.Reiter, for example Theorem 3.7. But, if the condition of the exchanged beliefs varied from Definition 2.2, the identity does not hold. It is interesting to discuss the relation between the identity and the condition.

When a large scale default reasoning system (deductive database) is constructed from the small scale systems, as stated before, it is necessary to analyze the interactions of the systems. The interactive extension for the systems is one of the most significant concept to show the relations of the systems. In this paper we discussed the interactions of only two interconnected default reasoning systems. In practice, however, it is necessary to discuss the interactions of many systems. But the architecture of the systems will seem in incredibly complicated artifice. The definition of the interactive extension for such systems and its analysis are the subject for a future study.

REFERENCES

1) Minker J. ed.:"Foundations of Deductive Database and Logic Programming", Los Altos, Calif., Morgan Kaufmann Publishers, Inc. (1988).

2) Ohosuga S.:"Knowledge Acquisition and Machine Learning", J. of Information Processing Society of Japan, Vol.26, No.12, pp.1520-1528 (1985-12).

3) Doyle J.:"A Truth Maintenance System", Artif. Intell., Vol.12, No.3, pp.231-272 (1979).

4) McCarthy J.:"Circumscription- A Form of Non-monotonic Reasoning", Artif. Intell., Vol.13, No.1/2, pp.27-39 (April 1980).

5) McDermott D. and Doyle J. : "Non-Monotonic Logic I", ibid., pp.41-72 (1980).

6) McDermott D. : "NonmonotonicLogic II : Nonmonotonic Modal Theories", J. ACM, Vol.29, No.1, pp.33-57 (1982).

7) Reiter R.:"A Logic for Default Reasoning", Artif. Intell., Vol.13, No.1/2, pp.81-132 (1980).

8) Aibara T., Murakami K., Babaguchi N. and Shitanda H.:"A Model Theoretic Approach for Default Logic", Trans. of Information Processing Society of Japan, Vol.28, No.2, pp.109-116 (1987-02).

9) Murakami K., Aibara T. and Shitanda H. : "Modified Extension and Its Properties in Default Reasoning", Trans. of Information Processing Society of Japan, Vol.28, No.12, pp.1280-1287 (1987-12).

10) Murakami K., Aibara T. and Shitanda H. : "Nonrecursive Extension and Its Properties in Default Reasoning", Journal of Japanese Society for Artificial Intelligence, Vol.3, No.3, pp.359-367 (1988-05).

11) Murakami K. and Aibara T. : "Interactive Extension in Default Reasoning", 1987 National Conference Rec., Information and Systems, IEICE Japan, Part 1, p.1-130 (Nov. 1987).

12) Murakami K. and Aibara T. : "Some Properties of Interactive Extension in Default Reasoning", 1988 National Convention Rec., IEICE Japan, Part D-1, p.1-101 (Mar. 1988).

13) Murakami K. and Aibara T. : "Consolidation of Knowledge Bases in Default Reasoning", Information Processing Society of Japan, Technical Report, DBS 66-1 (July 1988).

A Framework for the Parallel Evaluation of Recursive Queries in Deductive Databases

Runping Qi*and Wolfgang Bibel†
Department of Computer Science
University of British Columbia
Vancouver B. C. Canada, V6T 1Z2

ABSTRACT

In this paper we present a parallel processing model for the evaluation of recursive queries in Deductive Databases. The model is based on what we call reduced rule dependency graph. For each group of mutually recursive predicates and each possible query mode on those predicates, a process class to compute the answer to the query mode is created by a compiler. The process instantiations are created dynamically. In this model three kinds of parallelism are exploited: and–parallelism, pipeline–parallelism and loop–parallelism. Or–parallelism is obtained implicitly by the set–oriented treatment of processes. Because the processes are responsible for a rather elaborated task, the overhead is significantly less than that in the models proposed so far for Horn logic programs. The model also allows optimization techniques to be incorporated as appropriate in a concrete situation.

1 INTRODUCTION

The efficient evaluation of recursive queries is one of the major problems in Deductive Databases. Following the conventional terminology, we consider a Deductive Database consisting of:

- An extensional database (EDB) consisting of ground atomic formulas, also called facts. It may be viewed as a conventional relational database.
- An intensional database (IDB) consisting of a set of Horn Clauses (that are not facts) called rules. For convenience the predicates of the heads of the rules in IDB are assumed to be different from those in EDB.

*Most of this work was done when the author was a visiting scholar at UBC supported by Changsha Institute of Technology, PRC. E-mail address: qi@cs.ubc.ca

†The author's current address is: FB Informatik, Technische Hochcchule, D-6100 Darmstadt, West Germany. E-mail address: XIISWBIB@DDATHD21.BITNET

For given EDB, IDB and a given query goal, we need to find all tuples t such that *goal(t)* is logically implied by the union of EDB and IDB. In terms of fix–point semantics of logic programs this is equivalent to asking for the minimal model of a logic program [16].

A way to increase the computational speed for complex recursive queries is to exploit the parallelism in the computation of queries and make use of multi–processing techniques. In this paper we develop a parallel model for the evaluation of recursive queries. The structure of this model is based on *reduced rule dependency graphs* (defined in Section 3). The computation in this model consists of three phases. In the first phase, the overall structure of the logic program is analyzed and forced binding information is propagated through the program. This is similar to the preprocessing phase in some theorem proving systems [3, 4, 5]. In the second phase, *program blocks* (defined in Section 3) are recognized and compiled into parallel target versions. For the purpose of this paper these parallel programs are presented in a semi–formal way. In the last phase the compiled version will be mapped to a multi–processor environment and executed in parallel. In this paper we focus on the first two phases. The idea for our compilation method is derives from the algorithm proposed by Henschen and Naqvi [7] that we refer to as HN–algorithm.

The first attempt to model the parallel processing of recursive queries appeared in [17]. The model is based on the ideas of message passing and data flow. But it is not clear how queries can be evaluated efficiently. Another data–flow model was given in [9]. The query is represented as a *System Graph*, which is a data flow graph and is more elaborated than that in [17]. Using filtering techniques this model can do some kind of optimization on the queries by the incremental construction of filters in the graph. In terms of relational algebra this kind of optimization amounts to pushing the selection and project operations as far down in the expression tree as possible. However both these two models are based directly on the AND/OR structure of logic programs so that the recursions cannot be handled as efficiently as in our model.

There are many parallel models for the execution of logic programs, such as the *goalframe rewriting model* proposed by Goto [6] and the *reduced-or process model* proposed by Kale [8]. These models exploit the AND/OR-parallelism based directly on the structure of logic programs. The main differences between these models and our model are:

- We are aiming at exploiting the parallelism in the *compiled versions* instead of in the original version of logic programs. Because the compiled versions are iterative, the parallelism in them can be exploited more easily and more naturally. We need not tackle the problems such as structure copying vs. structure sharing and environment copying vs. environment sharing as in other models.

- We take advantage of binding information in the query mode so that lots of irrelevant facts and rules need not be considered. This factor significantly contributes to the efficiency of our model.

The remainder of this paper is organized as follows. In Section 2 we give an analysis through an example of the parallelism in the target versions of logic programs produced by the HN–algorithm [7]. We also point out how the parallelism can be exploited. In Section 3 we introduce some necessary concepts and present our parallel model. The outline of a compilation method is also presented. Familiarity with [7] is quite helpful for the readers interested in the fine details of our method. In Section 4 we discuss the performance of our model in comparison with the model proposed by Goto [6] for Horn clause programs. Section 5 concludes the paper with a brief description of future work.

2 ANALYSIS OF PARALLELISM

In this section we demonstrate the parallelism in the compiled versions of logic programs produced by a compilation algorithm proposed by Henschen and Naqvi in [7]. This is one of the fastest methods for the sequential evaluation of a query. We refer to it as HN–algorithm.

Example 1

$r(X,Y)$:- $up(X,X1)$, $r(X1,Y1)$, $down(Y1,Y)$
$r(X,Y)$:- $flat(X,Y)$
?- $r(cc,Z)$

This program is to compute the set of brethren elements for a given element cc in a graph. Here up, $down$, and $flat$ are assumed to be extensional relations (the case of intensional relations defined in other program blocks will be discussed in Section 3). In order to make the ideas in HN–algorithm easy to understand, let us introduce some simple notations first. Since we only deal with binary relations here, we can view these as set–to–set mappings. That is, any relation r maps any subset of the domain into another set. We denote $A.r$ the image of A by r, defined as:

$$A.r = \{\ y \mid \exists x \in A \text{ such that } r(x,y)\ \}$$

The composition $r \circ s$ of r and s is defined by

$$A.(r \circ s) = (A.r).s$$

r^n denotes the n–fold composition of relation r. With this notation the answer to the query in Example 1 may be represented by the following formula.

$$\bigcup_{n=0}^{h} \{cc\}.up^n.flat.down^n \quad \text{for some } h$$

The equivalent iterative program produced by HN–algorithm is shown in Figure 1. The symbol $\|$ in the program is an operation for the conjunction of two symbolic expressions. The program maintains two variables V and E as its state, where the value of V is $\bigcup_{n=0}^{n=l}\{cc\}.up^n$ and the value of E is an expression $flat.down^l$ for some $l \leq h$. At each step, using V and E, we compute some new tuples and compute the new values of V and E.

Now we point out four observations. First, all the binding modes for every predicate in the logic program in Example 1 can be determined in advance by the propagation of the binding mode of the original query. In Figure 1 we need only to know how to compute the expressions such as $V.up$, $V.flat$ and $V.down$. According to the definition of the operation ".", that means we need only to know how to compute the query modes $up(b,?)$, $flat(b,?)$ and $down(b,?)$ (here b indicates that the respective argument is bound to a constant such as cc above). Second, the different invocations of the same query mode behave almost same. So we can establish a process class for this task. Third, the evaluations of $V.flat.E$ in different iterations are mutually independent. So the evaluations can be carried out in parallel. Fourth, because the result of an invocation of a query mode is a set, the evaluation of $V.flat.E$ can be carried out by a pipeline.

```
answer := { }
V := {cc}
E := λ
while "new tuples are generated in V" do
      begin
            answer := answer+V.flat.E
            V := V.up
            E := E||'.down'
      end
```

Figure 1: The iterative version of Example 1

In accordance with the second observation, we assume that there are three process classes **UP**, **FLAT** and **DOWN** corresponding to the three query modes: $up(b,?)$, $flat(b,?)$ and $down(b,?)$. The structure of thes classes will be addressed later. By the techniques presented in Section 3 we will be able to obtain a parallel version of the above program which is shown in Figure 2. There $\mathbf{up_i}$ and $\mathbf{flat_i}$ are the instantiation of process class **UP** and **Flat**, respectively, and $\mathbf{down_{ij}}$ are the instantiations of **DOWN**. Figure 2 describes the static structure (the definition) of the process class for the query mode $r(b,?)$. It specifies the task of its instantiations and the relationship among the processes created during execution of an instantiation.

```
i := 1
create a process to compute {cc}.flat
creat a process of UP, up1,
      to compute {cc}.up
while upi produce at least one result do
      begin
            create a pipeline upi → flati+1 →
                  down1i → ··· → downii
            create a pipeline upi → upi+1
            i := i+1
      end
When all pipelines produce the result "end"
put "end" at the end of answer.
```

Figure 2: The Parallel version of Example 1

Suppose for this query the sequential program stops after n loops, the dynamic structure of the multi-process can be expressed as in Figure 3.

Here the pipeline with $\mathbf{down_{ii}}$ as its last process is responsible for the computation of $\{cc\}.up^i.flat.down^i$. The merge of the outputs from all pipelines is the result of the query.

$\{cc\}.\ \mathbf{flat_1} \rightarrow$
$\{cc\}.\mathbf{up_1} \rightarrow \mathbf{flat_2} \rightarrow \mathbf{down_{11}} \rightarrow$
$\downarrow$
$\mathbf{up_2} \rightarrow \mathbf{flat_3} \rightarrow \mathbf{down_{12}} \rightarrow \mathbf{down_{11}} \rightarrow$
$\downarrow$

....

$\downarrow$
$\mathbf{up_{n-1}} \rightarrow \mathbf{flat_n} \rightarrow \mathbf{down_{1n-1}} \rightarrow \cdots \rightarrow \mathbf{down_{n-1n-1}} \rightarrow$
$\downarrow$
$\mathbf{up_n} \rightarrow \mathbf{flat_{n+1}} \rightarrow \mathbf{down_{1n}} \rightarrow \cdots \mathbf{down_{nn}} \rightarrow$
$\downarrow$
$\mathbf{up_{n+1}}$

Figure 3: The dynamic structure of the multi-processing for Example 1

This example shows the potential parallelism in the compiled versions of logic programs and suggests some possible ways to exploit it. Motivated by this example we have developed a general model for the parallel evaluation of recursive queries. This model is presented in the next section.

3 A MODEL FOR PARALLEL EVALUATION

In this section we will introduce some related concepts, then present the detail of our parallel model.

3.1 Recursion

We assume that there are no tautological cycles in a logic program [5]. Following a terminology similar to the one in [2], we introduce the following definitions. Let p and q be two predicates. We say that q *depends on* p (denoted $p \rightarrow q$) if there is a rule with head predicate q and with its body containing the predicate p. We define $\overset{+}{\rightarrow}$ to be the transitive closure of $\rightarrow$. A predicate p is said to be *recursive* if $p \overset{+}{\rightarrow} p$. Two predicates p and q are *mutually recursive* if $p \overset{+}{\rightarrow} q$ and $q \overset{+}{\rightarrow} p$. It is obvious that mutually recursiveness is an equivalence relation on the set of recursive predicates. Therefore the set of recursive predicates can be decomposed into disjointed blocks of mutually recursive predicates.

A rule p :- $p_1, p_2, \ldots, p_n$ is *recursive* if p and p_i are mutually recursive for some $i = 1, ..., n$.

A recursive rule p :- $p_1, \ldots, p_n$ is *linear* if there is exact one p_i in the body of the rule which is mutually recursive to p. A set of rules is *linear* if every recursive rule in it is linear.

For a predicate p, $p(b, X)$ is a query mode of p, whereby b (resp. X) represents a vector of variables, indicating that these variables will be bound (resp. free) when the query mode is instantiated during query evaluation.

3.2 Reduced Rule Dependency Graphs

For a given IDB we can construct a *reduced rule dependency graph* (RRDG) which reflects the data dependency in a Deductive Database. An RRDG consists of two parts: the node set **N** and arc set **A**. The node set **N** of the graph for a given IDB can be generated in the following way. Thereby readers should recall that only three kinds of predicates may appear in an IDB: the extensional predicates, the non-recursive intensional predicates the the recursive intensional predicates.

- Initially **N** is empty.
- For each extensional predicate occurring in the IDB, a new node associated with this relation is added to **N**.

- For each non-recursive intensional predicate p in the IDB, a new node is added to **N**. The node contains those rules which have p as their head predicate.

- For each set S of mutually recursive predicates, a new node is added to **N**. The node contains all those rules with the head predicates from S.

We say that a predicate p is *defined in* a node n if p is the relation name associated with n or is a head predicate of some rules in **n**. We call the set of the rules in a node a *program block*.

The arc set **A** is generated as follows. For any two different nodes $\mathbf{n_1}$ and $\mathbf{n_2}$ in the node set **N**, if there is a rule in node $\mathbf{n_2}$ with a predicate p in its body and p is defined in $\mathbf{n_1}$, then there is an arc from the node $\mathbf{n_1}$ to node $\mathbf{n_2}$. We say that the rules in node $\mathbf{n_2}$ depend on the rules in node $\mathbf{n_1}$ or simply say node $\mathbf{n_2}$ depends on node $\mathbf{n_1}$. The RRDG of Example 2 in Figure 4 is shown in Figure 5. We mention that the RRDG defined in this paper is simpler and more natural than the *goal/rule* graph in [1, 15].

r(X, Y) :- *flat*(X, Y)
r(X, Y) :- *up*(X, Z1), *flat*(Z1, Z2), *down*(Z2, Y)

flat(X, Y) :- *m*(X, Z), *t*(Z, Y)
t(Z, Y) :- *flat*(Z, W), *p*(W, Y)
t(Z, Y) :- *f*(Z, Y)

p(W, Y) :- *q*(W, Y)
p(W, Y) :- *s*(W, W1), *f*(W1, W2), *p*(W2, Y)

Figure 4: Example 2

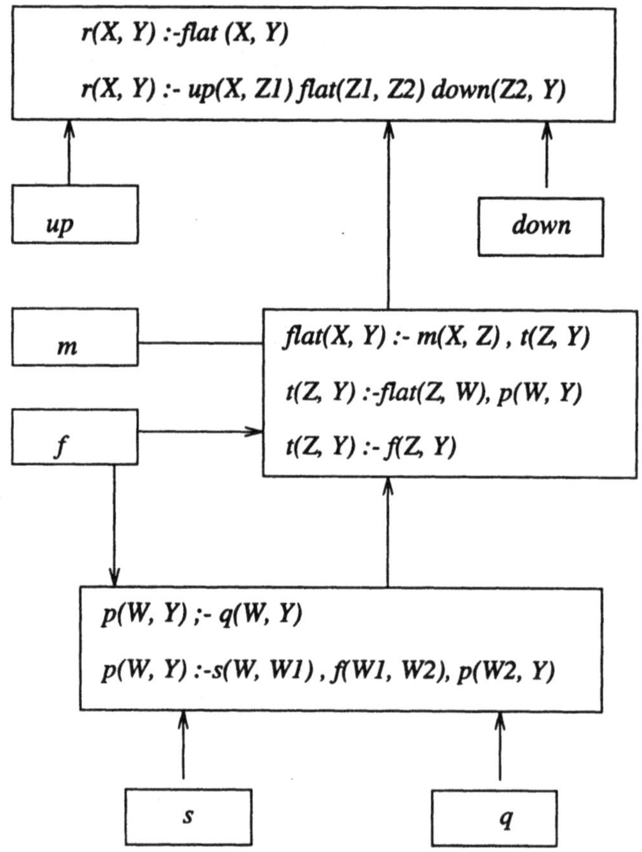

Figure 5: The RRDG of Example 2

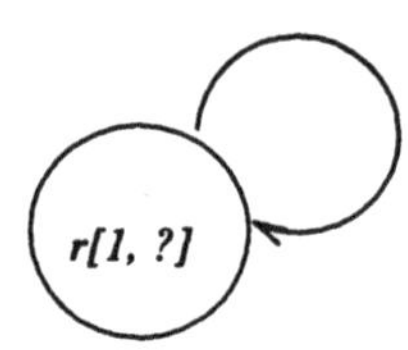

Figure 6: The binding graph of the query mode $r(b, ?)$

3.3 The Binding Passing

For a program block consisting of recursive rules and a query mode of a predicate defined in this program block, we can propagate the binding information in the query mode to obtain the *binding graph* for the predicates defined in the block, as defined in [2, 12, 13]. A binding graph indicates which query modes for the predicates occurring in the block are needed. In a binding graph, the nodes represent the query modes, the arcs represent the dependency relations. The binding graph of the program block in Example 1 in Section 2 is shown in Figure 6 (in this special case there is only one program block with only one binding graph. For the details on the binding graphs of queries readers may consult [2, 12, 13].

3.4 The Parallel Processing Model

The RRDG of an IDB and the binding graphs of the nodes for a query mode carry the information of data dependency in an IDB. The mutually recursive predicates should be evaluated simultaneously because they depend on each other. The evaluation of them depends only on those nodes from which there are arcs to this node. During evaluation of a query several query modes for a predicate and several instantiations for a query mode may occur. For every query mode we create a *process class*. The definition of each process class for a query mode specifies a scheme of computation for the query mode.

Informally, we require the definition of a process class consisting of the following parts:

- An *input process* responsible for collecting the input data into an input pool, providing primitives for the establishment of links between process instantiations.

- An *output process* responsible for dispatching the output data to certain channels linked to it. It gets the output data from an output pool. It will also provide some primitives for the establishment of links with other processes.

- A *process body* specifying how to compute the output data from input data. It determines which process instantiations should be created, and how they are organized. It gets input data from the input pool and puts the output data into the output pool. The details of this part reflects a computational scheme for the given query mode.

- Two *monitors* controlling the two pools. They provide exclusive-access primitives for the input process and process body, and for the process body and output process.

The introduction of an input process and an output process makes it possible to separate the work of data transmission from the work of data processing. This simplifies the control structure of the process body significantly. These two kinds of work are carried out in parallel. The two monitors coordinate the data passing between internal processes.

We assume that the instantiations of process classes can be created dynamically by other process instantiations through the execution of a primitive "create". Any two processes can be linked together by a pipeline. One process can receive inputs from and broadcast its outputs to many other processes.

Let us illustrate the dynamic structure and behavior of an instantiation of a process class. The process creates some new instantiations of other classes, organizes them in an appropriate way and collect output. Example 1 in Section 2 gives a good demonstration of the dynamic structure and behavior (see Figure 2). From that example we can see that two kinds of parallelism are exploited: the pipeline-parallelism among processes within a same pipeline and the loop-parallelism among pipelines. Each pipeline in Figure 2 corresponds to one execution of the loop body in the original sequential algorithm (whence loop-parallelism). The and-parallelism is not illustrated by that example. It can be observed in the Example 3.

The processes for the evaluations of query modes $g_1(b,?)$ and $g_2(b,?)$ are mutually independent and can be executed in parallel. The graph of process-network for the evaluation of the query mode $ss(b,?,?)$ is shown in Figure 8.

In summary, our approach to the evaluation of recursive queries in Deductive Databases is as follows.

1) The overall structure of the IDB is analyzed; then the RRDG of the IDB is created; then the binding information is propagated down-through the RRDG and the binding graphs created for each program block.

2) For each query mode in each binding graph a process class is created. The instantiations of a process class computes the answers to a concrete query mode instantiation.

3.5 The Outline of a Compilation Method

Now we present the program scheme for linear recursive queries. The structure of these scheme is similar to that in the HN-algorithm but expressed in terms of parallel processes.

$$ss(X,Y,Z) :- g_1(X,X1),\ g_2(X,X2),\ g_3(X1,X2,Y,Z)$$
$$:- ss(b,?,?)$$

Figure 7: Example 3

$g_1 \longrightarrow g_3$
$g_2 \nearrow$

Figure 8: Demonstration of and-parallelism

The main idea of the HN-algorithm is to identify a special loop in a linear recursive logic program, called *potential recursive loop* (PRL). This PRL consists of two parts: the *determined part* and the *induced part*. The only way to obtain an answer to a query is by evaluating the PRL zero or more times, and then evaluating the exit expression. The predicates in a PRL form a chain of natural joins, so, as pointed out in Section 2, we can use a pipeline to exploit the parallelism in the evaluation of the i-th unfold of the PRL. If $i \neq j$, the evaluation of the i-th unfold of PRL is independent of that of the j-th unfold of the PRL. Therefore, we can use n parallel pipelines to evaluate the n unfolds of the PRL respectively. For efficiency, we can also make use of the results of the determined part of the i-th unfold in the computation of the $i+1$-th unfold. The typical structure of a PRL is shown as follows.

$$q(W',Z') :- ipart(Y,W'), q(W'',Z''), dpart(X,Z')$$
$$q(W',Z') :- epart(U,V,W',Z')$$
$$:- q(?W',bZ')$$

Here $q(?W',bZ')$ is a query mode indicating that W' are free variables and Z' bound variables. The *epart*, *ipart* and *dpart* are extensional relations or predicates defined in other blocks. X, Y, Z', Z'', W', W'' represent vectors of variables. Z' represents the bound variables in the head predicate, X the variables determined by *dpart*, Z'' is a subset of X, Y a subset of W''. We now describe the general program scheme for performing the parallel computation of the answers.

We assume the existence of the *process classes* corresponding to the query modes $epart(-,-,?,b)$, $dpart(?,b)$ and $ipart(?,b)$. We denote these classes as **EPART**, **DPART** and **IPART**, respectively. At first we create two instantiations of **EPART** and **DPART** corresponding to the initialization phase in the HN-algorithm. We also initialize a formula variable, G, to be an expression from which the process pipelines for the evaluations of the induced parts can be created. The main part of the program scheme is a loop whose purpose is to create pipelines for the induced parts by evaluating G, further to modify G, and to determine the terminating condition. This leads to the semi-formal program scheme shown in Figure 9.

```
Loop
Z' := get-value-from input pool;
if Z' is not "end" then
   begin
   create a process of EPART with
       Z' as input;
   channel the results to the output process;
   G := a pipeline to evaluate
      epart(-,-,W2'',Z2'),ipart(Y2,W2');
   create a process wp of DPART
      to compute dpart(X2,Z2');
   While wp produces non-empty results do
      begin
      create a pipeline linking wp to G
      link G to the output process;
      create a process of DPART to compute
      dpart(X2,Z2'), linking wp to this process;
      use wp to denote this process;
      create another process ipart' of IPART;
      G := G o ipart';
      (o is an operator for pipeline combination)
      when some pipeline produced "end",
      stop the pipeline and
      release the resources occupied by it;
      endwhile;
   end;
exit(loop)
endloop
when all pipelines have produced results "end",
  put "end" into output pool;
when output process encounters "end",
  stop the output process
  stop the main process itself;
```

Figure 9: A general scheme for linear recursive queries

For special PRLs, the scheme can be adjusted as follows:

1. If the loop residue derived from a PRL has no induced parts, i.e. G is fixed, then we can modify the program scheme easily.

2. If the loop residue has no determined parts, then a rather different scheme shown in Figure 10 is applied. In this scheme, the results of working process wp are part of the final results, so they are channeled directly to the output process.

4 PERFORMANCE COMPARISON

In this section we discuss the performance of our model, comparing it with the *goalframe rewriting model* proposed by Goto [6] for the parallel execution of Horn clause logic programs. For both clarity and simplicity, we still use Example 1 in Section 2 with the extensional database shown in Figure 11.

```
Loop
Z' := get-value-from input pool;
if Z' is not "end" then
   begin
   create a process (denoted by wp) of EPART
   to compute answers to epart(-,-,?,Z')
   and channel the results to the output process;
   G:= a process to evaluate
     epart(-,-,?,Z'),ipart(Y2,W2');
   While wp produces non-empty results do
     begin
     channel the results of G to the output process;
     create another process ipart of IPART;
     G := G o ipart;
     (o is an operator for pipeline combination)
     use wp to denote new G;
     when some pipeline has produced result "end",
     stop the pipeline and release
     the resources occupied by it;
     endwhile;
   end;
exit(loop)
endloop;
when all subprocesses have stopped
  put the "end" into the output pool;
when the output process encounters "end",
  stop the output process then
  stop the main process itself.
```

Figure 10: A special scheme for the PRL without a determined part

$up(cc, cc_i)$	$1 \le i \le m$
$up(cc_i, cc_{ij})$	$1 \le i \le m,\ 1 \le j \le l$
$up(cc_{i1}, cc_{i1k})$	$1 \le i \le m,\ 1 \le k \le n$
$flat(cc_{1j1}, dd_{1j1})$	$1 \le j \le l$
$flat(cc_{1j}, dd_{1j})$	$1 \le j \le l$
$down(dd_{ijk}, dd_{ij})$	$1 \le i \le m,\ 1 \le j \le l,\ 1 \le k \le n$
$down(dd_{ij}, dd_i)$	$1 \le i \le m,\ 1 \le j \le l$
$down(dd_i, d_i)$	$1 \le i \le m$

Figure 11: An example of an extensional database

First consider the dynamic behavior of Goto's goalframe rewriting model [6] for this program.

At the very beginning, there is only one goalframe, the $r(cc, Y)$. It will produce two goalframes, $flat(cc, Y)$ and $up(cc, X_1), r(X_1, Y_1), down(Y_1, Y)$. We assume the controller to choose subgoals for subsequent reduction based on argument bindings.

The goalframe $flat(cc, Y)$ cannot produce any new goalframe while the goalframe
$up(cc, X_1), r(X_1, Y_1), down(Y_1, Y)$
will produce the following m goalframes.

$r(cc_i, Y_1), down(Y_1, Y) \quad 1 \leq i \leq m$

Each of these goalframes creates two new goalframes. So the following $2 \cdot m$ goalframes are produced.

$$up(cc_i, X_2), r(X_2, Y_2), down(Y_2, Y_1), down(Y_1, Y)$$
$$flat(cc_i, Y_1), down(Y_1, Y) \quad 1 \leq i \leq m$$

The latter m goalframes cannot produce any more goalframes while the former ones produce l goalframes each. So we obtain the following $m \cdot l$ new goalframes.

$$r(cc_{ij}, Y_2), down(Y_2, Y_1), down(Y_1, Y) \quad 1 \leq j \leq l, \; 1 \leq i \leq m$$

Each of them produces two goalframes. We get another $2 \cdot l \cdot m$ new goalframes as follows.

$$up(cc_{ij}, X_3), r(X_3, Y_3), down(Y_3, Y_2), down(Y_2, Y_1), down(Y_1, Y) \quad 1 \leq j \leq l, \; 1 \leq i \leq m$$
$$flat(cc_{ij}, Y_2), down(Y_2, Y_1), down(Y_1, Y) \quad 1 \leq j \leq l, \; 1 \leq i \leq m$$

At this point, each of the goalframes in the first group with literal $up(cc_{i1}, X_3)$ produces n goalframes. In the second group, each of the goalframes with literal $flat(cc_{1j}, Y_2)$ produces one. The number of the new goalframes shown as follows is $n \cdot m + l$.

$$r(cc_{i1k}, Y_3), down(Y_3, Y_2), down(Y_2, Y_1), down(Y_1, Y) \quad 1 \leq k \leq n, \; 1 \leq i \leq m$$
$$down(dd_{1j}, Y_1), down(Y_1, Y) \quad 1 \leq j \leq l$$

Each of the goalframes in the first group produces two goalframes. Each of the goalframes in the second group will produce one. The $2 \cdot m \cdot n + l$ new goalframes are shown as below.

$$up(cc_{i1k}, X_4), r(X_4, Y_4), down(Y_4, Y_3), down(Y_3, Y_2), down(Y_2, Y_1), down(Y_1, Y) \quad 1 \leq k \leq n, \; 1 \leq i \leq m$$
$$flat(cc_{i1k}, Y_3), down(Y_3, Y_2), down(Y_2, Y_1), down(Y_1, Y) \quad 1 \leq k \leq n, \; 1 \leq i \leq m$$
$$down(dd_1, Y) \quad 1 \leq j \leq l$$

The goalframes in the first group can produce no new goalframes. Each of the goalframes with literal $flat(cc_{11k}, Y_3)$ in the second group produces one new goalframe. All of the goalframes in the third group will produce the same result, that is d_1. So following n new goalframes are obtained.

$$down(dd_{11k}, Y_2), down(Y_2, Y_1), down(Y_1, Y) \quad 1 \leq k \leq n$$

All of these goalframes will produce the same goalframes in the form of:

$$down(dd_{11}, Y_1), down(Y_1, Y)$$

These will produce the same goalframe: $down(dd_1, Y)$ which produces one result for Y, that is, d_1.

In summary we can now easily see that the total number of the goalframes (including the initial one) is $3lm + 3mn + 2l + 3m + 2n + 3$ and the number of the failed goalframes (those can produce neither results nor new goalframes) is $1 + 2lm + 2mn - l - n$. In Goto's model, for every goalframe, there is one corresponding process. So the ratio between the number of failed processes and the total number of processes is about 2/3. These failed processes are waste of resources.

Suppose there are enough processors. Because the longest parent–child process chain is 8, the results could be computed in 16 logical time periods (a logical time period is the time for a process to create new goalframes or for sub-processes to report results to its parent–process). In reality if there are only s processes, the number of logical time periods for producing the results is about $16 \cdot 3 \cdot (nm + ml)/s$. This is in proportion with $m \cdot n$ and $m \cdot l$.

As the number of processes is so big, the overhead for scheduling must be very high. Another noticeable fact is that, whenever a new goalframe is produced, substantial work has to be done for the copying of the new goalframe.

Now we consider our model. For the same program and same query as the one just discussed for Goto's model, the dynamic structure of the multi-process network is shown in Figure 12. There are 4 pipelines with a total of 14 processes. We assume that a process can produce one result in a logical time period. The number of total logical time periods is in proportion with N where $N = \max\{s_i + r_i \mid 1 \leq i \leq h\}$, and s_i is the number of stages in pipeline i, r_i is the largest number of results produced by the processes in pipeline i. In this example, N is about $\max\{m \cdot n, m \cdot l\}$. So the number of logical time periods needed to produce the results in our model is in same order as that in Goto's model. But the number of processes created is significantly lower than that in Goto's model. Furthermore the processes in our model are organized into pipelines so there will be very little overhead for scheduling. The data transferred among processes are restricted to results so the communication load is much lower than that in Goto's model. If we make use of database techniques and package communication techniques, the performance of our model can even be further improved.

We should notice that duplicate results are produced in both models. However we can easily eliminate all duplicate results by attaching a filter to the output of each process (we can even ask the process class definition to specify this) in our model, but this seems hard to achieve in Goto's model.

Like other models, Goto's model is aiming at exploring the AND/OR parallelism inherent in the structure of logic programs. These models are all suffering some common drawbacks such as:

- They produce too many redundant processes so that the overhead for scheduling them becomes too high. The processes resulting in no results are waste of resources. The processes producing the same results are redundant as well.

$\{cc\}.\mathbf{flat}_1 \rightarrow$
$\{cc\}.\ \mathbf{up}_1 \rightarrow \mathbf{flat}_2 \rightarrow \mathbf{down}_{11} \rightarrow$
$\downarrow$
$\mathbf{up}_2 \rightarrow \mathbf{flat}_3 \rightarrow \mathbf{down}_{12} \rightarrow \mathbf{down}_{22} \rightarrow$
$\downarrow$
$\mathbf{up}_3 \rightarrow \mathbf{flat}_4 \rightarrow \mathbf{down}_{13} \rightarrow \mathbf{down}_{23} \rightarrow \mathbf{down}_{33} \rightarrow$
$\downarrow$
$\mathbf{up}_4$

Figure 12: The structure of the multi-process for example 1 with EDB

- The overhead caused by the communications among processes is too high. The information transferred among processes includes the copy of the subgoal-frame and the binding environment. The effective work done by a process is small in comparison with the overhead.

We think that the main reason for the above drawbacks is that the models are based directly on the recursive structure of logic programs. Our point is that exploiting the parallelism in an iterative program is much easier than that in a recursive program. The better performance of our model is mainly due to following facts.

- The processes in our model are set-oriented instead of tuple-oriented. This means that every process is responsible for a rather elaborated job so the number of processes can be reduced significantly without loss of parallelism. As a sequence, the overhead for scheduling is low.
- The compilation techniques make the recursive clauses easy to handle. Therefore the parallelism can be exploited easily.
- Redundancy is reduced by making use of global binding information.
- In our model we need not consider the problems such as backtracking, environment maintaining and frame copying, which are often trouble-making problems in the models for logic programs.

5 FUTURE WORK AND CONCLUSION

In this paper we analyzed the potential parallelism in the evaluation of recursive queries in Deductive Databases and presented a parallel model for it. Unlike traditional model for Logic Programs, our model aims at exploring the parallelism in the compiled and iterative versions of the recursive queries, and this turns out to be very natural and efficient. We also gave some program scheme of the compiled versions of a class of recursive queries. Through a rough comparison with Goto's model for a particular program, we found that the overheads in our model is much lower than in Goto's and we believe that the performance of our model is better than that of Goto's model for linear recursive logic programs without functional symbols.

We pointed out that the good performance of our model is due to two facts. One is that we have made a good use of binding information in query modes so that lots of irrelevant branches in the search trees are cut off in advance. The other is the compilation technique that translates the recursive structure of queries into an iterative structure so that the parallelism can be exploited more easily and naturally.

There are several problems to be solved. First, the application range of the program scheme presented in this paper is very restricted. More general scheme or approaches are to be developed. Second, a formal language should be developed so that the compiled versions of recursive queries can be expressed more accurately. Third, more analysis of the system performance and (simulated) experiments should be carried out so that we can get deeper understanding of our approach.

References

[1] F. Bacilhon and R. Ramamkrishnan, "Amateur's Introduction to Recursive Query Processing strategies" *ACM Proc. of SIGACT–SIGMOD Int. Conf. on Management of Data,* 16–52, 1986.

[2] F. Bancilhon, D. Maier, Y. Sagiv and J. Ullman, "Magic Sets and Other Strange Ways to Implement Logic Programs", *Proc. of the ACM SIGACT–SIGMOD Symp. on Principles of Database Systems,* 1–15, 1986.

[3] W. Bibel, R. Letz and J. Schumann, "Bottom–up enhancements of Deductive Systems", *Proc. of 4th International Conference on AI and Information–Control Systems of Robots,* 1987.

[4] W. Bibel, *Automated Theorem Proving,* Vieweg, Braunschweig, second edition, 1987.

[5] W. Bibel, "Advanced Topics in Automated Deduction", to appear in *Fundamentals of Artificial Intelligence II*, 1988, edited by R. Nossum, Springer, Berlin.

[6] A. Goto, H.Tanaka and T. Moto–Oka, "Highly Parallel Inference Engine PIE–goal rewriting model and machine architecture", *New Generation Computing,*2, 1984.

[7] L.J. Henschen and S. A. Naqvi, "Compiling Queries in Recursive First–Oder Databases", *J. ACM, 31, 1,* 47–85, 1984.

[8] L. V. Kale, "Reduced–Or Process Model", *Proc. of the 4th Int. Conf. on Logic Programming,* 616–632, 1987.

[9] M. Kifer and E. L. Lozinskii, "Filtering Data Flow in Deductive Databases", *ICDT'86*,1986, 186–202.

[10] D. P. McKay and S. Shapiro, "Using Active Connection Graphs for Reasoning with Resursive Rules", *Proc. 7th IJCAI*, 386–374, 1981.

[11] R. Ramamkrishnan, "Magic Templates: A Spellbinding Approach to Logic Programs", *Proc. of the 5th Int. Conf. on Logic Programming*, 140–159, 1988.

[12] D. Sacca and C. Zaniolo, "On the Implementation of a Simple Class of Logic Queries for Databases", *Proc. 5th ACM SIGACT–SIGMOD Symp. on Prinples of Database Systems*, 16–23, 1986.

[13] D. Sacca and C. Zaniolo, "The Generalized Counting Method for Recursive Logic Queries", *ICDT'86*, 31–53.

[14] J. D. Ullman, *Principles of Database Systems*, Computer Science Press, Rockville, Md., 1982.

[15] J. D. Ullman, "Implementation of Logical Query Languages for Databases", *TODS 10, 3*, 289–321, 1985.

[16] M. H. van Emden and R. Kowalski, "The Semantics of Predicate Logic as a Programming Language", *J. ACM 23, 4*, 733–742, 1976.

[17] A. van Gelder, "A Message Passing Framework for Logical Query Evaluation", *ACM Proc. of SIGACT–SIGMOD Int. Conf. on Management of Data*, 155–165, 1986.

[18] C. Zaniolo, "Safty and Compilation of Non–Recursive Horn Clauses", *Expert Database Systems: Larry Kerschberg, Editor*, 237–252, 1987.

COMPILATION AND EVALUATION OF ASYNCHRONOUS CHAIN RECURSIONS IN DEDUCTIVE DATABASES

Jiawei Han †
School of Computing Science
Simon Fraser University
Burnaby, British Columbia, V5A 1S6
Canada

Wen Yu Lu
Computer and Information Science
The Ohio State University
Columbus, Ohio 43210
U.S.A.

ABSTRACT

An asynchronous chain recursion is a recursion whose compiled formula consists of single chain or asynchronous chains. We study the compilation and evaluation of asynchronous chain recursions and show that many complex function-free recursions, which may contain single or multiple linear recursive rules, nonlinear recursive rules, mutually recursive rules and multiple-level recursions, can be compiled to asynchronous chain recursions. Our study on compilation methods, simplification of compiled formulas and query processing techniques shows that asynchronous chain recursions can be compiled to relatively simple compiled formulas and processed efficiently using transitive closure query evaluation techniques.

Keywords. *Deductive databases, compilation techniques, recursions, transitive closures, recursive query processing.*

1. Introduction

Transitive closure recursion is important in the development of deductive database systems because it is not only frequently used in practical applications but also requires relatively simple processing strategies which form a base for the study of complex recursions. Many techniques have been developed for the efficient processing of transitive closure queries [12, 14]. This motivates us to examine a related issue: *what kinds of complex recursions are compilable to the forms to which transitive closure processing techniques are applicable?*

This issue has been studied extensively on *single-linear (SL) recursions*, where *the recursion consists of one linear recursive rule and one or more nonrecursive rules.* Besides the pioneering studies by Aho and Ullman [1], Henschen and Naqvi [11], and others (see Bancilhon and Ramakrishnan [2]), Naughton endowed an interesting name, *one-sided recursions* [16], on such kind of recursions and showed that many interesting SL-recursions are one-sided recursions. Han and Luk [6] used a variable connection graph in the characterization of SL-recursions compilable to such kind of recursions (called *single-chain recursions*).

The issue is challenging when dealing with non-SL recursions (formally defined in Section 2). There have been some interesting studies on the compilation and transformation of some multiple linear recursive rules and nonlinear recursive rules, such as Minker and Nicolas [15], Henschen and Naqvi [11], Han and Henschen [5], Zhang et. al. [20], Ioannidis and Wong [13], and Naughton [17]. Their studies show that many non-SL recursions are compilable to the forms to which efficient algorithms are applicable.

This paper is a continued study on this topic. A special class of non-SL recursions, *asynchronous chain recursions (ACs)*, is identified. An asynchronous chain recursion is a recursion whose compiled formula consists of single chain or asynchronous chains. Our study contributes to the topic in several aspects: (1) it classifies non-SL recursions into several subclasses: multiple linear recursions, nonlinear recursions, mutual recursions and different-level recursions; (2) it presents some interesting results on compiling each class of non-SL recursions; (3) it studies the simplification of compiled formulas; and (4) it presents a quad-state query analysis method for efficient processing of versatile queries on asynchronous chain recursions.

† The work was supported in part by the Natural Sciences and Engineering Research Council of Canada under the Grant A-3723 and a research grant from Centre for Systems Science of Simon Fraser University.

The paper is organized as follows. Section 2 presents a classification of non-SL recursions and introduces the concept of asynchronous chain recursions. Section 3 is on the simplification of compiled formulas. Section 4 is on the compilation of non-SL recursions in linear variable patterns. Section 5 discusses the query processing of asynchronous chain recursions, and section 6 concludes our discussion.

2. Preliminaries

2.1. A Classification of Function-Free Recursions

Like most researchers, we assume that a deductive database consists of an *extensional database (EDB)* (a set of database relations) and an *intensional database (IDB)* (a set of intensional predicates defined by *function-free* Horn-clause rules). A predicate P is said to *imply* a predicate R ($P \Rightarrow R$) if there is a Horn clause in *IDB* with predicate R as the head and P in the body, or there is a predicate Q where $P \Rightarrow Q$ and $Q \Rightarrow R$ (transitivity). A predicate R is *recursive* if $R \Rightarrow R$. A **rule cluster** of a predicate R is the maximal subset of rules in *IDB* in which all the head predicates of the rules are either R or P where $P \Rightarrow R$. If R is recursive, the R-cluster is a **recursive cluster**, or simply, **recursion**.

A recursive rule is **linearly recursive** if the head predicate is the sole recursive predicate and appears exactly once in the body. It is **non-linearly recursive** if the head predicate is the sole recursive predicate but appears more than once in the body. It is **mutually recursive** if the head predicate, say R, is implied by another predicate S ($S \neq R$) in the body and S is also implied by R (i.e., $S \Rightarrow R$ and $R \Rightarrow S$). A set of mutually recursive rules forms a **clique**.

To facilitate our study of compilation of recursions, each predicate is associated with a **deduction level**. Each EDB predicate is at level 0. An IDB predicate is at the same level as its mutually recursive predicates, and is at least one level above the maximum level of all of its nonmutually recursive predicates in the bodies of the rules defining it. Such a deduction level assignment ensures that each IDB predicate can be computed using the lower-level predicates plus the computation of a recursion at its own level, if any. In this way, an IDB is stratified by deduction levels. Notice that such a deduction level-oriented stratification is based on the order of the computation of IDB predicates, which is different from the *stratified logic programs* by Ullman ([19]) in which the stratification of a database is based on the notion of negation.

A set of recursions are **different-levels of recursion** if the head predicate, say R, is implied by another recursive predicate S which is not implied by R (i.e., $S \Rightarrow R$ but $R \not\Rightarrow S$). That is, S is at a lower level of recursion than R.

Based on the above characteristics of rules, we classify function-free recursions into five classes:

1. **Single Linear (SL) Recursion**: if the recursion consists of *one linear recursive rule* and *one or more non-recursive rules* (*exit rules*);
2. **Multiple Linear (ML) Recursion**: if it consists of *multiple linear recursive rules* and one or more exit rules defining the same recursive predicate;
3. **Non-Linear (NL) Recursion**: if it consists of *one or more nonlinear recursive rules*, 0 or more linear recursive rules and some exit rules;
4. **Mutual Recursion (MR)**: if it consists of some *mutually recursive rules* but all the recursions are at the same level; and
5. **Different-Level Recursion (DL)**: if it consists of *more than one level of recursion*.

Recursions in classes 2 to 5 are **non-SL recursions**. According to our classification, a higher (latter) class may subsume the classes lower than it. For example, a different-level recursion (DL) may contain a mutually recursive (MR) sub-cluster which may in turn contain some nonlinear recursive rules (NL). Such a classification helps the development of compilation and processing techniques step by step, that is, the study of lower class recursions provides the basis for the study of higher class recursions.

2.2. Compilation of SL Recursions

Our study adopts the compilation approach [18]. The compilation of IDBs derives the processing outlines before accessing EDBs. In the compilation of an SL recursion, we consider that *the first expansion* of the recursive rule R is the recursive rule itself. The *k-th expansion* of R ($k > 1$) is the unification of the recursive rule of R with the predicate R of the $(k-1)$-th expanded rule. The *k-th compiled formula* is the formula generated by the unification of the exit rules of R with the predicate R in the body of the k-th expansion of R. The (complete) *compiled formula* of R is the union of the set of formulas generated by all the expansions of R.

As a notational convention, we use the upper case letters to denote predicates and the lower case letters to denote attributes with the those starting with t, ..., z indicating variables and all the others indicating constants.

Example 1. We examine the compilation of two typical SL recursions, *Ancestor* and *SG* (same generation relative), defined in Fig. 1, where P is for *Parent*.

(1a) $Ancestor(x,y) :- Ancestor(x,x_1), P(x_1,y).$
(1b) $Ancestor(x,y) :- P(x,y).$
(2a) $SG(x,y) :- P(x,x_1), P(y,y_1), SG(x_1,y_1).$
(2b) $SG(x,y) :- Sibling(x,y).$

Figure 1. Two typical single linear recursions

$$Ancestor(x_0,y) = \bigcup_{i=0}^{\infty}(P^i(x_{i-1},x_i), P(x_i,y)).$$

$$SG(x_0,y_0) = \bigcup_{i=0}^{\infty}(P^i(x_{i-1},x_i), P^i(y_{i-1},y_i), Sibling(x_i,y_i)).$$

Figure 2. Compiled formulas of the two SL recursions.

The compiled formulas of the two recursions are in Fig. 2, where $\cup$ denotes disjunction, and the notation, $P^i(x_{i-1},x_i)$, is defined as,

$$P^i(x_{i-1},x_i) = \begin{cases} true & \text{if } i=0, \\ P^{i-1}(x_{i-2},x_{i-1}), P(x_{i-1},x_i) & \text{if } i>0. \end{cases} \quad \square$$

In general, we have

Definition. A **chain** of *length* k ($k > 1$) is a sequence of k predicates with the following properties: (1) all k predicates have the same name, say P, and the l-th P of the chain is denoted as $P_{(l)}$, (2) there is at least one common variable in every two consecutive predicates, and if i is the variable position in the first predicate, j the variable position in the second, and the two positions contain the identical variable, then (i,j) is an invariant of the chain, i.e., the i-th variable of $P_{(l)}$ is identical with the j-th variable of $P_{(l+1)}$ for every l where $1 \le l \le k-1$. Each predicate of the chain is called a chain *element*. A chain element may also be formed by a sequence of connected predicates (i.e., predicates having shared variables). A unit-length chain is trivially a chain predicate, and a 0-length chain is defined as a *tautology*.

Definitions. A linear recursion is an **n-chain recursion** if for any positive integer K, there exists a k-th expansion of the recursion consisting of one chain (when $n = 1$) or n synchronous (of the same length) chains (when $n > 1$) each with the length greater than K, and possibly some other predicates which do not form a nontrivial chain. It is a **single-chain recursion** when $n = 1$, or a **multi-chain recursion** otherwise. The recursive rule of an n-chain recursion is called an **n-chain recursive rule.** A recursion is **bounded** if it is equivalent to a set of nonrecursive rules.

Variable connections among the predicates in a recursive rule strongly influence the expansions of the recursion. The simplest variable pattern of a recursive rule is *the linear variable pattern* [5] (or a *chain rule* [3]) where (i) all the predicates are binary and contain neither constants nor repeated variables, (ii) the predicates in the body of a rule form a well-formed join expression, that is, two consecutive predicates share variables at their neighboring argument positions and there is no other shared variable among predicates, and (iii) the two variables of the head predicate correspond to the starting and ending variables of the body. A recursive rule in the linear variable pattern preserves stability in the expansions [11], that is, variables at the corresponding argument positions in the recursive predicates of both head and body of the rule preserve the same corresponding positions at any expansion. For example, all the rules of Fig. 1 are chain rules.

As a notational shorthand, the variables inside the predicates of the rules and compiled formulas in linear variable patterns are omitted because they are implied by the predicate positions. For example, the formulas of Fig. 2 can be written as in Fig. 3.

$$Ancestor = Parent^+$$
$$SG = \bigcup_{i=0}^{\infty}(Parent^i \ Sibling \ Child^i).$$

Figure 3. Short form of the compiled formulas of Fig. 2.

It is a challenging task to compile the recursions in which some recursive rules are in nonlinear variable patterns. A study in [8] shows,

Theorem 1. *A single linear recursion is compilable to a bounded recursion or an n-chain recursion.*

Unfortunately, there is no such elegant property in non-SL recursions. This paper focuses on the recursions in which all the recursive rules are in linear variable patterns. The compilation of recursions in complex variable patterns is briefly discussed in section 5.

2.3. Asynchronous Chain Recursions

In the expansions of non-SL recursions, we adopt the breadth-first search philosophy. We consider that *the first expansion* of the recursive rule R is the set of recursive rules directly defining R. The *k-th expansion* of R ($k > 1$) is a set of rules each of which is obtained by the unification of one recursive definition in the recursion R with the corresponding recursive predicate in the body of one of the ($k-1$)-th expanded rules. If a newly generated rule is already in the current or previous expansions, it should be eliminated to avoid redundancy. The *k-th compiled formula* is the union of the set of expressions generated by the unification of the exit definitions in R with the recursive predicates in the bodies of the set of the k-th expanded rules of R. The (complete) *compiled formula* of R is the union of the set of formulas generated by all the expansions of R.

Definition. A recursion is an **asynchronous chain recursion (AC)** if its compiled formula consists of a finite number of asynchronous chains and possibly a small number of other predicates, where each chain element of the asynchronous chains may in turn consist of a finite number of asynchronous chains and possibly a small number of other predicates.

Notice in the definition that the length of each asynchronous chain is unbounded, that is, for any integer K, there exists a k-th expansion where the length of the chain is greater than K. However, the number of other predicates is *limited* (usually quite small), that is, there exist two integers M and m such that for any k-th expansion ($k > m$), the number of such predicates is less than M. Moreover, *asynchronous chains* means that the length of one chain is irrelevant to the lengths of the other chains in the formula.

Recursions can also be classified according to their compilation results. After compilation, a recursion belongs to one of the following four classes: (i) a *bounded recursion* (i.e., which is equivalent to a set of nonrecursive rules), (ii) a *synchronous chain recursion* (i.e., an n-chain recursion with n > 1), (iii) an *asynchronous chain recursion*, and (iv) a *complex nonlinear (non-SL) recursion beyond the first three classes.* An important implication of such a classification is that although a general evaluation algorithm, such as Semi-Naive algorithms [2, 18], or Generalized Counting and Generalized Magic Sets methods [4], can be applied to general function-free recursions, efficient evaluation algorithms can often be developed for special classes of recursions.

Many application-oriented examples are asynchronous chain recursions. Transitive closure recursions [1], one-sided recursions [16], single-chain recursions [6] and separable recursions [17] are typical asynchronous chain recursions. Here we present another example.

Example 2. Suppose a recursion *Know* is defined as follows: A thing is known by a person if it is discovered by him/her, or it is derivable from what he/she knows, or it is inherited from his/her ancestors' knowledge.

(3a) $Know(x,y)$:− $Discover(x,y)$.

(3b) $Know(x,y)$:− $Know(x,w), Derivable(w,y)$.

(3c) $Know(x,y)$:− $Ancestor(x,w), Know(w,y)$.

(3d) $Derivable(x,y)$:− $Derivable(x,w), Derivable(w,y)$.

(3e) $Derivable(x,y)$:− $Derive(x,y)$.

Figure 4. A non-SL recursion compilable to an AC.

The recursion is a DL (different-level) recursion. The lower level recursive predicates *Ancestor* and *Derivable* can be first compiled to $Parent^+$ and $Derive^+$, and then the higher level predicate *Know* is compiled to,

$$Know = (Parent^+)^*\ Discover\ (Derive^+)^*.$$

By simplification of compiled formulas (see section 3), we have

$$Know = Parent^*\ Discover\ Derive^*.$$

Since the compiled formula consists of two asynchronous chains, the recursion is an asynchronous chain recursion. □

Example 3. Not all non-SL recursions can be compiled to a finite number of chains. On such example is the recursion of Fig. 5.

(4a) R :− A, R, S, R, B.
(4b) S :− C, R, D, S.
(4c) R :− E.
(4d) S :− F.

Figure 5. A recursion which is not compilable to an AC.

This is because the first expansion of R is (4a) itself, the second expansion generates three expanded rules:

R :− $A, A, R, S, R, B, S, R, B$.
R :− A, R, C, R, D, S, R, B.
R :− $A, R, S, A, R, S, R, B, B$.

The third expansions generate more expanded rules. Obviously, the general expansions are not so regular to be expressed by a finite number of chains. □

3. Simplification of Compiled Formulas

The compiled formulas of non-SL recursions may contain complex chains of chains. It is necessary to simplify such formulas for efficient processing. Since predicates in each compiled chain form a well-formed join expression, we omit the variables inside the predicates in our presentation.

Theorem 2. (Simplification of nested single closures) *A compiled formula consisting of a (transitive and/or reflexive) closure of a one-level nested single closure is transformable to a single closure containing no nested closure(s).*

Proof.

The theorem can be proved by examining all of the possible cases of one-level nested single closures as below.

$$(A^*)^* \equiv (A^+)^* \equiv (A^*)^+ \equiv A^*A^* \equiv A^*$$
$$(A^+)^+ \equiv A^+A^* \equiv A^*\,A\,A^* \equiv A^+$$
$$(AB^*)^+ \equiv (A^+B^*)^+ \equiv A(A \cup B)^*$$
$$(B^*C)^+ \equiv (B \cup C)^*C$$
$$(AB^+)^+ \equiv A(BA \cup B)^*B$$
$$(B^+C)^+ \equiv B(B \cup CB)^*C$$
$$(AB^*C)^+ \equiv A(CA \cup B)^*C$$
$$(AB^+C)^+ \equiv AB(CAB \cup B)^*C$$

Notice that some of the above rules are presented only in transitive closure forms. Their corresponding transitive and reflexive closure forms can be represented by unioning with an identity relation, e.g.,

$$(AB^*)^* \equiv (A^+B^*)^* \equiv A(A \cup B)^* \cup I$$

We prove $(A^*)^* \equiv A^*$. The other equations can be proved similarly. First, A^* is contained in $(A^*)^*$, which can be shown by equating the outer star of $(A^*)^*$ to 1. Conversely, for any integers m and n, $E = (A^m)^n = A^{mn}$ is contained in A^*, which implies that $(A^*)^*$ is in A^*. Thus $(A^*)^* \equiv A^*$. □

Corollary 1. *A compiled formula consisting of multiple levels of nested closures where each level contains only a single closure is transformable to a single closure containing no nested closure(s).*

Proof.

Multiple levels of nested single closures can be transformed to simpler forms by performing reduction one level at a time. According to the formulas of Theorem 2, each nested single closure can be transformed to a non-nested single closure operation. Therefore, multiple level reduction will produce the formulas containing non-nested single closure operations as well. For example,

$$(((AB^+C)^+)D)^+ \equiv (AB(CAB \cup B)^*CD)^+$$
$$\equiv AB(CDAB \cup CAB \cup B)^*CD. \ \square$$

Corollary 2. *Compiled formulas containing nested multiple closures can be transformed to nonnested single closures by the following rules:*

$$(A_1^* \cdots A_n^*)^* \equiv (A_1^* \cdots A_n^*)^+ \equiv (A_1 \cup \cdots \cup A_n)^*$$
$$(A^+B_1^* \cdots B_n^*)^+ \equiv A(A \cup B_1 \cup \cdots \cup B_n)^*$$
$$(A_1^* \cdots A_n^* B^+)^+ \equiv (A_1 \cup \cdots \cup A_n \cup B)^*\,B$$
$$(A^+B^+)^+ \equiv A(A \cup B)^*B.$$

The correctness of the above rules can be proved similarly as the rules in Theorem 2.

The reduction of chains of chains to one level of chains is important because it reduces the computation of chain of chains to one or a few closure operations.

However, not all of the chains of chains can be reduced to non-nested closures. $(AB^+CD^+E)^+$ is one such example. Fortunately, many frequently used chains of chains can be transformed to non-nested closures by the above theorem and corollaries. Such transformations should be performed when possible in order to reduce the cost of the processing of nested closures.

4. Compilation of Non-SL Recursions in Linear Variable Patterns

We study the compilation of the recursions in which each recursive rule is in *linear variable patterns* (i.e., *chain rules*) and leave the compilation of recursions in complex variable patterns to a future paper.

To focus our attention on IDB predicates, a simplified *dependency graph* [19], an *IDB dependency graph* is introduced as follows.

Definition. An **IDB dependency graph** is a directed graph constructed as below. For each IDB predicate R, there is a vertex R in the graph. For the set of rules with head predicate R and defined solely by EDB predicates, we draw a small circle surrounding R (R is called a *circled node*). For each IDB predicate S in the body of a rule with the head predicate R, there is a directed edge $S \to R$. An edge or a circled node can be labeled by its corresponding rule identifier(s) when necessary.

4.1. Multiple Linear Recursions

A linear recursive chain rule is a *one-sided chain rule* if its body consists of a nonrecursive predicate joining with one side (one variable vector) of the recursive predicate. It is a *two-sided chain rule* if its body consists of two nonrecursive predicates, each joining with each side of the recursive predicate.

Example 4. We present an example of compiling an ML recursion (Fig. 6) in which each recursive rule is a one-sided chain rule. The example is taken from Han and Henschen [5].

(a_1) R :− A_1, R.	...	(a_i) R :− A_i, R.
(b_1) R :− R, B_1.	...	(b_j) R :− R, B_j.
(e_1) R :− E_1.	...	(e_k) R :− E_k.

Figure 6. A multiple linear (ML) recursion.

The IDB dependency graph of the recursion consists of multiple cycles shared with a single *pivot* (a **pivot** is a node shared by more than one cycle), as shown in Fig. 7.

The compilation of the recursion results in A^*EB^* where $E = E_1 \cup \cdots \cup E_k$, $A = A_1 \cup \cdots \cup A_i$, and $B = B_1 \cup \cdots \cup B_j$.

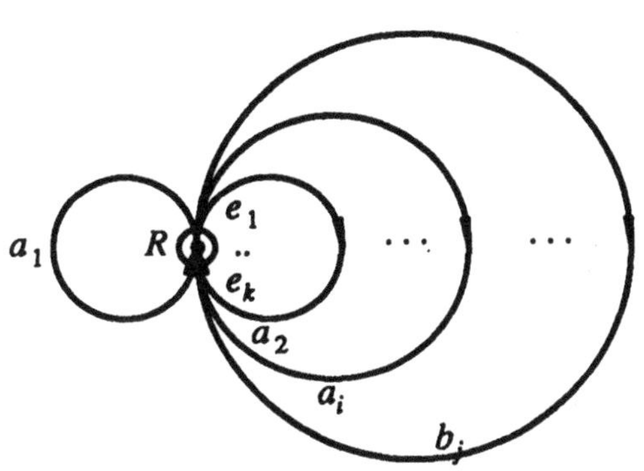

Figure 7. IDB dependency graph of the ML recursion.

Actually, even if there are some two-sided chain rules in such a recursion, it is still compilable to an AC if the relation at each side of every two-sided chain rule is contained in the union of the relations of the one-sided chain rules at that side. For example, if two two-sided recursive rules, "$R :- A_1, R, B_1.$" and "$R :- A_i, R, B_j.$", are added to the recursion of Fig. 7, the added rule will not change the compiled formula because all the tuples generated by expansions of the two-sided chain rules are contained in the formula. □

In general, we have

Theorem 3. (MLs in linear variable patterns) *An ML recursion in linear variable pattern can be compiled to AC if and only if each recursive rule in the recursion is a one-sided chain rule or the relation at each side of every two-sided chain rule is contained in the union of the relations of the one-sided chain rules at that side.*

Proof.

→ (if-part). Take the recursion in Fig. 6 as the typical case. The expansions of "$R :- A_1, R.$" and "$R :- A_2, R.$" derive the formula $(A_1^* A_2^*)^* R$, which is equivalent to $(A_1 \cup A_2)^* R$ according to Corollary 2. Obviously, it can be generalized to the case in which there are more than two such rules. Similarly, the compilation of the set of rules of (4c) derives $B = B_1 \cup \cdots \cup B_j$ associated with the other side of R. Therefore, the compiled formula is $A^* EB^*$. Similarly, if the relation at each side of every two-sided chain rule is contained in the union of the relations of the one-sided chain rules at that side (as shown in Ex. 4), all the synchronized tuples generated by two-sided recursions are contained in those generated by asynchronous chain recursions. Thus the resulting compiled formula remains the same.

← (only-if). We prove it by contradiction. If the relation at some side of a two-sided chain rule is not contained in the union of the relations of the one-sided chain rules at that side, some synchronized tuples generated by a two-sided recursion will not be contained in those generated by asynchronous chain recursions and cannot be processed without synchronization. Thus the recursion cannot be compiled to an AC. □

Example 5. A recursion consisting of a mixture of two-sided and one-sided chain rules may not be an AC. For example,

$$R :- A, R, B. \qquad R :- C, R. \qquad R :- E.$$

The compiled formula $R = \bigcup_{i=0}^{\infty}((C^* A)^i C^* E B^i)$ contains two synchronous chains. An interesting study of the evaluation of multiple linear recursions beyond the class of asynchronous chain recursions is in [9]. □

4.2. Mutual Recursions

It is challenging to compile mutual recursions. However, an important class of mutual recursions, *linear mutual recursion*, can be relatively easily compiled.

Definitions. A recursive rule is **linearly mutually recursive** if its body contains *exact one predicate* defined at the same deduction level as that of the head predicate, and the predicate is *not* the same as the head predicate. A set of rules forms a **linear mutual recursion** if it consists of linear mutual recursive rules, possibly some linear recursive rules, and one or more exit rules.

The IDB dependency graph of a linear mutual recursion contains cycles. A linear mutual recursion can be classified into the following five groups according to different kinds of cycles in its IDB dependency graph:

(1) *single cycle*: the graph consists of one cycle only;

(2) *multiple cycle, single pivot*: the graph consists of multiple cycles with only one *pivot*;

(3) *multiple cycle, ring pivots*: the graph consists of multiple cycles and the pivots form a ring along one cycle;

(4) *chain cycles*: the graph consists of a sequence of cycles which are connected as a chain, that is, each cycle is connected to two neighboring cycles except that at each end of the chain; and

(5) *complex cycle connections*: the graph cotains complex cycle connections beyond the above four classes.

In general, a lower numbered group can be considered as a special case of a higher numbered one. For example, Group 1 can be viewed as a special case of Group 2. However, in many cases, more efficient evaluation techniques can often be applied to a special class rather than a general one. We examine the compilation of linear mutual recursions group by group.

Example 6. The IDB dependency graph (Fig. 8) indicates its corresponding rule set (shown below) is in Group 1.

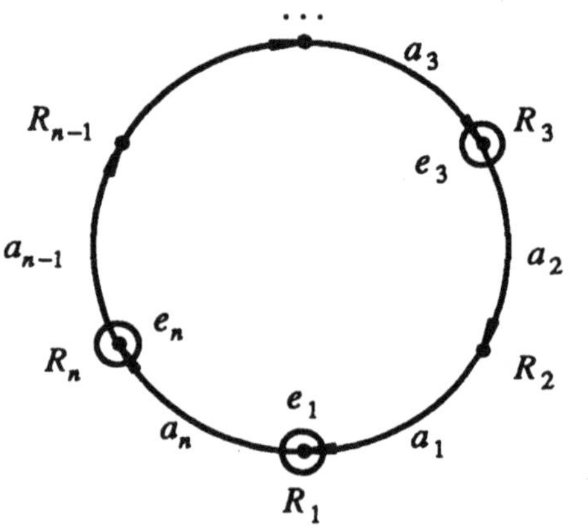

Figure 8. IDB dependency graph of a Group I recursion.

(a_1) $R_1 :- A_1, R_2.$
...
(a_n) $R_n :- A_n, R_1.$
(e_3) $R_3 :- E_3.$
(a_2) $R_2 :- A_2, R_3.$
(a_{n-1}) $R_{n-1} :- A_{n-1}, R_n.$
(e_1) $R_1 :- E_1.$
(e_n) $R_n :- E_n.$

The compilation is performed as follows. The set of compiled recursive rules of R_1 is the set of traversal paths starting at R_1 and going back to R_1 (without going through R_1 itself). There is only one such traversal path, "$a_1, a_2, ..., a_n$", in the IDB dependency graph, which indicates that the resolution is performed on the set of rules in the sequence of (a_1), with (a_2), ..., and with (a_n). Thus, there is one recursive rule *(5a)* which is obtained by performing a sequence of unifications of the recursive rules, that is, unifying R_i in the body with R_i in the head for $i = 2, ..., n-1$. The compiled exit rule of R_1 is a traversal from R_1 to a circled node without going through a cycle containing R_1. Since there are three circled nodes at R_1, R_3 and R_n, there are three such paths: "e_1", "a_1, a_2, e_3", and "$a_1, a_2, ..., a_{n-1}, e_n$". Therefore, the exit rule set of R_1 should contain three exit rules which can be unioned to one in the form of *(5b)*, where the notion "$R :- E_1; E_2; E_3.$" represents a set of exit rules, "$R :- E_1.$", "$R :- E_2.$", and "$R :- E_3.$".

(5a) $R_1 :- A_1, A_2, ..., A_n, R_1.$

(5b) $R_1 :- E_1;\ A_1, A_2, E_3;\ A_1, ..., A_{n-1}, E_n.$

Obviously, the compiled formula of R_1 is essentially a transitive closure

$$R_1 = (A_1 A_2 \cdots A_n)^* (E_1 \cup (A_1 A_2 E_3) \cup (A_1 ..., A_{n-1} E_n)).$$

The remaining IDB predicates in the clique can be derived from R_1 as shown below. Notice that the derivation of every other IDB predicate is a traversal from the corresponding IDB predicate to R_1.

(5c) $R_n :- A_n, R_1.$

. . . .

(5d) $R_2 :- A_2, ..., A_n, R_1.$ □

Theorem 4. *A Group I recursion is an AC if the nonrecursive predicates reside only at one side of the compiled recursive rule.*

Proof.

The IDB dependency graph of a Group I recursion consists of a single cycle. Suppose R_i is the head predicate and R_j the IDB predicate in the body of a rule. R_j can be defined either by a set of EDB predicates (when it is a circled node) or, otherwise, by another IDB predicate R_k, possibly with other EDB predicates. By resolution, the former generates a nonrecursive rule (with a set of EDB predicates in the body); while the latter generates a rule with the IDB predicate R_k in the body. Thus, the resolution on the whole cycle will generate one linear recursive rule with the IDB predicate R_i in the body (which is the compiled recursive rule), and a set of nonrecursive rules. If the nonrecursive predicates reside only at one side of the compiled rule, it can be compiled into a transitive closure. Thus, it is an AC. □

We examine Group 2 recursions. Example 2 is a Group 2 recursion, whose IDB dependency graph consists of multiple cycles with single pivot. By resolution, all the mutual recursions in Group 2 can be compiled into multiple linear recursions. Therefore, we have

Corollary 3. *A Group II recursion is an AC if the nonrecursive predicates reside at only one side in each cycle of the IDB dependency graph.*

We present an example of Group 3 recursion (*multiple cycle, ring pivots*).

Example 7. Let paternal and maternal ancestors be defined as in Fig. 9, where *PA* for *Paternal_Ancestor*, *MA* for *Maternal_Ancestor*, *F* for *Father*, and *M* for *Mother*.

(a_1) $MA :- M.$	(a_2) $MA :- M, MA.$
(a_3) $MA :- M, PA.$	(a_4) $PA :- F.$
(a_5) $PA :- F, MA.$	(a_6) $PA :- F, PA.$

Figure 9. Maternal/paternal ancestor recursion.

The IDB dependency graph of the recursion (Fig. 10) shows that it is in group 3. There are two cycles surrounding *MA*: (i) cycle a_2, and (ii) cycle $a_3 a_5$ on which there is one more cycle a_6. There are two exit paths for *MA*: (i) a_1, and (ii) a_3, possibly a cycle a_6 without going through *MA*, and then a_4. Thus we have,

$$
\begin{aligned}
MA &= (M \cup (M\ F^*\ F))^*\ ((M\ F+) \cup M) \\
&= (M \cup (M\ F+))^*\ ((M\ F^*) \\
&= (M\ F^*)^*\ ((M\ F^*) \\
&= (M\ F^*)^+ \\
&= M\ (M \cup F)^* \\
&= M\ P^*
\end{aligned}
$$

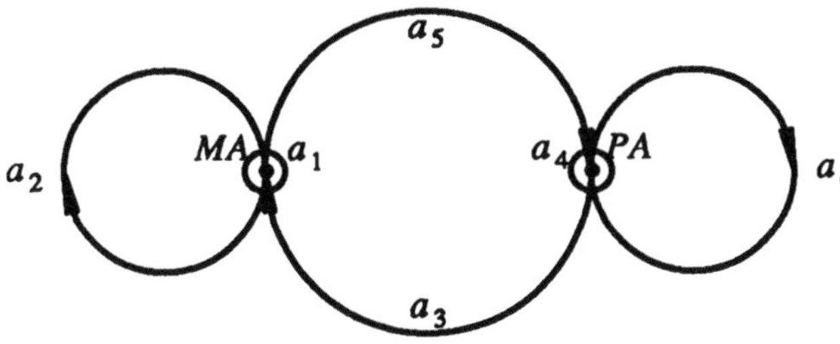

Figure 10. The IDB dependency graph of the recursion.

Notice that the transformation, "$(M\ F^*)^+ = M\ (M \cup F)^*$", is based on the nested closure transformation rules in Section 2. Let "$P = M \cup F$", where P is for *Parent*, and "*Parent* = *Father* ∪ *Mother*". The rule implies that *y is a maternal ancestor of x if y is x's mother or the mother of an ancestor of x.* Similarly, we have "$PA = F, P^*$". The compiled rule set is not only succint in semantics but also efficient in processing since there is only one transitive closure operation necessary. □

Other groups of linear mutual recursions can be compiled similarly. A detailed study of compilation and evaluation of linear mutual recursions is in [10].

4.3. Nonlinear Recursions

A general nonlinear recursion is not compilable to an AC, but some special ones are.

Example 8. Suppose R is defined by Fig. 6 and one nonlinear recursive rule,

(6) $R :- R, C, R, \ldots, C, R.$

where there are k R's and there is either a C between each pair of R's, or *no* C between any pair of R's. The n-th expansion on itself is in the form of $((RC)^{k-1})^n R$. The compiled formula of the recursion below shows that it is an AC.

$$R = ((A^* EB^* C)^{k-1})^* A^* EB^* .\ \square$$

From Ex. 8, we have

Theorem 5. (NLs in linear variable patterns) *An NL recursion in linear variable pattern can be compiled to an AC if each linear recursive rule in the recursion is a one-sided chain rule and there is only one nonlinear recursive rule in the form of (6d) in the recursion.*

The theorem provides a sufficient but not a necessary condition for compiling nonlinear recursions to ACs. It is easy to show that other nonlinear recursions may or may not be compilable to ACs. For example, it is not compilable to an AC by swapping exactly one C to D in (6) (where C ≠ D and k > 2). However, it is still compilable to an AC by adding to the recursion a nonlinear recursive rule,

$$R :- R, C, A, R, \ldots, C, A, A, R, B, B.$$

The rule happens to be an expanded rule of the original recursion. This is because the inclusion of such a rule will not change the compiled formula.

The compilation and evaluation of mutual recursions beyond linear ones can be treated in a way similar to nonlinear recursions. An interesting study on linearization of nonlinear recursions in nonlinear variable patterns is in [20].

4.4. Different-Level Recursions

There are also some interesting behaviors of different-level recursions related to ACs.

Example 9. A DL recursion of Fig. 11 can be compiled by first compiling the lower level recursion S and then treating the compiled formula as one EDB predicate in the compilation of the higher level recursion R.

$R :- R, S, A.$	$R :- E_1.$
$S :- B, S.$	$S :- E_2.$

Figure 11. A different-level recursion.

The compilation of S results in $B^* E_2$, and that of R results in $E_1(B^* E_2 A)^*$, which is still an AC. □

In general, we have

Theorem 6. (DL in linear variable patterns) *A DL (different-level) recursion is an AC if (1) the lowest level is compilable to an AC, and (2) every level other than the lowest level is compilable to an AC by treating the lower level recursive predicates as EDB predicates.*

Proof.

Each level of a recursion can be compiled by treating the lower level recursive predicates as EDB predicates. If each level can be compiled to an AC, the general compiled formula will contain asynchronous chains of chains, which is an AC. □

5. Query Processing in Asynchronous Chain Recursions

The compiled formulas of ACs span a wide spectrum, from simple transitive closures to complicated chains of chains. Since most frequently encountered chains of chains can be simplified to non-nested chains, our discussion is confined to the processing of non-nested chains.

Example 10. We examine the processing of a canonical ML recursion of Fig. 12.

(7a) $R(x,y,z,w) :- R(x_1,y,z,w), A(x,x_1).$
(7c) $R(x,y,z,w) :- R(x,y_1,z,w), B(y,y_1).$
(7d) $R(x,y,z,w) :- R(x,y,z_1,w), C(z,z_1).$
(7e) $R(x,y,z,w) :- E(x,y,z,w).$

Figure 12. A canonical ML recursion.

The compiled formula of the recursion consists of three asynchronous chains as below:

$$(8a) \quad R(x_0,y_0,z_0,w_0) = \bigcup_{i=0}^{\infty} \bigcup_{j=0}^{\infty} \bigcup_{k=0}^{\infty} ((A^i(x_0,x_i), B^j(y_0,y_j), C^k(z_0,z_k), E(x_i,y_j,z_k,w_0))$$

Since the three chains are independent of each other, it requires no chain synchronized processing. Thus it can be processed by transitive closure algorithms [2, 5, 16, 17]. However, in order to efficently evaluate vesatile queries on asynchronous chain recursions, different query processing strategies should be studied in detail. □

5.1. Quad-State Variable Binding Analysis

Versatile queries may have diverse instantiations and inquiries. An efficient query evaluation plan should be adaptible to versatile queries. Similar to [7], four states are associate to each variable in a query predicate based on the notion of *instantiation* and *inquiry*:

1. "p" — partially bound (instantiated and inquired),
2. "c" — query constant (instantiated but not inquired),
3. "u" — unbound (uninstantiated but inquired), and
4. "i" — irrelevant to the query (uninstantiated and not inquired).

We examine some versatile queries on the recursion *Know*.

Example 11. The predicate $Know(x,y)$ (Ex. 2) can be instantiated and inquired in many different ways. For example,

1. *"Is there anybody in AI group who knows something related to database?"*

(q_1) $?- Group(x, ai), Know(x, y), Related\_To(y, db).$

2. *"Print the names of the people in AI group who knows something related to database."*

(q_2) $?- Group(x, ai), Know(?x, y), Related\_To(y, db).$

3. *"Is there anyone who knows quack (a basic particle in Physics)? "*

(q_3) $?- Know(\_, quack).$

4. *"Print all the things that John knows."*

(q_4) $?- Know(john, ?y).$

Notice that a "?" mark is used in front of an inquired variable of a query to distinguish it from an uninquired one. The two arguments of *Know* are in the states of "c" and "c" in (q_1), "p" and "c" in (q_2), "i" and "c" in (q_3), and "c" and "u" in (q_4) respectively. □

A *distinguished variable* is a variable in the *head predicate* of a recursion. We classify distinguished variables of an asynchronous chain recursion into two categories: *chain-variables* and *exit-variables*. We refer the *near* end of a chain being the end of the chain linked to the exit expression in a compiled formula, and the *far* end of the chain is the other end of the chain. A *chain-variable* is the distinguished variable appearing in the *far end* of the chain, and an *exit variable* is the one appearing only in the exit expression. For example, in (8a), x_0, y_0 and z_0 are chain-variables, and w_0 is an exit-variable.

If there is more than one variable at the same end of a compiled chain, they should be folded (vectorized) into one vector for query analysis. We present the following folding rules.

(i) $c + u = p$,
(ii) $p + x = p$,
(iii) $x + i = x$, and
(iv) $x + x = x$

where $x \in \{c, p, u, i\}$ and "+" is a binary state-folding operator. Notice that "+" is commutative and associative. The folding of more than two variables at the same end of a chain can be done by repeatedly applying the folding rules.

5.2. Discard Irrelevant Chains in Query Processing

A chain of an AC is *irrelevant* to a query if and only if its folded chain-variable vector is in the state of "i". We show that query irrelevant chains should be discarded in the processing, that is, the number of transitive closures to be processed should be equivalent to the number of chains *relevant* to the query.

Lemma 1. (Discard Irrelevant Chains) *If the query is irrelevant to some chain vector of a canonical ML recursion, the answer to the query remains the same if the irrelevant chain is discarded in the processing.*

Proof.

Suppose the query is irrelevant to the C-chain of the formula (8a), i.e., z_0 is in the state of "i". If $(a, b, \_, d)$ is an answer to the query, it satisfies the formula regardless whether there is a C-chain in the formula. Therefore, the removal of the C-chain will not influence the correctness and completeness of the answer. □

This property can be demonstrated by (q_3) where the first argument is irrelevant to the query. The chain $Parent^*$ should be discarded in the processing.

Corollary. *If a query is irrelevant to all of the chain variables of an AC, its processing is confined to the set of exit rules only.*

5.3. Processing Directions

Since a query may be instantiated and inquired in different ways, the processing may proceed in different direction combinations. A general heuristic is that the processing should start at highly selective points. The precise processing plan should be determined by a quantitative analysis based on EDB statistics. We present the following four cases, which are also shown in two figures.

1. *Exit-chain processing*: If a query is highly selective at the exit-variables, processing should start at the center (E) and expand along the relevant chains.
2. *Chain-exit processing*: If all the query-relevant chain-variable vectors are highly selective, processing may start at each relevant chain and proceed in parallel towards the center.

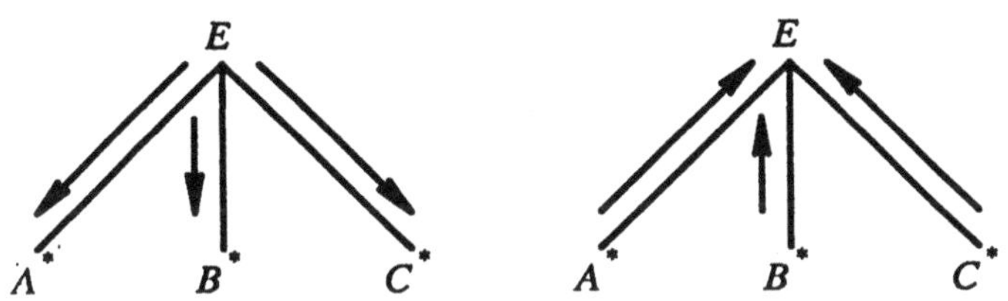

1) *Exit−chain processing* 2) *Chain−exit processing*

Figure 13. Exit-chain processing and chain-exit processing.

3. *Chain-exit-chain processing*: If the query provides highly selective information on some chain-variables, processing should start at those chain variables to derive the closures of such chains in parallel and merge those closures at the center (E). The merged results are used for the processing of other relevant chains.
4. *Bi-directional search only for "c"-"c" states*: If the query provides highly selective information on both ends of a chain, processing may start at both ends and perform a bi-directional search only when both ends are in the state of "c". Otherwise, a bi-directional search cannot guarantee the completeness of the answer by finding several meeting points.

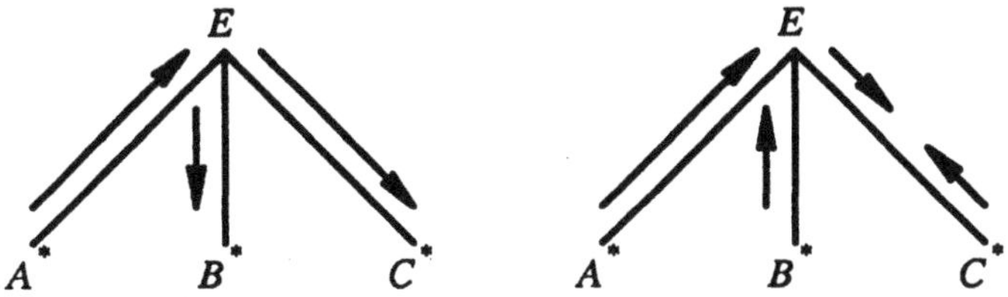

3) *Chain−exit−chain* 4) *Bi−directional*

Figure 14. Chain-exit-chain and bi-directional processing.

5.4. Processing Methods

Similar to n-chain recursions [7], there are four processing strategies for ACs:

1. A **nonrecursive strategy**, which uses only conventional nonrecursive (i.e., noniterative) algorithms. This is the case when all the chain variables are irrelevant to the query.
2. A **total closure strategy**, which derives the whole closure of a recursive relation. This is the case when all the variables are inquired but no instantiation information is provided.
3. A **query closure strategy**, which derives a query-related closure, i.e., the portion of the closure derivable from query constants; and
4. An **existence checking strategy**, which checks the existence of an answer in the database for either a driver set or each driver in a driver set. The search following a driver set or an individual driver terminates when it derives one answer or it determines that no such answer exists.

Furthermore, we distinguish *unary* algorithms from *binary* ones. A **unary algorithm** does not trace *driver* → *result* (i.e., *source* → *sink*) pairs in the processing while a **binary algorithm** does.

We provide the following algorithm selection table for the selection of binary vs. unary and query closure vs. existence checking algorithms. Notice that each state in the table is a folded state if there are more than one variable at the end of a chain.

State and Direction	Processing Algorithm
$c \rightarrow$	*unary*
$p \mid u \rightarrow$	*binary*
$\rightarrow c$	*existence checking*
$\rightarrow i$	**-portion of the chain discarded*
$\rightarrow p \mid u$	*query closure*

Table 1. Selection of processing algorithms for ACs

Theorem. 7. (Asynchronous chain processing theorem) *Table 1 represents the correct selection of algorithms for the processing of multiple asynchronous chains of an AC.*

Proof.

We prove the correctness of each entry in Table 1.

1. "c →" indicates that the processing starts at the end of a chain in the state of "c". Since the variable is instantiated but not inquired, it is unimportant to know that the value is derived from which initial drivers. Therefore, a unary algorithm can be used in the processing.
2. "p | u →" indicates that the processing starts at the end of a chain in the state of "p" or "u". Since the variable at the start end is inquired, the driver-result pair must be traced in the derivation in order to tell which driver derives what result or whether it may derive a result. Therefore, a binary algorithm must be used in the processing.
3. "→ c" indicates that the processing proceeds towards the end of a chain in the state of "c". Therefore, the processing started from a driver can terminate as long as the search determines whether the driver can derive an answer at the driven end. Therefore, an existence checking algorithm can be applied.
4. "→ i" indicates that the processing is irrelevant to the chain. The chain should be discarded according to Lemma 1. Notice that for a chain with +-portion, such as A^+, only the *-portion (A^*) is discarded. For example, for the formula BA^+, only BA need to be evaluated.
5. "→ p | u" indicates that the processing proceeds towards the end of a chain in the state "p" or "u" (inquired). Thus the processing must find all of the possible values at this end satisfying the query. Therefore, the query closure algorithm must be applied. □

Notice that in the analysis of queries on multiple asynchronous chains, the folding of variables may need to be performed across more than one chain, which is shown by the following example.

Example 12. Suppose for a query on the canonical ML recursion of Fig. 12, the state of A-chain is "p", that of B-chain is "i", that of C-chain is "u", and that of the exit variable is "c". Moreover, suppose the highly selective point of the query is at the chain variable of A-chain, that is, the processing should start at the A-chain. The processing can then be described by Fig. 15.

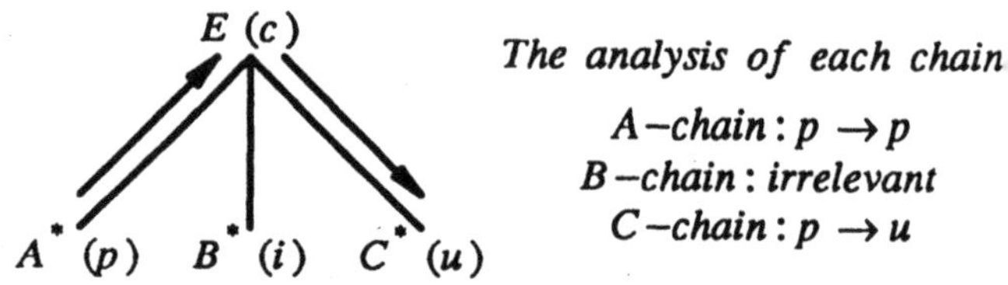

Figure 15. Query analysis for an AC.

As shown in Fig. 15, B-chain can be tossed away since it is irrelevant to the query. A-chain is characterized by "p → p" where the second "p" is obtained by folding the states of both the exit variable and the chain variable of the chain to be processed (i.e, C-chain), and "c + u = p". Simiarly, C-chain is characterized by "p → u" where "p" is obtained by folding the states of both the exit variable and the chain variable of the chain have been processed (i.e, A-chain), and "p + c = p". □

Finally, we study each query of Ex. 11 using our query analysis method.

Example 13. We analyze the queries in Ex. 12 using the above algorithm selection table.

1. In (q_1), the processing may start at both chain-variables. Both chains, *Parent** and *Derive**, are characterized by "c → c". Thus unary existence checking and bi-directional processing can be applied, i.e., the discovery of anybody in the AI group who knows something related to DB may terminate the query.
2. In (q_2), x is in the state of "p" and y is in "c". We may either (i) start at x and proceed toward the center and then to the other end of the chain where the search following each source driver x terminates as soon as it finds the first y satisfying the query (existence checking), or (ii) start at y and derive the query closure for the chain *Derive** ("c → p"), then start at x and for each source driver x the search terminates as soon as it finds the first y satisfying the query (existence checking). The search terminates when everyone in the AI group is examined (verified that he/she knows something or nothing related to DB).
3. In (q_3), the processing should start at the second argument. The first chain is irrelevant to the query, thus ignored in the processing. The second chain is characterized by "c → i", which should be processed using the unary existence checking algorithm. That is, processing terminates as soon as we find "quack" in "*Discover Derive** ".
4. In (q_4), the processing is chain-exit-chain processing. Both chains are characterized by "c → u" and requires the query closure algorithm. The processing starts at "*john* ", derives all of his ancestors, crosses *Discover*,

and then processes the second chain $Derive^*$ to derive all the things derivable from those discovered by John and his ancestors. It involves the processing of two transitive closures. □

6. Conclusion

We have studied an important class of function-free recursions, asynchronous chain recursions, whose compiled formulas consist of single-chain or asynchronous chains. Our study shows that many interesting function-free recursions can be compiled to asynchronous chain recursions and processed by transitive closure query processing strategies. Versatile queries on asynchronous chain recursions should be analyzed by the quad-state variable binding analysis.

Asynchronous chain recursions represent an important class of recursions which can be processed using efficient query evaluation methods. The study of the compilation of different classes of function-free recursions in complex variable patterns to asynchronous chain recursions and the exploration of other classes of complex recursions which can be processed by efficient query evaluation methods are interesting topics for the future research.

References

1. A. Aho and J. D. Ullman, Universality of Data Retrieval Languages, *Proc. 6th ACM Symp. Principles of Programming Languages*, San Antonio, Texas, January 1979, 110–120.
2. F. Bancilhon and R. Ramakrishnan, An Amateur's Introduction to Recursive Query Processing Strategies, *Proc. 1986 ACM-SIGMOD Conf. Management of Data*, Washington, DC, May 1986, 16–52.
3. C. Beeri, P. Kanellakis, F. Bancilhon and R. Ramakrishnan, Bounds on the Propagation of Selection into Logic Programs, *Proc. 6th ACM Symp. Principles of Database Systems*, San Diego, CA, March 1987, 214–226.
4. C. Beeri and R. Ramakrishnan, On the Power of Magic, *Proc. 6th ACM Symp. Principles of Database Systems*, San Diego, CA, March 1987, 269–283.
5. J. Han and L. J. Henschen, Handling Redundancy in the Processing of Recursive Database Queries, *Proc. 1987 ACM-SIGMOD Conf. Management of Data*, San Francisco, CA, May 1987, 73–81.
6. J. Han and W. S. Luk, What Kinds of Recursions Can Be Processed by Transitive Closure Strategies?, in Z.W. Ras and L. Saitta (eds.), *Methodologies for Intelligent Systems, 3, North-Holland, 1988, 170–179.*
7. J. Han, Multi-Way Counting Method, *Information Systems*, **14**(3), 1989, 219–229.
8. J. Han, Compiling General Linear Recursions by Variable Connection Graph Analysis, *Computational Intelligence*, **5**(1), 1989, 12–31.
9. J. Han and L. Liu, Efficient Evaluation of Multiple Linear Recursions, *IEEE Trans. Software Engineering*, **17**(12), 1991, 1241–1252.
10. J. Han, Compilation and Evaluation of Linear Mutual Recursions, *Information Sciences*, **56**, 1992.
11. L. J. Henschen and S. Naqvi, On Compiling Queries in Recursive First-Order Databases, *J. ACM*, **31**(1), 1984, 47–85.
12. Y. E. Ioannidis and R. Ramakrishnan, Efficient Transitive Closure Algorithms, *Proc. 14th Int. Conf. Very Large Data Bases*, Long Beach, CA, August 1988, 382–394.
13. Y. E. Ioannidis and E. Wong, Towards an Algebraic Theory of Recursion, *J. ACM*, **38**(2), 1991, 329–381.
14. B. Jiang, A Suitable Algorithm for Computing Partial Transitive Closures, *Proc. 6th Int. Conf. Data Engineering*, Los Angeles, CA, February 1990, 264–271.
15. J. Minker and J. M. Nicolas, On Recursive Axioms in Relational Databases, *Information Systems*, **8**(1), 1983, 1–13.
16. J. F. Naughton, One-Sided Recursions, *Proc. 6th ACM Symp. Principles of Database Systems*, San Diego, CA, March 1987, 340–348.
17. J. F. Naughton, Compiling Separable Recursions, *Proc. 1988 ACM-SIGMOD Conf. Management of Data*, Chicago, IL, June 1988, 312–319.
18. J. D. Ullman, *Principles of Database and Knowledge-Base Systems, Vol. 1*, Computer Science Press, Rockville, MD, 1988.
19. J. D. Ullman, *Principles of Database and Knowledge-Base Systems, Vols. 1 & 2*, Computer Science Press, Rockville, MD, 1989.
20. W. Zhang, C. T. Yu and D. Troy, Necessary and Sufficient Condition to Linearize Doubly Recursive Programs in Logic Databases, *ACM Trans. Database Syst.*, **15**(3), 1990, 459–482.

OBJECT-ORIENTED AND ADVANCED DATABASE SYSTEMS

METHOD MAINTENANCE ISSUES IN DYNAMIC OBJECT-ORIENTED DATABASES

Hyoung-Joo Kim, Suk-Ho Lee
Dept. of Computer Engineering
Seoul National University
San 56-1, Shinlim-dong Kwanak-gu
Seoul, Korea

and

Hernan Astudillo R.
College of Computing
Georgia Institute of Technology
Atlanta GA30332

ABSTRACT

Object-oriented database schemas are dynamically modified because object-oriented database applications are dynamically evolving. As schema definitions are modified, existing methods for previous schemas may not be valid. It is important to be able to achieve compatibility of methods in the face of changing schemas. In this paper, we analyze the effects of schema changes on object-oriented database methods in order to come up with a reasonable framework for method coversion.

1 Introduction

Object-oriented databases, originally developed to meet the specific needs for computer-aided design and manufacturing (CAD/CAM)[1] also becoming increasingly important as a means for reusing software description [6].

Most of object-oriented systems allow for *object* to be defined in terms of *classes*. These classes define *members*, which are either *methods* (procedures) or *instance variables*. Classes may *inherit* members from other classes [5]. This inheritance relationship defines a *class lattice*. This set of graph, classes and class members make the *schema*.

In most of their target areas(CAD, CAM, exploratory programming), object-oriented applications must support a working style where schema changes are rather frequent and with potentially far-reaching effects (such as invalidating previously valid source code). Schema changes and schema invariants have been studied elsewhere [3] but the effect of schema changes on class members has not received that much attention.

In some cases the consistency of a member can be automatically restored, but in other cases no such option is available. Most of the schema changes do not affect variables, but we will use a uniform treatment for both variables and methods. A very useful tool would be one that allowed the schema manipulator to evaluate quickly the impact of his/her changes on the validity of all the already existing source code.

This paper proposes a mechanism for providing automatic support to evaluate the side effects of programmer modifications to the schema on the validity of existing source code. We make the following assumptions:

- syntactic and semantic errors in source code are detected by other tools, like compilers or checkers; i.e. the system only accepts source code that is valid.
- our mechanism only *detects* newly created invalid situations, but it does not take any actions by itself. Hence, it might be applied to do anything from advise the programmer to force recompilations of invalid components.
- programs cannot modify the schema directly; programmers must do it by themselves.

Since the system does not accept invalid source code, all source code is valid in the absence of changes. Clearly, changes may (and do) affect this situation, and our mechanism indicates to the programmer which code may have become invalid and why. *We are only concerned with changes to the validity of source code previously valid.*

The paper is organized an follows: Section 2 develops a simple but general enough framework for object-oriented systems; Section 3 extends on the requirements for the validity of the code in the schema; Section 4 describes the higher-level structures used for registering the information necessary to determine the validity for code and the effect of schema changes on it; Section 5 describes in detail schema changes and how they affect the validity of methods; Section 6 presents some examples of schema changes and hypothetical system reaction to them; Section 7 illustrates a possible implementation of the validity information structures; finally, Section 8 gives the conclusion and delineates future work.

2 Schema Model

In this section we discuss the programming model and the schema entities. The database under study stores definitions and instances of classes. These classes are written in some language where the main data type are typed *references*, which may denote any instance. The type (class)[1] of the reference restricts this instance to belong to this class or to any of its subclasses. A class can redefine some or all of the members

[1] In this paper, *class*, *type* and *domain* will be interchanged freely, even if it may not be the most puristic approach.

that is inherits. (Allowing only references as data is particularly well suited to languages like Smalltalk [2] or Eiffel [4], but it can also be applied to subsets of languages like C++ [7].)

The schema entities are the class lattice, the classes and their members. Classes provide templates for building instances, and their members define the data and operations available to each instance. The declaration of each member is separated into two parts: definition and implementation.

2.1 Class Lattice

The class lattice is a rooted and connected directed acyclic graph (DAG), with nodes corresponding to classes and edges indicating inheritance.

Multiple inheritance allows for a class to inherit members defined in one or more classes (hereafter called its *ancestor* classes).

2.2 Class Definition

Each class is identified only by its (unique) literal name (i.e. a string). Notice that this does not imply dynamic binding or interpretation, since the mechanism here proposed allows to preserve type consistency in the presence of schema changes in a system with static binding.

The class definition indicates its ancestor classes and contains a set of definitions for its local members (defined shortly). Members can be either *inherited members*(i.e. defined in some ancestor class) or *local members*(i.e. defined in the current class). The set of all members of a class (except the ambiguous and redefined ones, see nest subsection) is called the *scope* of the class. Each local member has a *signature* (definition) and a (possibly null) *body* (implementation).

Members can be *methods* or *instance variables*. A method describes a procedure that is applicable to all instances of the class. An instance variable describes a reference that can be found in all instance of the class.

2.3 Member Definition

Each member signature consists of a fixed number of parameters (possibly zero) and a result; for the purpose of our mechanism, instance variables can be treated as parameterless members. We will use the following notation:

- method definition:
  $< member > (< listofparameters >) :< result >$

Each *parameter* is a pair $< label, domain >$, where each label is a unique literal and each domain is the name of a class. The *result* of the member is the name of a class. Languages where arguments are positional rather than named can be dealt with by replacing the label with its positional index.

Each local member has a name unique in its class (i.e. all local members have different names). This implies that two types of name conflict can occur:

- among inherited members:
  The conflicting members are not added to the scope of the class. To reference such a member, a *long name* like $C.M$ must be used, where M is the member name and C is the name of some ancestor class where the desired does belong to the scope. (The class C does not need to be the class where the member was originally defined.)
- among local and inherited members:
  The local member "hides" all conflicting inherited members, i.e. all calls to this member are understood to mean the newly defined local member. The inherited members are still accessible, but a long name must be used for them.

2.4 Member Implementation

For generality, we consider instance variables as methods with an empty body. Instead, method bodies are sequences of statements in some programming language. Without loss of generality, we will consider that this language has only *references* as data type. Methods can have *local references*, and can also access the instance variables. There are only two operations:

- assignment:
  $< reference >:=< expression >$
  (an *expression* is a method call or a reference)
- method call:
  $< reference > . < member > (< listofarguments >)$
  (each *argument* is a pair $< label, reference >$; and the *member* denotes unambiguously a method.

A member name M may be prefixed by a class name C using $C :: M$; if no prefix is given in the source code, the current class is assumed.

This model is less restrictive that it seems to be, because assignment and method call are enough to model complex control structures [8].

We will see in the following section the requirements that the schema components must meet and maintain to represent a valid software system.

3 Validity of Schema

A schema will be said *valid* iff the followings hold:

1. the class lattice is valid
2. each class definition is valid
3. each member definition is valid
4. each member implementation is valid

To make this definition meaningful, we need to precise the above enumerated terms.

As explained before, we assumed that no invalid components (say syntactically or semantically incorrect) are accepted to the system, so we do not care of this aspect of validity.

3.1 Validity of Class Lattice

The changes to a class lattice and the invariants to be maintained have been thoroughly reviewed in [3]. We propose the following invariants:

1. the class lattice is a rooted and connected DAG
2. all classes have a distinct name
3. all members of a class scope have a distinct name
4. all members of a class scope have a unique origin
5. all members of a class scope have one (or no) implementation
6. a class inherits *all* members from its superclasses (possibly redefining some of them)

This paper does not go further regarding the integrity of the class lattice, but it concentrates on the novel aspects of the maintenance of components integrity.

3.2 Validity of Class Definition

A class definition is valid if:

1. all local members have a distinct name
2. all member definitions are valid

This definition entails that a class definition may be valid even if its implementation might be wrongful, or perhaps unexistent!! This allows to check for and maintain the validity of new source code even before any of the members it calls be actually implemented. This property of encapsulation is extremely important when developing large software systems.

3.3 Validity of Member Definition

A member definition is valid if:

1. all parameters have a distinct label
2. all parameters have an existing domain
3. the result has an existing domain

The enforcement of distinct label can be done by mere inspection of the source code of the class. However, the *existence* of the domains of the parameters and result can only be derived by inspecting the schema. Our efforts are directed to simplify and make feasible the enforcement of this property at any point in the schema evolution (excepts perhaps in some necessary intermediate states).

3.4 Validity of Member Implementation

A member implementation is valid if:

1. it matches its signature
2. all local references have an existing domain
3. all assignments are valid
4. all method calls are valid

To deal with type-compatibility problem, we introduce the notion of *fitness*. An expression E is said to *fit* to a reference R if the domain of E is the same as or a subclass of the domain of R (remember that an expressing is either a reference of a member call). Similarly, a class C_i fits to a class C_j iff C_i is the same as or a subclass of C_j.

In other words, fitness determines when an object of a given class is also "acceptable" in another class.

We are now ready to define the validity of the parts of a member body. As before, we assume syntactic correctness:

1. an *assignment* < *reference* >:=< *expression* > is valid if:
   - the expression fits the reference
2. a *member call* is valid if:
   - the called member is indeed a member of its prefix class (of the current class if there is no prefix class in the source code)
   - the number of call arguments and of called member parameters are equal
   - for each parameter there is one argument with equal label, where the argument domain fits to the parameter domain

The scope of names is static, in the sense that all references and calls in a member body are understood in the context of the class where it was defined, not of the class where it is called from.

In the next section we study the possible schema changes and how they may affect the validity of schema components.

4 Taxonomy of Schema Changes

This section presents a simple classification of the changes that a programmer can make to an existing, valid schema.

4.1 Changes to the Class Lattice

1. add class C
2. delete class C (like in [3], all ancestors of C become ancestors of C's descendants)
3. rename class C as D (considered as deletion of C followed by insertion of D)
4. add a class as ancestor of another
5. remove a class from the ancestors of another

4.2 Changes to a Class Definition

1. add local method
2. delete local method
3. rename local method

4.3 Changes to a Member Definition

1. change result domain
2. add parameter
3. delete parameters
4. change parameter name
5. change parameter domain

4.4 Changes to a Member Implementation

Since the validity of member calls is derived only from the called members definition, the alteration of implementation source code doesn't affect any other component. These changes might be plausibly followed by recompilation (or at least re-generation of the validity information), but that triggering is beyond the scope of this paper.

5 Structures for Side Effects Detection

We have seen the criteria used for assessing the validity of a schema component. These criteria can be used to detect side effects of schema changes, but this requires the the bookkeeping of cross references. We define a minimal set of structures per schema component, which allows to detect when some cross references become void (signaling newly invalid schema components).

As an aside, this approach also has the advantage that an implementation of our mechanism can be object-oriented, by considering each kind of schema component as a class by itself.

From the discussion in previous sections, the following cross information must be kept (explicitly or derivable):

1. domain existence
2. domain fitting
3. member existence
4. argument/parameter label matching
5. argument/parameter domain fitting

The "tables" defined in the following subsections do not need to be implemented as such, but they can be derivable from some other stored data.

5.1 Tables for the Class Lattice

For the class lattice, the following tables are kept:

- *ancestor*
  Each entry $< C_i, C_j >$ indicates that class C_i is a direct ancestor of C_j.

5.2 Tables for each Class

For each class C_i, the following tables are kept:

- *members*:
  Each entry $< M_j, S_j >$ indicates that member M_j is locally defined in class C_i with signature S_j. The signature is in some format (text, tokenized, etc.) that allows to determine the fitting calls to it.

- *member aliases*:
  Each entry $< M_j, C_k :: M_k >$ indicates that member M_j of class C_i *denotes*(i.e. is an "alias" of) the member M_k defined locally in class C_k (clearly, if C_i has not inherited M_j from C_k, then both C_i and C_k will be the same). This table maps all member names "known" to C_i into the actual members they denote.

5.3 Tables for each Member

For each member M_j, the following tables are kept:

- *parameter domains*:
  Each entry $< C_k >$ indicates a class C_k that is the domain of a member parameter.

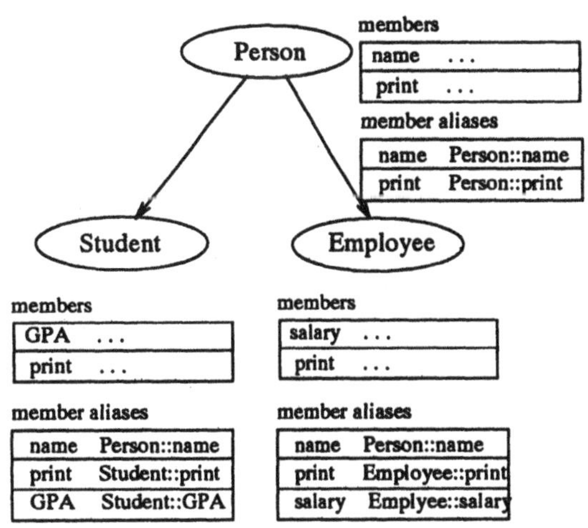

Figure 1: Example of Table Contents

- *result domain*:
  An entry $< C_k >$ indicates a class C_k that is the domain of the member result.

- *reference domains*:
  Each entry $< C_k >$ indicates a class C_k that is the domain of a local variable of the member body.

- *call prefixes*:
  Each entry < C_k > indicates a class C_k that is the prefix a member call in the member body.

- *body calls*:
  Each entry < $C_k :: M_k$ > indicates that the body source code of member M_j contains a call to member M_k of class C_k. (Notice that M_k may be just an alias for a member inherited by C_k from another class, but this is transparent to the calling member M_j.) As indicated before, the local class is assumed by default.

5.4 Example of Table Contents

Figure 1 illustrates the use of these structures to describe a simple schema, where class *Person* has subclasses *Student* and *employee*.

We will expand on this example later, but for now let's just remember that the fact that it is stored implies that is has been checked for syntactic and semantic validity.

All of these structures are updated every time that a schema components is compiled or checked, detecting side effects and alerting of possible invalidity situations. The next section explains how schema changes reflect in updates to these tables.

6 Detecting Side Effects of Schema Changes

When the mechanism detects a newly created situation that a schema component invalid, two things are done:

- *mark* the components as invalid, for modification by the programmer (and recompilation if needed)
- *suggest* a possible solution to the programmer (e.g. disambiguated calls to a given member)

The following subsection classify the change to the schema and for each change explain how the tables are updated, how the validity checking is done (and propagated if needed), and the action performed upon detection of invalid situations.

6.1 Changes to the Class Lattice

1. Create class C
   The only way effect of this creation of new structures; there are no side effects on other schema components.

   - create empty "members" and "member aliases" tables for C

2. Delete class C
   The deletion of a class has a double effect: where it is used as a domain, and where its members are call. To simplify the validity checking, the schema updating and checking are performed incrementally.

   - for each class C_i ancestor of C:
     apply class "drop ancestor" to drop C_i as ancestor of C (three operations trigger further checking)
   - for each class C_i descendant of C:
     apply "add ancestor" using all ancestor as C as new ancestors for C_i (those operations trigger further checking)
   - for each local "member" M_i from C:
     apply "delete local member" to delete M_i from C (those operations trigger further checking)
   - for each member M_i where C is a "parameter domain" or "result domain":
     mark the definition of M_i; no suggestion can be done
   - for each member M_i where C is a "reference domain" or a "call prefix":
     mark the implementation of M_i;no suggestion can be done

3. Rename class C_{old} as C_{new}
   simple updating of table entries is not enough, because in the process some name conflicts can appear; instead, the updating and validity checking are done incrementally.

   - create empty "members" and "member aliases" tables for C_{new}
   - for each class C_i ancestor C_{old}:
     apply "add ancestor"C_i and then apply "drop ancestor" C_i from C_{old}
   - for each class C_i ancestor of C_{old}:
     apply "drop ancestor" C_{old} from C_i and then apply "add ancestor" C_{new} to C_i (these operations trigger further checking)
   - for each local member M_i of C_{old}:
     apply "add local member" M_i to C_{new} and then apply "delete local member" M_i from C_{old} (these operations trigger further checking)
   - for each member M_i where C_{old} is a "parameter domain" or a "result domain":
     mark the definition of M_i; suggest to replace C_{old} with C_{new} in the source code
   - for each member M_i where C_{old} is a "reference domain" or a "call prefix":
     mark the implementation of M_i;suggest to replace C_{old} with C_{new} in the source code

4. Add ancestor A to class C
   Some names can now conflict (e.g. a member with the same happens to be inherited from two ancestors) and then reference must become explicitly disambiguated.

   - update the "member aliases" table of C to reflect the newly inherited members (remember that only local member s and unambiguous inherited members join this table; conflicting inherited members are not aliased)
   - for each alias M_i that was eliminates from the "member aliases" table of C(i.e. all inherited members that were unambiguous but now have conflicts):
     mark all members M_i where M_i is "called member"; suggest to disambiguate the original call

- for all descendants C_i to C:
  apply "add ancestor" C to C_i (the only effect of this will be to propagate any conflicts down the class lattice)

5. Drop ancestor A of class C
   Members inherited from A will become undefined in C and its descendants; also, C won't fit to A, nor will C's descendants.

   - update the "member aliases" table of C to eliminate the formerly inherited members and to add inherited members that have become unambiguous
   - for each name M_i that was eliminated from the "member aliases" table of C
     mark all member M_j where M_i is a "called member"; no suggestion can be done
   - for each member M_i where C is a "parameter domain" or their "result domain":
     apply "change parameter (result) domain" to M_i (this will propagate the fitness checking to all calls of M_i)
   - for each member M_i where C is a "reference domain" or "call prefix":
     check for fitness (remember that C will fit only if it is still a descendant of the class of the receiving reference or parameter); if check fails, mark the method implementation; no suggestion can be done

   - for all descendant C_i of C:
     apply "drop ancestor" C from C_i (this will propagate any aliases updates down the class lattice)

6.2 Changes to a Class Definition

1. Create local member M in class C
   The name M may become ambiguous in some descendant of C (due to multiple inheritance); or the new member M may hide some inherited M, forcing its caller to explicit naming.

   - create empty tables "parameter domains", "result domain", "reference domains","call prefixes" and "body calls"
   - update the "member aliases" table of C by removing M as alias of any inherited member (which becomes hidden) and defining instead M as alias C::M
   - for each alias M_i that was redefined in the "member aliases" table:
     check all members M_i where M_i is a "called member" to ensure that calls to M_i are still valid; if they are not, mark; no suggestion can be done

2. Delete local member M of class C
   member M will become undefined in C and its descendants.

   - update the "member aliases" table of C by removing M as alias of C::M; if there is an unambiguous inherited member C::M, then define M as its alias (i.e. a hidden member becomes visible)
   - if alias M was eliminated from the "member aliases" table of C:
     since now M is ambiguous, mark all members M_i where M is a "called member"; no suggestion can be done
   - if alias M was redefined in the 'member aliases" table of C:
     since now M denotes a different member, check all members M_i where M is a "called member" to ensure that calls to M are still valid; if they are not, mark; no suggestion can be done

3. Rename local member M_{old} of class C as M_{new}
   Since a member is identified only by its name, renaming it is equivalent to creating a new member and deleting the old one.

   - apply "create local member" M_{new}, with same parameters and result as M_{old}(this will take any name conflicts and hiding)
   - apply "delete local member" M_{old} (this will take care of any call to M_{old}

6.3 Changes to a Member Definition

1. Change result domain of member M of class C

   - modify "members" table of C to reflect the new signature
   - check the value returned in M implementation; if it does not fit M result domain anymore, mark M implementation; suggest changing returned value to fit result domain
   - for each member M_i where M is a "called member":
     check all calls to M for fitness to their assignments or parameters; mark those that are not valid anymore; suggest to change the use of the member

2. Add/Delete parameter in member M of class C

   - modify "members" table of C to reflect the new signature
   - mark the implementation of M (necessarily invalid); suggest updating to new parameter list
   - for each member M_i where M is a "called member":
     check all calls to M for parameter/argument call to new signature

3. Change parameter name in member M of class C

   - modify "members" table of C to reflect the new signature

- check the use of the old parameter in the implementation of M; if any is found, mark M implementation; suggest changing the old parameter by the new one
- for each member M_i where M is a "called member":
  mark M_i implementation (which uses the old parameter name in the call arguments); suggest changing the old parameter name by the new one in the call

4. Change parameter domain in member M of class C
   - modify "members" table of C to reflect the new signature
   - check the use of the parameter in the implementation of M; if any is found, check that they still fit; if some does not, mark M implementation; suggest changing the old use of the parameter
   - for each member M_i where M is a "called member": check all calls to M for fitness of the argument to the parameter; mark those M_i with calls that are not valid anymore; suggest changing the argument

7 Examples

In this section we present a series of changes performed to the original schema shown in Figure 1 and illustrate how these changes are reflected in the proposed tables.

7.1 Multiple Inheritance

In Figure 1, two subclasses of Person were identified, namely Student and Employee. If we now decide to allow for a Person to be both a Student and an Employee at a time (say working as a Teaching Assistant), a new class Assistant can be created, which inherits the members from both classes. Ambiguity appears here in two forms:

- Both superclasses of Assistant provide a member Print, so according to out rules no implicit alias is generated for Print; any attempt to use these members must be distinguished.

- The Name is unique, despite being inherited from both superclasses, because they both denote the same member $< Person, name >$; thus the ambiguity is just apparent.

The resulting schema and the updated members and aliases tables are shown in Figure 2.

7.2 Class Renaming

If a class is renamed (say, Person becomes Active), then its members are inherited by its former subclasses, but under its new name. In Figure 3 the updated tables show the new meaning for the aliases.

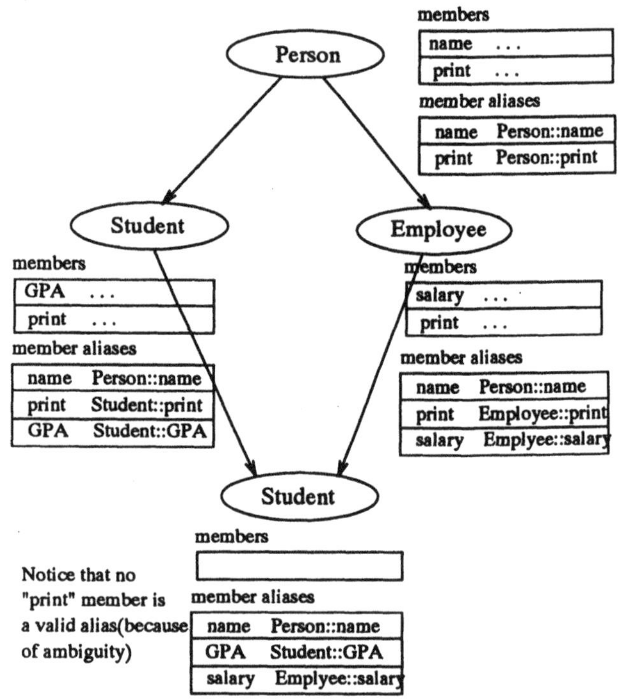

Figure 2: Multiple Inheritance

7.3 Creation of New Classes

Now we go into a bolder change to the schema. We will define a Person as either an Active or as a Retired, with proper members for ad-hoc printing. Here, Active is the renamed class of the previous example. Figure 4 shows the schema right after creating the two new classes.

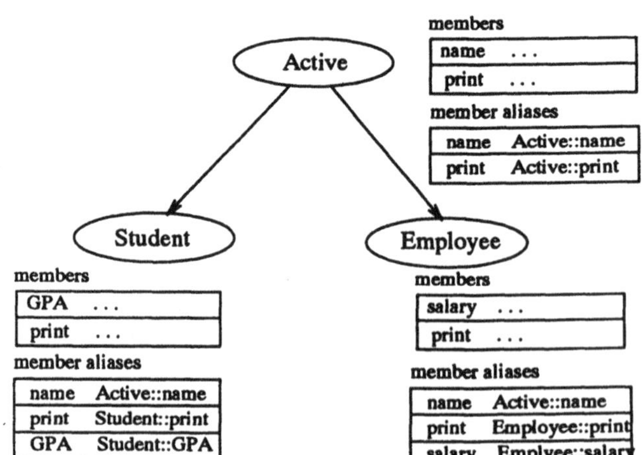

Figure 3: Class Renaming

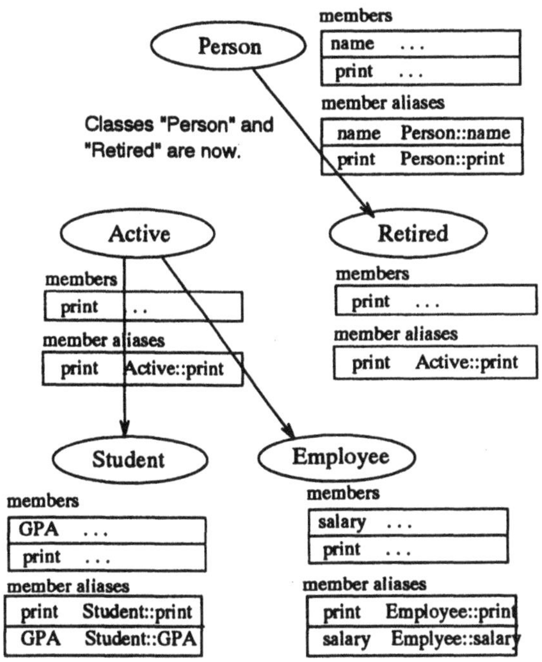

Figure 4: Creation of New Classes

7.4 Addition of Another Superclass

In this step, we add the just created class Person as superclass of Active, and this changes the aliases down the inheritance hierarchy, as shown in Figure 5.

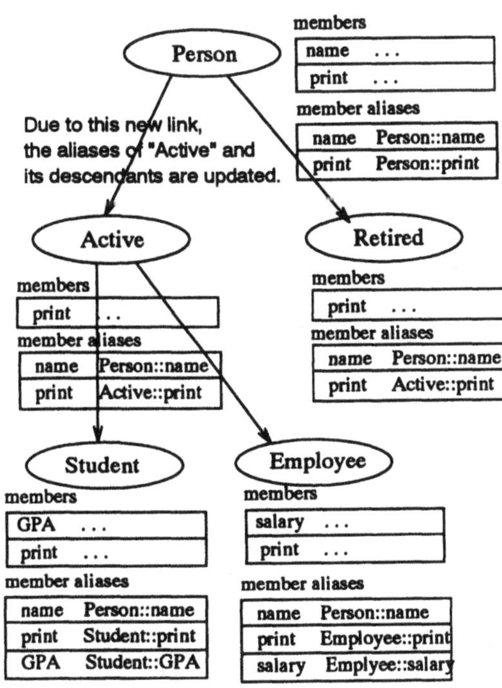

Figure 5: Addition of Another Superclass

7.5 Deletion of a Member

Finally, if the member "print" is deleted from class Active, the schema and the associated tables are modified as detailed in Figure 6.

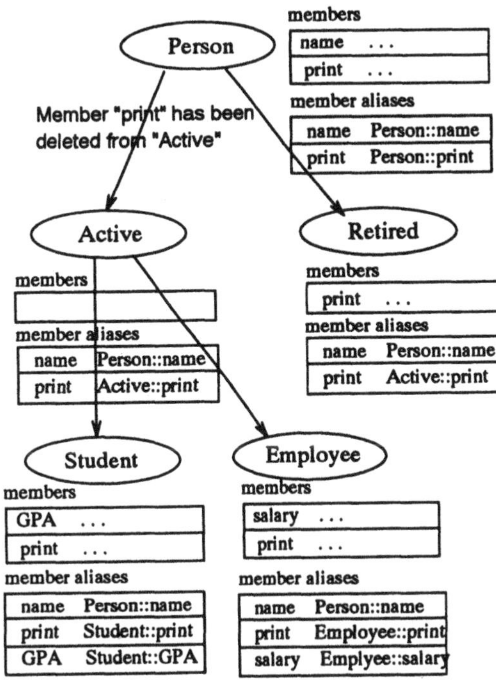

Figure 6: Addition of Another Superclass

8 Conclusion

Several of the described changes point to the need of keeping track of the validity of *expressions* through schema changes. However, if the only allowed means of class interaction are inheritance and messages (even for constructing objects), then this mechanism is powerful enough to take account of *all* effects of schema changes on the validity of member implementations.

References

[1] F. Bancilhon. "Object-Oriented Database Systems". In *Proceedings 7th ACM SIGART/SIGMOD/SIGACT Symposium on Principles of Database Systems*, December 1987.

[2] A. Goldberg and D. Robson. *Smalltalk 80: The Language and its Implementation.* Addison-Wesley, 1983.

[3] H.J. Kim J. Banerjee, W. Kim and H. Korth. "Semantics and Implementation of Schema Evolution in Object-Oriented Databases". In *Proceedings of ACM SIGMOD'87*, pages 311–322, December 1987.

[4] B. Meye. *Object-Oriented Software Construction.* Prentice Hall, 1988.

[5] B. Meyer. "Genericity versus Inheritance". *ACM SIGPLAN Noices*, (11):391–405, November 1986.

[6] B. Meyer. "Reusability: The Case for Object-Oriented Design". *IEEE Software*, (2):50–64, March 1987.

[7] B. Stroustroup. *The C++ Programming Language.* Addison-Wesley, 1986.

[8] D. Ungar and R. Smith. "Self: The Power of Simplicity". In *OOPSLA'87 Conference Proceedings*, pages 227–247, December 1987.

NICE-OS: an object server for persistent programming in NICE-C++*

E. Vittori, N.Le Thanh, G. Mopolo, S. Miranda

University of NICE- CNRS, I3S, 250 Avenue A.Einstein, bat. 4,
06560 Sophia-Antipolis - Valbonne, FRANCE
Tel. (33) 92 94 26 28 - telex GRP 970 006 - télécop. (33) 92 94 28 98

ABSTRACT :

This paper presents the NICE-OS object server of the system NICE-C++, an environment for persistent programming with the C++ language. NICE-OS has four main goals : persistent object management, multi-device storage, efficient access, and multi-user environment. This object server implements logical independance of the NICE-C++ persistency model. It can be used for supporting other object programming model. On the first hand NICE-OS is an object manager and on the other hand a set of tools for persistent programming in C++ language.

I - INTRODUCTION

Persistent programming [2), 3)] consists in introducing into a programming language the capability of defining and manipulating data whose life time is longer than those of the active programs which manipulate them.

Making a language persistent involves on one hand the definition of a model of persistency integration within the target language, and on the other hand designing a persistent data management system dedicated to the persistency model, for example Ps-Algol [19)].

Object programming approach [10),16)] can be seen as a new programming style increasing program quality by spliting program complexity between several software components called objects. So, it provides a support for integrating persistency within a uniform programming methodology. This approach has been studied in several works such as: E [20)], O++ [1)], Presto[9)] PC++[18)] which are based upon C++ language extensions.

Our work is included into this trend. It aims at designing and implementing a persistent object programming environment founded on C++ and called NICE-C++.

Regarding the above mentionned works, originality of our approach focus on the following three key points [17)]:

- NICE-C++ persistency model supports association links between persistent classes;
- its associated object server called NICE-OS has a double purpose:
  (i) total sharing of persistent objects between several active programs through a transactional communication protocol;
  (ii) providing efficient tools to make conditional as well as direct access to persistent objects thanks to strict management of persistent classes and access path towards their objects.
- persistency support is basically founded on the use of C++ genericity capabilities. This solution prevents us from modifying directly the C++ compiler. Management data structure are automatically generated by the NICE-C++ pre-processor so keeping flexibility and simplicity of C++ programming methodology.

This paper summarizes some researchs and developments made within NICE-OS server. In section I, we give a general overview of the NICE-C++ system. Then we will concentrate on the description of its object server NICE-OS, an object oriented DBMS kernel. Section III presents the NICE-OS architecture and advantages. Section IV deals with persistent object storage performed by two system managers : the segment manager and the device manager. Section V presents the tools used for object processing; these tools are gathered into three system managers : the virtual memory manager, the object manager, and the transactional communication manager.

II - PRESENTATION OF NICE-C++

II.1 - NICE-C++ Persistency Model

Persistency is introduced in NICE-C++ through the concept of **Pclass**. A Pclass is a C++ class whose instances can be persistent. A Pclass instance is called **candidate-object** if it is not persistent and **persistent-object** if it does persist. Each time a candidate-object becomes persistent, a persistent pointer called **POI**(persistent object identifier) is attached to it during all its life time. This persistent pointer is used for referencing the corresponding persistent object within all programs which are dealing with it.

NICE-C++ persistency model does not support the type orthogonality rule mentionned in [2)]. This restriction comes from our choice of avoiding any modification of the C++ compiler which would have been cumbersome and expensive. Contrary to the approach used in PC++ [18)], our

* Work supported by the ESPRIT II project n°2109

solution allows to support a scanning mecanism of persistent objects which is useful to use all the capabilities of the object server from an application program.

NICE-C++ only supports sets of persistent objects attached to a single class (while supporting inheritance). These sets are represented by the concept of **collection**. An object collection is a set of object associated with the same class and which are similar in nature (persistent or not). Moreover, the collection concept allows to represent association links between object classes. This link is traduced in NICE-C++ by two clauses: LINK et COMPONENT.

The following example illustrates the Pclass concept:

```
pclass Schema
{
   private
          key : char name[30];
   public
          indexed : int number;
          component:
             Collection_of_Hosts contains <=>
                   Collection_of_Schema is_contained;
...
}
pclass Host
{
   private
          key : char name[30];
          link :
             POI_Schema is_contained <=>
                   Collection_of_Hosts contains;
   public :
          text description;
          collection_of_string prompt;
          collection_of string filter;
```

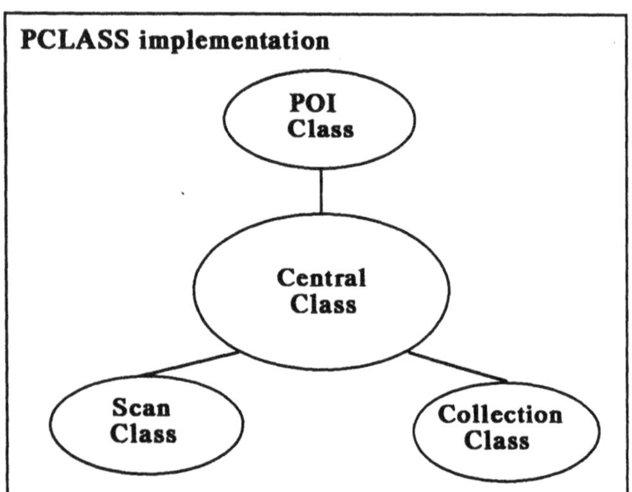

Figure 1: Pclass implementation in C++

The Pclass concept is implemented by using genericity capabilities provided by C++. A Pclass is defined by four C++ classes, one central class and three satellite classes (cf. figure 1):

- the central class includes object characteristics: attributes and methods;
- the satellite class POI represents the persistent pointers associated with persistent objects of the Pclass;
- the satellite class COLLECTION defines all the association links and persistent object sets attached to the Pclass;
- the satellite class SCAN is used to define conditional scans within the set of persistent object attached to the Pclass.

II.2 - Architecture of NICE-C++

The NICE-C++ system is implemented by using the client/server architecture. NICE-C++ architecture is defined by two software components [17]:

- an active component allowing persistent class implementation within each C++ program and providing communication tools with the server;
- a persistent component dedicated to persistent object description and manipulation from the object server NICE-OS.

The pre-processor purpose is four fold:

- it turns all the Pclasses included in a NICE-C++ programm into the corresponding central and satellite C++ classes by using a specification library. If the programm uses an existing Pclass, its associated specifications will be extracted from the library and all possible errors will be detected;
- it prepares integration of communication tools and specific methods associated with Pclasses, into the programs which are using them;
- it makes calls to the C++ compiler and linker in order to get a running program;
- if no syntaxic error is detected, it updates the class schema within the server according the new specifications introduced by the program.

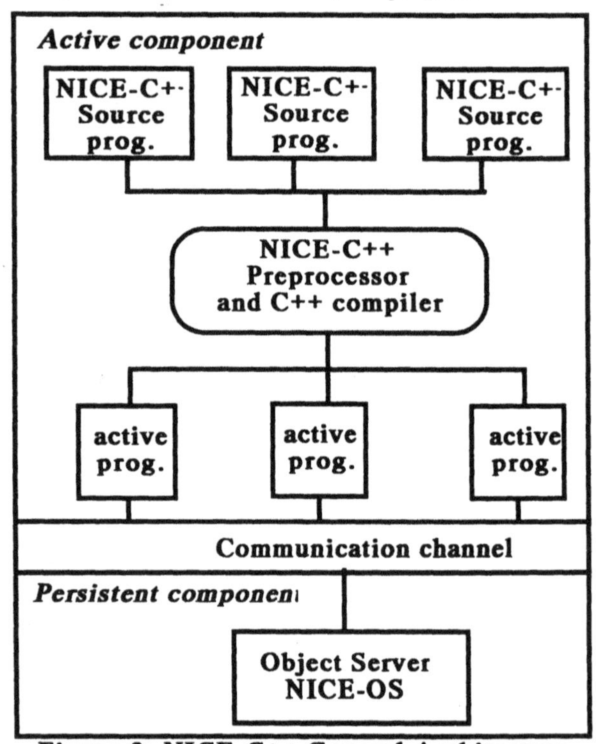

Figure 2: NICE-C++ General Architecture

Contrary to the general approach of object oriented DBMS [11], the object server NICE-OS has been designed as a specific object oriented DBMS dedicated to the C++ environment . It is managed by a transactional monitor able to treat messages coming form several active programs.

Persistent object are so shared by all active programs. Pclass specification is stored by the server so as to be compatible with the new ones defined within active programs. This double definition allows the server to perform scans on objects to be transfered into active programs. The scanning method relies on index structures availables within the server. This allows to reduce answering time of messages sent by active programs. In the following sections, we give a more detailed presentation of NICE-OS architecture.

Figure 2 present a synthetic schema of NICE-C++ general architecture .

III - NICE-OS GENERAL ARCHITECTURE

NICE-OS represents NICE-C++ DBMS level; it has been defined by enhancing the physical DBMS kernel NICEMP [6] with object and communication management facilities.
It is an object server which has three basic functions :

(i) storage of persistent and temporary objects that consist in managing several device types as well as system storage logical organization,
(ii) complex object restructuration in volatile memory which includes the three following aspects:
 * virtual memory management allowing dynamic and efficient space allocation for objects to be built,
 * types and persistent classes management for object interpretation,
 * data structures allowing conditional scanning of objects attached to a persistent class,
(iii) uniform communication transactional interface provided to NICE-OS users in a client/server mode.

NICE-OS is on the one hand an object server[13], and on the other hand a tool box allowing complex systems development. It represents the internal level of the DBMS in charge of object storage and physical acces as well as concurrency and failure recovery. Moreover, it provides virtual memory management mechanism not only for datas but also for working areas used for the development of higher system levels.

Figure 3 presents NICE-OS general architecture. It is defined by five managers that can be classified into two levels according to the task they deal with:

(i) Object Storage Tools

- The **Device Manager** is in charge of the management of the different device types connected to the system and so allows new device integration. It ensures physical storage of persistent objects.

- The **Segment and Virtual Table Manager** supports the management of:
 • segments allowing logical storage of data and system objects;
 • virtual tables allowing temporary working areas management.

This manager includes conversion functions that allow logical/physical mappings of object addresses. Object storage or access within segment/virtual tables is done by their physical object identifier (surrogate) called POI. POI consists of the segment or virtual table identifier and the object identifier inside the segment or virtual table.

(ii) Object Processing Tools

(ii) Object Processing Tools

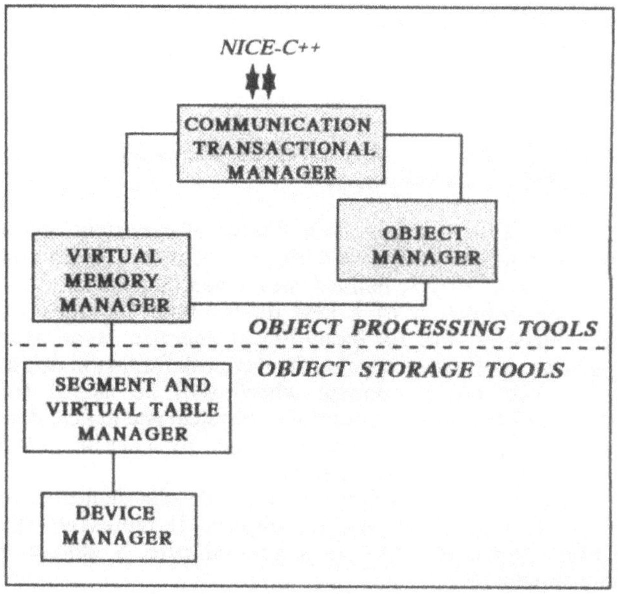

- **The Virtual Memory Manager** sets up links between storage and object processing levels. It dynamically manages volatile memory in order to avoid saturation during simultaneous manipulation of several objects. Therefore, virtual memory includes two parts :
 *persistent virtual memory associated with physical object (data) management,
 *dynamical virtual memory associated with logical object management.

- **The Object Manager** represents the logical level of NICE-OS. It supports three kinds of functions:
 * management of the persistent classes attached to NICE-C++ p-classes and organized in an inheritance hierarchy based on a set of predefined persistent types,
 * creation and update of objects within persistent classes,
 * sequential and conditional access to objects within a persistent class by using indexing techniques (*B-tree, hashing, A-graph, multi-list ...*).

- The **Communication Transactional Manager** has a double purpose:
 * supporting communication between NICE-OS and several client processes in a client/server mode,
 * managing concurrent accesses and running serialization.

IV - OBJECT STORAGE MANAGEMENT

Concerning data storage, two main aspects are pointed out : data physical storage with multi-device management ensured by the device manager and data logical storage based upon segment and virtual table concepts.

IV.1 - Device Manager

NICE-OS supports several storage and communication device type connections. Our Goal is to manage different device types connected to the system and to allow device dynamic integration. We take into account not only the *input/output* devices but also the *storage* devices that can be classified in two categories :

(i)*numerical devices* on which informations are stored in the form of digital data.

Example : magnetic disks, numerical optical disks, CD-ROM, ...

(ii) *non-numerical devices* : all the other kinds of device.

Example : videodisks, ...

The device manager is in charge of persistent object physical storage. It allows definition of new devices and suppression of already defined ones within the system .

The definition of a new device type includes its characteristics and its input/output *specific associated operations.* Before introducing the device definition in detail, let us point out a concept which will be useful for understanding notions connected to physical and logical data storage. A *physical object* is defined by a set of coded informations addressable on a device.

A device is considered as a set of cells dedicated to persistent storage of physical objects. It represents the storage physical unit. As a general rule, a device is characterized by :

(i) an identifier,
(ii) the smallest area addressable on the device,
(iii) a transfert unit : input/output atomic part addressable by the system,
(iv) a set of specific input/output operators.

Our first idea was to standardize the management of any device connected to the system, but this approach included several constraints. Actually, according to the type of device, characteristics are very different, mainly those concerning input/output operations. This is why a device definition includes its specific characteristics along with associated input/output operations.

For example, operations attached to a videodisc player may be:

- random access to a picture,
- variable scrolling thru the pictures (slow and fast / forward and reverse),
- audio handling,
- access to the current picture number,
- ...

We call "main device", the device the system is defined upon; it is considered as a predefined device.

IV.2 - Segment and Virtual-Table Manager

This manager is in charge of persistent object logical storage.This storage is founded on logical identification references - called POI (Physical Object Identifier) - to physical objects stored on the associated device. POI may be seen as a basic predefined type identifying an object during its manipulation within the whole NICE-OS system. It is settled by two logical structures:

- segments for storage of persistent data associated with the system different databases,
- virtual tables for temporary data storage.

We are going to present them in turn.

IV.2.1 - Segments and storage management

A segment represent the storage logical unit for persistent data. It is composed by a set of POI and characterized by:

(i) an identifier,
(ii) an associated physical device,
(iii) the smallest addressable area in the segment,
(iv) a transfert unit: segment logical division,
(v) a processing unit: elementary information processing unit. For segments associated with some devices (videodisc for instance) this characteristic is not applicable,
(vi) addressing mechanisms: they include a couple of bidirectionnal logical/physical mapping functions that insure the interface between physical and logical data storage.

We distinguish two kinds of segment according to the associated device type: pageable segments and non-pageable segments.

Pageable Segments

Pageable segments are associated with numerical devices. In a pageable segment, informations are stored in digital form and may be broken down into elementary units in order to facilitate their transfer and manipulation in volatile memory. Due to this splitting, we can point out two other concepts associated with pageable segments:

(i) the Block concept (related to the device): physical unit of data transfer to volatile memory; its size is a system parameter;
(ii) the Page concept (connected to the segment): logical unit of data transfer composedwith a set of contiguous blocks. The number of blocks in a page is variable.

A pageable segment consists of a set of (unnecessary) contiguous and variable-sized pages. Pages are connected together in a segment with a permanent logical order. We call logical address of a page in a segment, its ordering number in the ordered set of associated segment pages. This address is fixed. The page physical address refers to the physical page cell on the associated segment device it belongs to. This logical address varies dynamically with the pages updates.

Non-pageable Segments

They are segments associated with non-numerical devices. In such a segment, informations are not stored in digital form. Consequently, they can not be split up and can just be processed as a whole. A non-pageable segment is stored on its associated device, outside the reserved space of the database it belongs to. Let us take for example the associated segments of a videodisc like device: an associated non-pageable segment represents a set of picture references. As for pageable segments,addressing concepts are also defined.

A Non-pageable segment consists of a set of elements (picture references in the videodisc case). We call element logical address in a non-pageable segment, its ordering number in the ordered reference set the segment is composed of. The element physical address refers to the physical cell information on the associated device of the segment it belongs to.

Data Base Composition

A NICE-OS database is a storage area managed by the DBMS itself. It is composed with a segment set identified as follows:

(i) System Segments related to the database control informations (bloc0 and tables); these segments are necessarily pageable ones.
(ii) Main Data Segments corresponding to the database and defined inside the area reserved for the database by the DBMS. These segments are also necessarily pageable ones.
(iii) Annex Data Segments also related to data corresponding to the database but defined outside the reserved database area. They can be pageable or non-pageable ones.

Therefore, a database is inevitably composed with pageable segments (system segments and main data segments), along with data annex segments which can be non-pageable or pageable. The concept of data annex segment allows us to talk about an open DBMS. Actually, it permits the connection between a database and an external DBMS environment, and the integration of various device types. Annex segments can then be controlled by other access methods independent from those which are defined inside the DBMS. If they are related, for example, to a videodisc or a file defined by the file management system, they are then to be controlled by the corresponding specific system methods. Figure 4 presents the integration of multi-device aspect and the persistent memory organization.

The major segment manager role is to perform data logical storage in pageable or non-pageable segments. As such, it permits:
(i) new segment creation in the database,
(ii) segment suppression,
(iii) addition, modification and suppression of an element in a segment.

An element in a segment is viewed as a variable-sized byte string; this size may be changed during update operations. Each object stored in a segment is identified by a POI.

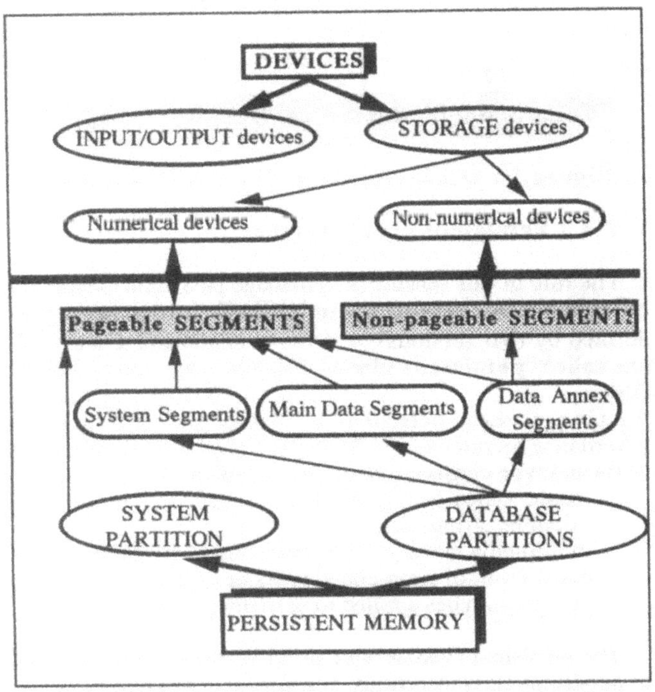

Figure 4 : Uniform Management of Different Device Types and Persistent Memory Partition

Data logical storage is only related to pageable segments. As we mentionned previously, a pageable segment is composed with a set of pages which consist of a set of contiguous blocks.

IV.2.2 - Virtual tables

NICE-OS allows managing both persistent data storage memory and virtual working memory. In an object programming and management environment, management of virtual dynamic memory is crucial [23]. Actually, the storage and working structures of complex objects are generally different and therefore require mappings during object loading in a working area. This mapping is independent from the physical storage mechanism. Consequently, it cannot be done generally, inside the loading area of the data extracted from the database. Furthermore, in a long transaction, an object may have gone thru several temporary modifications that are not to be recorded in the database. This(ese) working version(s) of an object ought to be saved during the global duration of the transaction, regardless of the initial object implementation in persistent memory...

A virtual table represents the logical unit of the system working virtual memory overflow area. Contrary to the segment management mechanism, virtual-table management requires simplicity in order to meet the goal of efficiency. First, the shadow mechanism [15] cannot be used for virtual tables. Furthermore, allocation units used for virtual tables must be related to the smallest allocation size of volatile memory.

A virtual table encompasses some fixed-sized elements themselves composed with a set of cells - the smallest volatile memory reservation unit for a working area (64 bytes in the present MS-DOS version). As for segments, each virtual-table element is related to a physical identifier (POI) which is permanent throughout table life.

This table management is performed by the following functions :
(i) creation of new virtual tables,
(ii) suppression of virtual tables,
(iii) granting an element in a table,
(iv) loading of an element in a table,
(v) revoking an element in a table.

Virtual tables take part in bringing into play the mechanisms of dynamic virtual memory (context stacks) allocation and management mechanisms. These aspects are detailed in section V.1.

V - OBJECT MANIPULATION

In this section, we present the three managers in charge of object processing within NICE-OS.

V.1 - Virtual Memory Manager

In DBMS, the use of persistent memory is absolutely necessary to allow the management of large amount of data. During a database manipulation, data must be loaded in volatile memory and saved in persistent memory after modification. The virtual memory manager performs data continuous exchanges in order to hide the limited size of volatile memory. Everything behaves just as if the user had a very large volatile memory, able to contain the whole database: the virtual memory.

As a general rule, virtual memory management requires development of stack management mechanisms performing data transfers between persistent memory and volatile memory. Different kinds of mechanisms have been proposed in litterature: LRU, LFU, FIFO, CLOCK, ... [7]. A thorough study of these methods points out LRU ("Last Recently Used") types algorithms as the simplest and, consequently the most used. Our approach implements a modified form of this method: the DLRU technique detailed below.

V.1.1 - The DLRU (Double LRU) technique

One of the problems not solved by the LRU technique is the lack of preventing a page from "going out" of the stack if we know that it will be often swapped in memory during a given transaction processing. As the stack capacity in page number is limited, it is not really desirable to see some of them going out of the working area before the end of the processing. In order to solve this problem, some commands were defined. They enable:

(i) to lock a page in a stack;
In order not to alter the page replacement mechanism, locked pages are not considered as being in the stack. This operator is useful when loading pages which are to be modified.
(ii) to unlock a locked page;
It is the locking inverse mechanism; unlocked pages will be put back into the stack and handled by the replacement mechanism.
(iii)to remove the top page into the bottom of the stack;
This operator is useful when we know in advance if the given page will not be used anymore during the current processing of a transaction.

The control of these functions is in charge of the user. The system operates at the end of the working session in order to free the pages (locked or no) that have been loaded exclusively by the session.

The implementation methodology of these mechanisms in NICE-OS presents a particular characteristic. There is a control stack named the Stack of Stacks (justifying the term "Double LRU") whose purpose is to apply the LRU mechanism to the stacks themselves (cf V.1.2). Actually, the stacks are not part of volatile memory (except the stack of stacks); they are loaded and saved dynamically in persistent memory. This permits to optimize the occupied space in volatile memory and to improve virtual memory mechanism performance [8].

V.1.2 - The two types of memory stacks

In NICE-OS system, volatile memory encompasses two parts:

(i) Persistent Data Memory: it represents the loading and saving areas for persistent object in volatile memory. It is directly related to data segments and used for data page exchanges coming from different databases.Such memory is managed by data stacks that constitute the data virtual memory.

(ii) Working Dynamic Memory: it provides the working areas allocated dynamically by a process. It is related to the virtual tables in order to constitute working virtual memory. This memory management is done thru the object stacks.For example, let us assume there exists a persistent object called TUPLE. For the tuple (instance of TUPLE) object manipulation, two stacks may be defined:
- the TUPSTACK stack, a data stack in which the tuple values saved in data segments will be loaded;
- the TUPVTAB stack, an object stack in which will be loaded the working areas necessary to the tuple manipulation.

As a general rule, data stacks are universal, that means a data stack may be used for different database object types. In the opposite, object stacks are often either specialized according to the class of the processed object , or private for a given transaction. If data stacks come from a DBMS environment, object stacks allow integration of NICE-OS into a programming environment.

V.2 - Object Manager

The Object Manager interprets commands comming from the communication transactional manager. These commands are calls to primitives attached to persistent class and persistent object updates, and to conditional scan of persistent classes involving (indexed or sequential) access to the corresponding set of objects.
Figure 5 presents the three components of the object manager.

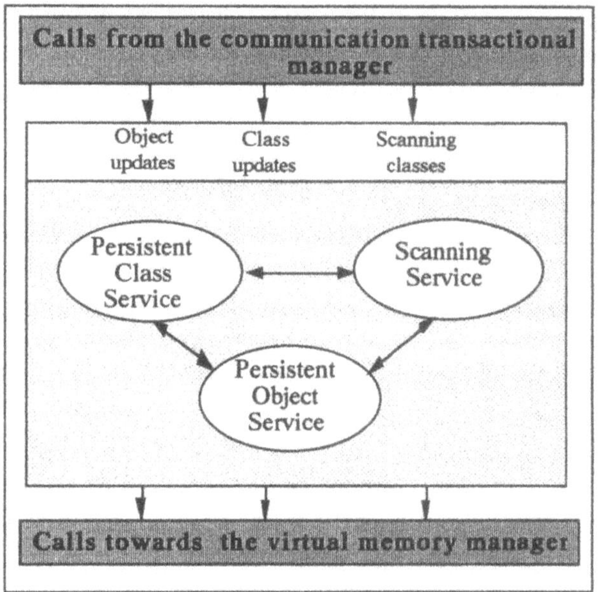

Figure 5 : Organization of the object manager

V.2.1 - Persistent class service

The role of this service is to manage persistent classes. In order to manage persistency in NICE-C++, each "pclass" is defined by two versions [17] : a C++ version and a persistent one called "**persistent class**" which is supported by NICE-OS.
As C++ classes, persistent classes are organized in an inheritance hierarchy which is founded on a set of persistent types and type constructors defined as follows:
- basic types (char, boolean, short, int, long, real, double, string, date, ...);
- multimedia types (text, image, sound, video);
- constructor of enumerated types defined on basic types;
- collection types applied to persistent classes.

The persistent class service provides primitives dedicated to persistent class insertions, deletions and updates including attribute insertion, modification and deletion. A class deletion is possible only if the concerned class is a leaf within the inheritance hierarchy and it is not already referenced in another class.

Other persistent language like PC++18) or PS-Algol 19) do not allow the schema to persist, they only support object persistency. In NICE-C++, we choose to make both objects and classes persistent in order to allow:

- object sharing by more than one user while type checking is done within the object server;
- object indexation which is crucial for efficiency in a persistent environment.

Each persistent class has a double dimension:

- an intensional one defined within the persistent class service,
- an extensional one defined by its set of instances called persistent objects.

Management of persistent class extensions is out of the scope of the persistent class service, it is the persistent object service which is in charge of their definition and update while the scanning service provides tools to have access into them .

V.2.2 - Persistent object service

A persistent object includes two parts:

- a fixed size part containing values defined on a basic type and a persistent identifier associated to the variable part. This part is stored within the data-segment attached to the corresponding persistent class;
- a variable part which is used to store complex attribute values such as text, collection,... This part is stored on the special segment attached to the complex type (ex: text segment).

The persistent object service provides a set of primitives functions for manipulating and updating objects attached to persistent classes. The four basic ones are the following:

- insertion of a new persistent object into a persistent class;
- modification of a persistent object;
- deletion of a persistent object;
- direct access to a persistent object.

At the internal level, these functions make calls to :

- the persistent class service in order to get information about classes and attributes,
- the virtual memory manager for main memory allocation,
- the scanning service to perform a selection each time there is a conditional modification or deletion request.

The main implementation problem attached to this service is the management of component and link properties during updates. We overcome this difficulty by using object keys as object names.

Let us illustrates this isssue with the example of section II.1. Classes Host and Schema both have "name" declared as a key field. Let us insert a new persistent object into the class Schema:

name = HAWKS
contains = {QUESTEL, ALL}

If QUESTEL and ALL do not already exist, the system will create them into the class Host:

name = QUESTEL	name = ALL
is_contained = HAWKS	is_contained = HAWKS

The other attributes attached to these two objects will be initialized with null values.
This technique allows us to avoid object cycles or recursivity.

V.2.3 - Scanning service

The purpose of this service is threefold:

(i) defining index structures attached to persistent clas attributes,
(ii) having sequential access to objects within a given collection of POI (or persistent class).
(iii) having conditional access to objects within a given collection of POI (or persistent class) by using index structures.

External interface of the scanning service is defined by a single function involving two parameters:

- a simple or complex condition involving attribute names, constants, comparison operators, logical connectors, method calls, ...
- a collection of POI or a persistent class.

In a complex type real world, traditional access methods (hashing, B-tree, ...) may be inadequate. For example, for three-dimensionnal objects, R-trees[12),22)] are more suitable while for a "text" type B^+-trees[5)], will be a well adapted mechanism. The technique of index used in NICE-OS is the B+-tree technique with the possibility to make index on multivalued attributes ("collection-of..." attributes). The index is created on a given attribute of the concerned class. On the opposite of the approach of ORION[14)], our indexingapproach is not based upon the class hierarchy and does distinguish between two types of index : the main index and the secondary index.

The scanning service make calls to the persistent object service, to the persistent class service and to the virtual memory manager in order to accomplish its tasks.

Similarly, both the persistent object service and the persistent class service alo make calls to the virtual memory manager.

During initialization of the NICE-OS working environment, information about object persistency management is loaded into main memory. For each persistent class, a working stack, called object buffer, is reserved. These buffers works in cooperation with NICE-OS data stacks, which can access directly to persistent data. The loading unit in the page stacks is the page (a page can contain several objects), while the loading unit in object buffers is the object. An object is an image of the class to which it belongs.

As an example, a request for an object of the PERSONN class by a scanning function involves loading of the required object into the BUF_PERSONN buffer associated with the PERSONN class. The concerned object or its physical identifier can be returned into a variable defined by the calling user's program.

In the same way, insertion of a new object into the PERSONN class involves, first, the reservation of an entry in the BUF_PERSONN object buffer. At logical storage level the concerned object will be inserted into a page and saved, after validation, into the SEG_PERSONN segment associated with the PERSONN class.

Object buffers contain in-memory copies of objects. Therefore, they play a crucial role for communications between the object manager and the object storage managers.

V.3 - Communication Transactional Manager

The goal of this manager is to etablish the connection between NICE-OS and any client process while supporting concurrency.

This dialogue is supported by integration of a communication layer into each client process.

Communication interface functions allow to create new communications channels, to send a message through an existing communication channel and to receive a message coming from NICE-OS through a specified communication channel.

A communication channel is defined by two message files attached to the two existing communication directions (NICE-OS ->Application and Application -> NICE-OS).

The communication transactional manager also supports concurrent access to persistent data. It is in charge of avoiding update loss, reading errors, inappropriate reads, bogus tuples or objects and identity mistakes.

Managing concurrency so involves the following tasks:

- transaction file management which consists in inserting or deleting a transaction within the file, loading a transaction into main memory ;
- locking management policy founded on both the double phase locking mechanism [4] and the WOUND-WAIT technique [21];
- calling the object manager in order to execute actions attached to the concerned messages.

VI - CONCLUSION

NICE-C++ persistent programming model is based on the one hand on an enhancement of the C++ class concept by the concept of persistent class and on the other hand on the extension of C++ type system. This double extension allows us to integrate in C++ a minimum set of concepts coming from the database world (indexing, constraints, association links, transactions) as well as a set of types dedicated either to persistency management (persistent object identifiers, conditional scanning) or to C++ programming (specific basic types, multimedia types) or even to both of them (collection of objects or values).

In this paper, we concentrated our description of NICE-C++ prototype in its underlying object server. It provides primitive attached to management of communications, transactions, schema , persistent objects, indexes, conditional scanning and persistent object storage. This object server implements logical independance of NICE-C++ persistency model. It can be used for supporting other object programming model.

A NICE-C++ prototype is already available on SUN-Sparc Unix and on PC-AT 486 under Unix-sco. This prototype has been used in the TOOTSI ESPRIT II project for implementing the global dictionary which contains meta-informations about TOOTSI applications.

Work on NICE-C++ is to be continued in the research direction as well as in the implementation way.

In the research field, we can mentionned the two following key points:

- finding an optimization technique for evaluating conditional expressions by reorginizing them according to the indexed conditions.
- increasing the system flexibility and adaptability at the level of transaction management and object physical grouping.

VII - BIBLIOGRAPHY

1) Agraval R., Gehani N.H., "ODE(Object Database and Environment): the language and the data model", Proc. of the ACM SIGMOD Int. Conf. on the Management of Data, Vol. 18, Portland Oregon-USA, June 1989

2) Atkinson M.P., Bailey P.J., Cockshott W.P. Chisholm K.J. and Morrison R., "An Approach to Persistent Programming", Computer Journal, Vol.26, No. 4, Nov. 1983, pp. 360-365.

3) Atkinson M.P. and Morrison R., "Procedures as Persistent Data Objects", ACM Transactions on Programming Languages and Systems, Vol.7, No.4, Oct. 1985, pp. 539-559.

4) Bernstein P.A., Hadzilacos V. and Goodman N., "Concurrency control and recovery in database systems", Addison-Wesley, Readings, MAss. 1987

5) Carey M., DeWitt D.,"The architecture of the EXODUS extensible DBMS", Proc. of the international workshop on object-oriented database systems, Pacific Grove, 1986

6) Dong J.T., Le Thanh N., Salgado C., Vittori E., , Mopolo G. and Miranda S., "Virtual-paged memory management in NICEBD", International Symposium on Database Systems for Advanced Applications, Seoul, Korea, April 1989, pp. 359-366.

7) Effelsberg W., Haerder T., "Principles of database buffer management", ACM TODS, Vol. 9, N° 4, December 1984

8) Ernst C., "Conception et implantation d'un système de gestion de bases d'objets de structure complexe. Application aux images", Thèse de Doctorat en Informatique, Université de Nice, March 1987

9) Giavitto J.L., Devarenne A. and Rosuel G., "PRESTO: des objets C++ persistants pour le système d'information d'Adage", Journées d'étude "Bases de Données Déductives et Bases de Données Orientées Objets", Paris, Dec. 13-14 1988, pp. 42-55.

10) Goldberg A., Robson D. "SMALLTALK: the language and its implementation", Addison Wesley, 1983.

11) Gruber O., Amasaleg L., Daynès L., Valduriez P., "Eos, an environment for object-based systems", INRIA Rocquencourt, Research report N° 1499.

12) Guttman T., "R-tree : a dynamic index structure for spatial searching", Proc. of the SIGMOD Conference, Boston, May 1984

13) Hornick M.F., Zdonik S.B., "A shared, segmented memory system for an object-oriented database", ACM Transactions on Office Information Systems, Vol. 5, N° 1, January 1987

14) Kim W., Garza J., Ballou N. and Woelk D., "Architecture of the Orion Next- Generation Database System", IEEE Transactions on Knowledge and Data Engineering, Vol.2, No.1, Mar. 1990, pp. 109-124.

15) Lorie R.A., "Physical integrity in a large segmented database", ACM TODS, Vol. 2, N° 1, March 1977

16) Meyer B., "Object-oriented software construction", Prentice Hall, 1989.

17) Mopolo-Moke G., " NICE-C++: une extension C++ pour la programmation persistante à partir d'un serveur de bases d'objets", Thèse de Doctorat en Informatique, Université de Nice et Sophia-Antipolis, December 1991.

18) Nguyen T.A., Wagner M., Hoffman B., "PC++: an object-oriented database system for C++ applications", 2nd Int. Symposium on Database Systems for Advanced Applications, April 2-4, Tokyo, Japan 1991

19) Persistent Programming Research Group, "The PS-Algol reference manual, 4th edition", Persistent Programming Research Report 12, february 1988, Computing Science

Dept., Univ. of Glasgow, Glasgow G12 8QQ
20) Richardson J.E. and Carey M.J., "Persistence in the E Language: Issues and Implementation", *Software - Practice and Experience*, Vol 19, No. 12, Dec. 1989, pp. 1115-1150.
21) Rosenkrantz D.J. and al., "System level concurrency control for distributed data base systems", ACM-TODS, Vol.3, N°2, June 1978
22) Sellis T., Roussopoulos N., Faloutsos C., "The R^+-Tree: a dynamic index for multi-dimensional objects", Proc. of the 13th VLDB Conference, Brighton 1987
23) Williams I., Wolczko M., Hopkins T., "Dynamic grouping in an object oriented virtual memory hierarchy", Proc. of the European Conference on Object-oriented Programming, Paris, June 1987.

ADVANCED FEATURES OF INTEGRATED DB/DC SYSTEM "XDM"

Kazuo Masai, Shoji Yamamoto, Hiromichi Ishikawa,Takashi Sumiyoshi
Mitsuo Miyazaki, Masato Saito,Toshikazu Hiramoto*,Shigeru Yoneda**

Software Development Center ,Hitachi Ltd.
*Hitachi Software Engineering Co.,Ltd.
**Systems Development Laboratory, Hitachi Ltd.

ABSTRACT

As the applications of DB/DC(Data Base /Data Communication) systems expand, DB/DC systems are growing very rapidly in terms of size and functionality. Distributed database and composite subsystem management facilities are developed in XDM,[1] the strategic DB/DC system program product of Hitachi,Ltd., to meet recent users' requirement. As a result of these functional extensions of XDM, it is possible to construct a large-scaled distributed DB/DC system with high performance and reliability.

1. INTRODUCTION

According to recent trends of internationalization of enterprises and intensification of relationships among companies, information systems with databases like banking on-line systems are required to handle following situations:

(1) progress of distributed information processing among geometrically distributed sites in VANs, including world-wide networks,

(2) progress of 24 hour continuous operation to improve service time,

(3) emergence of wide variety of application fields besides mainstay applications, e.g., office information systems, engineering information systems, micro-main-frame linked information systems, etc.,

(4) increase in size of a database from around 100GB to near 1000GB and transaction traffic from around 100trans/sec to about 500trans/sec.

To handle above situations, DB/DC systems have to furnish following facilities:

- distributed database system,
- composite system configuration composed of multiple DB/DC subsystems,
- relational database system based on the ISO standard SQL.

Providing above facilities, a large-scaled distributed database system with high performance and reliability can be constructed. This paper describes advanced features of the extended version of the integrated DB/DC system "XDM"(eXtensible Data Manager), named "XDM E2".[2] The objectives of XDM extension and its features are described in section 2. Configuration of XDM E2 is shown in section 3. And section 4 describes main facilities of XDM E2.

2. THE OBJECTIVES OF XDM EXTENSION AND ITS FEATURES

2.1 Realization of The Composite DB/DC Environment

The composite DB/DC environment conducts the following capabilities.

(1) Sharing databases in all processing environments.

Application programs under the following environments can share same XDM databases in the composite DB/DC system.

(a) General purpose DC environment

This environment is supported by XDM/DCCM3

(Data Communication and Control Manager 3), Hitachi's main TP monitor.

Ordinary online systems such as manufacturing control and/or inventory control can be built with this DC subsystem.

(b) DB/DC environment for financial and security system

TMS-4V/SP(Transaction Management System-4V/System Product) supports special DB/DC environment for very high traffic environment.

(c) Interactive and batch processing environment

XDM databases can be accessed from batch jobs or interactive jobs (TSS:Time Sharing System).

(d) Systemized Office Automation environment

XDM databases can be accessed from work-stations using micro-mainframe link(MML) connection.

Each access is conducted through the DB server HOAPDBS(High-level-object Management and Processing DataBase Server).

(2) Dual databases

An application program of each processing environment can access multiple databases such as structural database and relational database.

(3) Integrated management and independent operations

Management functions such as system control, journaling, and concurrency control are integrated for the purpose of easy and flexible system operations. At the same time, the DC(XDM/DCCM3) subsystem can be asynchronously operated in terms of system initiation, recovery, and system termination from other subsystems.

XDM E2 control that realizes the above facilities is named "composite subsystem control".

2.2 XDM Extension for Network Environments

XDM E2 can distribute functions, loads, and risks, using communication method among multiple DB/DC systems. Followings are the main extended facilities.

(1) Distributed database support among structural databases and among relational databases on host computers. (horizontally distributed database).

(2) Distributed database support between host computer system and work-station system (vertically distributed database).

2.3 Standardization of application interfaces

The database language SQL standardized by ISO is adopted as an application interface of XDM for accessing database. It provides common operating environment from large scale host computers to work-stations.

2.4 Performance Improvement of XDM E2 System

(1) Performance of concurrent processing

Concurrent processing mechanism of DB/DC processing is implemented to improve efficient use of the tightly coupled processors, e.g., M-684H quadruple processor system.

Following processes are performed in the concurrent fashion:

*accessing structural database ,

*accessing relational database ,

*journaling ,

*accessing a queue of sending and/or receiving messages.

Efficiency on the multiple processor environment is remarkably improved due to these concurrent processing.

(2) Hardware assist for relational database management system XDM/RD

Using hardware accelerator for relational database manipulation IDP(Integrated Database Processor),[3] XDM/RD can improve its performance remarkably.

Under multiple processor environment, XDM/RD can use multiple IDPs which leads to further performance improvement.

(3) Performance improvement of journaling

A number of I/Os occurred for the journaling can be reduced by buffering multiple journal data.

When a process makes a journaling request and have to wait for the completion of the previous journaling I/O, journal data is accumulated into a buffer and will be written to the journal file by a single I/O. All journaling requests are suspended until the corresponding journaling I/O completion. This buffering mechanism is particularly effective in the high traffic processing environment.

3. CONFIGURATIONS OF XDM EXTENDED VERSION XDM E2

XDM E2 is a composite system composed of multiple DB/DC subsystems. Its main component is the system controller:
XDM/BASE E2:system control, data dictionary/directory, and system operation services.
And its subsystems are as follows:
*XDM/DCCM3: data communication services (TP monitor),
*XDM/SD E2: structural database services,
*XDM/RD: relational database services,
*XDM/DF: distributed database services,
*ARF: higher-level reliable services for DB/DCs, which supports hot-standby (duplex system) feature,
*TMS-4V/SP: DB/DC services for financial and security system,
*HOAPDBS : database accessing services for work-stations.

Each subsystem is independent and can be selected according to the requirement. Figure 1 shows an example of XDM E2 configuration.

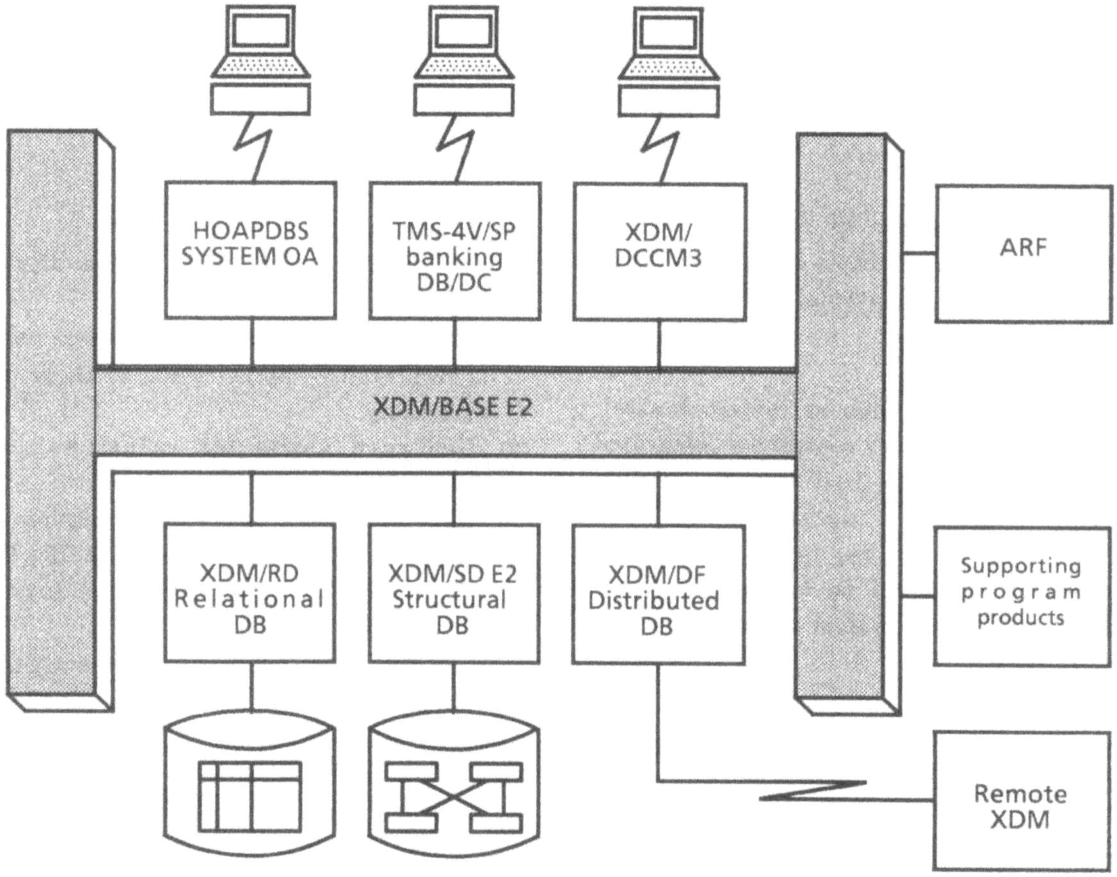

ARF:Advanced Reliability Feature
TMS-4V/SP : Transaction Management System-4V/System Product
HOAPDBS : High-level Object Management and Processing DataBase Server
XDM/BASE E2:XDM/Base E2
XDM/DCCM3:XDM/Data Communication and Control Manager 3
XDM/SD E2:XDM/Structured Data Base E2
XDM/RD:XDM/Relational Data Base
XDM/DF:XDM/Distributing Facility

Figure 1. XDM E2 system configuration

4. FACILITIES OF XDM E2 SYSTEM

4.1 Composite Subsystem Control Facilities

The most important feature of XDM E2 is the composite DB/DC environment. Composite DB/DC environment enables several DC subsystems such as general purpose data communication system and DB subsystems such as structural database and relational database to be connected to the system. Application programs under each DC subsystem can share one DB subsystem, and one DC subsystem can access all DB subsystems.

One subsystem's failure is confined within this subsystem and the whole system can continue to operate without this subsystem. After the subsystem recovery process, this subsystem can join the system without stopping the whole system.

The composite DB/DC system environment conducts the following matters:

(1) subsystem coexistence and operation independence among subsystems,

(2) improvement of the system operation and maintenance, and integration of system operations among DB/DC subsystems,

(3) acception of different demands among multiple processing environments,

(4) integrity management for the database update operation among subsystem independently controlling databases and XDM controlling databases.

To support composite DB/DC system, initiation, recovery, and termination of each subsystem must be done independently. Each subsystem's resources are controlled separately by the XDM E2 controller or by each subsystem.

Recovery information collected in a journal file must be separated to perform independent subsystem recovery. Journal file cannot be separated to each subsystem, as database recovery has to be done by DC subsystem while journal data must be taken by a DB subsystem. This means that even though recovery information should be separated, it cannot be separated from the beginning. Moreover, it is desirable to have single set of journal for whole system. XDM E2 supported the way to have single set of journal and independent recovery procedure by the subsystem recovery file and transaction recovery file as shown in Figure 2.

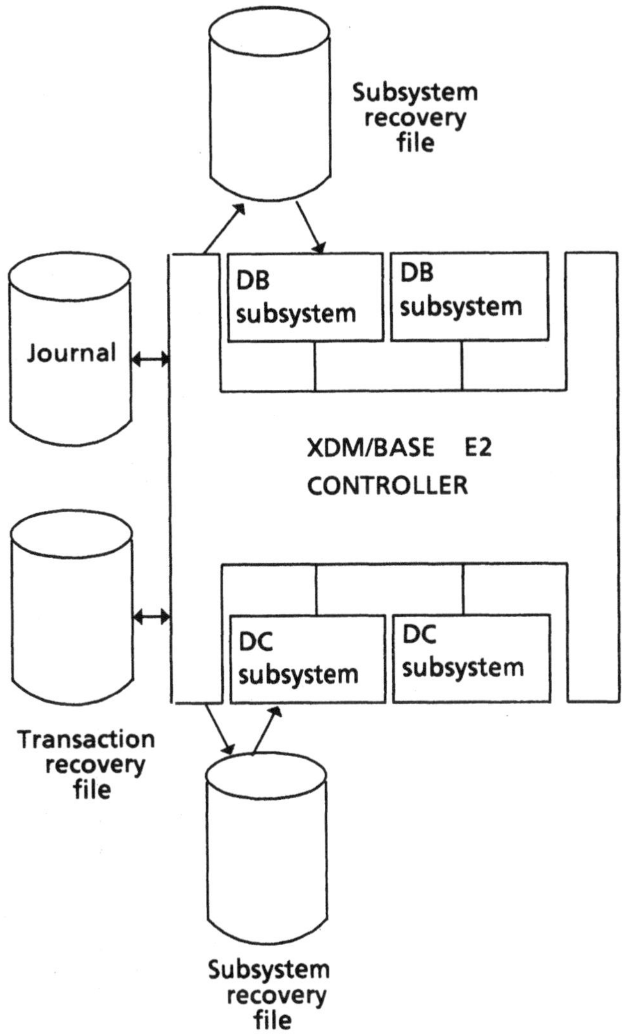

Figure 2. Recovery files

Subsystem recovery file is a file which contains recovery information for each subsystem. Transaction recovery file is a file which contains recovery information for each transaction. Information accumulated in journal file is selected and distributed to each subsystem recovery file and transaction recovery file by the XDM E2 controller.

The recovery after whole system's failure is done as shown in Figure 3. At first, the XDM E2 controller reads the system status file which maintains the system status information and recovers its status. Then, it reads the journal and distributes the journal data to each subsystem's recovery file and transaction recovery file. After this journal input process, each subsystem is initiated. The initiated subsystems recover their own status through the subsystem recovery files, and as soon as the status is recovered, each DC subsystem starts its online service independently.

The suspended transactions are recovered later using the information accumulated in transaction recovery file. This recovery can be done at any time after the DB subsystem initiation is completed.

This is called "delayed recovery", for the recovery
is processed after the online function's initiation. This enables each subsystem to recover asynchronously and even though some DB subsystem fails to recover, the remaining DC and DB subsystems can start their services.

It is important to integrate the management of system operations to reduce the maintenance cost of the composite subsystem environment. Journal file is integrated for easiness of handling. Entering a command is controlled by the XDM E2 controller and distributed to each subsystem according to its demanding resource.

Another important feature is two-phase commitment control.[4] The two-phase commitment among different DC subsystems supports multiple journal environment. Two-phase commitment is essential to assure integrity among geometrically distributed databases.

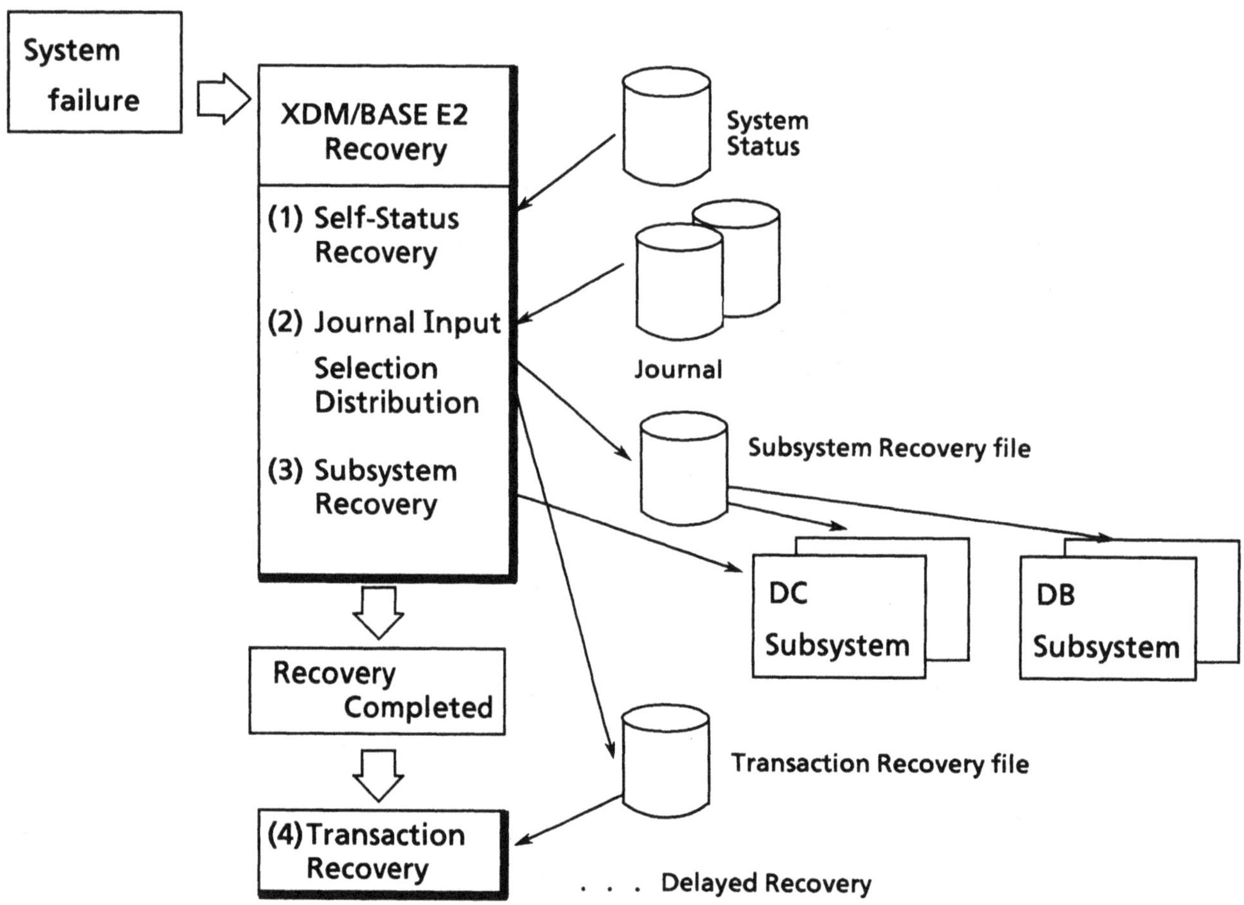

Figure 3. System Recovery Process

4.2 Distributed Database Access Facilities

The following requirements must be satisfied to realize a distributed database system:

- establishment of location transparency of databases to users,
- providing a unified access interface to distributed databases,
- integrity management against many types of failures in the distributed database environment.

To meet above requirements, XDM/DF(XDM Distributing Facility)[5] has been developed and has following features:

(1) Ease of creation and maintenance of user application programs.

A concept of Global Schema and Distribution Schema makes a UAP independent from locations of distributed DB. And one can create UAPs without knowing the location of the distributed DB. Global schema describes the logical database structure which is independent from the CPU node location. Distribution schema describes the node location information of the data which is determined by a key value. Definition of the distributed database is shown in Figure 4.

According to this independency, it is possible to change the location of data without any modification of the UAP.

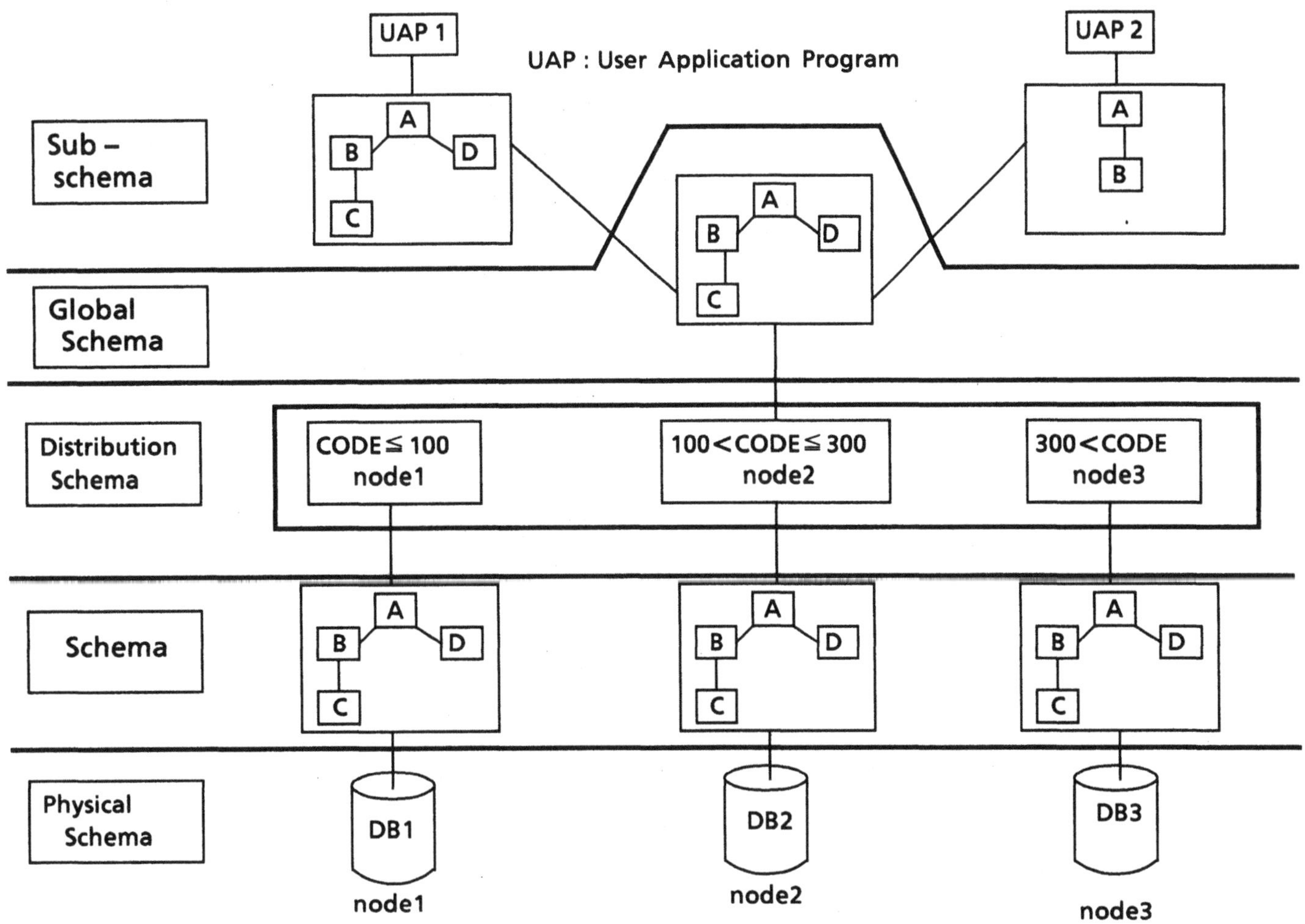

Figure 4. Definition for distributed DB

(2) Highly reliable system.

It is possible to keep the integrity of the distributed DB using the two-phase commitment mechanism. XDM/DF is implemented as a subsystem having both DB and DC characteristics within the composite subsystem environment. As XDM/DF is a subsystem, its failure is localized to itself.

And moreover, adopting hot-standby feature (duplex system), it is possible to restart the distributed DB without any operation after a switch over to the standby system.

(3) To support very large databases, data can be distributed up to 255 host computers.

4.3 Relational Database Facilities

XDM/RD is the relational database management system which provides the ISO standard database language SQL. Followings are XDM/RD functions:

(1) database organization facility for production applications:
   *adapting to variations of application scales,
   *adapting to very large-scaled databases,
      - up to 64 GB/table
      - up to 12.8TB/system
   *row-based clustering and key-range partitioning,
   *adapting to the variety of application fields.

(2) high-speed database access facility
   Following functions make it possible to access databases with high-speed:
   *concurrent access,
   *dedicating buffer pools to each database,
   *residing data dictionary data and SQL object code data on virtual memory.

(3) database language support based on the ISO standard SQL

(4) SQL support within language compilers, e.g.,COBOL 85, OPL1 E2

(5) support of module language

(6) XDM/RD performance improvement with IDP
   Following functions can be accelerated with IDP (Integrated Database Processor)hardware assist:
   *retrieval using extended SQL statements,
   *searching with multiple indexes,
   *sorting,
   *join operation,
   *index creation.

5. CONCLUSION

This paper described advanced features of the extended version of the DB/DC system XDM, i.e., XDM E2. This system can handle the enlargement and advancement of DB/DC systems according to the evolution of application fields, and has following functions:

(1) composite subsystem management,
(2) distributed database accesses,
(3) high performance transaction processing,
(4) relational database accesses based on ISO standard database language SQL.

REFERENCE

1) Sumiyoshi,T.,et.al.,"New integrated DB/DC system "XDM" to realize the very large databases", Hitachi Hyouron, 68, 5, 1986, pp.421-426(in Japanese).
2) Yamamoto,S.,et.al.,"Extension of Integrated DB/DC System "XDM" for a Distribution and Composition of System Components", Hitachi Hyouron, 70,7,1988, pp.93-100(in Japanese).
3) Torii,S.,et.al."Accelerating Nonnumerical Processing by an Extended Vector Processor", Proceedings of Fourth International Conference of Data Engineering, 1988, pp.194–201.
4) Date,C.J., An Introduction to Database Systems (Addison–Wesley Publishing Company), Vol.1,pp.594–595.
5) Yamamoto,H., "Discussion of Ensuring Data Integrity in Distributing Facility XDM/DF",4B–3, Proceedings of Sixth Joint Workshop of Computer Communications, IPSJ,1991.

ENGINEERING DATABASES

A SURVEY OF INTEGRITY CONSTRAINT CHECKING METHODS IN RELATIONAL DATABASES

Tok Wang LING and Sin Yeung LEE

Department of Information Systems and Computer Science
National University of Singapore
Lower Kent Ridge Road, Singapore 0511, Republic of Singapore.
email : lingtw@iscs.nus.sg, jlee@iscs.nus.sg

ABSTRACT

Constraint validation, an essential feature of any database system, is a process of guaranteeing and maintaining a set of semantic invariants across database state transitions. This process has been studied by many authors and various simplification methods have been proposed. This survey describes recent developments in the field of integrity constraint checking methods. We first give a review on different characteristics of methods for enforcing integrity constraints, followed by a survey of different methods to perform and simplify integrity checking in relational databases, and the corresponding ways to express integrity constraints.

1.0 INTRODUCTION

An **integrity constraint** is a formula which governs the database state [Eswa75, Hamm78]. When a database state is consistent with all the specified integrity constraints, we say that the database is consistent. Otherwise, when the database state does not obey some integrity constraints, the database state is said to be inconsistent. One of the major functions of a database management system is to ensure that the database is consistent. However, when a database is changed from the current database state to a new database state, there is no guarantee that the new state will obey the integrity constraints. A test is therefore necessary to ensure that the update does not create an inconsistent database state. Since the checking is done as often as transactions are performed, the test must be efficient. In other words, the integrity checking problem is basically the minimization of computation effort as well as database accesses for integrity checking.

One of the classical solutions to this problem is to extend the relational model to include modeling of certain common integrity constraints such as unique key constraints, referential constraints [Date86], domain constraints and nonnull constraints. Instead of developing a general algorithm to handle every possible integrity constraint, this method provides different solutions for different classes of constraints. These classes of constraints were introduced into the relational model to enrich the semantics data modeling capabilities. One of the major strengths of this method is that those common constraints have been fully studied by many authors and various efficient methods have been developed and implemented in a number of database systems. In [Beve87], the author discussed a new storage structure which can speed up the validation of referential constraints. In [Cass88], the author addressed the integrity problem concerning inclusion dependencies and referential constraints with a discussion on how his monitor system can handle some other kinds of database updates such as block deletions and cascade deletions efficiently. Another advantage of this method is that most of these constraints can be easily specified or derived in the database schema definition. For example, METUGDBMS has an automatic update integrity subsystem that is evolved from a multi-level DBMS software implementation based on the Entity-Relationship model. Constraints like "A staff cannot be both a clerk and a lecturer" can be easily specified using a mutually exclusive "IS-A" relationship.

However, extending the relational model alone to handle integrity checking is by no means a complete solution. Constraints which can be handled by this method are usually not sufficient to model real-world data semantics. For more complex constraints such as "The salary of every employee cannot be higher than that of his supervisor", it is the responsibility of the application programs to ensure the database integrity. This will produce redundant application program codes. Any modification to a database constraint will require the modification of every application program that updates the database. Hence, it is necessary to have a general integrity checking ability added to the conventional DBMS so that it can handle various types of user defined constraints.

2.0 CHARACTERISTICS OF INTEGRITY CHECKING

For each general integrity checking method, we can easily classify them by the major properties which the methods demonstrate. For example, some methods may only be able to handle single-update operations. They differ from those which can handle general transactions. In the following subsections, we shall give a summary of some major characteristics of integrity checking methods.

2.1 DECLARATIVE VERSUS PROCEDURAL

Integrity checking can adopt either the declarative approach or the procedural approach. Under the procedural approach, constraints are enforced mainly by procedures which are explicitly coded by the users. For example, triggers [Coda73, Eswa75, Eswa76] as well as validation programs maintain integrity constraints by the procedural approach. Under the declarative approach, on the other hand, each integrity constraint is specified as a logic assertion. Each assertion can be specified in many different ways such as domain calculus [Nico82], tuple calculus [Hsu85, Koba87], IC-formula [Ling87], Query-by-example [Zloo78], etc. Based on the input set of assertions, the integrity checking system will automatically generate the checking procedure.

Under the procedural approach, integrity checking can be very efficient because ad-hoc optimization can be easily incorporated for simple integrity constraints. However, to decide whether a set of procedures correctly enforces a given set of constraints is generally undecidable. Hence, the procedural approach is most suitable if the constraints are not too complicated as that the correctness of the procedures can be proven by the users. However, to deal with more general constraints, most of the integrity checking methods, as we shall see later, usually adopt the declarative approach.

2.2 TIMING OF INTEGRITY CHECKING

Integrity constraint checking can be classified according to the time of the checking of constraints with respect to the time of the actual physical update. We have identified three classes of execution :

1. Detection method : Checking is performed after the actual physical update, but before COMMIT.
2. Prevention method : Checking is performed before the actual physical update.
3. Delayed method : Checking is delayed if the current application does not make use of the updated data.

These three methods are summarized in the following sub-sections.

2.2.1 Detection approach

Integrity constraint checking can be based on detection of inconsistencies. A transaction *TR* is executed and the database state *S* is changed to another state *S'*. The constraint enforcement process verifies that all relevant constraints hold in state *S'*. If state *S'* is inconsistent, then the enforcement process can either change the state *S'* to a consistent state *S''* by some compensation actions, or restore to the original state *S* by undoing the transaction *TR*. This type of checking is also known as **after-checking.** This method is simple in implementation. There is no need to transform a constraint into some other special form to perform checking. The constraint itself is the test query, which can be evaluated directly or simplified as in [Nico82] before evaluation. It does not matter how many update operations have been performed to the database in the transaction because the checking can be postponed until just before the commitment of the transaction. This concept has been adopted by the timing type TT in E.F.Codd relational model version 2 [Codd90]. After-checking is also found in most of the trigger systems [Eswa75, Eswa76, Syba87, Daya88a, Daya88b]. Authors such as Nicolas [Nico82] have provided some algorithms to simplify after-checking.

This approach requires an updated database for the constraint evaluation. Therefore, the database must be first updated before any checking is possible. If the database is found to be inconsistent during the checking, all the updates must be undone. Such ROLLBACK is very costly in general.

2.2.2 Prevention approach

Integrity checking can be performed before the actual

update is performed on the database. This kind of preventive checking is also known as **before-checking**. This approach has the advantage of early detection of transactions which lead to inconsistent database state and such unnecessary physical database updates are avoided. In general, the prevention approach is less expensive than the detection approach since it is never necessary to undo the entire transaction if the transaction violates some integrity constraints.

However, methods employing this approach always need to reformulate each constraint into a set of pre-tests, which depends on the operations in the transaction. Different transactions can result in totally different sets of pre-tests. For example, given a constraint "there are at least two suppliers in the database", an insertion of one supplier and an insertion of two suppliers will result in two different pre-tests. Such tight dependency on the transaction makes prevention approach hard to adopt the compiled approach entirely. Another draw back is the high computation cost. Given any pre-test generating algorithm, it can be easily proven by the differential method that the number of conditions needed to be checked is exponential related to the number of tuple/domain variables being updated. For example, given that there are n insertions on the supplier relation, n^2 simplified pre-tests are generated if the required integrity constraint contains two instances of the supplier relation. The key constraint of the supplier relation is such an example. In general, n^r pre-tests are generated if there are r instances of the updated tuple/domain variables in the constraint and there are n updates in the transaction. Even thought after optimization according to methods such as those described in [Hsu85, Koba87, Ling87], each pre-test can have at least O(size of the supplier relation) reduction in the number of tuple accesses as compared to the direct checking, the cost reduction may be counter-balanced by the large number of pre-tests when the values of n and r are large. For a transaction which contains a large number of updates, and a constraint which contains many instances of the same relation such as in the multi-value dependency constraint (four instances in this case), the prevention approach can result in the combinatorial explosion of computation cost during the formulation of the pre-tests. However, as such worst case is hardly found in daily applications, and the cost of undoing database updates are much higher than the cost of CPU computation in formulation of the pre-tests, it is still beneficial to avoid undoing transactions in most of the time. Hence, lots of recent checking methods such as [Hsu85, Koba87, Ling87] adopt the prevention approach.

2.2.3 Delay approach

For certain applications like CAD (Computer-Aided Design) , there are some object instances which depend on the existence or values of other object instances. If these dependent object instances are of no interest to the current users/applications, then those constraints which govern the relations between instances of those dependent objects and their corresponding independent object instances may not need to be checked immediately when operations are performed on those independent object instances. For example, for the CASE (Computer-Aided Software Engineering) design application, structure chart design is usually based on some dataflow diagrams (DFD). When the DFD design is changed, the corresponding structure chart design may need to be updated. It is however unreasonable to expect the users to update the dependent structure chart design for every modification operation on the dataflow diagram design just because some integrity constraints are violated. The checking, however, can be activated much later after the design of the DFD process is completed. This type of checking is also known as **lazy evaluation**, and is supported in the triggers in Postgres. Another advantage of this method is that since real-time processing of integrity checking is reduced, those checking which can be delayed can be scheduled later so as to maximize the system performance.

While this approach cuts down a large amount of checking, its application is quite limited. Firstly, since checkings are delayed after the commitment of transactions, when some constraints are later found to be violated, we cannot abort the transaction but can only provide some recovery actions. Secondly, there must be a non-cyclic dependent graph for all the object instances in the application with respect to the entire integrity specifications of the system. For general databases such as the supplier-part database [Date86], where values of suppliers are independent from the values of parts and vice versa, we cannot apply this method.

2.3 SINGLE-UPDATE VERSUS MULTIPLE-UPDATE

Integrity constraint checking methods can be classified according to the types of transactions they can handle. The first group of methods can only handle single-update transactions. A single-update transaction is a transaction which contains only one database update operation, i.e., an insertion, a deletion or a modification of a single tuple. The other group of methods handle transactions which contain more than one database update. [Nico82, Ling87] discuss the integrity constraint checking for single-update. While these methods have their theoretical value, most of them cannot be easily extended to transactions containing multiple-update operations. The main difficulty is that although a database is consistent before and after the execution of a transaction, the database state can be inconsistent during the execution of the transaction. Reordering of the update operations may solve this problem for some instances, however, there are some transactions and set of constraints such that every ordering of the update operations in these transactions can create temporary inconsistent database states. Hence, methods that can only handle single-update cannot be applied to general transactions.

2.4 ACTION AFTER CHECKING

When a constraint is violated after a given transaction is executed, there are basically two different approaches in maintaining database consistency. One approach is to provide some recovery actions such as modifying the original transaction. Another approach is simply to reject the transaction. These two approaches are summarized in the following two subsections.

2.4.1 Transaction Recovery

When a constraint is violated, the integrity checking system will perform some recovery actions such as generating extra updates onto the database so that its integrity can be restored. For example, in the supplier-part database [Date86], when a supplier is deleted, it may violate the referential constraint. Under the transaction recovery approach, extra deletions of the supplier-part tuples which have the same supplier-id as the deleted supplier are generated. Since this class of strategy provides some automatic recovery mechanism, special update such as cascade deletion is well supported.

However, this class of strategy has the following drawbacks :

1. Each recovery action can induce new updates to the database, which may violate yet another constraint in the database. Upon such violation, another new set of updates will be introduced. This process can continue indefinitely and infinitely many new updates comprising insertion and deletion can be generated. It is generally undecidable if an arbitrary set of recovery actions will always terminate for a given set of input transactions.
2. Even if the set of recovery actions can be proven that their executions will always terminate for all inputs (transactions), it is difficult to ensure that the generated recovery actions actually restore the database integrity.
3. There are many possible recovery actions that can restore an inconsistent database. For example, given that the constraint "The salary of the president cannot be less than that of any employee" is violated, to restore the consistency of the database, we can either decrease some employees' salaries or increase the president's. However, such decision is up to the user, not the DBMS, to choose a solution. Hence, it is generally hard to specify which recovery actions should be used except for some trivial cases.

2.4.2 Transaction Rejection

For the transaction rejection approach, when an integrity constraint is violated, the checking system simply rejects the transaction and outputs the constraint which was violated. It is therefore the user's responsibility to modify the transaction. In this case, the checking method does not suffer the undecidable problem experienced in the recovery method. However, simply rejecting a transaction may not be a good solution for many applications. For example, just for the referential constraint alone, execution of the deletion of a supplier requires separate effort to include all the corresponding supplier-part tuples into the submitted transaction.

2.5 MAINTENANCE OF EXTRA KNOWLEDGE

Certain checking methods such as [Nico82, Koba87, Ling87] perform integrity checking only based on the constraint formula itself. One of the drawback of this approach is that in general it cannot provide much simplification for $\exists$-constraints in the form $\exists x\, W(x)$ where $W(x)$ is a well-formed formula. The reason is clear. To validate this constraint, we are required to find some values c which satisfy $W(c)$. Without extra information, such search is essentially the direct evaluation of the constraint itself. Besides ∃-constraints, there are constraints which involve aggregate functions such as SUM and COUNT. With these functions, simplification of checking is difficult without extra information. For example, given the constraint which states "The sum of the quantities of parts which a supplier supplies cannot be more than 1000". Without extra information, the total supplying quantity for a supplier must be re-evaluated every time some related supplier-part tuples are updated.

On the other hand, there are methods which make use of extra information to improve the performance of checking for certain types of constraints. For example, [Paig84] introduces the concept of concrete view and the use of auxiliary variables such as the number of red parts in the database to improve constraint checking. With these extra summarization, many integrity checkings are simplified. In the previous example, [Paig84] remembers for each supplier its sum of supplying quantities. The checking then becomes a trivial numeric comparison instead of searching through the entire database. [Hsu85] makes use of the concept of effective range, which is a view of a relation which contributes to the satisfiability of a constraint. This extra information is shown to reduce the number of tuples accessed during constraint evaluation. [Qian87] makes use of extra knowledge which includes physical access paths, validated constraints and database structures to aid optimization.

While providing extra knowledge can improve integrity checking, the maintenance of such knowledge can easily offset such advantage. For example, [Paig84] enforces the constraint that "There is a red part which is supplied by all london suppliers" by maintaining the number of red part which is supplied by all london suppliers. The constraint is not violated if and only if the count does not drop to zero. When there is a deletion of london supplier, intuitively there is no need to check against the constraint as shown by [Nico82, Koba87, Ling87], however, [Paig84] requires the update of the count to cope with such change. To find out how many red parts is now supplied by all london suppliers is, however, as bad as the direct evaluation of the constraint. Hence, while this method reduces cost during deletion of red part, its efficiency is destroyed when the deletion of a london supplier takes place. On the whole, application of this method is beneficial for simple constraints but becomes undesirable when constraints contain many alternating ∀ and ∃ quantifiers.

2.6 COMPILED VERSUS INTERPRETED

Integrity constraint checking can adopt either a compiled approach or interpreted approach. Under the compiled approach, for each constraint, all classes of plausible transactions are first explored and optimization is performed to generate a formula to enforce the corresponding integrity constraint for each class of transactions. This process is done before any transaction takes place. During the update of the database, the corresponding formula will be selected according to the transaction type and integrity checking is then performed. One of the obvious advantage of this method is the reduction of the repeated computational cost of constraint reformulation and optimization. However, as the number of classes of transactions is generally enormously large, pure compiled approach is only applicable if the classes of plausible transactions is few. For example, methods which only handle single-update transaction can adopt compiled approach.

Another approach is the interpreted approach, where all the reformulations and optimizations are done only after a transaction is given. It is more flexible and does not incur any storage overhead in adopting the prevention approach. However, this approach incurs a higher computation cost because optimization of the pre-test for each constraint needs to be re-calculated for each constraint checking process.

3.0 SURVEY OF VARIOUS METHODS OF CONSTRAINT VERIFICATION

In this section, we shall investigate various methods of constraint verification proposed by different authors.

3.1 TRIGGER

Instead of simply rejecting a transaction which resulted an inconsistent database state, some DBMS's choose to provide some recovery actions so that execution of these actions will restore the database consistency. Such capabilities in DBMSs can be traced back to the "ON condition" of CODASYL [Coda73]. Triggers were proposed for system R [Eswa75, Eswa76] as a mechanism for enforcing integrity constraints ("assertions"). The use of triggers for maintaining materialized views, snapshots, and derived attribute values, and the algorithms for implementing them are described in [Bune79, Koen81, Rous82, Morg83, Blak86, Huds86, Lind86, Hans87].

In particular, a trigger is a rule which specifies an action to be activated when certain database condition is fulfilled. It is often expressed as a rule of the following form :

on <*event*> if <*condition*> then <*action*>.

An event can be primitive or composite. Primitive events are database operations that can be detected by a DBMS such as "DELETION OF TUPLE IN SUPPLIER", or external events that are signaled by external processes such as timer processes and hardware failures. Formal parameters may be supplied to the event but the values must be bound to the actual values at the time the event occurs. Composite events such as "INSERTION OF TUPLE IN EMP AFTER 1-MAY-1991" are constructed from primitive events using algebraic operations such as "AND", "AFTER".

A condition is a query on the database. If the evaluation of the query is true or returns a non-empty answer, then the condition is satisfied. An event specifies the external condition (event) for the rule to be triggered, while a condition specifies the internal condition which must be satisfied to trigger the rule. Actions are generally a set of database operations such as insertions, deletions and modifications. However, notification to the user, waiting for external inputs, and invocation of an application program can be part of the action. These operations are supposed to restore the database consistency automatically, or at least force the user to perform further actions. For example, in the supplier-part database [Date86], if we delete a supplier record, then the referential constraint may be violated because there may be some records in the supplier-part relation which refer to the deleted supplier. However, if we delete all the tuples that refer to that deleted supplier in the supplier-part relation, then the consistency of the referential constraint can be restored. Such a deletion is also known as **cascade deletion** [Codd90].

Trigger has been implemented in several database systems such as System R [Eswa75, Eswa76], Sybase [Syba87] and VAX Rdb/VMS SQL. Automatic enforcement of referential integrity constraints by the means of cascade deletion [Codd90] is also included in the ANSI SQL2 standard. The HiPAC project [Daya88a, Daya88b] has proposed an Event-Condition-Action (ECA) rule as a formalism for trigger capabilities [Denn89].

There are some variations in the method of specifying trigger rules as well as their functionality among various trigger systems. For example, in the TANGUY-system, trigger rules are classified into before-rules and after-rules. Each before-rule is fired before its associated event such as physical update is executed, while an after-rule is fired after the associated event is executed. Another variation in the TANGUY-system is that it provides a passivation function. During the execution of a trigger rule, it can activate and passivate dynamically some other rules in the system. The rationale behind them is to support different versions of the same rule-based system, as well as to cope with exception handling. For example, in a school administration system, in order to provide exception for the president's daughter, the TANGUY system proposed a passivate and activate pairs to handle such a condition. Two rules are added :

```
(rule-name: b-register-president's-daughter
context:    BEFORE  (mes.receiver belongs-to SECTION) AND
                    (mes.operation = insert-message)  AND
                    (mes.para-message = enrolls)
condition: (mes.para.instance is-president's-daughter)
action:     (RULES  passivate rule-inst:
                    (Rule-name IN :
                    {prevent-overbooking,
                     enforce-course-acceptance-policy}
                    is-name-of)
priority:  1000
continuation: CONTINUE)

context:    AFTER   (mes.receiver belongs-to SECTION) AND
                    (mes.operation = insert-message)  AND
                    (mes.para-message = enrolls)
condition: (mes.para.instance is-president's-daughter)
action:     (RULES  activate rule-inst:
                    (Rule-name IN :
                    {prevent-overbooking,
                     enforce-course-acceptance-policy}
                    is-name-of)
priority:  1000
continuation: CONTINUE)
```

By this pair of rules, if the student is found to be the daughter of the President, then TANGUY will passivate the rule which specifies that every enrolled students should meet certain qualifications and the rule to prevent overbooking. After the transaction is finished, the two rules are re-activated.

The execution order of trigger after-rules also varies in various systems. It can be operated in the following different ways :

1. Rule can be executed *eagerly* just after each single operation is performed to the database. For example, triggers in Sybase and System R.
2. Rules are executed *patiently* only after all the actions specified in a transaction has been performed but before the commitment of the transaction. For example, assertions in System R.
3. Rules are executed *lazily* such that their executions can be deferred even after the commitment of transactions. This approach cannot undo a

committed transaction, but instead it will perform other delayed actions to restore the database consistency. This restoration of database states will be activated whenever demand arises. Postgres has implemented such execution mode.

In [Ceri90], the *eager* execution mode is used. The author described the order of rule execution as follows : after an application has issued a transaction, it will be executed until the commit point of that transaction. Then, the system starts to process the trigger rules. Based on the database operation in the transaction and the change in the database state, a set of rules is triggered. One rule is chosen from this set for evaluation. The selection of rules can be arbitrarily random, or based on a priority scheme such that one of the highest priority rules can be selected to execute first. If the rule's condition is evaluated to be false, then the semantic integrity enforced by that rule is not being violated at that point of the database. In this case, another triggered rule will be selected for evaluation until all trigger rules have been examined. On the other hand, when the condition of a triggered rule is evaluated to be true, the database consistency has been violated. In this case, its associated action will be executed to recover the consistency. If the action is simply a ROLLBACK, the transaction is rollback and the checking process is terminated. Otherwise, assume the rule being processed is R and the database operations in the action part of R is A, then A combined with the current transaction T_i forms another transaction T_{i+1}, that is, the checking system will consider the action from the trigger rule R as if it were executed as part of the user-specified transaction. Rules that have already been evaluated are considered to have already "processed" by the old transaction T_i and therefore will not be triggered again unless A contains some database operations which trigger them. The rest of the unprocessed rules will be triggered by the new transaction T_{i+1} resulted from combining the current transaction T_i with A. This process is applied recursively until either there is no more rule being triggered or no triggered rule has its condition satisfied. In this case, the entire transaction is then committed.

3.2 NICOLAS'S METHOD

[Nico82] adopts the after-checking and interpreted approach, and is targeted at single-updates. The method is declarative and does not maintain extra knowledge. [Nico82] uses closed well-formed formulas to express integrity constraints in relational databases. For example, the following expresses the referential constraint for the supplier-part relation :

$$\forall S\# \forall P\# \forall Qty \exists Loc \exists Color$$
$$(\neg sp(S\#, P\#, Qty) \vee (s(S\#, Loc) \wedge p(P\#, Color)))$$

One of the major contributions of [Nico82] is the recognition of the assumption that each constraint was satisfied before each transaction. By using this assumption, constraint checking for $\forall$-constraints can be greatly simplified. This thought has then been continued and used by almost every subsequent research on this area. Basically, the method tries to optimize the checking process by converting each constraint into a simplified formula based on the database operation. The method finds a set of substitutions γ_i based on the inserted/deleted tuple. With the set γ_i, the author further described how to construct simplified formulas for after-checking.

However, the substitution set γ_i is defined for those variables which are universally quantified but not governed by any existentially quantified variable. Therefore, no simplified version can be generated if the constraint is of the form $\exists x \forall y\ W(x,y)$. Furthermore, since modification is treated as a deletion followed by an insertion, unnecessary checkings may be required in certain modifications of attribute values of relation tuples.

3.3 HENSCHEN'S THEOREM PROVING METHOD

[Hens84] adopts the compiled, declarative, and after-checking approach. This method is targeted at single-updates and some particular kinds of transactions such as "Delete all red parts". Integrity constraints are expressed by first order formulas. This method is based on resolution proving procedure. [Hens84] first constructs a set of axioms based on the set of updates in a given transaction. These axioms define the relationship between all the updated relational predicates in the old database and the same predicates in the updated database. For example, if a tuple $r(a)$ is deleted in the database, [Hens84] will define $r_{OLD}(x)$ as the predicate before the transaction and $r_{NEW}(x)$ as the predicate after the transaction. Three related axioms added are as follows,

$$\neg r_{OLD}(x) \vee (x=a) \vee r_{NEW}(x)$$
$$\neg r_{NEW}(x) \vee (x \neq a)$$
$$\neg r_{NEW}(x) \vee r_{OLD}(x)$$

The first axiom states that each tuple found in the relation

r_{OLD} before update either appears in the updated relation r_{NEW} or is $r(a)$. The second axiom states that $r(a)$ is not in the new relation r_{NEW}. The last axiom states that all tuples in r_{NEW} are also in r_{OLD}.

Another set of axioms is constructed based on each integrity constraint. This set of axioms combined with the set of axioms generated by the given transaction becomes the basis of Henschen's proving procedure. To validate an integrity constraint, [Hens84] proposes to show a contradiction arises if we deny that the constraint holds in the new database. For example, to validate the constraint "Every company supplies nuts must also supply bolts", we add an axiom which indicates that the constraint holds in the old database :

$$\neg s_{OLD}(X, nuts) \vee s_{OLD}(X, bolts)$$

and deny that the constraint holds in the new database with the following two new axioms :

$$s_{NEW}(k, nuts)$$

$$\neg s_{NEW}(k, bolts)$$

where k is a Skolem constant.

During the resolution process, all the NEW relations are first eliminated. Further transformation of axioms can be done by making use of the fact that the constraint is satisfied prior updates, the equality axiom : $(\forall x)$ $(x=x)$, and paramodulation [Chan73] until no more axioms can be eliminated. In the case of the update CHANGE $s(a, nuts)$ to $s(b, nuts)$, after the elimination process, [Hens84] yields three axioms :

$$\neg s_{OLD}(b, bolts)$$

$$\neg s_{OLD}(b, nuts)$$

$$s_{OLD}(a, nuts)$$

To complete the refutation, it is required that either company b supplies bolts (so that company b can now supply nuts), or company b supplies nuts or company a does not supply nuts (where the modification is unsuccessful). This generates three queries to the database. If either one of the queries is success, then a contradiction arises and the constraint is satisfied.

However, his method is not complete. When no contradiction is found, it does not imply that the constraint is violated. Even there is a contradiction, it is not necessary that the refutation process is able to find such contradiction.

3.4 FINITE DIFFERENCING METHOD

R. Paige and S. Koenig have introduced an integrity checking method known as finite differencing method [Paig84]. It is a compiled approach which can handle single-updates. The method basically converts each integrity constraint into set operations. For example, the constraint that "there exists a red part" is converted to "If S denotes the set of all red parts, then the size of S must be greater than zero." The size of S, in this case, is explicitly stored as a variable in the database. In the case where a red part is inserted/deleted, this variable will only need to increase/decrease by one. The authors have identified this class of integrity constraints and called it 1DP which would require only O(1) time for integrity checking. The authors further discussed some transformations which can convert those integrity constraints outside the class of 1DP into several 1DP constraints.

However, given a more general constraint, the reformulated set test may involve a membership deciding procedure, which may not be O(1). Furthermore, when there are conjunctions of conditions, the set decision cost grows in the same rate as the traditional evaluation method. For example, to define a set of tuple S from relation r which satisfies both condition c_1 and c_2, the following set is defined

$$S = \{x \in \{y \text{ if } c_1(y)\} \text{ if } c_2(x)\}$$

Exactly how these two sets (concrete views) are being maintained is not stated. Should the set $\{y \text{ if } c_1(y)\}$ be explicitly stored, which demands too much space overhead, and requires high maintenance cost. Should it be re-calculated each time, which makes the method computationally expensive and is no better than a direct constraint evaluation.

3.5 HSU'2 AND-OR ALGORITHM

[Hsu85] is a declarative method which uses closed formulas of tuple calculus in the prenex normal form to express integrity constraints. The method adopts the before-checking approach and is applicable for general transactions. The method makes use of the differential method to construct a formula, known as the updated constraint, to be tested before the actual update. In particular, [Hsu85] provides a fast tool for a preliminary but fast simplification of a constraint when not much of the detail of a transaction is known. In case further simplification is needed, one must look for other methods requiring more information about updates and constraints.

The major contribution of the method is to reduce the search space during constraint evaluation for $\exists$-constraints.

It introduces a notion called effective range. In each constraint, each ∃-quantified tuple variable which is not governed by any ∀-quantifier has an effective range. It is a set of tuples in the corresponding relation table which contributes to the satisfaction of that particular constraint. Checking against certain ∃-constraint is therefore limited only to the tuples in effective ranges, instead of the corresponding entire relations. For example, given a constraint which states that "There is a red part which is supplied by all london suppliers", the corresponding effective range is the set of all red parts which satisfy the constraint. When some red parts are deleted, it is sufficient to check if the effective range is not empty after the deletion. [Hsu85] further proposes four rules and two decomposition processes to simplify constraints. It finally concludes with a complete algorithm to perform first-phase simplification on transactions during compiled-time. By his method, given a transaction which inserts a set of tuples Δr_3 into relation r_3, a constraint of the form of

$$\exists t_1 \in r_1 \exists t_2 \in r_2 \forall t_3 \in r_3 \; A(t_1, t_2, t_3)$$

can be simplified into

$$\exists t_1 \in Vr_1 \exists t_2 \in Vr_2 \forall t_3 \in r_3 + \Delta r_3 \; A(t_1, t_2, t_3)$$

where Vr_1 and Vr_2 are effective ranges of the tuple variables t_1 and t_2 respectively.

While this method has its own theoretical value, however, there is no mention on how an effective range should be computed or stored. It only assumes such a range exists and can be computed as fast as a normal tuple query. In general, the maintenance of an effective range can be even more costly than a direct evaluation of the constraint. Another draw back of [Hsu85] is that the simplification process can only be applied to certain types of ∃-constraints. For those constraints which are quantified by more than one ∃-quantifier, [Hsu85] will run into the combination problem and fail to simplify them for general transactions.

3.6 QIAN'S CONSTRAINT REFORMULATION

Instead of evaluating the integrity constraint itself, [Qian87] adopts a constraint reformulation approach. It converts each integrity constraint into another constraint which is supposed to be cheaper to evaluate. Strictly speaking, this reformulation process is done without considering any particular transaction, nor accessing the database.

In [Qian87], by making use of the external knowledge K, a constraint P is reformulated into P', known as antecedent of P, such that

1. K together with P' implies P
2. P' is both computationally cheaper than P and semantically as weak as possible.

For example, given the extra knowledge that

> "Every employee only works on those projects of the department he belongs to"

the constraint which states that

> "The salary of an employee cannot be higher than the budget of the department which contains some projects that the employee is working on"

is transformed into

> "The salary of an employee cannot be higher than the budget of the department which he belongs to"

The knowledge K used by the method includes cardinalities of relationships, other validated integrity constraints, database structures, physical organization and access paths, which includes materialized links and indexes. After describing the process which can derive multiple choices of antecedents, the paper further describes a heuristic search based on some guidelines and a cost function to find the best reformulation P' of a given constraint P. The cost function used in the search is based on two components : the computational cost of P', and the semantic weakness measure of P'.

One major drawback of the reformulation method is that the antecedent of the original constraint may be semantically too strong. In the above example, the antecedent restricts the salary of every employee while the original constraint does not restrict the salary of an employee who is not working on any project. This implies that failure of the test does not necessarily mean the constraint is violated. Furthermore, the reformulation only works for constraints which are ∀-quantified.

3.7 KOBAYASHI'S METHOD

[Koba87] uses declarative method and integrity constraints are expressed in tuple calculus. The checking adopts the compiled, before-checking approach and is capable of handling certain types of multiple updates without using of extra knowledge. The author classified integrity constraints according to the patterns of the combinations of ∀-quantifiers and ∃-quantifiers. For each pattern, the author stated a set of rules which reduces the integrity checking. For example, given a constraint $\forall t_{\in R} \; W(t)$ where $W(t)$ is a well-formed formula and contains no tuple variable ranged over relation R, an insertion of tuple c into relation R will not violate the constraint if and only if $W(c)$ is true in the current database.

One of the major contributions of [Koba87] is the introduction of some elementary checkings for ∃-constraints during deletion. Given an integrity constraint $\exists t_{\in R} W(t)$ where $W(t)$ is a well-formed formula and contains no tuple variable ranged over relation R, when a tuple c is deleted from the relation R, [Koba87] will not immediately check against the pre-test $\exists t_{\in R-\{c\}} W(t)$, instead, it will first evaluate $W(c)$. If it is false, then no checking is necessary. Otherwise, direct checking is performed. This principle can be further illustrated by the following example :

Given a constraint "There is a red part which is supplied by a london supplier", when a red part is deleted, the method will check first if the deleted part has been supplied by a london supplier, if the answer is negative, then no checking is required.

However, [Koba87] does not offer any improvement over constraint-types such as ∀∃∀ and ∃∀∃.

3.8 LING'S IC-FORMULA METHOD

[Ling87] is a declarative method where integrity constraints are expressed by well-formed formulas known as IC-formulas. An IC-formula is in the form $not(F)$ where F is a conjunction of positive literals and/or IC-formulas. It is relational complete and is capable of specifying integrity constraints. For example, the key constraint of the supplier-id in the supplier relation can be written as,

$$not(\, s(S\#, L_1) \wedge s(S\#, L_2) \wedge not(L_1 = L_2)\,)$$

The method adopts the compiled and before-checking approach. However, it is only targeted for single updates. One merit of the method is the elimination of unnecessary checkings in the case of modifications. Methods such as [Nico82, Hsu85] treat each modification as a deletion followed by an insertion. However, [Ling87] shows that there are unnecessary checkings which can be avoided if we consider each modification as a single atomic operation. Furthermore, the proposed IC-formula is Prolog-like, and constraint checking can be easily incorporated with any conventional Prolog system. The method is complete in the sense that it can be applied to all types of constraints. However, it cannot handle multiple-update transactions in general.

4.0 CONCLUSION

We have described a variety of principles behind integrity checking for relational databases. Each integrity constraint checking method can be classified according to the following characteristics : the declarative versus procedural nature, the timing of the actual checking process (i.e. detection, prevention, and delayed approaches), single-update versus multiple-update, the action after checking (i.e. transaction recovery and transaction rejection approaches), the inclusion of extra knowledge, and the compiled versus interpreted to perform optimization. We have identified various methods proposed by different authors [Nico82, Hens84, Paig84, Hsu85, Qian87, Koba87, Ling87], as well as a description of some trigger systems. The characteristics, the way to express integrity constraints and the application domain of each method together with its merits and short-comings are discussed. It is, however, possible to combine different characteristics in devising an integrity checking method, for example, many trigger systems adopt both before-checking and after-checking. Further research can also investigate the possibility to combine methods which perform well for ∀-constraints such as [Nico82, Ling87] with methods which perform well for ∃-constraints such as [Hsu85]. The challenge for finding a good combination of characteristics and methods for a given class of constraints and transactions is still wide open.

REFERENCES

[Beve87] M. Bever and R. Lorie, "An enhanced referential integrity scheme supporting complex objects", *IBM Research Report*, RJ-5585 (1987).

[Blak86] Blakely, J.P. Larson, and F.Tompa, "Efficiently Updating Materialized Views,", *Proceedings ACM SIGMOD on Management of Data*, 61-71, 1986.

[Bune79] Buneman, P. and E. Clemens, "Efficiently Monitoring Relational Databases", *ACM Transaction of Database Systems*, 4, 3, Sept 1979, 368-382.

[Cass88] Marco A. Cassanova, Luiz Tucherman and Antonio L. Furtado, "Enforcing Inclusion Dependencies and Referential Integrity", *Proceedings of the 14th VLDB Conference*, Los Angeles, California (August 1988) 38-49.

[Ceri90] Stefano Ceri and Jennifer Widom, "Deriving Production Rules for Constraint Maintenance", *Proceedings of the 16th VLDB Conference*, Brisbane (1990) 566-577.

[Chan73] Chang, C. and Lee, R.C., "Symbolic Logic and Mechanical Theorem Proving", *Academic Press*, New York, 1973.

[Coda73] CODASYL Data Description Language Committee. *CODASYL Data Description Language Journal of Development June 1973* NBS Handbook 113, 1973.

[Codd90] E.F. Codd, *The Relational Model for Database Management Version 2*, Addison-Wesley, 1990.

[Date86] C.J. Date, *An introduction to database systems, Vol. 1* 4th edition Addison Wesley 1986.

[Date90] C.J. Date, *Relational Database Writings 1985-1989*, Addison-Wesley, 1990.

[Daya88a] U. Dayal, "The HiPAC Project : Combining Active Databases and Timing Constraints", *Special Issue of Real Time Data Base Systems, SIGMOD Record*, 17, 1, March 1988.

[Daya88b] U. Dayal, "Active Database Systems", *Proceedings of third International Conference on Data and Knowledge Bases*, Jerusalem Israel, June 1988.

[Denn89] Dennis R.McCarthy and Umeshwar Dayal, "The Architecture of An Active Data Base Management System", *Proceedings of the 1989 ACM SIGMOD International Conference on the Management of Data* Vol 18, Number 2, June 1989, 215-224.

[Eswa75] K.P. Eswaran and D.D.Chamgerlain. "Function Specifications of a Subsystem for Data Base Integrity", *Proceedings of the 1st International Conference on VLDB* (September 1975).

[Eswa76] K.P. Eswaran. "Specifications, Implementations, and Interactions of a Trigger Subsystem in an Integrated Data Base System." IBM Research Report RJ1820 (August 1976).

[Hans87] Hanson, E., "A Performance Analysis of View Materialization Strategies." *Proceedings of the ACM SIGMOD Conference on Management of Data*, May 1987, 440-453.

[Hens84] Henschen, Mccune and Naqvi, "Compiling constraint-checking programs", *Advances in database theory*, Vol. 2, ed. H. Gallaire, J.Minker and J.M.Nicolas, Plenum Press, N.Y. 1984, 171-210.

[Hsu85] A. Hsu and T. Imielinski, "Integrity Checking for Multiple updates, *Proceedings of ACM-SIGMOD*, May 1985, 152-168.

[Koba87] Isamu Kobayashi, "Database Consistency and Update Validation", *Sanno College Bulletin* Vol 7 No 2 Mark 1987, 105-129.

[Koen81] S. Koening and R.Paige, "A transformational framework for the automatic control of derived data", *Proceedings of the seventh VLDB Conference*, Cannes, France (Sept. 1981). 306-318.

[Lind86] Lindsay, B.L. Haas and C. Mohan., "A Snapshot Differential Refresh Algorithm", *Proceeding on ACM SIGMOD Conference on Management of Data*, 1986, 53-60.

[Ling87] T.W. Ling, "Integrity constraint checking in deductive database using Prolog not-predicate", *Data and Knowledge Engineering* Vol 2, 1987, 145-168.

[Morg83] Morgenstern, M., "Active Databases as a Paradigm for Enhanced Computing Environments", *Proc 9th Internal Conference on VLDB*, 1983, 34-42.

[Nico82] J.M. Nicolas, "Logic for improving integrity checking in relational databases", *Acta Informatica* 18,(3), 1982, 227-253.

[Paig84] R. Paige, "Application of finite differencing to database integrity control and query/transaction optimization", *Advances in database theory*, Vol. 2, ed. H. Gallaire, J.Minker and J.M.Nicolas, Plenum Press, N.Y. 1984, 171-210.

[Qian87] X. Qian and D.R. Smith, "Integrity constraint reformulation for efficient validation", *Proceedings of 13th VLDB Conference*, Brighton, UK, Sept 1987, 417-425.

[Rous82] Roussopoulos, N., "View Indexing in Relational Databases", *ACM Transaction on Database Systems 7*, No. 2, June 1982, 258-290.

[Syba87] Sybase, Inc. *Transact-SQL User's Guide* (1987).

[Zloo78] M.M. Zloof, "Security and Integrity Within the Query-By-Example Database Management Language", *IBM Research Report*, RC6982, Feb 1978.

Realization of Composite Relationship Views Utilizing Regular Expressions

Haiyan XU

Department of Electronics
Fukuoka Institute of Technology
Fukuoka 811-02, Japan

Yahiko KAMBAYASHI

Integrated Media Environment Experimental Lab.
Faculty of Engineering, Kyoto University
Kyoto 606-01, Japan

Abstract

In design database systems, design objects as well as various kinds of binary relationships should be handled. In order to support the cooperation of many designers, flexible views are essential. Views required by designers, however, cannot be defined by subgraphs, because composite relationships not explicitly expressed must be considered. As conventional relational algebra lacks the capability of handling recursive operations, to use a powerful language like Datalog or Prolog is a very common approach. Since use of such a language results in systems with poor efficiency, we take an approach to utilize labeled directed graphs and regular expressions. Query processing on views can be achieved by conversion of regular expressions. As regular expressions are closed under most common operations and there are efficient algorithms to manipulate them, view handling procedures based on regular expressions are efficient, yet keeping enough expressive power.

1 Introduction

During the design process, large amount of design objects are created and there are various kinds of relationships among them, such as history relationships, aggregate relationships, correspondence relationships, exchange relationships, etc. So design database systems (DDBSs) must handle design objects together with relationships among them [Katz90]. Each kind of relationships satisfies a set of axioms, and the composition of more than one kind of relationships may correspond to another relationship. If such composition relationships are physically stored, however, we will have a storage cost problem as well as a maintenance problem of redundant relationships. As a result, it is necessary not to store composition relationships physically, and to make composition relationships available to designers by views and queries. To define such views and queries, use of a powerful language like Datalog or Prolog is a very common approach, since conventional relational algebra lacks the capability of handling recursive operations. Such an approach, however, will result in systems with poor efficiency except when special optimization procedures can be applied.

In this paper, we take the approach to use labeled directed graphs and regular expressions, which have the following advantages:

(1) Transitive relationships, or composite relationships generated by more than one kind of relationships, can be defined.

(2) Regular expressions are closed under most commonly used operations. Especially we will use closure properties under set operations and substitution.

(3) There are efficient algorithms to handle regular expressions. Furthermore, as each regular expression is related to a finite automaton, graph algorithms can be applied.

Our language consists of two parts: relational algebra (or SQL) and graph manipulation language, as discussed in [KaTY77]. The major difference from the approach reported in [KaTY77] is that the capability to define composition relationship views. The difference is similar to view definition capabilities of the network data model and the relational data model. Views of the former model correspond to subgraphs of underlying schema, while relational views can be joined from several relations.

Design objects and relationships among them can be naturally represented in term of labeled directed graphs (where vertices express design objects and edges represent relationships between design objects), if we restrict relationships to be binary. The following examples illustrate the requirements of views.

Example 1.1 (Transitively defined relationships)
Suppose a VLSI circuit design project is carried out by a logic circuit design group and a layout group, which cooperate in the following way: If the products designed by the logic circuit design group pass the logical simulation test, they can be submitted to the layout group.

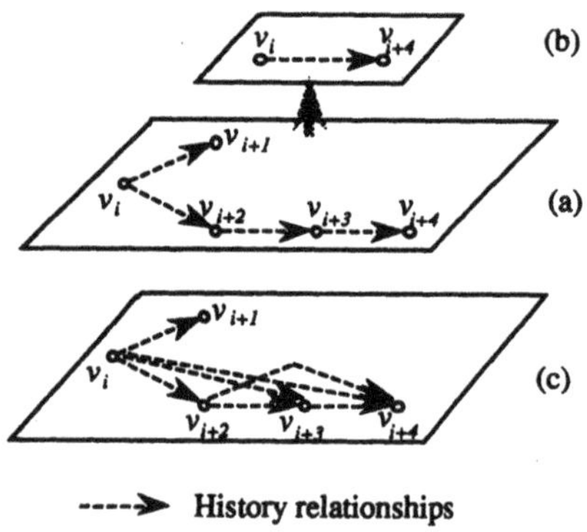

Figure 1: The view required by the layout group

Suppose the layout group finds a problem in design object v_i for layout, then the logic circuit design group must redesign it. Suppose it is done as shown in Figure 1 (a) (a history relationship from v_k to v_j is used to describe that design object v_j is created by refining design object v_k), and the problem is finally resolved in design object v_{i+4}. Obviously, the designers of layout group do not need to access design objects v_{i+1}, v_{i+2} and v_{i+3}. In order to understand the course of design object changes, however, the transitive history relationship from v_i to v_{i+4} should be shown to the layout group (Figure 1 (b)). The view of Figure 1(b) is not a subgraph of Figure 1 (a), although it is a subgraph of Figure 1 (c) which is generated from Figure 1 (a) by adding all transitive relationships. □

Example 1.2 (Composite relationships)
In the hierarchies of Figure 2 (an aggregate relationship from v_k to v_j is used to describe that design object v_k uses design object v_j as a component), suppose that designer B only wants to use design objects whose levels in the hierarchies are higher than or equivalent to the level of v_{i3}. In this case, however, the history relationship between the hierarchies may be lost in designer B's working environment. In order to fill it up, it is necessary to map history relationships in the conceptual schema into designer B's working environment in the following way: if history relationships are found between descendants (components or sub-components, etc.) of objects whose levels in the hierarchy are equivalent to the level of v_{i3}, a history relationship between them should be supplied in the view. □

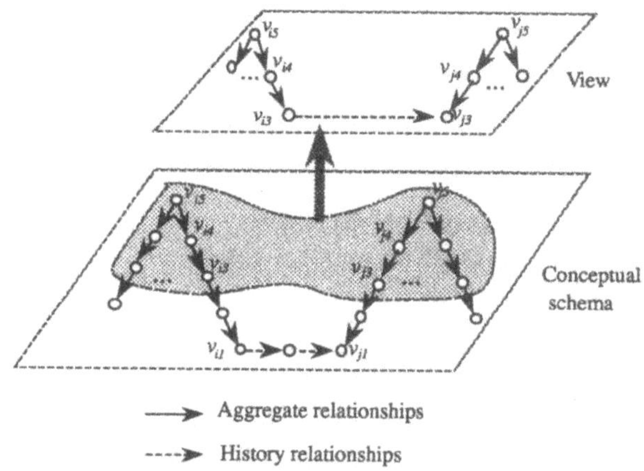

Figure 2: A view providing mapped history relationships

The above examples show typical requirements of views in DDBSs: It requires to map some paths in the conceptual schema (whose length is not fixed) into edges in a view. Although it is possible to express these properties by Prolog, efficiency of computation is a problem. Conventional DDBSs, on the other hand, physically store composite relationships [ChoK86, KaCB86]. So modification of relationships in the conceptual schema may cause some inconsistency problem between them and the composite relationships obtained by them. In this paper, we utilize automata theory to generate and manipulate such kinds of views. The major results are as follows.

(1) View definition functions are introduced, which can map the paths (composite relationships) in the conceptual schema into the edges in views.

(2) Methods to translate queries on views into their equivalent queries on the conceptual schema as well as to process the queries on the conceptual schema, are shown.

The paper is organized as follows: In Section 2, we discuss basic properties of four typical kinds of relationships and use object relationship graphs to represent such relationships. In Section 3, regular expressions on object relationship graphs are formalized. Based on regular expressions, in Section 4 the definition function for composite relationship views is introduced. How to translate queries on views into their equivalent queries on the conceptual schema, is discussed in Section 5. The well-known property: 'regular sets are closed under substitution', is used. We also show the outline of query processing on the conceptual schema in the section. Section 6 is concluding remarks.

2 Relationships Represented by Object Relationship Graphs

It is well known that a non-binary relationship can be represented by binary relationships by introducing an additional variable. In order to simplify the discussion, in this paper we will only use binary relationships to represent relationships between design objects. If all relationships are binary, design data can be represented naturally in term of labeled directed graphs, where vertices express design objects, edges represent relationships between the design objects, and labels of edges show the corresponding relationships for the edges.

Definition 2.1 An *object relationship graph* G is specified by (V, E), where $V = \{v_i \mid v_i$ corresponds to an ID of a design object$\}$ is called the vertex set of G and $E = \{v_i R_k v_j \mid$ there is relationship R_k from v_i to $v_j\}$ is called the labeled edge set of G (The label of edge from v_i to v_j is R_k, for edge $v_i R_k v_j \in E$). □

The typical kinds of relationships between design objects are as follows and Figure 3 shows examples of these relationships.

(1) History relationship $v_i H v_j$:
Design in general is under continuous revision. History relationship $v_i H v_j$ is used to record the history that design object v_j was refined from v_i.

(2) Aggregate relationship $v_i A v_j$:
Since design descriptions form component hierarchies, a given object may be described in terms of its component objects. Aggregate relationship $v_i A v_j$ is used to record the information that design object v_j is a component object of v_i.

(3) Correspondence relationship $v_i C v_j$:
Design descriptions exist across representation levels from a specification level (the top level) to an implementation level (the lowest level). For example, a VLSI circuit is specified by transistor circuits, functional block diagrams, and a functional description. Correspondence relationships $v_i C v_j$ is used to record the information that design objects v_i and v_j describe the same design in different representation levels and v_j is in a lower (i.e., detailed) representation level than v_i.

(4) Exchange relationship $v_i E v_j$:
Design objects can be classified by their functionality, interfaces and implementations [BatK86] and the design objects which have identical functionality and interface may be used interchangeably. Exchange relationship $v_i E v_j$ is used to record such an information between objects v_i and v_j.

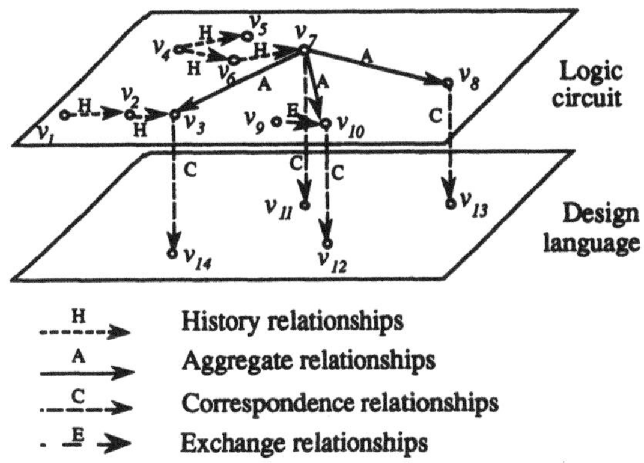

Figure 3: A structure of design data

Binary relationships can be classified by axioms they satisfy. Typical ones are listed as follows, where S is a set and R is a binary relationship on S.

Symmetry: For every a, b in S, aRb implies bRa.

Antisymmetry: For every a, b in S, only one of the three cases is satisfied: aRb, bRa, a and b are not related by R.

Transitivity: For every a, b, c in S, if aRb and bRc, then aRc.

According to the definitions of the four typical kinds of relationships, we can see that they have the following properties: History, aggregate and correspondence relationships are antisymmetric and transitive, while exchange relationships are symmetric and transitive.

A user can also define new kinds of relationships. For example, there may be the case that a circuit A can be replaced by B, B can be replaced by C, but A cannot be replaced by C. In such a case, users can define a new kind of relationship to represent the connection between circuit A and C. New relationships, furthermore, may also be defined by composition of several kinds of relationships. Example 1.2 showed one of such cases. Figure 4 (a) shows the case of composition of correspondence and exchange relationships: suppose v_3 and v_4 are in a same representation level, then there is an induced exchange relationship between v_3 and v_4. The composition of correspondence and history relationships are shown in Figure 4 (b): If two design objects (e.g.,v_1' and v_2') are related with history relationships, then there should be the same relationships between the objects (e.g., v_3' and v_4') which are in the same representation level and have transitive correspondence relationships with the above two objects.

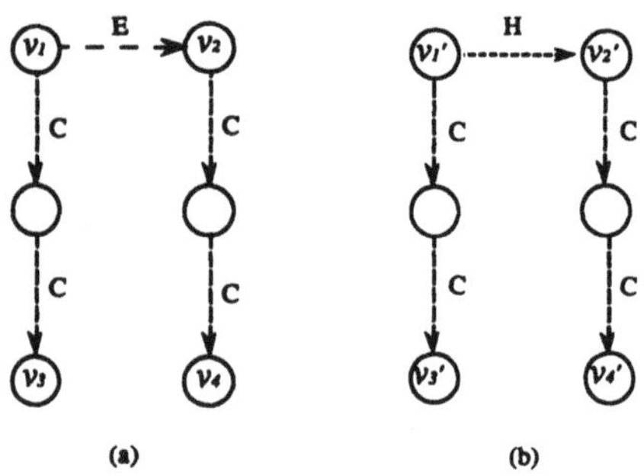

Figure 4: Composition of correspondence and other ones

In general, if we have a set T of relationships, we can get its closure T^* which contains T and all relationships calculated from T by their properties. There may be another set U such that $U^* = T^*$. U is called a minimum cover, if the number of elements in U is minimum (there is no V such that $V^* = T^*$ and $|U| > |V|$, where $|S|$ is the numbers of elements in set S). In order to save the space of DDBSs as well as to avoid the maintenance problem of redundant relationships, in this paper we assume that only the minimum cover of each kind of relationships are stored in the conceptual schema (these relationships are called primitive relationships). Note that a minimum cover is not always unique.

As a result, views of DDBSs cannot be defined by subgraphs, since only the minimum cover of each primitive kind of relationships is stored in the conceptual schema.

3 Regular Expressions for Object Relationship Graphs

Since transitive relationships are required to be provided into views, conventional view functions clearly do not suffice. To handle transitivity, the $*$ operation of regular expressions can be used. In this section, we give the definition of a special form of regular expressions: regular expression for object relationship graphs.

Definition 3.1 Let Σ be a finite alphabet set disjoint from $\{\varepsilon, \phi, +, \cdot, ^*, (,)\}$. A *regular expression* over Σ and the sets that they denote are defined recursively as follows.

(1) ϕ is a regular expression and denotes the empty set.

(2) ε is a regular expression and denotes the null sequence, a sequence of length 0, corresponding to the set $\{\varepsilon\}$.

(3) Each $a \in \Sigma$ is a regular expressions and denotes the set $\{a\}$.

(4) If r and s are regular expressions denoting the language $||r||$ and $||s||$, respectively, then $r + s$, $r \cdot s$ and r^* are regular expressions that denote the sets $||r|| \cup ||s||$, $||r||||s||$(concatenation), and $||r||^*$(closure), respectively. □

In general, a designer only concerns on some design objects which have some specific properties, e.g., the design objects whose designer is "John", the design objects which are updated at July 17, 1989. In order to satisfy such requirements of designers, we introduce the notion of labeling function.

Definition 3.2 Let $G = (V, E)$ be an object relationship graph, Σ be a set of finite alphabets. Then, a *labeling function* L on G is a function from V to Σ, representing by $\{(\gamma_i, Cond_i) \mid \gamma_i \in \Sigma,\ Cond_i$ is the condition for elements of $V\}$, which satisfies:

(1) $L(v_i) = \gamma_k$, if v_i satisfies condition $Cond_k$.

(2) $\forall v_i \in V(\exists \gamma_j \in \Sigma$ s.t. $L(v_i) = \gamma_j)$.

(3) if v_i satisfies $Cond_j$, then v_i does not satisfy $Cond_k(k \neq j)$. □

(2) means that every vertex has to be labeled and (3) means no vertex has more than one label. (2) and (3) are required to simplify the discussion. We can define a label corresponding to no vertex and a label corresponding to a set of vertices. For object relationship graphs, regular expressions in the following form are used (for set $T = \{t_1, t_2, \cdots, t_n\}$, the set notion T in regular expression describes $(t_1 + t_2 + \cdots + t_n)$).

Definition 3.3 Let $G = (V, E)$ be an object relationship graph, L be a labeling function on G. A *regular path expression* q for G and L is a regular expression over $\Sigma_v \cup \Sigma_v$ and $||q|| \subseteq ||(\Sigma_v\Sigma_e)^*\Sigma_v||$, where $\Sigma_{v1} = \{L(v) \mid v \in V\}$, $\Sigma_v = V \cup \Sigma_{v1}$, $\Sigma_e = \{R_k \mid v_iR_kv_j \in E\}$. □

That is, in the sets denoted by regular path expressions, labels for vertices and edges appear alternatively. For example, we give a labeling function L on G as $\{(\gamma_0,\ designer\ is\ \text{"}John\text{"})\cdots\}$. Then, $v_0 H \gamma_0$ is a regular path expression which describes the following kind of paths:

(1) The starting vertex is v_0.

(2) The terminating vertex has label γ_0 determined by L.

(3) There is the history relationship from v_0 to the terminating vertex.

Here $v_0 \in V$, $H \in \Sigma_e$, and $\gamma_0 \in \Sigma_{vl}$. From this example, we can see that labeling functions can be used to simplify the notation of regular expressions. Here, if the notation γ_0 is not used, we have to list all the objects created by *John* for the regular path expression.

For the path P from v_{i1} to v_{ij} in the object relationship graph G: $v_{i1}R_{i1}v_{i2}, v_{i2}R_{i2}v_{i3}, \cdots, v_{ij-1}R_{ij-1}v_{ij} (v_{ik}, v_{ik-1} \in V,\ v_{ik-1}R_{ik-1}v_{ik} \in E)$, we call $(v_{i1} + L(v_{i1}))R_{i1}(v_{i2} + L(v_{i2}))R_{i2} \cdots R_{ij-1}(v_{ij} + L(v_{ij}))$, as the regular expression q_p represented by P. That is, to simplify the definition, we use both vertex names and vertex labels. For this purpose, the set of all the symbols for vertex names and vertex labels are disjoint.

Definition 3.4 A query q is a regular path expression on object relationship graph $G = (V, E)$ and its labeling function L, represented by (G, L, q). The answer of the query is the set: $\{(v_i, v_j) \mid$ in G there is a path P from v_i to v_j which satisfies $||q_p|| \cap ||q|| \neq \phi\}$.

4 Definition of Composite Relationship Views

In this section, based on regular path expressions the definition functions to provide composite relationship views of DDBSs, are introduced and formalized.

In the above section, we have defined the regular path expressions for object relationship graphs. Using regular path expressions, not only transitive relationships can be represented, but also symmetric relationship R can be handled by introducing a new relationship R' and replacing each $\alpha R \beta$ by $(\alpha R' \beta + \beta R' \alpha)$ in the regular path expressions. By using the information of design objects, furthermore, we will see that even composite relationships created by several kinds of relationships can also be represented by regular path expressions. As a result, a view in DDBSs is specified in the following way:

(1) Select a set of vertices from its underlying schema (the conceptual schema or a view) by specifying their IDs or the properties they satisfies,

(2) Give regular path expressions to map the paths in its underlying schema into edges in the view.

(3) Assign the labels for each kinds of edges in the view.

Definition 4.1 *View definition function* is expressed by (G, L, S_v, Q_e, L_e), where

(1) $G = (V, E)$ is the underlying schema of the view.

(2) L is a labeling function on G.

(3) $S_v \subseteq \Sigma_v$.

(4) $Q_e = [q_1, q_2, \cdots, q_m]$ is a list of regular path expressions for G and L.

(5) $L_e = [l_1, l_2, \cdots, l_m]$ is a list of edge labels. □

Definition 4.2 Let (G, L, S_v, Q_e, L_e) be a view definition function. Then, *view* $G' = (V', E')$ defined by the view definition function is constructed in the following way:

$$V' = \{v_i \mid v_i \in V \wedge (v_i \vee L(v_i)) \in S_v\},$$

$$E' = \left\{ v_i R_k v_j \;\middle|\; \begin{array}{l} v_i, v_j \in V',\ \text{there is a path } P \text{ in } G \\ \text{from } v_i \text{ to } v_j, \text{ satisfying} \\ ||q_p|| \cap ||q_k|| \neq \phi, R_k = l_k (1 \leq k \leq m) \end{array} \right\}.$$

□

That is, a path in G, satisfying regular expression q_i (the i-th member of Q_e), is mapped to an edge in the view with label l_i (the i-th member of L_e).

We will show the ways to define views for Examples 1.1 and 1.2.

Example 4.1 View definition for Example 1.1

$$\begin{array}{lcl} G & : & \text{conceptual schema}, \\ L(v) & = & \left\{ \begin{array}{l} (X, \text{test result of } v = \text{"ok"}), \\ (Y, \text{test result of } v \neq \text{"ok"}) \end{array} \right\} \\ S_v & = & \{X\}, \\ Q_e & = & [\ XH(YH)^*X\ ], \\ L_e & = & [H]. \end{array}$$

$XH(YH)^*X$ defines the paths each of which connects two vertices with label X and does not go through another vertices with label X. Such a path is labeled into H in the view. □

Example 4.2 View definition for Example 1.2 (A^r is the edge label of reverse aggregate relationships; *level*(v) represents the level of design object v in its component hierarchy)

$$\begin{array}{lcl} G & : & \text{conceptual schema,} \\ L(v) & = & \left\{ \begin{array}{l} (T_+,\ level(v) > level(v_{i3})), \\ (T,\ level(v) = level(v_{i3})), \\ (T_-,\ level(v) < level(v_{i3})) \end{array} \right\} \\ S_v & = & \{T_+, T\}, \\ Q_e & = & [T(AT_-)^*H(T_-H)^*(T_-A^r)^*T,\ T_+AT_+ + T_+AT], \\ L_e & = & [\ H,\ A\ ]. \end{array}$$

The meaning of $q_1 = T(AT_-)^*H(T_-H)^*(T_-A^r)^*T$ is as follows.

(1) T: starting from one of the vertices with label T in some a hierarchy,

(2) $(AT_-)^*$: go down the hierarchy,

(3) $H(T_-H)^*$: related by H or transitive related by H,

(4) $(T_-A^r)^*$: go up another hierarchy,

(5) T: terminating at one of the vertices with label T (in the another hierarchy). □

5 Query Processing on Composite Relationship Views

In Section 4, we introduced the view function which can extract composite relationships by regular path expressions. After views are defined, designers can apply queries to views. Since views are logical schemata, it is necessary to convert queries on views into their equivalents on the conceptual schema. In conventional databases, the conversion process for retrieval operations is quite straightforward. The system needs only merge the retrieval operations and the view definitions. In DDBSs, however, the problem is not so simple, since a view is not a subgraph of the underlying schema. Furthermore, since views in general may be defined hierarchically (see Figure 5, a view can be defined using another views), it is also necessary to convert queries on hierarchical views efficiently.

In this section, let us first consider the problem of how to convert queries on the views defined directly on the conceptual schema.

Definition 5.1 A *substitution* f is a mapping of Σ_1 onto Σ_2^*. The mapping f is extended to strings as follows: $f(ax) = f(a)f(x)$ and $f(\varepsilon) = \varepsilon$. □

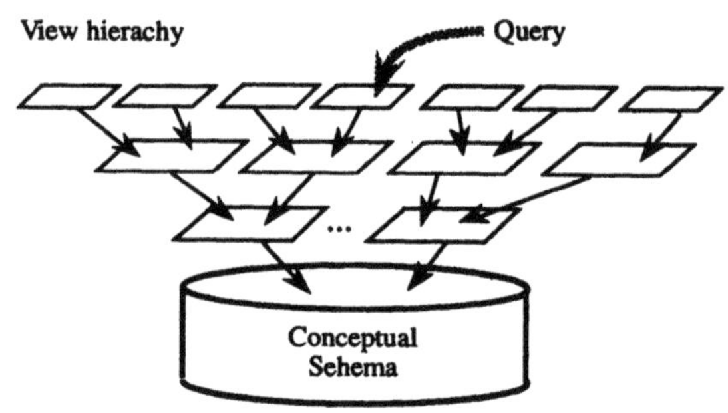

Figure 5: View hierarchies of DDBSs

It is known that regular sets are closed under substitution [HopU79]. Furthermore, given a regular expression r, an nondeterministic finite automaton (NFA for short) which accepts the language $||r||$, can be constructed in polynomial time [AhHU74]. Based on these properties, a query on a view G' can be converted into an equivalent query on its underlying schema. Let us first use an example to show the process of query conversion.

Example 5.1 Suppose a designer expects to construct a view G' by selecting design objects whose designer is *Smith* and transitive history relationships between them. G' can be defined by (G, L, S_v, Q_e, L_e), where

$$\begin{array}{lcl} G & & \text{conceptual schema,} \\ L(v) & = & \left\{ \begin{array}{l} (X, \text{designer of } v = \text{"Smith"}), \\ (X_-, \text{designer of } v \neq \text{"Smith"}) \end{array} \right\} \\ S_v & = & \{X\}, \\ Q_e & = & [\ X(HX_-)^*HX\ ], \\ L_e & = & [\ H'\ ]. \end{array}$$

On the view, suppose a designer expects to retrieve the transitive history relationships between the design objects which have passed their tests. Such a requirement can be represented by the following query on the view G'.

$$\begin{array}{lcl} L'(v_i) & = & \left\{ \begin{array}{l} (X_t, \text{test result of } v_i = \text{"ok"}), \\ (X_n, \text{test result of } v_i \neq \text{"ok"}) \end{array} \right\} \\ q' & = & X_t(H'X_n)^*H'X_t \end{array}$$

The process of conversion of the query on the view into its equivalent query on its underlying schema are graphically indicated in Figures 6, 7 and 8. Figure 6 (b) and (a) show two NFAs which accept the language denoted by the view definition and the query on the view, respectively. The substitutions are illustrated in Figure 7.

Figure 8 (a) shows the result of substitution, that is an NFA including ε-transition. Its ε-free equivalent machine

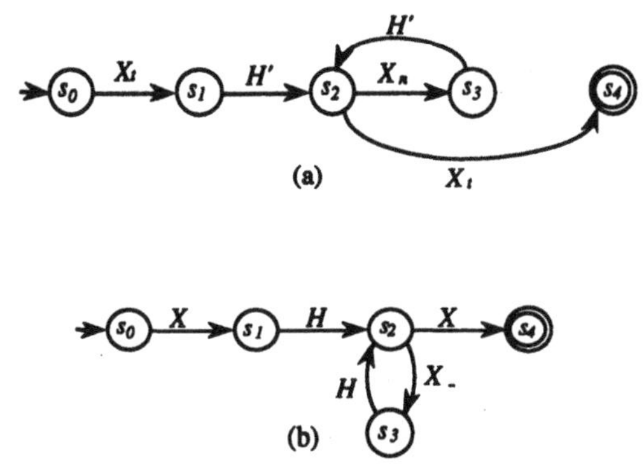

Figure 6: NFAs of a view definition and a query on the view

is shown in Figure 8 (b) †. From Figure 8 (b), we can see that vertex labels in adjoining transitions belong to Σ'_v and Σ_v respectively, e.g., X_t and X in the adjoining transitions from s_0. It is necessary to merge the labels of Σ_v and Σ'_v. The relabeling function for this example is:

$$L''(v_i) = \left\{ \begin{array}{ll} (X^N, & \text{designer of } v_i = \text{“Smith”} \\ & \quad \wedge \text{ test result of } v_i \neq \text{“ok”}, \\ (X^T, & \text{designer of } v_i = \text{“Smith”} \\ & \quad \wedge \text{ test result of } v_i = \text{“ok”}), \\ (Y, & \text{designer of } v_i \neq \text{“Smith”} \\ & \quad \wedge \text{ test result of } v_i \neq \text{“ok”}), \\ (Z, & \text{designer of } v_i \neq \text{“Smith”} \\ & \quad \wedge \text{ test result of } v_i = \text{“ok”}) \end{array} \right\}.$$

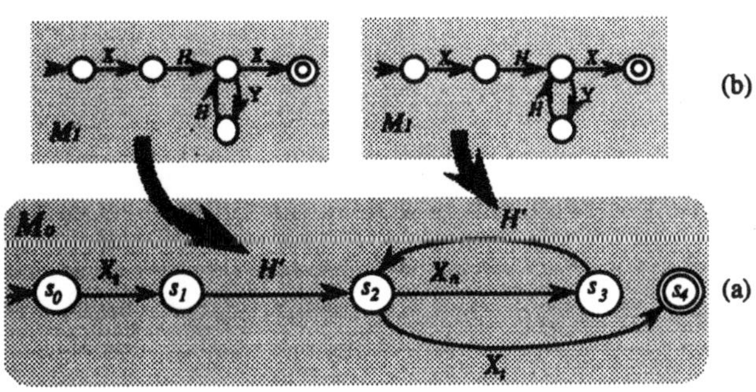

Figure 7: The substitution of Example 5.1

Using the relabeling function above, the ε-free NFA in Figure 8 (b) is converted into the NFA shown in Figure 8 (c), which accepts the language denoted the regular path expression on G (the underlying schema of the view). Now, we have constructed the NFA_1 accepting the language denoted query on G equivalent to the view query q'_1 of Q'_e. □

†For an NFA $M = (S, \Sigma, \delta, s_0, F)$, if $(\delta(s_i, \varepsilon) = s_j) \wedge (\nexists s_k \in S\ \nexists b \in \Sigma(\delta(s_k, b) = s_j)) \vee ((\forall d \neq \varepsilon \in \Sigma(\delta(s_i, d) = \phi)) \wedge (\delta(s_i, \varepsilon) = \{s_j\}))$, then for simplicity, we merge s_i and s_j into a single state.

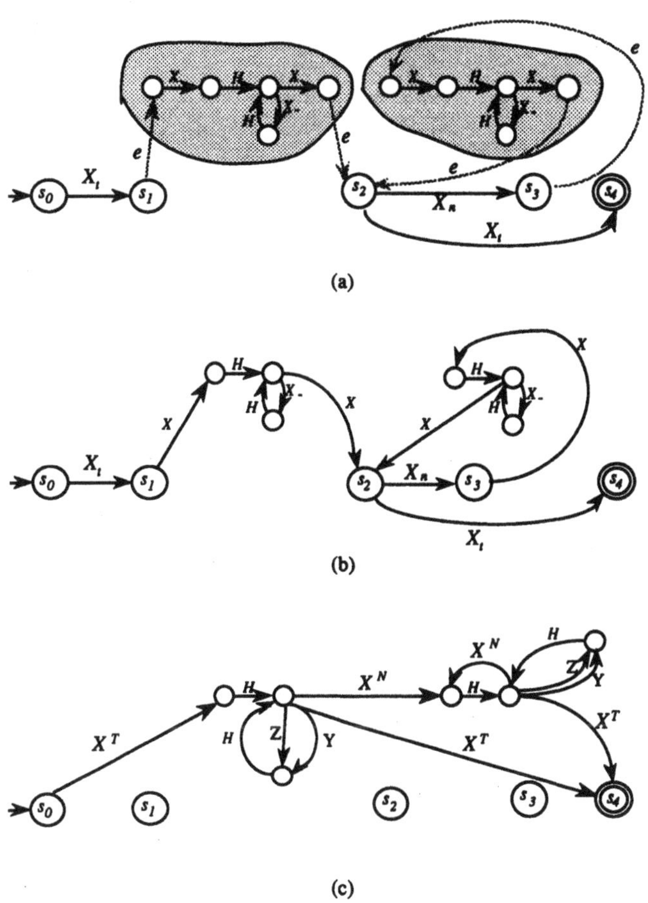

Figure 8: The conversion processes of query on a view

Algorithm 5.1: Query processing on views.
Input: Definition of view G': (G, L, S_v, Q_e, L_e),
a query on the view: (G', L', q') .
Output: a query on G: (G, L'', q'').
Method:
for each l_i in L_e **do** $f(l_i) := q_i$;
for each vertex label $x \in \Sigma'_v$ **do** $f(x) := x$;
for each $q'_i \in Q'_e$ **do**
  calculate $f(q'_i)$;
  construct NFA= $(S, \Sigma, \delta, s_0, F)$ accepting $||f(q'_i)|| - \{\epsilon\}$;
  for each $\delta(s_0, y) = s_j, \delta(s_j, x) = s_k$, $x \in \Sigma_v, y \in \Sigma'_v$ **do**
    $z := relabel(x, y, \Sigma_v, \Sigma'_v)$;
    if $z \neq$ " " **then**
      $\delta'(s_0, z) := s_k$; *change*(s_k) **end if**
  end for
end for
convert the NFA' into the regular expression q'',
  where NFA' accepts $||q''||$.
procedure *change*(s);

```
for each δ(s, w) = s1, w ∈ Σe do
  δ'(s, w) := s1;
  for each δ(s1, x) = sj, δ(sj, y) = sp, x ∈ Σv, y ∈ Σe do
    if x ∈ V then δ'(s1, x) := sj else
      for each w ∈ Σ'v1 do
        z := relabel(x, w, Σv, Σ'v);
        δ'(s1, z) := sj;
      end for
    end if
    change(sj);
  end for
  for each δ(s1, x) = sj, δ(sj, y) = sp, x ∈ Σv, y ∈ Σ'v do
  if sp ∈ F then
    z := relabel(x, y, Σv, Σ'v);
    if z ≠ " " then δ'(s1, z) := sp end if
  end if
  for each δ(sp, w) = sk, w ∈ Σv do
    if x = w then z1 := x else
      if (x ∈ V) ∧ ((w, Cond) ∈ L)∧ (x s.t. Cond)
        then z1 := x;
      if (w ∈ V) ∧ ((x, Cond) ∈ L)∧ (w s.t. Cond)
        then z1 := w;
      z := relabel(z1, y, Σv, Σ'v);
    end if
    if z ≠ " " then δ'(s1, z) := sk; change(sk) end if
  end for
end for
end procedure
function relabel(x, y, Σv, Σ'v);
/* construct relabeling function by merging L and L'; */
relabel := " ";
if ((x, Cond1) ∈ L)∧ ((y, Cond2) ∈ L') then
  L'' := L'' ∪ {(a new label, Cond1 ∧Cond2)};
  relabel := the new label;
end if
if (x ∈ V) ∧ ((y, Cond) ∈ L')∧ (x satisfies Cond)
  then relabel := x;
if ((x, Cond) ∈ L) ∧ (y ∈ V') ∧ (y satisfies Cond)
  then relabel := y;
if (x ∈ V) ∧ (y ∈ V') ∧ (x = y) then relabel := x
end function
```

According to the property: regular sets are closed under substitution [HopU79], we can proof the following theorem.

Theorem 5.1 *Algorithm 5.1 correctly converts a query* (G', L', q') *on view* G' *(defined by* (G, L, S_v, Q_e, L_e)*) into its equivalent on the underlying schema* G.

Proof: For q', after substitution f each edge label in Σ'_e is converted into a regular path expression which represents the corresponding paths in its underlying schema G. Since the regular set is closed under substitution, $f(q')$ is also a regular expression. $f(q')$, however, is not a regular path expression, because in NFA= $(S, \Sigma, \delta, s_0, F)$ accepting $||f(q')||$, there may be the following three cases which do not satisfy the definition of regular path expression.

(1) labels in adjoining transitions beginning from s_0 belong to Σ'_v, Σ_v and Σ_e.

(2) labels in adjoining transitions terminating at $s_f \in F$ belong to Σ_e, Σ_v and Σ'_v.

(3) Otherwise, labels in adjoining transitions may belong to (a) Σ_v, Σ'_v and Σ_v, or (b) Σ_e, Σ_v and Σ_e.

In order to convert $f(q')$ into a regular path expression, Algorithm 5.1 merges the vertex labels in the following way: In the cases 1, 2 and 3(a), Algorithm 5.1 merges the vertex labels in adjoining transitions into a new vertex label in Σ''_v and changes these adjoining transitions into a new transition with the merged vertex label in Σ''_v. In the case 3(b), Algorithm 5.1 changes the transition with the vertex label in Σ_v into transitions with equivalent vertex labels in Σ''_v. As a result, the NFA is converted into the one which accepts $||q''||$, where q'' is the regular path expression for G and L'', equivalent to q'. □

We have seen how queries on a view may be converted into their equivalents on the underlying schema. Queries on hierarchical views, of course, can be converted recursively. The cost of such a conversion, however, may be expensive. Since many views may be defined in DDBSs, converting hierarchical view definitions into their equivalents on the conceptual schema is very important. By using the query conversion algorithm recursively, we can convert a hierarchical view into an equivalent view on the conceptual schema (Figure 9). Such conversion is necessary only once per view; the product can usually be utilized many times. As a result, designers can define hierarchical views according to their requirements; the DDBSs however, can convert queries directly.

Using formal language theory, on the other hand, the processing query q on the conceptual schema G can be done in the following way [Wood88]:

(a) Construct an NFA= $(S, \Sigma, \delta, s_0, F)$ accepting $||q|| - \{\epsilon\}$ [AhHU74].

(b) Construct an intersection graph of the NFA and the conversion graph $G^c = (V^c, E^c)$ of the object relation-

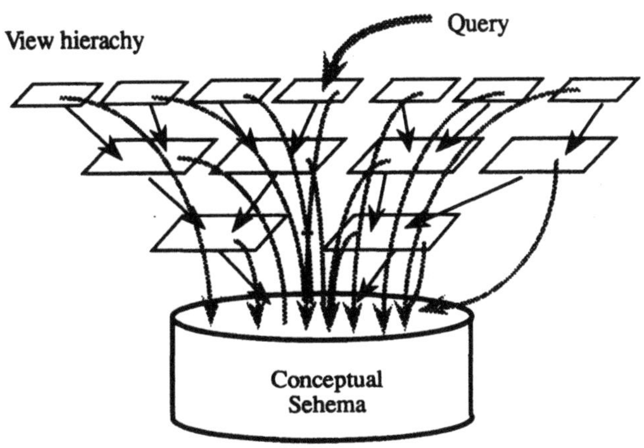

Figure 9: Conversion queries on hierarchical views directly

ship graph $G = (V, E)$ where $V^c = \{v_i^b \mid v_i \in V, b = 1, 2\}$, $E^c = \{v_i^2 R_k v_j^1 \mid v_i R_k v_j \in E\} \cup \{v_i^1 R_k v_i^2 \mid L(v_i) = R_k\} \cup \{v_i^1 v_i v_i^2 \mid v_i \in V\}$

(c) Find the paths in the intersection graph starting from (v_i^1, s_0) and terminating at (v_j^2, s_f), where $s_f \in F$. If there is such a path in the intersection graph, there is a path from v_i to v_j in the object relationship graph G, which satisfies the regular path expression q.

Let n be the number of the vertices of the object relationship graph G, the processing time of such regular path expressions can be bounded by $O(n^3)$ [HopU79]. Furthermore, there is much scope for possible improvements to the query processing.

6 Concluding Remarks

In this paper, we have established the necessity of composite relationships views in DDBSs, introduced view definition functions to provide them, and given the method to process queries on such views. Although in general, designers only need to access a subset of design objects, we have shown that the composite relationships between them satisfying certain properties may be important in their working environments. We indicated our view function is a very useful tool to provide such working environments and it can overcome many problems of previous work. By using results of the formal language theory, we showed that queries on these views can be converted into equivalent queries on the conceptual schema.

Future work includes expanding the view definition function to provide a working environment based on several existing views, discussing the method to optimize queries.

Acknowledgments

The authors are grateful to Associate Professor Tetsuya FURUKAWA of Kyushu University for many valuable discussions.

References

[AhHU74] A. V. Aho, J. E. Hopcroft, and J. D. Ullman, *The Design and Analysis of Computer Algorithms,* Addison-Wesley, Reading, MA, 1974.

[Bern87] P. A. Bernstein, "Database Systems Support for Software Engineering - An Extended Abstract," *Proc. of the 9th Software Engineering Conf.*, 1987, pp.160-178.

[BatK86] D. Batory and W. Kim, "Supporting Version of VLSI CAD Object," *IEEE Trans. Software Eng.*, 1986.

[ChoK86] H.-T. Chou and W. Kim, "A Unifying Framework for Version Control in a CAD Environment," *Proc. of the 12nd Int. Conf. on Very Large Data Bases*, Kyoto, Japan, Aug. 1986, pp. 336-344.

[HopU79] J. E. Hopcroft and J. D. Ullman, *Introduction to Automata Theory, Languages, and Computation,* Addison-Wesley, Reading, MA, 1979.

[KaTY77] Y, Kambayashi, K, Tanaka and S. Yajima, "A Relational Data Language with Simplified Binary Relation Handing Capability," *Proc. of the 3th Int. Conf. on Very Large Data Bases*, pp.338-350, 1977.

[Katz90] R. H. Katz, "Toward a Unified Framework for Version Modeling in Engineering Databases", *ACM Comput. Surv.*, Vol. 22, No. 4, 1990, pp. 375-408.

[KaCB86] R. H. Katz, E. Chang, and R. Bhateja, "Version Modeling Concepts for Computer-Aided Design Databases", *Proc. of ACM-SIGMOD Int. Conf. on Management of Data*, 1986, pp. 379-386.

[Wood88] P. T. Wood, "Queries on Graphs", Ph.D Thesis, University of Toronto, 1988.

A NESTED TRANSACTION MODEL FOR ENGINEERING APPLICATIONS

Rainer Unland

University of Hagen, Department of Computer Science
P.O. Box 940, D-5800 Hagen 1
Germany

Abstract

Before database systems are suitable to support new application areas, like for example CAD / CAM or CASE, they have to consider the special requirements of these environments. Main characteristics are the long duration of a design process, group-oriented division of areas of responsibility, and cooperative work between and within these groups. Due to the complexity, the group-orientation, the long duration of design processes and the enormous number of objects involved, a nested hierarchical transaction model seems to be absolutely necessary. In this paper we will present such a concept. The suggested transaction model supports several levels (transaction types) which, among others, allow to naturally reproduce the hierarchy within a design process: On the one hand a design team has to be protected from the outside world. This is done with the help of a so called database transaction. This transaction corresponds to a conventional transaction. On the other hand mechanisms are provided which not only permits to express the hierarchy within a project but also support a controlled cooperative work on common objects. For these purposes group transactions and user transactions are introduced. Group transactions are especially tailored to the cooperative kind of work of a group. The real development process, however, takes place in user transactions which are installed as childs of group transactions. Both kinds of transactions do avoid the rigid serializability criterion of conventional database systems. Instead, they offer some flexibility in working cooperatively on and with data. A first prototype of this transaction model was implemented on a VAX on top of the ORACLE relational database system.

1. Introduction

The conventional model of transactions as it was proposed by /Gray79/ is based on the ACID principle (/HäRe83/) which, in short, means that a transaction is an atomic unit of reads and writes against a database. To support atomicity and isolated execution a transaction is not allowed to see changes executed by a concurrent transaction. Additionally, the all or nothing principle must be obeyed. Either all changes are reflected in the database or none. As long as transactions process within a few seconds this model is suitable. Because transactions are short-lived little work will be lost in case of a reset process. Additionally, transaction have to wait only for a short period of time if they are blocked due to a conflict to a concurrent transaction.

Non standard applications, like e.g. CAD/CAM or software development, behave totally different. Typically, transactions are interactive and of long duration. Most of the work performed by a designer is only expressed within this transaction and documented nowhere else. Therefore, of course, long waits or rollback in case of a transaction or system failure arenot acceptable. Another important point is that design projects are usually performed by groups of experts who want to work in a cooperative fashion. These requirements led to some proposals of new transaction models which we will discuss in short. We lump together design, engineering, and software development projects under the term design projects.

/HaLo81/ propose the CHECK-OUT/CHECK-IN mechanism. The main idea of this approach is that objects are no longer directly modified within the (public) database (update in place). Instead, a copy of every object of interest is CHECKed OUT of the database into a private database. These private copies can be modified arbitrarily. After all modifications are performed the modified objects are written back into the database by CHECK-IN. Long-lived locks are imposed on the objects checked out from the public database. Other transactions can read these objects in the state before the check-out.

The CHECK-OUT/CKECKIN model offers the following advantages:

* objects can be read in their former state while being modified
* objects are modified in private workspace. Therefore, these modifications are not visible to other users.

This idea was improved in /LoPl83/. They distinguish between a public and several private databases in which objects can be copied from the public database. Every private database is associated with a conversational transaction. It provides shelter for a number of conventional transactions running on the data of the private database. Conventional transactions are provided to support a finer granule of recovery. The unit of consistency is the conversational transaction, while the unit of recovery is the conventional transaction.

A similar model is presented in /KaWe83/ and /Katz84/. For reasons of recovery they don't use conventional transaction but introduce savepoints.

These proposals already take the long duration and interactivity of design processes into consideration. Therefore, they are fully appropriate when users work in an isolated manner on objects of the public database. However, they do not sufficiently support those (many) environments where users do work cooperatively on a common set of objects.

/KLMP84/ remove this deficiency by the introduction of a hierarchy of transactions.

Since /BaKK85/ refine this proposal we will only discuss their model here. A design environment consists of a number of independent project transactions, which are protected against each other like conventional transactions. A project transaction consists of a number of cooperative transactions. Each cooperative transaction is responsible for a (complex) subtask. To fulfill this job a cooperative transaction can be subdivided into several client / subcontractor transactions (C/S transaction). Each C/S transaction deals with a well defined part of the original subtask. If this part is still very complex a C/S transaction is allowed to form a hierarchy of C/S transactions. Finally, each C/S transaction is divided into several designer's transactions each of which is associated with exactly one designer. A designer fulfills his task by starting a number of conventional short-duration transactions. The way transactions are associated with each other is very similar to the model of nested transactions presented in /Moss81/ or /Moss86/. Although cooperative work is supported to a certain degree the transaction model still has some weakness:

Usually a complex design process is subdivided into a (great) number of (small) subtasks which are executed by one or a couple of designers. But these small subtasks are still long duration subtasks. To modify a chip will take days or even weeks but not seconds. That means that a designer's transaction will work on a (maybe) small number of objects but for a longer period of time without wanting these objects to be released and thereby visible to other designers (even of the same design team). Therefore, from our point of view, this kind of splitting might cause some problems for the user especially because objects might be available to other designers between such short transactions. As one reason for providing this concept the need for an introduction of a formal model of consistency was mentioned. Without any doubt, the proposed model provides an elegant solution, but, from our point of view, only on the formal level. The pure splitting of long duration transactions into a number of short duration transactions doesn't really reflect the way designers want to work. The notion of transaction and the notion of consistency are tightly coupled. Therefore, we think that designers' transactions should still be long term transactions which should be treated as such.

Another drawback of this approach is that it doesn't support an appropriate recovery mechanism. For example, it is allowed to back up a C/S transaction. As a consequence all already committed short duration transactions of the project transaction are backed up, too. Since these transactions might already have released some updates (even in the public database) a rollback propagation might occur.

2. Demands on new transaction models

A major problem of new database applications is that they need an appropriate environment for their complex and lengthy design process. Within such a process a numerous number of users work for a long time (days, weeks or evem months) on a comparatively large, common set of objects. However, often complex tasks can be subdivided into more graceful subtasks which only require a subset of the objects.

Usually, the set of users split into (sub)groups. Each group covers an area of responsibility. To solve problems groups are further subdivided into subgroups, etc., until, at the end of the line, one or a couple of designers are responsible for the solution of a special problem. Each user works on a well-defined part of the problem within the environment. The members of the group work cooperatively, rather than competitively, they coordinate their work. In particular, the users know to what degree their work overlaps and whether they may proceed in parallel without endangering the consistency of the common data or not.

For environments like this strict serializability, as is provided by traditional concurrency control schemes, is too strict. Instead, it is also necessary to support cooperative work within groups of users.

The set of groups forms a tree-like hierarchy. Groups which are located below another group but on the same path to the root are called **subgroups** and define specializations of the work of the superior group. Subgroups are **tightly coupled** with there (unique) superior group (parent). On the other hand, groups of different branches of the hierarchy are usually involved in different problems. Therefore, these groups are only **loosely coupled**. Of course, cooperative work between tightly coupled groups has to be supported more intensively than cooperation between loosely coupled groups.

No question, an advanced transaction model for design-like applications should provide enough flexibility to support a more cooperative style of work. However, a large number of proposals to advanced transaction modeling concentrate first of all on modularity, failure handling and parallelism while a support of cooperative work is subordinated to serializability. Often, the assumption is still made that (sub)transactions are competitors rather than partners. However, appropriate support of cooperative work can only be achieved if the still predominant rigid concurrency control measures (strict isolation) are weakened, e. g., by moving some responsibility for the integrity of the data from the database management system to the application. Of course, this has to be done in a controlled way and the database management system has to offer as much help as possible. Especially, users should be able to influence the setting and releasing of locks in to cooperate and communicate in a more flexible way with each others.

In the next sections a transaction model will be presented

* which allows to reproduce the above mentioned complex hierarchies within large design divisions and
* which is capable to support the different kinds of cooperation between differently coupled groups.

Other essential concepts of non standard databases like e.g. versions and alternatives or a flexible synchronisation mechanism will not or only rudimentary be discussed. The interested reader is referred to the following (exemplary) literature:

version concept: /DiLo85/, /KaCB86/, /KlSW86/
concurrency control: /GaKi88/, /Unla90/, /UnSc92/

3. The nested transaction model

In order to provide the right fitting for a cooperative style of work the proposed transaction model offers several layers in a tree-like style (expressed by the provision of several transaction types, see figure 1): Firstly, users are to be shielded from the outside. This is done by the database transaction (**DBT**). This type of transaction realizes the one and only gateway of the design team to the public database. Protected by the DBT the design process can take place in a more convenient and suitable atmosphere. For this purposes an arbitrary number of (hierarchically structured) group transactions (**GT**) can be established. They serve the individual groups as private databases. The real work on objects, however, is done within user transactions (**UT**) which are always leaves of the group hierarchy tree. Of course, user transactions as well as group transactions support a controlled cooperative work on common objects within groups as well as between different groups (however, in a more restricted way). This paper is a refinement of the two-level transaction model presented in /KSUW85a/.

The unique direct path from a transaction T to the public database will be called the **direct path of T** in the following.

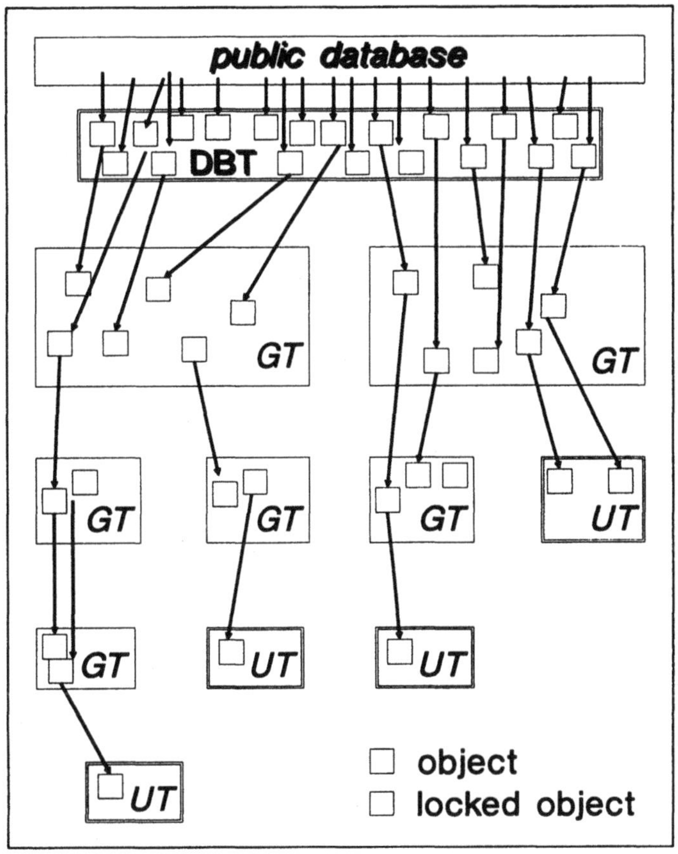

Figure 1: Representation nested transaction model

The following holds:

1. The set of all transactions forms a strict tree-like hierarchy. The database transaction acts as the root and the user transactions represent the leaves. All inner nodes are group transactions. Of course, while the tree is constructed, a group transaction may also be (temporarily) a leaf transaction. But since a group transaction is not allowed to manipulate objects (see (3)) it makes no sense to create a group transaction without any child transaction. The tree is built up from the root to the leaves and taken down in reverse order.
2. For each transaction T an **object pool** is established. The object-pool is a temporary database in which all objects necessary at that level are checked in. It exists only as long as T exists. It represents the "work environment" for the group. DBT and all GTs only serve as a kind of (more

DBT: database tr; GT: group tr; UT: user tr; CT: child tr; FT: father tr

suitable) database for their inferiors; they do not any manipulation of data (objects). UTs, additionally, allow users to operate on objects. An object pool can be logically subdivided into several subpools each of which includes the objects of exactly one child transaction. This view supports an easy assignment of objects to child transactions. The only way of how transactions can aquire objects is by the use of the CHECK-OUT command.

3. Each transaction is associated with exactly one user group. Here, the term group also comprises a single user.

4. GTs and UTs can operate concurrently; they are well-formed and - unless the user intervenes - two-phase. But they allow users to influence the concurrency control.

5. Transactions are object-oriented in the sense that they realize the principle of information hiding. Only members of the group which is associated with the transaction are allowed to operate on objects of the object pool. If non-members needs objects from an object pool they can communicate with the corresponding transaction by the sending of messages. The transaction can either reject or comply with the request. If the requested objects are not available in the object pool the transaction can send a message to its parent transaction in order to acquire the missing objects. The requesting user is not aware from which pools the objects of interest are taken.

6. By default every user is allowed to see at each time each object which belongs to the public database or any object pool on the direct path even if it is checked out by another transaction (dirty read). But the object won't be copied into the user's object pool. Instead, it remains in its original place. The user has to take into account that this kind of read is a dirty read.

Outline of a design process

Let a **design team** be the set of all users who are involved in a design process. For this team, as the root of their design environment, the database transaction (DBT) with its common object pool has to be installed. Under shelther of the DBT an arbitrary number of group transactions (GT) can be established. Each group transaction provides the object pool for the level it shall represent. The DBT as well as all GTs only serve their groups as a private object pool. No update-operations on objects are directly performed within such transactions. Modifications are completely performed in user transactions (UT).

Every transaction is associated with exactly one group or one designer. Only members of this group are allowed to access the object pool of that transactions. Therefore, the individual view of each designer can be defined. He is only allowed to lock objects

* in object pools which are on the direct path from his (user) transaction to the DBT
* and, additionally, he has to be member of the group associated with the corresponding object pool.

In the following an (informal) outline of a design process will be presented. The syntax used is exemplary and shall help the reader to understand the semantics of the commands. { } labels alternatives while [ ] describes optional parts of a command.

In our model every subject can uniquely be identified either by a system defined identifier or by a user defined name. For reasons of simplicity we will only use the identifier in the following although the use of the corresponding name would be possible, too.

Definition of groups

As already mentioned a design team can be subdivided into a number of subgroups. Each subgroup may run an arbitrary number of transactions. is a function in which If transactions represent the domain and groups the range of a function then the mapping between the transactions

DBT: database tr; GT: group tr; UT: user tr; CT: child tr; FT: father tr

and the user groups is surjective: Transactions are associated with exactly one group. Groups can be related to none up to an arbitrary number of transactions. Therefore, firstly user groups have to be defined:

CREATE_USER_GROUP *<group_name>* WITH_-MEMBERS *<user_id_list>*.

User_id_list can include a special user identification as well as a group identification which means that the group as a whole is part of the newly defined group.
The structure of a group can be modified at any point of time - even while an associated transaction is running- by:

CHANGE_USER_GROUP *<group_id>* $\left\{ \begin{array}{c} \text{ADD} \\ \text{REMOVE} \end{array} \right\}$ *<user_id_list>*.

By DELETE_USER_GROUP *<group_id>* a user group can be deleted. This command is only allowed if all transactions associated with the group have terminated.

Creation of a transaction

In the following we will sometimes use the terms *view of a designer* or *accessible objects*. By this we always mean the default view or the default access right to an object. No attention is paid to the fact that this view can be restricted by access control mechanisms.

Any designer can start a new transaction in his name or in the name of a group he is member of. A new GT or UT is always a **child transaction** (**CT** for short) of an already existing transaction (the **father transaction** (**FT** for short)). Therefore, the transaction tree is built up from the root to the leaves (top-down). Let T be an arbitrary transaction within the hierarchy. Each transaction on the direct path from T to the root is called **superior** to T while each transaction on a lower level which can be reached on a path starting at T is called **subordinate** to T. All superior transactions of T form a path, the **direct path**, while all subordinate transactions form a (sub)tree with T as its root (called **subtree of T** in the following).

The following command allows the user to start a new transaction:

CREATE_TRANS *<trans_name>* [FOR *<group_id>*] [AS_CHILD_OF *<trans_id>*] AS $\left\{ \begin{array}{c} \text{GT} \\ \text{DBT} \\ \text{UT} \end{array} \right\}$

Each transaction is associated with exactly one group which will be called **associated group** in the following. For reasons of simplicity we will call members of the associated group of a transaction T **members of T**. The associated group includes all members of that group that is declared in the FOR part. As already mentioned, the transaction model is in a sense object-oriented. Only members of the associated group have access to the interior of a transaction T. To assure that all members of T have also access to all subtransactions of T they are implicitly added to the associated group of any child transaction of T. Since this definition is recursive each member of T is implicitly also member of all transactions in the subtree of T. Of course, it is possible to explicitly remove a user from an associated group.

Let T be a transaction a designer D is currently working with. The most comprehensive transaction of D with regard to T (called **top transaction of D for T**) is that transaction T^t which is located on the direct path of T and which fulfills the following conditions:

* D is member of T and
* D isn't member of any transaction on the direct path of T^t.

In other words, the top transaction of D for T is that transaction on the direct path of T which is located nearest to the DBT (or the DBT itself). Of course, the top transaction of D may change if T changes.

DBT: database tr; GT: group tr; UT: user tr; CT: child tr; FT: father tr

If the FOR part of the CREATE_TRANS command is omitted only the user who has delivered the command represents the explicit part of the associated group.

If the AS_CHILD_OF part is omitted the new transaction represents a database transaction (DBT). In this case the AS part is redundant.

<trans_id> must not identify an UT since it is not allowed to create a transaction as a subtransaction of an UT.

CREATE_TRANS not only starts a new transaction but also creates the object-pool. Additionally, a new logical **subpool** is added in the object-pool of the FT (if the new transaction is not the DBT). The name of this subpool is identical to the name of the CT. The subpool serves as an input area for the CT. Not only all objects checked out by the CT are registered here but also those which are considered for the CT but which were not explicitly checked out by the CT yet.

Thus, the object pool is logically subdivided into a number of input areas, one for each child transaction, and a general area (called **common pool**). The common pool includes all objects which are still available. That are all objects which are not assigned to any CT yet as well as objects which are already locked by at least one CT, but only in a shared lock mode. Of course, objects with shared lock mode may occur in several subpools.

The following commands can be used by any member of a transaction T to add or remove objects to or from a subpool:

ADD *<object_id_list>* TO *<subpool_id>*

REMOVE *<object_id_list>* FROM *<subpool_id>*

As already mentioned the subpool name is identical with the transaction name of the CT.

The REMOVE command can only be applied if the appropriate objects are not checked out by the CT yet.

A subpool only serves as a check-in area for a CT. Modified objects which are to be written back to the FT have to be copied into the common pool of the FT.

Every transaction T can only be active on behalf of one member of the associated group at a time. The user who has control of T can perform each command associated with T until he explicitly suspends the transaction by the SUSPEND command:

SUSPEND *<trans_id>* suspends the transaction *<trans_id>* currently active for the user.

CONTINUE_TRANS *<trans_id>* reactivates the specified transaction.

A user may run several transactions at the same time. This enables him to work on different objects simultaneously, and to use transactions alternatively.

Different types of access

During a design process a lot of objects are needed for different reasons. The most important objects are those which are the basis of the design process. They have to be accessible during the complete process or, at least, for a considerably long period of time. Another group of objects are those which are only needed during a relatively short period. Examples for this type are objects which are used to to come to a decision or which were considered in a selection process but were excluded. Mostly, these objects have only to be read; often a dirty read is sufficient. A third group are objects which are accessed in a rather conventional way, for example administrative data.

In order to support these different kinds of demands three types of access are provided:

1. *Check-out / Check-in*

This mechanism is appropriate for all those objects which are needed for a long period of time and which are to be protected from modification by a lock.

2. *Dirty read*

A dirty read permits the read of any object at any time even if the object is locked exclusively. Therefore,

DBT: database tr; GT: group tr; UT: user tr; CT: child tr; FT: father tr

this type of access is appropriate for each read which doesn't require a fully consistent view of the objects read (e.g. browsing).

3. *Conventional access*

This kind of access is appropriate for all operations which have to work for a short period of time on a consistent set of objects. It employs the traditional two-phase lock protocol.

Check-out / check-in

Check-out / check-in are the one and only commands by which objects can be transferred from one object pool to another. By check-out a long-lived lock is imposed on the object which can, at the earliest, be released by an appropriate check-in. In the following we will describe the syntax of the command. We don't consider restrictions to access here. This will be done in a later section.

CHECK_OUT *<object_id>* [FROM { *<trans_id1>* PUBLIC DATABASE }]

[TO *<trans_id2>*] WITH *<lock_mode>*

CHECK_IN *<object_id>* [IN { *<trans_id1>* PUBLIC DATABASE }]

With the help of a check-out command a member of a transaction T checks out an object from an object pool (or the public database) and copies it into the object pool of another transaction. As already mentioned the object is at least logically included into each object pool of any transaction on the direct path between *<trans_id>* and T. A check-out always transfers an object from one level to a deeper level (from a superior to a subordinate transaction) while a check-in transfers it to a higher level (from a subordinate to a superior transaction).

We can distinguish between two types of check-out: a leaving one and a one coming in. Let T be a transaction a designer D is currently working with. The **check-out** is **coming in** if T wants to get an object O from any superior transaction. In this case the FROM part can be specified while the TO part can not be used since the destination transaction is T itself. O is copied from *<trans_id1>* to the common pool of T. If the FROM part is omitted then an object is requested from which the location is unknown. If O is part of the current access view of D the request will be granted if O is not locked in an incompatible mode. Otherwise, two possibilities exist. If O is located in an object-pool of any other branch the request is rejected. In the other case, that O is located on the direct path of T (but not in the access view of D for T) the request will be judged by each transaction on the path from the top transaction of D for T to the transaction which contains O. Therefore, the request moves up and requires each transaction on the path to agree. If any transaction does not comply with the request it is rejected. To reduce overhead it is possible to lay down a default behaviour (e. g. reject/agree in any case).

By a **leaving check-out** an object of the object pool of T is copied into the object pool of any subordinate transaction. Since now the initial transaction is fixed the FROM part can not be used.

A check-out coming in always copies an object of a higher level into the object pool of T while a leaving check-out copies an object of the object pool of T to a lower level transaction.

Each object is transmitted from up (e. g. public database) to down (e.g. UT). In this process the object O is copied into any object pool 'on the way' forming at least a continous path (exclusive lock) or a tree (shared lock). Since, therefore, a lot of copies can exist the question arises which transaction has which rights on O. The answer is that the rights on O depend on the type of lock. An exclusive lock only allows one transaction to modify O or to move O further on: the most subordinate transaction which possesses O. Therefore the right to move on or modify an object moves down with the object. Since the object can only be copied into the object pool of one child transaction a path is formed.

DBT: database tr; GT: group tr; UT: user tr; CT: child tr; FT: father tr

In case of a shared lock an arbitrary number of transactions are allowed to read the object. In this case every transaction which houses the object in its object pool is allowed to move it on to as many CTs as wished. Now, a tree is formed.

A transaction which is allowed to move on (and to modify) an object O is called **owner of O**.

Since in our model transactions are independent a 'long distance' check-out shouldn't be possible without the permission of every transaction T^i involved. To satisfy this requirement it has to be fulfilled that the user who delivers the check-out command is member of every T^i. In case of a leaving check-out this is, by default, always fulfilled. In the other case the designer has to be member of the starting transaction T^s (specified in the FROM part) and every transaction T on the direct path from T^s to the requesting transaction T.

The check-in command is similar to the check-out. However, it is always upward. A user checks in an object from the transaction T into the object pool of T's father transaction (default value if the TO part is omitted) or the transaction specified (*<trans_id1>*). A check-in does not automatically release the lock on the object. Locks can only be released by the special RELEASE command (RELEASE-LOCK *<lock_mode>* ON *<object_id>*) or by the AND-RELEASE-LOCK supplement to the CHECK-IN clause. Of course, the release of a lock is only allowed if all subordinate transactions have already released their lock on the object.

Dirty read

Each designer D is allowed (by default) to read every accessible object at any time in an unprotected mode. If D is currently an active user of transaction T then the accessible objects of D with regard to T are all those objects which are part of any object pool on the direct path or which belong to the public database. Objects in different branches of the tree are not accessible. A dirty read only allows to read the object. It is not copied into the object pool of T. The user has to be aware of the fact, that he might see objects in an inconsistent state.

READ *<object_id>* [FROM { *<trans_id>* / PUBLIC DATABASE }]

Conventional access

A conventional access is only defined on the public database and is realized by a traditional transaction. This kind of transaction can be started at any time inside of a design transaction T (UT, GT or DBT). It works directly on the public database and doesn't copy any object into the object pool of T. The user has to be aware of the fact that all objects accessed by a traditional transaction T^T are only locked during the run-time of T^T.

The access view of a designer

According to his function in the design team each designer has an individual view of the set of all objects accessible to him (called **access view**). In this context the right to access an object means to have the permission to check-out the object in any mode currently permissible or to check it in.

The access view depends on the transaction T the designer D is currently working with. If T is a user transaction then the view of a designer is established by the object pool of T and the appropriate subpool of the father transaction. Additionally, a designer has access to the object pool of every transaction on the direct path up to the top transaction of D for T. As an active user of a transaction T he doesn't have direct access to object pools of transactions which don't belong to the direct path of T even if he is member of these transactions.

If T is a group transaction (or the DBT) then D additionally has access to the subtree of T (by default).

The public database is generally accessible to everybody.

Therefore, the upward part of the access view of D always forms a path (and includes the public database), the downward part forms a tree.

Of course, each designer is only allowed to work with a transaction he is member of. In this context to work with a transaction T means to have access to the interior of T. The interior of all other transactions is invisible. If a user wants access to an object which is not accessible to him (is not in his view) he has to send a request to his FT. The FT decides whether it accepts or rejects the request. In case it accepts the request it has to check whether the object is already in its object pool. If not the FT has to send a request to its FT and so on. Let the transaction whose object pool contains the requested object be the **destination transaction**. Due to the procedure described above every transaction on the direct path up to the destination transaction is involved in the decision whether an object shall be granted to the user or not. Additionally, after a grant the object will at least be logically included in every object pool on the direct path from the destination transaction to the user's transaction. Nothing is said about how a transaction makes its decision. This can either be done automatically or by default or by a decision of any member of the associated group or in any other way.

Savepoints

Although we don't want to consider recovery mechanisms in more detail a short discussion seems to be necessary.

In our model we support the concept of savepoints (for further details see /KSUW85b/). Savepoints serve two different aims:

* they describe a checkpoint at which the system can restart in case of a system crash.
* they constitute a state to which a user can voluntary reset the transaction (or object modifications).

We can distinguish between two different kinds of savepoints: strong savepoints and weak savepoints.

A **strong savepoints** sets up an irrevocable state. Neither the system nor the user are allowed to reset a transaction beyond this point. The only way to attain to any further state is to start a compensation operation (transaction).

Weak savepoints, however, allow a voluntary reset to a state beyond them. They only serve the system as restart point whereas users may ignore them if they want to reset their work to an earlier state.

Transferring objects between transactions

To support the cooperation a transfer of objects between transactions is supported which belong to different branches of the transaction tree. Generally, only a transaction which is owner of an object is allowed to transfer it. Additionally, the current state of the object has to be protected by a strong savepoint. By this rollback propagation is prevented.

Lending of objects

For a number of reasons it might be desirable to let a user transaction UT^1 work on an object O for a certain period of time, although this object is exclusively locked by a transaction T^2. As long as UT^1 is member of the subtree of T^2 such a conduct does not cause any problems. But, in case this is not fulfilled (e. g. T^2 is a user transaction, too) a new mechanism has to be introduced. For this purpose we suggest the concept of lending of objects. With the lending of an object O to a user transaction UT^1, all rights are assigned to the borrower UT^1, except the right to check-in the object into the object pool of any other transaction. As soon as UT^1 has finished its work, it returns the control over O to the owner of the lock, i. e. to T^2. This concept allows an alternating work of UT^1 and T^2 on O, with either UT^1 or T^2 working at one time.
The lender T^2 uses the operation

DBT: database tr; GT: group tr; UT: user tr; CT: child tr; FT: father tr

GRANT <*object_id*> TO <*trans_id*>

Grant makes the object O to be lent available to the transaction <*trans_id*> (here: UT^1) in its present state. But, O is not directly copied into the object pool of UT^1. Instead, it is copied in the appropriate subpool of UT^1's father transaction. UT^1 can copy the borrowed object into its object pool by the CHECK_OUT command.

When UT^1 has finished its work, it releases the modified object by

RETURN <*object_id*>

for the original transaction. Again, O is not directly copied into the object pool of T^2 but into the appropriate subpool of T^2's FT. T^2 can fetch back the object by a check-out into its object pool.

Transfer of objects

If the owner transaction T^1 of an object O is not interested in getting the object back later, (e.g. another transaction continues its working unit), it can transfer it to another transaction T^2. The receiver transaction subsequently may work with the object at will, especially, it may check it in.

The transfer is realized by:

PASS <*object_id*> TO <*trans_id*>

The PASS command is not allowed in any case. Instead, two conditions have to be satisfied. Let D be the designer who wants to pass O from T^1 to T^2. Let T^R be the root of the smallest subtree which contains T^1 as well as T^2. To pass O from T^1 to T^2 means to remove O from every subpool on the direct path between T^1 and T^R and to add it to every subpool on the direct path between T^R and T^2. This is only allowed if

* T^R is part of the access view of D with regard to T^1 and
* every transaction on the direct path between T^R and T^2 permits the insertion of O in its object pool.

Communication system

Let D be a designer who is currently working with transaction T^1. If an object O is owned by a transaction T^2 in a different branch of the transaction tree it is, by default, not accessible for T^1 since it doesn't belong to the access view of D with regard to T^1. If D nevertheless wants to access O he has the possibility to ask a member of T^2 whether he is in the position to pass the object to T^1. In the same way D can ask for a dirty read. For this purposes a communication system is installed which allows every user to communicate with every other user or transaction. By this requests like the one above can be handled. Every member of a transaction is able to comply with or reject any request automatically or to make an individual decision.

Information system

In order to explore all possible avenues of cooperative work inside and between groups the user has to be in a position to get all information he needs. For this purposes a comprehensive information system is available. Among others this system enables the user to get the following informations:

* a list of all groups he is member of
* a list of all transactions to which he is associated
* a list of all members of a special group
* a list of all objects which belong to a given object pool
* a list of which transaction currently owns which object
* a presentation of the present transaction tree

Information board

Every object O which is checked out for modification or which was created by any transaction is supplied with an information board. Every owner O can stick information e. g. about the actual state of O or about recommended subsequent operations on the board. Therefore, this board is an important component which supports the users in their effort to work on the object in a consistent way.

EOT processing

Any transaction can be finished by the END_TRANS *<trans_id>* command. When the group or designer has reached his aim, the results (as well as any intermediate state the user wants to make visible to others) are written into the object pool of the FT (or the public database in case of the DBT).

Of course, this command is only allowed if all subordinate transactions have already finished their work.

The following principle is applicable to objects borrowed or checked out:

Only the objects which are rewritten explicitly (RETURN), survive the end of the transaction. EOT processing has to consider this principle:

In case that the transaction has lent individual objects to other users by GRANT and did not get it back, END_TRANS will be rejected, since the objects lent could not be written into the FT.

Every object the transaction has borrowed of other transaction and which has not been returned yet, is returned at END_TRANS. In this case the performed modifications are void, and the object is returned in its original state.

Concurrency control aspects

Of course, concurrency control aspects are an essential part of a transaction model. Nevertheless, we don't want to handle them here. The interested reader is refered to /Unla90/. In this paper

* a number of necessary lock modes are introduced
* the effect of a lock is split into
  - the effect for the owner of a lock (called internal effect) and into
  - the effect for concurrent transactions (called exetrenal effect).

The integration of both concepts leads to a general lock mechanism which supports the adaptation of concurrency control measures to the special needs of the individual applications.

4. CONCLUSIONS

This paper introduced a transaction model which is especially tailored to the requirements of design-like environments. A main objective of the model is a support of cooperative work. The proposed transaction model permits a natural reproduction of design processes. A database transaction acts as the basis for the design process. It shields the design team from the outside and, therefore, offers the possibilities for a convenient and suitable atmosphere in which designers can work in a cooperative way.

A first prototype of the transaction model was implemented on top of the relational database system ORACLE.

Literature

/BaKK85/ Bancilhon, F.; Kim, W.; Korth, H.: *A Model of CAD Transactions*, Proc. VLDB, Stockholm, 1985

/DiLo85/ Dittrich, K.R.; Lorie, R.A.: *Version Support for Engineering Database Systems.* IBM Research Report RJ 4769, San Jose, 1985

/GaKi88/ Garza, J; Kim, W.: *Transaction Management in an Object-Oriented Database System*, Proc. ACM-SIGMOD, Chicago, Illinois, 1988

/Gray79/ Gray, J.: *Notes on Data Base Operating Systems*, from 'Operating Systems', R. Bayer, R. Graham, G. Seegmüller (Editors), Springer Verlag, 1979

/HaLo81/ Haskin, R. L.; Lorie, R. A.: *On Extending the Functions of a Relational Database System*, IBM Research Report RJ3182; 1981

/HäRe83/ Härder, Th.; Reuter, A.: *Database Systems for Non-Standard Applications.* Proc. International Computing Symposium (ICS), 1983, Nürnberg, Teubner-Verlag.

/KaCB86/ Katz; R.H.; Chang, E.; Bhateja, R.: *Version Modeling Concepts for Computer-Aided Design Databases.* Proc. ACM-SIGMOD 1986.

/Katz84/ Katz, R.H.: *Transaction Management in the Design Environment,* aus 'New Applications of Data Bases', G. Gardarin, E. Gelenbe (Hrsg), Academic Press, 1984

/KaWe83/ Katz, R.; Weiss, S.: *Transaction Management for Design Databases*, Computer Sciences Technical Report No. 496, University of Wisconsin Madison; February 1983

/KLMP84/ Kim, W.; Lorie, R.; McNabb, D.; Plouffe, W.: *A Transaction Mechanism for Engineering Design Databases,* Proc. VLDB, 1984

/KlSW86/ Klahold, P., Schlageter, G., Wilkes, W.: *A General Model for Version Management in Databases*, Proc. VLDB, Kyoto, 1986

/KSUW85a/ Klahold, P.; Schlageter, G.; Wilkes, W.; Unland, R.; *A Transaction Model Supporting Complex Applications in Integrated Information Systems,* Proc. ACM-Sigmod 1985

/KSUW85b/ Klahold, P.; Schlageter, G.; Wilkes, W.; Unland, R.; *A Transaction Model Supporting Complex Applications in Integrated Information Systems,* (in German) Proc. GI Conference on Database Systems for Office Automation, Engineering, and Scientific Applications, Karlsruhe, West-Germany, 1985

/LoPl83/ Lorie, R.; Plouffe, W.: *Complex Objects and their Use in Design Transactions,* Proc. Databases for Engineering Applications, ACM-Database Week 1983

/Moss81/ Moss, J. E.: *Nested Transactions: An Approach to Reliable Distributed Computing*, PhD Thesis, Departement of Electrical Engineering and Computer Science, Massachusetts, Institute of Technologie; April 1981

/Moss86/ Moss, J.E.B.: *An Introduction to Nested Transactions*, COINS Technical Report 86-41, University of Massachusetts at Amherst, 1986

/Unla90/ Unland, R.: *A Flexible and Adaptable Tool Kit Approach for Concurrency Control in Non Standard Database Systems*; Proc. 3rd Int. Conf. on Database Theory (ICDT); Paris, France; Dec. 1990

/UnSc92/ Unland, R., Schlageter, G.: *A Transaction Manager Development Facility for Non Standard Database Systems*; in: "Transaction Models for Advanced Database Applications"; A. Elmargarmid (ed.); Morgan Kaufmann Publishers; to appear 1992 (in print)

DISTRIBUTED DATABASE AND REAL-TIME DATABASES

Seamless Interconnection in Federated Database Systems*

Douglas Fang Dennis McLeod

{dfang,mcleod}@usc.edu
Computer Science Department
University of Southern California
Los Angeles, CA 90089-0781

Abstract

An approach and mechanism to support the seamless interconnection of federated database systems is described. In the context of autonomous but interconnected database systems, it is necessary to accommodate the efficient sharing and transmission of information across database system boundaries. Towards achieving the goal of seamless interconnection, it is desirable to insulate a given database system from unnecessary detail of remote database systems, allowing users to utilize local tools for database management. A core object database model is used as a framework in which to provide techniques to support the sharing of information units (objects) at various levels of abstraction as well as the sharing of behavior.

1 Introduction

Consider an environment consisting of a collection of autonomous databases and their supporting systems, in which it is desired to support the controlled sharing and exchange of information among the collection. We use the term *federation* for this environment, and refer to the individual database systems as *components*. Such environments are increasingly common in various application domains, including office information systems, computer-aided design and computer-integrated manufacturing, personal computing, scientific information, etc. Effective principles, techniques, and mechanisms are required to support the construction and efficient operation of *federated database systems* to support the sharing and interconnection needs in these environments.

*This research was supported in part by NSF grant IRI-9021028, and in part by IMAR and NSF grant ECD-8717322.

The research described in this paper is a part of the Remote-Exchange project at USC [4]. Remote-Exchange considers three aspects of sharing and interconnection in the federated database environment. These may be viewed in the context of a given component (C), which intends to import and/or export information of other ("nonlocal") components:

1. the *discovery and identification* by component C of relevant nonlocal information;
2. the *resolution* of the similarities and differences between C's information and relevant nonlocal information ("semantic heterogeneity" [18]);
3. the efficient realization and implementation of actual *sharing and transmission* of information to and from C and other components.

This paper specifically explores the variety of sharing patterns that can occur in such an environment, and focuses on the third aspect above. A core object database model is used as a framework in which to provide techniques to support the sharing of information units (objects) at various levels of abstraction as well as the sharing of behavior. Significantly, we address this in the context of a further important goal: to make remote information as seamlessly integrated into C's local database as possible.

We use the term *seamless cooperative database system (SCDS)* to refer to the approach taken here. In the SCDS context, component autonomy and seamless integration are fundamental goals. This implies that we desire to provide users of a component with the flexibility of structuring and integrating remote information autonomously and independently, rather than for example imposing a single, global structure that all components must use for viewing remote information. In order to maintain this transparency, efficient access to remote information is critical. Otherwise, remote information will not appear transparent to users since access to remote information will be much slower than access to local information. Further, we must allow the users of a component to use its local tools to manipulate information.

Our approach to seamless cooperative database systems can be illustrated through an example, phrased in terms of an object-based database model as an inter-component communication forum. Consider the following scenario of two collaborating researchers. Two researchers, Researcher-A and Researcher-B, maintain separate databases of journal and conference publications. Each researcher uses a different underlying schema to model this information. Difficulties arise when Researcher-B wants to include a particular publication of Researcher-A's into his/her own database for viewing purposes. In traditional approaches, Researcher-B must first structurally integrate [2, 21] the two researchers' representations of publications (i.e., conceptual schemas). Researcher-B would then be required to import all of the publications that Researcher-A exports rather than just the single publication in which s/he is interested. Not only is this level of granularity course, it is potentially inefficient since extraneous data may also be retrieved.

Further, Researcher-A must typically keep multiple formatted versions of the same publication such as simple text, postscript and dvi formats so that Researcher-B can view it depending on whatever format his/her local system supports. In our approach, Researcher B can selectively import the exact publication in which s/he is interested. Further, since Reseacher-A encapsulates the publication object by a set of methods, Researcher B need not be aware of its internal representation. In particular, Reseacher-A might supply the method for displaying publication objects. This is advantageous for both Reseacher A and Researcher B. Reseacher A only needs to manage one format of the publication (e.g., dvi). Researcher B in turn, uses the method provided by Reseacher A (e.g., xdvi) for displaying the publication. More importantly, by using our approach Reseacher A's publication will appear completely local to Reseacher B. Researcher A can then manipulate and display this publication using the same local database management systems (DBMS) tools and application programs that s/he has invested much time and effort in learning and developing.

The remainder of this paper is organized as follows. Section 2 compares and contrasts our approach with previous work. Section 3 briefly describes the generic object-oriented database model in terms of which our work is couched and the variety of sharing patterns that may occur in object-based seamless cooperative database systems. Section 4 presents our mechanisms to supporting object-based sharing. Finally, Section 5 presents concluding remarks.

2 Related Research

Previous work in the area of distributed and heterogeneous database systems has proposed a variety of architectures for sharing in a distributed environment. Research in the area of *heterogeneous* database systems began over a decade ago [6, 21]. The term "heterogeneous databases" was originally used to distinguish work which included database model and conceptual schema heterogeneity from work in distributed databases[1] which addressed issues solely related to distribution. Recently, there has been a resurgence of research in the area of heterogeneous database systems. Systems using this architecture are characterized by the (possibly partial) integration of several compo-

[1]The term distributed database is used here as it has been mainly used in the literature, denoting a relatively tightly coupled, homogeneous system of logically centralized, but physically distributed component databases.

nent database schemas into one centralized global schema [19, 21, 22, 23]. In this approach, different user views can be defined. However, they must all be derived from the same global schema. While this approach supports pre-existing component databases, it falls short in terms of flexible sharing patterns; the integration process is very expensive and tends to be difficult to change. There is also a new layer of abstraction that the user must learn in order to pose queries on the global schema. To help alleviate this transition, various front ends can be placed on top of the global schema to emulate the user's local environment. Nevertheless, the user must alternate between his/her own local database and this new "virtual" database (distinct from his/her own local database) whenever s/he wants to consider any remote sharing. Orion-2 [12] for instance, uses the notions of a *private database* and a global *shared database*. The users then explicitly pose their queries against the private database or the shared database or the combination of private and shared database.

It is possible to observe some similarities between the heterogeneous database approach and the work described in this paper. In some sense, an implementation of a central node with a global schema can be considered to be a local database system that is incorporating remote data from external systems. However, there are three important differences. First, the global schema holds no local data. Rather, it is the (possibly partial) integration of remote schemas. There are no instantiations of local or remote data other than meta-data (i.e., schema and component information). Second, the database system used for constructing and maintaining the global schema is a system designed specifically for use in a distributed environment. Third, sharing patterns are not flexible. Importing individual instances or behavioral objects is not possible. Sharing patterns are usually restricted to high level, set oriented queries that are are passed over the network (e.g., expressed in SQL).

The *federated* architecture proposed in [10] involves loosely coupled collection of database systems, stressing autonomy and flexible sharing patterns through inter-component negotiation. Rather than utilizing a single, static global schema, the federated architecture allows multiple *import schemas*[2] which are stored in the *federal dictionary*. The rationale here is that the resolution of conflicts (e.g., structural, naming, and scale) during the schema integration process is a subjective, application dependent process. Accommodating multiple integrations (i.e., import schemas) allows flexibility and autonomy. Furthermore, once a particular import schema is chosen, data is retrieved directly from the exporter and not indirectly through some central node as in the heterogeneous database architecture.

The *multidatabase* architecture of [15]) is in a sense similar to the federated architecture. The observation here is that the integration process is too complicated and ultimately infeasible. In this architecture there is no global schema; the integration process is simply not supported. Rather, emphasis is placed on the *interoperability* among component databases based on a flexible, common multidatabase language. In this approach, the user is responsible for keeping track of the various databases and their schemas in order to navigate and manipulate data. In addition, the user utilizes a new multidatabase language. For example, in MRSDM [15] the multidatabase language provided, MRDS (based on the tuple calculus), introduces the notions of multiple queries, multiple identifiers, and semantic variables. These additional constructs are intended as tools for helping users to manipulate relations with multiple semantic interpretations.

3 Sharing Patterns in the Object Database Context

The conceptual database model employed in this research is based on the functional database models proposed in Daplex [20], Iris [7], and Omega [8]. This functionally object-oriented model (FOOM) contains features common to most semantic [9, 11] and object-oriented database models [1] such as GemStone [17], Orion [13], and O2 [14]. In particular, FOOM supports complex objects (aggregation), type membership (classification), subtype to supertype relationships (generalization), inheritance of functions (and attributes) from supertype to subtypes, run-time binding of functions (method

[2]These are sometimes referred to as federated schemas.

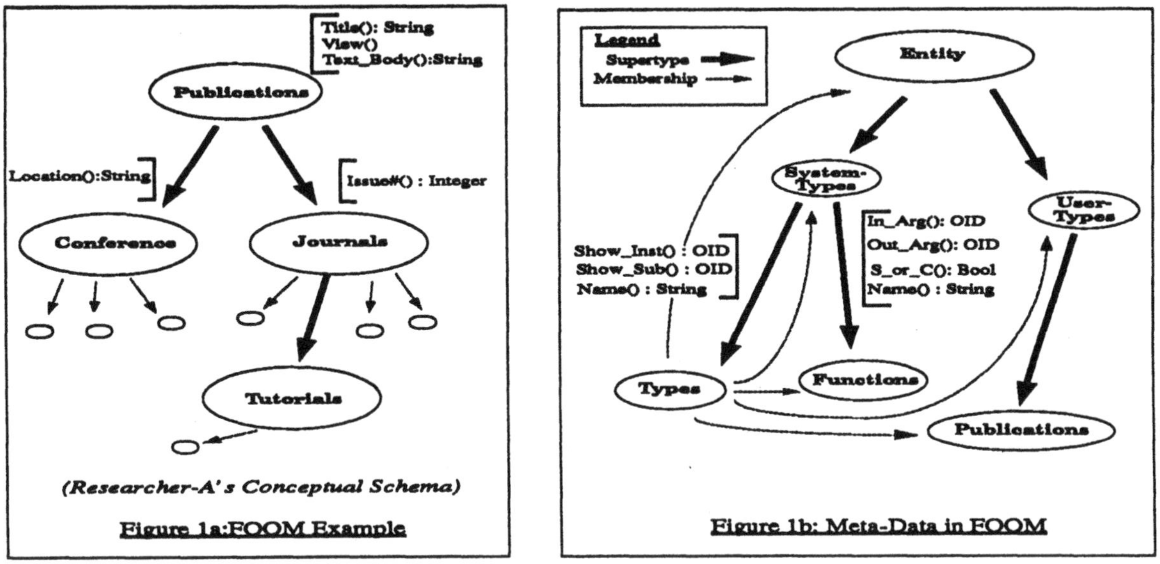

Figure 1a:FOOM Example

Figure 1b: Meta-Data in FOOM

Figure 1: FOOM Database Example

override), and user-definable functions (methods).

Everything in FOOM, including meta-data, is modeled as objects. There are three primary kinds of objects: instances, types, and functions. Functions operate on instances, types and possibly on other functions. Types constrain the objects on which functions can operate. Types also serve to encapsulate objects by defining the set of functions which operate on members of the type (as in abstract data types). Instances are classified into types and represent real world entities or values. All objects have a unique system generated object identifier (OID).

Functions are used to model attributes (or more generally inter-object relationships). These functions can be broken down into two categories: stored and computed. Stored functions loosely correspond to the traditional notion of stored attributes. Computed functions can be used to calculate values instead of simply retrieving stored values from the database.

Figure 1a represents the conceptual schema of Reseacher-A's database that was originally introduced in the collaborating researchers example described above. It serves to illustrate the simple diagrammatic notation we will use for depicting conceptual schemas in FOOM. In our diagrammatic notation, instance and type objects are depicted as bubbles. For type objects, the name of the type is placed within the bubble. There are four types depicted in Figure 1a: **Publications, Conferences, Journals**, and **Tutorials**[3]. Each type has a set of functions defined on it. The signature of each of these functions is placed immediately above the type. The input arguments of each of these functions, are instance objects of the type upon which the function is defined. Hence, the input argument type of functions is not shown in their signatures; it is assumed to be of the type on which the function is defined[4]. Hence, in Figure 1a, the functions defined on the type **Publications** are: *Title()*, *View()*, and *Text_Body()*. *Title()* is applied to an instance of type **Publication** and returns the ASCII string corresponding to the title of the publication. Similarly, *Text_Body()* returns a string representing the actual body of text. *View()* is used to display instances of **Publication** and does not return a value.

Two kinds of inter-object relationships are explicitly modeled in FOOM and have corresponding diagrammatic notation: the supertype to subtype (with inheritance) interclass relationship and the type membership relationship. All other inter-

[3] **Conferences** refers to conference papers, **Journals** denotes journal publications, and **Tutorials** refers to journal papers that are tutorial.

[4] The function is also defined on its subtypes through inheritance.

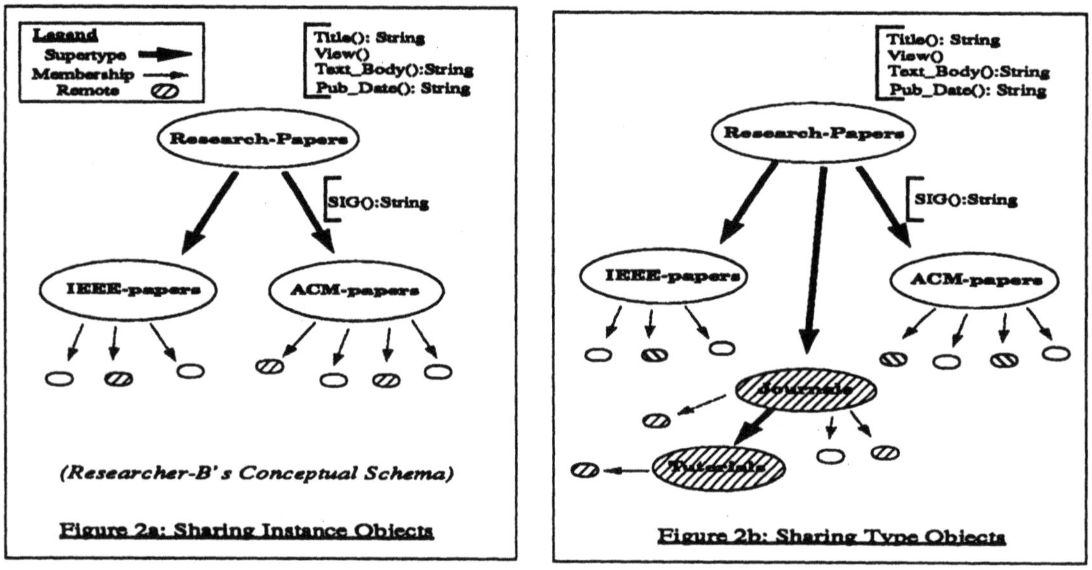

Figure 2: Sharing Pattern Example

object relationships are modeled through functions. The supertype to subtype relationship is depicted with thick dark lines from supertype object to subtype object. In Figure 1a, **Conferences** and **Journals** are subtypes of the type **Publications**. Further, through inheritance, not only do instances of **Conferences** have the *Location()* function defined on them, but they inherit the functions of their supertype, **Publications**. Hence the functions *Title()*, *View()*, and *Text_Body()* are also defined on instances of **Conferences**. Type membership is depicted with thin dotted lines from type objects to its members (i.e., instances). In Figure 1a, the **Journals** type has four instances: three directly created as **Journals** and one from the **Tutorials** subtype.

Meta-data about the model itself is also modeled in FOOM (see Figure 1b). **Entity** is the root of the type hierarchy and has as its subtypes **System-Types** and **User-Types**. **System_Types** in turn, defines two subtypes, **Types** and **Functions**. Note that all types are instances of the type **Types** as depicted by the thin dotted lines from **Types** to all other type objects. In fact, all of the types in Figure 1a are also instances of the type **Types**. The root of the hierarchy starting at **Publications** is also shown in Figure 1b, where the remainder of it is as shown in Figure 1a. **Types** has the three functions, *Show_Inst()* *Show_Sub()*, and *Name()* defined on it. *Show_Inst()* and *Show_Sub()* return the OID's of the instances and subtypes of a type respectively. *Name()* simply returns the ASCII string of a type. All functions are instances of the type **Functions** and have a corresponding set of functions defined on them. *In_Arg()* and *Out_Arg()* return the OID of the types of the input and output arguments of the function. *S_or_C()* returns true or false depending on whether the function is stored or computed. *Name()* simply returns the name of the function. These "meta-functions" may vary depending on the actual implementation but serve to illustrate the kinds of functions that might be defined on the meta-data (i.e., **Functions** and **Types**). Notice that the function *Name()* is overloaded; both the type **Types** and the type **Functions** have a function called *Name()* defined on them. This function overloading is not ambiguous since each function has its own unique OID; further, each function is distinguished by its input argument type. Also, to make conceptual schemas more legible, we do not always show all the functions defined on types nor do we draw all the thin dotted lines denoting type membership.

Since every object is treated uniformally in FOOM, it is natural to investigate the sharing of individual objects (instances), meta-data objects (e.g., types), and behavioral objects (functions). Returning to the previous example of collaborating researchers, recall that Researcher B would like to import some specific publications from Researcher

A. This situation corresponds to instance level sharing. In order to illustrate this more clearly, Figure 2a depicts the conceptual schema of Researcher B. Notice that Reseacher-B models publications differently than Reseacher-A (Figure 1a). Imported instance objects are denoted by the hashed bubbles in Figure 2a. Hence, Researcher B now sees four instances of **ACM-papers** where originally there were only two and three instances of **IEEE-papers** where originally there were only two. Even though Figure 2a depicts the remote instances differently than local ones, they all appear local (i.e., transparent) to Researcher B in our approach.

Existing approaches have concentrated on what corresponds to type level sharing [22, 24]. These systems focus on the sharing of entire collections (e.g., relations), rather than members of the collection (e.g., tuples). By contrast, importing a remote type in FOOM naturally leads to importing the subtree of the remote type hierarchy rooted at that type. Again, using the collaborating researchers example, assume Researcher B would also like to have access to all of Researcher A's journal publications. Figure 2b illustrates this situation. In this case, Researcher B also imports the **Tutorials** type by virtue of the supertype-subtype relationship. The principal advantage of this kind of sharing is that it allows Researcher B to use Reseacher-A's database without integrating Researcher A's conceptual schema with his/her own conceptual schema; Reseacher B simply uses the part of Researcher A's original schema rooted at **Journals**. Another way of looking at this is that Researcher B can now move from his/her own context to Researcher A's context. Researcher B can even add or delete instances from his/her own context of Researcher A (note that one of the instances of **Journals** in Figure 2b is local) without really adding or deleting it in Researcher A's database. This is a useful feature when the autonomy constraints of Researcher A prohibit any addition or deletion of its instances.

In addition to simply sharing objects representing information units, it is also possible to share behavioral objects. The importer may then access services not provided by his/her local system. For example, in the collaborating researchers scenario, assume Researcher B has a dvi previewer method but no latex compiler on his/her local system. Further, Researcher A has latex available by virtue of a function, *latex()*, which takes ASCII text with latex commands as input, and outputs dvi format. In this case, our approach allows Researcher B to share the function *latex()*. Sharing functions in this way is very natural in FOOM because functions are objects.

4 A Mechanism to Support Object-Based Sharing

One of the main goals of our SCDS mechanism is to provide the seamless integration of remote objects with local objects. The federated environment we are considering, however, places two significant restrictions on our implementation: no global schema and no global OID space. The lack of a global schema results in the possible absence, ambiguity, or conflict among type and function definitions of components. Issues such as these are addressed during the *resolution* phase [18]. We assume at this stage that the resolution phase has already occurred. Our concern here is with seamless operation of the sharing patterns described in Section 4 where any meta-data conflicts have been resolved.

At this stage, difficulties arising from the lack of a global OID space are the source of the major obstacles to providing seamless operation. The purpose of OIDs is to give each object a (system-wide) logically unique identifier. Since each component is autonomous, there is no way to guarantee that OIDs generated independently on separate components will be globally unique. Previous approaches simply construct unique global OIDs by concatenating a local OID and the database identifier uniquely identifying a site [12, 16]. However, this requires modification to local systems in order for them to be able to interpret the global OIDs. While this approach guarantees globally unique OIDs, it is not a tolerable here since existing components should operate without modifications to their local DBMS software. Our solution is to create surrogate objects locally for objects which exist remotely. Since these surrogates are created locally, the local DBMS is able to interpret and manipulate remote objects as usual through the surrogates. When it is necessary to retrieve the actual state of a remote object, using surrogates alone is

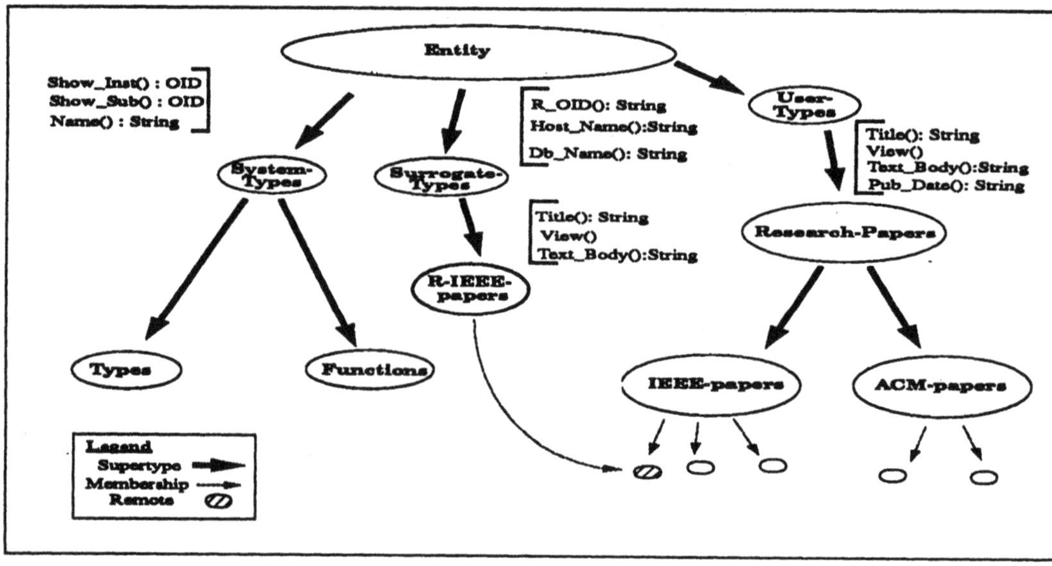

Figure 3: Sharing Instance Objects

not sufficient. Our implementation exploits the extensible nature of FOOM by rewriting the functions encapsulating surrogate objects as computed functions that then retrieve the results of applying the function on the remote component where the object is actually stored. This does not require modification to existing DBMS software. We simply provide computed functions to override the stored functions at run-time. In order for the overloading to perform correctly, function naming, binding, and placement in the type hierarchy are critical. Below, we discuss in more detail our technique for placing objects and overloading functions so as to preserve the seamless operation of a component.

4.1 Instance Level Sharing

The key to incorporating remote instance objects seamlessly into a local component is determining in which local component functions of the local component the remote instance participates, and then insuring that these functions operate transparently when surrogate objects are involved. Below we first consider the two kinds of functions in which instance objects participate and our approach for preserving transparency for them. Next, we discuss how we handle remote instances that have additional or missing functions defined on them by the remote component.

Functions in which instance level objects participate fall into two categories: functions that operate on the actual type object of which the instance is a member (e.g., *Show_Inst()*), and functions that are defined directly by the types of which the instance is a member (e.g, *Title()*). Hence, we must make sure that both of these kinds of functions operate correctly on surrogate instance objects.

When a type level function (e.g., *Show_Inst()*) is invoked, the function executes properly since the surrogate is created as a member of that very type. For example, in figure 2a, if we invoked the type level function *Show_Inst()* on **IEEE-papers**, the function would return three OIDs: two local instances and one surrogate. In general, all type level functions will have their transparency preserved by using surrogates.

For instance level functions, however, we need to introduce a surrogate type in order to preserve transparency. The purpose of this new surrogate type is to override the local functions that surrogates inherit from the local type of which they are a member. By additionally creating the surrogate as a member of this surrogate type, the functions that the surrogate instance originally inherited are overridden. This approach is illustrated in Figure 3. There are two thin dotted arrows from **R-IEEE-papers** ("R" for remote) and **IEEE-papers** to the surrogate instance. This indicates that surrogate instances (i.e., remote instances) of **IEEE-papers** are created as members of both **IEEE-papers** and **R-IEEE-papers**. Thus these (remote) instances inherit functions multiply from both **R-IEEE-papers** and **IEEE-papers**; any duplicately named function from the two types is overridden by the function defined by **R-IEEE-papers**. Surrogates are created as members of both types simultaneously because we need a surrogate to sometimes act as a member of **IEEE-papers** (for type level functions such as *Show_Inst()*) and sometimes as a member of **R-IEEE-papers** (for instance level functions such as *Title()*).

The approach we have just described for transparently sharing instances exploits the feature in FOOM that allows objects to be members of more than one type. We briefly describe here an alternative approach that we find inferior due to transparency considerations. The key to providing transparency involves the overriding of functions. In Figure 3, we accomplished this by creating the type **R-IEEE** and creating surrogates as members of both **IEEE-papers**and **R-IEEE-papers**. An alternative approach might be to create **R-IEEE-papers** as a subtype of **IEEE-papers** and create the local surrogates as instances of **R-IEEE-papers**. One major drawback with this approach is that remote instances are no longer transparent members of **IEEE-papers**. The user is now made aware of the **R-IEEE-papers** subtype in his/her conceptual schema. A second drawback is that in this approach surrogate types appear scattered throughout the user's conceptual schema. In our approach we are proposing all remote surrogate types are contained to a single branch of the type hierarchy under **Surrogate-Types**.

Functions that are locally defined but do not exist on the remote component from which instances are being imported should not pose any problems with respect to transparency. For example, *Pub_Date()* is not defined in the surrogate type **R-IEEE-papers** in Figure 3. Local queries involving *Pub_Date* will simply return null values for local surrogates' *Pub_Date* value. When the results of queries are passed back to the user, these null values are filtered out and discarded.

The reverse situation, where the remote component defines additional functions that do not exist locally is slightly more complicated; this depends upon the signatures of the functions on the remote component. Most of the functions presented in the examples return literal values such as strings or integers. Such literal types do not have OIDs associated with them. They form the atomic types upon which other user-defined abstract types can built. In addition to functions returning literal types, there are some functions that return abstract objects, as represented by OIDs. For example, one such function might be: *Author()*:**Publications->Persons**. *Author()* takes in an instance of type **Publications** and returns an instance of type **Persons**.

When signatures of additional functions defined by a remote component on an instance return simple atomic types, queries against the local instances should return null values (analogous to previous situation of missing functions), which are then discarded in the results. However, some problems occur when the result type of the function is non-atomic types and is not defined locally. For example, when trying to import the function *Author()*, two problems arise. First, the type **Persons** is not defined locally. Second, the OID returned by the overridden function will return a remote OID that the local system cannot interpret. The solution to the first problem is to create a local **Person** type by importing the meta-data from the remote component (see type level sharing in Section 5.2). For the second problem, a local surrogate must be created for the person who is the author of the instance publication being imported.

4.2 Type Level Sharing

There are two aspects to sharing type level objects. The first is to share only the meta-data associated with the type being imported. The second aspect is to also include all the members and subtypes of the type being imported.

The meta-data associated with a type consists of the signatures of the functions that serve to encapsulate the members of that type. Hence, all that is needed to import the meta-data of a remote type is create a local surrogate type with the same functions. The only real complication occurs when one of the functions has a signature whose result type

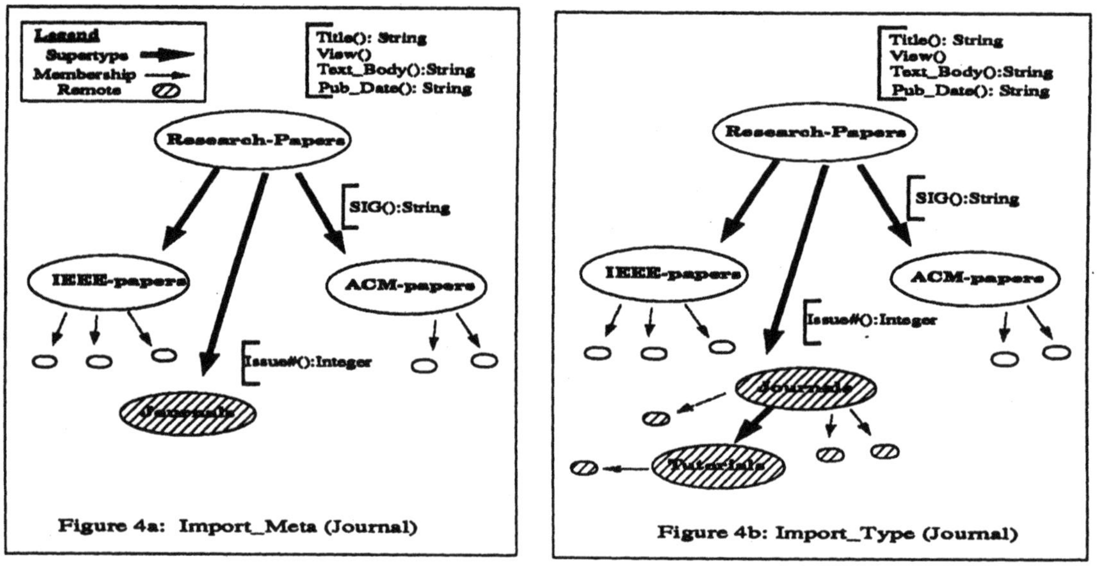

Figure 4a: Import_Meta (Journal)

Figure 4b: Import_Type (Journal)

Figure 4: Sharing Type Objects

is not known locally. Conceptually it is not difficult to apply this simple rule recursively to create a surrogate type for the closure of this type. However, the entire closure may not necessarily be required. The results of importing only the meta-data is illustrated in Figure 4b for the type **Journal**.

In addition to importing meta-data, the second aspect of type level object importation, involves also importing the remote members and subtypes of the type. This is the kind of type level sharing illustrated in Figure 2b. To accomplish this, we essentially use the same paradigm as described earlier: 1) Import meta-data of a type and 2) Import all the instances of the meta-data as in instance level sharing. To include subtypes, this rule can be applied recursively. Figure 4b illustrates this kind of type level sharing for the type **Journal**.

4.3 Behavior Level Sharing

The goal of supporting the sharing of behavioral objects is to allow a component to utilize remote services that may not be available locally. This corresponds to sharing *computed* functions. For example, suppose that Researcher B would like to share Reseacher A's *latex()* function. Normally, Researcher B views a publication object, say *inst*, by simply invoking the composed function, e.g., **emacs(Text_Body(*inst*))**. Now let us further assume that Reseacher B has the dvi literal type already defined and that s/he has the local function *xdvi* available for viewing dvi format. In order to generate dvi format from *Text_Body()* (in latex format), s/he imports the *latex()* function from Reseacher A. Now in order to preview the publication all that is necessary is to invoke the composed function: **xdvi(latex(Text_Body(*inst*)))**.

Importing functions as behavioral objects is relatively simple. All that must be done is to create a computed function that makes the appropriate RPC request to a remote component. We anticipate that the most useful functions will operate on literal types as in the *latex()* example. However, functions involving signatures with complex/abstract data can also be useful. This kind of sharing is discussed in detail in [3].

5 Concluding Remarks

In this paper, we have described an approach and mechanism for supporting seamless, transparent interconnection in federated database systems. This work is couched in the context of the Remote-Exchange project at USC. A functional object-oriented database model was employed as an inter-component communication forum. Sharing of meta-data objects (types), individual instance objects, and functions/methods has been explored. We have built an experimental testbed[5] with Iris[7] and Omega [8] DBMS components, which we are using to refine and evaluate our technique.

References

[1] M. Atkinson, et al. The Object-Oriented Database System Manifesto. In *Proceedings of the 1st Intl. Conf. on Deductive and Object-Oriented Databases*. Kyoto, Japan, December 1989.

[2] C Batini, M. Lenzerini, and S. Navathe. A Comparative Analysis of Methodologies of Database Schema Integration. *ACM Computing Surveys*, 18(4):323–364, 1986.

[3] D. Fang, J. Hammer, and D. McLeod. An Approach to Behavior Sharing in Federated Database Systems. In *Proceedings of the 3rd International Workshop on Distributed Object Management*, August 1992 (to appear).

[4] D. Fang, J. Hammer, D. McLeod, and A. Si. Remote-Exchange: An Approach to Controlled Sharing among Autonomous, Heterogenous Database Systems. In *Proceedings of the IEEE Spring Compcon, San Francisco*. IEEE, February 1991.

[5] D. Fang and D. McLeod. A Testbed and Mechanism for Object-Based Sharing in Federated Database Systems. Technical Report USC-CS-92-507, Computer Science Department, University of Southern California, Los Angeles CA 90089-0781, February 1992.

[6] A. Ferrier and C. Stangret. Heterogeneity in the Distributed Database Mangagement System SIRIUS-DELTA. In *Proceedings of the International Conference on Very Large Databases*. VLDB Endowment, 1983.

[7] D. Fishman, D. Beech, H. Cate, E. Chow, T. Connors, T. Davis, N. Derrett, C. Hoch, W. Kent, P. Lyngbaek, B. Mahbod, M. Neimat, T. Ryan, and M. Shan. Iris: An Object-Oriented Database Management System. *ACM Transactions on Office Information Systems*, 5(1):48–69, January 1987.

[8] S. Ghandeharizadeh, et al. The Design and Implementation of OMEGA. Technical report, USC, September 1991.

[9] M. Hammer and D. McLeod. Database Description with SDM: A Semantic Database Model. *ACM Transactions on Database Systems*, 6(3):351–386, September 1981.

[10] D. Heimbigner and D. McLeod. A Federated Architecture for Information Systems. *ACM Transactions on Office Information Systems*, 3(3):253–278, July 1985.

[11] R. Hull and R. King. Semantic Database Modeling: Survey, Applications, and Research Issues. *ACM Computing Surveys*, 19(3):201–260, September 1987.

[12] W. Kim, N. Ballou, J. Garza, and D. Woelk. A Distributed Object-Oriented Database System Supporting Shared and Private Databases. *ACM Transactions on Office Information Systems*, 9(1):31–51, January 1991.

[13] W. Kim, J. Banerjee, H. T. Chou, J. F. Garza, and D. Woelk. Composite Object Support in an Object-Oriented Database System. In *Proceedings of the Conference on Object-Oriented Programming Systems, Languages, and Applications*, pages 118–125, 1987.

[14] C. Lecluse, P. Richard, and F. Velez. O2, an Object-Oriented Data Model. In *Proceedings of the ACM SIGMOD International Conference on Management of Data*. ACM SIGMOD, June 1988.

[15] W. Litwin and A. Abdellatif. Multidatabase Interoperability. *IEEE Computer*, 19(12), December 1986.

[16] P. Lyngbaek and D. McLeod. Object Management in Distributed Information Systems. *ACM Transactions on Office Information Systems*, 2(2):96–122, April 1984.

[17] D. Maier, J. Stein, A. Otis, and A. Purdy. Development of an Object-Oriented DBMS. In *Proceedings of the Conference on Object-Oriented Programming Systems, Languages, and Applications*, pages 472–482. ACM, 1986.

[18] D. McLeod, D. Fang, and J. Hammer. The Identification and Resolution of Semantic Heterogeneity. In *Proceedings of International Workshop on Interoperability in Multidatabase Sytems*. Kyoto, Japan, April 1991.

[19] M. Shan. Unified Access in a Heterogenous Information Environment. *IEEE Office Knowledge Engineering*, 3(2):35–42, August 1989.

[20] D. Shipman. The Functional Data Model and the Data Language DAPLEX. *ACM Transactions on Database Systems*, 2(3):140–173, March 1981.

[21] J. Smith, P. Bernstein, U. Dayal, N. Goodman, T. Landers, K. Lin, and E. Wong. Multibase: Integrating Heterogeneous Distributed Database Systems. In *Proceedings of the National Computer Conference*, pages 487–499. AFIPS, June 1981.

[22] M. Stonebraker and E. Neuhold. A Distributed Database Version of INGRES. In *Proceedings of the Berkeley Workshop on Distributed Data Management and Computer Networks*, pages 19–36. University of California, Berkeley, May 1977.

[23] T. Templeton, et al. Mermaid: A Front-End to Distributed Heterogenous Databases. In *Proceedings of IEEE*, pages 695–708, 1987.

[24] R. Williams. R*: An Overview of the Architecture. Technical Report RJ3325, IBM, February 1981.

IN SUPPORT OF OPTIMISM IN A DISTRIBUTED DATABASE SYSTEM

Junguk L. Kim
Department of Computer Science
Texas A&M University
College Station, TX 77843–3112

ABSTRACT

This paper presents a novel mechanism which can be used to support the optimistic approach to network partitioning problem in distributed database systems. Our protocol provides the partitioning point effectively, by checking the status of the network only when necessary, and the system reconfiguration is performed in a highly reliable way. Its correctness for providing necessary changing points for partition operation is presented.

Key Words. Consistency, Distributed database systems, Network partitioning, Surveillance, Election.

1 INTRODUCTION

Data items in a distributed database system are replicated on different sites to provide better reliability and availability tolerating site and communication failures. When a distributed database system is installed on a network, in which several subnetworks are interconnected, it is possible that the network is partitioned so that a group of nodes cannot communicate with another. If uncoordinated updates are applied to different copies of a data item, it is quite possible that the values of the copies are not mutually consistent, and hence, for mutual consistency on the values of the copies, an update to them must be *atomic*.

Davidson *et al.*[1] surveyed the strategies proposed in the literature for the mutual consistency problem. Basically, there are two different approaches: the pessimistic approach [17,18,19,20,21,22,23,24,25] which guarantees the mutual consistency losing data availability and the optimistic approach [2,12,16] which allows data inconsistency for better availability assuming low probability of occurrences of the mutual consistency problem.

In the optimistic approach, while the network is partitioned, the system processes all transactions, but commitment becomes temporary until partitions are merged, even though actual copies of data items are updated. After the partitions are merged, possible inconsistencies among data item values are detected by using a global precedence graph, which checks for the serializability of the transactions executed in different partitions. This means that some transactions may have to be rolled back after partitions are merged, since the transactions which read or wrote a data item at any of the sites that did not have the value selected to be kept should be undone in order to make the database correct. The serializability of the executions of the transactions over the copies of the data items within one partition must be guaranteed.

We call the operation that supports the optimistic approach the *partition operation*. The partition operation includes a mechanism to detect changes in the status of the network, since a site in the partition may not realize the changes as they occur. In addition, the partition operation should have a mechanism to elect one coordinator to broadcast the new view to all sites in the partition. The election mechanism must be robust against all kinds of failures during its operation. Moreover, the view distribution process must deliver the same view to all sites in the partition. Unfortunately, it is not easy to cope with failures such as message loss, during the election process [3,6].

When all sites in a partition have the same view of the availability of the other sites, the partition operation is much more efficient. The system must know when and how the partition is formed. By "when" we mean not clock time, but the point within the execution schedule of transactions. Further, the status change of the network must be discovered as soon as possible.

In order to detect a status change in loosely coupled distributed system, a site may periodically send messages to check for network status changes or the status may be checked only when necessary. If such surveillance mechanism which operates only as needed is adequate to support partition operation, then the number of required messages can be reduced considerably. Essentially, we only need to know about status changes that can affect the consistency of the database. A number of protocols for failure and recovery detection, based on periodic checking, have been proposed in the literature (e.g., [5,9,10,14,15]).

This paper presents a protocol which supports the partition operation. In our protocol, each site monitors other sites only when necessary, as proposed in [7,8]. Specifically, if a transaction includes operations to be carried out at remote sites, its home site then checks the status of the other sites. A *Status Monitor* resides in each site to detect status changes (failure or recovery) of other sites and to coordinate the construction of a consistent view of the membership of a partition. In addition, the problem of synchronizing multiple state-change detection problem in system reconfiguration (basically the election problem) is handled in a particularly robust way, as proposed in [6]. The protocol consists of two subprotocols - the Failure and Recovery Detection Protocol (FRDP) and the Status Change Protocol (SCP). In summary, our algorithm provides the following facilities:

1. Detection of the status change of the network efficiently and correctly in a systematic way,
2. Correct provision of the necessary partitioning and merging points of the network to support data consistency mechanisms.
3. System reconfiguration by electing a coordinator in a partition in a robust way against message loss and processor failures.

In our model, we make the following assumptions: The message-communication subsystem is not completely reliable, meaning that message delivery is not guaranteed, but when a message is delivered, it is guaranteed to be uncorrupted (no Byzantine failures); When a node fails, it simply stops participating in the protocol (fail-stop); The time of message delivery between two nodes can be arbitrarily long, but it is bounded; The messages sent from one node to another are received in the order that they were sent; Any sequence of failures continually interrupting the system is finite, that is, eventually the system will remain failure-free for a long enough time; For simplicity, we assume that the merging is done between two partitions. For example, if partitions P_1, P_2, and P_3 are merged into partition P, we assume that P_1 and P_2 are merged into, say, P_{temp}, and then P_{temp} and P_3 are merged.

This paper is organized as follows. In section 2, basic concepts about transactions and serializability are presented. The theoretical background for the optimistic approach and partition history management is then introduced. Basic assumptions about communication facilities and the system model are presented. The description of the proposed protocol is presented in section 3. Section 4 shows that the protocol works correctly. The performance of our protocol is discussed and compared with other protocols in section 5. Finally, a summary of this paper and our conclusions are presented in section 6.

2 BACKGROUND

Partitions are assumed to be changed dynamically in this paper. Hence, a site must keep a partition history so that it knows when the state of data items in the sites in a newly merged partition was consistent, for detection of the mutual inconsistencies among data items. The partition that included the latest consistent copies of the data items, *nearest common father partition*, can be found if the partition history is kept by the sites. Here, we use a data structure called the *partition history graph* defined by [9].

Definition: Let P_0 be a partition where all sites in the system were active. A *Partition History Graph* of a partition P is a digraph $PHG(P)$ = (V,E) where

V = $\{P_i$— a site in P was in $P_i\} \cup \{P\} \cup \{P_0\}$, and

E = $\{P_i \rightarrow P_j$— a site in P_j was a member of P_i and P_j is the first active partition that the site joined after leaving $P_i\}$.

$PHG(P)$ is rooted at $Psub0$. □

Let us, for example, suppose that sites in P_0 = {A,B,C,D} are partitioned into two partitions P_1 = {A,B} and P_2 = {C,D}. They are then merged into P_3 = {A,B,C,D}. The $PHG(P_3)$ then consists of $V = \{P_0, P_1, P_2, P_3\}$ and $E = \{P_0 \rightarrow P_1, P_0 \rightarrow P_2, P_1 \rightarrow P_3, P_2 \rightarrow P_3\}$.

The transactions processed in the partitions formed after the nearest common father partition are examined for consistency. It is assumed that each partition has a unique coordinator. When a partition merge is detected, local transaction executions in the partition are stopped, and a new coordinator is elected. The coordinator then derives the total ordering of the transaction execution history, which is the collection of the read sets and the write sets of transactions processed in partitions formed after the nearest common father of the partitions being merged. Hence, partition P_i being merged has its own execution history called *a global history* of P_i. It is assumed that a global history of each partition being merged has the total ordering between the transactions processed, since a precedence order has been defined each time partitions are merged. Basically, the precedence is defined in a way that the read action must precede write action if they are executed in different partitions. It is also assumed that the transaction must read a data item before it writes the data. Thus, if two write operations in different partitions are applied to the same data item, then we cannot find the precedence.

A global precedence graph is generated from these global histories of the partitions being merged. The global precedence graph was defined by [2] and [14], where the conflicts between the transactions processed in different partitions being merged are detected. In the definition, partitioning was assumed to be pairwise, meaning that the partitioning subdivides one old partition into two subpartitions and merging combines the subpartions into the same old partition. Therefore, the global precedence graph is slightly modified as follows so that the conflicts across partition histories can be detected.

Definition: Let $H_1 = T_{11}, T_{12}, ..., T_{1n_1}$, and $H_2 = T_{21}, T_{22}, ..., T_{2n_2}$ be global histories of partitions P_1 and P_2 respectively. *The global precedence graph* $G(H_1, H_2) = (V, E)$ is a digraph where

$V = \{T_{11}, ...T_{1n_1}\} \cup \{T_{21}, ..., T_{2n_2}\}$

E = Dependency Edges ∪ Precedence Edges ∪ Interference Edges

1. A dependency edge exists between two transactions processed in one global history, $T_{li} \rightarrow T_{lk}$, iff i ¡ k and there is a data item $d \in WS(T_{li}) \cap RS(T_{lk})$, such that for all j, i¡j¡k, $d \notin WS(T_{lj})$.
2. A precedence edge exists between two transactions processed in one global history, $T_{li} \rightarrow T_{lk}$, iff i ¡ k, and there is a data item $d \in RS(T_{li}) \cap WS(T_{lk})$, and for all j, i¡j¡k, $d \notin WS(T_{lj})$, and there is no dependency edge $T_{li} \rightarrow T_{lk}$.
3. An interference edge exists between two transactions processed in different partition histories, $T_{li} \rightarrow T_{kj}$, iff there is a data item $d \notin RS(T_{li}) \cap WS(Tsubkj)$ and $T_{li} \neq T_{kj}$.

Before the global precedence graph is formed, the coordinator rolls back the transactions in one global history that were previously rolled back in the other global history. Conflicting transactions are detected as a cycle in the global precedence graph. If there is such a cycle, conflicting transactions are rolled back and this process continues until all cycles are eliminated. Then the remaining transactions are executed at sites that have copies of the data items for them but have not yet executed them, yielding a consistent database in the newly formed partition. If the newly formed partition consists of all sites in the system, then the database is completely consistent. We call the above actions to resolve data inconsistencies, the *merge process.* A set of transactions to be examined in the global precedence graph is called the *merge set.* When P_i and P_j are merged into P, the transactions processed in $PHG(P_i)$ and the ones processed in $PHG(P_j)$ form the merge set for P.

Since our protocol does not detect all network status changes, we define a *logical view* (or just view) of a partition which is defined as being the subset of sites with which communication is thought to be possible, and is denoted by $V(i)$. Note that a site may think that it cannot communicate with certain other sites even if they are available. Similarly, a site may be unavailable when it is thought to be available. But, if communication is needed with such a site, our protocol will detect the status change. Thus, a site's view of the network may be updated only when knowing the status of the network is necessary. A site S_i is considered to be *active* at site S_j if S_i and S_j are in the same logical partition in S_j's view. Otherwise, it is considered to be *inactive.* A site status table is maintained by each site to maintain its current view. The status table at each node has a partition identifier associated with it. $G(i)$ and $C(i)$ denote the identifier of the partition to which node i belongs and i's view of the elected coordinator of that partition, respectively.

A node in our model is a finite state automaton with three basic states: "Reconfiguration", "Normal", or "Failed". Let $S(i)$ denote the state of node i. When the state of a node is set to "Failed", the node is not in execution. The state "Reconfiguration" of a node indicates that the node is participating in the election of a coordinator. Between reconfigurations, the state of an active node is "Normal".

One of the constraints that the SCP subprotocol must follow is that all of the members of a partition must be in agreement as to the new leader after the election completes. Moreover, the views of any two nodes in different partitions must be disjoint in order for the nodes in different physical partitions to perform consistent actions. Further, overlapping partitions occur when the system state is changed by the reconfiguration to a state in which one or more members of one partition appear in the view of a node in another partition. Hence, the reconfiguration process must guarantee that all partitions (logical partitions) are disjoint. Formally, these constraints are stated as follows:

Definition: The system state is said to be *complete* in P, if and only if the following conditions are satisfied:

For any two nodes i and j in P:

1. $C(i) = C(j)$, when $S(i) = S(j) =$ "Normal" and $G(i) = G(j)$.
2. $V(i) \cap V(j) = \emptyset$, when $S(i) = S(j) =$ "Normal" and $G(i) \neq G(j)$.

3 THE FAILURE AND RECOVERY DETECTION PROTOCOL

In this section, a description of the proposed Protocol which consists of FRDP and SCP is presented. In determination of a consistent view of the network to support partitioned operation, the state of the partition must be monitored and a new state of the partition must be broadcast to all members of the new partition. The FRDP detects any status change caused by failure or recovery of the system, and the SCP elects one coordinator and distributes the consistent view of the partition. Before presenting the protocol, we describe the messages and data structures needed.

3.1 Messages And Data Structures

To facilitate the operation of the FRDP and the SCP, the following messages are used.

- The site status checking message (CHECK) - It is used to check the status of a site during normal FRDP operation.
- The status response message (RESPONSE) - It is used to reply to the CHECKs.
- E-COLLECT - It is used by the SCP to initiate an system reconfiguration when a status change is detected.
- E-RESPONSE - It is used to respond to E-COLLECT.
- E-ACK - It is used to acknowledge the status table in the SCP.
- E-FINISH - It is used to finish a system reconfiguration.

To maintain a current, consistent view of a partition, and to support the exchange of status messages, each site maintains a Site Status Table (SST). The SST is shared with local transactions but is updated only by the Status Monitor (SM). Each entry in the SST represents a site (S_i) in the network and has four fields:

- Request_Set : The set of local transactions requesting message exchange with site S_i.
- Received_Flag : Set when a RESPONSE is received from site S_i.
- Sent_Flag : Set when a CHECK is sent to site S_i.
- Status : UP if S_i is available, DOWN if not.

In order that a consistent timeout period be used throughout the network, it is assumed that each site owns a physical clock and that all clocks run at close enough to the same rate so that there is no discernible difference between timeout periods.

3.2 Description Of The FRDP

When a transaction sends a request (*Read* or *Write* request) to remote sites, it submits the *watch* request to the SM to monitor failure of any of the remote sites. When the SM receives a watch request from a local transaction, it puts the transaction identifier (TR_j) into the Request_Sets of the sites from which that transaction is requesting service. While a local transaction is waiting for service from remote sites, its SM periodically sends CHECKs to the sites involved and receives RESPONSEs from those sites.

When the SM sends out a CHECK, it resets the Received_Flags of all sites in the SST, sets the Sent_Flag of each site to which the CHECK is sent, restarts the timer, and waits for the RESPONSEs from the sites. When a RESPONSE is received, the SM sets the Received_Flag of the source site entry in the SST. The SM responds with a RESPONSE as rapidly as possible upon receiving a CHECK. When the timer expires, the SM checks whether the sites responded. If the SM receives a CHECK from a site to which it sent its CHECK, then the received CHECK is treated as a RESPONSE from the site.

The sites with nonempty Request_Sets in the SST comprises a set to be monitored for failure and recovery. Thus, if the sites marked UP responded and none marked DOWN responded among the ones with nonempty Request_Sets, then the SM generates the next CHECK and sends it to the sites. If any site marked DOWN responded or any site marked UP did not respond, then a status change is detected and the status reconfiguration mechanism takes over to get the new view about the new partition. While the SM is waiting for the timer to expire,

When the timer expires, the SM responds to the CHECKs received, examines the SST to check if there has been a status change, and generate the next CHECKs.

After the transaction receives its service from remote sites that are UP, it submits the *watch-release* request to the SM to indicate that it does not need to check the status of those sites any more. The SM then deletes this transaction identifier (TR_j) from the Request_Sets of the sites. If some sites marked UP do not respond, the SM marks thoses sites DOWN. The transaction does not submit the watch-release request for those sites assuming those sites are now separated into a different partition(s). Thus, when those DOWN sites respond, the merge of the partitions is detected. The SM checks local transaction requests for watch continually, except when it is performing other actions.

When a status change is detected, the SM sets the state to "Reconfiguration", and executes the SCP. The merge process defined in section 2 then takes over to reconcile inconsistencies among data items. The merge set is derived using the partition history graph. The conflicting transactions in the merge set are detected by the global precedence graph and rolled back until the database is consistent.

3.3 Description Of The SCP

When a site detects a status change, it initiates the SCP which consists of three phases and becomes a candidate itself. A site which receives a candidacy message becomes a cohort unless it has already become a candidate. However, even though it is already a candidate, it may decide to withdraw its candidacy and become a cohort, depending upon the priority of the sender of the message.

Basically, the candidate broadcasts its candidacy to all sites in the system. If there is no failure during execution of the SCP, then all candidates become aware of each other and the highest ranked candidate can declare that it is the coordinator of the new partition. However, when there is a failure during the SCP, electing one coordinator may not be possible as shown in [26]. With one failure, state of the system can be inconsistent. Hence, the approach adopted here in the SCP is to detect such inconsistency and re-executes the SCP with the assumption that such failure during the SCP is finite.

In the first phase, a candidate broadcasts E-COLLECTs to all sites in the system; and a non-candidate site (cohort) sends E-RESPONSE to the candidates, which carries the rank of the highest candidate seen by the site. A candidate receiving E-COLLECT from a higher-ranked candidate or E-RESPONSE with higher rank would withdraw its candidacy.

In the second phase, a candidate forms a new SST for its new partition and send it to all sites in its partition. After this point, it rejects any further E-COLLECTs. A cohort, on receiving the SST, it checks if the SST is from the highest ranked candidate seen by itself. If so, it accepts the SST and sends back an E-ACK.

In the third phase, the candidate which received E-ACKs from all members of its new partition, commits the SST into the partition history log, and sends E-FINISH to all of its members. On receiving such E-FINISH, a cohort commits the SST into the partition history log and sets its state to "Normal".

If a site does not receive a desirable message in each phase, it aborts the SCP, becomes a candidate, and re-execute the SCP.

4 CORRECTNESS

Let $PHG(P)$ be actual the partition history graph of P. Because of the way it works, the FRDP might have seen a different partition history graph of P from $PHG(P)$. We first prove that a partitioning can be detected exactly when some site in one partition checks the status of a site in the other partition.

Lemma 4.1: Suppose that partition P is partitioned into two partitions, P_i and P_j. The status monitors of the sites in P_i detect the partitioning if and only if there is a transaction in P_i which needs a copy of a data item in P_j.

Proof: It follows by the definition of our protocol. □

Lemma 4.2: Suppose that partition P is divided into two partitions, P_i and P_j. If there was no transaction in P_i which requested a copy of a data item in P_j, then there is no serializability conflict between transactions processed in P_i and P_j.

Proof: It follows from the definition of the global precedence graph, since there can be no interference edge from transactions processed in P_i to those processed in P_j. □

Corollary 4.1: If no site in a partition P detects a partitioning, transactions processed in P do not have any serializability conflicts with those processed in other partitions. □

To prove that the FRDP is correct (from the consistency point of view) we need to prove that all the serializability conflicts are detected under the FRDP. Since the serializability conflicts between transactions executed in different partitions are shown in cycles in the global precedence graph, it suffices to show that the global precedence graph derived from the merge set of $PHG(P)$ has a cycle if and only if the global precedence graph derived from the merge set of $PHG_{FRDP}(P)$ has a cycle, where $PHG_{FRDP}(P)$ is the ***partition history graph*** of P as seen by the FRDP.

In order to process the merging in the optimistic approach, the merge set must be derived. Although the FRDP cannot reflect the physical situation exactly, we can do the merging correctly, as long as all cycles are shown in the precedence seen by the FRDP.

Definition 4.1: Two merge sets MS_1 and MS_2 are equivalent, written $MS_1 \equiv MS_2$, if the global precedence graph derived from MS_1 has a cycle iff the global precedence graph derived from MS_2 has a cycle. □

Since the FRDP is not adequate to ensure that a log can be kept which reflects the actual history of partitioning and merging, we must show that a correct partitioning and merging history can be derived from the logs. Since some sites may not detect partitioning, they may consider that there has been no change in their partition, while sites that detected the partitioning know about it. After the execution of the system reconfiguration mechanism, it is possible that some sites see no difference between the old view and the new view, while other sites see the change. In order to record partitioning history, each partition must have its unique identifier. For example, let us suppose that partition A,B,C,D is split into two partitions A,B and C,D and that sites A and B know about the partitioning and sites C and D do not. When the partitions A,B and C,D are merged into a new partition A,B,C,D, Sites C and D do not see the difference between the new view and the old view. The old partition A,B,C,D has an identifier (A;i) and partition A,B has (A;$i+1$) (Concatenation of a sequence number with the coordinator site identifier provides a unique partition identifier.) All sites must record the new partition as (A;$i+2$) so that all four sites record the new partition with the same partition identifier.

Now, we show that the correct merge set can be derived from the FRDP. Note that the global precedence graph is used to detect serializability conflicts between the transactions processed in different partitions. Hence, if $MS_1 \equiv MS_2$, the two merge sets have the same effect in the optimistic approach.

Theorem 4.1: MS($PHG(P)$) $\equiv$ MS($PHG_{FRDP}(P)$).

Proof: Assume that we are merging P_i and P_j into P and there is a cycle in $PHG(P)$. We represent the cycle as $P_i \rightarrow \ldots \rightarrow P_n \rightarrow P_i$; that is, some transaction executed in P_{i+1} is dependent on the one executed in P_i and so on. We are going to prove that the same cycle is in $PHG_{FRDP}(P)$. Now, assume that P_j is missing in $PHG_{FRDP}(P)$. Then, $P_{j-1} \rightarrow P_j$ cannot be an interference edge, due to Lemma 4.1. Since $P_{j-1} \rightarrow P_j$ is not an interference edge, P_{j-1} must be an ancestor of P_j. So, in $PHG_{FRDP}(P)$, P_{j-1} and P_j are merged. Now, if $P_j \rightarrow P_{j+1}$ is an interference edge, then it should be in $PHG_{FRDP}(P)$, and there is nothing else to be proven. If $P_j \rightarrow P_{j+1}$ is not an interference edge, then P_j now must be an ancestor of P_{j+1}, and an argument similar to the one we used for P_j works here as well.

Since it is not difficult to prove that there are at least two interference edges in the above cycle, our above proof is sound. The proof that a cycle in $P_{FRDP}(P)$ implies a cycle in $PHG(P)$ is similar to the one above. □

We now argue that when sites in the system finish the SCP, the state of the system is complete.

Lemma 4.3: The state of a system that has employed the SCP is safe from physical partitioning.

Proof: Let us suppose that $C(i) \neq C(j)$ when $i \neq j$, $S(i) = S(j) =$ "Normal" and $G(i) = G(j)$. Each coordinator candidate generates a unique partition identifier and a cohort only accepts the SST (including unique partition identifier) from a candidate whose rank matches $R(C)$; i.e., whose candidacy it has accepted. Since $G(i) = G(j)$, i and j received and accepted the SST from the same candidate. Therefore, the assumption contradicts the specification of the protocol. □

Theorem 4.2: The state of a system that has employed the SCP is complete.

Proof: Let us suppose that $V(i) \cap V(j) \neq \emptyset$ when $S(i) = S(j) =$ "Normal", $i \neq j$, and $G(i) \neq G(j)$. Since $G(i) \neq G(j)$, there must have been two candidates, one for each partition. Suppose that node m is in both $V(i)$ and $V(j)$. For i and j to be in state "Normal" they must have accepted SSTs from their coordinators, $C(i)$ and $C(j)$, and later received FINISHs from them. But $C(i)$ and $C(j)$ would not have sent FINISHs to members of their partitions unless they had received acknowledgements from all partition members (including m). But the protocol prevents m from acknowledging more than one table.

With Lemma 4.3, the system state is complete. □

5 DISCUSSION

In this section, we compare the FRDP protocol with several existing protocols. In the RELNET subsystem[5], each site is associated with a group of guardians. A site sends messages called TIMESIGNAL to its guardians periodically. Failure of a sender of the TIMESIGNAL is detected by its guardians and failures of guardians are detected when they fail to respond within a timeout period. Additionally, a PROBE message is sent to sites to check the availability upon request from local processes. Therefore, the RELNET system requires $kn+\delta$ messages in one message cycle, where k is the number of guardians for one site and δ is the number of PROBE messages. The number of PROBE messages δ can be $n(n-k-1)$ in the worst case when each site must send PROBE messages to $n-k-1$ other sites. Thus, the number of messages required for one message cycle in the RELNET system is at most $M = n(n-1)$. In the best case when the system has a small constant k and no transaction wants PROBE messages to be sent out, $M = O(n)$. If all guardians fail, the RELNET system is not guaranteed to operate correctly.

The RSC protocol[14] passes messages around a virtual ring in the network. Each site sends an 'I-AM-ALIVE' message to its immediate neighboring site (the guardian site) periodically. If the guardian site does not receive an 'I-AM-ALIVE' message within some time interval, it executes the protocol for system reconfiguration. The RSC protocol requires n messages for network status checking in one message cycle. However, if there are n partitions and each partition consists of one site, each must check for the recovery of $n-1$ sites in the BROADCAST-AREA. In this case, $n(n-1)$ messages are required in one message cycle.

The number of messages required in the FRDP operation depends on the number of transactions in the system and how much remote site status checking is requested by those transactions. In the worst case, when all sites send status checking messages to the rest of the sites in the network, $n(n-1)$ messages are transmitted during each message cycle. In the best case, the FRDP requires no messages.

For simplicity, let $P(\tau)$ be the probability that τ transactions are active at one site in one message cycle, $\sum_{\tau=0}^{B} P(\tau) = 1$, where B is the maximum number of transactions which one site can process at one time. The average number of messages which one site must send for status checking can be expressed by a fan-out function $f(\tau)$, $0 \leq f(\tau) \leq (n-1)$. Therefore, the expected number of messages, N, which one site sends in one message cycle is: .br $N = \sum_{\tau=0}^{B} f(\tau)P(\tau)$. .br Any protocol that detects status changes by periodic polling of sites requires at least $n-1$ messages to be sent in each message cycle (period), since at least one site must poll each of the $n-1$ other sites. In such a protocol, the coordinator in a partition must send $n-1$ checking messages to detect the status changes of the remote sites. Thus, if k sites must send checking messages (k partitions); then the protocol requires $k(n-1)$ messages in one message cycle. However, the FRDP sends checking messages only when necessary. If there is no transaction involved with remote copies of data items, no checking messages are to be sent to failed sites (possibly in different partitions). The FRDP requires $N \times n$ messages in one message cycle, since there are n sites in the system. Therefore, the FRDP requires fewer messages in one message cycle (on the average) than other protocols when $N(\frac{n}{n-1}) < k$.

Now, we briefly analyze the message complexity of the SCP for one successful round. When all N nodes become candidates nearly at the same time, they all broadcast E-COLLECTs. Each node responds to every other, hence $N(N-1)$ E-RESPONSEs are generated. After this message exchange, all nodes, except for the highest ranked one, become cohorts and wait for the SST and FINISH. The highest ranked node generates at most N messages carrying the SST and N FINISHs. Therefore, the total number of messages is $O(N^2)$ for one successful round.

6 Conclusions

In this paper, we have considered status change surveillance issues supporting the optimistic approach to the network partitioning problem. Basically, the status change surveillance mechanism detects changes in the status of the network.

Protocols based on periodic status checking require considerable overhead. Even when the system is lightly loaded or idle, the status of the network is periodically checked. Therefore, the system may do unnecessary work to detect failures and to reconfigure the system. Our protocol detects a status change only when necessary. With our protocol, a status change may not be detected right after a site crashes or the network partitions, but it is detected later and system reconfiguration is initiated when the cooperation of that site is needed by a transaction. However, the whole system does not have to pay the cost of periodic checking.

Our protocol is attractive even in a busy system, since there may be no transactions needing remote service. One desirable aspect of the FRDP is that performance does not degrade when network partitioning occurs, while the others tend to require more messages than in the normal situation. The SCP correctly elects the coordinator of a newly formed partition and distributes a consistent view to the members of the partition. Unlike other protocols proposed in the literature, the SCP is particularly robust against network partitioning.

In summary, our protocol correctly supports efficient detection of status changes, and correctly provides the necessary configuration change points.

REFERENCES

1) Davidson, S.B., Garcia-Molina, H., and Skeen D., "Consistency in Partitioned Networks," ACM Computing Surveys, Vol. 17, No. 3, Sept. 1985, pp. 341-370.

2) Davidson, S.B., "Optimism and Consistency in Partitioned Distributed Database Systems," ACM Trans. on Database Systems, Vol. 9, No. 3, Sept. 1984, pp. 456-481.

3) Garcia-Molina, H., "Elections in a Distributed Computing System," IEEE Trans. on Computers, Vol. C-31, No. 1, Jan. 1982, pp. 48-59.

4) Gray, J.N., "Notes on Data Base Operating Systems," in R. Bayer, R.M. Graham, and G. Seegmuller (eds.), Operating Systems: An Advanced Course, Springer-Verlag, New York (1979), pp. 398-481.

5) Hammer, M. and Shipman, D., "Reliability Mechanism for SDD-1: A System for Distributed Database," ACM Trans. on Database Syst., Vol. 5, No. 4, Dec. 1980, pp. 431-466.

6) Kim, J.L. and Belford, G.G., "A Robust, Distributed Election Algorithm", Proc. IEEE 7th Symposium on Reliable Distributed Systems, Oct. 1988.

7) Kim, J.L., "A Protocol for Consistent Surveillance of Partitioned Network for Distributed Database Systems," Proceedings of International Symposium on Database Systems for Advanced Applications, April 1989, pp. 259-265.

8) Kim, J.L. and Hernandez, H., "A Network Surveillance Protocol for Distributed Database Systems," Journal of Data and Knowledge Engineering, North-Holland, Vol. 6, No. 5, September 1991, pp. 409-420.

9) Kim, W., "AUDITOR: A Framework for High Availability of DB/DC systems," IBM Res. Rep. RJ3512, 1982.

10) Ma, A.V. and Belford, G.G., "A Failure and Recovery Detection Protocol for Optimistic Partitioned Operation in Distributed Database Systems," Proc. 6th Int. Conf. on Distributed Computing Syst., May 1986, pp. 540-547.

11) Ma, A.V., "Optimistic Partitioned Operation in Distributed Database Systems," Ph.D. Thesis, Dept. Computer Science, University of Illinois at Urbana-Champaign, May 1986.

12) Parker, D.S., Popek, G.J., Rudisin, G., Stoughton, A., Walker, B.J., Chow, J.M., Edwards, D., Kiser, S., and Kline, C., "Detection of Mutual Inconsistency in Distributed Systems," IEEE Trans. on Software Engr., Vol. SE-5, No. 3, May 1983, pp. 240-246.

13) Skeen D. and Stonebraker, M., "A Formal Model of Crash Recovery in a Distributed System," IEEE Trans. on Software Engr., Vol. SE-9, No. 3, May 1983, pp. 219-228.

14) Walter, B., "A Robust and Efficient Protocol for Checking the Availability of Remote Sites," Proc. 6th Berkeley Workshop on Distributed Data Management and Computer Networks, 1982, pp. 45-67.

15) Walter, B., "Network Partitioning and Symmetric Surveillance Protocols," Proc. 5th Int. Conf. on Distributed Computing Systems, May 1985, pp. 124-129.

16) Wright, D.D., "Managing Distributed Databases in Partitioned Networks," Ph.D. Thesis, Dept. of Computer Science, Cornell University, Sept. 1983.

17) Skeen D. and Wright, D.D., "Increasing Availability in Partitioned Database Systems," ACM SIGMOD-84, Apr. 1984, pp. 290-298.

18) Thomas, R.H., "A Majority Consensus Approach to Concurrency Control," ACM Trans. Database Syst., Vol. 4, No. 2, June 1979, pp. 180-209.

19) Alsberg P. and Day, J., "A Principle for Resilient Sharing of Distributed Resources," Proc. 2nd Int. Conf. Software Eng., San Francisco, CA., Oct. 1976, pp. 562-570.

20) Stonebraker, M., "Concurrency Control and Consistency of Multiple Copies of Data in Distributed INGRES," IEEE Trans. Soft. Eng., Vol. SE-5, No. 3, May 1979, pp. 188-194.

21) Lelann, G., "Algorithms for Distributed Data-sharing Systems which Use Tickets," Proc. 3rd Berkeley Workshop on Distributed Data Management and Computer Networks, 1978, pp. 259-272.

22) Ellis, C., "A robust algorithm for updating duplicate databases," Proc. 2nd Berkeley Workshop on Distributed Data Management and Computer Networks, Berkeley, CA., May 1977, pp. 146-158.

23) Eager D.L. and Sevcik, K.C., "Achieving Robustness in Distributed Database Systems," ACM Trans. on Database Systems, Vol. 8, No. 3, Sept. 1983, pp. 354-381.

24) Gifford, D.K., "Weighted Voting for Replicated Data," Proc. 7th Symposium on Operating System Principles, Asilomar, CA., Dec. 1979, pp. 150-162.

25) Menasce D.A. and Muntz, R.R., "Locking Protocol for Resource Coordination in Distributed Databases," Proc. SIGMOD Int. Conf. on Management of Data, 1978, pp. 1-14.

26) Fischer, M., Lynch, N., and Paterson, M., "Impossibility of Distributed Consensus with One Faulty Process," J. ACM, Vol.32, No. 2, April 1985, pp. 374-382.

APPROACHES TO DESIGN OF REAL-TIME DATABASE SYSTEMS

Sang Hyuk Son, Juhnyoung Lee, and Hyunchul Kang†

Department of Computer Science, University of Virginia, Charlottesville, VA 22903, USA

† Department of Computer Science, Chung-Ang University, Seoul, Korea

ABSTRACT

Real-time database systems support applications that have severe operational constraints such as transaction deadlines and continued operation in the face of failures. In designing real-time database systems, there can be two approaches to meet those constraints. First approach is to redesign policies for scheduling transaction accesses to system resources, which is the primary determinant for real-time performance of the database system. Second approach is to trade desired features, such as serializability, or exploit semantic information of transactions and replicated data for high performance and reliability. In this paper, we discuss issues involved in these approaches, and present algorithms to solve problems in real-time database systems.

1. INTRODUCTION

As computers are becoming essential part of real-time systems, *real-time computing* is emerging as an important discipline in computer science and engineering [SHI87]. Since any kind of computing needs to access data, methods for designing and implementing database systems that satisfy the requirement of timing constraints in collecting, updating, and retrieving data play an important role in the success of real-time computing. In the recent workshops [IEEE91, ONR91], developers of "real" real-time systems pointed to the need for basic research in database systems that satisfy timing requirements in processing shared data. Further evidence of its importance is the recent growth of research in this field and the announcements by some vendors of database products that support features for high availability and predictability [SON88].

Compared with traditional database systems, a Real-Time Database System (RTDBS) have a distinct feature: they must satisfy not only the database consistency constraints but also the timing constraints associated with transactions. In other words, "time" is key factor to be considered in RTDBS. Transactions must be scheduled in such a way that they can be completed before their corresponding deadlines expire. For example, both the update and query on a tracking data of a missile must be processed within the given deadlines: otherwise, the information provided could be of little value. How to specify or determine deadlines is a relatively unexplored but difficult problem. It is even harder to guarantee that transactions can meet their deadlines due to dynamic nature of conflicts on shared data objects.

Conventional database management systems are typically not used in real-time applications due to poor performance and lack of predictability. Although conventional database systems provide efficient ways to store and retrieve data through user-friendly interface, they rely on secondary storage to store the database. In conventional database systems, transaction processing requires accessing database stored on the secondary storage; thus transaction response time is limited by disk access delays, which can be in the order of milliseconds. Still these databases are fast enough for traditional applications in which a response time of few seconds is often acceptable to human users. However, those systems may not be able to provide a response which is fast enough for high-performance real-time applications that require responses in the order of micro-seconds. Consequently, requirements and design objectives of real-time database systems widely differ from those of conventional database systems. A natural question is how should we redesign conventional database systems so that its performance and reliability can be acceptable for real-time applications.

One approach is to tinker with features of conventional database systems. For example, by combining priority-based real-time scheduling with concurrency control in database system, we can increase the possibility of urgent transactions meeting their deadlines. Also, by exploiting semantic information associated with transactions and data objects, we can use the notion of correctness different from the serializability of transaction execution. Another approach is the effective use of data replication to improve performance as well as reliability. In this paper, we discuss issues and approaches to the design of high-performance real-time database systems, and present algorithms to solve problems in those approaches.

This work was supported in part by the ONR by NRaD, by DOE, and by IBM.

2. CONCURRENCY CONTROL IN RTDBS

The real-time performance of an RTDBS depends on several factors such as the database system architecture and the underlying processor and disk speeds. For a given system configuration, however, the primary real-time performance determinants are the policies used for scheduling transaction accesses to system resources, since these policies determine when service is provided to a transaction. A special feature of "database" systems is that, in addition to standard hardware resources such as processors, memory and disks, data objects stored in the database form a set of logical resources. Therefore, the data accesses of transactions also have to be scheduled in accordance with real-time performance objectives. The data access scheduling mechanisms used in RTDBS's are commonly referred to as *real-time concurrency control* (RTCC) protocols.

Real-time concurrency control has two components: real-time scheduling and concurrency control. While both concurrency control and real-time scheduling are well-developed and well-understood, there is only limited knowledge about the integration of concurrency control and real-time scheduling. Though recently the problem has been studied actively, the solution proposed is still at an initial stage. A major source of problems in integrating the two is the lack of coordination in the development. They are developed on different objectives and incompatible assumptions [BUC89].

A simple integration method of real-time scheduling and concurrency control, called *pure method*, utilizes one concurrency control scheme as the base of RTCC protocol, and then integrates this basic concurrency control scheme with a priority-based conflict resolution mechanism such as *priority abort* and *priority wait* for real-time scheduling [HUA90]. The priority-based conflict resolution mechanism synchronizes concurrent data access operations of transactions in accordance with the priority of operations inherited from the timing constraints of transactions.

Most of the proposed RTCC protocols are developed using this pure method. Some of them employ pessimistic concurrency control schemes such as two-phase locking (2PL), and timestamp ordering (TO), where conflicts are resolved during data operation execution, while some of them depend on optimistic concurrency control (OCC), where conflicts of a transaction are validated only when it finishes its computation and is ready to commit.

In this section, we first summarize the proposed protocols developed under the pure integration method, and discuss informally their potential strengths and weaknesses. Then, we present a new approach to real-time concurrency control, that depends on *hybrid method*, i.e., a combination of both pessimistic and optimistic approaches. The goal of the hybrid method is to increase predictability and performance of real-time concurrency control protocols by avoiding problems of the pure method.

2.1. Protocols Based on Pessimistic Approach

Most of the initial work on RTCC has been conducted on utilizing 2PL as the base of RTCC. This is not surprising because 2PL has been well studied in traditional database systems and is being widely used in commercial database systems. Besides, recovery mechanisms for use with 2PL are well understood. 2PL uses pure blocking as its conflict resolution scheme. The beneficial effect of blocking is conservation of resources, which makes 2PL advantageous particularly under resource-limited situations. However, blocking results in prevention of the progress of transaction execution. Subsequently, a low degree of concurrency and a high probability of conflict are resulted. Moreover, 2PL has some inherent problems such as the possibility of deadlocks and unpredictable blocking times, which become even more serious for real-time transaction processing.

When 2PL protocol and priority-driven preemptive scheduling for CPU scheduling are simply integrated together in a RTDBS, a problem, known as *priority inversion*, can arise. A priority inversion occurs when a higher priority transaction must wait for the execution of lower priority transaction(s). Because higher priority transaction is blocked by lower priority transaction(s), this problem operates against the purpose of priority assignment in a RTDBS. Even worse, the blocking delay may be unbounded [SHA91]. Obviously, the blocking resulted from priority inversion is a serious problem to RTCC.

Priority inheritance is a scheme which eliminates the problem of CPU resource blocking and attempts to reduce the period of blocking. Under priority inheritance, when a priority inversion occurs, the low priority transaction holding the lock will execute at the priority of the highest priority transaction waiting for the lock, until it releases the lock. Because of the priority upgrading, the lock-holding transaction may not be preempted by a transaction with a priority lower than that of the waiting high priority transaction (but higher than that of the lock-holding transaction). Hence, it can execute faster than it will without priority upgrade, and release its lock quickly. As a result, the blocking time for the high priority transaction may be reduced.

2PL Wait Promote (2PL-WP) [ABB89] scheme is based on 2PL and employs priority inheritance for conflict resolution. 2PL-WP retains the resource-conservation feature of 2PL. However, under 2PL-WP, the duration of blocking of transactions is still uncertain, because under high data contention, priority inheritance could actually result in most or all of the transactions in the system executing at the same priority. Under this situation, the behavior of the RTDBS would effectively reduce to that of a conventional database system. Experimental performance evaluation of RTCC schemes shows that the performance of 2PL-WP degrades rapidly under high data contention [HUA91].

Priority ceiling protocol is another scheme developed to solve the priority inversion problem. Integrating the priority ceiling protocol with 2PL for real-time transaction processing results in a RTCC protocol, *2PL Priority Ceiling* (2PL-PC) [SHA91]. Under this scheme, the priority inversion is bounded to no more than one transaction execution time. Besides, the scheme is deadlock free. However, this scheme requires a prior knowledge about data objects to be accessed by each transaction. This condition appears to be very restrictive in many application. Moreover, the scheme becomes extremely conservative, with respect to the degree of parallelism, if transactions can access any data objects in the database.

2PL High Priority (2PL-HP) scheme [ABB88] is a real-time concurrency control method that is based on 2PL and employs priority abort policy for conflict resolution. When a transaction requests a lock on a data object held by other transaction(s) in an incompatible mode, priority of the requesting transaction is compared with that of the holding transaction(s). If the priority of requesting transaction is higher than that of all lock-holding transactions, the holding transactions are restarted and the requesting transaction is granted the lock; if the priority of requesting transaction is lower, it waits for the lock-holding transaction(s) to release the lock.

2PL-HP ensures that high priority transactions are not delayed by low priority transactions, i.e., no priority inversion is allowed. Under this scheme, priority abort conflict resolution scheme can also serve as a deadlock prevention mechanism, if the priority assignment mechanism assigns unique priority values and does not dynamically change the relative priority ordering of concurrent transactions. However, 2PL-HP scheme loses some of beneficial blocking factor of 2PL - conservation of resources. Another problem of this scheme is the possibility of *wasted restarts* [ABB88]. A restart of a transaction is wasted when the higher priority transaction which has given the source of the restart is later misses its deadline and is discarded. A restart caused only by eventually committed transactions are useful.

Several RTCC schemes based on TO have also been proposed [MAR89, SON90, ULU91]. In timestamp-based concurrency control protocols, scheduling decisions for conflicting operations are made using the timestamp values assigned to each transaction, typically at its startup time. TO protocols are aggressive schedulers depending on restarts to synchronize concurrent data access. Each data operation from a transaction is validated for conflict immediately when it is carried out to the scheduler, and if the operation cannot be validated, the transaction is aborted. This early detection and resolution for conflicts can be considered as an advantage of timestamp-based control compared with OCC. A problem of using TO in a prioritized transaction execution environment is so-called *priority inversion for timestamp-based protocols* [MAR89, ULU91], which indicates a situation that a high priority transaction T_H attempting to access a data item is aborted because a lower priority transaction T_L with a higher timestamp has accessed the data item earlier than T_H. In order to control the priority inversion problem of TO protocols, several methods have been proposed. The basic idea of these methods is to make use of transaction priority for scheduling decisions, and for this, the timing constraints of transactions are involved in the timestamp assignment procedure.

In *Priority Timestamp Ordering* (PTO) protocol [MAR89], a timestamp for each transaction is uniquely allocated from a total order of priority of transactions. Furthermore, to reduce the number of aborts, it uses a multiversion database that stores histories of data objects, and maintains a list of read timestamps and write timestamp for each data object. In order to avoid priority inversion, the commit of each transaction is delayed until all transactions with smaller timestamps, i.e., higher priorities have committed. This protocol ensures that no priority inversion can occur. The main weakness with this protocol is that transactions with low priority can be excessively blocked.

Another priority-based timestamp ordering protocol introduced in [ULU91] schedules transactions that arrive almost at the same time (within a small time interval δ) based on their timing constraints. The basic idea is that if a transaction can afford to wait up to δ time units before obtaining its timestamp, the scheduler can get a chance to involve timing constraints in ordering conflicting operations. With this protocol, each transaction is assigned a group timestamp and an individual timestamp within its group. The transactions that are submitted within a time interval δ are all placed in the same group and obtain the same group timestamp. Individual timestamps within the same group are determined based on the priorities of transactions. A transaction with higher priority obtains a larger timestamp so that it may not be aborted by lower priority transactions in the same group.

2.2. Protocols Based on Optimistic Approach

In the previous section, we have discussed some of the limitations of 2PL and TO protocols to be used as the base of RTCC. Within the framework of the pure integration method, a natural alternative for the base of RTCC would then be optimistic concurrency control [KUNG81]. An optimistic scheduler aggressively schedules all operations, hoping that nothing will go wrong, such as a non-serializable execution. Later when the transaction is ready to commit, conflicts are validated and a conflict resolution scheme is then applied to resolve the conflicts, if any. Most conflict resolution schemes associated with OCC schedulers employ restart to serialize concurrent data operations, thereby avoid blocking. Subsequently, OCC has the properties of non-blocking and deadlock freedom. In addition, it has a potential for high degree of parallelism. These features of OCC make it promising particularly for real-time transaction processing. However, the restart-based conflict resolution of OCC induces to wasted resources, because previously performed work has to be redone. This problem becomes even more serious for real-time transaction scheduling.

A group of real-time OCC schemes based on *forward validation* has been proposed [HAR90, HUA91]. The validation phase in OCC is where a test is performed to check whether updates made by the transaction would cause a loss of consistency. In forward validation, the validation test is conducted against active transactions in their read phase. When a conflict is detected, either the validating transaction or the conflicting active transaction can be aborted. It is this property that makes OCC with forward validation flexible and easily combined with priority mechanism. Besides, it provides the capability of early detection and resolution of conflicts that can reduce the wasted resources and time. However, OCC with forward validation is known to be difficult to implement, because it has to check dynamic read set of active transactions in the validation phase [HAE84]. Hence, the performance of OCC with forward validation depends heavily on the implementation of the protocol. Only when the protocol is implemented efficiently, the beneficial properties of non-blocking and deadlock-freedom of OCC can be useful.

OPT-ABORT protocol [HUA90] is an OCC with forward validation, and it utilizes transaction priority for conflict resolution. With this protocol, when a transaction reaches its validation phase, it is aborted if its priority is less than that of all the conflicting transactions. If not, it commits and all the conflicting transactions are restarted immediately. This protocol utilizes the priority of transactions during data conflict resolution, but the power of discriminating transactions is not strong because the condition for the restart of validating transaction is too strict and inflexible.

In OPT-SACRIFICE protocol [HAR90], when a transaction reaches its validation phase, it is aborted if at least one conflicting transaction has a higher priority than the validating transaction; otherwise it commits and all the conflicting transactions are restarted immediately. This protocol uses transaction priority in such a way that the validating transaction sacrifices itself for the sake of conflicting transactions with higher priority. With this scheme, many validating transactions may end up aborting after having paid for most of the transaction's execution, because of a conflicting high priority transaction still in its read phase. Another problem of this scheme is *wasted sacrifice*. A wasted sacrifice occurs when a transaction is sacrificed on behalf of another transaction that is later discarded.

In OPT-WAIT protocol [HAR90], when a transaction reaches its validation phase, if its priority is not the highest among the conflicting transactions, it waits for the conflicting transactions with higher priority to complete. This scheme gives the higher priority transactions a chance to make their deadlines first. While a validating transactions is waiting, it may be restarted due to the commit of one of the conflicting transactions with higher priority. This scheme keeps the original goal of real-time conflict resolution in that precedence is given to high priority transactions. There is no wasted restart in this scheme, because all restarts are made on demand. The blocking effect derived from delaying the validating transaction instead of immediately committing or aborting, results in the conservation of resources. However, the blocking effect also brings drawbacks as well as advantages. If a transaction finally commits after waiting for some time, it causes all its conflicting transactions with lower priority to be restarted at a later point in time, hence decreasing the chance of these transactions meeting their deadlines, and thus wasting resources. This problem can become worse because with this scheme, chained blocking is possible. Moreover, while a validating transaction waits, new conflicts can occur and the number of conflicting transactions is increased, hence resulting in more restarts.

WAIT-50 protocol [HAR90] uses a variation of priority wait strategy. With this protocol, a validating transaction will wait if at least 50% of conflicting transactions have a higher priority over the validating transaction, but otherwise it commits and all the conflicting transactions are restarted immediately. The purpose of WAIT-50 protocol is to maximize the beneficial effects of blocking, while reducing the effects of its drawbacks.

2.3. Hybrid Protocols

We have discussed some problems and limitations of 2PL, TO, and OCC to be used as the base of real-time concurrency control design. In this section, we present a new design method of real-time concurrency control, called *hybrid method*, that combines pessimistic and optimistic concurrency control schemes. The goal of this new design method is to increase predictability and performance of RTCC protocols by avoiding problems such as excessive and unpredictable blocking, and wasted restarts.

The hybrid method is divided into two categories according to the method of integrating pessimistic and optimistic concurrency control: *hybrid method using small integration*, and *hybrid method using large integration*. With small integration hybrid method, a new protocol is obtained as the result of the combination of two original protocols. On the contrary, with large integration hybrid method, we have a combined protocol, that uses original protocols as parts of the resultant protocol, and provides different protocol to transactions with different level of urgency. In this section, we present two protocols based on small integration hybrid method, and one protocol based on large integration hybrid method.

2.3.1. Hybrid Protocols Using Small Integration

Concurrency control protocols induce a serialization order among conflicting transactions. For a concurrency control protocol to accommodate the timing constraints of transactions, the serialization order it produces should reflect the priority of transactions. However, this is often hindered by the past execution history of transactions. A higher priority transaction may have no way to precede a lower priority transaction in the serialization order due to previous conflicts. For example, let T_H and T_L be two transactions with T_H having a higher priority. If T_L writes a data object x before T_H read it, then the serialization order between T_H and T_L is determined as $T_L \rightarrow T_H$. T_H can never precede T_L in the serialization order as long as both reside in the execution history. Most of the current (real-time) concurrency control protocols resolve this conflict either by blocking T_H until T_L releases the writelock or by aborting T_L in favor of the higher priority transaction T_H. Blocking of a higher priority transaction due to a lower priority transaction is contrary to the requirement of real-time scheduling. Aborting is also not desirable because it degrades the system performance and may lead to violations of timing constraints. Furthermore, some aborts can be wasteful when the transaction which caused the abort is aborted due to another conflict. The objective of the protocols presented in this section is to avoid such unnecessary blocking and aborting.

2.3.1.1. Integrated Real-Time Locking Protocol

The first protocol, *Integrated Real-Time Locking*, combines locking and OCC. By using a priority-dependent locking protocol, the serialization order of active transactions is adjusted dynamically, making it possible for transactions with higher priority to be executed first. Higher priority transactions are not blocked by uncommitted lower priority transactions, while lower priority transactions may not have to be aborted even in the face of a conflict. The adjustment of the serialization order can be considered as a mechanism to support real-time scheduling.

This protocol is an integrated protocol because it uses different solutions for read/write (rw) and write/write (ww) synchronization, and integrates the solutions to the two sub-problems to yield a solution to the entire problem.

The protocol is similar to OCC in the sense that each transaction has three phases, but unlike other OCC protocols, there is no validation phase. Three phases of this protocol are read, wait, and write phases. The read phase is similar to that of OCC wherein a transaction reads from the database and writes to its local workspace. In this phase, however, conflicts are also resolved by using transaction priority. While other optimistic protocols resolve conflicts in the validation phase, this protocol resolves them in the read phase. In the wait phase, a transaction waits for its chance to commit. Finally, in the write phase, updates are made permanent in the database.

(1) Read phase

The read phase is the normal execution of a transaction except that all writes are on private data copies in the local workspace of the transaction instead of on data objects in the database. Such write operations are called *prewrites*. The prewrites are useful when a transaction is aborted, in which case the data in the local workspace is simply discarded. No rollback is required.

In this phase read-prewrite and prewrite-read conflicts are resolved using a priority based locking protocol. A transaction must obtain the corresponding lock before it reads or prewrites. According to the priority locking protocol, higher priority transactions must complete before lower priority transactions. If a low priority transaction does complete before a high-priority transaction, it is required to wait until it is sure that its commitment will not lead to the higher priority transaction being aborted.

Suppose T_H and T_L are two active transactions and T_H has higher priority than T_L, there are four possible conflicts as follows.

1. $r_{T_H}[x]$, $pw_{T_L}[x]$
The resulting serialization order is $T_H \rightarrow T_L$, hence satisfies the priority order, It is not necessary to adjust the serialization order.

2. $pw_{T_H}[x]$, $r_{T_L}[x]$
Two different serialization orders can be induced with this conflict; $T_L \rightarrow T_H$ with immediate reading, and $T_H \rightarrow T_L$ with delayed reading. Certainly, the latter should be chosen for priority scheduling. The delayed reading in this protocol means blocking of $r_{T_L}[x]$ by the writelock of T_H on x.

3. $r_{T_L}[x]$, $pw_{T_H}[x]$
The resulting serialization order is $T_L \rightarrow T_H$, which violates the priority order. If T_L is in read phase, abort T_L. If T_L is in its wait phase, avoid aborting T_L until T_H commits in the hope that T_L gets a chance to commit before T_H does. If T_H commits, T_L is aborted. But if T_H is aborted by some other conflicting transaction, then T_L is committed. With this policy, we can avoid unnecessary and useless aborts, while satisfying priority scheduling.

4. $pw_{T_L}[x]$, $r_{T_H}[x]$
Two different serialization orders can be induced with this conflict; $T_H \rightarrow T_L$ with immediate reading, and $T_L \rightarrow T_H$ with delayed reading. If T_L is in its write phase, delaying T_H is the only choice. This blocking is not a serious problem for T_H because T_L is expected to finish writing x soon. T_H can read x as soon as T_L finishes writing x in the database, not necessarily after T_L completes the whole write phase. If T_L is in its read or wait phase, choose immediate reading.

As transactions are being executed and conflicting operations occur, all the information pertaining to the induced dependencies in the serialization order needs to be retained. In order to maintain this information, we associate the following with each transaction: two sets, *before_trset* and *after_trset*, and a count, *before_cnt*. The *before_trset* (respectively, *after_trset*) of a transaction contains all the active lower priority transactions that must precede (respectively, follows) this transaction in the serialization order. The *before_cnt* of a transaction is the number of the higher priority transactions that precede this transaction in the serialization order. When a conflict occurs between two transactions, their dependency is determined and then the values of their *before_trset*, *after_trset*, and *before_cnt* are changed accordingly.

(2) Wait Phase

The wait phase allows a transaction to wait until it can commit. A transaction in the wait phase can commit if all transactions with higher priority that must precede it in the serialization order, are either committed or aborted. Since the *before_cnt* of a transaction is the number of such transactions, the transaction can commit only if its *before_cnt* becomes zero. A transaction in the wait phase may be aborted due to two reasons; if a higher priority transaction requests a conflicting lock or if a higher priority transaction that must follow this transaction in the serialization order commits. Once a transaction in its wait phase finds a chance to commit, then it commits and switches to its write phase and releases all readlocks. The transaction is assigned a final timestamp which is the absolute serialization order.

(3) Write Phase

Once a transaction is in the write phase, it is considered to be committed. All committed transactions can be serialized by the final-timestamp order. In the write phase, the only work of a transaction is making all its updates permanent in the database. Data items are copied from the local workspace into the database. After each write operation, the corresponding write lock is released. The Thomas' Write Rule (TWR) [BERN87] is applied here. The write requests of each transaction are sent to the data manager, which carries out the write operations in the database. Transactions submit write requests along with their final-timestamps.

In summary, the protocol proposed in this section is a concurrency control protocol which integrates a priority-dependent locking mechanism with an optimistic approach. It works when no information about data requirements or execution time of each transaction is available. By delaying the write operations of transactions, the restraint of past transaction execution on the serialization order is relaxed, allowing the serialization order among transactions to be adjusted dynamically in compliance with transaction timeliness and criticality. The proposed protocol allows transactions to meet timing constraints as much as possible without reducing the concurrency level of the system or increasing the restart rate significantly.

2.3.1.2. Real-Time OCC Protocol Using Timestamp

The second protocol is a combination of OCC and timestamp ordering. This protocol guarantees serializability using dynamic timestamp ordering mechanism as well as validation test of OCC. This protocol has several advantages over other real-time OCC protocols proposed in [HAR90, HUA91]. First, in this protocol, the ability to detect and resolve nonserializable execution is further improved by timestamp interval facility. The ability of early detection and resolution of nonserializable execution is one of the primary merit of forward validation-based OCC. Early restart is especially important for RTDBS's, because it can increase the chances of meeting deadlines of transactions. The proposed protocol utilizes forward validation, and with the timestamp interval facility, it can check easily and detect early nonserializable execution. Second, the proposed protocol can avoid unnecessary aborts in other real-time OCC protocols with a refined categorization of conflict types, a timestamp interval facility, and a dynamic adjustment of serialization order mechanism. In this section, instead of describing the protocol in a formal way, we explain briefly the idea of each component of the protocol.

(1) OCC with Forward Validation

This protocol is an OCC protocol. The execution of each transaction in this protocol consists of three phases: read, validation, and write phase, as in other OCC protocols. This protocol uses forward validation scheme, rather than backward validation scheme. As mentioned earlier, in forward validation, the validation test is conducted against active transactions in their read phase. The phase-dependent control of OCC and the property of forward validation scheme provide a framework for the following components of the protocol.

(2) Categories of Conflicting Transactions

Since this protocol uses forward validation, when a validation test is performed for a transaction, say T_v, active transactions in the system can be divided into several sets according to their execution history (with respect to that of T_v). First, the set of the active transactions are divided into two sets: *conflicting set*, that contains transactions in conflict with T_v, and *nonconflicting set*, that contains transactions not in conflict with T_v. The conflicting set can be further divided into two sets: *Reconcilably Conflicting set* (RC) and *Irreconcilably Conflicting set* (IC). Transactions in the RC set are in conflict with T_v, but the conflicts are reconcilable, i.e., the conflicting operations can be made serializable. However, transactions in the IC set are in conflict with T_v, and the conflicts are irreconcilable, i.e., it is impossible to make the conflicting operations serializable. The formal description of the conditions to categorize these sets of active transactions is not provided in this paper due to space limit. Interested readers should refer to [SON92].

The RC transactions do not have to be aborted, but their execution history have to be adjusted with timestamp interval facility of this protocol, which is the topic of the subsection (4) below. The IC transactions should be handled with priority-based real-time conflict resolution, as discussed in the subsection (5) below.

(3) Dynamic Timestamp Allocation

Another important aspect of this protocol is dynamic timestamp allocation. Most timestamp-based concurrency control protocols use static timestamp allocation scheme, i.e., each transaction is assigned a timestamp value at its startup time, and a total ordering instead of a partial ordering is built up. This total ordering does not reflect any actual conflict. Hence, it is possible that a transaction is aborted even when it requests its first data access [BAY82]. Besides, the total ordering of all transactions is too restrictive, and degrades the degree of concurrency considerably. With dynamic timestamp allocation, serialization order among transactions are dynamically constructed on demand whenever actual conflicts occur. Only necessary partial ordering among transactions is constructed instead of a total ordering from the static timestamp allocation.

This dynamic timestamp allocation scheme is feasible, because OCC provides a phase-dependent structure of transaction execution. During the read phase, a transaction builds gradually its serialization order with respect to committed transactions on demand whenever a conflict with such transactions occurs. Only when the transaction commits (after passing the validation test), its permanent timestamp, i.e., the final serialization order is determined.

(4) Dynamic Adjustment of Serialization Order with Timestamp Interval

The dynamic timestamp allocation scheme is made further efficient with timestamp interval facility [BOK87]. More flexibility to adjust serialization order can be obtained using a timestamp interval (initially, the entire range of the timestamp space) assigned to each transaction instead of single value for timestamp. The timestamp intervals of active transactions preserve the partial ordering constructed by serializable execution. The timestamp interval of each transaction is adjusted (shrunk) whenever the transaction reads or writes a data object to preserve the serialization order induced by committed transactions. When the timestamp interval of a transaction shuts out, it means that the transaction has been involved in a nonserializable execution, and that the transaction should be restarted. With this facility, it is possible to detect and resolve nonserializable execution early in read phase.

Besides, when a transaction, say T_v, commits after its validation phase, the timestamp intervals of those transactions categorized as *reconcilably conflicting* are adjusted, i.e., the serialization order between the validating transaction T_v and its RC transactions are determined. Since the permanent serialization order (final timestamp) of these active transactions is not determined, all we have to do is just determine the partial ordering between T_v and these active transactions by adjusting their timestamp intervals. Thereby these transactions do not have to be aborted though they are in conflict with the committed transaction, i.e., unnecessary aborts are avoided, unlike other OCC protocols.

(5) Real-Time Conflict Resolution

In order to resolve irreconcilable conflicts of active transactions with validating transaction, either one has to be aborted. Because this protocol is based on OCC with forward validation scheme, either the validating transaction or the conflicting active transaction can be aborted. Hence to determine which transaction to abort, we can employ priority-based conflict resolution schemes such as *priority abort*, *priority sacrifice*, and *priority wait* [HAR90, HUA91]. With these schemes, we can extend our protocol to RTCC protocols, that are corresponding to the real-time OCC protocols such as OPT-ABORT, OPT-SACRIFICE, and OPT-WAIT [HAR90, HUA91].

2.3.2. Hybrid Protocols Using Large Integration

The main purpose of the hybrid method using large integration is to overcome inherent limitations of pure concurrency control schemes such as 2PL, TO, and OCC. The basic idea is that the combination of restart-based control and blocking-based control can compensate for the problems and limitations of one concurrency control method operating by itself.

Figure 1 illustrates the basic structure of the RTCC developed using the large integration hybrid method. With this method, a RTCC protocol consists of three units: two concurrency control units, *primary concurrency control* (PCC) and *secondary concurrency control* (SCC), and a dynamic timing analysis unit called *urgency test* (UT). We use a restart-based concurrency control for the PCC and a blocking-based concurrency control for the SCC. More specifically, we use an OCC protocol for the PCC, and a locking scheme for the SCC. The UT unit classifies dynamically the urgency of transactions, and behaves as a switch which routes the given transaction either to PCC or SCC for re-execution. With this setting, we can utilize the high degree of parallelism of the OCC in the first execution of a transaction, and the conservative guarantee of locking scheme for the last execution of the transaction only when it is classified urgent by the UT.

With this scheme, a transaction is executed in the following manner. First, the OCC protocol executes the data operations from a transaction. If all the operations are executed without any conflict, and the transaction is validated, then the execution is completed. In this case, we have taken the advantage of the high degree of parallelism of OCC. If the transaction is aborted due to conflicts, then it is passed to the UT, and its urgency is determined for the re-execution. If the transactions is determined to be urgent, i.e., its timing constraints can allow only one more execution time, then the transaction is passed to the locking scheme. The locking protocol can guarantee the completion of the transaction by a *lock pre-claiming* strategy [FRAN90]. If the aborted transaction is not urgent, then it is passed to the OCC protocol again. The re-execution of a transaction with the OCC protocol continues until it is scheduled successfully with the OCC protocol, or it becomes urgent, and is passed to the locking protocol. Figure 2 shows the states of transactions executed with the large integration scheme.

Figure 1. Structure of Protocol Using Large Integration

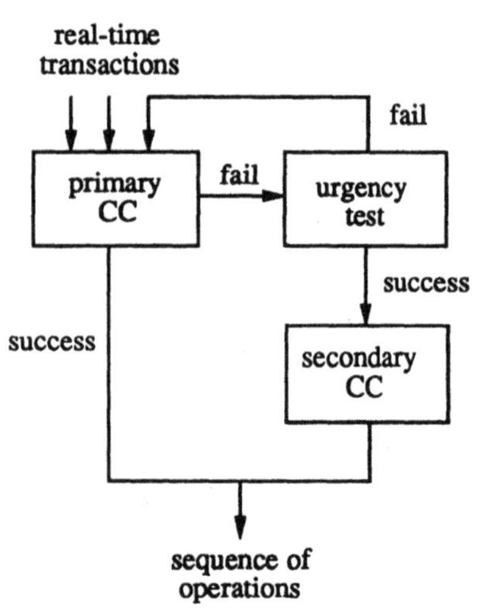

The basic idea is that as long as a real-time transaction is not urgent, it is advantageous to execute the transaction with an OCC protocol, exploiting its high degree of parallelism, but once it becomes urgent, it should be executed by the locking protocol, which guarantees the completion of the execution. The purpose of this RTCC scheme is to allow only bounded number of restarts for real-time transactions. It allows only as many restarts as the timing constraints of a transaction can tolerate.

The proposed RTCC protocol of large integration hybrid method offers substantial benefits over other RTCC protocols. To summarize, the protocol exhibits the following characteristics:

(1) The protocol can limit the number of restarts for high priority transactions, and allow only bounded blocking time for high priority transactions. Thus we can expect bounded execution time of real-time transactions, i.e., the completion of a high priority transaction is guaranteed.

(2) The protocol is also free from deadlock, though it employs locking as a part of the scheme. With the pro-

Figure 2. States of a Transaction

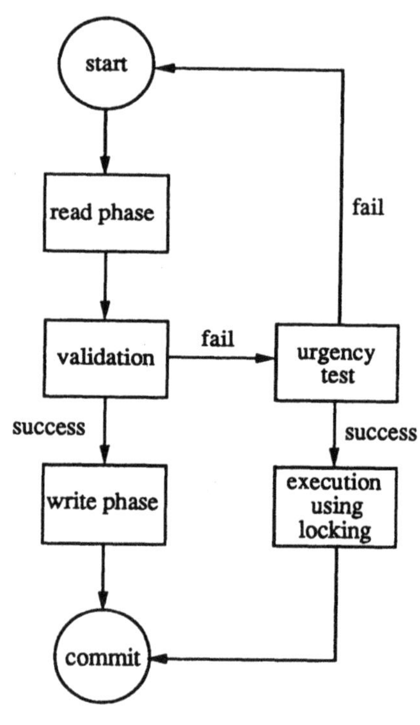

tocol, the validation order is the order by which locks are requested. Because the validation of transactions in the OCC is conducted one at a time in the critical section, the validation order does not introduce any cycle in the execution history, and hence deadlocks are avoided.

(3) With the dynamic analysis of the urgency of transactions, the protocol is flexible and dynamically adapt to the current system workload to obtain an optimal performance. This dynamic adaptivity of the protocol can be especially useful to stabilize the rapid performance degradation under overload situation. The dynamic adjustment of the urgency test condition can be easily implemented with low overhead.

3. DISTRIBUTED REAL-TIME DATABASE SYSTEMS

Falling cost of hardware and advances in communication technology over the last decade have triggered considerable interests in distributed database systems. In such systems, data objects are spread over a collection of autonomous computer systems (called *sites)* that are connected via a communication network. Since the physical separation of sites ensures the independent failure modes of sites and limits the propagation of errors throughout the system, distributed database systems must be able to continue to operate correctly despite of component failures. However, as the size of a distributed system increases, so does the probability that one or more of its components will fail. Thus, distributed systems must be fault tolerant to component failures to achieve a desired level of reliability and availability. Asserting that the system will continue to operate correctly if less than a certain number of failure occurs is a guarantee independent of the reliability of the sites that make up the system. It is a measure of the fault tolerance supported by the system architecture, in contrast to fault tolerance achieved by using reliable components.

Distributed database systems are of great importance to real-time applications because they offer several advantages such as higher system availability, over a single-site database system. In many situations, real-time systems naturally include distributed database systems because they are inherently distributed. In distributed real-time database systems, the main issue is how to make several sites work collectively so that a high level of performance is obtained. In this section, we discuss approaches to the design of high-performance distributed real-time database systems.

3.1. Using Semantic Information

We can enhance the performance of distributed real-time database systems by exploiting semantic information of transactions. A read-only transaction is a typical example of the use of transaction semantics. A read-only transaction can be used to take a checkpoint of the database for recovering from subsequent failures, or to check the consistency of the database, or simply to retrieve the information from the database. Since read-only transactions are still transactions, they can be processed using the algorithms for arbitrary transactions. However, it is possible to use special processing algorithms for read-only transactions in order to improve efficiency, resulting in high performance. With this approach, the specialized transaction processing algorithm can take advantage of the semantic information that no data will be modified by the transaction.

Serializability has been accepted as the standard correctness criteria in database systems. It means that the concurrent execution of a group of transactions is equivalent to some serial execution of the same group of transactions. However, people actually developing large real-time systems are unwilling to pay the price for serializability, because predictability of response is severely compromised due to blocking or preemption. For read-only transactions, correctness requirements can be divided into two independent classes: the currency requirement and the consistency requirement.

The currency requirement specifies what update transactions should be reflected by the data read. There are several ways in which the currency requirement can be specified; we are interested in the following two:

(1) Fixed-time requirement: A read-only transaction T requires data as they existed at a given time *t*. This means that the data read by the transaction must reflect the modifications of all update transactions committed in the system before *t*.

(2) Latest-time requirement: A read-only transaction T requires data it reads reflect at least all update transactions committed before T is started, i.e., T requires most up-to-date data available.

The consistency requirement specifies the degree of consistency needed by read-only transactions. A read-only transaction may have one of the following requirements:

(1) Internal consistency: It only requires that the values read by each read-only transaction satisfy the invariants (consistency constraints) of the database.

(2) Weak consistency: It requires that the values read by each read-only transaction be the result of a serial execution of some subset of the update transactions committed. Weak consistency is at least as strong a requirement as internal consistency, because the result of a serial execution of update transactions always satisfies consistency constraints.

(3) Strong consistency: It requires that all update transactions together with all other read-only transactions that require strong consistency, must be serializable as a group. Strong consistency requirement is equivalent to serializability requirement for processing of arbitrary transactions.

We make a few comments concerning the currency and consistency requirements. First, it might seem that the internal consistency requirement is too weak to be useful. However, a read-only transaction with only internal consistency requirement is very simple and efficient to process, and at least one proposed algorithm [FIS82] does not satisfy any stronger consistency requirement. Second, it is easy to see that strong consistency is a stronger requirement than weak consistency, as shown by the following example. Suppose we have two update transactions, T_1 and T_2, two read-only transactions, T_3 and T_4, and two data objects, X and Y, stored at two sites A and B. Assume that the initial values of both X and Y were 0 before the execution of any transactions. Now consider the following execution sequence:

T_3 reads 0 from X at A.
T_1 writes 1 into X at A.
T_4 reads 1 from X at A.
T_4 reads 0 from Y at B.
T_2 writes 1 into Y at B.
T_3 reads 1 from Y at B.

The values read by T_3 are the result of a serial execution of $T_2<T_3<T_1$, while the values read by T_4 are the result of a serial execution of $T_1<T_4<T_2$. Both of them are valid serialization order, and thus, the execution is weakly consistent. However, there is no single serial execution of all four transactions, so the execution is not serializable. In other words, both read-only transactions see valid serialization orders of updates, but they see different orders.

Clearly, strong consistency is preferable to weak consistency. However, as in the case of internal consistency, it can be cheaper to ensure weak consistency than to ensure strong consistency. For the applications that can tolerate a weaker requirement, the potential performance gain could be significant.

Finally, one might wonder why fixed-time requirement is interesting, since most read-only transactions may require information about the latest database state. However, there are situations that the user is interested in looking at the database as it existed at a given time. For an example of a fixed-time read-only transaction, consider the case of a general in the army making a decision by looking at the database showing the current position of the enemy. The general may be interested in looking at the position of the enemy of few hours ago or few days ago, in order to figure out the purpose of their moving. A read-only transaction of a given fixed-time will provide the general with the desired results.

3.2. Using Replication and Multiversion

An obvious approach to improve system availability is to keep replicated copies of critical data at multiple sites so that the system can access the data even if some of the copies are not available due to failures. In addition, replication can enhance performance by allowing transactions initiated at sites where the data are stored to be processed locally without incurring communication delays, and by distributing the workload of transactions to several sites where the subtasks of a transaction can be processed concurrently. These benefits of replication must be seen in the light of the additional cost and complexities introduced by replication control.

A major restriction of using replication is that replicated copies must behave like a single copy, i.e., *mutual consistency* of a replicated data must be preserved. By mutual consistency, we mean that all copies converge to the same value and would be identical if all update activities cease. The inherent communication delay between sites that store and maintain copies of a replicated data makes it impossible to ensure that all copies are identical at all times when updates are processed in the system [SON87].

Maintaining multiple versions of data objects is another approach to improve system responsiveness by increasing the degree of concurrency. The objective of using multiple versions is to reduce the conflict probability among transactions and the possibility of rejection of transactions by providing a succession of views of data objects. One of the reasons for rejecting transactions is that its operations cannot be serviced by the system. For example, a read operation has to be rejected if the value of data object it was supposed to read has already been overwritten by some other transactions. Such rejections can be avoided by keeping old versions of each data object so that an appropriate old value can be given to a tardy read operation. In a system with multiple versions of data, each write operation on a data object produces a new version instead of overwriting it. Hence, for each read operation, the system selects an appropriate version to read, enjoying the flexibility in controlling the order of read and write operations.

There are several problems that must be solved by an algorithm that uses multiple versions. For example, selection of old versions for a given read-only transaction must ensure the consistency of the state seen by the transaction. In addition, the need to save old versions for read-only transactions introduces a storage management problem, i.e., methods to determine which version is no longer needed so that it can be discarded. In the next section, we focus our attention on these problems.

4. A RESILENT SYNCHRONIZATION ALGORITHM

In the algorithm to be presented below, we use the notion of *tokens* to support fault-tolerant distributed real-time database systems in increasing both the availability of data and the degree of concurrency, without incurring too much storage and processing overhead. Each data object has a predetermined number of tokens. Tokens are used to designate a read-write copy, and a token copy is a single version representing the latest value of the data object. The site which has a token copy of a data object is called a ***token site***, with respect to the data object. The number of tokens for each data object can be used as a tuning parameter to adjust the robustness of the system.

Multiversions are stored and managed only at read-only copy sites. For read-only copies, each data object is a collection of consecutive versions. A read-only transaction does not necessarily read the latest committed version of a data object. The particular old version that a read-only transaction has to read is determined by the timestamp of the read-only transaction (for the latest-time requirement) or by the given time (for the fixed-time requirement). The timestamp is assigned to a read-only transaction when it begins, while the timestamp for an update transaction is determined as it commits. When a read-only transaction with timestamp T attempts to read a data object, the version of the data object with the largest timestamp less than T is selected as the value to be returned by the read operation.

We assume that update transactions use two-phase locking, with exclusive locks used for write operations, and shared locks for read operations. Lock requests are made only to token copies, and there is no locks associated with read-only copies. In addition, update transactions use the two-phase commit protocol and stable storage [LAM81] to achieve fault-tolerance to site failures. When a new version is created, it is created at all copy sites, including read-only copy site. However, any new versions are not accessible to other transactions until they are finalized through the two-phase commit protocol. Upon receiving the commit message from the coordinator, new versions of data objects created by the transaction replace the current versions at token sites, while they are attached to the multiple versions at read-only sites.

Operations invoked by update transactions are processed using ordinary two-phase locking: when an update transaction invokes a read operation on a data object, it waits until it can lock the data object in shared mode. When an update transaction invokes a write operation, it locks the data object in exclusive mode, and then creates a new version. If the transaction later aborts, the newly created version will be discarded. Our algorithm follows the *read-one/write-all-available* paradigm [BHA86] in which a read lock request succeeds if at least one of the token copies can be locked in shared mode, and a write lock request fails if at least one of the available token copies cannot be locked in exclusive mode. To achieve the high performance by reducing the cost of write operations in our algorithm, the level of synchronization between write operation and its physical implementation can be relaxed by allowing physical write operations to be completed by the commit time of the transaction. A write operation is considered completed when the required update messages are sent. This eliminates the delay caused by waiting for confirmation messages before the next operation can proceed.

4.1. Timestamp Management

As noted above, the algorithm combines timestamp ordering and locking. To generate timestamps for update transactions, a timestamp is maintained for each data object. The timestamp for data object X represents the maximum of the timestamps of update transactions that have accessed X and committed, and the timestamps of read-only transactions that have accessed X. Timestamps for update transactions are generated during the commit phase as follows:
In the first phase of the two-phase commit protocol, each participant attaches to the precommit message the maximum timestamps of all data objects that it accessed. Upon receiving precommit messages from the participants, the coordinator chooses a unique timestamp greater than all the timestamps received. This is the timestamp for the transaction. Then, in the second phase of the commit protocol, this timestamp is broadcast to all participants (piggybacked on the commit message). Each participant, upon receiving this message, updates the timestamp of each data object to the maximum of its current value and the received timestamp, and releases any locks held by the transaction. Any version written by the transaction is marked with the timestamp of the transaction. Note that timestamps are piggybacked on the precommit and commit messages, hence no additional messages are introduced here.

When a participant searches for the maximum timestamp to attach to a precommit message, read-only copies are also included in the set of copies for the search. By including the timestamps of read-only copies in determining the timestamp for an update transaction, the system can ensure that any potential conflicts between read-only transactions and the current update transaction are resolved in the correct order of their timestamps.

Timestamp assignment for read-only transactions with latest-time requirement is quite different from that for update transactions. When a read-only transaction begins, the coordinator sends messages to the participants telling them the data objects the transaction needs to read. When a participant receives such a request, it checks the current timestamp of each data object at the site, and sends the maximum timestamps among them to the coordinator. Each data object accessed by a read-only transaction in this way records the pair of the identifier of that transaction and the current timestamp it reported. After receiving responses from all participants, the coordinator chooses a unique timestamp greater than all the responses. The timestamp recorded for the read-only transaction at each object is thus a lower bound on the timestamp of the transaction, and it will be used in making a decision to discard or retain versions of the data object. For a fixed-time read-only transactions, timestamp is provided by the user, and hence the system needs not bother to assign a new timestamp for it.

When a read-only transaction with timestamp TS invokes a read operation on a data object, the participant chooses the version of the data object with the largest timestamp less than TS. This invocation of read operation is nothing but sending the timestamp TS to the participants, since each participant already knows which data object to read. If TS is larger than the current timestamp of the data object, it will be updated as TS. This will force update transactions that commit later to choose timestamps larger than TS, ensuring that the version selected for the read-only transaction does not change.

It is easy to show that the above algorithm ensures strong consistency. The mechanism for generating timestamps for update transactions ensures that any conflicting update transactions are ordered according to their timestamps, and hence they are serializable in the timestamp order. Read-only transactions then read versions of data objects consistent with all transactions executing in their timestamp order.

4.2. Version Management

To this point we have assumed that all versions are retained forever. We now discuss how versions can be discarded when they are not needed by read-only transactions. Recall that each data object keeps track of the read-only transactions that have accessed the data object, along with a lower bound on the timestamp chosen by each transaction. Data objects can use the following rule to decide which versions to keep and which to discard.

Rule for retention:

A version with timestamp TS must be retained if

(1) there is no version with timestamp greater than TS (i.e., current version), or

(2) there is a version with timestamp TS' > TS, and there is an active read-only transaction whose timestamp might be between TS and TS'.

By having a read-only transaction inform data objects when it completes, versions of data objects that are no longer needed can be discarded. This process of informing data objects that a read-only transaction has completed need not be performed synchronously with the commit of the transaction. It imposes some overhead on the system, but the overhead can be reduced by piggybacking information on existing messages, or by sending messages when the system load is low.

When a read-only transaction sends a read request to an object, the read-only site effectively agrees to retain the current version and any later versions, until it knows which of those versions is needed by the read-only transaction. When the read-only site finds out the timestamp chosen by the transaction, it can tell exactly which version the transaction needs to read. At that point any versions that were retained only because the read-only transaction might have needed them can be discarded. By minimizing the time during which only a lower bound on the transaction's timestamp is known, the system can reduce the storage needed for maintaining versions. One simple way of doing this is to have each read-only transaction broadcast its timestamp to all read-only sites when it chooses the timestamp.

The version management described above is effective at minimizing the amount of storage needed for versions. For example, unlike the "version pool" scheme in [CHA85], it is not necessary to discard a version that is needed by an active read-only transaction because the buffer space is being used by a version that no transaction wants to read. However, ensuring that each read-only site knows which versions are needed at any point in time has an associated cost; a read-only transaction cannot begin execution until it has chosen a timestamp, a process that requires communicating with all data objects it needs to access.

Because the timestamp for a fixed-time read-only transaction is determined by the user, the number of versions that needs to be retained to process fixed-time read-only transactions cannot be bounded as in the case for latest-time read-only transactions. In order to process all the potential fixed-time read-only transactions, the system must maintain all the versions created up to the present, which may require huge amount of storage. There are several alternatives to keep a history instead of saving all the versions created for each data object. One of the simplest and efficient alternative would be to keep a log of all the update transactions. Fixed-time read-only transactions can be processed by examining the log in reverse chronological order until the desired version of the data object can be reconstructed. Since fixed-time read-only transactions must examine the log, their execution depends on the availability of the log, and their execution speed would be slower than that of latest-time read-only transactions. One important advantage of the transaction log mechanism is that in many systems the log is required anyway for crash recovery. Thus, in these systems, keeping the log for fixed-time read-only transactions represents no real overhead.

Read-only transactions are never aborted and their response time is reduced because they do not need to go through two-phase commit protocol. Furthermore, access requests from read-only transactions do not require to access token copies, and hence no blocking is introduced by update transactions. This results in further reduction of response time of read-only transactions. In general, the number of aborts and average transaction response time for a given set of transactions depend on system parameters and read-set/write-set of transactions, making analytical evaluation complicated.

5. CONCLUDING REMARKS

A real-time database system supports applications which require severe performance constraints such as fast response time and continued operation in case of subsystem failures. Real-time database systems are still in the state of infancy, and issues and alternatives in their design are not very well explored. In this paper, we have addressed two approaches to design of real-time database systems. The first approach is aiming to increase predictability by combining priority-based real-time scheduling with concurrency control. The second approach calls for exploiting semantic information and data replication especially in distributed environments.

High performance and high reliability do not come for free. There is a cost associated with each approach: storage requirement and complicated control in synchronization and recovery. For appropriate management of multiple versions, some communication cost is inevitable to inform data objects about activities of read-only transactions. There is also a cost associated with maintaining the data structures for keeping track of versions and timestamps. In many real-time applications of database systems, however, the cost of those approaches is justifiable. Further work is clearly needed to develop alternative approaches for scheduling and recovery in real-time database systems and for exploiting semantic information of transactions, and to investigate performance of different approaches.

REFERENCES

ABB88 R. Abbott, H. Garcia-Molina, "Scheduling Real-time Transactions: A Performance Evaluation," *Proceedings of the 14th VLDB Conference*, 1988.

ABB89 Abbott, R., and H. Garcia-Molina, "Scheduling Real-time Transactions with Disk Resident Data," *Proceedings of the 15th VLDB Conference*, 1989.

BAY82 Bayer, R., K. Elhardt, J. Heigert and A. Reiser, "Dynamic Timestamp Allocation for Transactions in Database Systems," *Proc. 2nd Int. Symp. Distributed Data Bases*, September 1982, pp 9-20.

BERN87 Bernstein, P. A., V. Hadzilacos, and N. Goodman, *Concurrency Control and Recovery in Database Systems*, Addison-Wesley, Reading, Mass., 1987.

BHA86 Bhargava, B., Ruan, Z., Site Recovery in Replicated Distributed Database Systems, *Proc. 6th International Conference on Distributed Computing Systems*, Cambridge, Massachusetts, May 1986, pp 621-627.

BOK87 Boksenbaum, C., M. Cart, J. Ferrie, and J. Pons, "Concurrent Certifications by Intervals of Timestamps in Distributed Database Systems," *IEEE Transactions on Software Engineering*, Vol. SE-13, No. 4, April 1987.

BUC89 Buchmann, A. et al., "Time-Critical Database Scheduling: A Framework for Integrating Real-Time Scheduling and Concurrency Control," *5th Data Engineering Conference*, February 1989.

CHA85 Chan, A. and Gray, R., Implementing Distributed Read-Only Transactions, *IEEE Trans. on Software*

Engineering, Feb. 1985, pp 205-212.

FIS82 Fischer, M. J., Griffeth, N. D. and Lynch, N. A., Global States of a Distributed System, *IEEE Trans. on Software Engineering*, May 1982, pp 198-202.

FRAN90 Franaszek, P. A., J. T. Robinson, and Alexander Thomasian, "Access Invariance and Its Use in High Contention Environment," *Proceedings of 7th International Conference on Data Engineering*, Los Angeles, CA, February, 1990, pp. 47-55.

HAE84 Haeder, T., "Observations on Optimistic Concurrency Control Schemes," *Information Systems*, Vol. 9, No. 2, 1984.

HAR90 Haritsa, J. R., M. J. Carey, and M. Livny, "Dynamic Real-Time Optimistic Concurrency Control," *11th IEEE Real-Time Systems Symposium*, Orlando, Florida, December 1990.

HUA90 Huang, J., J. A. Stankovic, D. Towsley, and K. Ramamritham, "Real-Time Transaction Processing: Design, Implementation, and Performance Evaluation," Univ. of Massachusetts, COINS Technical Report 90-43, May, 1990.

HUA91 Huang, J., J. A. Stankovic, K. Ramamritham, and D. Towsley, "Experimental Evaluation of Real-Time Optimistic Concurrency Control Schemes," Univ. of Massachusetts, COINS Technical Report 91-16, January 1991.

IEEE91 *IEEE Workshop on Real-Time Operating Systems and Software*, Atlanta, Georgia, May 1991.

KUNG81 Kung H. T., and J. T. Robinson, "On Optimistic Methods for Concurrency Control," *ACM Transactions on Database Systems*, Vol. 6, No. 2, June 1981, pp 213-226.

LAM81 Lampson, B., Atomic Transactions, Distributed Systems: Architecture and Implementation, *Lecture Notes in Computer Science*, Vol. 105, Springer-Verlag, 1981, pp 246-265.

MAR89 Marzullo, K., "Consistency Control for Transactions with Priorities," *Technical Report*, Department of Computer Science, Cornell University, 1989.

ONR91 *ONR Foundations of Real-Time Computing Workshop*, Washington, D.C., Oct. 1991.

SHA91 Sha, L., R. Rajkumar, S. Son, and C. Chang, "A Real-Time Locking Protocol," *IEEE Trans. on Computers*, Vol. 40, No. 7, July 1991, pp. 793-800.

SHI87 Shin, K. G., Introduction to the Special Issue on Real-Time Systems, *IEEE Trans. on Computers*, Aug. 1987, 901-902.

SON87 Son, S. H., Synchronization of Replicated Data in Distributed Systems, *Information Systems 12*, 2, June 1987, 191-202.

SON88 Son, S. H., Guest Editor, *ACM SIGMOD Record*, Special Issue on Real-Time Database Systems, Vol. 17, No. 1, March 1988.

SON90 Son, S. H., and J. Lee, "Scheduling Real-Time Transactions in Distributed Database Systems," *7th IEEE Workshop on Real-Time Operating Systems and Software*, Charlottesville, Virginia, May 1990.

SON92 Son, S. H., J. Lee, and Y. Lin, "Hybrid Protocols Using Dynamic Adjustment of Serialization Order," *Technical Report TR-92-07*, Department of Computer Science, University of Virginia, March 1992.

ULU91 Ulusoy, O. and G. G, Belford, "Concurrency Control in Real-Time Database Systems," *Technical Report*, Department of Computer Science, University of Illinois at Urbana-Champaign, 1991.

PERFORMANCE EVALUATION OF REAL-TIME LOCKING PROTOCOLS

Sang H. Son, Chun-Hyon Chang†, and Young-Kuk Kim

Department of Computer Science, University of Virginia, Charlottesville, VA 22903, USA

† Department of Computer Science, Kon-Kuk University, Seoul, Korea

ABSTRACT

Real-time systems must maintain data consistency while minimizing the number of tasks that miss the deadline. To satisfy both the consistency and real-time constraints, there is the need to integrate synchronization protocols with real-time priority scheduling protocols. In this paper, we address the problem of priority scheduling in real-time database systems. We first present a prototyping environment for investigating distributed software. Specific priority-based real-time locking protocols are then discussed, together with a performance study which illustrates the use of the prototyping environment for evaluation of synchronization protocols for real-time database systems.

1. INTRODUCTION

The growing importance of real-time computing in a wide range of applications such as aerospace and defense systems, industrial automation, and nuclear reactor control, has resulted in an increased research effort in this area. Distributed systems greatly exacerbate the difficulty of developing real-time systems as delays associated with interprocess communications and remote database accesses must be taken into account [16]. Researchers working on developing real-time systems based on distributed system architecture have found out that database managers are assuming much greater importance in real-time systems. In the recent workshops [6, 8], developers of real-time systems pointed to the need for basic research in database systems that satisfy timing constraint requirements in collecting, updating, and retrieving shared data. Further evidence of its importance is the recent growth of research in this field [3, 12].

Compared with traditional databases, real-time database systems have a distinct feature: they must satisfy the timing constraints associated with transactions. In other words, "time" is one of the key factors to be considered in real-time database systems. The timing constraints of a transaction typically include its ready time and deadline, as well as temporal consistency of the data accessed by it. Transactions must be scheduled in such a way that they can be completed before their corresponding deadlines expire. For example, both the update and query on a tracking data of a missile must be processed within the given deadlines: otherwise, the information provided could be of little value. In such a system, transaction processing must satisfy not only the database consistency constraints but also the timing constraints.

In addition to providing shared data access capabilities, distributed real-time database systems offer a means of loosely coupling communicating processes, making it easier to rapidly update software, at least from a functional perspective. However, with respect to time-driven scheduling and system timing predictability, they present new problems. One of the characteristics of current database managers is that they do not schedule their transactions to meet response time requirements and they commonly lock data tables to assure database consistency. Locks and time-driven scheduling are basically incompatible. Low priority transactions holding locks required by higher priority transactions can and will block the higher priority transactions, leading to response requirement failures. New techniques are required to manage data consistency which are compatible with time-driven scheduling.

One of the primary reasons for the difficulty in successfully developing and evaluating new database management techniques suitable for real-time applications is that it takes a long time to develop a system, and evaluation is complicated because it involves a large number of system parameters that may change dynamically. For example, although new approaches for synchronization and database recovery have been developed recently [13, 14], experimentation to verify their properties and to evaluate their performance has not been performed due to the lack of appropriate test tools.

A prototyping technique can be applied effectively to the evaluation of database management techniques for distributed real-time systems. A *database prototyping environment* is a software package that supports the evaluation of database management techniques in an environment other than that of the target database system. The advantages of such an environment are obvious [15]. Although there exist tools for system development and analysis, few prototyping tools exist for distributed database experimentation, especially for distri-

This work was supported in part by ONR, by NRaD, and by DOE.

buted real-time database systems. Recently, simulators have been developed for investigating performance of several priority-based concurrency control algorithms for real-time applications [1, 2, 9]. However, they do not provide a module hierarchy composed from reusable components as in our prototyping environment. Software developed in our prototyping environment will execute in a given target machine without modification of any layer except the hardware interface. In the operating system area, the ARTS real-time kernel and its toolset, being developed at Carnegie-Melon University, attempts to provide a "predictable, analyzable, and reliable distributed real-time computing environment" which is an excellent foundation for a real-time system [18]. It implements different prioritized and non-prioritized scheduling algorithms and prioritized message passing. The major difference between our prototyping environment from ARTS is that ours is portable since it is implemented in a host environment, and our environment can support a spectrum of distributed database system functions without much overhead.

This paper presents a database prototyping environment that supports evaluation of distributed real-time database systems. To illustrate its usefulness, a series of experimentation to evaluate priority-based real-time locking protocols has been performed.

One of the major problems in priority-based locking protocols is that, owing to the effect of blocking, a condition known as unbounded *priority inversion*, where a higher priority task is blocked by lower priority tasks for an indefinite period of time. To address this problem, the priority ceiling protocol was proposed in [11]. It tries to achieve not only minimizing the blocking time of a transaction to at most one lower priority transaction execution time, but also preventing the formation of deadlocks. In this paper, we investigate the performance of the priority ceiling protocol and compare it with other synchronization protocols. We also discuss the performance of real-time locking protocols in distributed database environments.

The rest of the paper is organized as follows. Section 2 presents the design principles and the current implementation of the prototyping environment. Section 3 discusses priority-based real-time locking protocols and presents their experimental performance results using the prototyping environment. Section 4 presents two different priority-based locking protocols and their performance in distributed environments. Section 5 is the conclusion.

2. STRUCTURE OF THE PROTOTYPING ENVIRONMENT

A prototyping environment, if properly structured, can reduce the time for evaluating new technologies and design alternatives. From our past experience, we assume that a relatively small portion of a typical database system's code is affected by changes in specific control mechanisms, while the majority of code deals with intrinsic problems, such as file management. Thus, by properly isolating technology-dependent portions of a database system using modular programming techniques, we can implement and evaluate design alternatives very rapidly. For this reason, our prototyping environment is designed as a modular, message-passing system to support easy extensions and modifications. Server processes can be created, relocated, and new implementations of server processes can be dynamically substituted. It provides a library of modules with different performance and reliability characteristics for an operating system as well as database management functions [15]. Operating system facilities are included in the library because the correct functioning and timing behavior of database control algorithms depends on the appropriate support of the underlying operating system. For experimentation, the module library facilitates the construction of multiple system instances customized according to application-dependent requirements without much overhead.

The prototyping environment provides support for transaction processing, including transparency to concurrent access, data distribution, and atomicity. An instance of the prototyping environment can manage any number of virtual sites specified by the user. Modules that implement transaction processing are decomposed into several server processes, and they communicate among themselves through ports. The clean interface between server processes simplifies incorporating new algorithms and facilities into the prototyping environment, or testing alternate implementations of algorithms. A separate process for each transaction is created for concurrent execution of transactions.

Figure 1 illustrates the structure of the prototyping environment. The prototyping environment is based on a concurrent programming kernel, called the StarLite kernel, which supports process control to create, ready, block, and terminate processes. Based on the StarLite kernel, the environment consists of the modules for user interface, configuration management and transaction generation, transaction manager, message server, resource manager, and performance monitor.

User Interface (UI) is a front-end invoked when the prototyping environment begins. UI is menu-driven, and

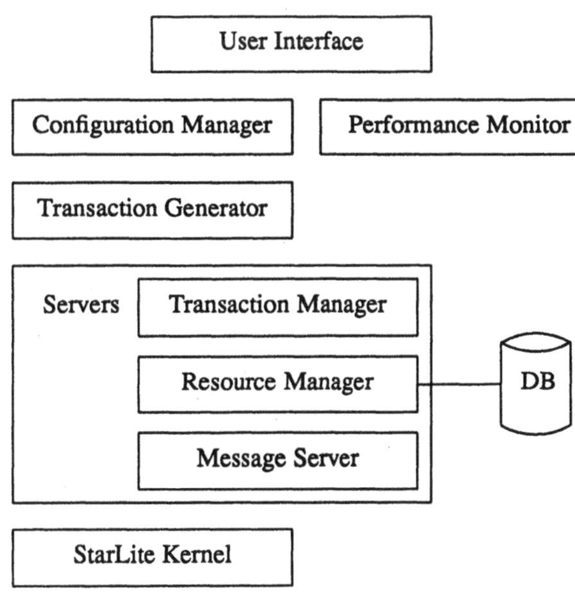

Fig. 1. Structure of the prototyping environment

designed to be flexible in allowing users to experiment various configurations with different system parameters. A user can specify the following:

- system configuration: number of sites and topology, and the relative speed of CPU, I/O, and communication cost.
- database configuration: database at each site with user defined structure, size, granularity, and levels of replication.
- load characteristics: number of transactions to be executed, size of their read-sets and write-sets, transaction types (read-only/update and periodic/aperiodic) and their priorities, and the mean interarrival time of aperiodic transactions.
- concurrency control: locking, timestamp ordering, and priority-based.

UI initiates the Configuration Manager (CM) which initializes necessary data structures for transaction processing based on user specification. CM invokes the Transaction Generator at an appropriate time interval to generate the next transaction.

Transaction execution consists of read and write operations. Each read or write operation is preceded by an access request sent to the Resource Manager, which maintains the local database at each site. Each transaction is assigned to the Transaction Manager (TM). The TM issues service requests on behalf of the transaction and reacts appropriately to the request replies. For instance, if a transaction requests access to a data object that is already locked, the TM executes either blocking operation to wait until the data object can be accessed, or aborting the transaction, depending on the situation. TM executes the two-phase commit protocol to ensure that a transaction commits or aborts globally.

The prototyping environment is currently implemented on a single host. The distributed environment is simulated by the Message Server (MS) listening on a well-known port for messages from remote sites. When a message is sent to a remote site, it is placed on the message queue of the destination site and the sender can block itself on a private semaphore until the message is retrieved by the MS at the receiving site. If the receiving site is not operational, a time-out mechanism will unblock the sender process. When the MS retrieves a message, it wakes the sender process and forwards the message to the proper servers or TM. The prototyping environment implements Ada-style rendezvous (synchronous) as well as asynchronous message passing. Inter-process communication within a site does not go through the Message Server; processes send and receive messages directly through their associated ports.

The Performance Monitor interacts with the transaction managers to record priority/timestamp and read/write data set for each transaction, time when each event occurred, statistics for each transaction in each node. The statistics for a transaction includes arrival time, start time, total processing time, blocked interval, whether deadline was missed or not, and the number of aborts.

3. PROTOTYPING REAL-TIME DATABASE SYSTEMS

In this section, we present a real-time database system prototyped using the prototyping environment. Two goals of our prototyping work are 1) evaluation of the prototyping environment itself in terms of correctness, functionality, and modularity, by using it in prototyping distributed database systems, and 2) performance evaluation of real-time locking and priority-based synchronization protocols through the sensitivity study of key parameters that affect performance.

Real-time databases are often used by applications such as tracking. Tasks in such applications consist of both computing (signal processing) and database accessing (transactions). A task can have multiple transactions, which consists of a sequence of read and write operations operating on the database. Each transaction will follow the two-phase locking protocol [4], which requires a transaction to acquire all the locks before it releases any lock. Once a transaction releases a lock, it cannot acquire any new lock. A high priority task will preempt the execution of lower priority tasks unless it is blocked by the locking protocol at the database. In this section we consider them in a single site environment. Real-time locking protocols in distributed environment is discussed in the next section.

3.1. Priority-Based Synchronization

In a real-time database system, synchronization protocols must not only maintain the consistency constraints of the database but also satisfy the timing requirements of the transactions accessing the database. To satisfy both the consistency and real-time constraints, it is necessary to integrate synchronization protocols with real-time priority scheduling protocols. Due to the effect of blocking in lock-based synchronization protocols, a direct application of a real-time scheduling algorithm to transactions may result in a condition known as *priority inversion*. Priority inversion is said to occur when a higher priority task is forced to wait for the execution of a lower priority task for an indefinite period of time. When two transactions attempt to access the same data object, the access must be serialized to maintain consistency. If the transaction of the higher priority task gains access first, then the proper priority order is maintained; however, if the transaction of the lower priority gains access first and then the higher priority transaction requests access to the data object, this higher priority task will be blocked until the lower priority transaction completes its access to the data object. Priority inversion is inevitable in transaction systems. However, to achieve a high degree of schedulability in real-time applications, priority inversion must be minimized. This is illustrated by the following example.

Example: Suppose T_1, T_2, and T_3 are three transactions arranged in descending order of priority with T_1 having the highest priority. Assume that T_1 and T_3 access the same data object O_i. Suppose that at time t_1 transaction T_3 obtains a lock on O_i. During the execution of T_3, the high priority transaction T_1 arrives, preempts T_3, and later attempts to access the object O_i. Transaction T_1 will be blocked, since O_i is already locked. We would expect that T_1, being the highest priority transaction, will be blocked no longer than the time for transaction T_3 to complete and unlock O_i. However, the duration of blocking may, in fact, be unpredictable. This is because transaction T_3 can be blocked by the intermediate priority transaction T_2 that does not need to access O_i. The blocking of T_3, and hence that of T_1, will continue until T_2 and any other pending intermediate priority level transactions are completed.

The blocking duration in the example above can be arbitrarily long. This situation can be partially remedied if transactions are not allowed to be preempted; however, this solution is only appropriate for very short transactions, because it creates unnecessary blocking. For instance, once a long low priority transaction starts execution, a high priority transaction not requiring access to the same set of data objects may be needlessly blocked.

An approach to this problem, based on the notion of *priority inheritance*, has been proposed [10]. The basic idea of priority inheritance is that when a transaction T of a task blocks higher priority tasks, it executes at the highest priority of all the transactions blocked by T. This simple idea of priority inheritance reduces the blocking time of a higher priority transaction. However, this is inadequate because the blocking duration for a transaction, though bounded, can still be substantial due to the potential *chain of blocking*. For instance, suppose that transaction T_1 needs to sequentially access objects O_1 and O_2. Also suppose that T_2 preempts T_3 which has already locked O_2. Then, T_2 locks O_1. Transaction T_1 arrives at this instant and finds that the objects O_1 and O_2 have been respectively locked by the lower priority transactions T_2 and T_3. As a result, T_1 would be blocked for the duration of two transactions, once to wait for T_2 to release O_1 and again to wait for T_3 to release O_2. Thus a chain of blocking can be formed.

One idea for dealing with this inadequacy is to use a total priority ordering of active transactions [11]. A transaction is said to be *active* if it has started but not yet completed its execution. A transaction can be active in one of two states: executing or being preempted in the middle of its execution. The idea of total priority ordering is that the real-time locking protocol ensures that each active transaction is executed at some priority level, taking priority inheritance and read/write semantics into consideration.

3.2. Total Ordering by Priority Ceiling

To ensure the total priority ordering of active transactions, three priority ceilings are defined for each data object in the database: the write-priority ceiling, the absolute-priority ceiling, and the rw-priority ceiling. The write-priority ceiling of a data object is defined as the priority of the highest priority transaction that may write into this object, and absolute-priority ceiling is defined as the priority of the highest priority transaction that may read or write the data object. The rw-priority ceiling is set dynamically. When a data object is write-locked, the rw-priority ceiling of this data object is defined to be equal to the absolute priority ceiling. When it is read-locked, the rw-priority ceiling of this data object is defined to be equal to the write-priority ceiling.

The priority ceiling protocol is premised on systems with a fixed priority scheme. The protocol consists of two mechanisms: *priority inheritance* and *priority ceiling*. With the combination of these two mechanisms, we get the properties of freedom from deadlock and a worst case blocking of at most a single lower priority transaction.

When a transaction attempts to lock a data object, the transaction's priority is compared with the highest rw-priority ceiling of all data objects currently locked by other transactions. If the priority of the transaction is not higher than the rw-priority ceiling, the access request will be denied, and the transaction will be blocked. In this case, the transaction is said to be blocked by the transaction which holds the lock on the data object of the highest rw-priority ceiling. Otherwise, it is granted the lock. In the denied case, the priority inheritance is performed in order to overcome the problem of uncontrolled priority inversion. For example, if transaction T blocks higher transactions, T inherits P_H, the highest priority of the transactions blocked by T.

Under this protocol, it is not necessary to check for the possibility of read-write conflicts. For instance, when a data object is write-locked by a transaction, the rw-priority ceiling is equal to the highest priority transaction that can access it. Hence, the protocol will block a higher priority transaction that may write or read it. On the other hand, when the data object is read-locked, the rw-priority ceiling is equal to the highest priority transaction that may write it. Hence, a transaction that attempts to write it will have a priority no higher than the rw-priority ceiling and will be blocked. Only the transaction that read it and have priority higher than the rw-priority ceiling will be allowed to read-lock it, since read-locks are compatible. Using the priority ceiling protocol, mutual deadlock of transactions cannot occur and each transaction can be blocked by at most by one lower priority transactions until it completes or suspends itself. For a more formal discussion on the protocol, readers are referred to [11]. The next example shows how transactions are scheduled under the priority ceiling protocol.

Example: Consider the same situation as in the previous example. According to the protocol, the priority ceiling of O_i is the priority of T_1. When T_2 tries to access a data object, it is blocked because its priority is not higher than the priority ceiling of O_i. Therefore T_1 will be blocked only once by T_3 to access O_i, regardless of the number of data objects it may access.

The total priority ordering of active transactions leads to some interesting behavior. As shown in the example above, the priority ceiling protocol may forbid a transaction from locking an unlocked data object. At first sight, this seems to introduce unnecessary blocking. However, this can be considered as the "insurance premium" for preventing deadlock and achieving block-at-most-once property.

Using the prototyping environment, we have been investigating issues associated with this idea of total ordering in priority-based scheduling protocols. One of the critical issues related to the total ordering approach is its performance compared with other design alternatives. In other words, it is important to figure out what is the actual cost for the "insurance premium" of the total priority ordering approach. In our experiments, all transactions are assumed to be *hard* in the sense that there will be no value in completing a transaction after its deadline. Transactions that miss the deadline are aborted, and disappear from the system.

3.3. Performance Evaluation

Various statistics have been collected during the experiments for comparing the performance of the priority ceiling protocol with other synchronization control algorithms. Transaction throughput and the percentage of deadline missing transactions are the most important performance measures in real-time database systems. This section presents these performance measures in a single site database system. Performance in distributed environments will be discussed in the next section.

Transaction are generated with exponentially distributed interarrival times, and the data objects updated by a transaction are chosen uniformly from the database. The total processing time of a transaction is directly related to the number of data objects accessed. Due to space considerations, we do not present all our results but have selected the graphs which best illustrate the difference and performance of the algorithms. For example, we have omitted the results of an experiment that varied the size of the database, and thus the probability of conflicts, because they only confirm and not increase the knowledge yielded by other experiments.

For each experiment and for each algorithm tested, we collected performance statistics and averaged over the 10 runs. The percentage of deadline-missing transactions is calculated with the following equation: *%missed* = 100 * (number of deadline-missing transactions / number of transactions processed). A transaction is processed if either it executes completely or it is aborted. In our experiments, all transactions are assumed to be *hard* in the sense that there will be no value in completing a transaction after its deadline. Transactions that miss the deadline are aborted, and disappear from the system.

We have used transaction size (the number of data objects a transaction needs to access) as one of the key variables in the experiments. It varies from a small fraction up to a relatively large portion (10%) of the database so that conflicts would occur frequently. The high conflict rate allows synchronization protocols to play a significant role in determining system performance. We also chose the average arrival rate so that protocols are tested in a heavily loaded rather than lightly loaded system. For designing real-time systems, one must consider high load situations. Even though they may not arise frequently, one would like to have a system that misses as few deadlines as possible when such peaks occur. In other words, when a crisis occurs and the database system is under pressure is precisely when making a few extra deadlines could be most important [1].

We normalize the transaction throughput in terms of data objects accessed per second for successful transactions, not in transactions per second, in order to account for the fact that bigger transactions need more database processing. The normalization rate is obtained by multiplying the transaction completion rate (transactions/second) by the transaction size (data objects accessed/transaction).

In Figure 2, the throughput of the priority ceiling protocol (C), the two-phase locking protocol with priority mode (P), and the two-phase locking protocol without priority mode (L), is shown for transactions of of different sizes. Since we chose the average arrival rate to make the system heavily loaded, both CPU and I/O were very heavily loaded when the average transaction size reaches 20. As the transaction size increases, there is little impact on the throughput of the priority ceiling protocol over a range of transaction sizes shown in Figure 2. This is because in the priority ceiling protocol, the conflict rate is determined by ceiling blocking rather than direct blocking, and the frequency of ceiling blocking is not sensitive to the transaction size.

However, the performance of the two-phase locking protocol with or without priority degrades very rapidly. This phenomenon is more pronounced as the transaction workload becomes more I/O bound, since there are few conflicts for the small transactions in the two-phase locking protocol, and the concurrency is fully achieved with an assumption of parallel I/O processing. Poor performance of the two-phase locking protocol for bigger transactions is due to the high conflict rate.

Another important performance statistic is the percentage of deadline-missing transactions, since the synchronization protocol in real-time database systems must satisfy the timing constraints of individual transaction. In our experiments, each transaction's deadline is set in proportion to its size and system workload (number of transactions), and the transaction with the earliest deadline is assigned the highest priority. As shown in Figure 3, the percentage of deadline-missing transactions increases sharply for the two-phase locking protocol as the transaction size increases. A sharp rise was expected, since the probability of deadlocks would go up with the fourth power of the transaction size [5]. However, the percentage of deadline-missing transactions increases more slowly as the transaction size increases in the priority ceiling protocol. Since there is no deadlock in priority ceiling protocol, the response time is proportional to the transaction size and the priority ranking.

4. PRIORITY CEILING IN DISTRIBUTED ENVIRONMENTS

In this section, we discuss the use of the priority ceiling approach as a basis for real-time locking protocol in a distributed environment. The priority ceiling protocol might be implemented in a distributed environment by using the global ceiling manager at a specific site. In this approach, all decisions for ceiling blocking is performed by the global ceiling manager. Therefore all the information for ceiling protocol is stored at the site of the global ceiling manager.

The advantage of this approach is that the temporal consistency of the database is guaranteed, since every data object maintains most up-to-date value. While this approach ensures consistency, holding locks across the network is not very attractive. Owing to communication delay, locking across the network will only enforce the processing of a transaction using local data objects to be delayed until the access requests to the remote data objects are granted. This delay for synchronization, combined with the low degree of concurrency due to the strong restrictions of the priority ceiling protocol, is counter-productive in real-time database systems.

An alternative to the global ceiling manager approach is to have replicated copies of data objects. An up-to-date local copy is used as the primary copy, and remote copies are used as the secondary read-only copies. In this approach, we assume a single writer and multiple readers model for distributed data objects. This is a simple model that effectively models applications such as distributed tracking in which each radar station maintains its view and makes it available to other sites in the network. For this approach to work, the following restrictions are necessary:

(1) Every data object is fully replicated at each site.

(2) Data objects to be updated must be a primary copy at the same site with the updating transaction.

(3) Every transaction must be committed before updating remote secondary copies.

Under these restrictions, the local ceiling manager at each site can enforce the priority ceiling protocol for the synchronization of not only the local data objects (primary or replicated copies), but also remote primary copies and local replicated copies. The first restriction is necessary because in a distributed database environment, holding locks across the network will occur if all the data objects requested by a transaction do not reside at the local site. If we allow each transaction to update its local copy without synchronizing with other transactions, transaction roll back and subsequent abort may result as in optimistic concurrency control. This situation is not acceptable in real-time applications. The second restriction prevents it by providing only a single primary copy.

If we insist that copies of a data objects must be identical with respect to all references, a transaction updating the primary copy cannot commit until all the remote copies are also updated. However, this solution requires locking data objects across the network, which can lead to long durations of blocking. The third restriction solves this problem by allowing remote copies to be historical copies of the primary copy; the primary and remote copies can be updated asynchronously. The third restriction, however, may cause a temporal inconsistency, owing to the delays in the network. That is, some of the views can be out of date. Even with this potential problem of reading out of date values, the third restriction is very critical in improving the system responsiveness in distributed environments. This also solves the problem of distributed deadlock. Since we do not have deadlocks at each site, and locks are not allowed to be held across the network, we cannot have distributed deadlocks.

We have investigated the performance characteristics of the global ceiling approach and the local ceiling approach with replication in a distributed environment. The real-time database system we have prototyped for the experiment consists of three sites with fully interconnected communication network. To focus on the impact of the transaction mix and the communication cost on the number of deadline-missing transactions, we did not include any I/O cost for the experiments. In other words, a memory-resident database system in a distributed environment was simulated. As in the single-site experiments, transactions enter the system with the exponentially distributed interarrival times and they are ready to execute when they appear in the system. Update transactions are assigned to a site based on their write-set, and read-only transactions are distributed randomly. The objects updated by a transaction are chosen uniformly from the database.

Figure 4 shows the ratio between the throughput of the global ceiling approach and that of the local ceiling approach, based on different transaction mix and communication delays. Even without considering the communication delay (i.e., communication delay = 0), the local ceiling approach achieves the throughput between 1.5 and 3 times higher than that of the global ceiling approach, over the wide range of transaction mix. The reason for this difference is that the degree of concurrency among the transactions at each site can be greatly improved due to the decoupling effect of data replication. If we consider communication delays, this performance ratio will increase according to the communication delay as shown in Figure 4.

Figure 5 illustrates the ratio of the percentage of deadline missing transactions between the global and the local ceiling approach, based on different communication delays for a specific transaction mix (50% read-only and 50% update transactions). There is a significant difference between the two approaches in the number of deadline missing transactions, although the increase rate of this performance ratio varies with the communication delay. In the range of small communication delays (up to 2 time units), this ratio increases rapidly, and then rather slowly after that. As the communication delay increases, the performance ratio increases beyond 16. This implies that the global ceiling approach is more than 16 times likely to miss the real-time constraints than the local ceiling approach, for a given set of real-time transactions. Performance improvement of the local ceiling approach is more substantial with small communication delays than with large delays. This is because as communication delay increases, the concurrency achieved by the local ceiling approach is limited by the the communication cost due to data replication. Figure 6 shows the percentage of deadline-missing transactions for two specific communication delays. As shown in Figure 5, the performance difference in terms of deadline-missing transactions between two approaches increases as the communication delay increases over a wide range of transaction mix. As the proportion of read-only transactions increases, the number of deadline-missing transactions decreases since the conflict rate will decrease.

Our performance results have illustrated the superiority of the local ceiling approach over the global ceiling approach, at least under one representative distributed real-time database and transaction model. Hence, from this experimentation, we believe that, even with the potential problem of temporal inconsistency (i.e., reading out of date values), the local ceiling approach is a very powerful technique for real-time concurrency control in distributed database systems.

There are applications where a temporally consistent view is more important than just the latest information that can be obtained at each site. For example, in an application like tracking, a local track would be updated periodically in conjunction with repetitive scanning. In order to provide a temporally consistent view in a distributed environment, we can utilize the periodicity of the update transaction as a timestamp mechanism. If the system provide multiple versions of data objects, ensuring a temporally consistent view becomes a real-time scheduling problem in which the time lags in the distributed versions need to be controlled. Once the time lags can be controlled by the timestamps of data objects, transactions can read the proper versions of distributed data objects, and ensure that decisions are based on temporally consistent data.

5. CONCLUSIONS

Prototyping large software systems is not a new approach. However, methodologies for developing a prototyping environment for distributed database systems have not been investigated in depth in spite of its potential benefits. In this paper, we have presented a prototyping environment that has been developed based on the StarLite concurrent programming kernel and message-based approach with modular building blocks. Although the complexity of a distributed database system makes prototyping difficult, current implementation of the prototyping environment has proven satisfactory for experimentation of design choices, different database techniques and protocols, and even an integrated evaluation of database systems. It supports a very flexible user interface to allow a wide range of system configurations and workload characteristics. Since our prototyping environment is designed to provide a spectrum of database functions and operating system modules, it facilitates the development of multiple system instances with different characteristics without much overhead. Expressive power and performance evaluation capability of our prototyping environment has been demonstrated by prototyping a distributed real-time database system and investigating its performance characteristics.

In real-time database systems, transactions must be scheduled to meet their timing constraints. In addition, the system should support a predictable behavior such that the possibility of missing deadlines of critical tasks could be informed ahead of time, before their deadlines expire. Priority ceiling protocol is one approach to achieve a high degree of schedulability and system predictability. In this paper, we have investigated this approach and compared its performance with other techniques and design choices. It is shown that this technique might be appropriate for real-time transaction scheduling since it is very stable over the wide range of transaction sizes, and compared with two-phase locking protocols, it reduces the number of deadline-missing transactions.

There are other technical issues associated with priority-based scheduling protocols that need further investigation. For example, the analytic study of the priority ceiling protocol provides an interesting observation that the use of read and write semantics of a lock may lead to worse performance in terms of schedulability than the use of exclusive semantics of a lock. This means that the *read* semantics of a lock cannot be used to allow several readers to hold the lock on the data object, and the ownership of locks must be mutually exclusive. Is it necessarily true? We are investigating this and other related issues using the prototyping environment.

Transaction scheduling options for real-time database systems also need further investigation. In priority ceiling protocol and many other database scheduling algorithms, preemption is usually not allowed. To reduce the number of deadline-missing transactions, however, preemption may need to be considered. The preemption decision in a real-time database system must be made very carefully, and as pointed out in [17], it should not necessarily based only on relative deadlines. Since preemption implies not only that the work done by the preempted transaction must be undone, but also that later on, if restarted, must redo the work. The resultant delay and the wasted execution may cause one or both of these transactions, as well as other transaction to miss the deadlines. Several approaches to designing scheduling algorithms for real-time transactions have been proposed [7, 17, 1], but their performance in distributed environments is not studied. The prototyping environment described in this paper is an appropriate research vehicle for investigating such new techniques and scheduling algorithms for distributed real-time database systems.

REFERENCES

[1] Abbott, R. and H. Garcia-Molina, "Scheduling Real-Time Transactions: A Performance Study," *VLDB Conference*, Sept. 1988, 1-12.

[2] Abbott, R. and H. Garcia-Molina, "Scheduling Real-Time Transactions with Disk Resident Data," *VLDB Conference*, August 1989.

[3] *IEEE Computer*, Special Issue on Real-Time Systems, vol. 24, no. 5, May 1991.

[4] Eswaran, K. P. et al, "The Notion of Consistency and Predicate Locks in a Database System," *Comm. of the ACM*, Nov. 1976, 624-633.

[5] Gray, J. et al., "A Straw Man Analysis of Probability of Waiting and Deadlock," *IBM Research Report*, RJ 3066, 1981.

[6] *8th IEEE Workshop on Real-Time Operating Systems and Software*, Atlanta, Georgia, May 1991.

[7] Liu, J. W. S., K. J. Lin, and S. Natarajan, "Scheduling Real-Time, Periodic Jobs Using Imprecise Results," *Real-Time Systems Symposium*, Dec. 1987, 252-260.

[8] *ONR Annual Workshop on Foundations of Real-Time Computing*, Washington, DC, Oct. 1991.

[9] Rajkumar, R., "Task Synchronization in Real-Time Systems," *Ph.D. Dissertation*, Carnegie-Mellon University, August 1989.

[10] Sha, L., R. Rajkumar, and J. Lehoczky, "Priority Inheritance Protocol: An Approach to Real-Time Synchronization," *Technical Report*, Computer Science Dept., Carnegie-Mellon University, 1987.

[11] Sha, L., R. Rajkumar, S. H. Son, and C. Chang, "A Real-Time Locking Protocol," *IEEE Trans. on Computers*, vol. 40, no. 7, July 1991, 793-800.

[12] Son, S. H., Guest editor, *ACM SIGMOD Record*, vol. 17, no. 1, Special Issue on Real-Time Database Systems, March 1988.

[13] Son, S. H. and A. Agrawala, "Distributed Checkpointing for Globally Consistent States of Databases," *IEEE Transactions on Software Engineering*, vol. 15, no. 10, October 1989, 1157-1167.

[14] Son, S. H., "Scheduling Real-Time Transactions," *Euromicro Workshop on Real-Time Systems*, Horsholm, Denmark, June 1990, 25-32.

[15] Son, S. H., "An Environment for Integrated Development and Evaluation of Real-Time Distributed Database Systems," *Journal of Systems Integration*, Kluwer Academic Publishers, vol. 2, no. 1, Feb. 1992, 67-90.

[16] Son, S. H. and S. Kouloumbis, "Replication Control for Distributed Real-Time Database Systems," *12th International Conference on Distributed Computing Systems*, Yokohama, Japan, June 1992.

[17] Stankovic, J. and W. Zhao, "On Real-Time Transactions," *ACM SIGMOD Record*, vol. 17, no. 1, Special Issue on Real-Time Database Systems, March 1988, 4-18.

[18] Tokuda, H. and C. Mercer, "ARTS: A Distributed Real-Time Kernel," *ACM Operating Systems Review*, vol. 23, no. 3, July 1989.

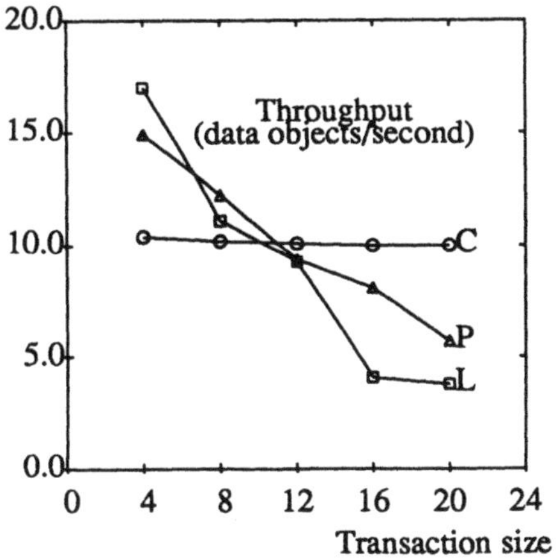

Fig. 2 Transaction Throughput.

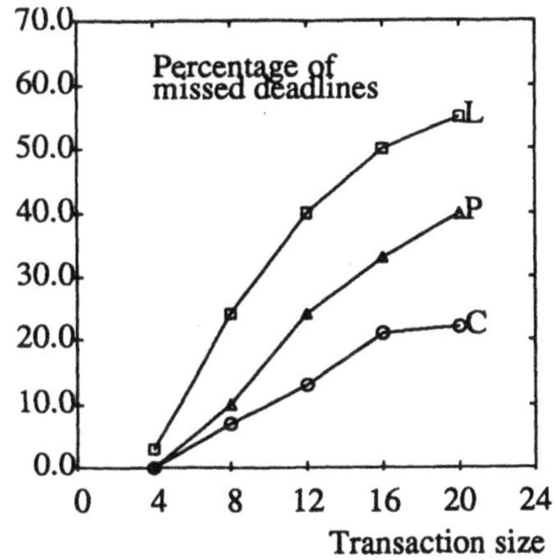

Fig. 3 Percentage of Deadline Missing Transactions.

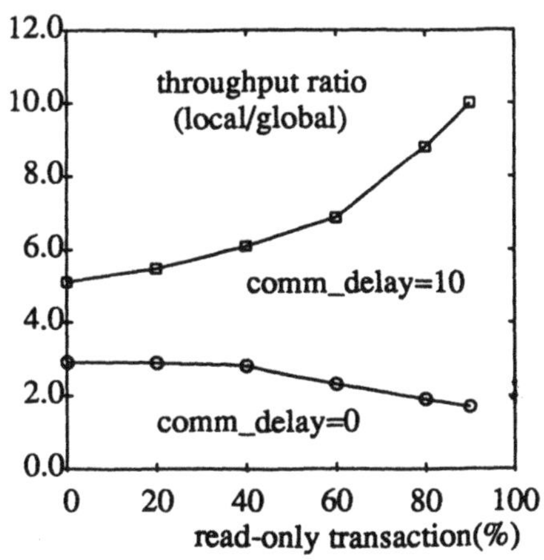

Fig. 4 Transaction Throughput Ratio

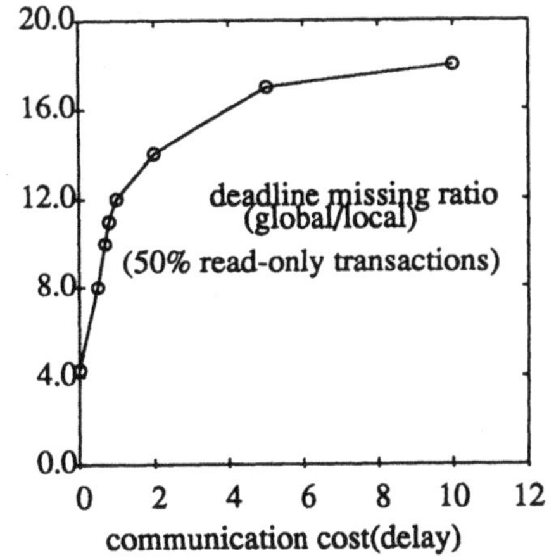

Fig. 5 Deadline Missing Ratio

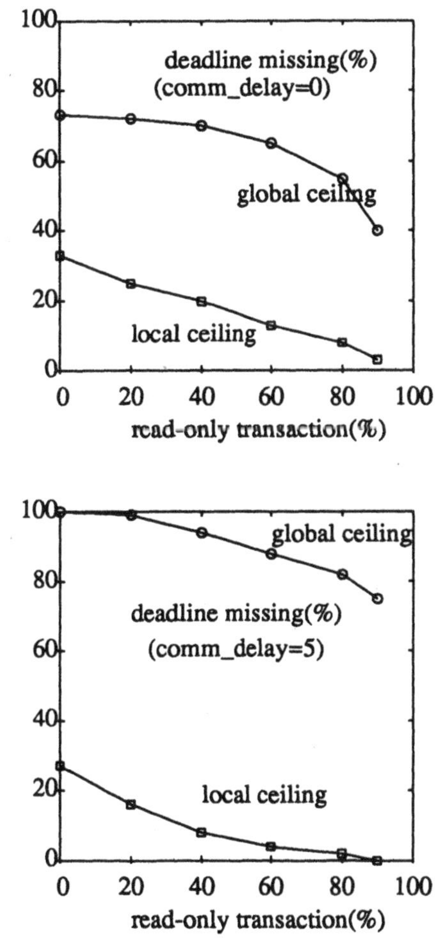

Fig. 6 Deadline Missing Transaction Percentage

DATABASE APPLICATIONS

CASE-BASED EVOLUTIONARY WORLD MODEL FOR ELECTRONIC SECRETARIES

Katsumi Kanasaki

Software Research Center
Ricoh Co., Ltd.
1-1-17, Koishikawa, Bunkyo, Tokyo 112, Japan

Tosiyasu L. Kunii

Department of Information Science
University of Tokyo
7-3-1, Hongo, Bunkyo, Tokyo 113, Japan

ABSTRACT

A world model for electronic secretaries is proposed to manage office procedures. Networks in a world hierarchy are used to store all past cases in addition to current activities and future plans. The model allows the user to modify the schema of the network whenever the office procedure changes. Moreover, the model can learn the schema also from actual cases.

Keywords: data model, object-oriented databases, schema evolution, learning, electronic secretaries

1 INTRODUCTION

This paper proposes a world model to manage *office procedures* for electronic secretaries. The model provides the basis to build an electronic secretary system that are used by secretaries and office workers as well.

Activities in recent offices range so wide that no individual understands all kinds of office procedures. Moreover, technical knowledge in each domain is expected for each activity. These circumstances call for computer-assisted secretary systems to professionally handle the office procedures.

Office procedures can be recorded in the system. However, it is not very useful to describe a fixed procedure for each task, because the procedure dynamically changes. The change cannot be predicted, because offices are *open systems* to dynamically upgrade the system functions [1]. In other words, our knowledge about office procedures is always *partial* and *incomplete,* and hence need to be integrated by the systems.

Instead of handling the fixed procedure for each task, our model dynamically creates database schemas and instances from all the past cases in addition to current activities and future plans of the task to integrate the knowledge. The past cases are exploited to this end to cover the various aspects of the knowledge related with the office procedures.

- A good procedure for each task can be chosen. Criteria for the selection depend on the current situation.
- It is possible to estimate how long the task takes.
- Forms, letters, and other materials and information can be reused. They can be also stored in the system.
- Repeated failures can be avoided, because possible problems can be predicted.
- A plan to cope with the problems can be found. The procedure can be changed before the change becomes too late.

Schemas of office procedures, or *classes* of office procedure *instances,* are also stored in the system. They are necessary to share knowledge among similar cases.

The office procedures are represented by networks that consist of labeled nodes and labeled links. This approach is also used in semantic networks and the entity-relationship model [2]. Basic semantic networks, however, lack the notion of schema. Although KRYPTON [3] and Sowa's conceptual graph [4] employ logic to represent constraints, it is not easy to represent data dependency in logic [5]. In the entity-relationship model, a schema must be defined before any data manipulation. This restriction is hardly accepted to describe office procedures, because the procedure always changes, and most office activities include tasks of a new kind. Section 2 presents the network representation of office procedures.

The office procedures must be classified so that past cases that are similar to present one can be searched and referred. A class hierarchy and inheritance are often used for this purpose. The classification of the real world always includes exceptions. In other words, non-monotonic reasoning is required, because our knowledge about a class is always incomplete. Inheritance hierarchies with exceptions have been studied [6,7,8)].

This paper introduces the concept of *worlds* and a *world hierarchy* to represent *inheritance of relationships*, which is not well handled in the current inheritance theories nor existing inheritance systems such as entity-relationship models with generalization and object-oriented database systems [9,10)].

The world concept is also useful to represent alternatives, versions, and beliefs. The world concept is introduced in Section 3.

The schema must be able to rapidly change when the office procedure changes; the schema *evolves*. Although the schema evolution in object-oriented database systems has been studied [11,12,13)], the systems create no instances when a new class is added. This paper attacks this problem using dependency constraints on relationships. Task instances can be automatically created when a new task class is added to the procedure. Section 4 presents an algorithm for the schema evolution.

This paper proposes to *learn* the schema from cases, because it is cumbersome for users to modify the schema whenever the procedure changes. In the early work, we have proposed to automatically generate relational schemas from instances by induction [14)]. However, it is difficult for our model to uniquely determine a schema from only instances, because our model is more flexible than the relational model. Instead, copying instances for instance creation, user operations guide the learning mechanism. This approach makes the learning process efficient. Section 5 presents an algorithm for the learning.

Instance creation by copying is adequate for learning, because the instance can be created before its class is determined and created. Objects are created by copying prototypical objects also in delegation [15)]. However, no concrete learning algorithms for delegation are proposed. Although delegation makes no distinction between instances and classes, this paper distinguishes them to use the result of learning.

2 NETWORKS FOR OFFICE PROCEDURE DESCRIPTION

Office procedures are, of course, a kind of procedures. However, procedural representation is not adequate to describe them, because it is not possible nor necessary to describe all co.ditions that will affect the procedures. Our knowledge is always partial and incomplete.

Instead of the procedural representation, constraints on tasks and related entities are described. When new information is given, new constraints can be added. The new information is often inconsistent with the current information. In this case, some constraints can be weakened or deleted. It is also possible to save the original constraints as another world.

A Node Denotes an Entity or an Entity Set

This paper distinguishes four entity sets: tasks, time intervals (or time points as special cases [16,17)]), persons (or organizations), and other entities. Instances of the entities are called *node instances*. Each entity set is further classified into *node classes*.

The constraints can be specified for each node. A label of the node implicitly works as a constraint. For example, a label Program-Committee-Member represents a constraint that the node corresponds to a program committee member. Explicit constraints are often specified for time intervals. For example, a time interval for a weekly meeting may start at 1 p.m. on Thursday, and another time interval for equipment purchase may last for three months.

The lowest number and the highest number of instances can be also specified for each class. This constraint is called the *cardinality constraint*.

A Link Denotes a Relationship

The following relationships between entities are considered.

PART-OF: For example, there is a PART-OF relationship between two tasks, one that organizes a conference and one that calls for papers. In this paper, this relationship is represented as

Call-for-Papers is-part-of Organize-a-Conference.

If A is-part-of B, where A and B are tasks, the period of B covers the period of A.

This relationship allows stepwise refinement of procedures. The PART-OF relationships between entities other than tasks can be also considered.

BEFORE: For example, Review before Select-Papers. Entities on both sides are tasks or time. This relationship restricts the order of tasks.

TIME: For example, November-30 is-time-of PC-Meeting. This relationship restricts the period of tasks.

AGENT: For example, Reviewer is-agent-of Review.

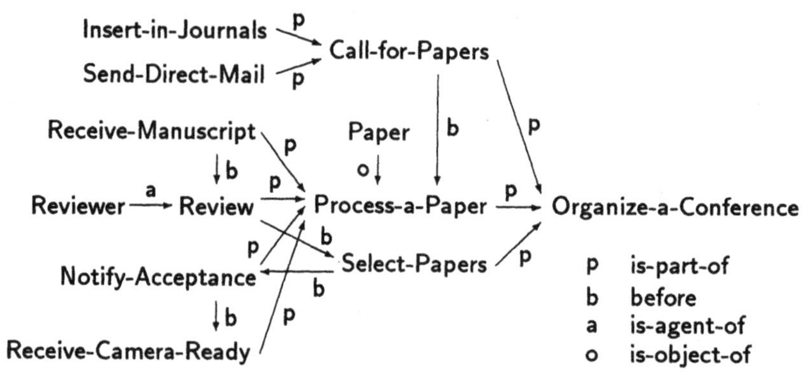

Figure 1: A part of the procedure to organize a conference can be represented as a network shown here.

OBJECT: For example, Paper is-object-of Process-a-Paper.

Instances of the relationships are called *link instances.* A link instance connects a pair of node instances. Classes of the relationships are called *link classes.* A link class connects a pair of node classes. A subset of node classes and link classes for the procedure to organize a conference is shown in Figure 1.

Dependency constraints are specified for link classes. This paper uses *mapping cardinality* to represent the constraints. For example,

Review $_3$ is-part-of $_1$ Process-a-Paper

denotes that there must be just three instances of Review for each instance of Process-a-Paper, and there must be one instance of Process-a-Paper for each instance of Review. Three instances of Review can be automatically created when an instance of Process-a-Paper is created.

Another example is

Reviewer $_1$ is-agent-of $_{1-\infty}$ Review.

In this case, a range of mapping cardinality is specified.

Alternatives of office procedures are described in different worlds as presented in Section 3. Knowledge, belief, and expectation of different persons are also described in different worlds. This makes constraints in each world consistent without describing complicated conditions.

The networks presented here are not intended to be complete. For example, a relationship that represents object equality may be necessary. Emotion of persons may also be necessary for some cases [18)].

3 WORLD MODEL

Class hierarchies can be used to inherit class properties. *Derived classes* (or subclasses) inherit properties of *base classes.* However, relationships between classes cannot be inherited according to the class hierarchies.

Let us consider a one-to-one relationship

Call-for-Papers $_1$ is-part-of $_1$ Organize-a-Conference.

Although Organize-DASFAA[1] is a derived class of Organize-a-Conference, the derived relationship between Call-for-Papers and Organize-DASFAA is not one-to-one. A one-to-one relationship exists between Call-for-DASFAA-Papers and Organize-DASFAA, where Call-for-DASFAA-Papers is a derived class of Call-for-Papers. The new class must be created, and the PART-OF relationship must be redefined.

This derived class is also required to modify procedures for the derived cases. For example, there may be a relationship

Send-Direct-Mail $_{1-\infty}$ is-part-of $_1$ Call-for-Papers.

If the task Send-Direct-Mail is not necessary for the class of DASFAA symposiums, the class Call-for-DASFAA-Papers must be created to delete the relationship.

The concept of *world* is introduced to solve the problem. A *class world* contains a network of node classes and link classes. *Derived worlds* inherit their networks from *base worlds.* Derived classes inherit their properties from base classes. Derived links, however, connect derived nodes, instead of base nodes.

An *instance world* contains a network of node instances and link instances. A network in an instance world usually satisfies constraints described in the corresponding class world(s).

For example, a class world may contain a network

Send-Direct-Mail $_{1-\infty}$ is-part-of $_1$ Call-for-Papers

Call-for-Papers $_1$ is-part-of $_1$ Organize-a-Conference,

and its derived world may contain

Call-for-Papers $_1$ is-part-of $_1$ Organize-DASFAA.

The derived class does not contain the class Send-Direct-Mail.

[1]DASFAA is the abbreviated name of *International Symposium on Database Systems for Advanced Applications.*

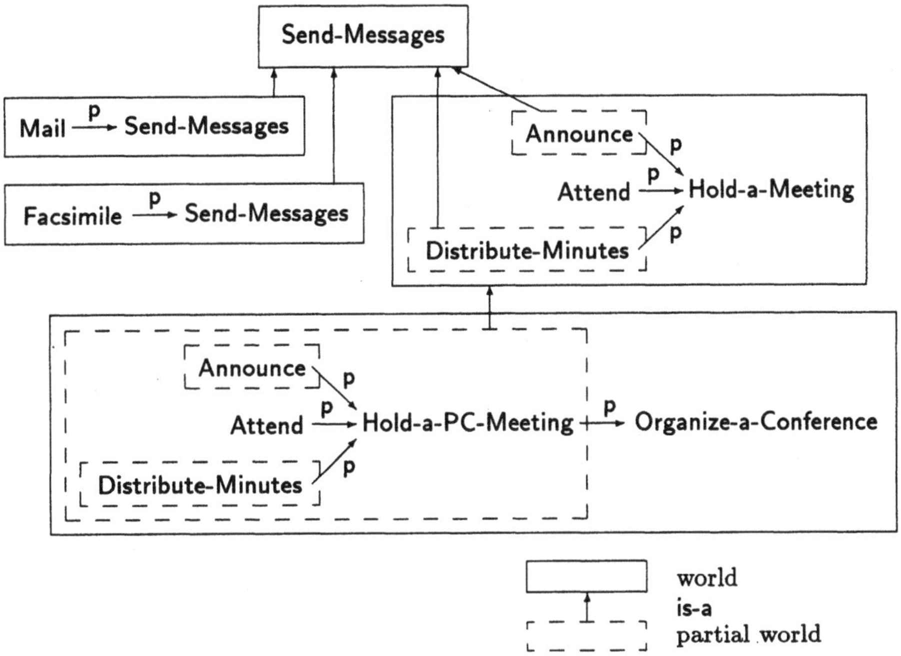

Figure 2: The procedure to hold a meeting is reused to hold a PC meeting. The procedure to send messages is also reused.

Call-for-Papers in the derived world is a derived class of **Call-for-Papers** in the base world. Although this paper does not present internal representation for worlds, it is expected that the derived class need not be physically created if the label and other properties are shared with the base class.

Construction of Class World

How are the worlds created? This section assumes that office procedures are given in advance. Section 5 deals with the learning process of office procedures. Here is the steps to construct a new class world.

1. A class world representing a procedure that is similar to the given one is chosen as a base world. If the given procedure is a completely new one, the root world, which is empty, is chosen.

2. A derived world of the base world is created. The derived world looks like a copy of the base world.

3. The derived world is modified. Node and link classes can be added and deleted. Properties (labels and constraints) of classes can be modified.

Repetition of these steps produces a simple hierarchy of worlds, which is not sufficient to reuse procedures. For example, we would like to reuse a procedure to hold a Program Committee meeting for an Organizing Committee meeting.

Let us call a subgraph of a world a *partial world*. For example, the procedure to hold a Program Committee meeting is represented by a partial world of the world that represents the procedure to organize a conference. The partial world can be derived from the world that represents the procedure to hold a meeting as shown in Figure 2.

If a world W contains a partial world PW, and a world DW is derived from W, DW contains a partial world DPW that is derived from PW.

Construction of Instance World

In an instance world, tasks of the same class may be repeated. For example, an instance of **Process-a-Paper** must be created for each paper. The instance world, in this way, grows on demand. The steps to construct an instance world follow:

1. A class world representing a procedure for the given tasks is chosen.

2. An instance world of the class world is created. The instance world is empty at first. If there are classes whose cardinality constraint requires a fixed number of instances, the instances are created.

3. New instances are created by specifying classes. The instances first look like copies of the classes.

4. The instance network is modified. Properties of the node instances, in particular, are specified. Step 3 and 4 are repeated on demand.

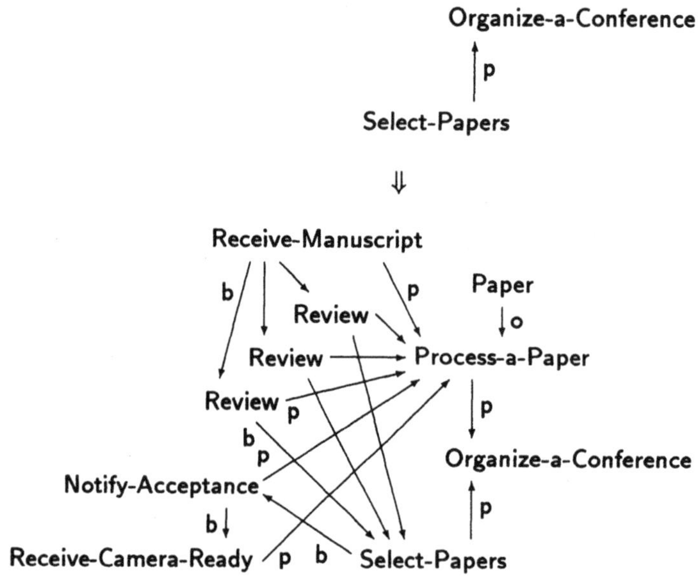

Figure 3: When the class **Paper** in the example is specified, the instance network changes as shown here.

An algorithm to create instances in Step 2 and 3 must be investigated. Let us start from an example.

When the class **Paper** in Figure 1 is specified, an instance of **Paper** and an instance of **Process-a-Paper** connected by an OBJECT link are created. A PART-OF link between the instance of **Process-a-Paper** and the instance of **Organize-a-Conference** is then connected. Three instances of **Review** are created and connected with the instance of **Process-a-Paper**. BEFORE links between the instances of **Review** and the instance of **Select-Papers** are also connected. AGENT links between the instances of **Review** and instances of **Reviewer** will be created in Step 4 when the reviewers are assigned. The changes are shown in Figure 3.

The following policy realizes the operation above:

1. In Step 2, the number of instances is specified by the cardinality constraint on the node class. In Step 3, a node class is specified by a user, and a node instance of the class is created at first.

2. If there is a constraint A $_1$ link $_n$ B, where A and B are node classes, and n is a constant such as 1 and 2, n new instances of B are created for each new instance of A. The corresponding instances are connected.

3. If there is a constraint A link $_1$ B, and B must have just one instance, new instances of A are connected with the instance of B.

4. Link instances in a world define a relation of the link. The relation of a path of link classes can be defined as the composition of the relations of the links.

   If there is a path from A to B such that link instances on the path have already reflected new instances, link instances between A and B are created so that they define the same relation.

   Although this policy assumes that all relations between the same nodes are the same, this condition does not always hold. If the path from A to B defines a relation that does not satisfy the constraint on the link between A and B, or two such paths define different relations, this policy should not be used.

Links that cannot be created by this policy must be interactively created so that constraints for the world are satisfied. This task, however, can be postponed until information enough to determine connected instances is available. The system can automatically register this task to remind users of postponed tasks.

Alternatives, Versions, and Beliefs

World hierarchies are also useful to represent various concepts such as alternatives, versions, and beliefs in addition to classification.

There are, in general, many alternatives for office procedures. For example, messages can be sent by mail, phone, facsimile, or E-mail. The alternatives can be represented as derived worlds of a world in this model as shown in Figure 2.

Recording of changes is an important job of secretaries. For example, failure of a task may demand a change of a plan. In this case, it is a bad idea to discard the original plan. The reason of the failure or the plan itself will be useful for future cases.

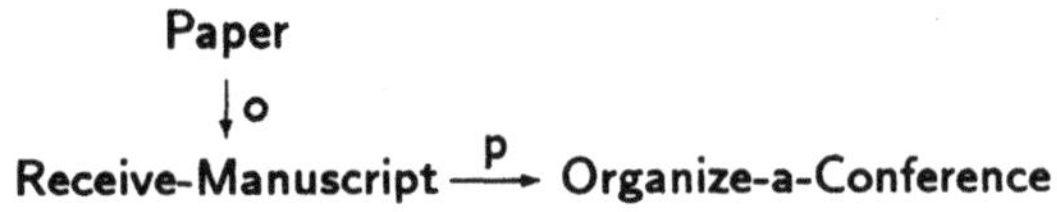

Figure 4: When the class world shown here is evolved to the original example, its instance worlds are reorganized.

The system can store versions of worlds to support this job. The world for a new version is derived from the world for its previous version. It is allowed that instance worlds are derived from an instance world. The reason of creating the version is described as a property of the world. Section 4 deals with the case that the schemas of two versions are different.

The concepts of contexts [19,20] and change propagation [20] have been proposed to deal with versions of complex objects. Multiple inheritance presented in Section 4 allows a world to represent a context. Although the context is a kind of views and difficult to update, the world can be modified. The change propagation is naturally realized by the world derivation, because it implies inheritance of relationships.

Communication is another important job of secretaries. The secretary system must be able to deal with knowledge, belief, and expectation of agents. Different persons, in general, believe or expect mutually inconsistent propositions. Hence, they are put into separate worlds to avoid confusing the system and users. If, for example, beliefs of a person are inconsistent with current facts, the secretary will send messages to correct the beliefs.

4 SCHEMA EVOLUTION

A network in a class world must be able to change easily when a rule of office procedure is modified, or a new viewpoint of the office procedure is adopted. If the viewpoint is modified, networks in the corresponding instance worlds must be also modified. If the rule is modified, instance worlds for future tasks and currently active tasks may be modified, but finished tasks are not modified.

The original network of the class world must be retained for the finished tasks. This is easily carried out; a derived class world can be created and modified instead of the original class world.

Now, let us consider how instance worlds are modified in the other cases. For example, imagine that the network in Figure 1 previously looked like the network in Figure 4. In the original world, only one class of tasks Receive-Manuscript was recorded together with Paper. When a new task class Review was introduced, the user decided to group the tasks into a task class Process-a-Paper.

In this example, an instance of Process-a-Paper must be created for each instance of Paper if there is a constraint Paper $_1$ is-object-of $_1$ Process-a-Paper. The instances are connected by OBJECT links. Three instances of Review are also created for each instance of Process-a-Paper if there is a constraint Review $_3$ is-part-of $_1$ Process-a-Paper. PART-OF links around Process-a-Paper must be connected so that the composition of PART-OF relations and an OBJECT relation does not change.

This modification of instance worlds can be formalized by multiple inheritance. The new instance world is created so that it inherits its network from both the original instance world and the new class world. When new instances are created, the policy to create instances presented in Section 3 is used.

The network in an instance world is also modified when its IS-A links to class worlds are explicitly added or deleted. The class world can be exchanged, because the user might not have information enough to choose a class when an instance was created.

For example, there are alternative ways such as Mail and Facsimile for the task Send-Messages as shown in Figure 2. An instance to announce a meeting may be created in a partial world that is derived from Send-Messages, because it has not yet decided how the messages will be sent. When it is decided that a facsimile is used, an IS-A link to the world that contains Facsimile will be added to the partial world.

Multiple Inheritance

As presented above, a derived world and a derived partial world must be able to have more than one base world. IS-A links to the base worlds can be added to make this situation possible.

Remark that the term "derived" is so generally used that new instance worlds can be derived from the existing class worlds and instance worlds. The term "object" is used here to represent both a class and an instance.

If the base worlds are completely independent, the derived world contains the networks of all the base worlds separately. However, if objects in two base worlds are derived from the same world, only one object may be present in the derived world.

The following algorithm is used when an IS-A link to a base world X is added to a world W. This algorithm is compatible with the theoretical work by Horty [8].

1. A world Y such that both W and X are derived from Y, and that no derived worlds of Y have this property is found. If there is more than one world that satisfies

this condition, the result of this algorithm may be ambiguous.

2. If there is an object in X that is not derived from Y, its derived object is created in W. When instances derived from classes are created, the policy presented in Section 3 is applied as if all existing instances have been created.

3. If an object in W is derived from an object in Y along with the path of world derivation, a copy of the object in W is created for each object in X that is derived from the object in Y. If no objects in X are derived, the object in W is deleted. The properties of the new objects are determined as follows:

   - If the original object in W and the object in X have the same property, the property is used.
   - If a property of original object in W is derived from Y, the property of the object in X is used.
   - If a property of the object in X is derived from Y, the property of the original object in W is used.
   - Otherwise, the result is ambiguous. A user should specify the property.

5 SCHEMA LEARNING

As described in Section 4, the schema of an office procedure can be modified any time. It is, however, cumbersome for users to modify the schema whenever the procedure changes. In fact, the user may not be able to position a new task in the world hierarchy, because the user does not well understand the task.

Our model allows the user to directly modify instance worlds. Their schemas are learned from the cases in the instance worlds.

If two instances are similar, the instances may belong to the same class. This is the basic idea for the learning. However, how can the system judge the similarity of the instances? This paper actually leaves the judgement to users.

The user creates instances by copying other instances. This method is, in fact, often used in the real world. For example, it is usual that a previously written letter is slightly modified and reused. The system assumes that the copy and the original of the instance belong to the same class.

Let us consider the learning process case by case.

Create: If a network of instances is created from scratch, the classes for the instances are created in the class world. If more than one class world is the base world of the instance world or its partial worlds, the system will ask the user to select one. If, however, a created link instance is connected with a node instance that has been present, only the class worlds that contain the class of the node instance are selected.

The cardinality constraints on the created classes are maintained so that they reflect the current status of the instance world.

For example, if a task instance **Announce** in Figure 2 was just added to hold the first Program Committee meeting, a task class **Announce** and a relationship **Announce** $_1$ **is-part-of** $_1$ **Hold-a-PC-Meeting** are also added to the corresponding class world.

Delete: If instances are deleted, their cardinality constraints are maintained. Classes are not deleted unless explicitly specified.

Copy: If a network of instances is copied from an instance world W to an instance world X (W and X can be the same world), they belong to the same classes. Let G and H be the original network and the new network, respectively. The copied network must be connected with nodes. Let S and T be the sets of node instances that are connected with G and H, respectively.

A class world Y that satisfies the following conditions is searched at first.

- Both W and X are derived from Y.
- Instances in S and T are derived from the same classes in Y.
- No derived worlds of Y satisfy these conditions.

If Y is found, instances in G and H are derived from classes in Y. If the classes are not present, they are created.

For example, when the instance **Hold-a-PC-Meeting** is copied to hold the second meeting, no classes are created, but a relationship **Hold-a-PC-Meeting** $_1$ **is-part-of** $_1$ **Organize-a-Conference** changes into **Hold-a-PC-Meeting** $_2$ **is-part-of** $_1$ **Organize-a-Conference**. If the instance **Announce** is copied to hold an Organizing Committee meeting, a class **Announce** and a PART-OF link between **Announce** and **Hold-a-Meeting** are created in the world to hold a meeting.

If Y is not found, a world Z that consists of the classes of G is searched. If such a world is not present, it is created. The class worlds of W and X are arranged so that G and H are derived from Z.

For example, if an instance **Mail** to announce a meeting is copied to distribute minutes, a class world to send messages that contains a network **Mail** $_{0-1}$ **is-part-of** $_1$ **Send-Messages** will be created.

The algorithm cannot produce a structure that represents alternatives such as one shown in Figure 2. The class world will, instead, contain **Mail** $_{0-1}$ **is-part-of** $_1$ **Send-Messages** and similar structures for other alternatives. Users can rearrange the structure any time.

6 CONCLUSION

A world model for electronic secretaries was proposed to manage office procedures. Office procedure instances and their classes are described as networks in a world hierarchy. Users interact with the system by modifying the network in a world. This eases the interaction, because the user need not worry about the other worlds.

The office procedure often changes in an unexpected manner, because offices are open systems. The model proposed in this paper allows the user to modify the definition of the office procedure. Cardinality constraints on relationships and entity sets are employed to automatically modify office procedure instances according to the new definition.

It is usual in offices as open systems that a new kind of tasks becomes required. This paper proposed to learn the definition and the constraints for the office procedures from actual cases. The user need not define the procedures.

This paper did not deal with data manipulation and reasoning on the model. Although they are future works, there are a number of ideas. The worlds may be considered as possible worlds in Kripke's model of modal logic. Assumption-based belief revision systems may be applicable to find and resolve contradiction. A plan may be constructed by constraint-based reasoning.

ACKNOWLEDGEMENTS

The authors would like to thank Hideko Kunii for her valuable comments on this research. Discussion with Nobuhiro Ajitomi, Naoko Ichikawa, Hiroyasu Kurose, and Hideaki Nakayama was also fruitful. This research is based on the experience of one of the authors as a secretary of *International Symposium on Database Systems for Advanced Applications.*

REFERENCES

1) Hewitt, C., "Offices are Open Systems," *ACM Trans. Office Information Systems 4,* 3 (1986) pp. 271–287.

2) Chen, P. P., "The Entity-Relationship Model—Toward a Unified View of Data," *ACM TODS 1,* 1 (1976) pp. 9–36.

3) Brachman, R. J., Fikes, R. E., and Levesque, H. J., "Krypton: A Functional Approach to Knowledge Representation," *IEEE Computer 16,* 10 (1983) pp. 67–73.

4) Sowa, J. F., *Conceptual Structures,* Addison-Wesley, 1984.

5) Davies, T. R. and Russell, S. J., "A Logical Approach to Reasoning by Analogy," *Proc. IJCAI* (1987) pp. 264–270.

6) Etherington, D. and Reiter, R., "On Inheritance Hierarchies with Exceptions," *Proc. AAAI* (1983) pp. 104–108.

7) Touretzky, D. S., *The Mathematics of Inheritance Systems,* Morgan Kaufmann, 1986.

8) Horty, J. F., Thomason, R. H., and Touretzky, D. S., "A Skeptical Theory of Inheritance in Nonmonotonic Semantic Networks," *Proc. AAAI* (1987) pp. 358–363.

9) Maier, D., Stein, J., Otis, A., and Purdy, A., "Development of an Object-Oriented DBMS," *Proc. OOPSLA* (1986) pp. 472–482.

10) Banerjee, J. et al., "Data Model Issues for Object-Oriented Applications," *ACM Trans. Office Information Systems 5,* 1 (1987) pp. 3–26.

11) Skarra, A. H. and Zdonik, S. B., "The Management of Changing Types in an Object-Oriented Database," *Proc. ACM OOPSLA* (1986) pp. 483–495.

12) Penney, D. J. and Stein, J., "Class Modification in the GemStone Object-Oriented DBMS," *Proc. ACM OOPSLA* (1987) pp. 111–117.

13) Banerjee, J., Kim, W., Kim, H. J., and Korth, H. F., "Semantics and Implementation of Schema Evolution in Object-Oriented Databases," *Proc. ACM SIGMOD* (1987) pp. 311–322.

14) Kunii, T. L., Weyl, S., and Tenenbaum, J. M., "A Relational Data Base Schema for Describing Complex Pictures with Color and Texture," *Proc. International Joint Conference on Pattern Recognition* (1974).

15) Lieberman, H., "Using Prototypical Objects to Implement Shared Behavior in Object Oriented Systems," *Proc. ACM OOPSLA* (1086) pp. 214–223.

16) Allen, J. F., "Maintaining Knowledge about Temporal Intervals," *Commun. ACM 26,* 11 (1983) pp. 832–843.

17) Shoham, Y., *Reasoning About Change,* MIT Press, 1988.

18) Sousa, R. de, *The Rationality of Emotion,* MIT Press, 1987.

19) Chou, H-T. and Kim, W., "A Unifying Framework for Version Control," *Proc. VLDB* (1986) pp. 336–344.

20) Katz, R. H. and Chang, E., "Managing Change in a Computer-Aided Design Database," *Proc. VLDB* (1987) pp. 455–462.

SUPPORTING THE CHARACTER SETS OF JAPANESE KANJI AND KOREAN HANGUL IN THE *ADABAS/NATURAL* SYSTEM

Masahiro Shimada [1)], Hideki Nishimoto [2)], Takashi Ishizaka [1)],
Andreas Schütz [3)], Yong-Soo Kim [4)] and Yoshioki Ishii [1)]

1) Software AG of Far East Inc., JAPAN   2) Ryukoku University, JAPAN
3) Software AG, GERMANY   4) Penta Computer Korea Co., Ltd., KOREA

ABSTRACT

Software AG of Far East (SAGFE) has established various system environments peculiar to Japanese use since Japanese Kanji was supported on ADABAS for the first time in 1978.

The supporting of Japanese language, which started by putting the character strings on a special Kanji printer, has recently been improving with the development of terminal equipment and controllers.

This paper describes the progress of our supports for Japanese language at SAGFE and Software AG (SAG) Germany and a study on Korean Hangul done by SAG and Penta Computer Korea as well as Japanese Kanji. Additionally, the method called DBCS (double-byte character set) support is proposed. We discuss the problems and solve those problems by adapting the fourth generation language, NATURAL, as a SAG product.

1 SUPPORTING JAPANESE KANJI ON ADABAS

The Japanese language borrowed extensively from the Chinese Hanzi by way of Korean to write their own language around 1,500 years ago. Later, the characters came to symbolize native Japanese words similar in meaning to that of the Chinese.

Modern Japanese is written as a mixture of ideograms, Kanji, and native phonetic letters, Kana. The Kana phonetic alphabet exists as Hiragana and Katakana, which serve different purposes and differ stylistically. A typical passage of Japanese writing contains Kanji, Hiragana, and perhaps also Katakana. Both Kana syllabaries consist of 46 basic symbols each, and Kanji characters are limited to about 2,000 symbols for official and daily use.

In the early Japanese computer market, there was intense interest in the establishment of a system to handle Kanji. However, it took a long time and a vast sum of money to create compatibility with existing systems and to develop devices peculiar to Japanese use. Generally one byte is used to denote a character, but the eight-bits byte provides for as many as 256 characters. Japanese Kanji must be represented by codes that are usually two bytes long because there are many different kinds of characters (Fig.1-1). This point is pressing computer manufacturers and vendors in Japan to greatly revise standard systems.

JAPANESE CHARACTER STRINGS	DATA	
日本語の文章	0E4562456648E7449A45CA476E0F	←IBM
	28C6FCCBDCB8ECA4CECAB8BECF29	←Fujitsu

Fig.1-1 Japanese character and code representation

A great number of Kanji typing methods have been developed to date, all of which fall into three main categories: two-dimensional selection array, coding scheme, and phonetic conversion[1)]. Currently phonetic conversion is the most popular method for general users in Japan by reason of its having so few rules to learn, its use of English-typing skills, and others.

The history of the supporting Kanji on the ADABAS system in Japan can be divided into four stages as follows: (Fig.1-2)

Stage I) Putting Kanji characters on a special printer by batch processing

In 1978, we supported the Japanese Kanji first on the law retrieval system developed with an ADABAS system at the Administrative Management Agency (the Management and Coordination Agency at present). The system is for retrieving the texts of laws and regulations, which the user does by specifying key words. The texts are then printed out on a printer. There was not any terminal equipment displaying the Kanji characters on the market; therefore, putting on a special Kanji printer after the retrieval by batch processing mode. To make the system more flexible, an option was built in allowing for the form of the Kanji text to be freely adjusted.

Stage II) Supporting early Kanji terminals

As soon as the early Kanji-supported terminal came onto the market in 1980, we tried using the user-friendly query system ADASCRIPT on ADABAS with the terminal. The fourth generation language NATURAL (Version1.1), to develop application programs on ADABAS, was released at the same time. Their terminal drivers were ought to be upgraded to process Kanji data on the screen.

Kanji terminals with different specifications were made by different manufacturers, so we had to cope with each model separately.

In 1981, we succeeded at Kyodo Oil Company in adopting a method in which a map with Kanji characters and ruled lines is created in advance. The map is synthesized with the NATURAL screen at run time in order to completely support "the Kanji ruled-line map facility" for the Fujitsu terminal. In the ensuing year the Hitachi terminal also was supported by this method.

Stage III) Providing the phonetic conversion typing method

Typing Kanji characters into the system is the job of the technical operators, done mainly by typing the Kanji codes or with a Kanji tablet.

In 1982, SAGFE succeeded in equipping the NATURAL system with a phonetic conversion method. The typist first enters its Hiragana spelling of the text directly enclosed with apostrophes, then the word-unit homophones are searched with the dictionary. After they appear on the screen, the operator can choose the number of the appropriate word. This is the same popular method used for personal computers in Japan. Additionally, our method can be implemented on all non-intelligent terminals because it does not require a special dictionary or an additional processor on the terminal.

Meanwhile, IBM started to support Japanese Kanji. Their system handled complex screen images with Kanji characters with difficulty, since it supported only the method identifying the Kanji mode as a field attribute. Therefore, it was not broadly accepted in the market place.

Stage IV) Developing the environment of the DBCS support

In 1982, an important problem arose when the new version NATURAL (V1.2) was released because it was equipped with the Map Editor facility for designing the direct output image on the screen.

The processing of the screen I/O is very difficult using our method in this case because the length of physical data going into the terminal is greater by some bytes of the control-codes than the length of characters displayed on the screen.

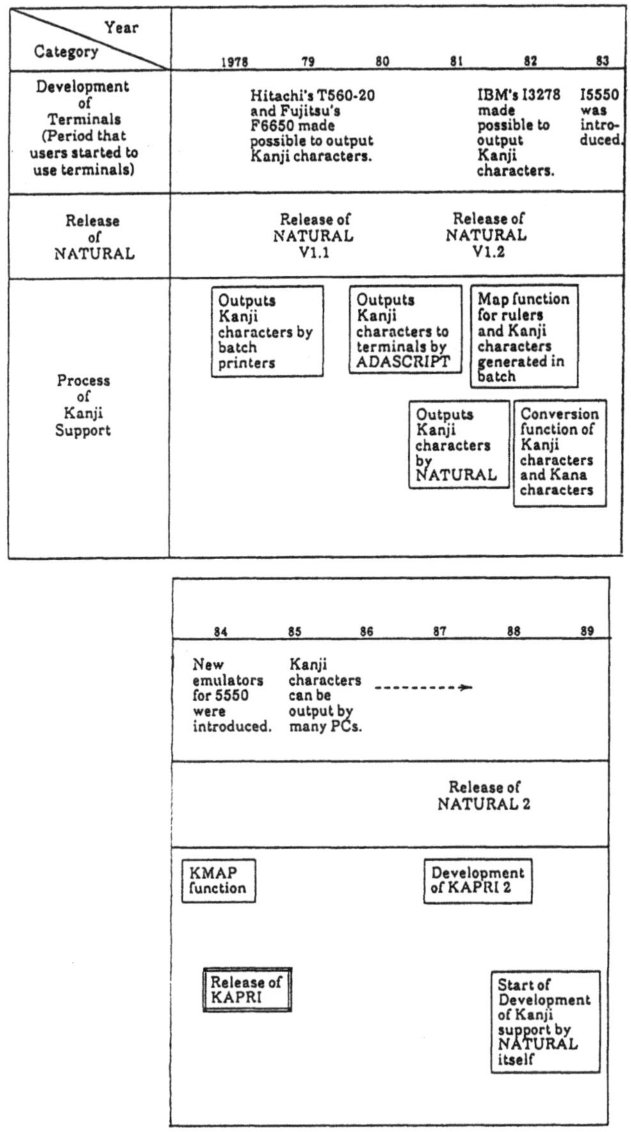

Fig.1-2 The history of Kanji Support in SAGFE

A new innovation of SAGFE was the development of the Kanji Proto-typing Interface (KAPRI) product with a KMAP facility which provides for adjusting the length of the data stream. Additionally, we succeeded in implementing KAPRI for the IBM 3278 terminal and it contributed to the NATURAL system's hot sales.

In 1984, IBM developed the virtual terminal emulator for the personal computer. This facility adapts the same Kanji shift code as Japanese products use. Since then, Kanji character data has been mostly put into the computer through the phonetic conversion processor on an intelligent terminal or on a work-station. Consequently, mainframes mainly undertake data manipulations after the Kanji has been put in.

The first version of NATURAL2 was formally released in 1987. Some of its screen operations were strongly reinforced. In the same year, SAGFE developed and released the KAPRI2[3] product corresponding to the NATURAL2 system. Recently, SAG has decided to design and develop the double-byte character set (DBCS) products in order to completely support all the multi-characters sets in the world. The specifications are discussed in Chapter 4.

There are, besides IBM, several manufacturers in Japan developing products compatible with IBM software. The products of the operating system, the TP monitor, and the terminal supported by the ADABAS/NATURAL system are shown in Fig.1-4. This demonstrates the high adaptability of ADABAS/NATURAL and the strength of SAGFE's support.

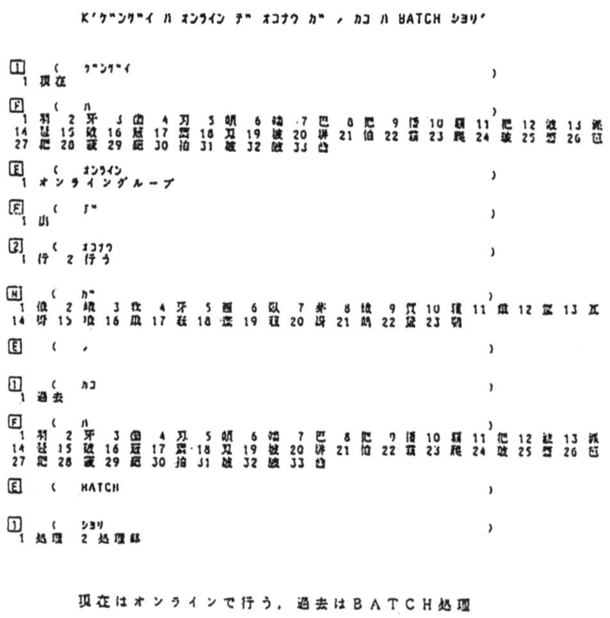

Fig.1-3 An example of the phonetic conversion method

Manufacturer	OS	TP monitor	Terminal (Note 1)
IBM	MVS, MVS/XA VS1 DOS, DOS/VSE VM/CMS	COM-PLETE TSO CICS IMS	I3270 I3278 I5550 (and other PCs with Japanese 3270 emulators) N6300 (I3270 compatible)
FUJITSU	OSIV/F4 MSP OSIV/X8 FSP	COM-PLETE TSS AIM	F9526 F665X F668X PCs with 6650 emulators (eg. FMR)
HITACHI	VOS 3 VOS 2 VOS 1	TSS ADM DCCM II DCCM III TMS/3V	H9415 T560-20 PCs with 560-20 emulators (eg. 2020)
MITSUBISHI	GOS/VS	TSS CIMS	M4378 PCs with emulators

Fig.1-4 ADABAS/NATURAL environments supported in Japan

2 AN OUTLINE OF KOREAN HANGUL

In Korean, the use of Hanzi is gradually being phased out, although the Korean language was also deeply affected by Chinese Hanzi characters. Now Korean is commonly written in a pure phonetic alphabet, called Hangul, with no Hanzi at all. Hangul was invented in 1446 during the reign of Sejong, the fourth King of the Yi dynasty. It is the only script known to have been designed by a committee.

This phonetic alphabet has 24 letters, consisting of 10 vowels and 14 consonants. The letters are designed to be grouped into square clusters of two, three, or occasionally four letters. Each cluster represents one spoken syllable of the language. The number of characters required for general use come to about 2,000 clusters (Fig.2-1).

A Hangul cluster may come in different shapes and positions, depending on its surrounding context. A computerized Hangul typing system can have a single generic key or a Romanized phonetic symbol for each Hangul letter. The computer is relied on to decide the proper graphical form and position for each letter in relation to the letter or letters surrounding it. Computer display is very good for "movable" typing because each new letter usually requires revising the form and placement of letters that have previously been typed[1] (Fig.2-2).

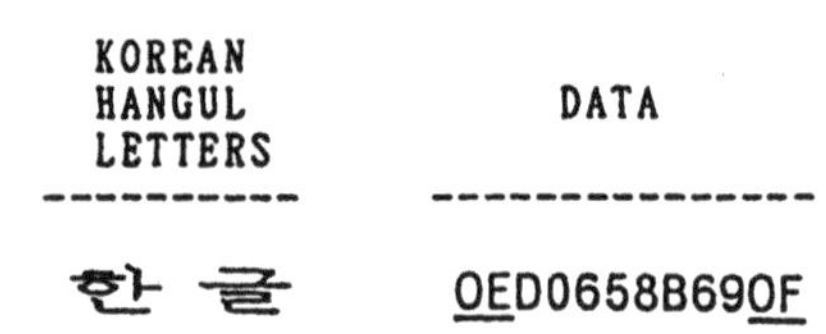

Fig.2-1 Korean Hangul and code representation

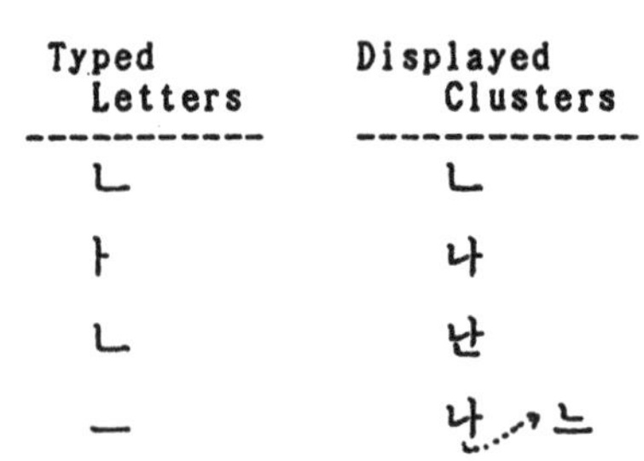

Fig.2-2 Movable typing of Hangul

3 PROBLEMS OF DOUBLE-BYTE CHARACTER SET SUPPORT

The common problems on the support of handling multi-characters are discussed in this chapter. The first problem is to create several code notations representing the same character set. Manufacturers naturally establish the original code specification before standards are completely set in the country for the computerized code notation of each character. The two types of code tables of Japanese Kanji are shown in Fig.3-1.

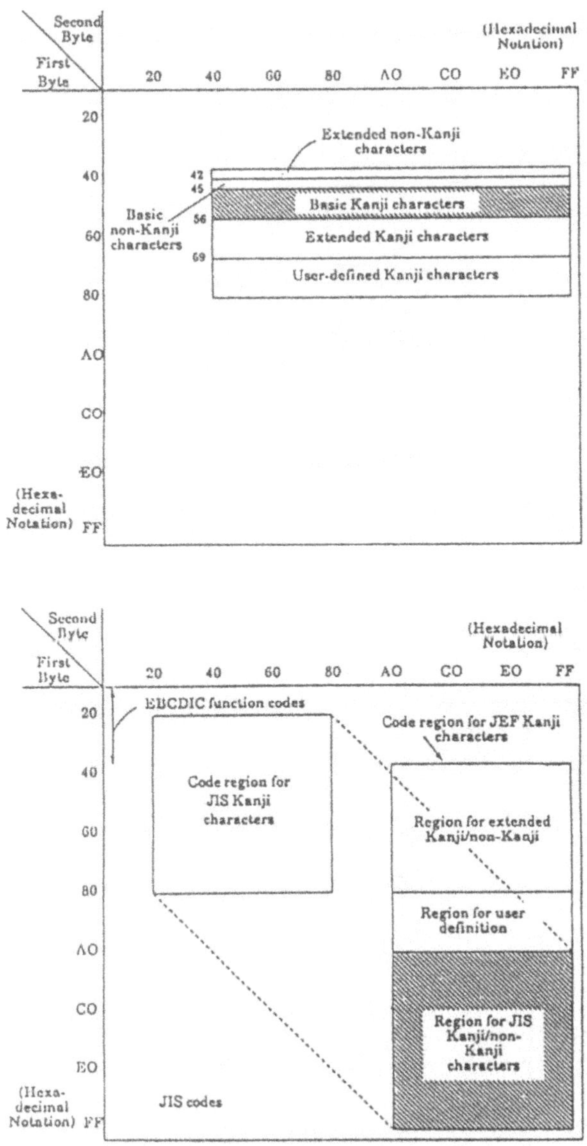

Fig.3-1 IBM and JIS Kanji codes

Although the IBM Kanji code is organized as an expansion of EBCDIC, the JEF code by Fujitsu and the KEIS code by Hitachi adopt the shifted JIS code. In an environment of distributed processing, the character strings belonging to the same character sets, even if each is based on different code notations, must be executed correctly in comparison or move operations. Consequently, a data transformation function may be additionally required, and this is seen to be a very important role of the database management system.

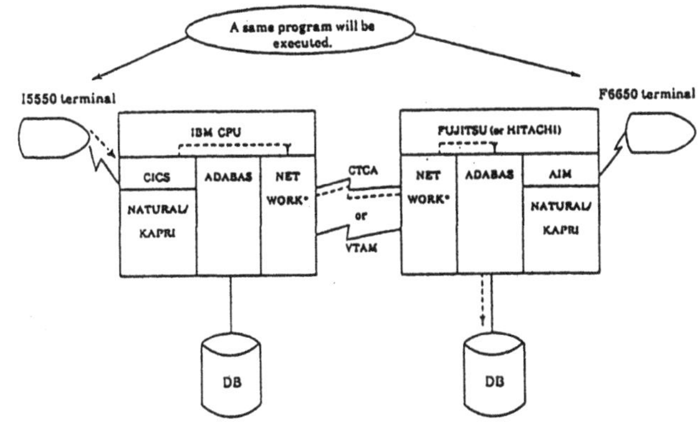

Fig.3-2 ADABAS/NATURAL distributed environment

```
0010 *
0020 *   NOT SUPPORTED DBCS FACILITY   PROGRAM SAMPLE
0030 *
0040 * MOVE
0050 *
0070 RESET #DATA1(A12) #DATA2(A6) #DATA3(A12)
0080 MOVE ' 日本語漢字 ' TO #DATA1
0090 MOVE #DATA1 TO #DATA2
0100 COMPRESS #DATA2 'ABCDEF' INTO #DATA3 LEAVING NO SPACE
0110 DISPLAY #DATA2 / #DATA2(EM = H(6)) #DATA3 / #DATA3(EM = H(12))
0120 END
```

```
      #DATA2                  #DATA3
--------------------  ---------------------

 日本                  日本[illegible]                →character representation
0E4562456648          0E4562456648C1C2C3C4C5C6       →HEX notation

    (after MOVE)              (after COMPRESS)
```

Some data may be currupted when SI code is truncated after executing MOVE statement and SI code of DBCS data is unable to be specified.

Fig.3-3 An Example of data manipulation with trouble

Second, there may be many difficulties in handling shift control codes. In the terminal data stream, double-byte characters are generally distinguished from single-byte characters by checking the beginning and end of strings with the Shift Out/Shift In (SO/SI) control code.

Each manufacturer has its own specifications of the SO/SI codes, and this is an important problem in the distributed processing environment.

The database management system should also be able to completely transform the control codes used by every site (Fig.3-2). Additionally, the internal procedures of the data manipulations - Search, Move, Edit and others - should be revised with various options to keep the results consistent (Fig.3-3).

4 THE DBCS SUPPORT ON THE ADABAS/NATURAL SYSTEM

The double byte character set (DBCS) support of ADABAS/NATURAL consists of two products, the ADABAS/NATURAL code standardization and the DBCS facility.

The former product is designed for correctly processing data manipulations, even among different code notations belonging to the same character set.

In the ADABAS/NATURAL world, all representation of character strings would usually conform to the standard code notation established for each character set in advance (Fig.4-1). DBMS should keep environments of every site and give proper code transformation during only the I/O communication. Consequently, the internal procedures of the data manipulation can keep the results consistent; additionally each site does not need any additional transformation program or huge table.

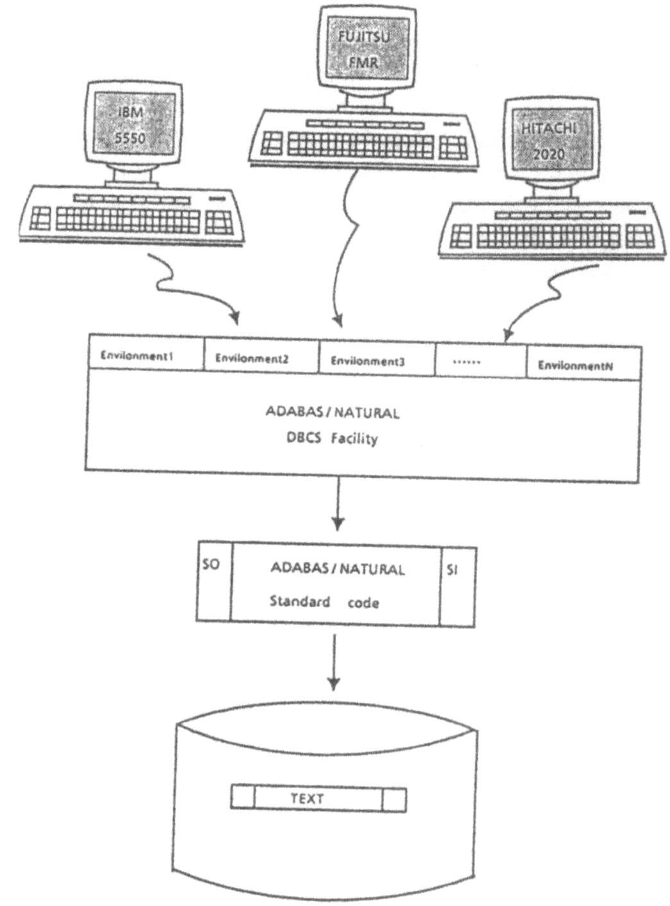

Fig.4-1 ADABAS/NATURAL standard codes

The latter product DBCS facility has been developed so that all NATURAL operations can completely accept every variable, name, and data value described in any double-byte character as well as single-byte character defined as EBCDIC or ASCII. The DBCS facility includes the following strong points:

a. Reinforced Editors

The NATURAL offers four types of editors[2]. The Edit commands affected by supporting DBCS completely are the Split, the Join, the Scan and the Change of any NATURAL editor mode.

All cursor-oriented commands (Join, Split) should be checked to see if the cursor is in the middle of a DBCS field. If so, the cursor has to be on an even byte boundary controlled by the terminal. Additionally, in the split function, the split fields have to be enclosed by SO/SI codes at the end of the split operation.

The Join command checks to see if the two new adjacent fields are both enclosed in SO/SI codes. If so, the terminating SI of the leading field and the starting SO

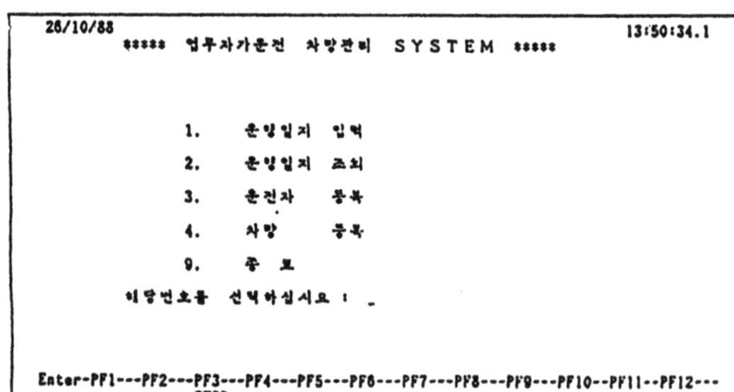

Fig.4-2 Screen supported DBCS

of the following field are eliminated (See Fig.3-3). The Scan and Change commands check to see if the argument strings are enclosed in SO/SI codes and will then locate targets only if the analysed strings are enclosed in SO/SI codes as well.

b. Names written in DBCS

The names of programs, data areas, database areas and others used in the NATURAL environment can be written in DBCS. It is important for the synthesized data management, documentation, and program maintenance. If each name cannot exceed n bytes, this means that names coded in DBCS can have up to n/2 characters, including SO/SI codes. These names always have to be enclosed in SO/SI codes to allow NATURAL editors, the NATURAL List functions and the Scan functions to work correctly.

c. DBCS field type

There are two ways for NATURAL to recognize the DBCS field. If a field value is represented in DBCS mode, it starts with the SO code and is terminated with a SI code. These SO/SI codes are part of the field value. Field values passed to or from NATURAL do not need special considerations, with the exception of the NATURAL editors and all possible value splits on an odd-byte boundary. The other possibility to identify field values in DBCS representation is the DBCS field type by the new print mode format 'D'. This format can be specified as a new value to the session parameter, PM (Print mode) = D, which indicates for the given field that the data of that field is completely in DBCS mode. At terminal I/O time NATURAL automatically will add the attribute for these fields to switch the terminal to the correct set. This technique will save two bytes for each field in the database but requires the knowledge of which data is in DBCS mode to process them correctly. The NATURAL data description module (DDM) will accept the specification of 'PM = D' as part of the ADABAS field description.

d. SO/SI preservation during data manipulations

The following main NATURAL statements for data manipulation can also deal with DBCS characters completely:

(1) Separate statement

The Separate function is used for dividing one character string into several other character strings. This statement checks the field contents for a starting SO. If found, all scanning will be done in two-byte steps; the resulting strings will all be enclosed in SO/SI codes.

(2) Compress statement

Compress is the function used for joining two character strings. This statement checks if two joining strings end and start with SO/SI codes and will eliminate them to form one complete DBCS character string. If the delimiter character used is space and the two joining strings are in DBCS mode, the SO/SI codes are removed from the end of the first field as well as from the start of the second field.

(3) Move statement

A check has to be performed if the source field contains data starting with SO when data is moved from one field type alphanumeric into another alphanumeric type field. If so, the resulting field value has to be enclosed in SO/SI codes.

5 CONCLUSION

So far, the handling of double-byte characters in the ADABAS/NATURAL system environment has been supported with an additional product, "KAPRI"[3], by SAGFE. However, it is for just putting the characters on specially designed terminal displays or printers used in Japan.

Recently we have planned to design a complete DBCS support and build it into the nucleus of the ADABAS/NATURAL system in order to deal with double-byte characters correctly for various data manipulations.

It may become easier to build applications for handling other multi-characters sets, in addition to Kanji or Hangul, if the character data are managed on the ADABAS/NATURAL standard code system and operated through the DBCS facility we have presented.

REFERENCES

1) J.D.Becker,"Typing Chinese, Japanese, and Korea", COMPUTER, Jan.1985, pp.27-34

2) Software AG, "Double Byte Character Set", Software AG Internal Document, 1988

3) Software AG of Far East, "KAPRI Reference Manual" (In Japanese), Tokyo, 1988

MARELA
A Matrix Relational Model for Statistical Database Management

Rosine CICCHETTI(1,2), Lotfi LAKHAL(1,3), Serge MIRANDA(1)

(1) Université de Nice-Sophia Antipolis, I3S-CNRS, Bât. 4, Rue A. Einstein, Sophia-Antipolis, 06560 Valbonne, FRANCE.
(2) CERAM, rue Dostoïevski, BP 085, 06902 Sophia-Antipolis
(3) Université de Nancy I-ESSTIN Sophia-Antipolis

Abstract
One of the important issues of statistical database management is to define a data model and language for modelling and manipulating complex statistical summaries in the database. This paper proposes a matrix relational model and language for statistical database management. The matrix relational data structure combines the relation and matrix organizations. It offers a natural and densly built-up representation of complex statistical summaries. It proposes new objects and constructors for statistical database organization. The matrix relational language is an algebraïc query language, using an extended relational algebra.

I. INTRODUCTION

Since the first LBL international workshop on statistical and scientific database management (Menlo Park, California, 1981), research efforts have started examining the basic problems associated with statistical database management systems [3], [8], [18], [21], [22], [24]. We refer to Statistical DataBases -SDB- as databases that contain statistical summaries. Some common examples are census data, mortality data, and environment data for socio-economic applications.
Before describing our contribution to the domain, we present the statistical database concepts and summarize the previous works dealing with SDB. We focus more particularly on relational and nested relational models and pay particular attention to their insufficiencies for statistical data management.

I.1. Statistical Database concepts

Statistical data are described in terms of two types of attributes : *category* and *summary attributes*. The latters are essentially numerical since they correspond to quantitative data being measured or summarized. Category attributes are descriptive fields that characterize summary attributes.
Statistical summaries or macro-data [24] are derived through a twofold operation over raw data (or micro-data [24]. Actually, micro-data are classified according to category attribute values. Then statistical aggregations (e.g. Count, Sum) or statistical analysis functions are applied. They achieve for each class of individuals a summary value. Each of these values is uniquely identified by a combination of category attribute values.
Criterium classification of statistical summary matches *multidimensional space*. Furthermore, since macro-data are dense, this space may be defined by the Cartesian-product of category attribute domains. A null value may be assigned, instead of a summary value, to missing combinations.
In statistical databases, two kinds of summaries may be distinguished :
- *Elementary statistical summaries* which have a unique summary attribute and one multidimensional space ;
- *Complex statistical summaries* grouping elementary summaries according to their common category attributes. Of course they have several summary attributes and are characterized by a set of multidimensional spaces.

At last, among semantical aspects of summaries to be noted, the "nature" of summary attributes is fundamental. It accounts for the fact that their values translate counts, sums, averages, standard deviations, and so on. This notion is essential in data interpretation. Furthermore it adds fundamental information on the possible summarizability of macro-data. Actually, summaries may be derived or not, according to the statistical function used to compute them. Derivable summaries are, in fact, limited to the ones achieved by applying an additive function (Count or Sum). But it is recognized that most of classical functions may be expressed in terms of additive ones [4]. When such an expression can be stated, then they are called calculable functions and their results are equivalent to those of an arithmetic calculation on summaries achieved by using their additive parameter functions. For example, the average may be achieved from "count" and "sum"; covariance parameter are "count", "sum of products" and "sum of squares" ; regression analysis is calculable according to "count", "sum", "sum of products" and "sum of squares". The statistical functions "min" and "max" extract some particular values of summary attributes. They may be considered as selection operations.

I.2. Statistical database example

To illustrate our intent, throughout this article, we consider a statistical database describing student census. Individuals of the examined population are students characterized in particular by their : sex (SEX), socio-professional class (CLASS), study year (YEAR), studied discipline (DISCIP), the fact they are or not grant-holders (GRANT_H) and the possible amount of their grant (GRANT). The four elementary statistical summaries A, B, C and D are supposed to be derived from an individual sub-set matching with the students of Nice University. A and C respectively permit to count Nice students :

- By sex, socio-professional class, study year and the fact that they are grant-holders or not ;
- By sex, discipline, study year and the fact that they are grant-holders or not ;

Summary attributes BTT_GRANT and DTT _GRANT of the summaries B and D correspond to the total amount of student grants. They are achieved by summing up values of attribute GRANT, for the considered individuals.

They respectively give this amount :

- By sex, socio-professional class and study year ;
- By sex, discipline and study year.

Let's consider, for example, the multidimensional space of A. It matches the Cartesian-product of attributes SEX, CLASS, YEAR and GRANT_H. The grouping of the two elementary statistical summaries B and D, according to their common category attributes SEX and YEAR, creates a complex summary, having two summary attributes and two multidimensional spaces that share these category attributes.

I.3. Related Works

Some statistical data models and query languages have been proposed in litterature. They may be classed in :

- Semantic data models such as SUBJECT [17] and SAM* [23]. They provide new concepts relevant to issues of statistical database design.
- Extended Relational Models and Languages, like ABE [12], QBSRT [10], Category-Summary-Statistical Function Model [4], Category-Numerical Relation Algebra [9], [7], and a user-friendly database query language, STBE [19]. They use relations as a statistical database management support.

Statistical query languages, such as ABE, QBSRT and STBE, extend relational algebra by integrating a few new Filter and Composition operations, like aggregation (in all mentionned languages), aggregation-by-template, i.e. aggregation on relation with multivaluate attributes (in STBE), bi-directional outer join (in STBE), restrictions and statistical procedures (in QBSRT, and Category-Summary Statistical Function Model). The two major attempts to define algebra for statistical database management have been proposed by Ghosh [8, 9], and by Fortunato, and al. [7]. They encompass a large number of suitable category numerical operators, with varying complexity, but they deal with elementary statistical summaries. None of these works include transposition operations, as query language primitives. Although these manipulations are considered (with aggregation) as some of the most common operations in statistical databases [18], [21].

I.4. Insufficiencies of relational and nested relational supports

The relational model and later the nested relational models [1] provide neither explicit concepts for statistical data representation nor efficient processing capabilities. Without involving physical support issues [18], we pinpoint some problems inherent in relational representation of statistical summaries.

A clear distinction between category and summary attributes cannot be stated. Nevertheless, such a distinction is fundamental for statistical data interpretation and also for manipulations. Actually, operations on category attributes are very different from summary attribute handling.

An another constraint of relational modelling concerns the representation of the summary attribute semantics. It cannot be entirely explicit even through the domain concept, for the "nature" of such attributes is untranslatable in this model. Nevertheless, it determines the summarizability of macro-data sets. Therefore, it is not possible to check the exacteness of derived summary values, specially when cascades of aggregations are realized.

The only complex summaries to be represented through relation must have a unique multi-dimensional space, i.e. their summary attributes must be described by the same category attributes. Therefore, in most common cases, several relations are required to represent statistical summaries in the database. This is very embarrassing specially when considering the problem of summary proliferation in statistical databases [22].

At last, the relational algebra cannot answer statistician's requests. No restructuring data capabilities (transposition) are supplied for relation data structure. Relation derivations are not controled and the interrogation primitives ought to be used in a more restrictive frame.

Example 1. The statistical database "student census" needs four 3NF relations (in each relation, category attributes are a key, and summary attribute a non-key). They are shown in figure 1.

Nested relational model has been developped in order to extend the applicability of the relational model to non-business applications, such as computer-aided design, image processing, office automation and text retrieval [1]. Nested relations have claimed that they are suitable for modelling and handling statistical data. This is true but nevertheless they are inefficient [8], in part, because they inherit some inadequacies of relational data structure. They also complicate the identification of elementary statistical summaries within a complex one. Nested relation algebra is very powerful for the mentionned applications that deal with individual or hierarchical individual records. However, statistical databases deal with summaries of raw data and lead to ignore the details of individuals [4].

Example 2. To illustrate our intent, we have chosen the nested relational model of (Abiteboul and al. [2]) called Verso model, since it integrates Transposition abilities.

A clear representation of the statistical database example needs two nested relations (illustrated in figure 2) in the Verso model. Actually this model does not allow attributes to be repeated.

I.5. Towards a statistical database model

The weaknesses of relational and nested relational models, pinpointed previously, have led some searchers to propose specific modelling approaches. In these works, the proposed data structures are defined by considering the summary characteristics. Thus, they are more satisfying than the examined models. Nevertheless, some problems are not solved. Among them, we already mention the structuration constraints (only elementary summaries may be represented) and the lack of transposition operations. Let's also note that summary attribute "nature" is not taken into account. Therefore derivations cannot be con-troled.

The objective of our approach is to avoid the limits given previously for summary modelling whilst preserving the strengths of specific structuration approaches.

The model that we define is called MAtrix RELAtional model -MARELA-. It makes use of relational structure in order to represent raw data and introduces a new data structure for summaries.

At last, it proposes a formal frame for the combined micro and macro-data management.

Later on, we describe the different aspects of our proposals. First of all, we present our structuration approach for statistical summaries. Then we detail the manipulation capabilities of our algebraïc language and pay particular attention to its most original possibilities for both raw and summarized data.
We conclude by giving a complementary approach of MARELA. It is based on the same concepts and aims at the same objectives. But it avoids, at least, two constraints inherent in MARELA.

SEX	YEAR	CLASS	BTT_GRANT
F	1	Farmers	23.625
F	1	Workers	45.000
F	1	Managers	1.000
F	2	Farmers	11.700
F	2	Workers	34.500
F	2	Managers	1.000
M	1	Farmers	13.220
M	1	Workers	60.200
M	1	Managers	7.700
M	2	Farmers	4.560
M	2	Workers	50.750
M	2	Managers	5.500

SEX	YEAR	DISCIP	DTT_GRANT
F	1	Computer science	26.250
F	1	Mathematics	27.000
F	1	Physics	37.125
F	2	Computer science	28.800
F	2	Mathematics	17.900
F	2	Physics	28.200
M	1	Computer science	46.740
M	1	Mathematics	23.630
M	1	Physics	27.250
M	2	Computer science	41.730
M	2	Mathematics	28.880
M	2	Physics	29.250

SEX	YEAR	GRANT_H	DISCIP	CNB
F	1	Yes	Computer science	25
F	1	Yes	Mathematics	18
F	1	Yes	Physics	27
F	1	No	Computer science	39
F	1	No	Mathematics	21
F	1	No	Physics	14
F	2	Yes	Computer science	24
F	2	Yes	Mathematics	15
F	2	Yes	Physics	20
F	2	No	Computer science	33
F	2	No	Mathematics	20
F	2	No	Physics	18
M	1	Yes	Computer science	38
M	1	Yes	Mathematics	17
M	1	Yes	Physics	25
M	1	No	Computer science	37
M	1	No	Mathematics	29
M	1	No	Physics	23
M	2	Yes	Computer science	29
M	2	Yes	Mathematics	19
M	2	Yes	Physics	25
M	2	No	Computer science	42
M	2	No	Mathematics	28
M	2	No	Physics	25

SEX	YEAR	GRANT_H	CLASS	ANB
F	1	Yes	Farmers	15
F	1	Yes	Workers	30
F	1	Yes	Managers	2
F	1	No	Farmers	14
F	1	No	Workers	25
F	1	No	Managers	5
F	2	Yes	Farmers	9
F	2	Yes	Workers	23
F	2	Yes	Managers	1
F	2	No	Farmers	12
F	2	No	Workers	29
F	2	No	Managers	5
M	1	Yes	Farmers	10
M	1	Yes	Workers	43
M	1	Yes	Managers	7
M	1	No	Farmers	9
M	1	No	Workers	40
M	1	No	Managers	8
M	2	Yes	Farmers	3
M	2	Yes	Workers	35
M	2	Yes	Managers	5
M	2	No	Farmers	5
M	2	No	Workers	42
M	2	No	Managers	8

Figure 1. Relational representation of statistical database "Student Census".

SEX YEAR GRANT_H(CLASS ANB)* (DISCIP CNB)*

SEX	YEAR	GRANT_H	CLASS	ANB	DISCIP	CNB
F	1	Yes	Farmers	15	Computer science	25
			Workers	30	Mathematics	18
			Managers	2	Physics	27
F	1	No	Farmers	14	Computer science	39
			Workers	25	Mathematics	21
			Managers	5	Physics	14
F	2	Yes	Farmers	9	Computer science	24
			Workers	23	Mathematics	15
			Managers	1	Physics	20
F	2	No	Farmers	12	Computer science	33
			Workers	29	Mathematics	20
			Managers	5	Physics	18
M	1	Yes	Farmers	10	Computer science	38
			Workers	43	Mathematics	17
			Managers	7	Physics	25
M	1	No	Farmers	9	Computer science	37
			Workers	40	Mathematics	29
			Managers	8	Physics	23
M	2	Yes	Farmers	3	Computer science	29
			Workers	35	Mathematics	19
			Managers	5	Physics	25
M	2	No	Farmers	5	Computer science	42
			Workers	42	Mathematics	28
			Managers	8	Physics	25

SEX YEAR (CLASS BTT_GRANT)*(DISCIP DTT_GRANT)*

SEX	YEAR	CLASS	BTT_GRANT	DISCIP	DTT_GRANT
F	1	Farmers	23.625	Computer science	26.250
		Workers	45.000	Mathematics	27.000
		Managers	1.000	Physics	37.125
F	2	Farmers	11.700	Computer science	28.800
		Workers	34.500	Mathematics	17.900
		Managers	1.000	Physics	28.200
M	1	Farmers	13.220	Computer science	46.740
		Workers	60.200	Mathematics	23.630
		Managers	7.700	Physics	27.250
M	2	Farmers	4.560	Computer science	41.730
		Workers	50.750	Mathematics	28.880
		Managers	5.500	Physics	29.250

Figure 2. Nested relational representation of statistical database "Student Census".

II. MATRIX RELATION MODEL

In most of the research works on advanced databases (including object oriented databases) [1], hierarchical data organization predominates so much that one may forget to wonder : is the hierarchical data organization a universal representation ? i.e is it suitable for all advanced database applications ?

In a SDB context and for the reasons given previously, few approaches have prefered a two-dimensional table organization [7], [10], [19]. In the same sense, we propose a *matricix data organization*, through a new data structure : Matrix Relation -MR- (also called Complex Statistical Table in [15, 16]). It combines relational and matrix organizations. Actually, it is inspired by concepts such as those of attribute, semantical domain and relation, which are adapted in order to represent category attributes and multidimensional spaces. It also makes use of a matrix organization for summary attribute values.
The aim of MR structure is to make explicit all the specific concepts of SDB. In the organization choices, we try to avoid the gap between the formal definition of the data structure and its perception by the user.

The MR structure may be seen as a modular one since the elementary summary representation, through Atomic Matrix Relation - AMR -, is a particular case of complex summary structuration. Futhermore any AMR may be identified within MRs. In the same way as AMRs may be grouped to achieve MRs, the latters may also be gathered within a more complex MR. The rules that allow such building up are based both on organization coherence and on AMR and MR semantics.
Except these integrity constraints, it does not exist limits in the complexity of summaries that may be represented through MRs. An another point to be noted is that MARELA model enables to capture the whole semantics of summary attributes, including their "nature".

In this section, we detail the objects and constructors of the model. Then we present AMR and MR in an intuitive and formal way. We also have a glance at their compatibility.

II.1. Objects and Constructors

The two basic objects in MARELA are those of category attribute and summary attribute. They can be perceived as atomic information of different types. To represent complex summaries, attribute organization requires the following constructors : Cartesian-Product, List and Union (of structures). Category attributes are organized according to a category attribute schema, i.e. a list of attributes. Its instances permit to represent a multidimensional space by using the Cartesian-Product constructor. Such schemas take place in the *row* and *column* dimension that structure an AMR. AMR allows the representation of elementary summary. The values of its unique summary attribute are organized in a matrix form, achieved by the List constructor. Any AMR is characterized by the statistical function used to compute its summary values.
AMRs are grouped to achieve MR representing complex summaries. Observed on the component elements of MR, such an organization process includes the Union constructor. This permits to define category attribute multi-schema, in an intensive and extensive way, from category attribute schemas of the AMRs components of the MR, and from their instances. The Union allows to represent data sets of different types. Through two multi-schemas, the row and column ones, achieved by the Union constructor, it is possible to represent heterogeneous and potentially shared multi-dimensional spaces. Summary attributes of the components AMRs are organized as a matrix in the MR. The summary-value structuring is based on List and Union constructors.

MRs have a schema and instances. They are characterized by the statistical functions that permit to derive their summary attributes. These functions are also organized in a matrix way.

II.2. Atomic Matrix Relation

The AMR schema may be perceived as an array in which category attribute names appear in the row and column headings, and the unique summary attribute matches the cell. The statistical function used to compute its values is associated to the AMR. Row and column dimensions of the AMR are organized according to category attribute schemas, defined as a list of category attribute names. The category attribute schemas may be perceived as relation schemas.

AMR schema is defined as follows :
SCHEMA(AMR) = (X_r, X_c, V, f) where :

- $X_r = [x_r^1, x_r^2, \ldots, x_r^m]$ is the row category attribute schema ;
- $X_c = [x_c^1, \ldots, x_c^m]$ is the column category attribute schema ;
- V is the summary attribute of the AMR and
- f is the function used to calculate V.

Futhermore, we have : $X_r \cap X_c \cap \{V\} = \emptyset$.

Example 3. Let's consider the representation of the statistical summaries A, B, C and D through AMRs. Their schemas are given below in textual form. Their tabular representations are illustrated in figure 3.
A = ([SEX, CLASS], [YEAR, GRANT_H], ANB, Count)
B =([SEX, CLASS], [YEAR], B_TT_GRANT, Sum)
C= ([SEX, DISCIP], [YEAR, GRANT_H], CNB, Count)
D = ([SEX, DISCIP], [YEAR], D_TT_GRANT, Sum)

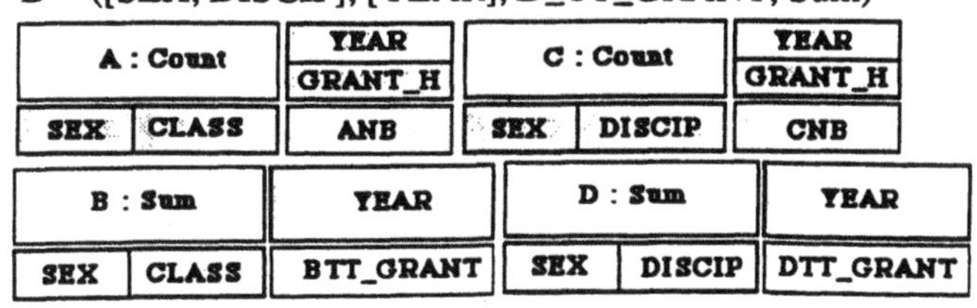

Figure 3. A,B,C,D schemas.

Later on, we just give the tabular representation, in order to illustrate MR structure.

AMR instances are seen as an array, filled up with category attribute values and those of the summary attribute. The latters are structured according to the instances of row and column category attribute schemas, defined by the cartesian-product of value sub-sets of their attributes.
AMR extension is defined as follows :
EXTENSION(AMR) =
(VAL(X_r), VAL(X_c), M(V)) where :

$$VAL(X_r) = [t_r \,/\, t_r \in \bigotimes_{i=1}^{m} DOM(x_r^i)]$$

$$VAL(X_c) = [t_c \,/\, t_c \in \bigotimes_{j=1}^{n} DOM(x_c^j)]$$

$M(V) = [v_{|VAL(Xr)|,|VAL(Xc)|}] \; / \; v_{P(tr),P(tc)} \in DOM(V)$

with $DOM(V) = REAL \cup NULL \mid INTEGER \cup NULL$;
$t_r \in VAL(X_r)$ and $t_c \in VAL(X_c)$.
$P : VAL(X_r|X_c) \rightarrow |VAL(X_r|X_c)|$.

Example 4. The instances of AMRs A, B, C, and D are shown in figure 4.
Let's consider the AMR B and more specially female students in the class "farmers". The total amount of their grants for the first and second study years are respectively 23.625 and 11.700.

A : Count		1 Yes	1 No	2 Yes	2 No
F	Farmers	15	14	9	12
F	Workers	30	25	23	29
F	Managers	2	5	1	5
M	Farmers	10	9	3	5
M	Workers	43	40	35	42
M	Managers	7	8	5	8

B : Sum		1	2
F	Farmers	23.625	11.700
F	Workers	45.000	34.500
F	Managers	1.600	1.000
M	Farmers	13.220	4.560
M	Workers	60.200	50.750
M	Managers	7.700	5.500

C : Count		1 Yes	1 No	2 Yes	2 No
F	Computer science	25	39	24	33
F	Mathematics	18	21	15	20
F	Physics	27	14	20	18
M	Computer science	38	37	29	42
M	Mathematics	17	29	19	28
M	Physics	25	23	25	25

D : Sum		1	2
F	Computer science	26.250	28.800
F	Mathematics	27.000	17.900
F	Physics	37.125	28.200
M	Computer science	46.740	41.730
M	Mathematics	23.630	28.880
M	Physics	27.250	29.250

Figure 4. A,B, C, D extensions.

II.3. Matrix Relation

MR is a grouping of AMRs. It allows the representation of complex statistical summaries. It is achieved by a twofold concatenation, according to rows and columns, of different AMRs. The row and column dimensions of MR are said to be structured according to row and column multi-schemas of category attributes (Union of category attribute schemas).
MR instances may be perceived as an array of category and summary attribute values, achieved by concatenation, according to rows and columns, of instances of its AMR components.

MR is defined as follows :
$MR = [AMR_{m,n}] \; / \; \forall \, i \in [1...m]$
Let's note $AMR_{ij}(X_r)$, the row category schema Xr in AMR_{ij} and $AMR_{ij}(X_c)$, the column category schema Xc in AMR_{ij}.
$AMR_{i1}(X_r) = AMR_{i2}(X_r) = ... = AMR_{in}(X_r)$.
$AMR_{i1}(VAL(X_r)) = ... = AMR_{in}(VAL(X_r))$.
and $\forall \, j \in [1...n]$
$AMR_{1j}(X_c) = AMR_{2j}(X_c) = ... = AMR_{mj}(X_c)$.
$AMR_{1j}(VAL(X_c)) = ... = AMR_{mj}(VAL(X_c))$.

Example 5. If the user whishes to work on summaries A, B, C and D, he may gather the corresponding AMRs, within MR Z1 whose schema is given in figure 5.
Z1 instances are illustrated in figure 5. Let's consider female students in the class "farmers", the following information is given :
- The population size in the first and the second study year respectively, for both grant-holders and non holders which are 15, 14, 9, and 12 ;
- The total amount of grants for the first and the second year are respectively 23.625 and 11.700.

Z1			
A : Count	B : Sum	YEAR	YEAR
C : Count	D : Sum	GRANT_H	
SEX	CLASS	ANB	BTT_GRANT
SEX	DISCIP	CNB	DTT_GRANT

Z1: A : Count, B : Sum / C : Count, D : Sum		1 Yes	1 No	2 Yes	2 No	1	2
F	Framers	15	14	9	12	23.625	11.700
F	Workers	30	25	23	29	45.000	34.500
F	Managers	2	5	1	5	1.600	1.000
M	Framers	10	9	3	5	13.220	4.560
M	Workers	43	40	35	42	60.200	50.750
M	Managers	7	8	5	8	7.700	5.500
F	Computer science	25	39	24	33	26.250	28.800
F	Mathematics	18	21	15	20	27.000	17.900
F	Physics	27	14	20	18	37.125	28.200
M	Computer science	38	37	29	42	46.740	41.730
M	Mathematics	17	29	19	28	23.630	28.880
M	Physics	25	23	25	25	27.250	29.250

Figure 5. Z1 schema and extension.

The tabular presentation, used in previous figures, shows the MR schema in form of an array (workable for a user-friendly interface) encompassing four areas :
- Title area, displays the MR name and component AMR identifiers in a matrix form. The statistical functions used to calculate its summary attribute is associated with each AMR ;

- Row heading area (in grey), allows the presentation of the row multi-schema of category attributes, in such a manner that any row i describes, from left to right, the ith schema of category attribute multi-schema ;
- Column heading area (in grey), permits in the same way to present the column multi-schema ;
- Cell area, groups summary attribute names as a matrix.

In the chosen presentation for AMR and MR instances, the four described areas are preserved. Any row (or column) of the row heading area describes, from left to right, one instance of row multi-schema of category attributes. The summary values appear in cells.

II.4. Compatibility of MR

Any two MRs are compatible according to rows (or columns) if their row (or column) multi-schemas encompass compatible category attributes. Moreover if their multi-schema instances are identical, they are said to be completely compatible. These two kinds of MR compatibility supply the semantical rules necessary to build up more complex MRs. Later on, these kinds of operations will be refered as compositions.

Example 6. The AMRs A et B are completely compatible according to row dimension. B and D are completely compatible according to column dimension.
MR Z4, whose schema and instances are shown in figure 6, represents the population of Nice students on one hand by sex and class (matching with AMR E), and on the other hand by sex and discipline (matching with AMR F). The MRs Z1 and Z4 are compatible according to rows but not completely. Actually, the category attribute CLASS does not have the same values in these MRs.

Z4		Ø
E : Count		
F : Count		
SEX	CLASS	ENB
SEX	DISCIP	FNB

Z4		Ø
E : Count		
F : Count		
F	Farmers	150
F	Workers	320
F	Tradesmen	405
M	Farmers	102
M	Workers	370
M	Tradesmen	390
F	Computer sciences	294
F	Mathematics	212
F	Physics	120
M	Computer sciences	350
M	Mathematics	195
M	Physics	164

Figure 6. Z4 schema and extension.

II.5. MR contributions

The MR structure is really suitable for summary representation. To make sure that its advantages are convincing, let's have a short comparison with the models examined in the first section.
On a semantical point of view, MR is beyond relation and nested relation, for at least two reasons. The first one concerns the distinction between category and summary attributes. The second refers to its ability to represent summary with unlimited complexity. This last argument may also be used in the comparison with specific modelling approaches. Furthermore, the latters do not offer a rigourous frame for summary representation. Nevertheless, we think that such a frame is strongly required, at least to be a solid base to define manipulation operators.
An another interesting point is that elementary summaries are explicit within MRs. This is important to make the structure easy to comprehend for the user and to facilitate his interpretation of data.
At last, MR proposes an original solution to capture summary attribute semantics, by integrating the functions used to calculate the macro-data sets.
We now are going to show how our manipulation proposals take advantage of MR contributions.

III MARELA LANGUAGE

Conventional database query languages are defined by taking into account the goals of management applications, and more specifically the detailed data retrieval. Nevertheless these kinds of operations play a minor part in statistical applications while new needs rise. This is why these languages cannot be satisfying in our context.
In this section, we describe our proposals but, first of all, in order to emphasize their interests, we give the functionnalities that a manipulation language for SDB must offer according to us.

III.1. Operation classes on SDB

To property achieve workable SDB, it is necessary to propose suitable summary manipulation capabilities. For this reason, an identification of specific needs of statisticians is essential. Some of them have been suggested in [17], [21], [24]. We keep and complete them through the following generic classification : Composition, Filter and Transposition operations.

Composition. In research works whose major objective concerns complex summary modelling, composition facilities are strongly required. They concern the building up of more complex summaries. We think that statisticians cannot satisfy their needs with elementary summary manipulation. A significant example, illustrating this need, is to consider an elementary summary and the totals derived from the aggregation of several (or all) category attributes. Associating these totals with the macro-data from which they are computed (in order to manipulate them as a whole), imperatively requires capabilities of complex summary modelling. A data structure allowing complex summary representation may be, if required compositions are supplied, an interesting tool for grouping elementary statistical summaries. Such groupings may be operated to make comparisons but also to optimize storage efficiently (by sharing common data). They also may be perceived as an organization tool for the database. Actually gathering coherent summaries can facilitate the retrieval of relevant ones. This last objective is particularly interesting when considering one characteristic of statistical databases being summary proliferation.

Filter. To allow users to select relevant data within a summary, filter operations must be supplied. They work on attribute value sets, by refining or enlarging them. They also permit to extract a summary belonging to a more complex one. The first purpose of these manipulations is macro-data retrieval but they also play a part in the joining of statistical summaries with homogeneous, but nevertheless different, multidimensional spaces. However the main operations in this class refer to summary aggregation. They consist in removing one or several category attributes whilst operating an aggregation of the corresponding summary values, in order to achieve a summary with a coarser level of detail than the initial one.

Transposition. One of the identified needs for summary manipulation is to introduce a dynamic aspect in summary structure [18]. Actually data structure must be able to change, i.e. be restructured according to user requests. These reorganizations, that we call transpositions, have a presentation goal, since they allow users to examine data exactly the way they want to. They also take an important part in the joining of statistical summaries that are organized in a different way but with homogeneous multidimensional spaces. Transpositions are also essential when combined with summary aggregation and composition.

III.2. MARELA manipulation principle

The goal of MARELA language is to allow the user to manipulate statistical data being raw or detailed. It operates on a twofold structure, relation and MR ones. Relations are used to represent micro-data and MR for macro-data. Its basic idea is to take advantage of all the capabilities of relational algebra while extending it in order to take new needs into consideration.
Based on relational primitives, MARELA makes also use of the relational aggregation operator, defined by Klug [12], and of the external joins [6]. The first one permits to create aggregated relations and the seconds play a part in MR compositions.
MARELA proposes an arithmetical aggregation

operator to complete Klug's one and two operators RELATION and TABLE, that realize translation between the two data structures being used. To prepare the conversion between relation and AMR, DPJOIN operator is proposed.
RELATION and TABLE seem, at least in their phylosophical existence, like Nest and Unnest operators, being proposed in N1NF relational models [1]. But the latters proceed to the creation of a hierarchical and then a "flat" structure even through the operators that we introduce create a matrix and then a "flat" structure.
Every time it is possible MARELA makes use of relational algebra to manipulate summaries and when this algebra cannot answer the needs, it proposes specific operators.
So we can offer the user possibilities to make aggregations which are controled and really adapted to summaries. We also come up to users' expectations in matter of summary re-organization. The different operators that we define for that, have few equivalents in the other approaches of summary management. Nevertheless, they answer a need considered as essential by the specialists.
MARELA encompasses possibilities of creation, transposition, composition and aggregation with additive functions, of complex statistical summaries. The principle of MARELA is illustrated in the figure 7.

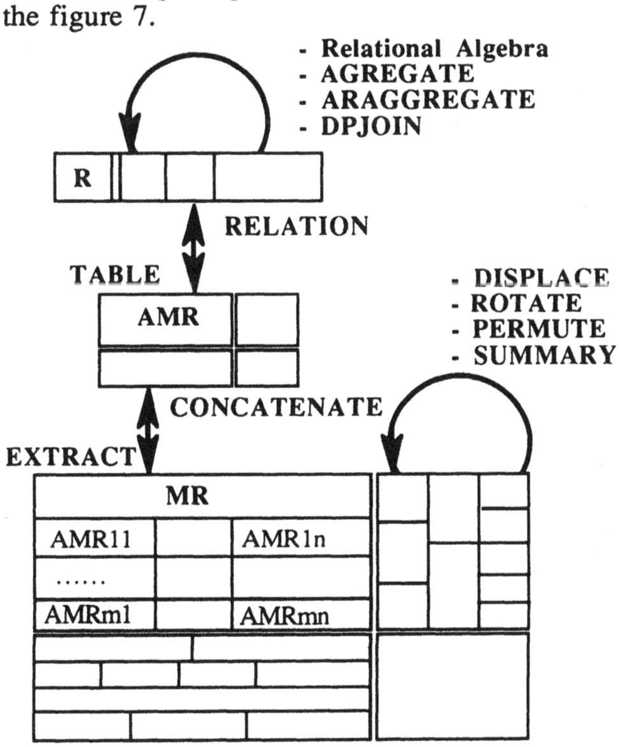

Figure 7. MARELA principle

III.3. Algebraïc operators

In this section, we have a survey on the three components of MARELA language, i.e. an extended relational algebra, primitives consecrated to structure translation and specific operators to manipulate MRs.
For each component, we pinpoint the more interesting operators.

Extended relationnal algebra :
Relationnal algebra is really suitable to manipulate raw data since they are not very different from classical data in management applications. However, the summary creation possibilities are too restrictive. Actually, in a statistical context, aggregations and arithmetical calculations must be combined to produce the required parameters of calculable functions (for example sum of products, sum of square, ...).
MARELA language offers this possibility through the ARAGREGATE operator. It is defined as follows :
let's have a relation R(U), X a subset of U attributes, t[X] the projected tuple t on X, f a statistical additive function, A and B two numerical attributes of U, that are not necessarily distinct.
ARAGGREGATE(R(X), f(op(A,B) = Y)
= R'(X,Y)
= {t[X] o y / t ∈ R and y = f(op(t'[A], t'[B]))/
t' ∈ R and t'[X] = t[X]}
where op is one of the basic arithmetical operators and o stands for concatenation.

Such an operator, after a preliminary grouping of tuples, makes for each tuple an arithmetical calculation from the values of two numerical attributes and adds up the achieved results for each stated classe of tuples.

To translate a relation R(X, Y, Z), with $|Z| = 1$, and $X \cup Y \rightarrow Z$, into an AMR(X_r, X_c, V, f), the join dependency $\otimes(X, Y)$ must be hold in $\Pi_{X,Y}(R)$, since there is a summary value $v_{P(t_r),P(t_c)}$ for each couple (t_r, t_c). If a relation does not satisfy this dependency, DPJOIN must be applied.
It is is defined as follows :
let's have a relation R(U), X, Y two subsets of U such as the join dependency $\otimes(X, Y)$ is not hold in R.

$$\mathrm{DPJOIN}(R(X, Y)) = R'(X, Y) = ® (R, \underset{X \cup Y = X \cup Y}{\otimes} \Pi_X(R), \Pi_Y(R)$$

where :

- ® is the symbol of the left outer join ;
- ⊗ stands for the cartesian product and
- Π is the projection operator.

The join dependency ⊗(X, Y) is hold in R'.

Example 7. The DPJOIN operator is illustrated in the following figure, by giving an example of relation (on the left) and the result of DPJOIN (on the right).

A	B	C	D
a1	b1	c1	1
a1	b1	c2	2
a1	b2	c1	3
a1	b2	c1	4
a2	b1	c1	5

A	B	C	D
a1	b1	c1	1
a1	b1	c2	2
a1	b2	c1	3
a1	b2	c1	4
a2	b1	c1	5
a2	b1	c2	NULL

Figure 8 : DPJOIN use

Translation operators :

To allow the AMR creation from relation and conversely, we introduce the primitives TABLE and RELATION. They make up a bridge between the relational structure and the MR one.

Aggregated relations, achieved by AGGREGATE or ARAGGREGATE, may be converted into AMRs using the TABLE operator. To realize such a translation, the aggregated relation must represent elementary summary and have to satisfy the two following constraints :

- it exists a functional dependency between all the category attributes and the summary one ;
- an embedded join dependency is satisfied in the relation.

The TABLE operator is defined as follows :

AMR = TABLE(R(X, Y, Z), f) with :

SCHEMA(AMR) = (X_r, X_c, V, f) and

$X_r = X$, $X_c = Y$, $V = Z$.

EXTENSION(AMR)

= (VAL(X_r), VAL(X_c), M(V)) where :

VAL(X_r) = $\Pi_X(R)$, VAL(X_c) = $\Pi_Y(R)$

and

$M(V) = [v_{P(tr),P(tc)}] \,/\, \forall\, t \in R,\ v_{P(tr),P(tc)} = t[Z]$.

$t_r = t[X]$, $t_c = t[Y]$.

When the DPJOIN result is converted into AMR, by TABLE, the introduced null values have the following semantics :

- they are considered like 0 if the statistical function used to aggregated the relation is Sum or Count ;
- they are similar to respectively to $-\infty$, $+\infty$ if the statistical function is Max, Min.

The RELATION operator realizes the inverse translation. It creates an aggregated relation from an AMR. It is defined as follows :

RELATION(AMR(X_r , X_c, V, f) = R(X, Y, Z)

$= \{t \,/\, t[X] = t_l,\ t[Y] = t_c,\ t[Z] = v_{P(tr),P(tc)}\}$

with $X \cup Y \rightarrow Z$.

Specific operator on MRs :

To manipulate summaries, MARELA makes use of relational algebra. But it cannot be sufficient to answer statisticians' needs. This is why we propose some additional possibilities.

In the composition class, we define the CONCATENATE operator. It allows to gather completely compatible MRs, in order to achieve a more complex one. It is defined as follows :

Let's have the two following MRs :

MR1 = [$AMR_{m1,n1}$] and MR2 = [$AMR_{m2,n2}$]

CONCATENATE(d, MR1, MR2)

= [$AMR_{m1+m2,n1}$]

if d = 'c', i.e. MR1 and MR2 are completely compatible according to columns.

or

= [$AMR_{m1,n1+n2}$]

if d = 'r', i.e. MR1 and MR2 are completely compatible according to rows.

The filter operators in MARELA are EXTRACT and SUMMARY. The first one extracts a MR from a more complex one. The latter provide MR aggregations, by removing one or several category attribute and summing up the associated summary values. Before realizing this calculation,

SUMMARY makes sure that an additive function characterized the MR to be aggregated.
The SUMMARY formal definition is given in [15]. The EXTRACT one is as follows :

Let's have the MR = $[AMR_{m,n}]$
EXTRACT(MR, $[AMR_{m1,n1}]$) = $[AMR_{m1,n1}]$ with $m1 \leq m$ and $n1 \leq n$.

The transposition class is made up of three basic operators : DISPLACE, ROTATE and PERMUTE. The first one modifies the order of category attributes within a schema. The second one changes the dimension to which a category attribute belongs. The latter inverse the two multi-schemas of a MR.
Let's note that CONCATENATE and EXTRACT may play a transposition part by offering possibilities of dynamic modifications of the schema order within a multi-schema.
We do not present here the formal definitions of the transposition primitives. They are given in [15]. But we emphasize their importance, particularly in a grouping process of MRs, with an example.

Example 8. Let's consider the AMR C' (the AMR C is supposed to be derived from C', and is informationnaly equivalent to it, i.e. RELATION(C') = RELATION(C)). Its schema and instances are given in figure 9.

C' : Count			GRANT_H
SEX	DISCIP	YEAR	C'NB

C' : Count			Yes	No
F	Computer sciences	1	25	39
F	Computer sciences	2	24	33
F	Mathematics	1	18	21
F	Mathematics	2	15	20
F	Physics	1	27	14
M	Physics	2	20	18
M	Computer sciences	1	38	37
M	Computer sciences	2	20	42
M	Mathematics	1	17	29
M	Mathematics	2	19	20
M	Physics	1	25	23
M	Physics	2	25	25

Figure 9. C' schema and extension.

Transposition possibilities allow to group together A and C', after having transformed C' into C, by using ROTATE operator. The resulting MR Z2 is illustrated in figure 10.

Z2		
A : Count		AN_ET
C : Count		GRANT_H
SEX	CLASS	ANB
SEX	DISCIP	CNB

Z2		1	1	2	2
A : Count					
C : Count		Yes	No	Yes	No
F	Farmers	15	14	9	12
F	Workers	30	25	23	29
F	Managers	2	5	1	5
M	Farmers	10	9	3	5
M	Workers	43	40	35	42
M	Managers	7	8	5	8
F	Computer sciences	25	39	24	33
F	Mathematics	18	21	15	20
F	Physics	27	14	20	18
M	Computer sciences	38	37	29	42
M	Mathematics	17	29	19	28
M	Physics	25	23	25	25

Figure 10. Z2 schema and extension.

At last, complementary filter operations are provided through relational primitives. For instance, outer joins may be used to produce aggregated relations which are completely compatible. This possibility is important particularly when considering the use constraint of CONCATENATE operator.

III.4. MARELA language contributions

On a functional point of view, we consider that MARELA reaches its objectives. Actually, it comes up to statisticians' expectations, pinpointed previously. MARELA encompasses operators for each class of SBD manipulations. We note that none satisfying answer is made in other approaches for transpositions and aggregations. Since these operations are the most common ones in SDB,

particular efforts have been made to integrate related primitives in MARELA. In our model, MR structure may be reorganized through the three transposition operators in order to satisfy statisticians' needs. Summary aggregations are intentionally limited to the correct ones, i.e. they cannot create wrong summary values.
An another strength of MARELA is the formal description of the combined use of relations and MRs. We propose conversion primitives and enrich the relational algebra to property achieve workable translations.
At last the following pratical advantage of our approach must be noted. MARELA may be implemented using a relational DBMS as support. A prototype has been developped on ORACLE with a dictionary approach. Nevertheless, MARELA has a constraint that we mention in the following section.

IV. CONCLUSION

The great difference between raw and detailed data has convinced us that a twofold structure is necessary to represent them in a suitable way. Furthermore they must be manipulated through adapted (and so different) operators. With MARELA, we propose a formal frame for SDB management. Without re-opening the whole question, we note a constraint inherent in MARELA approach : the resorting to relational algebra for summary handling is not an ideal solution. Actually, user may pay particular attention to the use of relational primitives for they may lead to create macro-data sets wrong semantically. Furthermore they imply multiple conversions between the two structures.
To avoid this difficulty, it is sufficient to propose some new operators on MRs (and to eliminate the RELATION operator). They would realize on summaries the operations made through relational algebra, i.e. filter operations as selections or additional composition facilities like outer joins. There is no particular difficulty to define and integrate them in MARELA. So, it is quite easy to avoid the mentionned constraint whilst preserving all the advantages detailed previously.

V. REFERENCES

[1] Abiteboul S., Fischer P. C., Schek H. J. (Eds), "Nested Relations and Complex Objects in Databases", Lecture Notes in Computer Science, Vol. 361, Springer Verlag, 1989.

[2] Abiteboul S., Bidoit N., "Non first normal form relation - An algebra allowing data restructuring", Journal of computer and system sciences, Vol. 33, 1986, pp. 361 -393.

[3] Adam N. R., Wortmann J. C., "Security-Control Methods for Statistical Databases : A Comparative Study", ACM Computing Survey, Vol. 21, 1989, pp. 514-556.

[4] Chen M.C., McNamee L., "On the Data Model and Access Method of Summary Data Management", IEEE Transaction on Knowledge and Data Engineering, Vol. 1, 1989, pp. 519-529.

[5] Cicchetti R., "Contribution à la modélisation des résumés dans les bases de données statistiques", Thèse de Doctorat, Université de Nice, Juin 1990.

[6] Codd E. F., "The relational model for database management. Version 2", Ed. Addison-Wesley , 1990.

[7] Fortunato E., Rafanelli M., Ricci F. L., Sebastio A., "An Algebra for Statistical Data" , in Proceedings of the International Conference on Statistical and Scientific Database Management, 1986, pp. 122-134.

[8] Ghosh S. P., "Statisticians and Statistical Database Management", IBM Research Report N° RJ 6975, San Jose, 1989.

[9] Ghosh S. P., "Category Numerical Relational Operators for Statistical Database Management", IBM Research Report N° RJ 5780, San Jose 1987.

[10] Ghosh S. P., "Statistical Relational Tables for Statistical Database Management", IEEE Transaction on Software Engineering, Vol. 12, 1986, pp. 1106 -1116.

[11] Hebrail G., "Définition de Résumés et Incertitude dans les Grandes Bases de Données", Thèse de Doctorat, Université de Paris-Sud, 1987.

12] Klug A, "Equivalence of Relational Algebra and Relational Calculus Query Languages Having Aggregate Functions", ACM Transaction On Database Systems, Vol. 29, 1982, pp. 699-717.

13) Lakhal L., Cicchetti R., "STAR+, un langage de manipulation de résumés statistiques structurés", Revue AFCET-DUNOD RAIRO-Recherche opérationnelle, Vol. 24 N°4, pp. 365-432, 1990.

[14] Lakhal L., Cicchetti R. , Miranda S., "STAR, un langage de manipulation de bases de données statistiques", Revue -AFCET, Modèles et Bases de Données 12, 1989, pp. 3-20.

[15] Lakhal L., Cicchetti R. , Miranda S., "Complex-Statistical-Table Structure and Operators for Macro Statistical Databases", Foundations of Data Organization and Algorithms. Lecture Notes in Computer Science, Vol. 367, Springer Verlag, 1989, pp. 421-438.

[16] Lakhal L., Cicchetti R. , Miranda S., "Relation and Table Language for Statistical Databases. Mathematical", Foundamentals of Database Systems. Lecture Notes in Computer Science, Vol. 364, Springer Verlag, 1989, pp. 285-300.

[17] Olken F., Rotem D., Shoshani A., Wong H. K. T., "Scientific and Statistical Data Management Research at LBL", Proceedings of the International Conference on Statistical and Scientific Database Management, 1986, pp. 1-20.

[18] Olken F., "Physical Database Support for Scientific and Statistical Database Management", Proceedings of the International Conference on Statistical and Scientific Database Management, 1986, pp. 44-60.

[19] Özsoyoglu G, Matos V., Özsoyoglu Z. M., "Query Processing Techniques in the Summary-Table-By-Example Database Query Language", ACM Transaction On Database Systems, Vol. 14, 1989, pp.526-573.

[20] Rafanelli M., Ricci F. L., "STAQUEL : a Query Language for Satistical Macro Database Management Systems", in Proceedings of Convention Informatique Latine, 1985, pp. 16-19.

[21] Shoshani A., Wong H.K.T., "Statistical and Scientific Database Issues", IEEE Transaction on Software Engineering, Vol. 11, 1985, pp. 1071-1081.

[22] Shoshani A., "Statistical Databases : Characteristics, Problems and some Solutions", in Proceedings of the International Conference on Very Large Databases, 1982, pp. 147-160.

[23] Su S. Y. W., "SAM* : A Semantic Association Model for Corporate and Scientific-Statistical Databases", Information Science, Vol. 29, 1983, pp. 151-199.

[24] Wong H. K.T., "Micro and Macro Statistical / Scientific Database Management", in Proceedings of the IEEE International Conference on Data Engineering, 1984, pp. 104-110.

FUNCTIONAL APPROACH TO CHEMICAL STRUCTURE DATABASES

Y.Q. Luan*, N.Ohbo**, H.Kitagawa**, X.Yu** and Y.Fujiwara**
*Program in Engineering Sciences
**Institute of Information Sciences and Electronics Univ. of Tsukuba

ABSTRACT

This paper presents a new scheme for design and implementation of a functional data model on top of the conventional relational DBMS. Motivation comes from the need for improved tools and techniques for the specification, design and implementation of chemical structure databases. The scheme provides a high-level user interface integrated into the programming language LISP. An extended relational DBMS with capabilities of handing ADTs(Abstract Data Types) is developed. A functional data model, called TIME data model, is designed and implemented as an external model of the extended relational DBMS. The scheme supports behavioral abstraction as well as structural abstraction. Implementation of some features has been completed on UNIX environments and they are put into experimental evaluation.

Key Words and Phrases: Chemical Structure, Abstract Data Type, Functional Data Model Relational Data Model.

1 INTRODUCTION

This paper presents a new scheme for the specification, design and implementation of chemical structure databases. The fundamental ideas are from hierarchical representation of chemical structures by means of the BCT(Block Cutpoint Tree)[16], ADT[12),13),18),21], relational database[4] and functional data model[19].

Information about chemical structures is essential in many engineering and scientific applications, such as substructure searches, structure elucidation from spectral data, drug design, and planning of synthesis. One of the major problems in computer handling of chemical structures is the explosion of time and space complexities caused by increase in the number of atomic combinators. Many attempts have been made to design and implement concise, highly descriptive and easy-to-manipulate models of chemical structures[7),9),17]. The BCT model adopted here is universal and independent of particular applications, and application systems based on it may substantially reduce time and space complexities.

Most of the works in chemical structures have adopted the approach of designing a system tailored to specific chemical applications. Relatively fewer attempts have been made to connect existing chemical structure models with conventional DBMSs, because conventional DBMSs do not allow the modeling of chemical structures in a natural way or at least they do not support the retrieval and manipulation of such structures in a way that is familiar to chemists.

In TIME project, we have designed the TIME chemical data management system, in which an extension of BCT representation model connects with a conventional relational DBMS. A relational DBMS is chosen because of its data-independent representation, and high-level information access facilities. However, straightforward application of the relational model to chemical structure databases lacks constructs in defining hierarchical nature of the decomposition of chemical structures naturally and in defining manipulation of chemical objects such as chemical formulas and chemical graphs in a succinct way.

However, developments in programming language area offer very promising prospects for modeling data accompanied by complicated chemical semantics. ADT in the programming language area facilitates uniform description of chemical structures and other data. An ADT is an encapsulation of a data structure along with a collection of operations for manipulating the data structure. The data language DAPLEX based on the functional data model supports a conceptually natural database interface. Especially it supports powerfully and flexibly the representation of hierarchical relationships. Our scheme is intended to support ADTs in a relational context and to support a functional data model as an external view on top of the relational DBMS. In relational context, ADTs are treated as individual columns of relations. The approach is similar to those of ADT-IN-INGRES[12),21)] and RAD[18)]. By adding ADTs for encapsulating chemical objects such as chemical graphs and chemical formulas to primitive types, sophisticated data structures can be more directly described in the relational framework. In the external view, we treat ADT as a user-defined primitive entity.

The hierarchical decomposition of a chemical structure is represented as a collection of tuples that belong to more than one relation. Therefore a chemical structure can be considered as a complex object[15)] or molecular object[3)]. Typical approaches are based on hierarchical extensions to the relational model such as XSQL[10)] or the nested relations[5),11),14)]. Functional data model as an external view provides facilities for mapping complex objects onto relational database structures and for retrieving these objects as single entities. It also supports traversal among a variety of relationships appearing in these objects.

The scheme proposed in this paper provides a sound basis for the specification, design and implementation for the chemical structure databases. The fundamental features of TIME chemical data management system are as follows.

a) It provides a high-level user interface integrated into the programming language LISP. LISP is used to implement chemical structure applications as well as to manipulate chemical structures in TIME databases.

b) The extended relational DBMS is implemented on the commercially available relational DBMS G-BASE*.

c) A functional data model, called TIME data model, is designed and implemented as an external model of an extended relational DBMS having capability of ADT manipulation.

Our scheme has been implemented on UNIX** environments as a part of the TIME project. Implementation of some features has been completed and they are put into experimental evaluation.

The remainder of this paper is organized as follows. Section 2 describes our model of chemical structures and its representation in the relational model. In section 3 we describe architecture of TIME chemical data management system and the basic semantics and the language interface of TIME data model. In section 4 we apply our scheme to an example chemical structure database to exemplify its applicabilities. Section 5 is devoted to conclusion and discussion of the future research topics.

2 MODELING OF CHEMICAL STRUCTURE

In this section, we present our conceptual database of chemical structures. First we describe a chemical structure model based on BCT. The relational schemas and an illustrative example of database instances are presented. Finally we briefly discuss our motivation for developing an external functional view.

2.1 Segmentation of Chemical Structure: Super Block Segmentation Method

Since many applications of chemical structure databases require substructure searches, an effective and powerful segmentation of a whole structure into meaningful units is a key to successful databases. The BCT representation of chemical stricture is a graph theoretical decomposition method, where intermediate descriptive units are introduced to facilitate substructure searches.

A chemical structure is regarded as a graph whose vertexes and edges correspond to atoms and bonds, respectively. The descriptive unit in the BCT scheme is called a block or a biconnected component of a graph and corresponds to what is called a ring system or a ring assembly, except for blocks that have only two vertexes. An example of the BCT tree is shown in Fig.1, where a cutpoint is defined as a vertex whose removal increases the number of connected components of a graph. This method is powerful for detecting ring systems in a chemical structure. However, it is

* G-BASE is a trademark of RICOH CO., Ltd.
** UNIX is a trademark of AT&T.

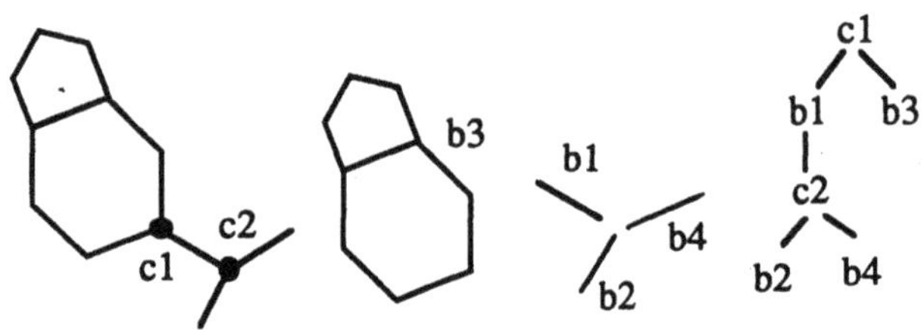

Fig.1 Cutpoints, Blocks and BCT of Chemical Structure

undesirable that too many separated blocks consisting only two vertexes are generated.

In order to overcome this difficulty, we introduce a new descriptive unit, called a supper block, which represents an acyclic part of a chemical structure as a single supperblock without any segmentation. So as a result, what we call a super block is either

a) cyclic supper block: a block whose number of vertexes is more than two, or

b) acyclic super block: a component of a graph generated by removing cyclic super blocks from the original graph.

A SC-tree(Super-block Connection tree) is constructed to represent the connections among super blocks by denoting super blocks as nodes and connections among them as edges. Fig.2(a) shows an example of the super block segmentation and an SC-tree. Cyclic super blocks can further be segmented into fundamental rings by the SSSR (Smallest Set of Smallest Ring) method[8]. An example is shown in Fig.2(b). These segmentation methods are universal and independent of particular applications, and can support manipulation of chemical structures in a way that is familiar to chemists.

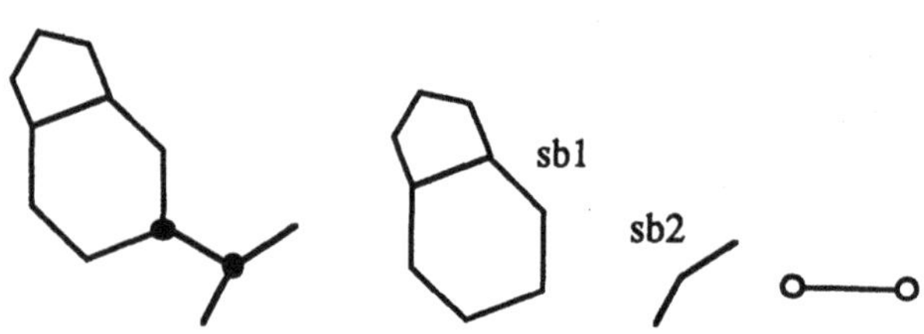

Fig.2(a) A Chemical Structure Graph, its Super Blocks and SC-tree.

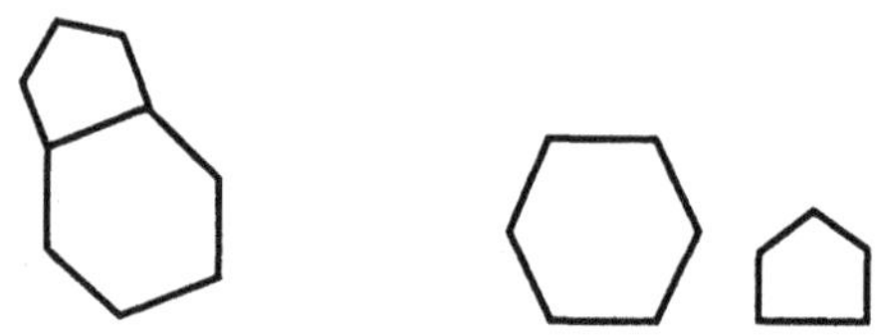

Fig.2(b) A Cyclic Super Block and its SSSR.

2.2 Representation Model of Chemical Structure

In designing a chemical structure database system, we first introduce a structural representation model which satisfies the following requirements.

a) It is able to describe the segmentation of any chemical structure into its substructures.

b) It is able to share common substructures in the database.

c) It is able to reconstruct the original chemical structure by combining all the segmented substructures together in a certain way.

Fig.3 illustrates a conceptual diagram of our representation model. The structural representation of the model is a DAG(Directed Acyclic graph), and can be defined as G = (N, E), where N represents the set of nodes and E represents the set of edges. N has three mutually disjoint subsets, i.e. $N = GN \cup CN \cup LN$. As shown in Fig.3, GN(Graph Node) corresponds to chemical structures and substructures; CN(Connection Node) represents the connections among substructures; and LN(Link Node) represents the correspondences between vertexes in chemical structures and vertexes in substructures.

Constraint imposed on the indegree and outdegree of these three kinds of nodes are listed below.

a) The indegree of GN is greater than or equal to 0, while the outdegree of it is 0 or 1. A graph node of indegree 0 is called a root graph node, and a graph node of outdegree 0 is called a leaf graph node.

b) The indegree of CN is 1, while the outdegree of it is greater than 0.

c) Both the indegree and outdegree of LN are 1.

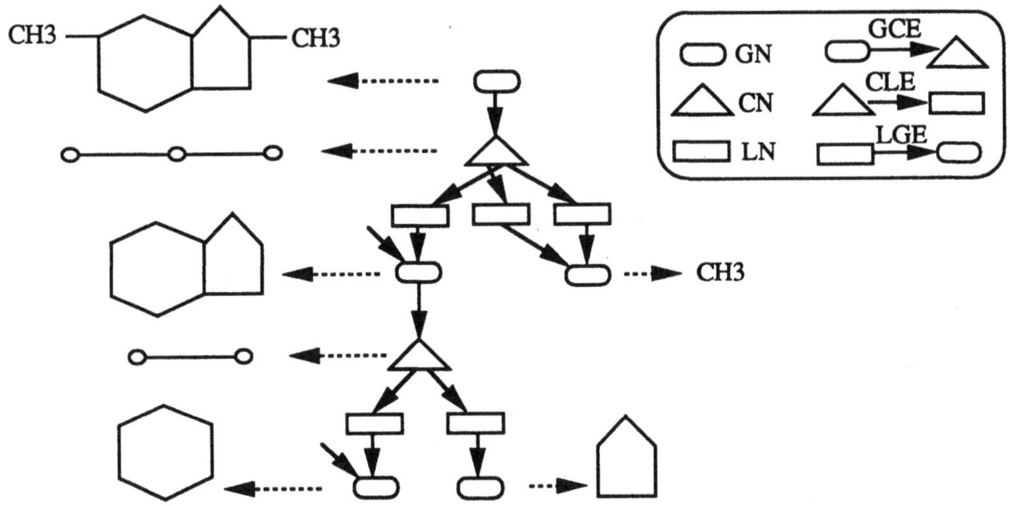

Fig.3 The Conceptual Diagram of the Representation Model.

E also has three disjoin subsets, i.e. E = GCE ∪ CLE ∪ LGE, where Graph-Connection-Edges GCE ⊆ GN × CN, Connection-Like-Edge CLE ⊆ CN × LN and Link-Graph-Edge LGE ⊆ LN × GN, respectively.

2.3 Relational Database Schema of Chemical Structure Database

TIME system has a layered architecture as elaborated in the next section. At the bottom of it lays the extended relational database management system with ADT handling capabilities. Here we show a relational database schema which represents aforementioned structural decomposition model of chemical structure.

R1: COMPOUND
(C#, NAME, NUM-OF-VERTEXES, NUM-OF-EDGES, CHEMICAL-FORMULA)

R2: SUBSTRUCTURES
(S#, NUM-OF-VERTEXES, NUM-OF-EDGES, CHEMICAL-GRAPH, TYPE, CHEMICAL-FORMULA)

R3: CONNECTION
(CG#, NUM-OF-NODES, NUM-OF-EDGES, GRAPH, TYPE, EDGE-MAPS)

R4: LINK
(L#, VERTEX-MAPS)

R5: COMPOUND-CONNECTION
(C#, CG#)

R6: SUBSTRUCTURE-CONNECTION
(S#, CG#)

R7: CONNECTION-LINK
(CG#, L#)

R8: LINK-GRAPH
(L#, S#)

Graph nodes in the structural decomposition model are divided into two types, i.e., chemical structure nodes and substructure nodes depending on their difference with respect to chemical meanings. R1 and R2 represent chemical structure nodes and substructure nodes, respectively. NUM-OF-VERTEXES and NUM-OF-EDGES are listed as examples of attributes that are used as keys for retrieval of structures. R3 and R4 correspond to connection nodes and link nodes, respectively. R5 and R6 correspond to GCE which describes the correspondence between a chemical structure and its segmentation. R7 corresponds to CLE and represents the correspondence between segmentation and its component. R8 corresponds to LGE and gives a relationship between nodes and substructures in segmentation. An example of database instances is shown in Fig.4.

R1: COMPUND

C#	NAME	NUM-OF-VERTEXES	NUM-OF-EDGES	CHEMICAL-FORMULA
c1	DL-GLYCERALDEMTDE-EYHYL ACETAL	12	13	$C_8H_3O_4$
c2	AZELAIC ACID	10	10	$C_7H_5O_2Cl$

R2: SUBSTRUCTURE

S#	NUM-OF-VERTEXES	NUM-OF-EDGES	CHEMICAL-GRAPH	TYPE	CHEMICAL-FORMULA
s1	9	10	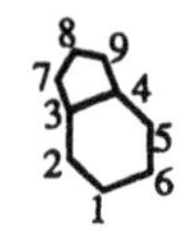	CYLIC-SUBER-BLOCK	$C_7O_2H_5$
s2	3	2	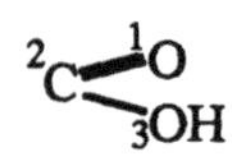	ACYCLIC-SUPER-BLOCK	COOH
s3	1	0	$_1$Cl	ACYCLIC-SUPER-BLOCK	Cl
s4	6	6	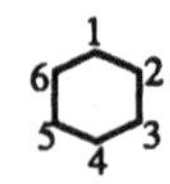	RING	C_6H_6
s5	5	5		RING	$C_3O_2H_2$

R3: CONNECTION

CG#	NUM-OF_NODES	NUM-OF_EDGES	GRAPH	TYPE	EDGE-MAPS
cg1	2	1	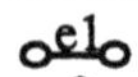	SC-TREE	(e1 (6 11))
cg2	2	1		RING-CONNECTION-GRAPH	(e2 (3 4))
cg3	3	2		SC-TREE	(e3 (2 7) e4 (1 8))

R4: LINK

L#	VERTEX-MAPS
l1	((c1.6 s2.6))
l2	((c1.11 s2.2))
l3	((s1.3 s5.4) (s1.4 s5.3))
l4	((s1.3 s4.6) (s1.4 s4.1))
l5	((c2.7 s3.1))
l6	((c2.2 s4.6) (c2.1 s4.1))
l7	((c2.8 s2.2))

R5: COMPOUND-CONNECTION

C#	CG#
c1	cg1
c2	cg3

R6: SUBSTRUCTURE-CONNECTION

S#	CG#
s1	cg2

R7: CONNECTIUON-LINK

CG#	L#
cg1	l1
cg1	l2
cg2	l3
cg2	l4
cg3	l5
cg3	l6
cg3	l7

R8:LINK-GRAPH

L#	S#
l1	s1
l2	s2
l3	s5
l4	s4
l5	s3
l6	s4
l7	s2

Fig.4 An Example of Chemical Structure Database.

2.4 Motivation for Developing the External Functional View

The scheme in the previous subsection assumes an extension of the conventional DBMS, namely uses of ADTs in individual attributes of relations. An ADT is a user-defined data type specified by the encapsulated data structure and externally visible operations for its manipulation. In the above scheme, new types such as CHEMICAL-FORMULA, CHEMICAL-GRAPH, EDGE-MAPS, GRAPH and VERTEX-MAPS have to be supported. Without attributes of ADT domains, those objects have to be encoded in flat tabular form only consisting of primitive data items such as integers, reals and character strings. However, this restriction makes database manipulation very irritating.

Chemists naturally views that a chemical structure has a number of substructures as its parts, and a part again has a number of substructures as its subparts. However, the scheme in the previous subsection does not necessarily model the decomposition of a chemical structure in a way that is familiar to chemists. The decomposition is represented by a collection of tuples that belong to different relations. Manipulation of the inclusion relationship appearing in the chemists' view requires users to write very lengthy and tedious operations over several relations such as LINK, CONNECTION, etc.

In order to support the chemists' natural view, an external model on top of relational database schema is required. The functional data model and the language DAPLEX proposed by Shipman seem to be a very promising candidate for implementing the external view. It is well known that DAPLEX supports the representation of hierarchical relationships. It provides the facility of nested functions to retrieve objects that are composed of several different entity types. DAPLEX is often accused that it does not allow the user to define computationally complex functions. In DAPLEX functions are merely used to define relationships. In order to support the manipulation of objects by application-specific operators, DAPLEX would have to be extended to provide user-defined operations on the entities[20),23)]. By adding ADTs defined in the underlying relational DBMS to standard data types in the scheme of the functional data model, application specific operations can be flexibly supported.

3 TIME SYSTEM

In this section, we present TIME functional data model. We first describe the layered architecture of TIME system. Then our model is presented with a simple example of a chemical structure database.

3.1 TIME System Architecture

Fig.5 is a depiction of the layered architecture of TIME chemical data management system. The Entity Handler implements TIME data model. It consists of the data modeler, function descriptor and the query processor. The data modeler defines a functional data model similar to that of DAPLEX. The function descriptor defines each function in TIME data model in terms of the language of the extended relational system, called ADT-QUEL. The query processor translates TIME queries into the ADT-QUEL formats. The extended relational system realizes the concept of "individual columns as ADTs" proposed by Stonebraker[12),21)] and Osborn[18)]. It has been developed by adding a module, called "ADT-QUEL interpreter"[13)], into the commercially available relational DBMS G-BASE.

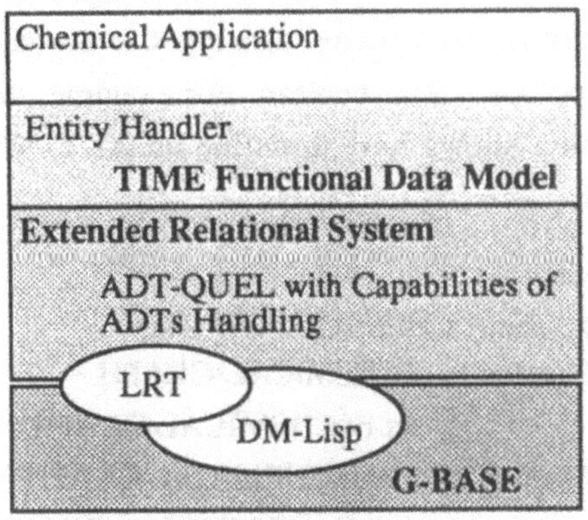

Fig.5 The Layered Architecture of TIME Chemical Data Management System.

G-BASE is distinguishable from other commercially available relational DBMSs by its LISP-based programming interface called DM-Lisp. DM-Lisp consists of usual LISP functions and database handling functions. LRT(Lisp-Run-Time), a set of functions, accepts S-expressions of queries and translates them into DB-Lisp forms. Then by evaluating those forms, database accesses are carried out.

ADT-QUEL interpreter provides users with capabilities to define ADTs. It also has a capabilities to translate the extended QUEL statements including user-defined ADT functions into LISP S-expressions. The S-expressions are further translated into DM-Lisp forms by LRT. LRT is also modified to accept ADT functions embedded in the extended QUEL statements.

3.2 ADT in the Extended Relational Model

In ADT-QUEL, ADT is defined along the line in programming language theory. An ADT is modeled as follows[13]: ADT = (N, S, F), where N is the name of ADT, S is the data structure specification and F is a set of ADT functions defined on it to manipulate objects. Only the name and ADT functions are externally visible, the data structure specified by S can be accessed only through ADT functions. ADT functions can be classified into the following three categories.

1. B-function: $A \times A_1 \times \ldots \times A_m \times P_1 \times \ldots \times P_n \rightarrow$ boolean
2. P-function: $A \times A_1 \times \ldots \times A_m \times P_1 \times \ldots \times P_n \rightarrow P'$
3. A-function: $A \times A_1 \times \ldots \times A_m \times P_1 \times \ldots \times P_n \rightarrow A'$

Here, A_i (i=1,...,m) ($m \geq 0$) and A' are ADTs which are not necessarily distinct from A. P_j (j=1,...,n) ($n \geq 0$) denotes a primitive data type. We designate integer, real, character string, boolean as primitive data types. P' denotes a primitive data type other than boolean. For example, the following expression shows how to define an ADT "CHEMICAL-GRAPH".

```
ADT-define(
    ADT-name CHEMICAL-GRAPH,
    B-function in is CHEMICAL-GRAPH ×
                    set-of CHEMICAL-GRAPH → boolean,
    B-function display is CHEMICAL-GRAPH → boolean,
    P-function num-of-C is CHEMICAL-GRAPH → integer,
     ......
    filename = "/adt/chemicalGraph")
```

Here, "set-of CHEMICAL-GRAPH" represents a set of CHEMICAL-GRAPH instances. "Filename" is the name of the file that contains the definition of ADT functions written in LISP. It is noteworthy that each function is defined in the programming environment, and therefore it is not stored in the persistent database environment.

3.3 TIME Data Model

TIME data model is based primarily on DAPLEX functional data model. The external schema consists of a set of entity types. The syntax of the definition of an entity type is shown as follows.

```
(def-entity-type E (Parent)
        ((F1 E1)
        (F2 E2)
         ......
        (Fm Em)))
```

Here Parent is the specification of the inheritance. In our scheme, a multiple inheritance hierarchy is supported which enables an entity type to have more than one parent. N_i(i=1, ..., m) is a function whose domain is the entity type E and whose range is E_i(i=1,..., m). E_i can be a user-defined ADT or a primitive entity type. An examples is shown below to illustrate entity type definition.

```
(def-entity-type COMPOUND ()
    ((ID               CHAR)
    (SEGMENTATION      SC-TREE)
    (STRUCTURE         CHEMICAL-GRAPH)
    (COMPONENT         set-of SUBSTRUCTURE)))

(def-entity-type SC-TREE ()
    ((ID        CHAR)
    (GRAPH      TREE)
    (INCUDE     set-of SUPER-BLOCK)))
```

Here, two entity types COMPOUND and SC-TREE are defined. The COMPOUND entity type has four function ID, SEGMENTATION, STRUCTURE and COMPONENT. CHAR is a data type, representing a surrogate, i.e., the unique identifier in the underlying database of the compound. So ID function returns a surrogate of a COMPOUND instance. SC-TREE is one of the other entity types of the schema, so SEGMENTATION models a relationship between entities. SUB-STRUCTURE is also an entity type. COMPONENT function is a multi-valued function, because a compound can be composed of many substructures. CHEMICAL-GRAPH is an ADT defined in the underlying extended relational system.

Functions defined on entity types are classified into the

following six categories.

1) entity type → primitive data type
2) entity type → ADT
3) entity type → entity type
4) entity type → set-of primitive data type
5) entity type → set-of ADT
6) entity type → set-of entity type

In the definition of entity type COMPOUND and SC-TREE shown above, the type of functions ID, SEGMENTATION, STRUCTURE, COMPONENT, GRAPH and INCLUDE is filled into the category of 1), 3), 2), 6), 2) and 6), respectively. Mapping from the external functional data model to the extended relational model is represented by the specification of functions. Functions are specified by giving a way to retrieve function definitions stored persistently in the database. For example, SEGMENTATION function is specified by the following def-attribute-function special form.

```
(def-attribute-function SEGMENTATION (COMPOUND i)
        (range-of t is COMPOUND-CONNECTION
         retrieve (cvt t.CG#)
         where t.C# = ID(i)))
```

The body of the special form is an ADT-QUEL expression, where i is an entity of COMPOUND type, ID(i) returns a surrogate of i in the database. The t.CG# column stores surrogates of SC-trees. Function cvt, an inverse function of ID: SC-TREE → CHAR, converts the internal representation of an entity, i.e., a surrogate, to an entity of SC-TREE type. Furthermore, by using ADTs, we can define functions which do not appear explicitly as attributes in the underlying database.

```
(def-attribute-function ATOMS (COMPOUND i)
    (range-of t is COMPOUND
     retrieve (set-of-attoms t.CHEMICAL-FORMULA)
     where t.C# = ID(i)))
```

Here t.CHEMICAL-FORMULA returns CHEMICAL-FORMULA ADT, and set-of-atoms is a function defined on it. Users can write a query as if there were the attribute ATOMS in the underlying database.

In addition to the functions given above, the def-derived-function special form provides a construct similar to the derived function in DAPLEX. The following form defines a function which computes a set of SUPER-BLOCK instances for a given COMPOUND instance.

```
(def-derived-function INCLUDE-BLOCK(COMPOUND i)
        (INCLUDE (SEGMENTATION i)))
```

Furthermore, operations on entity types can be defined by the def-operation special form. The function body of this special form is a valid LISP form. The following form computes the isomorphism between two SC-trees.

```
(def-operation SAME-STRUCTURE
        ((SC-TREE i) (SC-TREE j))
        (isomorphic (GRAPH i) (GRAPH j)))
```

where isomorphic is a function defined on TREE ADT.

3.4 Data Manipulation

The for-each special form provides a capability of manipulation of TIME data model. The form is similar to that of statice[22]. Here we will show a simple example of queries.

Query: Display all chemical structures of compounds which contain 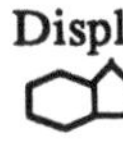 as a substructure.

```
(for-each ((COMPOUND i))
    (where (in (graph)
            (mapcar 'STRUCTURE (COMPONENT i))))
    (values (display (STRUCTURE i))))
```

In the above query, i stands for an entity of COMPOUND type. The content of "where" clause is always a valid LISP form that expresses the qualification of the query. The "(graph)" form is a constant function defined on CHEMICAL-GRAPH ADT. Here a value 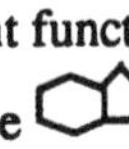 is assumed to be designated as a constant of CHEMICAL-GRAPH ADT. The function "in" is also defined on the CHEMICAL-GRAPH ADT. It returns true if the first argument is in the list specified by the second argument. The content of "values" clause must be a valid LISP form that expresses how to format the return values of the query. The function "display" is defined on CHEMICAL-GRAPH ADT, and it generates as side-effect a two-dimensional image of a given chemical graph.

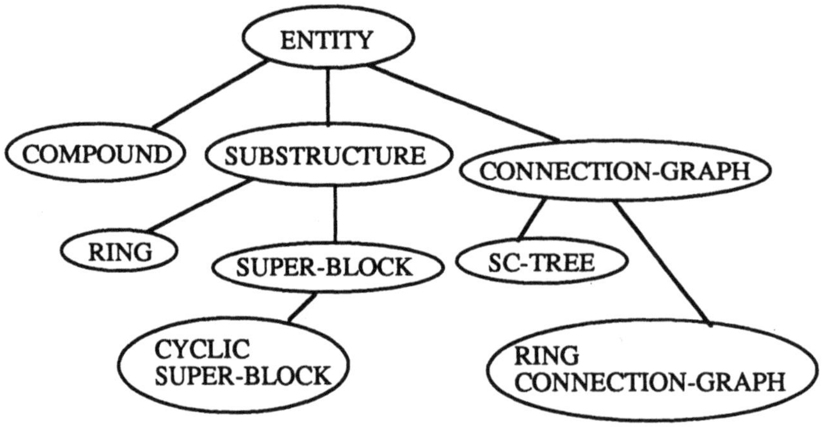

Fig.6 The Type Hierarchy of Chemical Structure Database.

4 FUNCTIONAL DATA MODEL OF CHEMICAL STRUCTURE DATABASE

In section 2, we described a chemical structure model based on the hierarchical decomposition, and presented a representation in the relational model. In section 3, we described our TIME data mode. In this section, we will present a chemical structure database in terms of the TIME data model and give some examples of queries.

4.1 Chemical Structure Database

TIME data model provides high-level information hiding facilities and powerful data manipulation capability. It handles complex objects and complex data such as graphs under the concepts of entity types and/or ADTs. Using TIME data mode, users can define their own view on application area data without the knowledge of representation details of these data in the database. In Fig.6 we show the type hierarchy of chemical structure database, and in Fig.7 we show an example schema defined as an external view on the relational database shown in section 2.3.

```
(def-entity-type COMPOUND()
    ((ID CHAR)
     (FORMULA CHEMICAL-FORMULA)
     (NAME CHAR)
     (NUM-OF-ATOMS INT)
     (NUM-OF-EDGES INT)
     (ATOMS set-of ATOMS)
     (STRUCTURE CEHMICAL-GRAPH)
     (SEGMENTATION SC-TREE)
     (COMPONENT set-of SUBSTRUCTURE)))

(def-entity-type SUBSTRUCTURE()
    ((ID CHAR)
     (FORMULA CHEMICAL-FORMULA)

     (NUM-OF-ATOMS INT)
     (NUM-OF-EDGES INT)
     (STRUCTURE CHEMICAL-GRAPH)))

(def-entity-type SUPER-BLOCK(SUBSTRUCTURE)
    ((INCLUDED-BY SC-TREE)
     (PARENT COMPOUND)))

(def-entity-type CYCLIC-SUPER-BLOCK
            (SUPER-BLOCK)
    ((SEGMENTATION RING-CONNECT-GRAPH)
     (INCLUDE set-of RING)))

(def-entity-type RING (SUBSTRUCTURE)
    ((INCLDED-BY RING-CONNECT-GRAPH)))

(def-entity-type CONNECTION ()
    ((ID CHAR)
     (NUM-OF-NODES INT)
     (NUM-OF-EDGES INT)))

(def-entity-type SC-TREE(CONNECTION)
    ((INCLDE set-of SUPER-BLOCK)
     (GRAPH TREE)))
```

```
(def-entity-type RING-CONNECT-GRAPH
        (CONNECTION)
        ((INCLUDE set-of RING)
         (GRAPH GRAPH)))

(def-ADT GRAPH() ...)
(def-ADT TREE() ...)
(def-ADT TREE() ...)
(def-ADT CHEMICAL-FORMULA() ...)
(def-ADT ATOMS () ...)
(def-ADT EDGE-MAPS() ...)
(def-ADT  VERTEX-MAPS() ...)
```

Fig.7 An Example Scheme of Chemical Structure Database

In Fig.7, the COMPOUND entity type corresponds to the relation COMPOUND in the underlying relational database. However, SEGMENTATION, STRUCTURE and COMPONENT functions access to other relations such as COMPOUND-CONNECTION, COONECTION-LINK, LINK-GRAPH, SUBSTRUCTURE and LINK. So it represents an object that falls into a category of a complex or a molecular object. The SEGMENTATION function computes a SC-tree as a result of the segmentation of a compound. Each entity of SC-TREE type corresponds to such a tuple in the CONNECTION relation that its TYPE value is "SC-TREE". The values in TYPE column in CONNECTION can be utilized to classify the type of CONNECTION into subtypes. It is noteworthy that STRUCTURE function in the definition of COMPOUND entity type computes a chemical graph from its components using connectivity information scattered over several relations.

4.2 Query Examples

Here we will show some examples of queries which access chemical structure database through the external view defined above.

Query 1

List compounds whose SC-tree is isomorphic to a given tree 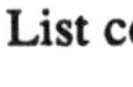.

```
(let ((result nit)
   (for-each ((COMPOUND i ))
      (where match (tree) (GRAPH (SEGMENTATION i))))
      (values (setf result (cons (NAME i ) result))))))
```

where, the function "match" is defined on the TREE ADT. The form (SEGMENTATION i) returns an entity of the SC-TREE type, and the function GRAPH defined on the SC-TREE returns an object of TREE ADT. The form (tree) is the constant function defined on the TREE ADT.

Query 2

Display all chemical structures which contain  and 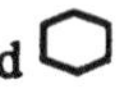 connected directly.

```
(for-each ((COMPOUND i))
      (where (CONTAIN (SEGMENTATION i) (sc-tree)))
      (values (display (STRUCTURE i))))
```

Here CONTAIN is a binary operation defined by the def-operation special form. It returns true if the first SC-tree contains the second SC-tree as its component. The form "(sc-tree)" is a constant function is a constant function defined on the SC-TREE entity type. A constant of entity type is defined by designating the function values explicitly.

Query 3

Display structures of compounds which contain a cyclic super block of size 5.

```
(for-each ((CYCLIC-SUPER-BLOCK i))
      (where (= 5 (NUM-OF_ATOMS i)))
      (values (mapcar 'display
            (mapcar 'STRUCTURE (PARENT i)))))
```

Here NUM-OF-ATOMS and PARENT are defined on SUBSTRUCTURE and SUPER-BLOCK entity types, respectively. These functions are inherited to CYCLIC-SUPER-BLOCK type, PARENT function returns a list of compounds having a given cyclic super block as its component.

5 CONCLUSION

This paper has proposed a new approach to design and implement chemical structure databases. We start from the hierarchical decomposition of chemical structures based on the super block decomposition and SSSR method. The basic motivation of this study has been to object-oriented and flexible manipulation of this hierarchical decomposition. Key construct of our scheme is the layered architecture consisting of the conventional relational DBMS, extended relational DBMS with capabilities of ADT handling and the functional data model as an external view.

The approach supports behavioral abstractions by introducing of ADTs as well as has capabilities to realize the structural abstraction such as generalization hierarchy and/or complex objects.

The fundamental features of our data model TIME are as follows.

a) It provides a high-level user interface integrated into the programming language LISP.

b) It is designed and implemented as an external view of the commercially available relational DBMS, G-BASE, so it provides logical data independence between views and the conceptual database.

There are some future works remaining.

a) So far we only support associative retrieval to the chemical structure database. Insertion and deletion of objects as well as the update of view are also needed to be supported.

b) In order to handle large amount of chemical structure data, considerable efforts for speed up are required.

ACKNOWLEDGEMENT

The authors wish to thank many members of database division of Ricoh Software Lab. for their helpful discussion on the design and implementation of TIME project. This work is partially supported by grants from University of Tsukuba Project Research.

REFERENCE

1) Banerjee, J., Chou, H. Tl, Barze, J.F., Kim, W., Woelk, D. and Ballou, N., "Data Model Issues for Object-Oriented Applications," ACM Trans. Office Inf. Syst., Vol.5, No.1, pp.3-26

2) Banerjee, J., Kim, W. and Kim, K.C., "Queries in Object-Oriented Databases," Proc. of IEEE Fourth Conference on Data Engineering, Los, Angeles, Feb. 1988, pp.31-38.

3) Batory, D.S. and Buchmann, A.P., "Molecular Objects, Abstract Data Types and Data Models: A Framework," Proc. of the Tenth International Conference on VLDB, Singapore, Aug. 1984, pp.377-387.

4) Codd, E.F., "A Relational Model of Data for Large Shared Data Banks," CACM, Vol.13, No.6, Jun. 1970, pp.377-387.

5) Dadam, P., et al., "A DBMS prototype to support extended NF2-relations: An Integrated View on Flat Tables and Hierarchies," Proc. of the ACM SIGMOD'86, 1986, pp.376-387.

6) Fishman, D.H., et al., "Iris: An Object-Oriented Database Management System," ACM Trans. Office Inf. Syst., Vol.5, No.1, Jan. 1987, pp.48-69.

7) Fujiwara, Y. and Nakayama, T., "A Graph Data Base for Storage of Chemical Structures Organized by the Block-Cutpoint Tree Technique," Analytica Chemica Acta, 133, 1981, pp.48-69.

8) Gasteiger, J. and Jochum, C., "An Algorithm for the Perception of Synthetically Important Rings," J. Chem. Inf. Comput. Sci., Vol.19, No.1, 1979, pp.43-48.

9) Graf, W., Kaindl, H.K., Kniess, H., Schmitd, B. and Warszawski, R., "Substructure Retrieval by Means of the BASIC Fragment Search Dictionary Based on the Chemical Abstracts Service Chemical Registry III System," J. Chem. Inf. Comput. Sci., Vol.19, No.1, 1979.

10) Haskin, R.L. and Lorie, R.A., "On Extending the Functions of a Relational Database System, ACM Proc. of the International Conference on the Management of Data," Jun. 1982, pp.207-212.

11) Jaeschke, G. and Schek, H.J., "Remarks on the Algebra of Non First Normal Form Relations," Proc. of ACM SIGACT/SIGMOD Symposium on Principles of Database Systems, Los Angeles, Mar. 1982, pp.124-138.

12) James, J., Fogg, D. and Stonebraker, M., "Implementation of Data Abstraction in the Relational Database System INGRES," ACM SIGMOD Record, Apr. 1983, pp.1-14.

13) Jiang, S.J., Kitagawa, H., Ohbo, N., Suzuki, I. and Fujiwara, Y., "Abstract Data Types in Graphics Database," Proc. of IFIP TC-2 Working Conference on Visual Database Systems, Tokyo, Apr. 1989.

14) Kitagawa, H., "Structured forms Handling by Nested Table Data Model," Ph.D. Dissertation, The University of Tokyo, Jan. 1987.

15) Lorie, R. and Plouffe, W., "Complex Objects and Their Use in Design Transactions," Proc. of ACM SIGMOD Conference on Engineering Design Applications, San Jose, May 1983, pp.115-121.

16) Nakayama, T. and Fujiwara, Y., "BCT Representation of Chemical Structures," J. Chem. Inf. Comput. Sci., 20, 1980, pp.23-28.

17) Nakayama, T. and Fujiwara, Y., "Computer Presentation of Generic Chemical Structures by an Extended Block-Cutpoint Tree," J. Chem. Inf. Comput. Sci., 23, 1983, pp.80-87.

18) Osborn, S.L. and Heaven, T.E., "The Design of a Relational Database System with Abstract Data Types for Domains," ACM Trans. Database Syst. Vol.11, No.3, Sept. 1986, pp.357-373.

19) Shipman, D., "The Functional Data Model and the Data Language DAPLEX," ACM Trans. Database Sys., Vol.6, No.1, 1981, pp.140-173.

20) Stehle, H., "EDAPLEX: An Extension of the Functional Data Model DAPLEX for Computer-Geometry Applications," Master's thesis, University Karisruhe, 1986.

21) Stonebraker, M., Rubenstin, B. and Guttman, A., "Application of Abstract Data Types and Abstract Indices to CAD Data," Proc. of the Annual Meeting Database Week, San Jose, May 1983, pp.107-115.

22) Weinreb, D., Feinberg, N., Gerson, D. and Lamb, C., "An Object-Oriented Database System to support an Integrated Programming Environment," IEEE Data Engineering, Vol.11, No.2, Jun. 1988, pp.33-43.

23) Yu, X., Ohbo, N., Kitagawa, H. and Fujiwara, Y., "Integration of Functional Data Model into Programming Environment: Application to Solid Databases," Proc. of IFIP TC-2 Working Conference on Visual Databases System, Tokyo, Apr. 1989.

VISUAL DATABASE LANGUAGES

Design and Implementation of a Visual Query Language for Historical Databases

Eitetsu Oomoto *
Division of Intelligence Science
Graduate School of Science and Technology
Kobe University

Katsumi Tanaka †
Dept. of Computer and Systems Engineering
Faculty of Engineering
Kobe University

Abstract

This paper describes the design and implementation of a visual query language *HistoryChart* for historical databases. The underlying data model for HistoryChart is a tuple-sequence data model, where each tuple allows set-valued attributes and contains a time-stamp attribute. A history of an object is represented by a sequence of these tuples. The major characteristics of the language HistoryChart are: (a) each historical (temporal) query is represented by a combination of visual symbolic patterns like time charts, (b) generalization hierarchies for attribute-names and attribute values are supported for specifying queries and displaying the retrieval results, and (c) the output of queries are also sequences of tuples, and are displayed in a visual form.

Keywords:
historical database, visual query language, generalization

1 INTRODUCTION

Recently, much attention has been focussed on the *historical* or *temporal* database systems [1][2][3]. As for query languages, for example, TQuel[4] and HTQuel[5] are historical database query language based on the relational data model. These query languages are basically extensions of the relational database language QUEL. Also, the algebra for historical relational databases was investigated in [6] by Clifford and Tansel. The underlying database consists of relations in which *time stamp* attributes or *time interval* attributes are embedded. Although these query languages offer useful functions to create historical (or temporal) queries, we consider the following problems still exist.

- **Need for understanding relation structures:** When creating a query, users are enforced to understand the structure of relations and where *time* attributes are attached.
- **Lack of visual interfaces:** Most of the conventional query languages for historical databases do not offer visual user interfaces. Since (1) current workstation technology offers a powerful facility for creating sophisticated and interactive user interfaces, such as bit-map displays, window software and graphics interfaces, and (2) the introduction of *time* into scheme structures and DBMS functions will make query formulation more complicated, we believe it is necessary to construct a visual query language or at least to add a visual interface on these command-oriented query languages.
- **No support of generalization hierarchy:** Conventional historical database query languages do not directly support the generalization[7] (is-a) hierarchy. Supporting these hierarchies is useful to formulate queries from the more abstract viewpoint. Furthermore, it is useful to output the resulting history consisting of detailed objects in a more abstract manner.

The usage of natural language interfaces is considered to be a candidate for constructing historical database user interfaces. However, from our experience, we found that it is not a easy task for users to formulate historical queries exactly in natural language.

This paper describes the design and implementation of a visual query language *HistoryChart* for historical databases. The underlying data model for HistoryChart is a tuple-sequence data model, where each tuple allows set-valued attributes and contains time-stamp attributes. Each object history is represented by a sequence of these tuples. The major characteristics of the language HistoryChart are:

*Author's address: Rokkodai, Nada, Kobe 657, Japan
E-mail: oomoto@in4wolf.in.kobe-u.ac.jp
†Author's address: Rokkodai, Nada, Kobe 657, Japan
E-mail: tanaka@icluna.kobe-u.ac.jp

- Each historical (temporal) query is represented by a combination of visual symbolic patterns.
- Generalization hierarchies for attribute-names and attribute values are supported for specifying queries and displaying the retrieval results.
- The output of queries are also sequences of tuples, and are displayed in a visual form.

Section 2 describes our motivations for designing HistoryChart query language. Section 3 describes basic constructs of HistoryChart. In section 4, we illustrate the usage of HistoryChart in specifying several types of historical queries together with examples. In section 5, the implementation issues are described. Section 6 is a concluding remarks.

2 MOTIVATIONS

In this section, we describe several motivations for designing and implementing our HistoryChart query language.

2.1 Oriental Medicine Expert System

We have developed an expert system[8] for Oriental Medicine, which consists of diagnostic knowledge and oriental drug information. The notable feature of the Oriental medicine is that it takes a relatively long time to cure patients, and that the histories of patients' symptoms, disease-names (called symptom complexes) and applied drugs are very important to decide a way for curing patients. This system also has a facility to store the historical records of patients in the form of Prolog facts. In order to see the patients' conditions or to acquire the diagnostic knowledge, a facility for retrieving and browsing patients' historical records is required. Since the users of this system are supposed to be doctors or nurses, an easy-to-use and user-friendly historical query language is required. The major requirements for such a historical query language are as follows:

- Easy-to-use facility to retrieve patients that satisfy a specified historical condition, for example, *find a patient who continued to take a drug A during the symptom B appeared.*
- Browsing capability of a patient's historical records. For example, *Display the relationship among a history of the appearance of symptom A, a history of taking a drug B, and a history of the appearance of diseases of category C.* In this case, the relationship of these histories is more important than the actual time or time interval of each component's appearance or detailed disease names of category C.
- A graphical interface, in which users have less opportunities to be enforced to type in commands, attribute-names and attribute values.

2.2 Time Charts for Specifying Queries

Even when people communicate with the other about historical or temporal issues, natural languages do not seem to be the easiest and the most accurate way. For specifying complicated conditions involving time, they usually use a visual tool, for example, time charts. Time charts are useful to understand the relationships among several time intervals. Our HistoryChart is based on these time charts, and historical (or temporal) queries are basically represented by several time charts.

Although time charts are useful to represent relationships among several histories, we often need further tools to specify the properties of time intervals: for example,*this is the first appearance of the entity*, or *the appearance of an entity during a certain time interval is not important* and so on. Therefore, we need some tool to add more meaning to time charts. In HistoryChart, we introduced several symbols as the components of each time line for this purpose.

2.3 Generalization of Histories

Suppose that $a_1, \ldots, a_n$ are drugs of category a and that $b_1, \ldots, b_m$ are symptoms of category b. Assume that a patient's history of applied drugs and a history of the appearance of symptoms are $a_1a_2a_3$ and $b_1b_1b_2$, respectively. It is very useful if the system supports the generalization of histories, since doctors may sometimes wish to issue queries from more abstract level. That is, the above histories can be generalized into aaa and bbb, respectively. For example, the query: *Find a patient such that the appearance history of symptoms of category b overlaps with the time interval during which he continuously took drugs of category a.* This facility is also useful when summarizing the retrieval result. HistoryChart supports the generalization of histories for both specifying queries and summarizing the results.

3 BASIC CONSTRUCTS

In this section, the basic constructs of HistoryChart are explained.

3.1 Underlying Data Model

A *historical database* $\mathcal{H}$ is a collection of *object histories*, where each object history is represented as a tuple-sequence[9]. For each tuple sequence s, all the tuples appearing in s are defined over the same domains. For a tuple sequence $s = t_1 \ldots t_k$ $(k \geq 1)$, each t_i $(1 \leq i \leq k)$ is assumed to be a tuple defined over $Dom(TIME) \times Dom(E_1) \times \cdots \times Dom(E_n) \times 2^{Dom(E_{n+1})} \times \cdots \times 2^{Dom(E_{n+m})}$ for some $n \geq 1$ and $m \geq 0$. Here, each E_i denotes the name of an *entity type*, and $Dom(E_i)$ denotes the set of all the possible entities of E_i. $Dom(TIME)$ is the infinite set of time points.

For example, John's history of taking drugs is a single object history $s = t_1 \ldots t_k$ such that each t_i is defined over $Dom(TIME) \times Dom(PATIENT) \times 2^{Dom(DRUG)}$. Here, the entities of the entity type $PATIENT$ are assumed to be patient names. The term *object* is used to denote a single existence who is an owner of several histories. Here, John is an object, and the above object history is a history of taking drugs owned by John. In this example, at each time point, John was provided with a set of drugs, and so, the domain about drugs is defined as the powerset of $Dom(DRUG)$. Furthermore, since the object history s is John's history, every $PATIENT$ value appearing in s must be the same value John.

In order to guarantee the above semantics of object histories, we need the notions of *keys* defined as follows:

Definition 1
A combination of entity types $\{E_1 \ldots E_i\} (1 \leq i)$ is said to be a *key* if it satisfies the following conditions:

1. For each object history s in $\mathcal{H}$, the values of $\{E_1 \ldots E_i\}$ must be the same for each tuple in s.
2. For each object history s and s' over the same domains in $\mathcal{H}$, if $s \neq s'$ then the values of $\{E_1 \ldots E_i\}$ of s and s' must be different.

In the above example, if we have several persons' histories of taking drugs, then the corresponding key for these object histories is $PATIENT$. Although the schema definition, including keys and other types of constraints for object histories, is an important issue, the topic is beyond the scope of this paper. We assume in this paper that for each set of object histories over the same domains, their key is predefined and is maintained by the system. Other important assumption is concerned with time, and in this paper, we assume that the $TIME$ values appear in increasing order.

3.2 Query Table

In HistoryChart, each query is represented as a *query table* filled with *historical symbolic patterns* and time specifications on the display (see Figure 1). A query table consists

time-specification column	condition column-1	. . . . . .	condition column-n	target column

Figure 1: *A query table*

of three kinds of columns: *time-specification column*, *condition columns* and *target column*. The meaning of these columns are as follows:

- *time-specification column*: In this column, users can specify a time-point value per a field. Each time-point value is used to represent that the time interval indicated by the *historical symbol* appearing in the same row contains this time-point. As time-point values, not only absolute dates, but also relative values can be used. For example, `'88/09/27'`, `1 month ago`, `2 weeks ago` and so on.
- *condition columns*: This column represents a history about the appearance of specified entities. Users can put a *historical symbolic pattern* into each condition column. Intuitively, each historical symbolic pattern represents a temporal condition about the appearance history of same entities.
- *target column*: This column is used to specify the histories to be output. In the header part of the target column, users specify an entity-type or an entity, the appearance history of which will be output. In the contents of the target column, users specify by the historical symbol ? what portion of the specified history is of interest. By this, users can obtain an arbitrary subhistory (some interval).

Each *historical symbolic pattern* appearing in a condition column is a sequence consisting of the following *historical symbols*:

- | symbol: This symbol denotes a time interval during which the entity specified in the header part of the condition column continuously exists.
- $\times$ symbol: This symbol denotes a time interval during which the specified entity does not exist.
- $\top$ symbol: This symbol denotes a time interval during which the specified entity appears at the first time.
- $\perp$ symbol: This symbol denotes a time interval during which the specified entity appears at the last time.
- ? symbol: This symbol denotes a time interval during which the specified entity of an object exists or does not exist. If this symbol appears in the target column, then it means that the time interval specified by this symbol should be output.

It should be noted that the length of the time interval represented by each of the above symbols is not fixed, and that each symbol corresponds to a consecutive subsequence of a tuple-sequence s. In each condition column, a single historical symbolic pattern is placed, and for each row of a query table, the length of the time intervals represented by several symbols are assumed to be the same. Suppose that a historical symbolic pattern $\vdash - - \dashv$ is placed in a condition column, and that `headache` is placed in its header part. Also, assume that John's symptom history is $t_1t_2t_3t_4$ such that:

t_1=(`'880301'`, `'John'`, { `fever` })

t_2=('880415', 'John', { **fever**,**headache** })

t_3=('880510', 'John', { **headache** })

t_4=('880525', 'John', { **fever** })

The time interval represented by ⊢ − − corresponds to the interval between t_2 and t_3 (more exactly, the semi-closed time interval ['880415','880510')), since **headache** appeared in t_2 at the first time. Also, the time interval represented by ⊣ corresponds to the semi-closed time interval ['880510','880525'), since after '880525', the symptom **headache** does not appear in this history. Therefore, this historical symbolic pattern corresponds to the tuple subsequence t_2t_3.

3.3 Generalization Hierarchies

Usually, in the header part of each condition column, users specify a certain entity (for example, **headache** which is an entity of the entity-type *SYMPTOM*). Also, in the header part of the target column, users can specify a certain entity type (for example, *SYMPTOM*). However, in general, users can specify either an entity or an entity-type in both of these header parts, since HistoryChart supports generalization (is-a) hierarchies consisting of entity-types and entities. Suppose that *SYMPTOM* is placed in the header part of a condition column. This means that the history represented by this column is a sequence of arbitrary entities of type *SYMPTOM*. Also, suppose that a user specifies the entity **headache** in the header part of the target column. This means that the desired output is a sequence of the existence or the nonexistence of the entity **headache**. In general, for each entity-type E_i, the *is-a* relationship is predefined over $Dom(E_i) \bigcup \{E_i\}$, where E_i is defined to be the most abstract one. Furthermore, it is allowed that for distinct entity-types E_i and E_j, $Dom(E_i) \bigcap Dom(E_j) \neq \phi$. Also, there is a special symbol *ENTITY* such that E_i *is-a ENTITY* for all i.

4 OVERVIEW OF HISTORY-CHART

4.1 Basic Queries

First of all, if users wish to see the whole history of the appearance of entities of entity type *SYMPTOM* for each object, the corresponding query is represented by the query table in Figure 2. The query table in Figure 2 uses two columns: one is for specifying the condition and the other is for specifying the target name *SYMPTOM*. The left column specifies a time interval during which at least one entity (of type *ENTITY*) appears in an object history. Since this condition-column specification is the most general one, users can abbreviate to specify this column. That is, the query table in Figure 3 is regarded as equivalent to Figure 2.

If users wish to retrieve the history of entities of entity type *DRUG* for each object until the entity **headache** first appeared, such a query is represented in Figure 4.

ENTITY	target(*SYMPTOM*)
⊤	?
∣	?
∣	?
∣	?
⊥	?

Figure 2: *Retrieve the whole history of sets of SYMPTOM entities for each object.*

target(*SYMPTOM*)
?
?
?
?
?

Figure 3: *The same query as Figure 2*

headache	target(*DRUG*)
	?
	?
	?
⊤	
∣	
∣	

Figure 4: *Retrieve the history of sets of DRUG entities until the headache appears at the first time for each object.*

This query table consists of two columns. The left column specifies the first appearance of entity **headache**, and the right column specifies to output the history of the appearance of sets of *DRUG* entities until **headache** first appeared.

In the similar manner, If users wish to output the history of sets of *DRUG* entities *since* the time when the entity **headache** disappeared. Such a query is represented in Figure 5. If there exist more than one entities e such that e *is-a* **headache** in the generalization hierarchy, the condition column indicates the history of the appearance of several headache entities until the last appearance.

Figure 6 shows a query involving two condition columns. This query table intends to retrieve a history of sets of *DRUG* entities, during which both **fever** and **headache** continuously appeared, for each object. More precisely, the resulting history should start from the time when **headache** appeared at the first time, and should end at the time when **fever** disappeared. As for the mathematical properties of these basic queries, see [10].

headache	target(*DRUG*)
|	
|	
⊥	
	?
	?

Figure 5: *Retrieve the history of sets of DRUG entities after the headache disappeared for each object.*

fever	headache	target(*DRUG*)
⊤		
|		
|	⊤	?
|	|	?
⊥	|	?
	|	
	⊥	

Figure 6: *Retrieve a history of sets of DRUG entities during which both* **fever** *and* **headache** *appeared.*

4.2 Using Other Symbols

By placing × symbols, it becomes possible to specify a time interval during which the specified entity did not appear at all.

fever	target(*DRUG*)
⊤	?
×	?
|	?
×	?
⊥	?

Figure 7: *An example query using × symbols.*

For example, Figure 7 shows a query table, in which × symbol appears twice in the condition column with the header **fever**. Since the target is *DRUG*, the resultant history is a sequence of sets of *DRUG* entities such that

- The start of the resultant history must coincide with the time when **fever** appeared at the first time.
- The end of the resultant history must coincide with the time when **fever**'s appearance was the last time.
- During the interval from the first appearance of **fever** to the last appearance of **fever**, there must be exactly two sub-intervals during which **fever** never appeared.

Only the object histories satisfying the above conditions are retrieved.

The next example illustrates the ? symbol. Figure 8 shows a query to retrieve the history of sets of *DRUG* entities for each object. The conditions which the resultant history should satisfy are as follows: (1) The start point should be the same time at which **fever** first appeared. (2) The end point should be the same time at which **fever**'s appearance was the last time. (3) During the time interval after the start point until the last point, the appearance of **fever** is immaterial. The difference between Figure 7 and Figure 8 should be noted.

fever	target(*DRUG*)
⊤	?
?	?
?	?
?	?
⊥	?

Figure 8: *An example query using ? symbols.*

As a general rule, the blanks in the query table are interpreted as ? (don't care) symbol. But, in the upper rows of the row containing ⊤ symbol and in the lower rows of the row containing ⊥ symbol, the blanks are interpreted as × symbol.

When users want to specify time-points in their query table, *time-specification column* is used. Once a time-point is given on this column, the row which contains the time-point corresponds to a single tuple of an object history. For example, in the query table shown in Figure 9, the first row represents the tuple of three months ago such that **fever** does not appear in this tuple, and the beginning of the

time	fever	target(*DRUG*)
3 months	×	?
	×	?
	?	?
	|	?
1 month	|	?

Figure 9: *An example query using time-specification column.*

output. The last row denotes a tuple of one month ago and also denotes the end of output. The condition column states that **fever** did not appear three months ago and existed one month ago. The query in Figure 9 returns the history of sets of *DRUG* entities from three months ago to one month ago.

For more complex example, the combination of above query is shown in Figure 10. this query has following meaning. *One month ago,* **fever** *existed and* **headache**, *which had already existed, disappeared. Two weeks ago,* **fever** *disappeared, and* **headache** *existed. For each object history satisfying these conditions, output the history of sets of DRUG entities from the first appearance of* **headache** *to the last appearance of* **headache**.

time	fever	headache	target(*DRUG*)
	|	⊤	?
1 month	|	×	?
	|	?	?
	|	?	?
	×	?	?
2 weeks	×	|	?
	?	⊥	?

Figure 10: *An example query using time-specification column.*

4.3 Visualizing Histories

After identifying a specific object, users can output several histories of the object at the same time in visual form. For this purpose, a query table consisting of only (multiple) target columns is used. For example, the query table in Figure 11 shows a demand to output three histories of a specific object o in a visual form. In this example, each of the following time intervals will be output by a historical symbolic pattern:

- the time intervals during which **Aspirin** was applied.
- the time intervals during which **fever** existed.
- the time intervals during which **headache** existed.

target(**Aspirin**)	target(**fever**)	target(**headache**)

Figure 11: *Output the* **Aspirin**, **fever**, **headache** *histories in a visual form for a specific object.*

Each historical symbolic pattern to be output will be the form of $\times - - \times \times - - \times \times - - - \times$. By this, users can easily understand the relationship among the above histories. It is also possible to specify entity-type names in the target columns. In this case, the generalization hierarchies are used.

4.4 Logical Connectives

In condition columns of a query tables, we can use *logical* connectives **AND** and **OR**. For example, the query table in Figure 12 outputs the history of sets of *DRUG* entities for the time interval since both of **fever** and **headache** appeared at the first time until the combination of the two symptoms disappeared.

Suppose that we have the generalization hierarchies shown in Figure 13. Here, let $S_1 = \{a_1, b, b_1, b_2, b_3, \ldots\}$, $S_2 = \{a_2, b, b_1, b_2, b_3, \ldots\}$ be sets of entities, in each of which the *is-a* relationships are defined as shown in Figure 13. Also, assume that $S = S_1 \bigcup S_2$ and $S_0 = S_1 \bigcap S_2$. If a_1**AND**a_2 is specified in a condition column, this means a combination of an arbitrary entity in S_1 and an arbitrary entity in S_2, for example, a_1**AND**b_3 is b_1**AND**b_2 and so on. It should be noted that a_1**AND**a_2 does not correspond to the set S_0. If a_1**or**a_2 is specified in a condition column, this means the appearance of an arbitrary entity in S.

fever and headache	target(*DRUG*)
⊤	?
|	?
|	?
|	?
⊥	?

Figure 12: *Output the history of sets of* DRUG *entities for the time interval since both* **fever** *and* **headache** *appeared at the first time until they disappeared.*

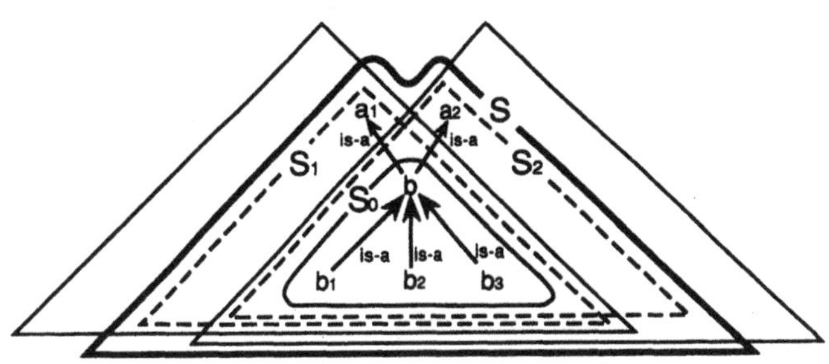

Figure 13: *Usage of logical connectives.*

5 Implementation

In this section, the implementation issues of HistoryChart are briefly described.

5.1 System Overview

HistoryChart was implemented in Prolog on a 16bits-personal computer, and it was used for retrieving and browsing patients' historical records for the Oriental Medicine. The historical records of objects (patients) and the dictionary of a generalization hierarchy of entities (symptoms, disease-names, and applied drugs) are stored on main memory as Prolog facts.

When a user formulates a query, most of operations are done easily with a pointing device and menu selections. Figure 14 shows the actual screen image of HistoryChart.

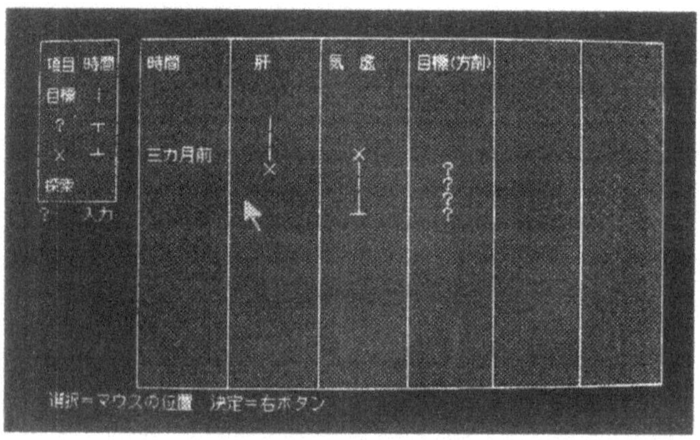

Figure 14: *A screen image of HistoryChart.*

5.2 Query Reduction

User-formulated query tables are stored into main memory as the form of Prolog facts. In the first phase of query processing, they are optimized to remove their redundancy. This process is shown in Figure 15.

The query table of Figure 15 (a) is divided into line by line, and they are compared with neighboring ones (Figure 15 (b)). If neighboring lines of the table are equal each other, they are reduced to one (Figure 15 (c)). This is the reason why the length of time span, which is denoted by a line of query table, is not fixed to a specific length. Therefore, the system replaces multiple rows having identical symbolic patterns by a single row with keeping the meaning of the query table preserved.

5.3 Query Processing

After the query reduction, the system begins to process the resultant query. Here, for simplicity, we show only an outline of our query processing algorithm.

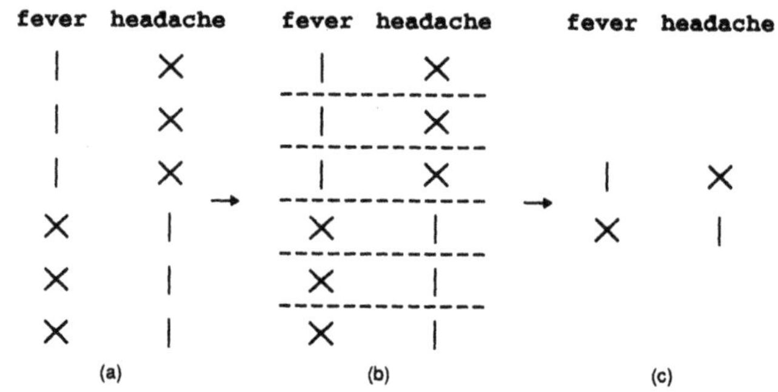

Figure 15: *Reduction of a query table*

For each object history, the system tries to divide the object's tuple sequence into several subsequences. As shown in Figure 16, an object history is divided according to a given query table so that each subseqence may correspond to one row of the reduced query table, respectively. If it is not able to divide the sequence so that each subsequence may correspond to a distinct row of the query table, the retrieval is failed. Otherwise, the subsequence which corresponds to ? symbol in the target column is created as a result.

The implementation techniques that we used are very simple, and no sophisticated methods for searching or indexing were used. The pattern matching and backtracking mechanisms of Prolog were used as the basis of current HistoryChart system.

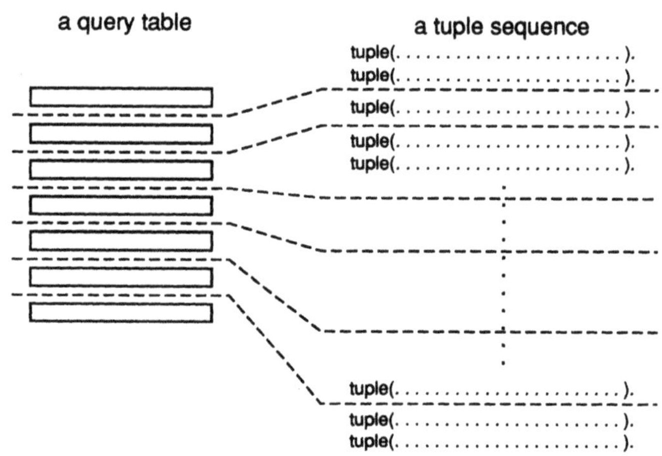

Figure 16: *Correspondence between a query table and a tuple sequence*

6 CONCLUDING REMARKS

In this paper, we described the design and implementation of a visual query language HistoryChart for historical databases. The major characteristics of HistoryChart are: (a) visualization of historical queries using time-chart like symbolic patterns, and (b) utilization of generalization hierarchy for specifying queries and abstracting the resulting histories.

HistoryChart was implemented in Prolog, and it is currently working. As described in Section 2, HistoryChart is currently used for retrieving and browsing patients' historical records for the Oriental Medicine.

Further improvements should be done concerned with the following issues:

- Currently, HistoryChart can not specify a query involving multiple object histories. That is, it is not possible to specify conditions concerned with more than one object histories.
- In order to make the meaning of a created query table more understandable to users, one possible approach is to transform the query table into the expression of natural languages. It seems to be useful to find users' mistakes in specifying queries. Also, the translation of output from chart forms into a natural language sentence seems to be an interesting research issue.
- In specifying conditions, HistoryChart can not specify a condition involving numerical data and comparison operators.
- In HistoryChart, if two consecutive tuples appear in a certain object history, the attribute values except TIME are assumed to have the same values as the first tuple during the time interval between these two tuples' time-stamps. In some situations, this approach may not be suitable.

Acknowledgement
The authors are grateful to the colleagues of Kitamura Lab. of our department for useful discussion. This work is partially supported by the Science Foundation Grant of the Ministry of Education, Science and Culture of Japan.

References

[1] Snodgrass, R. ed., *Research Concerning Time in Database: Project Summaries*, ACM SIGMOD RECORD, Vol.15, No.4, pp.19–39, Dec. 1986.

[2] Snodgrass, R., *Temporal Databases: Status and Research Directions*, ACM SIGMOD RECORD, Vol.19, No.4, pp.83–89, Dec. 1990.

[3] Soo, M.D. ed., *Bibliography on Temporal Databases*, ACM SIGMOD RECORD, Vol.20, No.1, pp.14–23, March 1991.

[4] Snodgrass,R., *The Temporal Query Language TQuel*, Proc. of 3rd ACM SIGACT–GIGMOID Symposium on Principles of Database Systems, pp.204–213, April 1984

[5] Gadia, S.K. *A Query Language for a Homogeneous Temporal Database*, Proc. of 4th ACM SIGACT–SIGMOD Symposium on Principles of Database Systems, pp.51–56, March 1985.

[6] Clifford, J. and Tansel ,A.U., *On Algebra for Historical Relational Databases: Two Views*, Proc. of ACM–SIGMOD International Conference on Management of Data, pp.247–265, May 1985.

[7] Smith, J.M. and Smith, D.C.P, *Database Abstractions: Aggregation and Generalization,* ACM Trans. on Database Systems, Vol.2, No.2, pp.105–133, June 1977.

[8] Tanaka, K. Tsuji, S. and Kitamura, S., *Visibility and Controllability in an Oriental Medicine Expert System*, Proc. of 11th Annual International Computer Software and Applications Conference (COMPSAC), pp.656–662, Oct. 1987.

[9] Ginsburg, S. and Tanaka, K., *Computation-Tuple Sequences and Object Histories*, ACM Trans. on Database Systems, Vol.11, No.2, pp.186–212, June 1986.

[10] Ginsburg, S. and Tanaka, K., *Interval Queries on Object Histories: Extended Abstract*, Proc. of 10th International Conference on Very Large Data Bases, pp.208–217, Aug. 1984.

Multi-Media Database Language SL/B5 based on Screen Flow

Fumio KITAGAWA *and* Hideto IKEDA

Information Processing Center, Hiroshima University
1-2-4, Kagamiyama, Higashi-Hiroshima 724 JAPAN

Abstract

A very significant goal for multi-media database systems (MMDBS) is the integrated management of unstructured data such as drawings, images, text and voice as well as formatted or structured data. So it is required for MMDBS to harmonize both multi-media data storage and processing capabilities. Traditional technology for data management is based on storage and retrieval of structured data of numerics and characters. But the current technological environment is not sufficient to implement practical application systems in the storage and processing of unstructured data. In order to overcome the problems involved in implementing MMDBS, this paper proposes a new multi-media data processing language SL/B5 based on screen flow. A program of SL/B5 is represented by a collection of screens which are connected through what we have termed "screen call". The specifications of each screen may be divided into four parts, IMAGE for formatting multi-media data on a display terminal with speakers, FUNCTION for data entries and transformations, DATABASE for database accesses and CALL for conditional call of other screens with parameters. The database is a collection of 5-tuple (value, data type, attribute, entity, term of validity) which can include multi-media objects, meta-data, user information, security and integrity specification. The special database structure is called B5 structure. SL/B5 provides us powerful, flexible and friendly multi-media data processing capabilities based on flexible database structure B5. SL/B5 was specially designed to support development of information systems by naive end-users in considering the harmonization to B5.

KEYWORDS : multi-media database system, screen language, screen flow control, multi-media data storage B5, end-user computing, 4th generation language.

1. Introduction

The majority of efforts in database research have been spent in developing database management systems (DBMSs) for traditional business applications, such as employer administration and inventory control that use well formattable or structurable data. The success of DBMS architecture is derived from various requirements that cannot be sufficiently satisfied in traditional DBMSs.

Some DBMSs were expanded to meet a part of the requirements from nontraditional applications, e.g., engineering database systems, image database systems, statistical database systems and knowledge-base systems. These expansions are basically made in two ways, i.e., data types and data manipulation capabilities. Improvement of performance and user interface are involved in the two expansions.

Some other DBMSs were expanded as total tools for developing and maintaining information systems by integrating application packages, report writers, query languages, statistical packages, data dictionary systems and end-user-oriented programming languages. Among these integrated software, some were improved for productivity of system development and were called fourth generation languages.

The two different trends of DBMSs suggest that a significant problem for future DBMSs is the harmonized integration of storage and processing for multi-media data. From these considerations, future DBMSs must satisfy the following requirements.

(1) ⟨ Meaningful integration of multi-media data ⟩
There are many requirements in multi-media database management (e.g. [*Christodoulakis et al 84 , Stonebraker and Rowe 85*]). Future multi-media DBMSs should support nontraditional data types, complex data types and abstract data types. Multi-media data is created from some other data by compositions. For example, a driver's license is a multi-media data which is composed of a photo and signature (image data) and some descriptions, ID number, name, data of issued type, class, data of expiry (character data) and so on. Although traditional DBMSs have tried to manage some relationships of data with integrity, they were not sufficient for nontraditional applications. Especially, hierarchical relationships by data abstraction. It is very important to support such hierarchical relationships of data because meaningful integration of various data types is one of the final goals for multi-media DBMSs.

(2) ⟨ Integration of preexisting applications ⟩
For future DBMSs, it is not a common recognized require-

ment but it is very important to continue the support to preexisting applications, and, if possible, to solve some practical problems of them; e.g., productivity, flexibility, maintainability, performance, reliability, usability of data and user-friendliness. Users want to use one DBMS to implement nontraditional application systems and to transfer their preexisting applications without changing programs and data.

(3) ⟨ Improvement of user interface ⟩

Multi-media user interface has some possibilities of improving user interface. The improvement can be achieved in each of the following processes: Design, programming, operation, maintenance, training, and documentation. The system can become more friendly, because it is more suited to humans than traditional technology.

(4) ⟨ Powerful and high-productivity language for manipulating multi-media data ⟩

The most significant problem of current information systems is the back-log. In order to solve the back-log problem, some successful approaches were proposed [*Martin 82, Martin 85*], e.g., fourth generation languages, information center, end-user computing and prototyping. On the other hand, many functions are needed to manipulate multi-media data. Multi-media data naturally involves higher complexity of data processing. It is important to reduce the complexity. This suggests a need for improvement of DBMSs and programming languages. Multi-media DBMSs as future DBMSs must meet these requirements completely.

There have been some efforts to develop a DBMS that satisfies such requirements, e.g., extended relational models [*Lorie and Plouffe 83, Stonebraker and Rowe 85, Schwarz et al 86*], object models [*Dayal et al 85, Woelk et al 86*]. These approaches focus only on problems which will occur when we expand data type, but we have not yet sufficiently treat them as integration problems of existing information systems and nontraditional application systems.

In order to solve these problems totally, this paper proposes a new multi-media data processing language SL/B5 based on multi-media data storage B5. A program of SL/B5 is represented a collection of screens which are connected through "screen call". Each screen is specified in four sections, IMAGE for formatting multi-media data on a display terminal with speakers, FUNCTION for data entries and transformations, DATABASE for database accesses and CALL for conditional call of other screens with parameters. The database is a collection of 5-tuple (value, data type, attribute, entity, term of validity) which can include multi-media objects, meta-data, user information, security and integrity specifications. The special database structure is called B5 structure. SL/B5 provides us powerful, flexible and friendly multi-media data processing capabilities based on flexible database structure B5. SL/B5 was specially designed to support development of information systems by naive end-users in considering the harmonization to multi-media storage B5.

Structure and basic features of multi-media storage B5 are presented in Section 2, where the concept of objects is also introduced. Section 3 provides syntax and semantics of language SL/B5 together with their design policies. Section 4 discusses how to implement SL/B5 with performance consideration.

2. Multi-media Storage

2.1 Structure of B5

We propose a new database storage B5 in this section. B5 is a (large) sheet which has five columns, (VALUE, TYPE, ATTRIBUTE, OBJECT, TERM-OF-VALIDITY). Our database is a collection of such 5-tuple, which is called a **fact**. An object to be managed in the system is identified by **object name**. A property of observed information of an object is distinguished by an **attribute value**. In order to store a fact of an object, it is necessary to express it as a manageable value in the computer, usually a bit string. We call it **object value**. There are various ways to express a fact, e.g., fixed point binary, floating point binary, packed decimal, unpacked numeric. If we treat the value meaningfully, we need description of the **data type** and **term of validity** for the fact. For example, a fact of B5 (H. IKEDA, CHAR(8), NAME, STAFF, 1988.4.1–*) means that character string "H. IKEDA" is a name of a staff member from April, 1st, 1988.

As a value, we can accept complex expressions of other objects be setting and listing. The previous example driver's license can be stored as a set of facts;

(I230-3204-8092, *, LICENSE#, 301332145,
10-31-87 to 03-30-91)

(ORIGINAL, *, TYPE, I230-3204-8092, *)

(A, *, CLASS, I230-3204-8092, *)

(NONE, *, RESTRICTION, I230-3204-8092, *)

( *, SIGNATURE, 301332145, *)

( *, PHOTO, 301332145, *)

where it is supposed that the following facts were already stored in advance;

(LICENSE#, CHAR(8), ID, LICENSE, *-*)

(CHAR(14), CHAR(8), DATA-TYPE, LICENSE#, *-*)

(301332145, NUM(9), ID, PERSON, *-*)

(CHAR(<= 10), CHAR(10), DATA-TYPE, TYPE, *-*)

(CHAR(1), CHAR(7), DATA-TYPE, CLASS, *-*)

(CHAR(<= 20), CHAR(10), DATA-TYPE,
RESTRICTION, *-*)

(IMAGE(200, 100, M), CHAR(16), DATA-TYPE,
SIGNATURE, *-*)

(IMAGE(200, 600, C), CHAR(16), DATA-TYPE,
PHOTO, *-*)

The later facts correspond to meta-data in traditional DBMSs. Such meta-data are also treated in B5. Attribute name ID has special meaning in B5, i.e., the corresponding value (301332145) is used as an identification of the object (PERSON). Such names are referred to "reserved words", that have special meaning and are attached special functions in B5. DATA-TYPE, NAME, OBJECT, ATTRIBUTE and TERM-OF-VALIDITY are also reserved words. The other reserved words include SYSTEM, ELEMENT, OCCURRENCE, FUNCTION, RELATION, FORMULA, USER, CONSTRAINT, EXPRESSION and so on.

2.2 Database Access in B5

The most simple query is a 5-tuple that is created from a fact by replacing some elements with variables. In the license example, the following tuples are queries:

(X, *, LICENSE#, 301332145, *)

(Y, *, PHOTO, 301332145, 12-01-88) ,

which have the meaning of:

What is the license number of driver #301332145?

Show me a photo of driver #301332145 at December 1st, 1988.

respectively.

Complex queries are available in B5, such as;

$\exists$ Y (X, *, name, Y, *)
& (Y, *, ID, person, *)
& (A, *, CLASS, Y, *) ,

which means that "List up all names of persons who have a driver's license of class A". The answer to this query is a set of names because the number of persons who satisfy the conditions is possibly two or more. A variable with quantifier, such as Y, is called a bounded variable and a variable without quantifier, like X in the above query is called unbounded. A 5-tuple which includes unbounded variables can be said to be a query. Symbol "&" means "and", which is one of the logical operators. The other logical operators are "or" and "not". The other quantifier than "$\exists$" is "$\forall$" in B5. A general query is composed with some simple queries, quantifiers, and logical operators.

Users can specify a query in a more simple way, e.g.,

(X, *, NAME, PERSON(Y), *)
& (A, *, CLASS, Y, *)

for the same query above because the reserved word ID plays a special role for such retrieval.

3. Screen Language SL/B5

3.1 General Concept of Screen Language SL/B5

SL/B5 is a programming language which is supported in multi-media storage B5. Traditional procedural languages focus to describe behavior of the target program in the computer. Generally, a program written in a procedural language, PL/1, COBOL and PASCAL is a sequence of instructions which are executable in the target computer.

A program written by SL/B5 is a collection of screens, which can be shown in the target display terminal with speakers. A screen is identified by a name and consists of four sections, i.e., IMAGE, FUNCTION, DATABASE, CALL. Figure 1 illustrates a screen.

A screen is a unit of execution of a program like a sentence of PL/1 or PASCAL. But the function is quite different from a sentence. PL/1 supports various sentences which have different functions. SL/B5 supports execution of screens which provide the same type of capabilities, that is, formatting data to be shown on the target display terminal with speakers, data transformations, database access and transfer the control to another screen. Namely, a program of traditional programming languages is a sequence of heterogeneous instructions, input/output sentences, data transformation sentences and control sentences. On the other hand, a program of SL/B5 is a collection of screens which have homogeneous functions. This is the most different feature of SL/B5. This difference is similar to that between "Blocks" and "Legos". "Blocks" are a set of pieces with different shapes, balls, rectangular plates, triangular plates, sticks and so on. "Legos" are a collection of same pieces. However both toys are for construction. As similar as a complex (toy) building can be constructed by some simple legos with the same shape, a complex program can be described by some simple screens with same type.

The other significant difference of SL/B5 from traditional programming languages is to create a program from external behavior of the target system. This approach is usually used in prototyping or requirement specification languages, and is advantageous in comparison to traditional ones.

3.2 Structure of B5-Screen

A screen of SL/B5 consists of four sections, i.e., IMAGE, FUNCTION, DATABASE and CALL. Appendix I defines the syntax of screen. In this section, we shall describe some semantics of each section.

The IMAGE Section specifies how to create a screen on a bit-mapped display with speakers. All data other than voice can be displayed on a bit-mapped screen. The major feature of IMAGE Section is to map displayable data as image data on a target screen. The Background can be modified for effective representation of data.

The FUNCTION Section plays the role of data transformations, e.g., arithmetic computations, format/data type transformations, image processing and even data entry from the keyboard, mouse, touch screen and microphone. Basically, all data must be transformed to image data or voice in this section. But a user can eliminate the last transformation to image data, only when it is natural and trivial one.

The DATABASE Section includes all updates of the database B5. We can specify them in a very simple way, because the database is organized in a B5 format. Conditional updates are also available by using IF clauses.

The CALL Section can be used for realizing a screen flow. IF a condition specified in IF clause of this section is satisfied, the control of execution is transferred to a corresponding screen with parameters.

```
DEFINE SCREEN study_of_flower 1024 × 760 ;
IMAGE
  X1 AT (0, 0) – (1023, 759) ;
  "STUDY OF FLOWER" AT (100, 100) – (880, 150) WITH SIZE(24), BASE(GREEN), BOX(SINGLE) ;
  X2("EXAMPLE") AT ( 40, 600) – (400, 650) WITH SIZE(24), BASE(BLUE), BOX(SINGLE) ;
  X3("STRUCTURE") AT ( 40, 700) – (480, 750) WITH SIZE(24), BASE(BLUE), BOX(SINGLE) ;
  X4("FAMILY") AT (600, 600) – (820, 650) WITH SIZE(24), BASE(BLUE), BOX(SINGLE) ;
  X5("END") AT (600, 700) – (770, 750) WITH SIZE(24), BASE(RED), BOX(SINGLE) ;
  X6      ;
FUNCTION
  X1 = SELECT(*, "picture", "blue capensis", *) ;
  X6 = TRANS("Select one subject by touching the screen", A), TYPE(FEMALE) ;
DATABASE
  SCR-NAME AS "history_of_study" OF USER-ID AT B5-TIME ;
CALL
  example_of_flower IF INPUT(TOUCH) .IN. X2 ;
  structure_of_flower IF INPUT(TOUCH) .IN. X3 ;
  family_of_flower IF INPUT(TOUCH) .IN. X4 ;
  EXIT IF (INPUT(TOUCH) .IN. X5) .OR. TIMEOUT(5 min) ;
```

FIGURE 1-a **An example of screen definition**

FIGURE 1-b **Behavior of the screen defined as Figure 1-a**

3.3 Special Features of SL/B5

In this section, we shall show some special features of SL/B5 as follows;

(1) **Higher modularity of information** is the most significant design policy of SL/B5. As we stated above, a program of SL/B5 is a collection of homogeneous screens. These characteristics derive from easy understanding and ease-of-use of information resources. It also makes ti easy to add a new resource by modifying some pre-defined resources. Another effort for higher usability of screens is recursive call capability. Figure 2 is an example of query screen, which asks the name of a flower on the display. When a flower is changed to one of another kind, the screen can be available because this screen is not dependent on a particular kind of flower. Figure 2 is also an example of recursive call capability. By parameterizing a name of a flower, we can use the same screen for both query and answer.

(2) **Audio-visualization of all information** is also a basic policy for SL/B5 design. All data can be mapped to a movie, that is, a series of image screens with synchronized voice. A traditional way how to store information in the computer is a coding representation. If we want to see the information, we must transform it to image data on a screen, paper, plotter or voice on a speaker. Characters are displayed as a font on a screen. A function can also be seen as a graph, that is to say a kind of image data. Therefore, true transformation of data is a mapping to image data. In the FUNCTION Section of SL/B5, all data to be displayed on a screen, which are also included in the IMAGE Section, must be mapped to image data. Figure 3 illustrates of conceptual diagram for data transformation in SL/B5.

(3) **Orthogonalization of functions** is important for design of every language. Especially, a multi-media DBMS requires many functions of data transformation, because it is necessary to support individual functions for each data type and data transformation for each other. If we would support simple union of individual functions for each data type, the number of all functions in the system would be very vast and we could not learn and use it. An approach to solve this problem is the orthogonalization of functions, that is, using the same name for functions having similar capabilities and different data types. It, however, is easier to preach than to practice this. Appendix II is the list of functions to be supported in SL/B5. The design policy was orthogonalization of functions.

4. Discussion and Conclusion

This paper proposed a new multi-media data processing language SL/B5. The special characteristics are :

(a) Screen-based language
(b) Multi-media database storage B5
(c) Orthogonal set of functions
(d) Audio-visual representation

On the other hand, we have discussed requirements that future DBMSs should satisfy in the Introduction. Now we shall check each requirement that can be attained by SL/B5. Meaningful integration of multi-media data can be implemented by the special multi-media storage B5 and functions given in SL/B5. Although we could not sufficiently present a detail of B5, it has enough capabilities for the integration. We believe that SL/B5 can support basically almost all preexisting applications of traditional DBMSs. But we will check the functional capabilities and performance by prototyping and carry out minor change if necessary. This requirement is a requirement which we cannot neglect from a practical point of view. Screen interface and multi-media support of SL/B5 will improve user interface and productivity of programs by end-users.

This language SL/B5 and database storage B5 are now developing a prototype system by the support from Tokyo Electric Company (TEPCO) in Japan. The first application of SL/B5 will be a CAI system of Hiroshima University.

References

1. [*Christodoulakis 85*] S. Christodoulakis, "Multimedia Database Management: Applications Problems (position paper)," *Proc. of the ACM SIGMOD Conf. on the Management of Data*, 1985.
2. [*Dayal et al 85*] U. Dayal, A. Buchman, D. Goldhirsch, S. Heiler, F. Manora, J. Orenstein and A. Rosenthal, "PROBE-A Research Project in Knowledge-Oriented Database Systems: Prelimary Analysis," Computer Corporation of America Technical Report CCA-85-03, July, 1985.
3. [*Lorie and Plouffe 83*] R. Lorie, and W. Plouffe, "Relational Databases for Engineering Data," *Proc. of the Second Intl. Conf. on Foundations of Computer Aided Process Design*, June, 1983.
4. [*Martin 82*] J. Martin, Application Development without Programmers, Prentice-Hall Inc., 1982.
5. [*Martin 85*] J. Martin, Forth-Generation Languages, Vol.1, 2, 3, Prentice-Hall Inc., 1985.
6. [*Schwarz et al 86*] P. Schwarz, W. Chang. J. C. Freytag, G. Lohman, J. McPherson, C. Mohan and H. Pirahesh, "Extensibility in the Starburst Database Systems," *Proc. 1986 International Workshop on Object-Oriented Database Systems*, September, 1986.
7. [*Stonebraker and Rowe 85*] M. Stonebraker and L. Rowe, "The Design of Postgres," Memo. No. UCB/REL 85/95, Electronics Research Lab., Univ. of California, November, 1985.
8. [*Woelk et al 86*] D. Woelk, W. Kim and W. Luther, "An Object Oriented Approach to Multimedia Databases," *Proc. ACM SIGMOD Conf. on the Management of Data*, May, 1986.

```
DEFINE SCREEN question_of_flower(&p1; &p2) 1024 × 760;
IMAGE
  X1 AT (0, 0) – (1023, 759);
  "Input the name of this flower." AT &c_adr WITH SIZE(24);
  X3 AT &i_adr WITH BOX(SINGLE), BASE(WHITE);
  X4      ;
  X5("END") AT (650, 700) – ( 820, 750) WITH BASE(RED), BOX(SINGLE);
FUNCTION
  X1 = SELECT(*, "picture", &p1, *);
  &c_adr = SELECT(*, "comment-area", X1, *);
  &i_adr = SELECT(*, "input-area", X1, *);
  X3 = INPUT(KEY), TYPE(ITALIC), EFFECT(RED);
  X4 = TRANS(&p2, A), TYPE(FEMALE) IF &p2 .NE. NULL;
DATABASE
  ⟨ SCR-NAME, X3 ⟩ AS "history_of_study" OF USER-ID AT B5-TIME ;
CALL
  question_of_flower(&p1; "GOOD!") IF &p1 .EQ. X3;
  question_of_flower(&p1; "BAD!") IF &p1 .NE. X3;
  study_of_flower IF (INPUT(TOUCH) .IN. X5) .OR. TIMEOUT(5 min);
```

When this screen is called with a parameter, the behavior of this screen is different from itself called with an another parameter (Figure 2-b, 2-c).

FIGURE 2-a An Example of definition for multi behavior screen

FIGURE 2-b One behavior of the screen called by 'CALL question_of_flower("lotus")'

FIGURE 2-c Another behavior of the screen called by 'CALL question_of_flower("orchid")'

form of object	*additional attributes by data transfer*	*specify*
code-data ↓ image-data	type {font, tone} effect {color, decoration, music-interval, tempo}	attributes in transform-formula
image-data ↓ screen	arrangement {position, time} font-size impose {replace, OR, AND, XOR} box of area base color of area	IMAGE Section
screen ↓ device	device number specify some windows effect {volume, surround, echo}	manual operation
device ↓ person		

FIGURE 3 Conceptual diagram for data transfer

Appendix I SYNTAX OF SL/B5

In the following description, a word enclosed "[" and "]" is omittable.

object := *numeric_character* | *character* | *sound_element* | *pixel* | *variable*
  | < *object*,... >
  | {*object*,...}
  | *function* [(*object*)] | *object function object*
function :=*character_string*
variable := &*character_string*
object_type := *N* | *C* | *A* | *I* | *L* | *S* | *D*
  | < *object_type*,... >
  | { *object_type*,... }

N : numerical value   *L* : list
C : character string   *S* : set
A : audio   *D* : database
I : image

SCREEN DEFINITION

screen := ***DEFINE SCREEN***
    screen_name (*parameters*; *recursive_parameters*) [*size*] ;
  IMAGE_Section
  FUNCTION_Section
  DATABASE_Section
  CALL_Section

screen_name := *character_string*
parameters := *image_id* | *variable*
  | *parameters*, *parameters*
size := *h_size* × *v_size*
image_id := X*numeric_characters*
(*h_size*, *v_size* : positive integer)

IMAGE_Section

IMAGE_Section := ***IMAGE*** *image_description_string* ;

image_description_string := image_description
| image_description_string ; image_description
image_description := image_id [(object)] image_environment
| object image_environment
image_environment := AT area [WITH d_attributes] [WHEN period]
| WHEN period
area := address[−address] | variable
address := (integer, integer)
d_attributes := display_attribute
| d_attributes, display_attribute
display_attribute := SIZE (s_parm) | IMPOSE (i_parm) | BASE (c_parm) | BOX (b_parm)
s_parm := integer
i_parm := REP | AND | OR | XOR
c_parm := WHITE | BLACK | RED | BLUE | GREEN | YELLOW | PURPLE
| PINK | BROWN | LIGHT_BLUE | LIGHT_GREEN
| LIGHT_YELLOW | THRU
b_parm := NONE | SINGLE | DOUBLE | BOLD
period := time , time
time := integer min integer sec
| integer min
| integer sec

FUNCTION_Section

FUNCTION_Section := FUNCTION transform_descriptions;
transform_descriptions := transform_formula [IF condition_formula]
| transform_descriptions ; transform_formula [IF condition_formula]
transform_formula := variable = object [, transform_attributes]
transform_attributes := [TYPE (t_parm)], [EFFECT (e_parms)]
t_parm := ITALIC | GOTHIC | MINCHO
| MALE |FEMALE | CHORUS | PIANO | VIOLIN | FLUTE
| BIRD | BELL | BUZZER | CHIME
e_parms := eparm | e_parms, eparm
eparm := c_parm
| UNDERBAR | SHADOW | SLANT | BOLD | EDGE | WIDE | SLIM
| OCTAVE | (integer) | TEMPO (integer)
condition_formula := object .relation. object | attention
| ($\exists$ variable) condition_formula
| ($\forall$ variable) condition_formula
| condition_formula .AND. condition_formula
| condition_formula .OR. condition_formula
| .NOT. condition_formula
| (condition_formula)
relation := EQ | GE | GT | LE | NE | INC | ELM | IN
attention := ATTEN | TIMEOUT (time) | ERROR

DATABASE_Section

DATABASE_Section := DATABASE update_description_string;
update_description_string := update_description
| update_description_string; update_description
update_description := value AS attribute OF entity AT term [If condition_formula]
(value, attribute, entity, term : object)

CALL_Section

CALL_Section := CALL screen_call_descriptions;
screen_call_descriptions := screen_name (put_parms ; put_r_parms) [IF condition_formula]
| screen_call_descriptions ; screen_name (put_parms ; put_r_parms) [IF condition_formula]
(put_parms, put_r_parms : object)

Appendix II THE LIST OF FUNCTIONS

TABLE 1. Functions

FUNCTION	object	role of function
SELECT	object, num, condition	Select num-elements from the object by condition. (num : integer)
APPEND	object1, object2, num	Append object2 to object1. When two objects are list-type, num indicates the order of insert position.
DELETE	object, condition	Delete elements by condition.
CHANGE	object1, object2, condition	Change a subset/sublist of object1 that is selected by the condition into object2.
*	object1, object2	Product of object1 by object2
+	object1, object2	Sum of object1 and object2
−	object1, object2	Difference between object1 and object2
/	object1, object2	Quotient (object1 divided by object2)
COUNT	object	The number of elements of the object
INDEX	object1, object2	Get the position of object2 in object1.
TRANS	object, parameters	Transform the object by the parameters.
EDIT	object, parameters	Edit the object by the parameters.
INPUT	device-name, range	Input data from device.
O-TYPE	object	Return the type of object.

TABLE 2. Functions to get a system value

FUNCTION	role of function
DATE	GET year, month, date
TIME	GET hour, minute, second
B5-TIME	GET DATE and TIME with B5 format
USER-ID	GET USER-ID
SCR-NAME	GET screen-name in which this function specified
SYS-NAME	GET system-name

Appendix III SPECIAL SCREENS

SCREEN	role of screen
EXIT	EXIT from SCREEN to OS
PAUSE(next-screen(parms))	PAUSE until to get a reply
SHELL(next-screen(parms), command)	execute OS command
RETURN(parm)	RETURN to called screen

Map-Oriented Visual Language : MOL

Masahide Ohtomo and Hideto Ikeda

Information Processing Center, Hiroshima University
1-1-89 Higashi-Senda, Naka, Hiroshima 730 JAPAN

Abstract

New technologies and instruments of computer are widely used, and it is the time to make efforts in shaping the computer world to the user's world. One of the efforts is improvement of a programming language. In the area of database systems, some fourth generation languages adopted visual representations in order to improve their user interfaces. These are, however, not sufficient for naive users because of poor capability for describing procedural programs and difficulty of understanding. This paper proposed a new visual language named MOL, which can be used by non-programmers to develop application systems. The structure of database is represented as a special diagram which is referred to a "map" in this paper. On the map, there are some information centers which manage a collection of data. These centers are connected by avenues, when there are certain relationships between respective data of two information centers. A program is represented as a trail of the map. In order to access data with MOL, a user orders a messenger to trace avenues, visit information centers, collect data, fill a reporting sheet with the data and bring back it. The collected data can be processed on a spread sheet. By using MOL, user interface can be improved to be more friendly for non-programmers than the other fourth generation languages without loss of powerful capability of procedural languages.

Keywords and key-phrases : visual language, fourth generation language, information retrieval language, user interface, end user computing

1. Introduction

E.F. Codd and J. Martin pointed out the effectiveness of the end user computing against the application backlog [5,6,11]. Many fourth generation languages (4GLs) has been developed to support end user computing [12]. One of the important problems of 4GL is improvement of the user interface. Visual representations are effective and promising approach to the problem. Wide use of workstation with a bit-mapped display and a pointing device accelerates visualization of programming languages. An icon technique is spread over various fields because icons make easy to find what can be done in the system.

A. Makinouchi and B.D. Yoon [10] classified 4GLs into three groups from the view point of user interface. A target of the first group, e.g., SNAP [1], Ski [9], GUIDE [15], QPE [3], is to support in making of a query. A focus of the second group, VIEW [14], MINOS [4], GRAIN [2] and TIMBER [13], is to present data in a visual way. An intention of the last group, e.g., LID [7] and ISIS [8], is to fulfill both targets at a time,

It is important to visualize various kinds of processes by some standardized and restricted ways. but in general, simplification of a visual language conflicts with variety of representable processes. Information retrieval is a kind of process. Practically, it is important to develop a language because a retrieval program is frequently used by end users and is a typical process.

On the other hand, J. Martin classified a 4GL into a procedural type and a non-procedural type. A non-procedural language has a merit in easiness for development of applications by end users. However, all applications, especially, complex ones, cannot be described with it.

SNAP [1] represents the structure of a database as an entity-relationship diagram. A user makes a graph with selection of entities and relationships, and specifications of retrieval conditions. Queries are generated from the graph. The graph is a visual representation of a retrieval process. Since an entity and a relationship are abstract notions, an end user feels not friendly in use of the language.

MOL is a new visual language based on a *map*. The map is composed of *information centers* which are connected by *avenues*. Each information center manages a collection of data. When there is a certain relationship between respective data of two information centers, the centers are connected by an avenue named after the relationship. A user calls a *messenger* on the map and directs him to visit information centers and collect data. The messenger traces avenues in the map, collects the data, fills a spread sheet with the data and returns it to the user. The user can manipulate the data on the spread sheet. A *trail* is a map in which the footprints of the messenger are marked. A user can save the trail which can be used when he executes the same process. A reuse of a trail corresponds to an automatic execution of the retrieval, and so a trail is a retrieval program.

MOL represents data and relationships as a map in familiarly to end users. Navigation is visualized as behaviour of a messenger. Such a representation helps a user in his intuitive understanding of a program. An interactive interface of MOL relieves an end user from tortures of describing a complex procedure.

MOL is implemented on a workstation with a bit-mapped display and a pointing device. MOL uses LU6.2 to access a remote database. LU6.2 established by OSI is a remote access protocol for database systems. MOL generates a sequence of commands to access a database corresponding to each action of a messenger. Data which are transferred to a workstation from a database system are processed by operations of spread sheet such as calculation, derivation and deletion.

Section 2 describes basic concepts of a map-oriented visual language MOL and Section 3 illustrates actions of MOL. Moreover an implementation of MOL is discussed in Section 4.

2. Basic Concepts of MOL

2.1 Map

MOL visualizes structure of a database as a map. A map is composed of information centers which are connected with avenues. An information center manages a collection of data, and has a name which shows a content of the data. When there is a certain relationship between respective data of two information centers, the centers are connected by an avenue. A map is drawn by a database administrator. Example of a map is shown in Figure 1. The map corresponds to an entity-relationship diagram shows in Figure 2. A building in the map shows an information center. In this example, CUSTOMER information center in Figure 1 corresponds to CUSTOMER entity in Figure 2. EMPLOYEE information center corresponds to three entities; SALESMAN, ACCOUNTANT and BUYER. It implies a possibility of one-to-N correspondence.

2.2 User

A user of MOL makes a *direction* for a messenger. A direction is represented by a map, *reporting sheets* and *security keys*. All information centers that the messenger should visit are marked. Reporting sheets include the data items to be collected and conditions of retrievals. A user has an office. A user calls a messenger to his office and gives a direction. The user receives a report from the messenger, check them, and modifies the direction. When the user gets final reports, he saves the map, security keys, result sheets and closes his office.

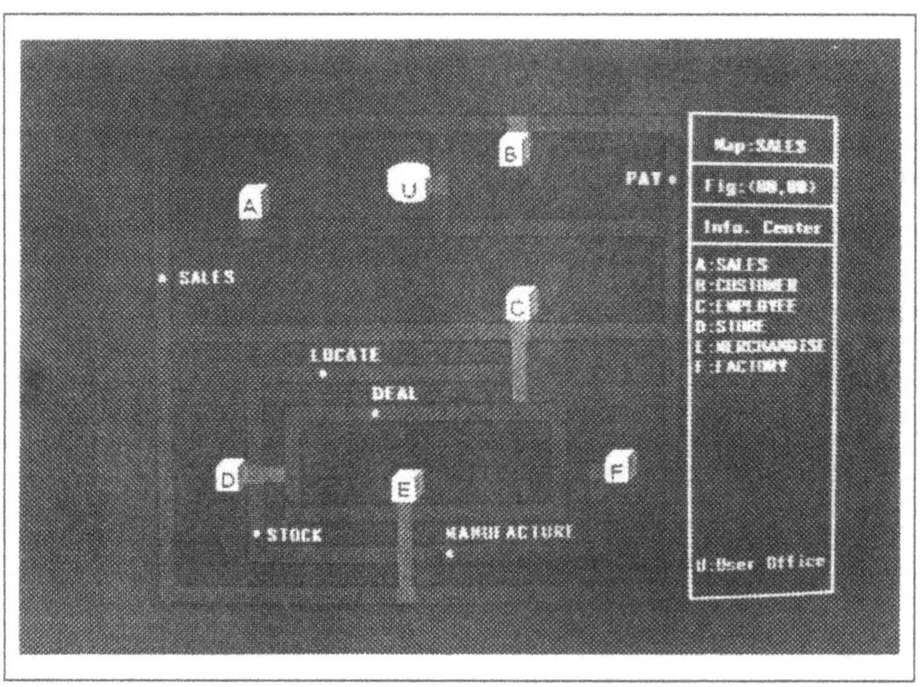

Figure 1. Map of SALES Management System

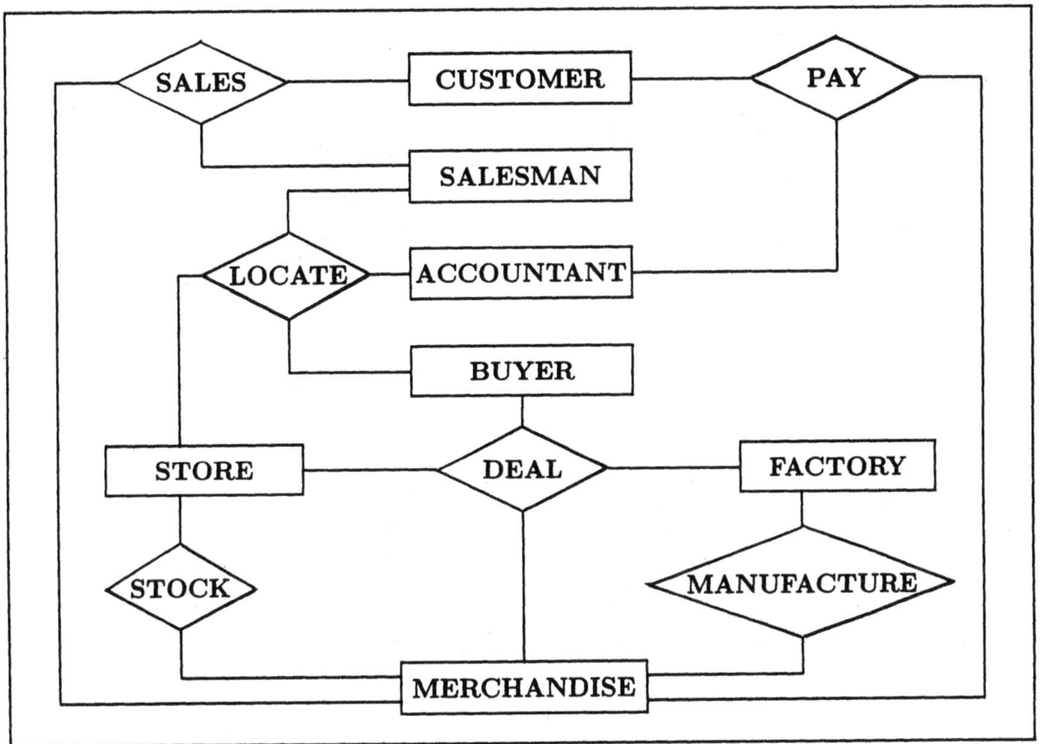

Figure 2. Entity-Relationship Diagram of SALES Management System

Figure 3. EMPLOYEE Information Center

2.3 Messenger

A messenger is a person who collects information under some directions of a user. He visits some information centers, collects data, fills sheets with the data and return them to his host. Figure 4 shows an interior of a user office and a messenger who has a sheet bag and a key bag. MOL represents a retrieval process as behaviour of a messenger on a map.

2.4 Information Center

An information center possesses a collection of data. Each information center has the same functions. Each center contains *a security control box, reception desks, a general information desk, a work desk, a mail box and a printer.* Figure 3 shows an interior of an information center. A privilege of a messenger is checked at a security control gate. Each reception desk corresponds to some entities. A messenger can get information of data managed in the center and how to use of the facilities from the general information desk. A work desk is used to verify and calculate the data. A mail box is used to send reporting sheets to and receive modified directions from his host.

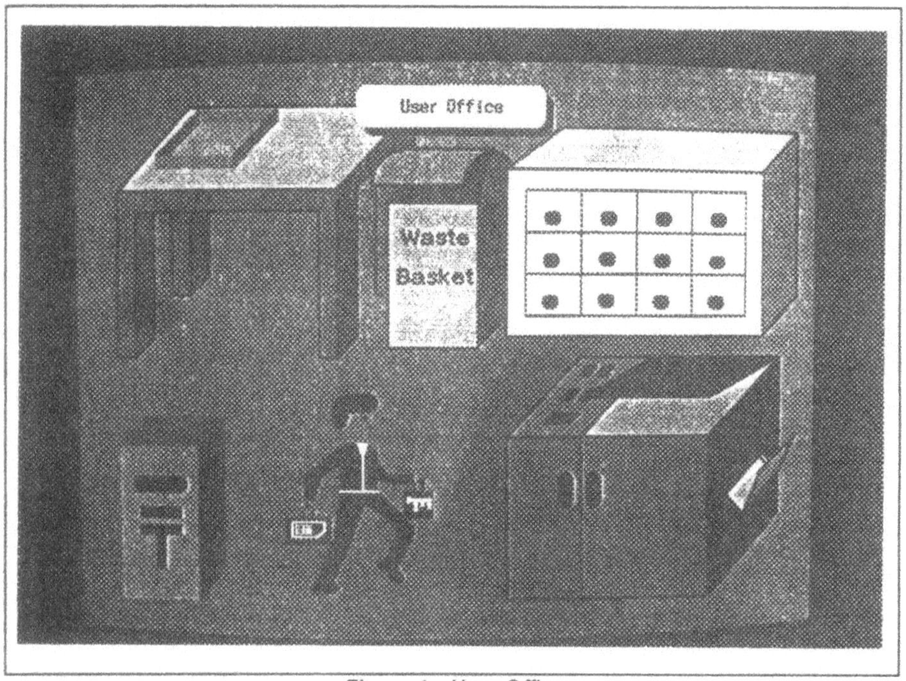

Figure 4. User Office

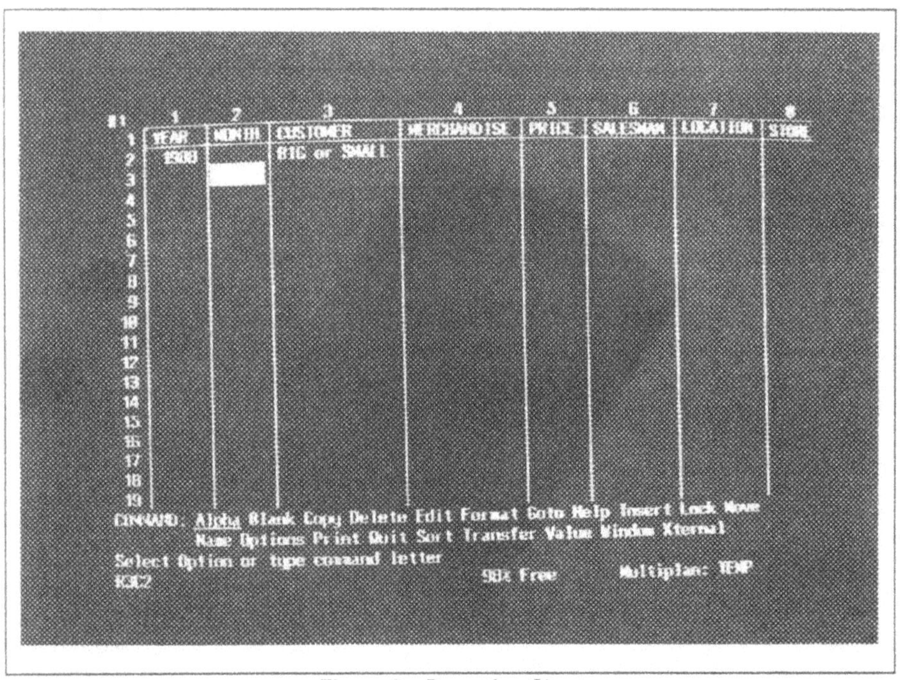

Figure 5. Reporting Sheet

2.5 User Office

Interior of a user office is shown in Figure 4. There is a *sheet box* on a *work desk*. The box is a container of mails from his messenger. A user saves reporting sheets, maps and trails in a *cabinet*. When a user wants to ask a messenger something, the user makes a direction and send it to the messenger. A *waste basket* contains reporting sheets which are discarded by the user. The contents of a waste basket is permanently disposed when the user closes his office.

2.6 Avenue

An avenue connects some information centers. Each avenue has a name which is corresponding to a relationship of data. Passing of the messenger on a avenue joins data in two centers. For example, in Figure 1, SALES avenue connects SALES and EMPLOYEE information centers and joins two sets of data by two items, salesman-name and employee-name.

2.7 Reporting Sheet

A reporting sheet is contained in a direction for a messenger from the user. A messenger fills a sheet with collected data and returns it to his host. Figure 5 shows a reporting sheet. The data items to be collected are noted in the first row. In the second row, the conditions of retrievals are noted. An example in Figure 5 implies directions; "Retrieve the sales data of BIG Co.,Ltd. or SMALL Co.,Ltd. in 1988 year and report the names of merchandise, price and names of salesmen." The messenger notes collected data in a sheet. Whenever there is a sheet on a work desk, a user can process data by operations of spread sheet, such as calculation, deletion, derivation.

2.8 Security

There is a security control gate in every information center to protect data from wrong accesses. A messenger needs a security key to pass a gate. A database administrator gives keys with a map to users.

2.9 Trail

A trail is a map in which some footprints of a messenger are marked. A user can save and reuse a trail to collect data along the same route. Figure 6 shows a trail. When the messenger receives a trail, he traces his footprints. A reuse of a trail corresponds to execution of a retrieval process. Thus, a trail is a retrieval program in MOL. There are two way to execute a trail. One is an *automatic execution*

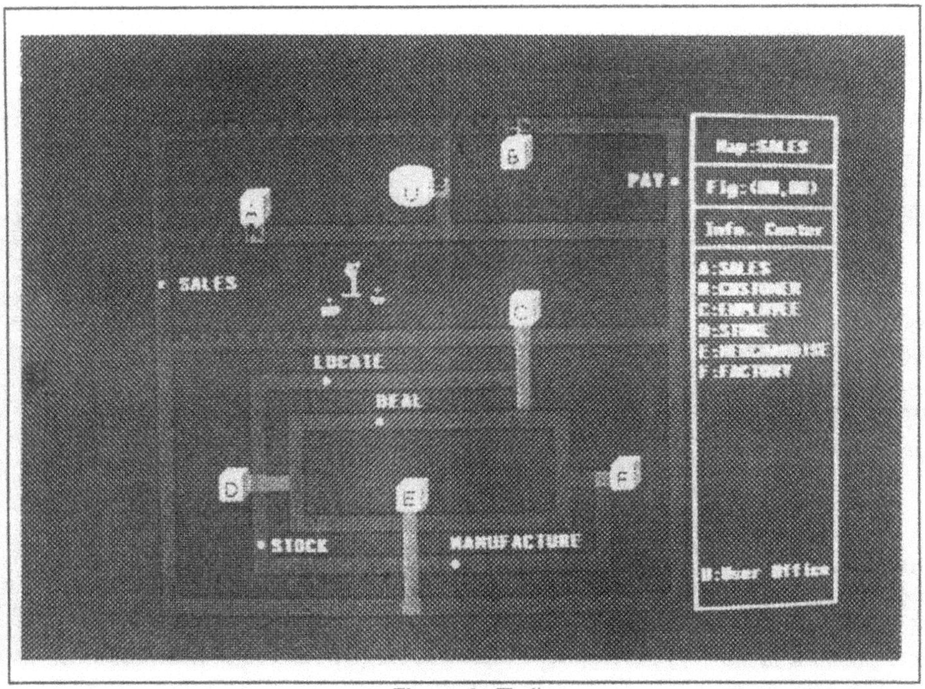

Figure 6. Trail

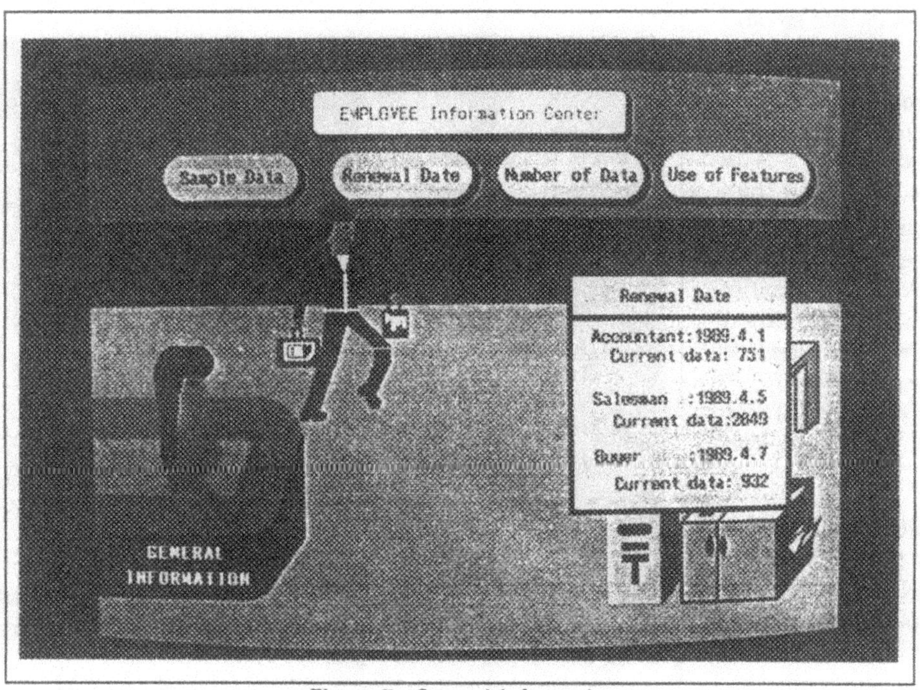

Figure 7. General Information

and the other is a *stepwise execution.* Under a *stepwise execution,* a messenger waits for a direction of his host in each information center. A user can terminate an action of his messenger any time.

3. ACTIONS of MOL

3.1 Direction

MOL starts from an user office. Figure 4 shows an user office. A user makes a direction on his desk. As shown in Figure 5, a direction is to collect data of sales for BIG Co., Ltd. or SMALL Co.,Ltd. in 1988. After making the direction, the user calls a messenger and gives him the direction. The messenger puts some reporting sheets and security keys in a sheet bag and a key bag respectively. He gets out of the user office with the bags.

3.2 Visiting

At first, the messenger goes to SALES information

center. He obtains data satisfying the condition shown in Figure 5. He puts a sheet on a reception desk. Then the sheet is filled with resultant data. He goes out from SALES information center, takes SALES avenue and visits EMPLOYEE information center.

3.3 Permission

Figure 3 shows the interior of EMPLOYEE information center. The messenger shows a security key at entrance gate of EMPLOYEE information center. He is permitted to enter the center.

3.4 Getting information

The messenger goes to a general information desk and asks about sales data in 1988. Figure 7 shows a menu of information. He selects data items following the characters i.e. the renewal date, the number of data, and so on.

3.5 Reception of data

The messenger takes out a reporting sheet from his sheet bag. A sheet shown in Figure 8 was filled with sales data at SALES information center. He puts a sheet on a reception desk. Since he comes out of SALES information center through SALES avenue, data of EMPLOYEE are joined with name of salesman. As shown in Figure 9, a sheet which is filled with data of EMPLOYEE is returned to the messenger.

3.6 Verification and calculation

The messenger puts a sheet on a work desk to show collected data to his host. He can manipulate the data in the spread sheet.

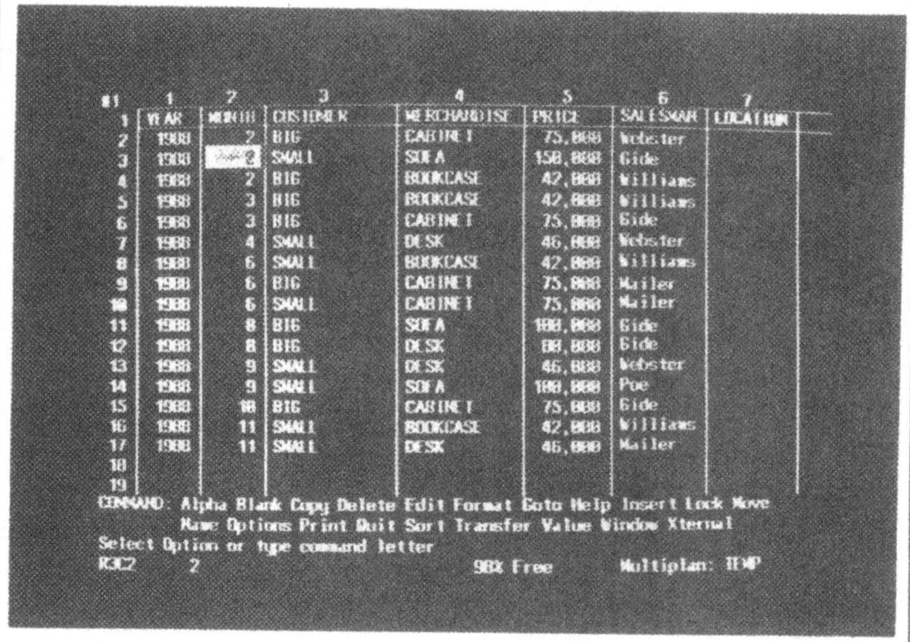

#1	1	2	3	4	5	6	7
1	YEAR	MONTH	CUSTOMER	MERCHANDISE	PRICE	SALESMAN	LOCATION
2	1988	2	BIG	CABINET	75,000	Webster	
3	1988	3	SMALL	SOFA	150,000	Gide	
4	1988	2	BIG	BOOKCASE	42,000	Williams	
5	1988	3	BIG	BOOKCASE	42,000	Williams	
6	1988	3	BIG	CABINET	75,000	Gide	
7	1988	4	SMALL	DESK	46,000	Webster	
8	1988	6	SMALL	BOOKCASE	42,000	Williams	
9	1988	6	BIG	CABINET	75,000	Mailer	
10	1988	6	SMALL	CABINET	75,000	Mailer	
11	1988	8	BIG	SOFA	100,000	Gide	
12	1988	8	BIG	DESK	80,000	Gide	
13	1988	9	SMALL	DESK	46,000	Webster	
14	1988	9	SMALL	SOFA	100,000	Poe	
15	1988	10	BIG	CABINET	75,000	Gide	
16	1988	11	SMALL	BOOKCASE	42,000	Williams	
17	1988	11	SMALL	DESK	46,000	Mailer	
18							
19							

COMMAND: Alpha Blank Copy Delete Edit Format Goto Help Insert Lock Move
Name Options Print Quit Sort Transfer Value Window Xternal
Select Option or type command letter
R3C2 2 98% Free Multiplan: TEMP

Figure 8. Reporting Sheet at SALES Information

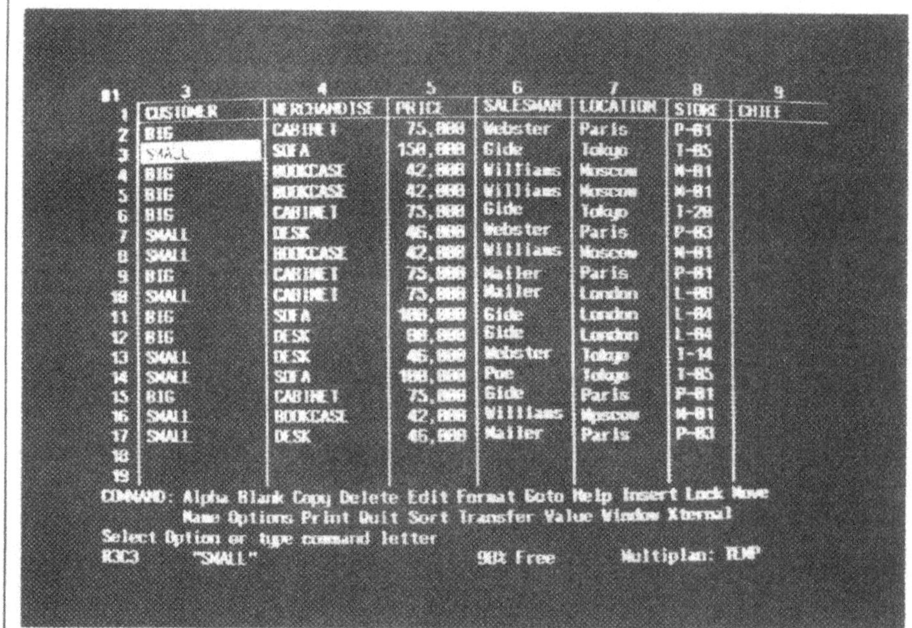

#1	3	4	5	6	7	8	9
1	CUSTOMER	MERCHANDISE	PRICE	SALESMAN	LOCATION	STORE	CHIEF
2	BIG	CABINET	75,000	Webster	Paris	P-01	
3	SMALL	SOFA	150,000	Gide	Tokyo	T-05	
4	BIG	BOOKCASE	42,000	Williams	Moscow	M-01	
5	BIG	BOOKCASE	42,000	Williams	Moscow	M-01	
6	BIG	CABINET	75,000	Gide	Tokyo	T-20	
7	SMALL	DESK	46,000	Webster	Paris	P-03	
8	SMALL	BOOKCASE	42,000	Williams	Moscow	M-01	
9	BIG	CABINET	75,000	Mailer	Paris	P-01	
10	SMALL	CABINET	75,000	Mailer	London	L-00	
11	BIG	SOFA	100,000	Gide	London	L-04	
12	BIG	DESK	80,000	Gide	London	L-04	
13	SMALL	DESK	46,000	Webster	Tokyo	T-14	
14	SMALL	SOFA	100,000	Poe	Tokyo	T-05	
15	BIG	CABINET	75,000	Gide	Paris	P-01	
16	SMALL	BOOKCASE	42,000	Williams	Moscow	M-01	
17	SMALL	DESK	46,000	Mailer	Paris	P-03	
18							
19							

COMMAND: Alpha Blank Copy Delete Edit Format Goto Help Insert Lock Move
Name Options Print Quit Sort Transfer Value Window Xternal
Select Option or type command letter
R3C3 "SMALL" 98% Free Multiplan: [illegible]

Figure 9. Reporting Sheet at EMPLOYEE Information Center

3.7 Printing

In order to print collected data, messenger picks a printer. Then the user gets the printed data.

3.8 Mailing

A mailing service is also applicable for sending reporting sheets and security keys to the user.

3.9 Save

When the user gets all reports, he saves the sheets, the security keys, the trails and the maps. He closes his office and MOL is terminated.

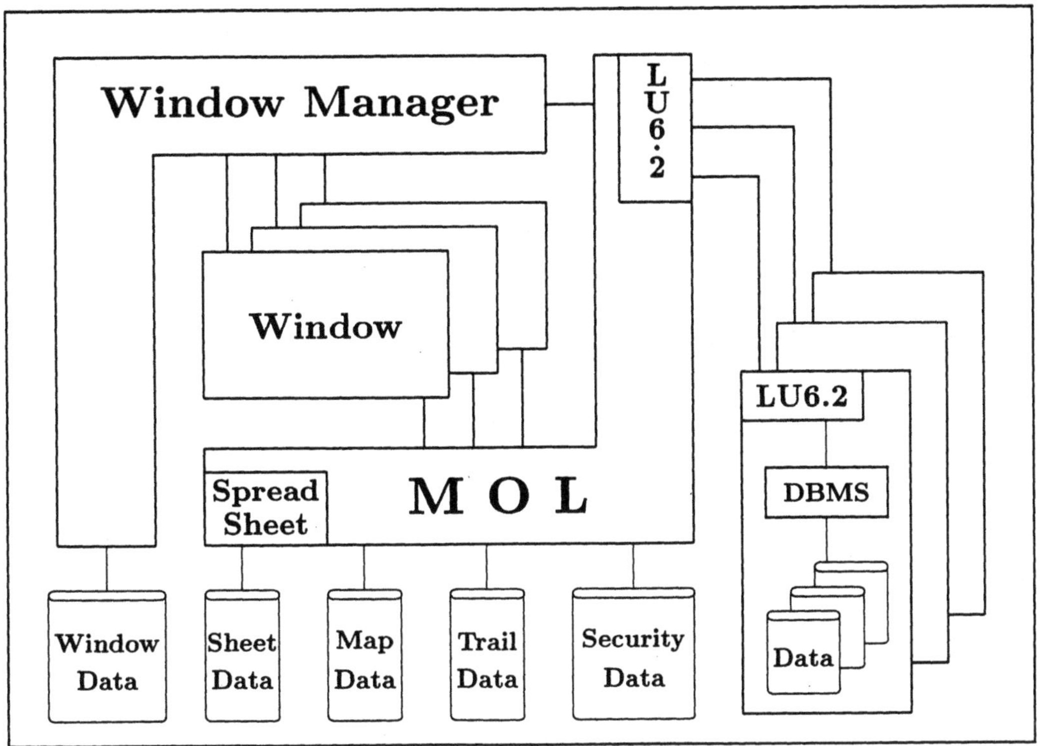

Figure 10. Configuration of MOL

4. Implementation

A configuration of MOL is shown in Figure 10. MOL is implemented based on three software tools, a window manager, a database access protocol (LU6.2) and a spread sheet. MOL is a program to control the three tools.

The window manager controls all windows used in MOL. A user specifies directions for a messenger in each window. By the specification, MOL decides a window to be active, generates a sequence of commands to access a database or transforms a format of received data into another format which spread sheet software can read.

LU6.2 is a remote access protocol for database systems. When a user requests to retrieve data, MOL generates a sequence of commands of LU6.2. By using LU6.2, the commands are transferred to a database and the result are sent back to LU6.2. The resultant data are transformed into a spread sheet by MOL.

A spread sheet is called by a window of MOL. In a window, a user can manipulate collected data by operations of the spread sheet software.

By use of the three tools, we can implement MOL as a local program of a workstation.

5. Discussion

In this paper, we proposed a map-oriented visual language MOL which is a procedural language for information retrievals. A structure of a database is represented as a map. A procedure is represented as actions of a messenger on a map. A map is well familiar and easy to understand for naive users. A map is also good to represent navigations.

A user sometimes gives a messenger a wrong instruction. Collected data are often so large beyond user's expectation. A user of MOL can see and process collected data any time even on a way of collection. An interactive interface of MOL enables a user to specify his requests step-by-step.

We use LU6.2 for remote database access and a spread sheet software for calculations and modifications. It is easy to implement MOL because the programs to be developed are only interfaces among LU6.2, a spread sheet software and a window manager.

A large map can be divided into some screens in MOL. But only one or two screens are used because almost practical applications of their database include up to 30 entities.

References

1. Bryce, D. and Hull, R., SNAP : A Graphic-Based Schema Manager, *Proceedings of the International Conference on Data Engineering, 151-164, 1986.*

2. Chang, S.K. et al., A Relational Database System for Pictures, *Proceedings of Workshop on Picture Description and Management, 1977.*

3. Chang, N.S. and Fu, K.S., Query Language for Image Database Systems, *Proceedings of Workshop on Picture Description and Management, 1980.*

4. Christodoulakis, S., Ho, F. and Theodoridou, M., The Multimedia Object Presentation Manager of MINOS : A Symmetric Approach, *Proceedings of ACM SIGMOD International Conference on the Management of Data, 295-310, 1986.*

5. Codd, E.F., A Relational Model of Data for Large Shared Data Banks, *Communication of ACM, Vol.13, No.6, 377-387, 1970.*

6. Codd, E.F., Relational Database : A Practical Foundation for Productivity, *Communication of ACM, Vol.25, No.2, 109-117, 1982.*

7. Fogg, D., Lessons from a 'Living in a Database' Graphical Interface, *Proceedings of ACM SIGMOD International Conference on the Management of Data, 100-106, 1984.*

8. Goldman, K.J., Goldman, S.A., Kanellakis, P.C. and Zdonic, S.B., ISIS : Interface for a Semantic Information System, *Proceedings of ACM SIGMOD International Conference on the Management of Data, 328-342, 1985.*

9. King, R. and Melville, S., Ski : A Semantics—Knowledgeable Interface, *Proceedings of the Tenth International Conference on VLDB, 30-34, 1984.*

10. Makinouchi, A. and Yoon, B.D., A Survey of Multimedia Database Interfaces, *Information Processing, Vol.28, No.6, 694-704, 1987. (In Japanese)*

11. Martin, J., *Application Development Without Programmers,* Prentice-Hall, Inc., 1982.

12. Martin, J., *Fourth-Generation Languages, Vol.1,2 and 3,* Prentice-Hall, Inc., 1985.

13. Stonebraker, M. and Kalash, J., TIMBER : A Sophisticated Relation Browser, *Proceedings of VLDB, 1-10, 1982.*

14. Wilson, G.A. and Herot, C.H., Semantics VS Graphics — To Show or Not to Show, *Proceedings of VLDB, 1980.*

15. Wong, H.K.T. and Kuo. I., GUIDE : Graphical User Interface for Database Exploration, *Proceedings of the Eighth International Conference on VLDB, 22-32, 1982.*

NAVIGATION IN THE VISUAL INFORMATION DATABASE WORLD

Hisashi Kasahara Tomio Kishimoto

NTT Human Interface Laboratories, Nippon Telegraph and Telephone Corporation

ABSTRACT

Some ideas on managing visual objects and their viewing environment are proposed as the navigational aids for multi-media databases. "Image Base Navigator", described in this paper, is an organized browsing environment, in which we can effectively see and examine a complex of visual objects and in which we can find out associative and related objects with less concern for query procedures. A new information complex modeling technology and a new information world viewing model are introduced. Prototype examples of navigational environment are given. This environment is implemented on the object-oriented data modeling basis.

[Keywords] image database, visual thinking, image retrieval, visual interface, database navigation, object oriented modeling

1. INTRODUCTION

An advanced database interface is needed to realize a "Visual Thinking" environment for creative work using visual materials, such as decision making in offices or laboratories, artistic or commercial design, coordination of interiors, and many other possible applications. For tasks such as these, it is usually the case that:

(1) Users have a definite objective in mind,

(2) but they are not sure about which materials are relevant to their task.

In this paper, we examine a viewing environment for users and propose a model for managing visual materials that would support such application tasks as sketched above.

This paper will describe what we call an "Image Base Navigator"; an organized database browsing environment, in which users can effectively see and examine a complex of visual materials. While browsing, it is quite possible for users to come across significant information unexpectedly and easily change their course of action to locate information which is more relevant to their objective. All these operations can be carried out without using any symbolic query procedures.

(In this paper, we use the terms "visual information", "visual materials", or "visual objects" to refer to pictures, texts, (3-D or 2-D) graphics, videos, animations, diagrams, and their combinations.)

In section 2, we survey the conventional visual information viewing and managing environments to clarify the position of our research work. Then, in sections 3 and 4, we propose a new viewing model and visual information managing model for complexes of visual information. In section 5, a prototype environment called "Image Base Navigator" is introduced and the application of our viewing/managing model is examined in detail. Section 6 summarizes our work.

2. USER-INFORMATION INTERFACE

The user-information interfaces for visual information systems can be roughly categorized into the following three types.

Type-1: is common in conventional file system environments, and also has been used for visual information systems. Users directly specify picture numbers (file numbers) or picture names (file names) to view visual objects. Some systems use a pictorial directory which is presented to the user as an index of picture information. They adapt the hierarchical tree structure for managing and viewing a number of visual objects.

Type-2: is common in conventional symbolic database management system (DBMS) environments, and has also been widely used for visual information systems. DBMS, or a database server, works as an agent of the user to locate significant information which matches user's query intention. In this interface, the media interworking mechanisms in DBMS were the key subjects for research. They need the intra-media connection between words (i.e. user's key-words) and words (i.e. database media), between sketches (user's key-images) and sketches (database media), etc., and the inter-media connection between words (user's key-words) and documents (database media), between words (user's key-words) and pictures (database media), between sketches (user's key-images) and pictures (database media), etc. The user-information interface applied in most conventional visual information systems has been composed of key-words provided by the user and symbolic matching by the database server using a symbolic index corresponding to each visual information type. Symbolic indexes are manually constructed for each piece of pictorial information in advance. Experiments have been carried out in some specific fields, in which key-images (sketches, graphics, etc.) are provided by the user and the pattern matching process is done by the database server using the original picture or iconic index (generally called similarity retrieval technology). However, such techniques still have a long way to go. Much progress must be made in the computer vision and pattern recognition fields before such inter-media searches will be feasible.

The most intractable problems for this type of interface are caused by the gap between the tremendous volume of information created by databased visual information and the limited capacity of the possible query description media of users. The variety of possible meanings of an image represents another problem. The interpretation of image meaning is dependent on the situational contexts which include, who views the image when and how it is displayed. Database servers are unable to specify tight indexes for such media. Nor are users able to specify tight filters for them.

Type-3: graphically shows the database structure to the user and the user browses through it to locate the information desired. For this kind of interface, a number of interesting studies have been carried out on information viewing environments for symbolic information systems. A pioneer work by Herot[1)] provided a graphically represented spatial data surface over a symbolic database. Other works by Fogg[2)] and Larson[3)] provided graphically represented entity-relationship networks or nested documents of data. Some related research has also been performed on visual information systems.[4,5)] This type of user-information interface is expected to solve the bottlenecks of the Type-2 interface for visual information retrieval systems, and appears to offer attractive and promising features for visual thinking.

This paper focuses on the Type-3 user-information interface which is most applicable to visual thinking tasks and matches the requirements mentioned in the previous section. Users who are not able to produce appropriate keywords to retrieve some indefinite target would prefer to take a directed stroll in the database world.

3. NAVIGATION CONCEPT

A new viewing model for a complex of visual information objects is proposed here. We will refer to this basic concept as "Navigation", as in navigating through a visual database world.

In the presentation to follow, we will pursue the navigation analogy; "World" will refer to the visual world of information being navigated through, "Scene" is the information surface which can be observed while navigating through the world, and "Viewer" is you the navigator. The basic navigational operations are as follows:

(1) Standing Viewer Operation (pan, zoom in/out)

In this operation, the viewer stays at a fixed location in the "World" and examines the information objects which he can see there.

(2) Spatially Moving Viewer Operation (parallel transfer, back-and-forth transfer, orbit transfer)

In this operation, the viewer moves from one location to another in the "World" to look at other complexes of information objects.

(3) Temporally Moving Viewer Operation (temporal transfer)

In this operation, the viewer moves from one period to another to look at information objects at different periods of time.

(4) Scene Operation (dynamic-scene, scene-change)

In this operation, the scene content changes dynamically.

The difference in the presentation medium of the visual world gives various properties to the viewing environment. However, we will pursue the "Navigation" model as in the following examples.

<ex-1> 2-dimensional text page or 2-dimensional image world

The viewer pans his view to see other scenes of the world when he can only see a portion of the 2-D text page or the 2-D image at a time. He zooms either in to see more detail or out for a wider perspective of the 2-D text page or the 2-D image.

<ex-2> 3-dimensional image world (such as CAD graphics)

The viewer pans his view to see other scenes of a 3-D image when he can only see some portion of it at a time. He zooms either in to see more detail or out to see a more inclusive view of the image. He transfers his view in parallel or back-and-forth or in orbit to see the 3-D objects from other directions or locations.

<ex-3> Motion imagery world

In this case, a scene is viewed as a dynamic-scene, or the viewer can transfer his view temporally to see arbitrary video frames as a new scene.

<ex-4> Document world (as a complex of formatted text pages)

The viewer pans his view to see other pages of a document when he can only see some portion of the document at a time. Or, the viewer transfers his view temporally to see older versions of the document.

(The filtering of the information world using some query procedures can also be stylized as a scene-change operation.)

The "Scenes" described in the examples above are composed of some objects which are related in a spatio-temporal manner. For example, a 2-D text page scene has some content portions (objects) in it and they have a relationship as a physical page layout (refer Fig. 1(a)). Or consider a 2-D image scene with some visual objects in it that are related in some spatial arrangement (refer Fig. 1(b)). The

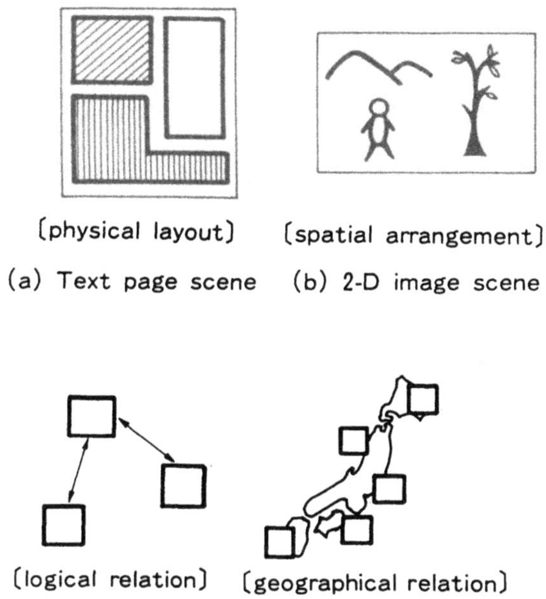

(□ ···visual objects in database)

(c) Visual information database scene

Fig. 1. Various Navigation Scenes

information objects in a multi-media database also have various properties, various operational features and a number of relationships with each other. Our "Navigation Concept" therefore defines the "Scene" of a visual information database "World" as a complex of visual information objects which have various relationships with each other (refer Fig. 1(c)).

Based on this "Navigation Concept", we have developed an "Image Base Navigator" to enable users to rapidly and easily navigate through the spatial complexes of multi-media visual information. The main features of the navigator are:

(1) All operations are based on images. Since no symbolic interactions are involved, we have coined the term "Image Base".

(2) A visual navigator is used as a cue to enable users to navigate through the space of databased information. Without cues, users would lose their orientation; hence, our designation "Navigator".

(3) Panning, zooming and transferring operations are provided.

In the following two sections, the mobility and orienting schema for the users working in this environment is described in detail.

4. INFORMATION MANAGING MODELS

"Grouping" and "Relation" structure is at the heart of the information complex modeling we propose here. The context of a visual information object in a visual information database world is determined through n objects "Grouping" and further through "Relation"s in a group. With these two parameters, it is easy to specify the meaning of a visual object in the world. In other words, this approach facilitates navigational indexing. This "Grouping" and "Relation" model is the basis of structuring navigational scenes for users.

From the examples shown in Table 1, it can be seen that there are various ways of grouping and relating to form an organized complex of visual objects. Visual objects can be

Table 1. Grouping and Relation Examples

Grouping Motivation \ Relation	Aggregate relation	Spatial-view relation	Visual-properties relation	Locational relation	Temporal relation	Semantic relation
Information related to specific OBJECT	CAD object	Multi-directional shots	Color/Shape coordination	Locational background coordination	Video cuts editing Periodical version management	Hypertext
Information related to specific SCENE	Graphically structured scene		—	Nation-wide aerial photographs		
Information related to specific EVENT	—		—	Nation-wide event overlook		
Information related to specific CATEGORY	—	—	Consumer goods design catalog	Real estate pictures		
Information related to other specific purposes	Research paper	Multi-directional montage pictures	CT(Computer Tomography) pictures of the same disease	CT pictures of the same patient's body		

related in a number of basic ways:

(a) Aggregate relation

Indivisible combination of several visual objects making up a unit of information.

(b) Spatial-view relation

The object relations derived, for example, from camera operations.

(c) Visual-properties relation

The object relations derived, for example, from image attribute.

(d) Locational relation

The object relations derived, for example, from geographical property.

(e) Temporal relation

The object relations derived from such temporal properties as afterward, beforehand, while, and so on.

(f) Semantic relation

The object relations derived from semantics of its content.

(g) Other relations

Arbitrary relations.

We have realized the mapping of these relationships onto the "Grouping" & "Relation" model based on the object-oriented data modeling paradigm.(for example, 6)) We have defined an "information unit" and a "link" as entities in the visual information database world. An information unit is composed of one or several visual objects and is the indivisible unit of information. This information unit is represented as a member (=instance) of a group (=class). A group defines the descriptions of attribute indexes (=properties) and possible operations (=methods) which can be applied to all the information units in that group. An information unit defines the values of indexes created for that unit. Groups can form a hierarchy representing their subordination relationships. As for a "link", it is also represented as a member (=instance) of a relation (=class). A relation has some attributes (=properties) and some operations (=methods) which can be applied to all the links in the same class. Relations can also form a hierarchy representing their subordination relationships. A link has two or more references to information units, which indicate the correspondence between the link and the information units.

We have allowed an information unit to be a member of more than one group, we call this a multiple membership, to make the "Grouping" model more flexible. Moreover, we have allowed arbitrary information units to be linked together by arbitrary relations. This function is quite important to ensure that databases are flexible and extensible for visual thinking. Not all information can be stylized in a "Grouping" framework especially when the database is in its growing process, in which new, isolated but significant information can be input in a serial fashion.

An example framework of information modeling for the "Image Base Navigator" is indicated in Fig. 2. The "Core Unit" indicated in Fig. 2(b) represents the user's present location in the database. A hierarchy of groups forms a navigation district. The links supply navigation paths between information units in a group or to information units in other districts. The roles of these in navigation will be described in detail in the next section.

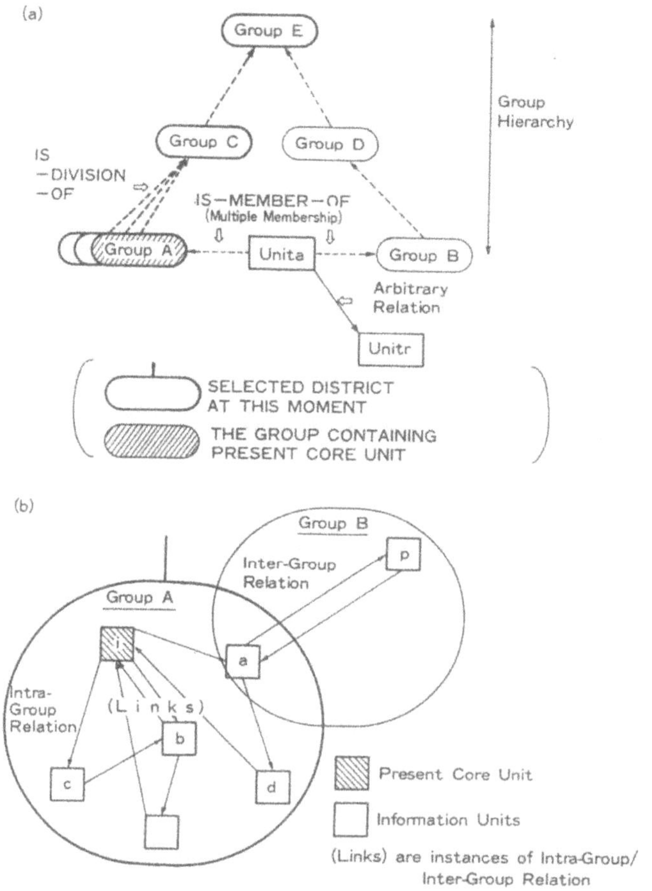

Fig. 2. Information Management Overview

5. NAVIGATION IN THE VISUAL INFORMATION DATABASE WORLD

The specific but basic (for the idea) appearance of the user interface in "Image Base Navigator" is indicated in Fig. 3. The formatted visual information objects in this display indicates the present view of the user as a scene in the visual information database world. The center window displays the "Core Unit". This unit indicates the user's present position in the visual information database world. The small windows on the upper part of the display indicate the "Navigators" to the information groups in the same district which the user can select as the next browsing direction at this time. The representative visual object of each group is displayed as a "Navigator". The small windows on the lower part of the display indicate the "Navigators" to the units which are members of the same information group with the "Core Unit" and are related to the "Core Unit" in some binary relation. Users can select one of them as the next browsing direction in the group. The small windows on the left side of the display

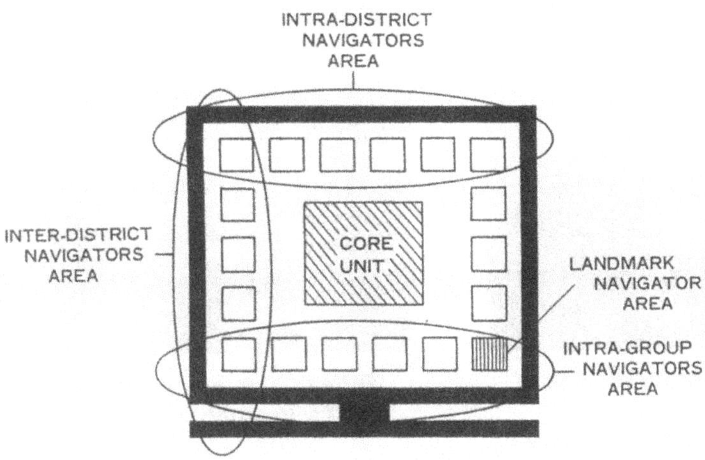

Fig. 3. Basic User Interface Appearance of the Image Base Navigator

indicate the "Navigators" to the information units providing scenes of other districts of the world to the viewer. The representative visual objects of other districts are displayed as "Navigators". They are primarily based on the multiple membership of the "Core Unit" to other visual information groups of other districts. Moreover, they can be visual objects which have some arbitrary relation with the "Core Unit" and at the same time, are not a member of the same group with it.

Users select one of the "Navigators" to walk around the visual information database world. The information unit which corresponds to the "Navigator" selected is newly displayed in the "Core Unit" area for further examination or operations. The "Navigators" are subsequently renewed to form the next scene of the world. They enable users to navigate further in one direction. When users walk across the district boundaries by selecting one of the "Navigators" on the left side, a landmark "Navigator" is displayed in the lower-right window. This landmark "Navigator" is the key to returning to the original group and prevents users from losing their way.

For example, let the shaded Unit i in Fig. 2(b) be the "Core Unit" at present. Unit i is displayed in the center area of the display in Fig. 3. Let the shaded Group A in Fig. 2(a) be the group containing the present "Core Unit" Unit i. The representative visual objects of the groups in the same district as Group A (bold lined ones on the lower left of Fig. 2(a)) are displayed in the upper "Navigators" windows, which include one for Group A. Group A is the group which is active as the users location in the world at this moment. Unit i has links to Unit a, b, and c which belong to the intra-group relation class (Fig. 2(b)). These linked units are displayed in the lower "Navigators" windows at this moment. Let the user select Unit a as the next browsing direction. Then Unit a is displayed in the center area of the display as the "Core Unit" instead of Unit i and new "Navigators" are displayed in the "Navigators" windows. They are:
Unit d of Group A which is linked from Unit a by an intra-group relation (Fig. 2(b)) and is displayed in a lower window;
Unit p of Group B which is linked from Unit a by inter-group relation (Fig. 2(b)) and is displayed in a left window;
and Unit r which is linked from Unit a by an arbitrary relation (Fig. 2(a)) and is displayed in another left window.
The inter-group relations such as between Unit a and Unit p originate from the multiple membership, in this case membership of Unit a to Group A and Group B (Fig. 2(a)). Next, let the user select Unit p as the next browsing direction. Then Unit p is displayed in the center area of the display as the "Core Unit" instead of Unit a and new "Navigators" are displayed in the "Navigator" windows. The lower righthand window shows the landmark "Navigator" Unit a which is linked by inter-group relation from Unit p. This link instance is a dynamic one. It is consequently regenerated from each new "Core Unit" while navigating through other districts.

The links described above inherit their properties or operational features from relation class definitions. The name of each link instance is presented on the upper portion of each "Navigator" screen as an additional symbolic aid for navigation. The upper "Navigators" present the name attribute of each group as symbolic navigational information.

One simple example of the "Image Base Navigator" environment is indicated in Fig. 4.(i)～(vii). It is an example of a light catalog database. "Grouping" is done according to light types and series, and "Relation" is defined according to the differences in visual properties of information units in a group, such as shape, color, size, and number property of lights. These strategies for creating a database environment are specified according to the requirements of each application. A multiple membership feature appears in Fig. 4.(iv) to (vii), which projects the membership of the present "Core Unit" belonging to stairwell-type-3 group and also to series-xx group. Users select their desired paths to navigate through and examine the information in the database. Users can select the path to the next light picture which is different in shape from the core light picture (Fig. 4.(ii) to (iii), and (iv) to (vi)), or select the path to one which is different in color from the core one (Fig. 4.(iv) to (v)), or move to one which is different in size from the core one, or move to one which is different in light number. They have various associative selectors for their navigation. They can wonder around other districts (i.e., district of information units of the series-xx group) according to their intention.(Fig. 4.(iv) to (vi)) Navigation based on the relation of visual property difference is useful for this kind of pictorial database.

This navigational style of walking around the information world is called the "Walk Through" mode. In this mode, the view of users is defined as the whole display including "Core Unit" and "Navigators". They pan their view to see other information units in the same information group. They zoom their view to see the information units in the group. They transfer their view and their location to walk across to the information units in different groups or districts.

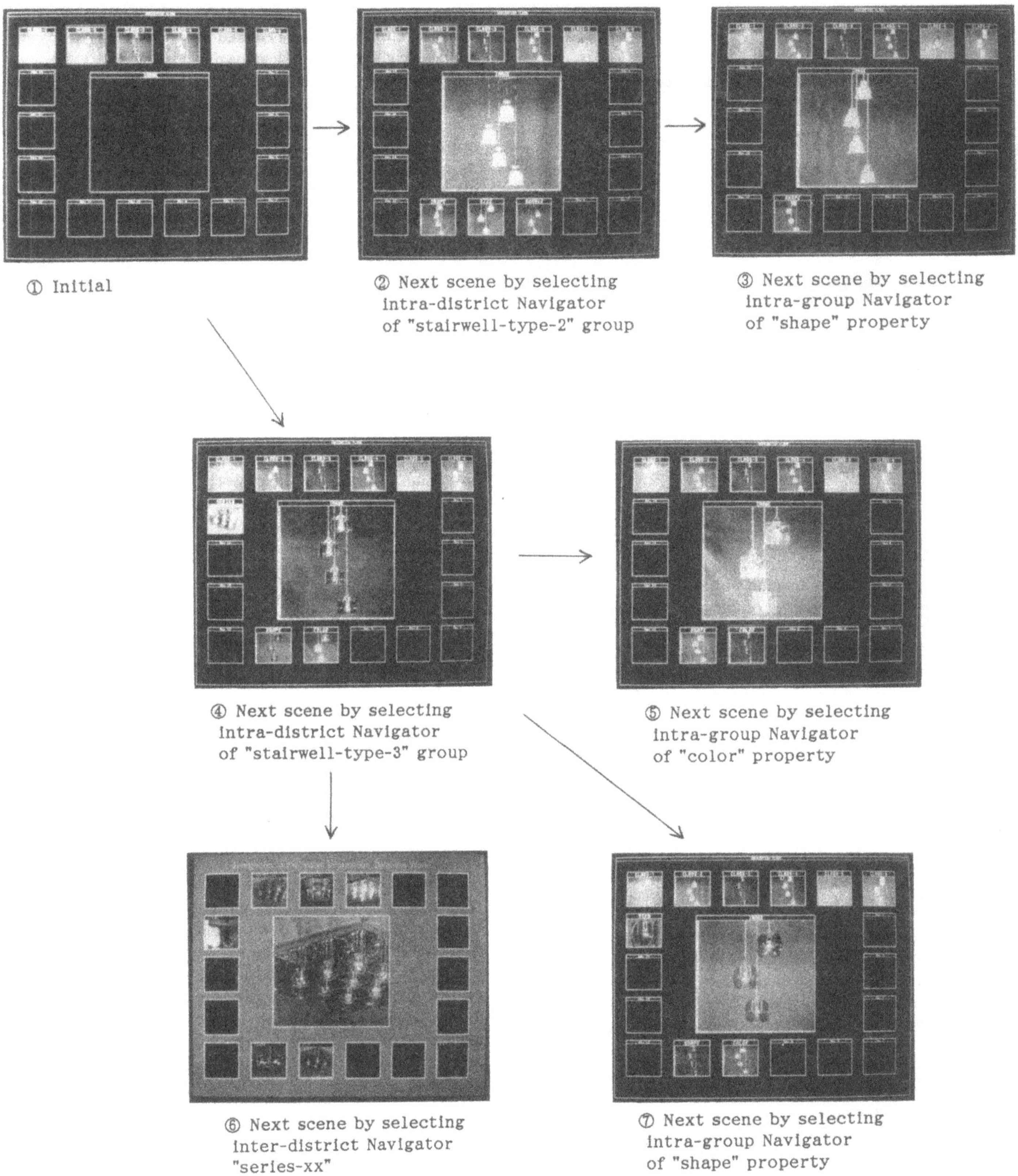

Fig. 4. The "Image Base Navigator" in Action
(for a light catalog database)

The other navigational mode is called the "Observation" mode, in which the users' view is restricted only to the "Core Unit". In this mode, the navigational operation depends on the presentation medium of the information unit. Users pan, zoom, or transfer their views, observe dynamic-scene, or drive scene-changes as the examples described in section 3. These operational menus, dependent upon each medium class, are defined by the inheritance of operations through visual media oriented class definitions.

The small windows on the right side of the display in Fig. 3 are reserved for the "Navigators" to the information units which are filtered by some query operations on the "Core Unit" in the "Observation" mode.

These organized displays and interaction with the information world provide a basic environment for users to navigate through visual information databases. The variations of the scene format in the display can be controlled according to the presentation property of relation in that group, but still the "Image Base Navigator" keeps on providing a scene of the information world as relational views of the "Core Unit", which is the body of a visual object at the present position, and the related "Navigators", which are representatives of the related objects.

Functions providing a wider view could be an option. Nevertheless, this basic scene efficiently provides a wide view of the information world by presenting representatives of groups and ones of other districts. From an operational point of view, some optional servers could be incorporated into this navigating environment. For example, the user may like to keep some information unit visible while browsing through other units for reference or for comparison. These functions are to be implemented as a customized service in the "Image Base Navigator".

How shall we handle content portion driven grouping? An information unit can be composed of several visual objects which are indivisible. Each object can compose an individual group according to its relation. The "Navigators" presented in this case are the content portions which have contributed to make up the group. The definition of the portion to be a "Navigator" is described as one of the properties of the information unit instance.

We have primarily used pictorial navigators to enable users to navigate in various directions. These navigators are from the original databased media, not reformed symbolic or iconic indexes. They work well especially in our prototype database of pictures of interior goods and pictorial materials for visual design. This is because, the relational path can not be precisely described by symbolic information in such systems. Pictorial representation enhances rapid recognition of ideas and memory recall. Some recent data on the value of these pictorial navigators can be seen in Egido[7)].

6. CONCLUDING REMARKS

We tried to introduce a database environment which can be applied to the visual thinking tasks utilizing visual materials. The best solution would be a loose and visual indexing of the databases and flexibility in structuring the scenario for interaction between users and database.

We tried to apply a modeling oriented approach. The visual information managing model was based on "Grouping" and "Relation" concepts and the new viewing model proposed here was based on "Navigation Concept". "Image Base Navigator" provides users with a structured view of the information world which is wide enough and relevant to spatio-temporal navigation. We tried to make good use of logically associative and visually associative connections to realize the mobility and the orientation schema for users to navigate through the database world. Users can select their route according to their personal cognition of the relationship between "Core Unit" and "Navigators" around it. They might happen to come across information initially unexpected, but quite significant for their work. Their thinking might be accelerated by associative reference to related information. They might gradually fix or modify their images of target information while walking through the database.

In our approach, the Type-3 navigational environment (refer to Section 2) is the basic user-information interface, but some Type-2 query procedures are possible depending on the type of information unit. Optional functions and future research results for Type-2 interfaces could be integrated to enlarge the interface channel in our visual thinking environment.

If the "Relation" function of the model presented is not used at all (in such a case, there can be no organized browsing path in a group nor to other districts), you would get a database of conventional hierarchical data structure which forms the Type-1 user-information interface referred in section 2.

The viewing environment presented in this paper was based on the premise that a database was organized in advance. On the other hand, the mechanism for a database to automatically and gradually reorganize its knowledge structure from its initial stages might conceivably be applied to an advanced visual thinking environment. This will be a subject for further study.

ACKNOWLEDGEMENTS

We are grateful to Dr. Hiroshi Yasuda, Executive Manager of Visual Media Laboratory, NTT Human Interface Laboratories, for his encouragement to this research work. We also thank Yoshinobu Tonomura, Hideki Koike, Shinji Abe and Tutomu Horikoshi for their technical advice and discussions on the handling of visual information.

REFERENCES

1) Herot, C. F., "Spatial Management of Data," ACM Trans. on Database Systems, Vol.5, No.4, 1980, pp493-514.
2) Fogg, D., "Lessons from a "Living in a Database" Graphical Query Interface," ACM SIGMOD, 1984, pp100-106.
3) Larson, J. A., "A Visual Approach to Browsing in a Database Environment," IEEE COMPUTER, June 1986, pp62-71.
4) Donelson, W. C., "Spatial Management of Information," ACM SIGGRAPH, 1978, pp203-209.
5) Christodoulakis, S. and Faloutsos, C., "Design and Performance Considerations for an Optical Disk-Based, Multimedia Object Server," IEEE COMPUTER, December 1986, pp45-56.
6) Woelk, D., Kim, W. and Luther, W., "An Object-Oriented Approach to Multimedia Databases," ACM-SIGMOD, 1986, pp. 311-325.
7) Egido, C. and Patterson, J., "Pictures and Category Labels as Navigational Aids for Catalog Browsing," CHI'88, 1988, pp. 127-132.

QUERY PROCESSING

A Survey of Some Spatial Match Query Algorithms

C. C. Chang and D. J. Buehrer

National Chung Cheng University
Chia Yi, Taiwan, R.O.C.

Abstract

This paper surveys recent research involving the retrieval of symbolic pictures from a large database. The symbolic pictures are composed of various types of icons that may represent either physical objects or the feature points of these objects in the original image. The queries to the database may involve the use of the operators <, =, and > to compare the X and Y coordinates of the icons. S.K. Chang [1] has defined several versions of the spatial match query problem, depending on exactly how the patterns are intended to match the subject pictures:

a. Type 2 - Does there exist an exact match which preserves distances?
b. Type 1 - Does there exist a match if rows and colums of the subject can be deleted?
c. Type 0 - Does there exist a match if rows and columns of the subject may be merged together?

Although the type 0 and type 1 problems generally have an exponential number of matches in the worst case, the above existential queries can usually be quickly answered by using a variety of techniques. We will survey some of these techniques in this paper.

Keywords: spatial match query, symbolic picture, icon, pattern match, algorithm

1. Introduction

With the advent of wide-spread use of hypermedia, image databases will become increasingly important. For example, large databases of satellite photographs (e.g. for weather prediction, mining, crop prediction, pollution control, astronomy) will be used by an increasingly large network of users. These users may desire to query this database of images to find all images satisfying certain constraints. Preferably, they will be able to use a query-by-example mode, moving around icons in a pattern picture, and having the system find all images that have the same spatial relationships among the objects [2].

There has recently been considerable research on such retrieval of symbolic pictures from an iconic image database. The icons are a symbolic representation of a part of the real image. They may represent, for example, certain feature points of certain objects. Assuming that each image has a corresponding symbolic iconized picture, the images may be retrieved by first searching the iconic database.

The Intelligent Image Database System (IIDS), proposed in 1988 by S.K. Chang et al. [3], provides for such a high-level iconic spatial query-by-example search mechanism. As spatial match queries were originally formulated by S.K. Chang [1] [4], only the spatial relationships among the icons are considered. Moreover, the pattern picture is assumed to be aligned with the pictures to be searched, so that rotations do not have to be considered. The queries for these retrievals are only permitted to include the 9 spatial relationships among pairs of icons, based on whether the X and Y coordinates of two icons are relatively <, =, or >. In the next section, we will present a more detailed description of the spatial match query problem as defined in [1]. In Section 3, various heuristic solutions to the basic problem are reviewed. In Section 4, other considerations, such as disk access time, are added into the problem, and various solutions are reviewed. Finally, Section 5 presents some conclusions and directions for future research.

2. Background and Definitions

Each symbolic picture is defined to consist of a two-dimensional array of spatial locations. Each location may contain an arbitrary number of "icons", where an icon represents a feature point of an object in the corresponding physical image. For instance, the feature points could be taken to be the centroids of the intersections of minimal rectangles which enclose the objects in the physical image. Each icon type has a name. Multiple icons with the same name are permitted, and they may be at the same location.

The spatial query match problem was originally defined in terms of the 2D string representation of these symbolic pictures [1]. So we will first present the definition of 2D strings.

Definition 1: (1D string) Let V be a vocabulary consisting of the union of a set of icons and the set of relation symbols R= {"<", ":", "="}, where these sets are disjoint. A 1D string over V is any string $v_1 v_2 \ldots v_n$, $n \geq 0$, where the v_i's are in V.

Definition 2: (2D string) A 2D string: (γ_x, γ_y) over V is defined as

$$(v_1 r_{1x} v_2 r_{2x} \ldots r_{(n-1)x} v_n,$$
$$v_{p(1)} r_{1y} v_{p(2)} r_{2y} \ldots r_{(n-1)y} v_{p(n)})$$

where

the string $v_1 \ldots v_n$ is a 1D string over V,

p: {1,...,n} --> {1,...,n} is a permutation over {1,...,n},

$r_{1x} \ldots r_{(n-1)x}$ is a 1D string over R,

and $r_{1y} \ldots r_{(n-1)y}$ is a 1D string over R.

Definition 3: (augmented 2D string) An augmented 2D string $(\gamma_x, \gamma_y, \gamma_p)$ over V is defined as

$$(v_1 r_{1x} v_2 r_{2x} \ldots r_{(n-1)x} v_n,$$
$$v_{p(1)} r_{1y} v_{p(2)} r_{2y} \ldots r_{(n-1)y} v_{p(n)},$$
$$p(1)p(2)\ldots p(n))$$

where the symbols are defined as in the definition of 2D strings.

In these definitions, the "<" symbol represents "to the left of" when used in the γ_x string, and it represents "below" when used in the γ_y string. The "=" symbol represents the "in the same spatial location as" relation, while the ":" symbol represents "in the same row as" or "in the same column as" relation, depending on whether it occurs in γ_x or in γ_y. For example, the 2D augmented string representation of the symbolic picture in Figure 2 is (a = d < a = b < c, a = a < b = c < d, [1,3,4,5,2]), where the vocabulary V is {a,b,c,d}.

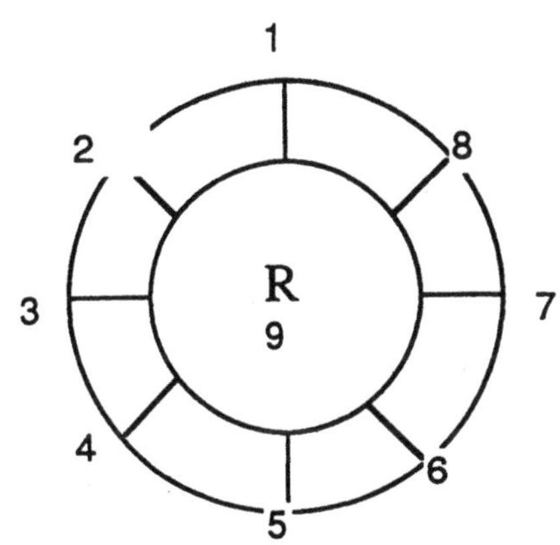

Figure 1
9 Directions

The permutation list of the augmented 2D strings is sometimes needed to be able to produce a unique picture from the 2D representation. That is, a 2D string without the permutation indices may correspond to more than one picture if several icons have the same name.

Notice that these definitions do not permit the picture to have any blank rows or columns. The above definitions can be extended to permit the v_i symbols to include the null string. Empty rows or columns in a pattern are taken to mean that the corresponding subject icons must necessarily be at least that many rows or columns apart. However, for most queries, the patterns are first reduced in size by deleting blank rows or columns. Notice that there is no need for the subject or pattern to be square.

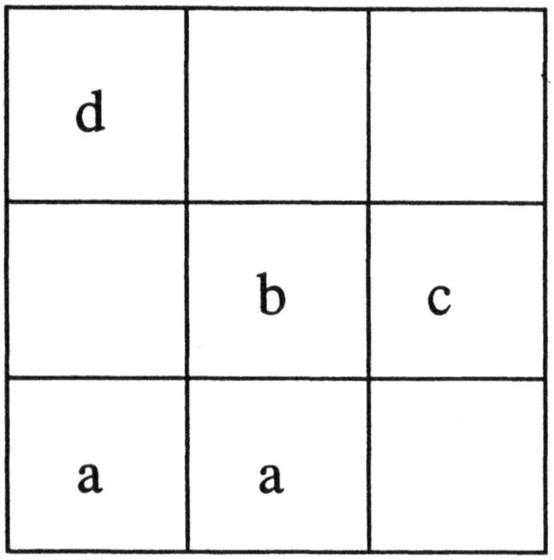

Figure 2
An Iconic Picture

We now go on to define three types of pattern matching. These types of pattern matching are illustrated in Figure 3. As mentioned in the abstract, Type-0 matches permit subject rows and columns to be merged, Type-1 matches permit only deletions of subject rows and columns, and Type-2 matches permit no merges or deletions.

Definition 4: (1D Types of matching) A string γ is a type-i 1D subsequence of a string α if (1) γ is contained in α, and (2) if $a_1 w_1 b_1$ is a substring of γ, a_1 matches a_2 in α, and b_1 matches b_2 in α, then type-i is

(type-0) if $r(b_2)-r(a_2) \geq r(b_1)-r(a_1)$ or $r(b_1) - r(a_1) = 0$

(type-1) if $r(b_2)-r(a_2) \geq r(b_1)-r(a_1) > 0$ or $r(b_2) - r(a_2) = r(b_1) - r(a_1) = 0$

(type-2) if $r(b_2) - r(a_2) = r(b_1) - r(a_1)$

where r(x), the rank of the symbol x, is defined as one plus the number of "<" symbols which precede the symbol x in the string γ.

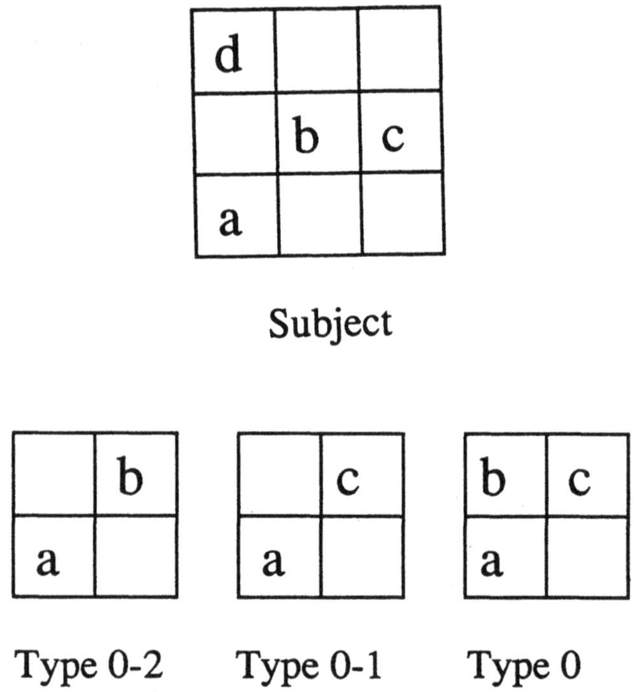

Figure 3
Sample Subject and Pattern Matches

Algorithm 1: (Simple spatial match retrieval algorithm)

1. Let $(\alpha_x, \alpha_y, \alpha_p)$ and $(\gamma_x, \gamma_y, \gamma_p)$ be the 2D string representations of symbolic pictures f and f', respectively.
2. For each 1D type-i subsequence γ_x of α_x until done (found by using a standard algorithm for finding a type-i subsequence of one string in another string).
   A. From the vector K of positions icons in α_x which are matched by the above 1D subsequence.
   B. From the vector P(K) of positions of these icons in α_y.
   C. From the substring β_y of α_y which contains the symbols at positions $P(K_i)$.
   D. If the 2D subsequence $(\beta_x, \beta_y, \gamma_p)$ is equal to the 2D string $(\gamma_x, \gamma_y, \gamma_p)$, then add this answer into the solution.

Definition 5: (2D Types of matching) Let $(\alpha_x,\alpha_y,\alpha_p)$ and $(\gamma_x,\gamma_y,\gamma_p)$ be the 2D string representations of symbolic pictures f and f', respectively. $(\gamma_x,\gamma_y,\gamma_p)$ is a type-*i* 2D subsequence of $(\alpha_x,\alpha_y,\alpha_p)$ if γ_x is a type-*i* 1D subsequence of α_x and γ_y is a type-*i* 1D subsequence of α_y. f' is said to be a type-*i* sub-picture of f.

The question of whether or not a pattern is contained in a subject picture is now reduced to the problem of checking whether or not the pattern is a 2D type-i subsequence of the subject. Notice that although it can be checked whether or not a 1D string is a type-i subsequence of another 1D string in O(n) time, the 2D subsequence problem is much more difficult. This is because there are a potentially exponential number of 1D subsequences. However, it is not evident which of those potential solutions will satisfy the 2nd dimension constraints.

A straightforward algorithm for trying all of the subsequences is given above. The problem with the above algorithm is, of course, that it takes a potentially exponential time to find a single solution. Depending on how the 1D algorithm generates solutions, the above algorithm may have to try all of these solutions before arriving at a correct solution for the 2D problem.

In the next section, we present algorithms which do better than Algorithm 1.

3. Some faster spatial query algorithms

In this section we present some algorithms for the spatial match query problem that have appeared in the literature. These algorithms are either based on a 2-dimensional version of the longest common subsequence problem, or else they are based on a fast subset-checking algorithm, for checking if all of the spatial relationships of the pattern picture are contained within the spatial relationships of the subject picture. In the latter case, the spatial relationships between the objects are usually stored in triples (O_i,O_j,R_{ij}), where the object O_i and the object O_j are related by one of nine spatial directions R_{ij}.

Lee et al. [5] proposed methods of finding "similar" pictures, based upon the 2D string encoding. By finding the 2D strings' longest common subsequences, the most "similar" pictures could be retrieved. That is, it produced the matching with the maximum number of icons having the same spatial relationships for the subject and pattern pictures. Notice that the 2D common subsequence problem is much more difficult than the 1-D common subsequence problem since the ordering is no-longer transitive. For instance, if icon A is north-east of B and C is south-east of B, then we do not know whether C is north or south of A. This makes the algorithm take non-polynomial time, which is unacceptable for large databases.

In [6], C.C. Chang proposed an algorithm for type-1 matching which is based on the 9DLT (9-Directional Lower Triangular) matrix representation, where each R_{ij} of the above triples is stored in row i and column j of a matrix. Since the spatial relation between O_i and O_j can be calculated from the spatial relation between O_j and O_i, only the lower left half of the matrix needs to be stored. The algorithm uses 1-dimensional string matching techniques to select rows and columns of the subject picture whose objects might match those of the pattern picture. Then the two 9DLT's are subtracted to see if all entries are 0, in which case the pattern picture is contained within the subject picture.

C.C. Chang and S.Y.Lee [7] then proposed using a hashing scheme to find all subject pictures which were similar to a pattern picture. In order to reduce the number of blank entries in the hash table, a nearly-minimal perfect hashing function was used. Each triple (O_i,O_j,R_{ij}) was hashed to a unique postion in this hash table, and a list of all subject pictures which contained that triple was stored at that position of the hash table. Since each list was sorted, the intersection of the lists could be efficiently computed. In this way, the pictures which had the most tuples in common with the pattern picture were computed.

Since the hashing scheme used in that paper could not easily accept new elements into the hash table, the scheme was modified by C.C. Chang and T.C. Wu [8] to make use of a more flexible method of table compression. Thus, symbolic image databases with a dynamically increasing number of icon types could be handled.

Later, Chang [9] proposed a very fast algorithm for type-1 matching. This algorithm is based on the use of the Chinese remainder theorem to encode the triples of the subject and pattern pictures. The algorithm runs in time $O(r \log(m))+O(r^2)$, where the subject has m objects and the pattern has r objects.

4. Other considerations

Since the number of images in a database may be very large, the efficiency of symbolic image retrieval becomes critical. Some techniques for improving disk access can be used. If the symbolic images are stored on one disk, the similar images can be "clustered" together. If the symbolic images are stored on 2 or more disks, they may be "declustered" in order to increase the amount of concurrency in their retrieval. This clustering and declustering depends on having a similarity measure between the symbolic pictures. Once this similarity measure is defined, a short spanning path, which is not necessarily the shortest spanning path, can be used to group similar pictures. Going in order according to this path, the pictures are distributed across disks, and then ordered within disks. The results of simulations for two such similarity measures are provided in [10] and [11]. They indicate that such clustering and declustering methods are effective for the symbolic image databases.

Most pattern-matching algorithms contain a pre-pass to check whether or not all of the pattern icons are at least contained somewhere in the subject. The constraints are essentially relaxed so that no location-checking is performed.

For Type-0 matching, where subject locations can be merged, this approach can be generalized to a form of successive relaxation, where successively precise location matching is performed at each step. First, all of the pattern icons are merged into 1 location by adding up their T vectors. The Type-0 algorithm will match iff the subject contains the pattern icons at any arbitrary locations. Then the pattern can be divided into 4 approximately equal-sized rectangles, and the icons in each rectangle can be merged. Type-0 pattern matching is now performed with this 2X2 pattern. Successively refined patterns of any size can be used, but we will assume that the patterns are of approximately sizes $2^i X 2^i$ positions. This successive relaxation will usually quickly eliminate many impossible matches, thus speeding up the average-case search time considerably, while at most doubling the worst-case runtime (assuming that the algorithm takes time which is at least linear in the size of the subject picture).

The above algorithms may be thought of as labeling problems [12], where each pattern location is labeled with the possible matching subject locations. These labels can be successively eliminated as more and more constraints are applied to the pattern position, until unique solutions are eventually found. Although there may be exponentially many solutions in the worst case, there may be a polynomial worst-case time bound from one solution to the next solution.

5. Summary and Conclusions

The formulation of the spatial match queries given by S.K. Chang [1] is a special case of more general pattern matching. It is essentially the case in which no rotations are permitted, but non-uniform horizontal/vertical expansions/contractions/translations are permitted (for types 0 and 1). There are many other special cases of spatial queries which still need to be studied. For example, spatial matching within given tolerances (for distances or angles) is a very important problem. Mixed-mode queries, using both positional and alphanumeric constraints among the icons, should also be a very important area of research. It is probable that efficient algorithms for these spatial query problems will turn out to be special cases of constraint-propagation algorithms, dynamic programming, and other fairly standard search techniques. Such techniques are being built into many of the newer constraint-based languages such as CLP [13] and Prolog III [14]. It is likely that such languages will have built-in algorithms that could prove to be very useful for answering generalized queries which involve both alphanumeric and spatial information.

References

1. S. K. Chang, Principles of Pictorial Information Systems Design, Prentice Hall International, Englewood Cliffs, New Jersey, 1989.

2. N.S. Chang and K.S. Fu, "Query-by-pictorial-example," *IEEE Transactions on Software Engineering*, Vol. SE-6, No. 6, pp.519-524, 1980.

3. S. K. Chang, C.W. Yan, D. C. Dimitroff, and T. Arndt, "An Intelligent Image Database System," *IEEE Transactions on Software Engineering*, Vol. 14, No. 5, pp. 681-688, May, 1988.

4. S. K. Chang, Q.Y. Shi, and C.W. Yan, "Iconic Indexing by 2D Strings," *IEEE Transactions on Pattern Analysis and Machine Intelligence*, Vol. PAMI-9, No. 3, pp. 413-428, May, 1987.

5. Suh-Yin Lee, Man-Kwan Shan, and Wei-Pang Yang, "Similarity Retrieval of Iconic Image Database," *Pattern Recognition*, Vol. 22, No. 6, pp. 675-682, 1989.

6. C.C. Chang, "Spatial Match Retrieval of Symbolic Pictures," *Journal of Information Science and Engineering*, Vol. 7, pp.405-422, 1991.

7. C.C. Chang and S.Y. Lee, "Retrieval of Similar Pictures on Pictorial Databases", *Pattern Recognition*, Vol. 24, No. 7, pp.675-680, 1991.

8. C.C. Chang and T.C. Wu, "Retrieving the most Similar Symbolic Pictures," to appear in *Information Processing and Management, an International Journal*, Pergamon Press, New York.

9. C.C. Chang, "A Fast Algorithm to Retrieve Symbolic Pictures", to appear in *International Journal of Computer Mathematics*, Gordon and Breach, New York.

10. C.C. Chang and D. J. Buehrer, "De-Clustering Image Databases", *Database Systems for Advanced Applications '91*, Advanced Database Research and Development Series, Vol. 2, World Scientific Publishing Co., Singapore, 1992.

11. C.C. Chang, S. J. Hwang, and D. J. Buehrer, "On the Design of Image Databases for Concurrent Spatial Match Retrieval", *Proceedings of Int'l Conf. on Information and Systems*, Hangzhou, China, pp.1034-1038, 1991.

12. D. J. Buehrer and C.C. Chang, "An O(N*M*T) Spatial Match Retrieval Algorithm", *Proceedings of the International Computer Symposium '90*, National Tsing Hua University, Hsinchu, Taiwan, December, 1990.

13. Catherine Lassez, "Constraint Logic Programming", BYTE Magazine, pp.171-176, August, 1987.

14. Alain Colmerauer, "Opening the Prolog III Universe", BYTE Magazine, pp. 177-182, August, 1987.

INTERSECTION OPERATIONS IN A MULTI-LAYERED SPATIAL DATA MODEL

David W. Embley

Brigham Young University
Provo, Utah 84602

George Nagy

Rensselaer Polytechnic Institute
Troy, New York 12180

ABSTRACT
A multi-layered, spatial, data model allows a user to operate at a high level of abstraction, yet allows efficient processing and storage of spatial data with finite-precision machinery. At the level just below the application layer, lexical and spatial objects are organized into object sets which, in turn, are represented as nested relations. While users view curves, regions, and images as continuous entities, all actual operations on the data take place at lower levels on discretized versions of idealized objects. Taking generalized intersection (relational join) as a prototypical operation, the concepts of completeness, homogeneity, regularization, interval arithmetic, round-off estimation, rational arithmetic, and topological data structures are examined in the context of the correspondence between the continuous- and the discrete-model representations.

1. INTRODUCTION

We have developed a multi-layer integrated data model that unifies digitized spatial data and related lexical information.[6)] The user level at the top allows customization of the system for specific applications. At the next layer (the conceptual model), generic spatial and lexical objects are classified into object sets organized in a semantic data model. In the third layer (the continuous database model), object sets and relationships among objects are represented as relations but, in contradistinction to the customary relational database convention, relations with an infinite number of tuples are allowed. For spatial data such as images, these infinite relations correspond to a continuous view of the world. Thus, at this layer and above users need not be concerned about sampling and quantization schemes used to acquire, store, and manipulate images under limitations imposed by finite machines. The infinite relations are translated into a discrete database model (the fourth layer). Abstract operations can be developed for each of these four layers. The actual data operations are performed at the level of the computational model (the fifth layer), where efficient, specialized data structures and algorithms can be applied to spatial and lexical objects. Data representation on physical mass-storage media is modeled in the last layer.

In each layer, there are objects, relationships among objects, and operations that can be applied to objects. At the higher levels, objects are abstract and operation behavior is ideal. Implementation of abstract objects with ideal behavior quickly becomes non-trivial, however, as the details of the abstract objects and the details of the implementation are exposed. We begin, in this paper, to explore the behavior and implementation of objects in our multi-layered model. We focus initially on object intersection, which is an important subclass of operations we wish to model.

Intersection is seen differently at each level of our multi-layered model. At the top level in our model, a user may be interested in bridges on a highway that cross a particular river or in studying the development of some town. In the conceptual layer these objectives may be achieved by finding the crossings of a highway and a river or restricting the coverage of several dated earth photographs to the boundaries of a particular town. For the continuous database model, we may consider the first of these requests as an intersection between a smooth, continuous curve representing the highway and a smooth, continuous curve representing the river and the second as having a fundamental operation that involves the intersection of a continuous region representing the area of a town and a smooth, continuous, bounded image of the town and surrounding area. At the discrete database level, however, these objects are no longer smooth, continuous, and bounded, but are finitely sampled and discretized points. Curves are conceptually represented as an ordered, discrete set of points with a 1-D interpolation schema, regions as the interior of closed curves, and images as coordinate-value pairs with a 2-D interpolation schema enclosed by a closed curve. These notions are elaborated in Section 4. Another example, routing a railroad through a hilly region, is discussed in some detail in Section 5.

We are particularly interested in expressing (intersection) operations in the continuous database model and mapping them to operations in the discrete database model. We begin in Section 2 by explaining how objects and operations are defined at the continuous database level. We then discuss, in Section 3 how the conceptual-model user expects idealized intersection at this level to behave, and we observe that intersection is well-defined for infinite representations. In Section 4, we discuss problems that arise when we must provide finite representations for conceptually continuous objects. We summarize and make some concluding remarks in Section 5.

2. OBJECT AND OPERATION DEFINITIONS FOR THE CONTINUOUS DATABASE MODEL

The continuous database model hides within it the inherent complexity of the discrete representation of continuous spatial objects such as images, regions, and curves. Hidden aspects include spatial sampling, amplitude quantization, choice of view point, and framing characteristics. At this level, continuous objects are represented as infinite sets of tuples. For instance, for an image we postulate a relation that contains an infinite number of tuples (one x–y–z-tuple for every pair of real numbers x and y). The continuous database model may also include naturally discrete objects such as individual points within an area and descriptive lexical data. Operations for the continuous database model, such as intersection, map these continuous or discrete objects to other continuous objects or to discrete objects.

Our continuous database model is a collection of objects grouped into object sets, a collection of relationships among the objects grouped into relationship sets, and a collection of applicable operations associated with each object set. Here we are only concerned with object sets and defined operations in object sets.

Object sets are described by object-set descriptors, defined as follows.

Object-Set: <name>
Domain: { <string list> } | **ISA** <object-set name>
| <object-set name list> | **P**(<object-set name>)
Properties: <constraint/property list>
Operations: <function-definition list>
End

Each object set has a unique name that identifies it. The domain of an object set can be defined in four ways: (1) by giving the elements of the domain as a set of lexical strings, (2) by stating that it "ISA" specialization of some other object set (which may either be built-in such as *Real* and *Integer* or defined in the model), (3) by listing its subcomponents when it is an aggregation, or (4) by designating an object set as the base set for an object set containing elements of a power set. Additional properties of the domain may be given to further constrain it. Finally, applicable operations may be defined for the object set.

A partial object-set descriptor for *Image* follows.

Object-Set: *Image*
Domain: **P**(*Image_Point*)
Properties:
1. FUNCTION: *Point* → *Intensity_Value*
2. CONTINUOUS: *Point*
3. CONTINUOUS: *Intensity_Value*
4. 0 ≤ *Intensity_Value* AND *Intensity_Value* ≤ 1

Operations:
Intersect(*Image*, *Region*) → *Region*
Intersect(*Image*, *Curve*) → *Image–Curve*
Intersect(*Image*, *Point*) → *Image–Point*
...
End

An image is defined as a power set of image points. An *Image_Point* is assumed to have been previously defined as a pair (*Point*, *Intensity–Value*) where a *Point* is a pair of reals (X, Y) and an *Intensity–Value* is a real Z. In the object-set descriptor, an image is further constrained to be a continuous function from a plane of points to a set of intensity values between zero and one. Of the many possible operations on images that can be defined, just a few of the intersection operations are listed.

From the perspective of the database, each object set and each relationship set represents a relation, which may be nested and thus may not necessarily be in first normal form. At this level, some of the relations may be considered to represent continuous objects. Images, regions, and curves are all considered to be continuous. In the conceptual database model these objects are thought of and operated on as if they had an infinite number of tuples. Thus, for example, when an operation takes the intersection of a region and an image, the user need not be concerned about whether the discrete points representing the region and the image plane are the same.

We observe that our intersection operations are broader than the class of intersection operations for standard sets. Indeed, from a database point of view the intersection operation we are considering is the *natural join*. Thus, for example when we intersect an image, whose database scheme is conceptually (X, Y, Z), and a region, whose database scheme is conceptually (X, Y), we are really joining on the common attributes (X, Y). This, of course, leaves the part of the image whose support region intersects with the region, which is precisely the intersection operation we want.

3. IDEALIZED INTERSECTION

The types of objects of interest here are points, curve-segments, region-segments, and image-segments. To avoid constant repetition, we abbreviate curve-segment to *curve*, region-segment to *region*, and image-segment to *image*. In this section, we discuss only ideal objects: smooth, continuous curves, bounded regions, and smooth, continuous, and bounded images.

In general a user may wish to intersect any two objects of these types. To accommodate the user, we wish to provide ideal intersection operations consistent with the user's point of view at the level of the continuous database model. We begin by giving a a table of expected results, but point out that problems quickly begin to surface, even in our ideal, continuous model. Table 1 shows a table of expected result types.

Table 1. Typical Expectations for Binary Intersections

	point	curve	region	image
point	point			
curve	point	point		
region	point	curve	region	
image	image-point	image-curve	image	-

Consideration of Table 1 immediately shows that our set of object types is not complete. When an image is intersected with a point, the expected result is a point with an intensity value, which we call an *image–point*. Similarly, when an image is intersected with a curve, the expected result is a curve with intensity values, which we call an *image–curve*.

Any intersection in Table 1 may also be empty. A point intersected with a point is only a point if the two points are the same, and a region intersected with an image is only an image if the region overlaps the image support region. Since the intersection of any two objects may be null, we assume this and omit mention of it in Table 1.

In Table 1, the intersection of two curves is given as a point. Curves, however, may intersect at one or more points, or overlap completely, or have some overlap and some crossings. We can capture this by allowing mixtures of objects. For the intersection of curves we need a set containing a set of points and a set of curves.

Mixed sets of objects also arise when we intersect an image with an image. In Table 1, this result is marked with a dash because it is not immediately obvious what the result type should be. Considering generalized intersection as a natural join (as we do) shows that the result should be the set of triples in the two images that are identical. The result is thus a (possibly empty) set of image-points. Depending on the intersection, however, the resulting object may be an image, an image-curve, an image-point, a set of images, a set of image-curves, a set of image-points, or a mixed set of image sets, image-curve sets, and image-point sets.

By considering all possible cases including pathological cases such as when the intersection of a region and an image is along touching edges, we conclude that a general object representing all possibilities is a set of six sets: (1) a point set, (2) a curve set, (3) a region set, (4) an image set, (5) an image-point set, and (6) an image-curve set. We call this general object an *intersection object*.

Since we assume here that an intersection object is created solely through intersections of basic points, curves, regions, and images, an intersection object has certain restrictions. There is no intersection object, for example, that has a non-empty curve set and at the same time a non-empty image-curve set. Indeed, if any one of the sets -- point set, curve set, or region set -- is non-empty, then all the sets -- image set, image-point set, and image-curve set -- must be empty. The converse of this statement is also true, so that if any one of the sets -- image set, image-point set, or image-curve set -- is non-empty, then all the sets -- point set, curve set, and region set -- must be empty. These restrictions are a consequence of using the natural join as our generalized intersection operation. Since our basic objects either have scheme (X, Y) or (X, Y, Z), a join of any two basic objects both with scheme (X, Y) results in an object with scheme (X, Y), and a join of any two basic objects that do not both have scheme (X, Y) has scheme (X, Y, Z). By induction, all generated schemes for intersection objects are either (X, Y) or (X, Y, Z) and cannot have contained sets with different schemes.

Because of these join restrictions, we can classify objects into a limited number of types based on whether contained sets are empty or non-empty. For intersection objects with scheme (X, Y), any of the 3 XY-scheme sets may be empty or not empty, and thus there are 8 $(=2^3)$ types of XY-scheme sets. Similarly, there are 8 types of XYZ-scheme sets.

We observe that the intersection operator is *closed* with respect to these 16 types of intersection sets and that these 16 types therefore constitute a *complete* set of intersection-object types. Let I_1 and I_2 be two intersection objects. We define $I_1 \cap I_2$ as follows. Let I_1*–elements* be the union of the sets contained in I_1. Similarly, let I_2*–elements* be the union of the sets contained in I_2. Let (e_1, e_2) be an element of I_1*–elements* $\times$ I_2*–elements*. Application of $e_1 \cap e_2$ produces sets with types as shown in Table 2. The intersection object $I_1 \cap I_2$ consists of the six sets each of which is the union of sets of the same type generated as a result of all the elementary intersections. As can be seen by inspecting Table 2, the result of intersecting any two of the 16 types is always one of the 16 types.

Of all the intersection objects that can be defined or generated, we are particularly interested in the following seven fundamental objects. (1) The intersection object whose contained sets are all null is the null object. (2) The intersection set whose only non-empty set is its point set and whose point set contains exactly one element is a point. Similarly (3, 4, 5, 6, 7), the intersection set whose only non-empty set is its curve (region, image, image-point, image-curve) set and whose curve (region, image, image-point, image-curve) set contains exactly one element is a curve (region, image, image-point, image-curve). We call these intersection objects *homogeneous intersection objects*.

It is of interest to observe that we can define intersection algorithms for intersection objects such that intersection on the set of homogeneous intersection objects is closed. One possible algorithm is to intersect the intersection objects as defined and then eliminate all elements from all but the most complex, non-empty contained set and select within the most complex, non-empty contained set (any) one of the "largest" elements. For regions, we choose "largest" by area, for images -- by area of support region, for curves -- by length, for image-curves -- by length of support curve, for points -- by sum of coordinate points, and for image-points -- by sum of support coordinate points. Another algorithm would force the selection to either be null or in the result set as designated in Table 1. Then, by disallowing the (potentially confusing) intersection of two images, it is possible to give only expected results according to Table 1.

It is also of interest to observe that spatial relations defined by others[4)] can be defined with intersection objects. For example, two regions are *disjoint* of their intersection is the null object. Two regions *meet* if all contained sets except the curve set are empty. Two regions *overlap* if all contained sets except the region set are empty. One region *covers* another if all contained sets except the region set are empty and the generated intersection object is identical to the covered object. Two regions R_1 and R_2 are *equal* if R_1 covers R_2 and R_2 covers R_1.

Table 2. Generated Set Types
(Table entries are sets, e.g., point = point set.)

	point	curve	region	image-point	image-curve	image
point	point					
curve	point	point curve				
region	point	point curve	point curve region			
image-point	N/A	N/A	N/A	image-point		
image-curve	N/A	N/A	N/A	image-point	image-point image-curve	
image	N/A	N/A	N/A	image-point	image-point image-curve	image-point image-curve image

4. FINITE OPERATIONS

Moving from the continuous, infinite domain of the third layer of our database model to the fourth, discrete layer poses two principal problems. The first problem is the treatment of region and image boundaries and other curves. This problem is a consequence of the finite amount of information obtained and retained, which precludes us from knowing whether certain points (indeed, almost all points) belong to a given object. The second problem is the accumulation of round-off or truncation error in performing arithmetic operations with finite-precision machines.

Geometry and topology play equally important roles in our definitions of spatial objects. To secure local consistency, we draw on solid modeling for the useful concept of regular sets (r-sets). A set is said to be *regular* if it is closed (i.e., it contains its boundary), and if every neighborhood of any point in it contains an element of its interior (i.e., it has no isolated or dangling points). A r-set need not be connected. R-sets are not closed under intersection (and boolean operations in general): for instance, the intersection of two adjacent squares would yield an edge. Therefore, to preserve regularity, a regularized counterpart of each boolean operation, similar to our homogeneous-object generation algorithms above, must be defined. In this example, the dangling edge would simply be removed. More precise definitions of these notions can be obtained elsewhere.[21,22] In the sequel, we shall consider only r-sets and regularized operations, with the practical consequence that in the discrete domain, regions and images cannot be represented simply as a set of points, but must include an explicit boundary. Boundary curves, in turn, which are discretely represented as a chain of points, must also include an explicit interpolation scheme.

The translation from the discrete representation to the continuous one is thus undertaken by interpolation. For curves, including boundaries, we use one-dimensional interpolation; for images, two dimensional interpolation. While in solid modeling non-linear polynomial interpolation (quadrics and splines) are frequently used, in geographic models the tradeoff between linear and polynomial methods favors the linear methods because the interval size is inversely proportional to at most the square of the number of points rather than the cube, as in solid modeling. Furthermore, unlike in machine design, circular arcs and other simple analytical curves are scarce. Linear interpolation results in piecewise linear approximations for curves and triangulated irregular networks (TINs) for topographic surfaces and images. (It is not possible to fit planar patches on a rectangular mesh of points).

Since piecewise linear representations of curves and surfaces (including images) are much more common in geographic information systems than polynomial representations, we will discuss possible approaches for overcoming the inaccuracies generated by finite computer precision only for the intersection of straight-line segments. Some general causes for numerical instability are subtracting comparable quantities, intersecting almost parallel lines, and non-uniform distribution of the floating-point grid.

The coupled issues of numerical error and topological consistency have been the subject of increasing attention in computational geometry. Examples of the effects that we are concerned with abound.[7,8] In computing multiple intersections of thematic overlays in cartography, for example, thin slivers that have no physical significance appear. Political boundaries, roads and rivers display unpredictable jags. Under rotation and, even more, under a change in map projection, entire towns may migrate from county to county or state to state. Parallel lines meet short of infinity. Area estimates become inconsistent: the parts no longer add up to the whole. In three dimensions, surfaces that should be smooth develop cracks and creases. Abutting objects do not quite touch. Some partitions in uniform subdivisions are larger than others.

Dobkin broadly classifies approaches to overcome these problems as being *geometric* or *numeric*.[2] The former consist of solutions that intentionally tolerate or even generate positional errors to accommodate imposed geometric constraints; the latter attempt to control computational precision independently of geometric or topological constraints. A somewhat parallel classification by Hoffman divides approaches into *perturbation* and *perturbation-free* methods.[12]

Some of the numerical options available to cope with cumulative round-off error are interval arithmetic,[19] statistical estimation of round-off error,[23] and rational arithmetic.[11]

In interval arithmetic, each value is represented as an ordered pair of numbers that correspond to upper and lower bounds. On each arithmetic operation, new bounds are computed. These bounds are, however, often far too pessimistic, and decisions based on value comparison become indeterminate as soon as the bounds of the two values being compared overlap. Interval operations on reals have been extended to matrices and vectors, and specifically to scalar products.[15] Ottman has shown how to evaluate many geometric primitives to least-significant-bit accuracy.[20]

Statistical methods of estimating round-off error are forced to rely on simplistic assumptions, namely independent and identical distribution of errors. While some predictions can be made for multiplication, division, and addition, subtraction tends to lead to unpredictable growth of errors.[16] Dobkin has shown the application of the permutation and perturbation method[23] to the interesting problem of reproducing pentagons that involves only line intersections.[2]

In rational arithmetic, each number is represented by a pair of integers p and q in the form p/q. If we allow integers of arbitrary length, each real can be approximated to arbitrary precision, but the major advantage of the method is that the arithmetic operations give exact results in rational form. Although at each step, the rationals can be checked for reducibility (i.e., common factors), they tend to grow rapidly. Franklin and his colleagues have extensively investigated the use of rationals in polygon intersections and also coded some of their algorithms in Prolog.[9,10] Finite fields for the numerator and denominator in "slash number arithmetic" have also been advocated: it can be shown that under some circumstances intermediate errors are cancelled.[14,17] Numerical accuracy problems arise normally only in iterated computations with accumulated round-off error. The representation of straight-line segments on a grid using rationals was demonstrated elsewhere.[3,18]

The explicit retention of topological relationships is more common in solid modeling than in GIS. For instance, various subsets of Euler operators are generally used to construct solids with guaranteed topological validity (i.e., no self-intersections) and data structures (for example, the popular winged-edge structure) with explicitly encoded redundant adjacency-topology relationships rather than simply vertex geometry.

In the same spirit, it is often useful to retain the ancestry of vertices created by intersection operations. For instance, if a vertex is created by the intersection of two line segments each defined by two vertices, then retention of the collinearity constraint can avoid problems downstream.[5] A natural consequence of this approach is that data points entered separately must always be treated as distinct points even if their coordinates are indistinguishable at the precision of the representation. Conversely, points with different coordinates must be considered identical even if their coordinates differ: this may arise, for instance in obtaining different values for the coordinates of line segment A intersected with line segment B than vice versa.

In practice, however, such problems are usually handled by resorting to double and even quadruple precision and the arbitrary introduction of epsilon-thresholds to determine coincidence and collinearity. Such an approach merely hides and postpones the problems, and cannot guarantee robust results.

A example of a geometric rather than numeric approach is Egenhofer's simplicial approach.[4] All objects are represented as minimal n-simplices (a 1-simplex is an edge, a 2-simplex is a triangle, a 3-simplex is a tetrahedron). The topological relationships of adjacent simplices are retained permanently.

5. EXAMPLE

As an example of a non-trivial intersection operation, consider the intersection of a curve with an image. We may be interested, for instance, in computing the amount of earth removal required to run a level railroad bed through a hilly area. In the discrete database model, the topographic surface is represented by a Digital Elevation Model. We may view such a model as an x-y-z image array, with the z-values corresponding to the elevation of the terrain above sea-level measured at uniformly spaced grid points. The elevations must be suitably scaled to restrict their range to [0,1]. It is assumed, of course, that the range of the digital elevation model spans the entire region to be traversed by the railroad.

The prospective path of the railroad, at constant elevation, is a smooth curve that is represented in the discrete database as a string of points (x-y pairs). We may assume that points are given more frequently wherever the tracks curve. In general, however, the x-y pairs describing the curve do not coincide with the grid coordinates of the digital elevation model of the terrain.

A first approximation to estimate the volume of excavation, perhaps to be used to compare alternative routings of the tracks, would require obtaining a profile of the terrain along the proposed route. In our terminology, the profile would be an image-curve. In three dimensions, the image-curve generates a vertical surface whose area, multiplied by the nominal width of the track-bed, would yield the required volume of excavation.

Assuming our continuous database model with idealized operations, we can write a relational-algebra query to solve our problem as follows.

$$\pi_{result}\,\chi_{result \leftarrow nominal\text{-}width \,\times\, area}\;\chi_{area \leftarrow image\text{-}curve\text{-}area}(amtrack\text{-}curve\text{-}1 \;|\times|\; terrain\text{-}1)$$

Here, *terrain*–1 is the digital elevation model and *amtrack–curve*–1 is the smooth curve. Their (idealized) join produces an image curve. We next use the χ operator[1,13)] to compute the line-integral area of the image curve, and then multiply this computed area by the nominal width of the track. Both of these operators are also idealized in our continuous database model. The result yields the required volume of excavation.

The first problem we face in the computation is to determine the elevation at points other than the given grid points. Linear interpolation is the simplest approach. Since four arbitrary points cannot be fitted by a plane, the entire area is triangulated by subdividing each rectangular element about a consistently-chosen diagonal. This is, of course, an example of a 2-D simplicial structure. The interpolated elevation of any point within a triangle is then given by a linear expression in the elevations of the three vertices of the triangle.

Note that the elevations could also have been represented at irregularly spaced points. In that case, the triangulation necessary to obtain a piecewise linear approximation (a TIN: cf. Section 4) would be much more complex than merely introducing diagonals in the uniform grid.

We also assume that between the given points, the locus of the railroad track may be approximated by a straight line segment linking each pair of points. We compute the elevation at each vertex of the polyline representing the curve using the linear expression derived from the digital elevation model. The final result is a piecewise-linear space curve (in our terminology, an image-curve).

The spatial resolution of the original data is usually determined by external considerations. However, for greater accuracy, the elevation could be interpolated by a bilinear function, which would result in a piecewise-quadratic surface. Such a surface does not, however, have continuous first derivatives. In order to guarantee continuous first derivatives, we would have to resort to cubic polynomials in x and y (for instance, bicubic splines), which have sufficient degrees of freedom to satisfy the additional constraints.

Similarly, the image-curve need not be restricted to a piecewise linear function, but could be interpolated by higher order polynomials or rational functions. In this case, we should perform the interpolation directly on the space curve, since performing it on the original planar curve would require computing the geometric intersection of two high-order curved surfaces. If an iterative algorithm is used, this could give rise to cumulative numerical error, as discussed in Section 4.

If the railroad tracks were not to be perfectly level, then the route itself would be represented by an image-curve whose z-values would correspond to the desired elevation at each x-y point. Now, to compute the volume of excavation, we would have to take the difference between this image-curve and another image-curve generated by the intersection of the projection of the track on the horizontal datum with the image. The difference operation is simplified by the fact that both image-curves have the same x-y coordinates. This sequence of operations would result in an image curve whose z-values correspond to the difference in elevation between the proposed track and the terrain.

The issues related to collinearity mentioned in Section 4 would arise if some segments of track are required to be absolutely straight. For example on a viaduct traversing a lake or a wide river gorge.

Note that all of the computational questions are completely hidden from the continuous database model. The required operations can be expressed simply as a relational query as shown above. An explanation of how such queries can be compiled is found elsewhere.[6)]

6. CONCLUDING REMARKS

We are committed to a database model for geographic information systems that allows the end user to manipulate the data in an application-oriented framework and ignore irrelevant artifacts, such as spatial sampling, amplitude quantization and the effects of finite precision processing. At the more user-oriented levels of the data model, we take advantage of the convenience of an object-oriented semantic model and the theoretical tractability of relational algebra. However, the data obtained from the real world, such as point data representing object location, line data representing rivers and roads, regions corresponding to political or natural (thematic) subdivisions, and generalized images such as digital elevation models and satellite pictures, must still be represented in a discrete form. The accuracy of such a representation is dictated by the instrumentation for acquisition, the storage and processing resources available, and the requirements of the application.

In the continuous model both objects and operations are considered to be ideal. Even under ideal conditions, however, the myriad of possibilities grows quickly, necessitating the introduction of restrictions to make problems tractable. The interface between the continuous model and the discrete model is by no means trivial. On the one hand, choices must be made regarding the preferred method of interpolation in translating the discrete data to the idealized data, and on the other, provisions must be made in guarding against the effects of cumulative arithmetic error due to finite machine representation.

We believe that both of these choices are dictated by the application, and therefore a useful system must incorporate entire families of interpolation algorithms and geometric processing algorithms, much as statistical packages incorporate numerous methods for the estimation of parameters (and for dealing with missing data), and numerical analysis packages provide many alternatives for finding the roots of equations, or for numerical integration and differentiation. We have focussed on the problem of generalized intersection (or join) to examine the issues presented by a prototypical geometric operation. References were provided to some of the principal candidates developed in computational geometry for dealing with finite data and finite-precision computers.

ACKNOWLEDGEMENTS

We are grateful for the assistance of Gabriella Dodero (University of Genova) and Maharaj Mukherjee (RPI) for calling our attention to some of the references in Section 4.

REFERENCES

1) B. Czejdo and D.W. Embley, "An approach to computation specification for an entity-relationship query language," *Proceedings of the Sixth International Conference on Entity-Relationship Approach*, pp. 307-321, New York, New York, November 1987.

2) D. Dobkin and D. Silver, "Recipes for geometry & numerical analysis - part I : a numerical study," *Proceedings of an ACM Symposium on Computational Geometry.*, pp. 93-105, 1988.

3) L. Dorst and A.W.M. Smeulders, "Discrete representations of straight lines," *IEEE Transactions on Pattern Analysis Machine Intelligence*, vol. 6, pp. 450-463, July 1984.

4) M.J. Egenhofer, "Topological relationships in spatial databases," Unpublished manuscript, National Center for Geographic Information and Analysis & Department of Surveying Engineering, University of Maine, pp. 1-26, Orono, Maine, 1989.

5) D.W. Embley, M. Mukherjee, and G. Nagy, "Making do with finite numerical precision in spatial data structures," *Fourth International Symposium on Spatial Data Handling,*, pp. 55-65, Zurich, Switzerland, 23-27 July 1990.

6) D.W. Embley and G. Nagy, "A multi-layered approach to query processing in geographic information systems," *Proceedings of the International Workshop on Database Management Systems for Geographical Applications*, pp. 214-238, Capri, Italy, 16-17 May 1991.

7) W.R. Franklin, "Efficient polyhedron intersection," *Proceedings of Graphics Interface '82*, pp. 73-80, Toronto, Ontario, May 1982.

8) W.R. Franklin, "Cartographic errors symptomatic of underlying algebra problems," *Proceedings of the International Symposium on Spatial Data Handling*, vol. 1, pp. 190-208, Zurich, Switzerland, August 1984.

9) W.R. Franklin and P.Y.F. Wu, "A polygon overlay system in Prolog," *Autocarto 8: Proceedings of the 8th International Symposium on Computer Assisted Cartography*, pp. 97-106, Baltimore, Maryland, April 1987.

10) W.R. Franklin, N. Chandrasekhar, M. Kankanhalli, M. Seshan, and V. Akman, "Efficiency of uniform grids for intersection detection on serial and parallel machines," *Proceedings of of CG International '88*, p. 51, Geneva, Switzerland, May 1988.

11) G.H. Hardy and E.M. Wright, *An Introduction to Theory of Numbers, 4th Edition,* Clarendon Press, Oxford, England, 1960.

12) C.H. Hoffman, "The problems of accuracy and robustness in geometric computation," *IEEE Transactions on Computers*, pp. 31-41, March 1989.

13) A. Klug, "Equivalence of relational algebra and relational calculus query languages having aggregate functions," *Journal of the Association for Computing Machinery*, vol. 29, no. 3, pp. 699-717, July 1982.

14) P. Kornerup and D.W. Matula, "Finite precision rational arithmetic: an arithmetic unit," *IEEE Transactions on Computers*, pp. 31-41, March 1983.

15) U. Kullisch and W.L. Miranker, *Computer Arithmetic in Theory and Practice,* Academic Press, 1981.

16) J.D. Marsa and D.W. Matula, "A simulative study of correlated error propagation in various finite precision arithmetics," *IEEE Transactions on Computers*, vol. c-22, pp. 587-597, June 1973.

17) D.W. Matula and P. Kornerup, "Approximate rational arithmetic systems: analysis of recovery of simple fractions during expression evaluation," *Lecture Notes on Computer Science*, vol. 72, pp. 383-397, Springer Verlag, 1979.

18) M.D. McIllroy, "A note on discrete representation of lines," *AT & T Technical Journal*, vol. 64, pp. 481-490, February, 1984.

19) R.E. Moore, *Interval Analysis,* Prentice Hall, Englewood Cliffs, New Jersey, 1966.

20) T. Ottman, G. Thiemt, and C. Ullrich, "Numerical stability of simple geometric algorithms in the plane," *Proceedings of a Symposium on Computational Geometry*, pp. 119-125, June 1987.

21) A.A.G. Requicha, "Representations for rigid solids: theory, methods, and systems," *ACM Computing Surveys*, vol. 12, no. 4, pp. 437-464, December 1980.

22) R.B. Tilove, "Set membership classification: a unified approach to geometric classification problems," *IEEE Transactions on Computers*, vol. c-29, pp. 874-883, October 1980.

23) J. Vignes and M.L. Porte, "Error analysis in computing," *Information Processing*, vol. 1, p. 710, 1974.

Processing Nondeterministic Queries Including Sets and Constraints Utilizing Data Dependencies

Mizuho Iwahara† and Yahiko Kambayashi‡

† Department of Computer Science and Communication Engineering,
Kyushu University, Fukuoka 812, Japan
‡ Integrated Media Environment Experimental Laboratory,
Kyoto University, Kyoto 606, Japan

ABSTRACT

In this paper, we will discuss processing methods for set constraint queries. Set constraint queries produce set-valued solutions, and their conditions are given as "constraints," which describe the solution sets using first-order quantified predicates on their member tuples. We shall examine a subclass of set constraint queries, called functional dependency (FD) set constraint queries. For a given set of FDs as query constraints, we will give a method to analyze query complexity using an FD-graph. We will show that certain classes of queries can be processed in time polynomial in the size of the database, and other classes are NP-complete. We also show that certain classes of NP-complete queries can be processed in polynomial time if certain data dependencies exist in the database.

1 INTRODUCTION

As database applications areas expand, many weak points of traditional query languages, such as the relational algebra, have been found, and many extensions to those languages have been proposed. A part of important notions in such extensions includes:

Handling sets and/or complex structures In Engineering databases, supporting complex objects and/or rich data types is quite important. As an extension to handle complex structures rather than flat relations, nested relations have been studied [10) 16)]. In logic programming, LDL1 [3)] and LPS [14)] allow the use of sets to represent a wider class of queries in a simple way.

Computational complexity of queries Introducing powerful operations for handling complex objects sometimes results in consuming prohibitively high amount of resources to process a query. For example, a user may issue a query which computes all the subsets of a given relation. Users must be careful to write queries to avoid such dangerous situations. Another way is to impose syntactic restrictions on the query language, so that all queries written in that language will be processed in reasonable time. A guideline for such safety is that queries which can be processed in time polynomial to the size of the database. Query languages that allow only polynomial time queries (P-time queries) have been widely investigated (see [5)] for a survey).

It is shown that a first-order language augmented with the fixed point operator (LFP queries) is incapable to express all P-time queries [4)]. Interestingly, if a total ordering of the universe of constants is given as a predicate, then LFP queries are exactly P-time queries [7)18)]. However, A total ordering is considered to be dangerous because evaluation of a query may depend on what total ordering is used. The language which expresses exactly all order-independent P-time queries is still an open problem [8)].

Nondeterminism A nondeterministic query does not necessarily give a unique answer from the same database, rather defines a set of answers, and only one answer is nondeterministically chosen from that set. A typical example of nondeterministic queries is sampling queries, such as choosing one employee from each department, where each department consists of a set of employees. Various nondeterministic query languages have been proposed for defining nondeterministic queries [1)13)17)].

Set constraint queries, which was proposed in an earlier version of this paper [9)], forms an important class of queries, and generates set-typed values as solutions. The conditions for a query are given as "constraints" that should be satisfied by the solution set as a whole, and not necessarily by each element of the set. Using such constraints, we can describe conditions of the form "each two elements of a solution must satisfy predicate α," or "there must exist an element of the solution satisfying predicate β."

Example 1 Let $R_p(PA)$ be a relation which has attribute P for a person's name, and attribute A for a person's age. Now we want to know a largest set of people where the difference of age of any two people in the set is less than r. We can express solution S as follows:

$$\text{maximize} \quad S \quad \text{such that}$$
$$(S \subset R_p) \quad \wedge \quad (\forall \tau \in S)(\forall \mu \in S)(\,|\tau[A] - \mu[A]| < r).$$

Example 2 Let $R_c(CT)$ be a relation that contains all classes with C for course names and T for teachers' names. A student intends to choose a largest set of classes that he can attend, by selecting tuples from R_c. Here we assume the constraint that he cannot take two classes having the same course name. We can describe possible solutions for the query as follows:

$$\{ S \mid (S \subset R_c) \wedge (\forall \tau \in S)(\forall \mu \in S) b(\tau, \mu)\},$$

where $b(\tau, \mu) = \neg(\tau[C] = \mu[C]) \vee (\tau[T] = \mu[T])$. We call binary predicates of the form $b(\tau, \mu)$ *binary constraints.*

In Example 2, suppose that the relation R_c consists of n tuples. Then it is easily shown that the number of the solutions of the query, or even that of the largest is not bounded by some polynomial of n. Thus it is not realistic to report all the (largest) solutions. However, queries whose output type is a set of (tuple) sets and that set variable ranges through all subsets of a tuple set, often have an exponential number of solutions. Thus for such queries, nondeterministically choosing one or several solutions out of all the solutions is essential. Such nondeterminism often increases the complexity class of the query language [1)12)]. We will discuss a nondeterministic version of set constraint queries that can be evaluated efficiently.

From Sections 4 to 6, we will consider a subclass of set constraint queries, namely *functional dependency (FD)* set constraint queries. These queries consist of binary constraints which correspond to FD sets. In Example 2, the binary constraints correspond to the FD set $\{C \to T\}$. An FD set constraint query is essentially the same as the choice operator in Datalog [13)]. However, evaluating a query of a set of FDs, or multiple choices on a relation becomes much complex than single FD queries. In Section 5, we will analyze the complexity of FD set constraint queries using FD-graphs [2)].

FD set constraint queries which are ordinarily NP-complete may be solvable in P-time if additional information can be obtained. In Section 6, we will show how FDs and JDs (join dependencies) maintained in the database may sometimes be used to achieve such complexity reduction. These techniques exploit P-time graph algorithms such as the maximum matching and maximum network flow algorithms.

2 PRELIMINARIES

For a given attribute set $X = \{A_1, A_2, \ldots, A_n\}$, a *relation* $R(X)$ on X is a finite set of mappings $\tau : \{A_1, A_2, \ldots, A_n\} \mapsto D_1 \times D_2 \times \cdots \times D_n$, where each D_i is the domain of attribute A_i, and each A_i is mapped to an element of D_i. Each mapping τ shall be called a *tuple* of $R(X)$. X shall be called a *relational scheme* of $R(X)$. In general, the relational scheme of a relation R shall be denoted by $\underline{R}$.

The relation R can be represented as a table which has attributes for rows, and tuples for columns. In this paper we use $A, B, C, \ldots$ for the names of single attributes, and $\ldots, X, Y, Z$ for the names of attribute sets. The union of two attribute sets is simply denoted by the concatenation of their names.

Relational algebra is a procedural language for relational databases. The three major operations of relational algebra are described as follows. The value for an attribute set X of a tuple μ is denoted by $\mu[X]$.
(Projection) For a relation $R(X)$ and an attribute set $Y (\subseteq X)$, $R[Y] = \{\mu[Y] \mid \mu \in R\}$ is called the *projection* of R onto Y.
(Selection) Let θ be one of the comparison operators $=, >, \geq, <, \leq, \neq$. For θ, a constant vector 'c', a relation $R(X)$ and an attribute set $Y (\subseteq X)$, $R[Y\,\theta\,\text{'c'}] = \{\mu \mid \mu \in R, \mu[Y]\,\theta\,\text{'c'}\}$ is called the *selection* of R on Y.
(Join) Let $R_1(X_1)$ and $R_2(X_2)$ be relations. The *(natural) join* of R_1 and R_2 shall be denoted as $R_1 \bowtie R_2 = R(X_1X_2)$, where $R(X_1X_2) = \{\mu \mid \mu[X_1] \in R_1, \mu[X_2] \in R_2\}$.

For a relation $R(X)$, R is said to satisfy the *functional dependency (FD)* $X_1 \to X_2$ $(X_1, X_2 \subseteq X)$, if for any two tuples μ_1 and μ_2 of R, $\mu_1[X_1] = \mu_2[X_1]$ implies $\mu_1[X_2] = \mu_2[X_2]$.

Let F be a set of FDs and U be an attribute set for which F is defined. We denote by F^+ the *closure* of F with respect to Armstrong's inference rules, described as follows:

Reflexivity: If $Y \subseteq X$, then $X \to Y$.
Transitivity: If $X \to Y$ and $Y \to Z$, then $X \to Z$.
Union: If $X \to Y$ and $X \to Z$, then $X \to YZ$.

For sets of FDs E and F, E is called a cover of F, if $E^+ = F^+$ holds. A set of FDs F is *nonredundant* if no FD in F can be inferred from the remaining ones. A *minimum cover* is defined as a nonredundant cover with the minimum possible number of FDs.

A relation R is said to satisfy a *join dependency(JD)* $\bowtie [X_1, X_2, \ldots, X_n]$, if $R = R[X_1] \bowtie R[X_2] \bowtie \cdots \bowtie R[X_n]$ holds. Here we call each X_i an *element* of the JD. A JD can be represented as a hypergraph $H = (V_H, E_H)$, where V_H is a set of nodes corresponding to single attributes of the JD, and E_H is a set of hyperedges, each of which corresponds to one of the elements of the JD.

We may prune a given hypergraph H by (1) removing any node incident to only one hyperedge, and (2) removing any hyperedge which is a subset of another hyperedge. By repeating steps (1) and (2) until no more nodes or hyperedges can be removed, if no more nodes remain, the join dependency corresponding to H shall be called *acyclic*, otherwise, it shall be called *cyclic*. Acyclic JDs form an important subclass of JDs.

3 SET CONSTRAINT QUERIES

3.1 The Definition

Definition 1 Let R and S be relations of the same scheme $\underline{R}$. The following formula $C(S)$ is called a *query constraint*:

$$C(S) = \bigwedge_{i=1}^{n} (\forall \tau \in S)(\forall \mu \in S)\, b_i(\tau, \mu) \wedge \bigwedge_{i=1}^{m} (\mathsf{Q}_i \tau \in S) u_i(\tau).$$

Here τ and μ are tuple variables with range S, and $\mathsf{Q}_i \in \{\forall, \exists\}$. Each $b_i(\tau, \mu)$ and $u_i(\tau)$ is a tuple relational calculus expression upon free variables. The expressions of the form $b_i(\tau, \mu)$ shall be called *binary* constraints; those of the form $u_i(\tau)$ shall be called *unary* constraints.

For a given relation R and a given query constraint C, the function Q_C defined below is a *set constraint query* on $\underline{R}$.

$$Q_C(R) = \{S \mid S \subset R \wedge C(S)\}$$

Each $S \in Q_C(R)$ is called a *solution* of $Q_C(R)$.

There are two types of complexity measures for database queries. For a set constraint query $Q_C(R)$, if $S \in Q_C(R)$ can be decided in time (or space) bounded by a function f of $|R|$, then $Q_c(R)$ is said to have time (or space) *data complexity* f. Alternatively, if f is a function of $|C|$, then $Q_C(R)$ has *expression complexity* f [18]. Here $|R|$ denotes the size of relation R, and $|C|$ denotes the length of expression C. In this paper, we will consider only the data complexity measure.

Note that a solution S of $Q_C(R)$ can be computed in NP-time by first guessing some S, and then evaluating $C(S)$. Note also that in the case of disjunction of query constraints, we can evaluate each conjunctive clause independently.

We could consider allowing ternary constraints or more complex constraints, or the use of arbitrary quantifications for binary constraints. For these cases, solutions may be obtained in NP-time. However queries of the form of Definition 1 are sufficiently complex to deserve special study. An example of a query with high complexity will be shown in Section 5.

In this paper, we will consider set constraint queries which consist of only binary constraints.

3.2 Nondeterminism in Set Constraint Queries

Let $Q_C(R)$ be a query consisting of binary constraints alone. Let G_1 be the directed graph in which its each vertex corresponds to a tuple of R, and there is an edge (u, v) if and only if the ordered tuple pair (u, v) satisfies all binary constraints. By the definition of solutions, the tuples of a complete subgraph of G_1 constitute a solution of $Q_C(R)$.

Since the number of complete subgraphs, or cliques, of a graph is exponential to the number of vertices, a single query may have an exponential number of solutions, too many to generate in practice. We should restrict solutions to reasonable or important solutions. Some possible restrictions are the following:

(1) Report all maximal solutions.
However, a graph which consists of n vertices may have up to $3^{n/3}$ cliques. It is not reasonable to generate all maximal solutions.

(2) Report one (or several) maximal solutions.
This can be achieved in P-time by adding a tuple to a solution one by one, subject to the query constraint, until no more tuples can be added. The resultant solution is dependent on the input order of the tuples. The query thus becomes nondeterministic.

(3) Report one (or several) largest solutions.
For combinatorial problems, a largest solution is often an optimal one. However, it is well known that the problem of determining whether a (undirected) graph has a clique of a given cardinality is NP-complete. It seems to be difficult to give an efficient algorithm for arbitrary constraints.

To obtain a reasonable size of solutions, producing only several solutions is necessary, and thus the nondeterminism of set constraint queries is essential and inevitable. In many cases, the nondeterministic choice of solutions is quite arbitrary and what solution is chosen is not so important, when the given constraints are satisfied.

Restriction (3) to one of the largest solutions is often useful and important. Restriction (2) can be implemented efficiently, but there is a possibility that the cardinality of the solution generated will be too small. In this paper, we will analyze the use of Restriction (3) for optimization problems.

Functional dependency (FD) is a well-known and important type of semantic constraint in relational databases. FDs can be expressed as symmetric and reflexive binary relations defined on tuple sets. Thus, through the use of Horn clauses, we may use FDs to describe binary constraints of queries. Such queries form a natural subclass of set constraint queries.

Definition 2 A set constraint query whose binary constraints can be expressed as a set of FDs, is called an *FD* set constraint query.

4 PROCESSING FD SET CONSTRAINT QUERIES

We consider here some methods for processing FD set constraint queries. The complexity of these methods depends on certain properties of the FD sets.

We illustrate these methods using a job assignment problem. Let $R_1(ETJ)$ be a relation consisting of attribute E for employee names, attribute T for time slots, and attribute J for types of jobs. A tuple of R_1 means that a certain employee can engage in a certain type of job at a certain time. A job assignment problem is finding a subset S of R_1 which satisfies some given constraints. Subset S is optimal if it is an assignment of the greatest possible number of jobs to employees.

The following examples show three different assignment constraints, their descriptions using FD sets, and methods for processing them.

Example 3 The constraint is that each employee can engage in only one type of job, and same type of job may be performed by an arbitrary number of employees at the same time. This constraint is described by the following FD set:

$$F_1 = \{ ET \rightarrow J \}$$

The collection of subsets of R_1 which satisfy F_1 form a (partition) matroid, since R_1 can be partitioned into tuple sets by the values of ET, and any solution may contain at most one tuple from each partition. We can solve this problem using a greedy algorithm for finding a largest independent subset [15].

Example 4 In addition to the constraint of Example 3, we assume that each type of job needs only one employee in a given time slot. This constraint is described by the following FD set:

$$F_2 = \{ ET \rightarrow J, \quad JT \rightarrow E \}$$

We can express R_1 as a bipartite graph B_1, whose two vertex sets correspond to the tuple sets $R_1[ET]$ and $R_1[JT]$, and whose edges join tuples common to both sets. A solution of the job assignment problem is then a subset of the edges of B_1. Constraint F_2 forces each vertex of B_1 to be incident to at most one edge of the solution. Thus, we can apply the maximum matching algorithm [15] for bipartite graphs to find a solution for query Q_{F_2}.

Example 5 We assume that each type of job has exactly one employee, and each employee is assigned only one type of job. This constraint can be denoted by following FD set:

$$F_3 = \{ E \rightarrow J, \quad J \rightarrow E \}$$

F_2 can be deduced from F_3 by the inference rules of functional dependencies. We can say that query Q_{F_3} includes the constraints of query Q_{F_2}.

Let B_2 be a bipartite graph whose two vertex sets correspond to the sets of E and J, respectively. B_2 includes an edge (e, j) of weight k, if there are k tuples of R_1 which have values e for E and j for J.

Similarly to Example 4, we can apply the weighted maximum matching algorithm [15] to B_2 to obtain a solution.

5 COMPLEXITY ANALYSIS OF FD SET CONSTRAINT QUERIES

In this section, we discuss the complexity of FD set constraint queries by analyzing properties of FD sets using FD-graphs.

5.1 FD-Graphs

The following definition of an FD-graph is taken from [2]. The FD-graph of an FD set F, denoted by G_F, has two kinds of nodes, *simple nodes* and *compound nodes*, defined as follows. Let U be the finite attribute set for which F is defined. With every attribute $A \in U$ we associate a simple node labeled A. For every FD: $X \rightarrow Y$ in F, where X consists of more than one attribute, we associate a compound node labeled X. There is an arc from a (compound or simple) node X to a simple node A if $X \rightarrow A$ is implied by the set F of FDs. There is an *FD-path* from node X to node Y, denoted by $< X, Y >$, if $X \rightarrow Y$ is implied by the set F of FDs.

Now we introduce several subclasses of FD sets. By restricting query FD sets to such subclasses, we can analyze complexity of FD set constraint queries in more simple way. We assume that the given query FD set has been converted into a minimum cover.

Definition 3

(1) A set F of FDs whose left-hand sides consist of single attributes, shall be called a *simply-covered FD set.*

(2) For an FD set F, if in its FD-graph there exists a node set $\{X_1, \ldots, X_n\}$, whose elements are pairwise disjoint, and a set of FD-paths between these nodes constitutes a cover of F, then F shall be called a *disjoint-covered FD set.*

(3) For an FD set F, if in its FD-graph there exists a node set $\{X_1, \ldots, X_n\}$ such that $X_i \not\subseteq X_j$ for all $i \neq j$, and a set of FD-paths between these nodes constitutes a cover of F, then F shall be called a *compound-covered FD set.*

The node set $\{X_1, \ldots, X_n\}$ in both (2) and (3) shall be called a *covering node set.*

In the FD-graph of an arbitrary FD set, there may exist two nodes having no FD-path between them, but there is a FD from one of these nodes to a subset of the other node.

A simply-covered FD set may be represented by an ordinary directed graph. The FD-graph of a disjoint-covered FD set may also be represented by a directed graph whose nodes corresponding to the covering node set, and whose arcs correspond to FD-paths between the covering node set. Compound-covered FD sets need restrictions before they can be handled as directed graphs. Such conditions will be discussed in Section 6.

We represent a disjoint or compound-covered FD set by its covering node set, and the FD-paths between nodes. We call such graphs "reduced" FD-graphs, or simply FD-graphs, and we call those FD-paths simply "arcs."

The FD set F_2 of Example 4 is a compound-covered FD set. We illustrate F_2 by the FD-graph of [2] in Figure 1-(a), and by the reduced FD-graph in Figure 1-(b).

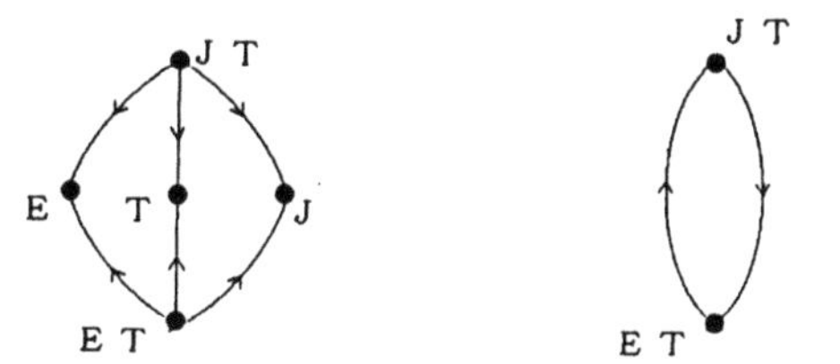

(a) FD-graph (b) Reduced FD-graph

Figure 1: Two representations of $\{ET \rightarrow J, \quad JT \rightarrow E\}$

In the following discussion, we consider only simply, disjoint, or compound-covered FD sets as constraints of FD set constraint queries. Obviously, a simply-covered FD set is disjoint-covered, and a disjoint-covered FD set is compound-covered.

We shall first discuss a special case of functional dependencies.

5.2 Null-Dependent FDs

An FD set constraint query whose FD set is $\{\emptyset \rightarrow X\}$ will be said to generate a solution which is the largest subset whose tuples all have the same X-value. In the job assignment problems of the previous examples, using such a *null-dependent* FD $\emptyset \rightarrow E$, we may express constraints that allow the selection of the employee who can handle the greatest number of different jobs.

A null-dependent FD is transitive, in addition to reflexive and symmetric. Such FDs therefore establish an equivalence relation on tuple sets. A given relation can be decomposed into equivalence classes based on a null-dependent FD. This operation corresponds to the operation "Group-by[X]" [11].

Theorem 1 Let $Q_F(R)$ be an FD set constraint query on $\underline{R}$ whose FD set F contains $\emptyset \rightarrow X$. Let $S_1, \ldots, S_k$ be relations obtained by partitioning the input relation R by the equivalence relation of $\emptyset \rightarrow X$. Then the maximum solutions of $Q_F(R)$ are the largest relations in the solutions of $Q_{F'}(S_1), \ldots, Q_{F'}(S_k)$, where $F' = F - \{\emptyset \rightarrow X\}$.

Let us suppose that in the input relation R, a JD $\bowtie[Y_1, \ldots, Y_n]$ and the set E of FDs hold. Then in each subrelation with respect to $\emptyset \rightarrow X$, $\bowtie[Y_1 - X, \ldots, Y_n - X]$ and the set $\{\emptyset \rightarrow X\} \cup E$ of FDs hold [11]. In Section 6, we will discuss the use of these dependencies for processing queries.

5.3 Analyzing Complexity Using FD-Graphs

We now consider the following FD set constraint queries whose FD-graphs consist of 2 or 3 arcs: Q_{F2eq}, Q_{Fout}, Q_{Fin}, Q_{Fchain}, Q_{F3eq}, Q_{F2eqin}, and $Q_{F2eqout}$. Each query is defined on the relational scheme $\underline{R_2} = XYZ$, where X, Y and Z are pairwise disjoint, as such, each query FD set is disjoint-covered. The FD-graphs of these queries except Q_{F2eqin} and $Q_{F2eqout}$ are illustrated in Figure 2.

(1) Q_{F2eq} (Two nodes are equivalent)
$F2eq = \{X \rightarrow Y, Y \rightarrow Z\}$

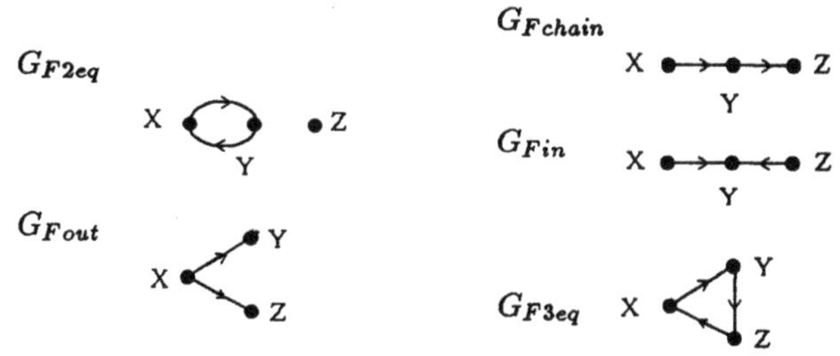

Figure 2: FD-graphs

This case is treated in the same manner as Example 5. G_{F2eq} is a strongly connected graph.

(2) Q_{Fout} (A node has two outgoing arcs)
$Fout = \{X \rightarrow Y, X \rightarrow Z\}$.
The dependency $X \rightarrow YZ$ can be deduced from the FD set, and this case is similar to Example 3.

(3) Q_{Fin} (A node has two incoming arcs)
$Fin = \{X \rightarrow Y, Z \rightarrow Y\}$.

(4) Q_{Fchain} (Chain structure)
$Fchain = \{X \rightarrow Y, Y \rightarrow Z\}$.

(5) Q_{F3eq} (3 equivalent nodes)
$F3eq = \{X \rightarrow Y, Y \rightarrow Z, Z \rightarrow X\}$.
The set $\{X, Y, Z\}$ is called a *equivalent* covering node set.

(6) Q_{F2eqin} (2 equivalent nodes plus 1 incoming arc)
$F2eqin = \{X \rightarrow Y, Y \rightarrow X, Z \rightarrow Y\}$.

(7) $Q_{F2eqout}$ (2 equivalent nodes plus 1 outgoing arc)
$F2eqout = \{X \rightarrow Y, Y \rightarrow X, Y \rightarrow Z\}$.
We can solve this query by projecting R_2 onto XY and YZ, then apply the matching algorithm for the two equivalent nodes, as in Example 4. After a largest solution on $R_2[XY]$ is obtained, join that solution with $R_2[YZ]$.

Q_{F2eq}, $Q_{F2eqout}$ and Q_{Fout} can be processed in P-time; on the other hand, Q_{Fin}, Q_{Fchain}, Q_{F3eq}, and Q_{F3equt} are NP-complete.

Theorem 2 The FD set constraint queries Q_{Fin}, Q_{Fchain} and Q_{F3eq} are NP-complete in data complexity.

Proof: First we show a reduction of 3SAT [15] to Q_{Fin}. For a given instance of 3SAT, let us construct $R_2(XYZ)$ for the input relation of Q_{Fin} as follows.

Let X-values correspond to the logical variables of the formula of 3SAT, Y-values to positive and negative literals of logical variables, and Z-values to disjunctive clauses of the formula respectively. Each Y-value should be matched to corresponding X-values (logical variable), and each Z-value (disjunctive clause) should be matched to three Y-values (literals) that the Z-value contains (Figure 3).

On this instance, $Y \to X$ holds. By the query FD $X \to Y$, we represent the assignment of *true* or *false* for each logical variable. By the query FD $Z \to Y$, we represent the selections of one literal from each disjunctive clause that causes the clause to be *true*.

The number of tuples of each solution corresponds to the number of Z-values of that solution, since $Z \to Y$ and $Y \to X$ hold on it. Therefore the solution which has all Z-values of $R_2(XYZ)$ is maximum, and if there exists such solution, the formula of 3SAT must have a satisfying truth assignment.

Conversely, if the formula has a satisfying truth assignment, we can form a maximum solution by choosing the literals of Y assigned *true*, and choosing one literal assigned *true* from each Z-value.

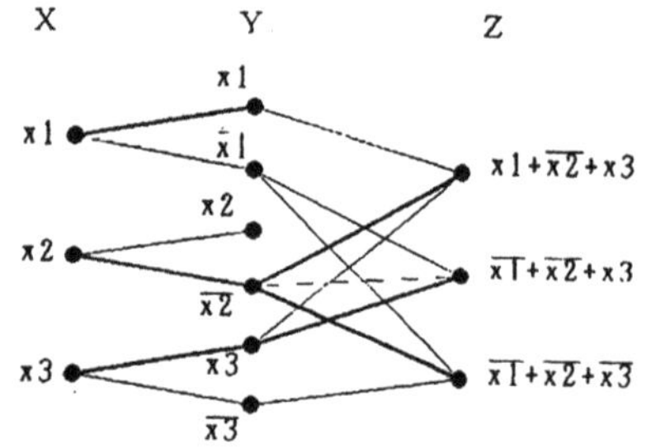

Figure 3: Reduction of 3SAT to Q_{Fin}

Since $Fchain$ contains $X \to Z$ by transitivity, the node Z has two incoming arcs on the FD-graph. The proof of Q_{Fchain} may therefore be constructed similarly to Q_{Fin}. The query Q_{F2eqin} also has two incoming edges at node Y in its FD-graph. In Figure 3, the relation R_2 reduced from a 3SAT instance satisfies the FD $Y \to X$. This implies that a solution of $Q_{Fin}(R_2)$ is also a solution for $Q_{F2eqin}(R_2)$ in this 3SAT instance, hence Q_{F2eqin} is NP-complete.

Q_{F3eq} is proved to be NP-complete by the reduction of 3D-MATCHING [15], that is described as follows:

Instance : Set $M \subseteq X \times Y \times Z$, where X, Y and Z are disjoint sets having the same number q of elements.

Question : Does M contain a *matching*, i.e., a subset $M' \subseteq M$ such that $|M'| = q$ and no two elements of M' agree in any coordinate?

For the relation $R_2(XYZ)$ as an instance of 3D-MATCHING, if the query $\{X \to Y, Y \to Z, Z \to X\}$ has a maximum solution of q tuples, R_2 contains the matching.

□

From the above discussions, it is a hard problem to process queries which contain Q_{Fin}, Q_{Fchain} or Q_{F3eq}.

6 PROCESSING FD SET CONSTRAINT QUERIES UTILIZING DATA DEPENDENCIES

In a given database management system, there may exist data dependencies, such as join dependencies (JDs) or functional dependencies (FDs), that are maintained in order to preserve semantic constraints. For example, on the relation $R_1(ETJ)$ of Section 4, if all employees care only about the time slots and don't care about the types of jobs, $\bowtie [ET, TJ]$ holds. On the other hand, if all employees care only about types of jobs, $\bowtie [EJ, JT]$ holds. In processing queries, the system should be able to take advantage of these dependencies.

We show that the NP-complete queries of the previous section can be processed in P-time if there exists certain types of dependency sets in the database.

6.1 JDs Corresponding to Equivalent Covering Node Sets

Let us consider as an example the query Q_{F3eq} of Subsection 5.3, with an additional join dependency $\bowtie [XY, YZ]$ constituting the database dependency set D (Figure 4). Note that $F3eq$ is a disjoint-covered FD set. The existence of D allows the decomposition of $R_2[XYZ]$ into $R_2[XY]$ and $R_2[YZ]$. This partition allows us to define a directed graph G_{XYZ}, which contains two bipartite graphs corresponding to $R_2[XY]$ and $R_2[YZ]$ respectively, and arcs that connect corresponding Y-values of the both bipartite graphs, as illustrated in Figure 5. The maximum solution of $Q_{F3eq}(R_2)$ may be represented as a maximum flow from the source node s to the target node t of G_{XYZ}. Then we can solve this problem using a maximum network-flow algorithm [15].

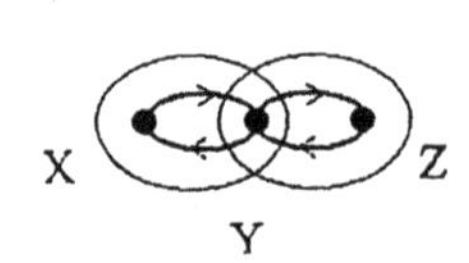

Figure 4: G_{F3eq} and the corresponding JD

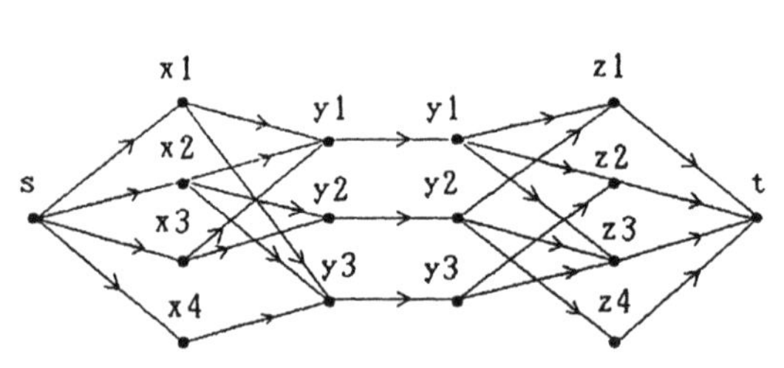

Figure 5: Reduction of Q_{F3eq} to a maximum flow problem

There may be a cyclic JD that decomposes equivalent covering nodes, such as $\bowtie [XY, YZ, ZX]$; in this case, however, the problem remains NP-complete. This can be shown by a reduction of a restricted form of the 3D-MATCHING problem.

The idea of Figure 5 may be extended to the case of a chain join dependency decomposing the equivalent covering node set (see Figure 6).

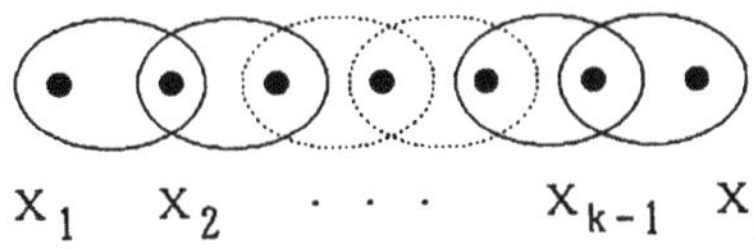

Figure 6: A chain join dependency

Theorem 3 Given a FD constraint query Q_F on $\underline{R}$ whose constraint F is a disjoint-covered FD set, representable as the equivalent covering node set $\{X_1, \ldots, X_k\}$ $(k \geq 2, X_i \cap X_j \neq \emptyset$ for $i \neq j)$, if there exists the join dependency $\bowtie[X_1X_2, X_2X_3, \ldots, X_{k-1}X_k]$ in R, a maximum solution of $Q_F(R)$ can be computed in P-time.

Proof: Let $G_R = (s, t, V, A)$ be a directed graph constructed as follows. Each $R[X_iX_{i+1}]$ is represented as a bipartite graph whose two node sets correspond to the set of X_i-values and X_{i+1}-values respectively. Each two nodes labeled with same X_i-value of two bipartite graphs are connected by an arc. The source node s is connected to all nodes of X_1-values by arcs, and the target node t is connected to all nodes of X_k-values. The directions of arcs follow the order $s \rightarrow X_1 \rightarrow X_2 \rightarrow \cdots \rightarrow X_k \rightarrow t$. The capacity of all arcs is 1.

For a maximum flow f_m of G_R, let S_{f_m} be the relation obtained by collecting tuples $(x_1x_2\cdots x_k)$ such that there is a flow in f_m that passes nodes $x_1, x_2, \ldots, x_k$, where each x_i belongs to the set of X_i values.

S_{f_m} is a maximum solution of $Q_F(R)$, since the JD $\bowtie[X_1X_2, X_2X_3, \ldots, X_{k-1}X_k]$ implies that each tuple of S_{f_m} is contained in R. Also, G_R is a ***simple network***; namely, one in which each node either has only one outgoing arc, or only one incoming arc, and the capacity of all nodes is 1. In a simple network, each node has at most one unit flow in any feasible flow, and any arc will be saturated to either 0 or 1 in any maximum flow. Therefore each X_i-value may appear at most once in any maximum flow of G_R. Hence the constraints of F hold for S_{f_m}, and the number of tuples of S_{f_m} equals the value of the flow f_m.

Conversely, from any solution S of $Q_F(R)$, we can produce a flow f whose value equals the number of the tuples of S. Therefore, S_{f_m} is the maximum solution of $Q_F(R)$. The maximum flow of simple networks can be computed in $O(|V|^{1/2}|A|)$ time [15). □

This method could not be extended to the case of compound-covered FD sets directly, since for a covering set $\{X_1, \ldots, X_k\}$ of a compound FD set, $\bowtie[X_1X_2, X_2X_3, \ldots, X_{k-1}X_k]$ may be a cyclic JD, and the maximum flow may have a tuple that does not exist in the input relation. This problem may be resolved by introducing another condition, called "attribute-connected."

In an attribute-connected JD $\bowtie[X_1X_2, X_2X_3, \ldots, X_{k-1}X_k]$, if an attribute A is contained in X_i and X_j, then A must also be contained in all components in the sequence between X_i and X_j. Such a JD still remains acyclic, but may not be a chain.

Theorem 4 Given a FD constraint query Q_F on $\underline{R}$, whose set of constraints F is a compound-covered FD set, representable as the equivalent covering node set $\{X_1, \ldots, X_k\}$ $(k \geq 2)$, suppose that there exists the join dependency $\bowtie[X_1X_2, X_2X_3, \ldots, X_{k-1}X_k]$ in R such that if $A \in X_i$ and $A \in X_j$ for $1 \leq i < j \leq k$, then $A \in X_l$ for $i \leq l \leq j$. Then, a maximum solution of $Q_F(R)$ can be computed in P-time.

The method of Theorem 3 could not be extended to the case of tree acyclic JDs, such as Figure 7, this is justified by the following theorem:

Theorem 5 Let $Q_F(R)$ be an FD set constraint query whose constraint set F is disjoint-covered, and F can be represented by the equivalent covering node set $\{X_1, X_2, X_3, X_4\}$. Then, $Q_F(R)$ is NP-complete in data complexity, even if there exists the join dependency $\bowtie[X_1X_4, X_2X_4, X_3X_4]$ in the input relation R.

Proof: Let $R_3(X_1X_2X_3)$ be the relation corresponding to the instance M of 3D-MATCHING. By giving each tuple of R_3 an unique identifier, let us construct the relation $R_4(X_1X_2X_3X_4)$, whose attribute X_4 represents these identifiers. FD $X_4 \rightarrow X_1X_2X_3$ holds in R_4, which implies that $\bowtie[X_1X_4, X_2X_4, X_3X_4]$. By testing the cardinality of the maximum solution of $Q_F(R_4)$, we can decide the 3D-MATCHING problem. □

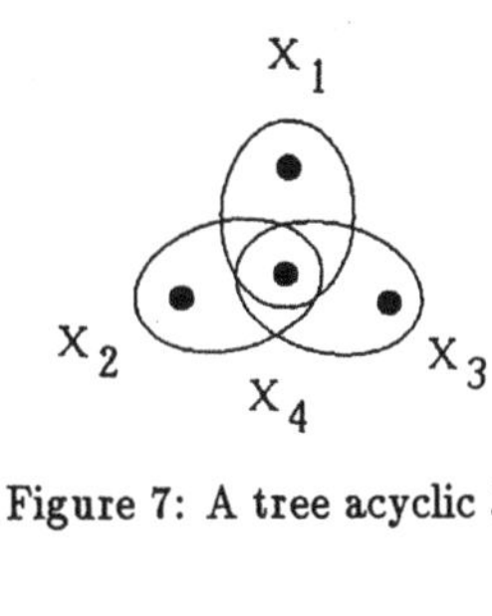

Figure 7: A tree acyclic JD

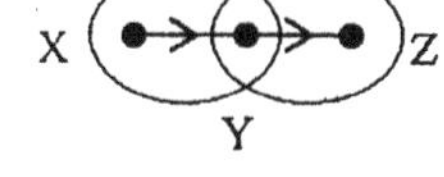

Figure 8: Q_{Fchain} and the corresponding JD

6.2 JDs Corresponding to Directed Trees

Let us suppose that for the query Q_{Fchain} of Section 5.3, there exists the join dependency $\bowtie[XY, YZ]$ (X, Y and Z are pairwise disjoint) as shown in Figure 8. In this case, we can decompose $R_2(XYZ)$ into $R_2[XY]$ and $R_2[YZ]$, and apply the greedy algorithm of Example 3 to $R_2[XY]$ and $R_2[YZ]$ respectively.

The relation $S(XYZ)$ obtained by joining the maximum solutions of $R_2[XY]$ and $R_2[YZ]$ is the maximum solution of Q_{Fchain}, since the maximum solution of $R_2[YZ]$ for $Y \to Z$ contains all Y-values of R_2. Hence, the choice of tuples from $R_2[YZ]$ according to $Y \to Z$ cannot influence the choice of tuples from $R_2[XY]$.

This idea may be extended to the cases of directed trees in disjoint-covered FD sets, and attribute-connected directed trees in compound-covered FD sets.

Theorem 6 Let Q_F be a FD set constraint query on $\underline{R}$ whose constraint set F is disjoint-covered or compound-covered, and whose FD-graph is a directed tree T_F in the covering node set. If F is compound-covered, then suppose that for each two nodes X_i and X_j of T_F, $X = X_i \cap X_j$ is contained in the node X_{ij} of the least common ancestor of X_i and X_j on T_F, and the nodes in the path from X_{ij} to X_i and from X_{ij} to X_j. If there exists an acyclic join dependency j whose components consist of a node and its children of T_F, then the maximum solution of $Q_F(R)$ can be computed in P-time.

Proof: For each non-leaf node X_i of T_F, let $X_{d(i,1)}, \ldots, X_{d(i,k_i)}$ be the children of X_i. Let $F_i\,(i = 1, \ldots n)$ be the FD set obtained by restricting F to $X_i X_{d(i,1)} \cdots X_{d(i,k_i)}$, and let S_i be a maximum solution of the query $Q_{F_i}(R[X_i X_{d(i,1)} \cdots X_{d(i,k_i)}])$. S_i can be computed in a manner similar to that of Q_{Fout} of Section 5.

Now we show that the relation $S = S_1 \bowtie S_2 \bowtie \cdots \bowtie S_n$, which is obtained by joining solutions of each node, is a maximum solution of $Q_F(R)$. S is a subset of R, because JD j exists in R. Since the union of all F_is implies F, S satisfies F, hence $S \in Q_F(R)$. Each S_i contains all values of $R[X_i]$ without duplication, where X_i is the root node of G_{F_i}. When each S_i is joined with its children $S_{d(i,1)}, \ldots, S_{d(i,k_i)}$, no tuple of S_i will be lost, since for each tuple μ of S_i, there exists exactly one tuple that can be joined with μ in each $S_{d(i,j)}$. This follows from the conditions for disjoint-covered and compound-covered FD sets. Therefore, S contains all the values of $R[X_R]$ without duplication, where X_R is the root node of G_F.

Conversely, since any solution has no duplicated X_R-values, and the cardinality of any solution cannot exceed the cardinality of $R[X_R]$, S is maximum. □

6.3 Utilizing FDs of Database Dependencies

Given a query and its FD set F, if there exists an FD corresponding to an FD in D, (the set of database dependencies), then it may be removed from F. Moreover, there are cases where NP-complete queries may be transformed into matching or maximum flow problems by adding FDs of D to the query FD set F. For example, consider the query Q_{Fchain} of Subsection 5.3. If D contains the FD $Z \to X$, then adding $Z \to X$ to $Fchain$ makes the nodes of $\{X, Y, Z\}$ mutually equivalent. Thus Q_{Fchain} is transformed to Q_{F3eq}. Since the chain JD $\bowtie[XY, YZ]$ may be deduced from $Z \to X$, we may transform Q_{Fchain} into a maximum flow problem similar to that of Subsection 6.1.

Theorem 7 Let Q_F be a FD set constraint query on $\underline{R}$. Suppose that the input relation R satisfies a set D of FDs. For a set E of FDs in R, if $(F \cup D)^+ = (E \cup D)^+$ holds, then $Q_E(R) = Q_F(R)$; that is, Q_F and Q_E are equivalent.

For a given compound-covered query FD set F, we can transform F into E applying the following operations on the FD-graph G_F, in accordance with the set D of database dependencies by Theorem 7.

We can compute arcs on the covering node set of G_F from FDs of D.

(1) For an arc f of G_F, if the corresponding arc can be derived from D, then the arc f can be removed from G_F.

(2) If a new arc f can be derived from D, then the arc f can be added to G_F.

(3) If an arc f of G_F can be derived from other arcs of G_F, then the arc f can be removed from G_F.

6.4 Combined Method

By combining the methods of Subsections 6.1–6.3, an FD set constraint query may be processed in P-time, if the following conditions are satisfied. For the FD-graph G_F of a FD set constraint query Q_F whose constraints F is disjoint or compound-covered,

(1) There may exist at most one equivalent node set C consisting of more than one node. If C consists of more than two nodes, then there exists a JD corresponding to C in the manner of Subsection 6.1,

(2) The arc set of G_F, minus the arcs of C, consists of a set $\{T_1, \ldots, T_k\}$ of pairwise-disjoint directed trees. For each T_i there exists a JD corresponding to T_i in the manner of Subsection 6.2,

(3) If (1) or (2) does not hold, then G_F can be transformed to satisfy (1) and (2) using the operations of Subsection 6.3.

□

The method of Subsection 6.1 may be applied to the equivalent covering node set C, and the method of Subsection 6.2 may be applied to each T_i. By joining the maximum solutions of these parts, we obtain the maximum solution of $Q_F(R)$.

7 CONCLUDING REMARKS

Handling sets in query languages often causes problems in query processing and optimization. In set constraint queries, by introducing useful notions, such as FD-graphs, analyzing the complexity of queries is possible.

The use of unary constraints, not discussed in this paper, does not raise the complexity of queries. If a query consisting of binary constraints can be computed in P-time, queries which consist of those binary constraints and arbitrary unary constraints can also be computed in P-time.

Acknowledgments

The authors are grateful to Hiroshi Imai and Tetsuya Furukawa for valuable discussions. The authors also thank Michael E. Houle for helpful comments on this paper.

References

(1) Abiteboul, S. and Vianu, V., "Procedural and Declarative Database Update Languages," Proc. 7th ACM PODS (1988), pp. 240-250.

(2) Ausiello, G., D'Atri, A. and Sacca, D., "Graph Algorithms for Functional Dependency Manipulation," J. of ACM, Vol.30, No. 4 (1983), pp. 752-766.

(3) Beeri, C., Naqvi, S., Ramakrishnan, R., Shmueli, O. and Tsur, S., "Sets and Negation in a Logic Database Language (LDL1)," Proc. 6th ACM PODS (1987), pp. 21-37.

(4) Chandra, A. K. and Harel, D., "Structure and Complexity of Relational Queries," J. Comp. System Sci., 25, 1 (1982), pp. 99-128.

(5) Chandra, A. K., "Theory of Database Queries," Proc. 7th ACM PODS (1988), pp. 1-9.

(6) Chen, W. and Warren, D. S., "C-Logic of Complex Objects," Proc. 8th ACM PODS (1989), pp. 369-378.

(7) Immerman, N., "Relational Queries Computable in Polynomial Time," Proc 14th ACM STOC (1982), pp. 147–152.

(8) Immerman, N. Patnaik and Stemple, D., "The Expressiveness of a Family of Finite Set Languages," Proc. 10th ACM PODS (1991), pp. 37–52.

(9) Iwaihara, M. and Kambayashi, Y., "Processing Set Constraint Queries Utilizing Data Dependencies," Proc. Int. Workshop on Discrete Algorithms and Complexity, pp. 269–276, 1989.

(10) Jaeschke, G. and Schek, H-J., "Remarks on the Algebra of Non-First-Normal-Form Relations," Proc. 1st ACM PODS (1982), pp. 124–138.

(11) Kambayashi, Y., Tanaka, K. and Takeda, K., "Synthesis of Unnormalized Relations Incorporating More Meaning," Information Sciences, Vol. 29 (1983), pp. 201–247.

(12) Kolaitis, P. G. and Papadimitriou, C. H., "Why not Negation by Fixpoint?," Proc. 7th ACM PODS (1988), pp. 231–239.

(13) Krishnamurthy, R. and Naqvi, S., "Nondeterministic Choice in Datalog," Technical Report ACA–ST–029-88, MCC, TX78759, 1988.

(14) Kuper, G. M., "Logic Programming with Sets," Proc. 6th ACM PODS (1987), pp. 11-20.

(15) Papadimitriou, C. H., Steiglitz, K., "*Combinational Optimization*," Prentice-Hall, 1982.

(16) Paredaens, J., "Possibilities and Limitations of Using Flat Operators in Nested Algebra Expressions," Proc. 7th ACM PODS (1988), pp. 29–38.

(17) Sheng, Y.-H., "A Non-deterministic Deductive Database Language," Proc. ACM SIGMOD (1991), pp. 188–197.

(18) Vardi, M. Y., "The Complexity of Relational Query Languages," Proc. 12th ACM STOC (1982), pp. 137–146.

AN ENHANCED RETE ALGORITHM FOR LARGE SCALE DATA ACCESS

Nobuhiro Ajitomi†, Hiroyasu Kurose‡

Software Research Center
Software Division
RICOH Co., Ltd.

1-1-17, Koishikawa, Bunkyo-ku, Tokyo, 112 JAPAN
†aji@src.ricoh.co.jp, ‡kurose@src.ricoh.co.jp

ABSTRACT

This paper introduces the OD-RETE pattern matching algorithm which is obtained by incorporating the on-demand evaluation mechanism into the RETE algorithm and which is suitable for production systems that access to large scale data. It allows to construct both of a "data-driven" network that simulates an ordinary RETE network and a "request-driven" network that performs on-demand formula evaluation. The latter network can treat large data without loading the whole data into the network. This paper describes the OD-RETE algorithm by defining nodes as "objects" that exchange messages with each other and discusses the ways to utilize this algorithm with DBMSs.

1 INTRODUCTION

RETE[8] is a well known pattern matching algorithm. It is efficient for comparing a large collection of patterns with a large collection of data. Many production systems such as OPS5[5,8] use this algorithm or its variants[9,15,19]. It is used to determine which rules satisfy condition parts.

The effectiveness of the RETE algorithm comes from sharing of pattern matching tests and storing the results of these tests. Storing the results makes re-evaluations of tests efficient.

The RETE algorithm which has these features is useful not only for production systems but also for database management systems. It can be used to validate integrity constraints of a database management system (DBMS) and to evaluate queries.

The RETE algorithm has been seldom used with a DBMS. With a DBMS, the original RETE algorithm has several problems such as shortage of memory and explosion of evaluation time. The RETE algorithm requires a very large memory area for the working memory (WM) because the records in a DBMS must be loaded into the WM. There are some attempts[10] in which only activated data are loaded in order to save the WM area.

The network in the RETE algorithm is reconstructed when rules are changed. It is difficult to keep the network and the WM consistent after reconstruction. Several production systems support incremental compilation of a RETE network [3,5,15]. It is not a crucial problem that the WM is cleared in reconstruction as far as a RETE network is seldom reconstructed. However it may be a severe problem when the network is often reconstructed or the recomputation cost of the WM is untolerable. The RETE algorithm with a DBMS has so large the WM that the re-evaluation requires a great deal of computation.

If the above problems are solved, the RETE algorithm increases efficiency of database queries and expert systems that use very large scale data. It is also applied to view update[4,12,17], snapshot update[1,11] and multiple query optimization[6,18]. It is also useful for inference procedures on a database such as checking database integrity [7,14].

The RETE algorithm works effectively only when data in a RETE network change relatively slowly. Because the RETE algorithm maintains states between production cycles, it is inefficient in such situations that most of the data change in each cycle. Intermediate results of matching can be stored in a RETE network so that all data in the WM need not be recomputed every time the WM is modified. But if there are a lot of data, the size of intermediate results may be combinatorially explosive. An algorithm named TREAT in which pattern matching is recomputed every cycle without intermediate results is proposed[13]. TREAT is better than RETE when data changes frequently. An algorithm that stores or recomputes the intermediate results in need is better than RETE and TREAT.

We solve these problems by adding special functions to each node in a RETE network. Our enhanced algorithm is called OD-RETE algorithm, where 'OD' stands for On-Demand evaluation mechanism.

In the OD-RETE algorithm, nodes in a network are

regarded as "objects" (in the sense of object-oriented programming paradigm), or processes communicating to each other. A node can send a *message* to another node. A node that receives a message will take some actions and return back some reply to the message sender. All interactions between nodes can be handled as messages. A downward data flow (seen in RETE) is simulated by "feed data" messages that are sent from upward nodes to downward nodes. A node can request to retransmit all data by sending a "request all data" message to its upward node. In general, data feeding messages flow downwards and data requesting messages flow upwards. An OD-RETE network can behave as an ordinary RETE network with using the former feature, and also perform on-demand formula evaluation, as a DBMS does, with using the latter feature. These features improve the efficiency of memory use and increase the computing speed.

The structure of this paper is as follows. In the next section, the OD-RETE algorithm is defined. In section 3, the features of this algorithm are described. In section 4, applications for a DBMS are exemplified. Section 5 concludes this paper and presents a discussion of future works.

2 ALGORITHM DESCRIPTION

This section describes the OD-RETE algorithm. An OD-RETE network is constructed from three types of nodes which are *test nodes*, *join nodes*, and *memory nodes*. Test and join nodes correspond to *one-input nodes* and *two-input nodes* in the original RETE algorithm [8] respectively. Memory nodes correspond to *left-* and *right-memories* of two-input nodes in [8]. A memory node has data storages, called a *token memories*, each of which can contain a token sequence. This section describes how these three nodes in our algorithm work.

Like an ordinary RETE network, an OD-RETE network has several entries (from which the network receives tokens from the outer world) and exits (i.e., goals, each of which corresponds to each production rule). In this paper, *downward* direction means the direction from entries to exits, and *upward* direction means the opposite direction.

2.1 Notation

This section introduces some concepts and notations that are necessary to describe our algorithm.

Let U be the set of all values we are concerned. When a set of *attributes* A is given, a *tupple on* A is defined as a mapping from A to U. We represent the set of all tupples on A by U^A. When A is empty, there exists only one tupple, denoted by 1 here.

A *token* is a signed tupple as defined in [8]. Tokens $+x$ and $-x$ denote an addition and a deletion of x respectively. A sequence of signed tupples on A is called a *token sequence on* A. In this paper, a token sequence $X = \langle \pm x_1, \pm x_2, \ldots \rangle$ is expressed by a summation form such as $X = \pm x_1 \pm x_2 \pm \ldots = \sum c_\alpha x_\alpha$ (where $c_\alpha = \pm 1$). When a token sequence X can be expressed as $X = x_1 + x_2 + \ldots = \sum x_\alpha$ (where $x_\alpha \neq x_\beta$ for all different α and β), X is interpreted as a relation $X = \{x_1, x_2, \ldots\}$. An empty sequence, denoted by 0, is regarded as an empty relation.

When x is a tupple on A and A' is a subset of A, its *projection* $x' = x|_{A'}$ is a tupple on A' that satisfies $x'(a) = x(a)$ for all $a \in A'$. For a relation $X = \sum x_\alpha$ on A, X's projection is defined by $X|_{A'} = \sum (x_\alpha|_{A'})$.

For a token sequence $X = \sum c_\alpha x_\alpha$ and a logical formula ψ, X*'s restriction by* ψ is defined by $\mathsf{Restrict}_\psi(X) = \sum c'_\alpha x_\alpha$ (where $c'_\alpha = c_\alpha$ if x_α satisfies ψ; $c'_\alpha = 0$ otherwise).

For a token sequence $X = \sum c_\alpha x_\alpha$ (where $x_\alpha \neq x_\beta$ for all different α and β), its *absolute value* is defined by $\mathsf{Abs}(X) = \sum |c_\alpha| x_\alpha$. Note that $\mathsf{Abs}(X)$ is a relation.

The *product* of two token sequences $X_1 = \sum c_{1\alpha} x_{1\alpha}$ and $X_2 = \sum c_{2\alpha} x_{2\alpha}$ is defined by $X_1 X_2 = \sum (c_{1\alpha} c_{2\beta}) y_{\alpha\beta}$ (where $y_{\alpha\beta} = x$ if $\{x_1\} \bowtie \{x_2\} = \{x\}$; $y_{\alpha\beta} = 0$ when $\{x_1\} \bowtie \{x_2\} = \{\}$). Obviously $1X = X1 = X$ and $0X = X0 = 0$ hold for any X. When all $c_{i\alpha}$ is 1, the product XY is equivalent to the natural join of two relations, i.e., $X \bowtie Y$.

A *message expression* $[R, M]$ denotes an action to send a message M to a node R and to wait its reply, and the returned value itself. A message expression (R, M) denotes an action to send a message M to a node R. In (R, M), the message sender does not wait a reply and the returned value is discarded. For ease of explanation, we introduce a dummy null node, denoted by 0. $[0, M]$ returns 0 and $(0, M)$ means no operation for any message M.

Each node has several *upward ports* and *downward ports* which contain information about the network structure. We represent the i-th upward port and the j-th downward port of a node R by $\langle i|R$ and $R|j\rangle$ respectively. An upward port can be connected to a downward port of another node, and a downward port can be connected to an upward port of another node. We represent a connection $R|i\rangle$ between $\langle j|S$ by a diagram:

$$R|i\rangle \longrightarrow \langle j|S$$

2.2 Messages

This section gives descriptions of messages that are exchanged between nodes in the OD-RETE algorithm. Those messages can be classified into three groups: network manipulating messages, data feeding messages, and data requesting messages. Network manipulating messages (M_{init}, M_{free}, M_{connect}, and M_{discon}) are used to grow or shrink networks. Data feeding messages (M_{feed}) are used to send data downward direction, as in a RETE network. Data requesting messages (M_{reqold} and M_{reqnew}) are used to request data. Data requesting messages flow upward and those replies flow downward in a network.

$M_{\text{init}}(R)$ —— Here R is a node. This message requests the receiver node to connect its first upward port to the appropriate downward port of R. This is used to add a test or memory node to a network. (A test/memory node has one upward port.)

$M_{\text{init}}(R_1, R_2)$ —— Here R_1 and R_2 are nodes. This message requests the receiver node to connect its first and second upward ports to the appropriate downward ports of R_1 and R_2. This is used to add a join node to a network. (A join node has two upward ports.)

M_{free} —— When this message is sent to a node in a network the receiver node is removed from the network.

$M_{\text{connect}}(R, m)$ —— Here R is a node and m is an upward port number of R. This message requests to connect $\langle m|R$ to some downward port in the message receiver. The receiver returns the downward port number.

$M_{\text{discon}}(i)$ —— Here i is a downward port number of the message receiver. This message requests to disconnect a connection on a downward port i.

$M_{\text{feed}}(m, X)$ —— Here m is an upward port number of the message receiver and X is a token sequence. When this message is sent, the receiver node will get X through its upward port m.

$M_{\text{reqold}}(i, X)$ —— Here i is a downward port number of the message receiver node and X is a relation. If the downward port i is defined to send tokens on A, X must be a relation on a subset of A. When $X = 1$, this message requests to transmit all data that have been sent through the downward port i of the receiver node. Sending this message simulates a memory-scan operation. When $X \neq 1$, XY will be returned, where Y is the returned value for $M_{\text{reqold}}(i, 1)$. Note that when M_{reqold} is sent twice the second execution will return the same value of the first execution (if there are no other activities in the network).

$M_{\text{reqnew}}(i)$ —— Here i is a downward port number of the message receiver node. This message requests to transmit all data that have arrived at the receiver node and have not been sent through the downward port i. Those data are sent through the downward port i. Note that when $M_{\text{reqnew}}(i)$ is sent twice the second execution will return 0, i.e., an empty token sequence (if there are no other activities in the network).

2.3 Nodes

We give complete definition of OD-RETE nodes here. First we explain variables allocated and maintained by each node. A node has several variables in it that contain state information of the node. Those variables are listed bellow.

Upward/downward ports —— An upward port is implemented as a pair of two variables R_i^{up} and m_i^{up} (where $i = 1$ in a test/memory node; $i = 1, 2$ in a join node). Similarly, a downward port is implemented as a pair of R_i^{down} and m_i^{down} (where $i = 1, 2, \ldots$). When there exists a connection between $R|m\rangle$ and $\langle n|S$, $R_m^{\text{down}} = S$ and $m_m^{\text{down}} = n$ hold in R, and $R_n^{\text{up}} = R$ and $m_n^{\text{up}} = m$ hold in S.

Token memories —— A memory node has one upward token memory X_1^{up} and several downward token memories $X_1^{\text{down}}, X_2^{\text{down}}, \ldots$. Each memory corresponds to each port. (A memory node has one upward port and several downward ports.) The X_1^{up} memory keeps the sum of all tokens that have arrived at the memory node and the X_i^{down} memory keeps the sum of all tokens that have departed through the i-th downward port. Since these token memories can be implemented to share stored data, the amount of the stored data is proportional to $\|\mathsf{Abs}(X_1^{\text{up}}) \cup (\mathsf{Abs}(X_1^{\text{down}}) \cup \mathsf{Abs}(X_2^{\text{down}}) \cup \ldots)\|$ which is less than $\|\mathsf{Abs}(X_1^{\text{up}})\| + (\|\mathsf{Abs}(X_1^{\text{down}})\| + \|\mathsf{Abs}(X_2^{\text{down}}\| \ldots)$, where $\|X\|$ denotes the number of tupples contained in a relation X.

Working variables —— Some working areas are temporarily needed.

The self node —— In the description of each node, the node itself is referred as a special variable R^{self}.

$$
\begin{array}{lcll}
\mathsf{Feed}(i, X) & = & (R_i^{\text{down}}, M_{\text{feed}}(X)) & (\text{when } X \neq 0) \\
 & & \text{do nothing} & (\text{when } X = 0) \\
\mathsf{ReqOld}(i, X) & = & (R_i^{\text{up}}, M_{\text{reqold}}(m_i^{\text{up}}, X)) & \\
\mathsf{ReqNew}(i) & = & (R_i^{\text{up}}, M_{\text{reqnew}}(m_i^{\text{up}})) &
\end{array}
$$

Figure 1: Procedures used in node descriptions.

For ease of node description, we define three procedures as shown in Fig.1. Procedure $\mathsf{Feed}(i, X)$ feeds data X to $R^{\text{self}}|i\rangle$: procedure $\mathsf{ReqOld}(i, X)$ requests $\langle i|R^{\text{self}}$ to retransmit all data: procedure $\mathsf{ReqNew}(i)$ requests $\langle i|R^{\text{self}}$ to transmit new data.

Test node —— Let A be a set of attributes, and ψ be a logical formula. The test node for ψ restricts a token sequence on A by ψ. The description of this test node is shown in Fig.2. When receiving $M_{\text{feed}}(1, X)$, this node behaves like a one-input node in [8], i.e., this node feeds $\mathsf{Restrict}_\psi(X)$ to all downward nodes. When receiving M_{reqold} or M_{reqnew}, this node forwards this message to its upward node, restricts the value returned from the upward node by ψ, and replies the restricted data.

Join node —— Let A_1, A_2 be sets of attributes. The *join node on A_1 and A_2* joins two token sequences on A_1 and A_2 and generates a new token sequence on $A_1 \cup A_2$. For $M_{\text{feed}}(i, X)$, this node behaves like a two-input node in [8], except that it sends M_{reqold} message upward instead of scanning left- or right-memory. For $M_{\text{reqold}}(i, X)$ and $M_{\text{reqnew}}(i)$

$M_{init}(R)$	$R_1^{up} \leftarrow R,\ \ m_1^{up} \leftarrow [R, M_{connect}(R^{self}, 1))]$
M_{free}	$[R_1^{up}, M_{discon}(m_1^{up})]$
$M_{connect}(R, m)$	find i such that $R_i^{down} = 0$ $R_i^{down} \leftarrow R, \quad m_i^{down} \leftarrow m$ reply i
$M_{discon}(i)$	$R_i^{down} \leftarrow 0$
$M_{feed}(1, X)$	$\mathsf{Feed}(i, \mathsf{Restrict}_\psi(X))$ (for all i)
$M_{reqold}(i, X)$	$Y \leftarrow \mathsf{Restrict}_\psi(\mathsf{ReqOld}(1, X))$ $\mathsf{Feed}(j, Y)$ (for all j such that $j \neq i$) reply Y
$M_{reqnew}(i)$	$X \leftarrow \mathsf{Restrict}_\psi(\mathsf{ReqNew}(1))$ $\mathsf{Feed}(j, X)$ (for all j such that $j \neq i$) reply X

Figure 2: Test node for ψ.

$M_{init}(R_1, R_2)$	$R_1^{up} \leftarrow R_1,\ \ m_1^{up} \leftarrow [R_1, M_{connect}(R^{self}, 1)]$ $R_2^{up} \leftarrow R_2,\ \ m_2^{up} \leftarrow [R_2, M_{connect}(R^{self}, 2)]$
M_{free}	$[R_1^{up}, M_{discon}(m_1^{up})]$ $[R_2^{up}, M_{discon}(m_2^{up})]$
$M_{connect}(R, m)$	same as $M_{connect}$ for a test node
$M_{discon}(i)$	same as M_{discon} for a test node
$M_{feed}(i, X)$	$Y \leftarrow \mathsf{ReqOld}(2 - i, X\|_{A_1 \cap A_2})$ $\mathsf{Feed}(j, XY)$ (for all j)
$M_{reqold}(i, X)$	reply $\mathsf{ReqOld}(1, X\|_{A_1})\,\mathsf{ReqOld}(2, X\|_{A_2})$
$M_{reqnew}(i)$	$X_1 \leftarrow \mathsf{ReqNew}(1)$ $Y_2 \leftarrow \mathsf{ReqOld}(2, \mathsf{Abs}(X_1)\|_{A_1 \cap A_2})$ $X_2 \leftarrow \mathsf{ReqNew}(2)$ $Y_1 \leftarrow \mathsf{ReqOld}(1, \mathsf{Abs}(X_2)\|_{A_1 \cap A_2})$ $\mathsf{Feed}(j, X_1Y_2 + X_2Y_1)$ (for all $j \neq i$) reply $X_1Y_2 + X_2Y_1$

Figure 3: Join node for A_1 and A_2.

messages, the node generates data requesting messages to compute $X\,\mathsf{ReqOld}(1,1)\,\mathsf{ReqOld}(2,1)$ and $X(\mathsf{ReqNew}(1)\,\mathsf{ReqOld}(2,1) + \mathsf{ReqNew}(2)\,\mathsf{ReqOld}(1,1))$ respectively. The detailed algorithm is shown in Fig.3.

Memory node —— A memory node has token memories $X_1^{up}, X_1^{down}, X_2^{down}, \ldots$ as explained before. Each memory node runs in either of two modes: *buffering mode* and *non-buffering mode*. When receiving a M_{feed} message, a non-buffering memory node sends the received data to all downward nodes immediately, while a buffering memory node does not send them until required by an M_{reqnew} message. Token memories are scanned when actions for M_{reqold} and M_{reqnew} messages are taken. The detailed algorithm is shown in Fig.4.

3 FEATURES AND USAGE

This section shows how networks are constructed from nodes defined in the previous section.

$M_{init}(R)$	$R_1^{up} \leftarrow R,\ \ m_1^{up} \leftarrow [R, M_{connect}(R^{self}, 1)]$ $X_1^{up} \leftarrow \mathsf{ReqOld}(1, 1)$ $X_i^{down} \leftarrow X_1^{up}$ (for all i)
M_{free}	$[R_1^{up}, M_{discon}(m_i^{up})]$
$M_{connect}(R, m)$	same as $M_{connect}$ for a test node
$M_{discon}(i)$	same as M_{discon} for a test node
$M_{feed}(1, X)$	$X_1^{up} \leftarrow X_1^{up} + X$ ($X_i^{down} \leftarrow X_1^{up}$, $\mathsf{Feed}(i)$(for all i) - in non-buffering mode)
$M_{reqold}(i, X)$	reply XX_i^{down}
$M_{reqnew}(i)$	$X_1^{up} \leftarrow X_1^{up} + \mathsf{ReqNew}(1)$ $X \leftarrow X_1^{up} - X_i^{down}$ $X_i^{down} \leftarrow X_1^{up}$ reply X

Figure 4: Memory node.

3.1 Data-Driven Network

Suppose there are relations $X_1^{db}, X_2^{db}, \ldots$ on $A_1, A_2, \ldots$, and $A \subset \bigcup A_i$. When a logical formula ψ is given, a *query by* ψ means to compute $X_\psi = \{x \in U^A \mid x \text{ satisfies } \psi;\ x|_{A_i} \in X_i^{db} \text{ holds for all } i\}$ from $X_1^{db}, X_2^{db}, \ldots$. If the formula ψ is simple enough, it is possible to construct a RETE network that processes this query. This RETE network can be considered as a data-driven computing system. Since each node is programmed to take an action when a token arrives at the node, the whole computation process will be completed just after tokens are fed to the network.

The OD-RETE algorithm is designed as an extension of the RETE algorithm, and it is possible to construct a data-driven OD-RETE network as follows. First, a network is constructed from the given condition ψ according to the ordinary RETE algorithm; test nodes are used instead of one-input nodes, join nodes connected to non-buffering memory nodes are used, i.e.:

$$\begin{matrix} \longrightarrow \langle 1|R_1^{mem}|1\rangle \longrightarrow \langle 1| \\ \longrightarrow \langle 1|R_2^{mem}|1\rangle \longrightarrow \langle 2| \end{matrix} \Big\} R^{join}|m\rangle \longrightarrow$$

instead of two-input nodes (where R_1^{mem} and R_2^{mem} are non-buffering memory nodes, and R^{join} is a join node). The network will have several ports of entry nodes $\langle m_1^{ent}|R_1^{ent}, \langle m_2^{ent}|R_2^{ent}, \ldots$ that correspond to $X_1^{db}, X_2^{db}, \ldots$ respectively, and one exit node R^{exit} that corresponds to X_ψ. The next step is to add a buffering memory node R_*^{exit} to the exit node by sending $M_{init}(R^{exit})$ message to R_*^{exit}. The final step is to execute:

$$m_*^{exit} \leftarrow [R_*^{exit}, M_{connect}(R^{dummy}, m^{dummy})]$$

to allocate an upward port in R_*^{exit} (where R^{dummy} is a non-null dummy node and m^{dummy} is an arbitrary integer). As shown in Fig.5, $R_*^{exit}|m_*^{exit}\rangle$ is used to retrieve X_ψ.

Whenever a tupple is added to or deleted from a relation X_i^{db}, the memory in R_*^{exit} is recomputed and updated automatically. The resulting relation X_ψ is simply

$$\begin{array}{ll}\text{Initialize :} & (R_i^{\text{ent}}, M_{\text{feed}}(m_i^{\text{ent}}, X_i^{\text{db}})) \;\; \text{(for all } i\text{)} \\ & X_\psi \leftarrow [R_*^{\text{exit}}, M_{\text{reqold}}(m_*^{\text{exit}}, 1)] \\ \text{Add } x \text{ to } X_i^{\text{db}} : & (R_i^{\text{ent}}, M_{\text{feed}}(m_i^{\text{ent}}, +x)) \\ \text{Delete } x \text{ from } X_i^{\text{db}} : & (R_i^{\text{ent}}, M_{\text{feed}}(m_i^{\text{ent}}, -x)) \\ \text{Update } X_\psi : & X_\psi \leftarrow X_\psi + [R_*^{\text{exit}}, M_{\text{reqnew}}(m_*^{\text{exit}})]\end{array}$$

Figure 5: Usage of a data-driven network.

$$\text{Initialize : } \; X_\psi \leftarrow [R_*^{\text{exit}}, M_{\text{reqold}}(m_*^{\text{exit}}, 1)]$$

Figure 6: Usage of a data-driven network when $X_i^{\text{db}} = 0$.

updated by data transmission between R_*^{exit} to X_ψ. If X_ψ is implemented as a reference to X_1^{up} in R_*^{exit}, even this transmission will be unnecessary.

Here we present examples of data-driven OD-RETE networks. Suppose $X_1^{\text{db}}, X_2^{\text{db}}$ are relations on A_1, A_2, and $\psi \equiv P_1(A_1) \wedge P_2(A_2) \wedge Q(A)$ where $P_1(A_1), P_2(A_2)$ and$Q(A)$ are atomic formulas on A_1, A_2, and $A = A_1 \cup A_2$, respectively. In this case, a data-driven OD-RETE network for ψ will be created as in Fig.7. Here $R_{P_i}^{\text{test}}s$ and R_Q^{test} are test nodes for $P_i(A_i)$ and $Q(A)$, $R_{P_1 \wedge P_2}^{\text{join}}$ is a join node, $R_{P_i}^{\text{mem}}$ is a non-buffering memory node, and R_ψ^{mem} $(= R_*^{\text{exit}})$ is a buffering memory node. Next suppose $\psi' \equiv P_1(A_1) \wedge P_2(A_2) \wedge Q'(A)$. Since formulas ψ and ψ' have a common subformula, these two formulas can share a subnetwork for the common subformula, as shown in Fig.8.

In most cases where RETE networks are used, $X_i^{\text{db}} = 0$ holds for all i in the initial state. In such a situation, the initialization step is simplified as Fig.6.

3.2 Request-Driven Network

The design goal of the OD-RETE algorithm is to incorporate the request-driven query evaluation mechanism into the RETE algorithm, which is based on data-driven query evaluation. When tokens are fed to a request-driven RETE network, the network stores those tokens into memories in it and does no more processing until it is requested to evaluate queries.

Let $X_1^{\text{db}}, X_2^{\text{db}}, \ldots$ be relations on $A_1, A_2, \ldots$ and ψ be a logical formula on a subset of $\bigcup A_i$. A request-driven OD-RETE network for ψ can be constructed according to the ordinary RETE algorithm; In construction, test nodes are used instead of one-input nodes, join nodes are used instead of two-input nodes, and buffering memory nodes $R_1^{\text{db}}, R_2^{\text{db}}, \ldots$ are used as entry nodes corresponding to $X_1^{\text{db}}, X_2^{\text{db}}, \ldots$ respectively. The port to retrieve X_ψ, the result of the query, is allocated by:

$$m^{\text{exit}} \leftarrow [R^{\text{exit}}, M_{\text{connect}}(R^{\text{dummy}}, m^{\text{dummy}})]$$

Here, R^{exit} is the exit node of the network. Thus the port $R^{\text{exit}}|m^{\text{exit}}\rangle$ for X_ψ is obtained. The usage of this network is shown in Fig.9.

In this network, requesting data to R^{exit} triggers all necessary computations and causes X_1^{up} in R^{exit} to be updated. This happens in the initialization step and the updating step by M_{reqold}. If X_1^{up} in each R_i^{db} is implemented as a reference to a relation X_i^{db} in a DBMS, the initialization step is simplified as Fig.10, which is the same as the initialization step of a data-driven OD-RETE network as shown in Fig.6.

Fig.11 is a request-driven OD-RETE network for $\psi \equiv P_1(A_1) \wedge P_2(A_2) \wedge Q(A)$ and $\psi' \equiv P_1(A_1) \wedge P_2(A_2) \wedge Q'(A)$.

Networks discussed in the previous section and here are to be called totally-data-driven OD-RETE networks and totally-request-driven OD-RETE networks. There are various ways to construct networks besides these two extreme strategies, since it is possible to make partially-data-driven/partially-request-driven OD-RETE networks in which both of data-driven subnetworks and request-driven subnetworks exist. Such mixed OD-RETE networks can be used to integrate production systems and DBMSs.

Fig.12 is an example of the mixed network. Here R_1^{db} is a non-buffering memory node, and R_2^{db} and $R_{P_1 \wedge P_2}^{\text{mem}}$

$$\left.\begin{array}{l}(X_1^{\text{db}}) \longrightarrow \langle 1|R_{P_1}^{\text{test}}|1\rangle \longrightarrow \langle 1|R_{P_1}^{\text{mem}}|1\rangle \longrightarrow \langle 1| \\ (X_2^{\text{db}}) \longrightarrow \langle 1|R_{P_2}^{\text{test}}|1\rangle \longrightarrow \langle 1|R_{P_2}^{\text{mem}}|1\rangle \longrightarrow \langle 2|\end{array}\right\} R_{P_1 \wedge P_2}^{\text{join}}$$

$$R_{P_1 \wedge P_2}^{\text{join}}|1\rangle \longrightarrow \langle 1|R_Q^{\text{test}}|1\rangle \longrightarrow \langle 1|R_\psi^{\text{mem}}|1\rangle \longrightarrow (X_\psi)$$

Figure 7: A data-driven network for $\psi \equiv P_1(A_1) \wedge P_2(A_2) \wedge Q(A)$.

$$\left.\begin{array}{l}(X_1^{\text{db}}) \longrightarrow \langle 1|R_{P_1}^{\text{test}}|1\rangle \longrightarrow \langle 1|R_{P_1}^{\text{mem}}|1\rangle \longrightarrow \langle 1| \\ (X_2^{\text{db}}) \longrightarrow \langle 1|R_{P_2}^{\text{test}}|1\rangle \longrightarrow \langle 1|R_{P_2}^{\text{mem}}|1\rangle \longrightarrow \langle 2|\end{array}\right\} R_{P_1 \wedge P_2}^{\text{join}}$$

$$R_{P_1 \wedge P_2}^{\text{join}} \left\{\begin{array}{l}|1\rangle \longrightarrow \langle 1|R_Q^{\text{test}}|1\rangle \longrightarrow \langle 1|R_\psi^{\text{mem}}|1\rangle \longrightarrow (X_\psi) \\ |2\rangle \longrightarrow \langle 1|R_{Q'}^{\text{test}}|1\rangle \longrightarrow \langle 1|R_{\psi'}^{\text{mem}}|1\rangle \longrightarrow (X_{\psi'})\end{array}\right.$$

Figure 8: A data-driven network for $\psi \equiv P_1(A_1) \wedge P_2(A_2) \wedge Q(A)$ and $\psi' \equiv P_1(A_1) \wedge P_2(A_2) \wedge Q'(A)$.

$$\begin{array}{ll}\text{Initialize :} & (R_i^{\text{db}}, M_{\text{feed}}(1, X_i^{\text{db}})) \;\; \text{(for all } i\text{)} \\ & X_\psi \leftarrow [R^{\text{exit}}, M_{\text{reqold}}(m^{\text{exit}}, 1)] \\ \text{Add } x_i \text{ to } X_i : & (R_i^{\text{db}}, M_{\text{feed}}(1, +x_i)) \\ \text{Delete } x \text{ from } X_i : & (R_i^{\text{db}}, M_{\text{feed}}(1, -x_i)) \\ \text{Update } X_\psi : & X_\psi \leftarrow X_\psi + [R^{\text{exit}}, M_{\text{reqnew}}(m^{\text{exit}})]\end{array}$$

Figure 9: Usage of a request-driven network.

$$\text{Initialize : } \; X_\psi \leftarrow [R^{\text{exit}}, M_{\text{reqold}}(m^{\text{exit}}, 1)]$$

Figure 10: Usage of a request-driven network when R_i^{ent} is implemented on a DBMS.

$$\left.\begin{array}{l}(X_1^{db}) \longrightarrow \langle 1|R_1^{db}|1\rangle \longrightarrow \langle 1|R_{P_1}^{test}|1\rangle \longrightarrow \langle 1| \\ (X_2^{db}) \longrightarrow \langle 1|R_2^{db}|1\rangle \longrightarrow \langle 1|R_{P_2}^{test}|1\rangle \longrightarrow \langle 2|\end{array}\right\} R_{P_1\wedge P_2}^{join}$$

$$R_{P_1\wedge P_2}^{join}\left\{\begin{array}{l}|1\rangle \longrightarrow \langle 1|R_Q^{test}1|\rangle \longrightarrow (X_\psi) \\ |2\rangle \longrightarrow \langle 1|R_{Q'}^{test}|1\rangle \longrightarrow (X_{\psi'})\end{array}\right.$$

Figure 11: A request-driven network for $\psi \equiv P_1(A_1)\wedge P_2(A_2)\wedge Q(A)$ and $\psi' \equiv P_1(A_1) \wedge P_2(A_2) \wedge Q'(A)$.

$$\left.\begin{array}{l}(X_1^{db}) \longrightarrow \langle 1|R_1^{db}|1\rangle \longrightarrow \langle 1|R_{P_1}^{test}|1\rangle \longrightarrow \langle 1| \\ (X_2^{db}) \longrightarrow \langle 1|R_2^{db}|1\rangle \longrightarrow \langle 1|R_{P_2}^{test}|1\rangle \longrightarrow \langle 2|\end{array}\right\} R_{P_1\wedge P_2}^{join}$$

$$R_{P_1\wedge P_2}^{join}|1\rangle \longrightarrow \langle 1|R_{P_1\wedge P_2}^{mem}\left\{\begin{array}{l}|1\rangle \longrightarrow \langle 1|R_Q^{test}|1\rangle \longrightarrow (X_\psi) \\ |2\rangle \longrightarrow \langle 1|R_{Q'}^{test}|1\rangle \longrightarrow (X_{\psi'})\end{array}\right.$$

Figure 12: Another network for $\psi \equiv P_1(A_1) \wedge P_2(A_2) \wedge Q(A)$ and $\psi' \equiv P_1(A_1) \wedge P_2(A_2) \wedge Q'(A)$.

are buffering memory nodes. Suppose X_2^{db} is a large relation in a DBMS. When a token $\pm x_1$ is fed to $\langle 1|R_1^{db}$, R_2^{db} receives $M_{reqold}(1, y)$ (where $y = x_1|_{A_1\cap A_2}$) and will return yX_1^{down}. If X_1^{down} has an index whose key is $A_1 \cap A_2$, yX_1^{down} can be retrieved easily by utilizing the index. Thus, only required data in X_2^{db} flow into the network.

3.3 Dynamic Network Construction

In section 3.1 and 3.2, networks are constructed statically, i.e., no tokens are fed to a network during network construction. However, our OD-RETE algorithm allows to feed tokens to a network under the construction. Networks can grow (or shrink) even after it has been initialized and fed some data.

For any node R in a OD-RETE network, it is possible to grow the network by sending $M_{init}(R)$ message to a new test/memory node S. Similarly, for any nodes R_1, R_2 in a OD-RETE network, it is possible to grow the network by sending $M_{init}(R_1, R_2)$ message to a new join node S. The newly created part of the network is initialized by M_{reqold} message toward the downward end, same as in Fig.6 and Fig.10. Once initialized, there are no differences between the older part and the newly created part of the network. Thus, in our algorithm, usage of a network is independent of the way how the network has been constructed, in data-driven manner or request-driven manner, statically or dynamically, etc.

For example, the network in Fig.7 can grow up to the network in Fig.8 by $[R_{Q'}^{test}, M_{init}(R_{P_1\wedge P_2}^{join})]$ and $[R_{\psi'}^{mem}, M_{init}(R_{Q'}^{test})]$. The newly created part is initialized by $X_{\psi'} \leftarrow [R_{\psi'}^{mem}, M_{reqold}(1, 1)]$.

A network can shrink by an M_{free} message. A node R is *removable* when R has no downward nodes (i.e., $R_i^{down} = 0$ for all i). The M_{free} message to a removable node removes the node from a network. If S is the only downward node of R, removing S makes R removable.

$M_{recfree}$ if there exists i such that $R_i^{down} \neq 0$
then return immediately
$(R_h^{up}, M_{discon}(m_h^{up}))$, $(R_h^{up}, M_{recfree})$
(for all upward port h)

Figure 13: $M_{recfree}$ message to recursively free nodes.

Fig.13 is a definition of the "recursive free" message to remove the receiver node and all other nodes that become removable.

4 APPLICATION FOR DBMS

OD-RETE may be applied to several kinds of problems for which RETE is inefficient. The OD-RETE algorithm loads data into the WM as little as possible. It can be applied to rule bases with very large data. Especially, it is useful for productions that refer a lot of objects in a database.

In RETE, even invariable records such as code tables, must be loaded into the WM. OD-RETE makes the WM small. It also improves the speed of inferences. Therefore, inferences on a database can be executed with OD-RETE at an enough speed. Checking database integrities is an example of productions on a database.

OD-RETE can connect and disconnect its network without clearing the WM. It can add or delete rules dynamically. The property of the dynamic reconstruction is useful for query optimization of a database.

Checking integrity, materialized view, and query optimization are illustrated in this order as examples of its applications.

4.1 Checking Database Integrity

Database integrity is concerned with ensuring that the database is correct even though users or application programs try to incorrectly modify it. It is desirable to be able to describe integrity constraints on any combination of records. Most DBMSs, however, allow users to constrain only values of fields and referential integrities.

In order to check the database integrity, an OD-RETE network is constructed from the negation of the integrity constraint. The network has a buffered memory node as its exit node. While the database satisfies the integrity constraint, no tokens reach the exit node of the network. At the end of each transaction, the exit node is checked whether its memory is empty or not. If the memory is not empty, the integrity constraint is not satisfied in the current state and its corresponding transaction must be rollbacked.

4.2 Materialized View

View materialization means to evaluate a view definition and store its results. The resulting relation is called a *materialized view*. As the database changes because

$$
\left.\begin{array}{l}
(X_1^{\mathrm{db}}) \longrightarrow \langle 1|R_1^{\mathrm{db}}|1\rangle \longrightarrow \langle 1|R_{P_1}^{\mathrm{test}}|1\rangle \longrightarrow \langle 1| \\
(X_2^{\mathrm{db}}) \longrightarrow \langle 1|R_2^{\mathrm{db}}|1\rangle \longrightarrow \langle 1|R_{P_2}^{\mathrm{test}}|1\rangle \longrightarrow \langle 2|
\end{array}\right\} R_{P_1\wedge P_2}^{\mathrm{join}}
$$

$$
R_{P_1\wedge P_2}^{\mathrm{join}} \left\{\begin{array}{l}
|1\rangle \longrightarrow \langle 1|R_Q^{\mathrm{test}}|1\rangle \longrightarrow \langle 1|R_2^{\mathrm{mem}}|1\rangle \longrightarrow (X_2^{\mathrm{view}}) \\
|2\rangle \longrightarrow \langle 1|R_Q^{\mathrm{test}}|1\rangle \longrightarrow \langle 1|R_3^{\mathrm{mem}}|1\rangle \longrightarrow (X_3^{\mathrm{view}})
\end{array}\right.
$$

$$
R_{P_1}^{\mathrm{test}}|2\rangle \longrightarrow \langle 1|R_{P_1'}^{\mathrm{test}}|1\rangle \longrightarrow \langle 1|R_1^{\mathrm{mem}}|1\rangle \longrightarrow (X_1^{\mathrm{view}})
$$

Figure 14: A network for materialized views.

$$
\begin{array}{ll}
\text{Initialize :} & (R_h^{\mathrm{db}}, M_{\mathrm{feed}}(1, X_h^{\mathrm{db}})) \\
 & X_i^{\mathrm{view}} \leftarrow [R_i^{\mathrm{mem}}, M_{\mathrm{reqold}}(1,1)] \\
 & \qquad (\text{for } \; h = 1,2; i = 1,2,3) \\
\text{Add } x \text{ to } X_h^{\mathrm{db}} : & (R_h^{\mathrm{db}}, M_{\mathrm{feed}}(1, +x)) \\
\text{Delete } x \text{ from } X_h^{\mathrm{db}} : & (R_h^{\mathrm{db}}, M_{\mathrm{feed}}(1, -x)) \\
\text{Access } X_i^{\mathrm{view}}: & X_i^{\mathrm{view}} \leftarrow X_i^{\mathrm{view}} + [R_i^{\mathrm{mem}}, M_{\mathrm{reqnew}}(1)] \\
\text{Remove } X_i^{\mathrm{view}}: & [R_i^{\mathrm{mem}}, M_{\mathrm{discon}}(1)] \\
 & [R_i^{\mathrm{mem}}, M_{\mathrm{recfree}}]
\end{array}
$$

Figure 15: Usage of the network for materialized views.

of updates applied to the base relations, the materialized view also changes. A materialized view can always be brought up to date by re-evaluation. However, complete re-evaluation is often inefficient, and the cost involved may be untolerable The problem addresses how to quickly update a view in response to database changes. This problem is different from the traditional view update problem. User can only update base relations and direct update to views are not considered.

It is possible to construct an OD-RETE network from the condition that defines a view. If this network has a memory node as its exit node, it works as a materialized view. The access to the materialized view is performed by sending M_{reqnew} to the memory node.

For example, Fig.14 is a network for multiple views. In this figure, X_i^{db} is a database relation. R_i^{db} is a non-buffering memory node. R_i^{mem} is a buffering memory node. The conditions corresponding to the views are as follows:

$$
\begin{array}{lcl}
X_1^{\mathrm{view}} : \psi_1(X_1^{\mathrm{db}}) & \equiv & P_1(X_1^{\mathrm{db}}) \wedge P_1'(X_1^{\mathrm{db}}) \\
X_2^{\mathrm{view}} : \psi_2(X_1^{\mathrm{db}}, X_2^{\mathrm{db}}) & \equiv & P_1(X_1^{\mathrm{db}}) \wedge P_2(X_2^{\mathrm{db}}) \wedge Q(X_1^{\mathrm{db}}, X_2^{\mathrm{db}}) \\
X_3^{\mathrm{view}} : \psi_3(X_1^{\mathrm{db}}, X_2^{\mathrm{db}}) & \equiv & P_1(X_1^{\mathrm{db}}) \wedge P_2(X_2^{\mathrm{db}}) \wedge Q'(X_1^{\mathrm{db}}, X_2^{\mathrm{db}})
\end{array}
$$

In this network, requesting data to R_i^{mem} only causes the access to the memories in R_i^{mem} because R_i^{mem} is re-computed when a tupple is added to or deleted from X_i^{db}. X_i^{view} is accessed as fast as an ordinary materialized view.

When a database is updated, new tokens corresponding to the update flow into the network and views are differentially updated. This is faster than complete re-evaluation. Multiple views can share intermediate results of sub-conditions. The total throughput of multiple view evaluation is higher than that of individual evaluation of views.

When a view is added or deleted, the OD-RETE network is reconstructed. The network is reconstructed dynamically without interfering another view access. Even after the reconstruction, the speed of view access does not slow down. A partial change of view schemas does not cause complete re-evaluation of the whole view.

4.3 Query Optimization

The method of view optimization applies to ordinary query optimization. The result of queries is stored in an OD-RETE network in the same way as the materialized views. The result gives a possibility of improvement of response time of a DBMS. However, there are a lot of various queries in retrievals. It is impossible that the network for all queries is made in advance. In each retrieval, the sub-net corresponding to the query is added to the OD-RETE network. After a retrieval is executed, identical retrievals are executed only by accessing to the WM. It is useful for queries which are partially equivalent to the previous queries.

The method is also applicable to multiple query optimization. If there are queries that contain common sub-queries, it is not efficient to process them individually. The process can share intermediate results of the sub-patterns.

By the existence of various patterns of retrievals, the network may grow unlimitedly. This explosion can be avoided by removing rarely used sub-networks using strategies such as LRU. The removal causes no effect to other parts of the network. Queries that are not related to the removed sub-networks can be answered quickly after the removal.

5 CONCLUDING REMARKS

A new approach, the the OD-RETE algorithm, has been proposed to adapt the RETE algorithm to DBMSs. This algorithm has been obtained by incorporating an on-demand evaluation mechanism into the RETE algorithm and treating all control/data flows as "messages" exchanged between RETE nodes.

The OD-RETE algorithm is an extension of the original RETE algorithm and has all advantages that the RETE algorithm has. Besides those advantages, the OD-RETE algorithm has the "request-driven" feature. This feature enables to avoid feeding all contents of a database into an OD-RETE network. It also enables incremental query addition/deletion. The OD-RETE algorithm, which has the "data-driven" feature that comes from the RETE algorithm and the "request-driven" feature that fits DBMSs, is a relevant solution for integrating production systems and DBMSs.

Finally we mention future plans relating to this research. The first plan is to implement an experimental OD-RETE -based production system to evaluate the OD-RETE algorithm. The second is to enhance the algorithm and to make it possible to remove and reconstruct a branch of a network while the branch is in use. The last is to incorporate an on-demand evaluation mechanism into other extensions of the RETE algorithm. Specifically we plan to integrate the OD-RETE and an enhanced RETE algorithm that is designed to treat quantified logical formulas [2].

6 Acknowledgements

The authors would like to express their gratitude to Dr. Hideko Kunii for her invaluable suggestions. The authors would also like to thank Mr. Katsumi Kanasaki. The authors are grateful to Ms. Naoko Ichikawa and Mr. Hideaki Nakayama for their helpful assistance and kind criticism.

REFERENCES

1) Adiba, M. E. and Lindsay, B. G., "Database snapshots," *Proc. VLDB '80* (1980), pp.86–91.

2) Ajitomi, N., "An Enhanced RETE Algorithm and Its Formal Description," *RICOH Technical Report*, No.18 (1988), pp.24-27

3) Araya, S. et al., "Incremental Structuring of Knowledge Base," *Trans. of Inst. of Electronics, Information and Communication Engineers* Vol.J71-D, No.6 (1988), pp.1100–1108.

4) Blakeley, J. A., Larson, P. A. and Tompa, F. W., "Efficiently updating materialized view," *Proc. ACM SIGMOD Int. Conf. Manage. Data* Vol.1986 (1986), pp.61–71.

5) Brownston, L., *Programming expert systems in OPS5*, Addison-Wesley (1985).

6) Chakravarthy, U. S. and Minker, J., "Multiple Query Processing Databases using Query Graphs," *Proc. VLDB '86* (1986), pp.384–391.

7) Fernandez, E. B., Summers, R. C. and Wood, C., *Database Security and Integrity*, Addison-Wesley (1981).

8) Forgy, C. L., "Rete: A Fast Algorithm for the Many Pattern / Many Object Pattern Match Problem, " *Artificial Intelligence*, Vol.19 (1982), pp.17–37.

9) Forgy, C. L., *The OPS83 User's Manual*, Production Technologies, Inc. (1986).

10) Langley, P., "Exploring the Space of Cognitive Architectures," *Bahavior Reseach Method and Instrumentation*, Vol.15 (1983), pp.289–299.

11) Lindsay, B., Haas, L., Mohan, C., Pirahesh, H. and Wilms, P., "A snapshot differential refresh algorithm," *Proc. ACM SIGMOD Int. Conf. Manage. Data* Vol.1986 (1986), pp.53–60.

12) Medieros, C. and Tompa, F. W., "Understanding the implications of view update policies," *Proc. VLDB '85* (1985), pp.316–323.

13) Miranker, D. P., "TREAT: A Better Match Algorithm for AI Production Systems," *Proc. AAAI-87* (1987), pp.42–47.

14) Nicolas, J. M., "Logic for Improving Integrity Checking in Relational Data Bases," *Acta Informatica*, Vol.18, No.3 (1982), pp.227–253.

15) Schor, M. I., Daly, T. P., Beth, H. S. L. and Tibbitts, R., "Advances in RETE Pattern Matching," *Proc. Natl. Conf. Artif. Intell.*, Vol.1 (1986), pp.226–232.

16) Sellis, T. K., "Multiple Query Optimization," *ACM TODS*, Vol.13, No.1 (1988), pp.23–52.

17) Shmueli, O. and Otai, A., "Maintenance of views," *ACM SIGMOD Rec* Vol.14, No.2 (1984), pp.240–255.

18) Subieta, K. and Rzeczkowski, W., "Query Optimization by stored queries," *VLDB '87* (1987), pp.369–380.

19) Tano, S., Masui, S., Sakaguchi, S. and Funabashi, M., "A Fast Pettern Match Algorithm for A Knowledge Based Systems Building Tool - EUREKA," *Trans. on Info. Proc. Soc. of Japan*, Vol.28, No.12 (1987), pp.1255–1268.

File Organization and Database Machines

Partial-match Retrieval using Multiple-key Hashing with Multiple File Copies

Kotagiri Ramamohanarao
Dept. of Computer Science
The University of Melbourne
Parkville 3052, Australia

John Shepherd
Dept. of Computer Science
The University of Melbourne
Parkville 3052, Australia

Ron Sacks-Davis
Dept. of Computer Science
R.M.I.T.
Melbourne 3001, Australia

ABSTRACT

The average cost for answering partial-match queries can be dramatically reduced by storing multiple copies of the data, each with a different clustering. We analyse the cost benefits (in terms of disk accesses) of this arrangement and present algorithms for determining a minimal cost file organisation for a given probability distribution of queries. We also show how constraining the range of values for specific attributes affects the usefulness of maintaining multiple copies.

1 Introduction

The performance of partial-match retrieval systems depends on two factors: how quickly the system can locate the matching records and how long it takes to actually retrieve these records from the data file. Modern partial-match indexing algorithms [4, 14, 13] address the first problem, and their performance is now very good. In fact, their cost is generally dwarfed by the cost of reading the pages indicated by the indexing algorithm. This indicates that clustering methods, whose job it is to keep sets of related records together on a small number of pages, are not as well-developed as indexing methods.

One method for clustering records in the data file to minimise query cost is based on multi-attribute hashing [13, 1]. In this method, the address of the page where a record is stored is determined by the attribute values of the record. For a file containing 2^d pages, the page address of a record is represented by a d-bit long address string; the hash code for each attribute value contributes some of these bits. The clustering of records in the data file depends on the number of bits which each attribute contributes to the address. The problem of determining an optimal clustering boils down to determining how many bits should be allocated to each attribute and this depends on the query distribution. For example, if attribute A_i is more commonly specified in queries than attribute A_j, then attribute A_i should contribute more address bits than attribute A_j.

While we can find a clustering which minimises the *average* query cost, for some queries the matching records may still be scattered over many pages. This is because the clustering will be "biased" towards the most common queries. Given that different queries have significantly different clustering requirements, any single clustering is at best a compromise. The only way to further reduce the average query cost is to store several copies of the data, each of which is clustered differently. Assuming that there are k copies of the data file, we can partition the queries into k disjoint subsets and associate a copy with each subset. Queries from a given subset are answered using the associated copy, and the records in the copy can be clustered to give the best performance for these queries. Since the number of queries in each subset is smaller than for a single data file, we can achieve better clustering.

In addition to considerably improving the average query cost, there are a number of other advantages to this approach. Nowadays, the cost overhead in storing multiple data copies is no longer prohibitive because the storage cost per unit data of mass storage devices is decreasing rapidly. Having multiple copies ensures data redundancy, and the existence of data redundancy increases the reliability of the system. In distributed systems, multiple copies of data are useful in order to reduce traffic on the communication channel and increase the available parallelism.

In this paper, we analyse the cost benefits to the partial-match retrieval problem of storing multiple copies of the data when the probability distribution of queries is known. This effectively involves determining a suitable partitioning of queries over the copies of the data and determining bit-allocations for each copy. To our knowledge, this problem has not been previously addressed.

In the next section we introduce the partial-match retrieval problem and analyse the cost of partial-match retrieval using multi-attribute hashing when we have only a single copy of the data. In section 2, we analyse the cost of partial-match retrieval using multi-attribute hashing when we have multiple copies of the data. In section 3, we describe several heuristic algorithms for allocating bits in a near-optimal manner. Section 4 presents results which show the performance improvements which can be expected by using a multiple copies of the data. In section 5 we give some intuition on the complexity of the problem of determining bit-allocations to optimise retrieval performance for multiple copies. Section 6 compares multi-attribute hashing to other indexing schemes in the context of multiple copies of the data. Section 7 discusses related file organisations for partial-match retrieval which also employ redundancy to improve retrieval performance. In section 8, we examine our bit-allocation algorithms in the context of dynamic files.

1.1 Partial-Match Retrieval Using Multi-attribute Hashing

Each *record* in the data file consists of a number of *attributes* which may be specified in a query, plus other fields which are irrelevant to the considerations here. Let us assume that there are n attributes, $A_1, A_2, ..., A_n$. A *partial-match query* is a specification of the values of zero or more of these attributes. The answer to a partial-match query is a set of records in the data file which have the specified values for the specified attributes. .pp While there are a number of file organisations to handle such queries, there are essentially three distinct approaches: *inverted file organisations*, *multi-attribute hashing*, and *binary coding* (*descriptor*) *schemes* [4, 14, 13]. Here we deal primarily with methods relevant to multi-attribute hashing. Note that *grid files* [10] while appearing to be a distinct class of file organisations, are closely related to multi-attribute hashing, and, for our purposes, the properties of the multi-attribute hashing schemes hold equally for grid files.

In a multi-attribute hashing scheme, the records of a file are stored in a number of pages, where each page holds a number of records. Let us assume that the data file contains 2^d pages, where $d > 0$. Each record has n attributes and n associated hashing functions, h_i. Each h_i provides a mapping from the key space of attribute A_i to the set of all possible strings of bits of length d_i, where $d_i >= 0$ and $d_1 + d_2 + ... + d_n = d$.

The page in which a particular record is stored is computed as follows: For each attribute A_i, its value is hashed to a bit-string of length d_i bits using the hashing function h_i. The bit-string resulting from the concatenation of these bit-strings for the individual attributes gives the page number. Of course, we should choose the hash functions so that they distribute the records evenly among the pages. In situations where the data file size varies significantly, we require dynamic hashing functions for partial-match retrieval based on *linear hashing* or *extendible hashing* [6, 12]. In this case, we interlace the bits of the attribute hash bit-strings using a *choice vector* that specifies which bit of which attribute contributes to each bit of the page number bit-string.

A partial-match query is answered in a multi-attribute hashing scheme using the following method. For each specified attribute A_i we generate a bit-string containing d_i bits using the hash function h_i and the specified value. For each unknown attribute A_i we form a string containing d_i $*$'s. We then form the concatenation of these strings, which gives a string containing 1's, 0's and $*$'s. Substituting all possible combinations of bit-values for the $*$'s generates the set of all addresses for the candidate pages. We then fetch each of these pages from the data file to examine them for matching records. Consider, for example, a data file containing three attributes $A_1A_2A_3$, with the bit-allocation $d_1 = 3, d_2 = 2, d_3 = 2$. If a query specifies attributes A_1 and A_3, we first construct bit-strings for these attributes. Let these bit-strings be 010 and 11 respectively. The concatenated bit-string for the query is denoted by $010**11$, where the $*$'s are the unknown bit values due to the unspecified attribute A_2. Substituting all possible bit-values for the positions containing $*$'s generates the four candidate page addresses: 0100011, 0100111, 0101011 and 0101111.

The distribution of records among the pages of the data file (*clustering*) depends on the choice of the values of the d_i. For example, if $d_1 = d$, then the clustering is determined solely by the value of attribute A_1. The *optimal clustering* is the one which gives the minimum average query cost.

An important aspect of our approach is that we take account of the probability distribution of *query types* in computing optimal bit-allocations. Let $Q \subset \{A_1, A_2, ...A_n\}$. A query q is of type Q if the set of attributes specified in q is equal to Q. A relation with n attributes thus has 2^n query types. Let p_Q be the probability that a query of type Q is made; then the set of p_Q values for all query types defines the ***probability distribution of query types*** (which we will abbreviate to *query distribution*) for the relation. The p_Q values for a particular relation can be determined by collecting statistics on the types of queries made on that relation (although when the system is being designed we may have to estimate the expected usage of the various query types). Given a query distribution and a bit-allocation for a relation, the average cost of a query, C_{av}, and the average insertion cost, I_{av}, are defined as follows:

$$C_{av} = us.2^d \sum_Q p_Q \prod_{A_i \in Q} 2^{-d_i} \qquad (1)$$

$$I_a v = in.1 \qquad (2)$$

where the summation is over all query types and us and in are constant factors which take into account the length of overflow chains. The values for these constants depend on several factors, such as the load factor and the number of records per page, and can be derived using the formulae given in [6]. For example, a file containing 50 records per page with a load factor of 0.75 has $us = 1.0284$ and $in = 2.474$. As these factors do not influence which clustering is optimal, we treat them as unit factors for the remainder of this paper.

The problem of minimising the average query cost is studied in [1, 6, 5]: given values for the p_Q's, we wish to find $d_1, d_2, ..., d_n$ which minimises the average query cost and satisfies the constraint that $d_1 + d_2 + ... + d_n = d$. Aho and Ullman [1] give formulae to derive the optimal values of the d_i's in terms of the probability distribution in the *independent case*, that is, when the probability of specifying a particular attribute does not depend on the specification of any other attribute. This problem was shown to be NP-hard for non-independent query probability distributions [8]. However, in this case, there are heuristic algorithms that give good solutions [5, 6]. We conjecture that the problem of determining optimal bit-allocations for the case of multiple copies is NP-hard, even when the attributes are independently specified (see section 5). As we show, despite the complexity of the problem, there are heuristic algorithms which give good solutions for general query distributions even over multiple copies.

2 Multi-attribute Hashing with Multiple Copies

While an optimal multi-attribute hashing scheme gives a clustering that minimises the *average* query cost for a given query distribution, it does not necessarily give good performance for each individual query type. In fact, it can be very expensive when the selectivity of the queries is high (that is, when specifying a small number of attributes yields only a few matching records). In this case, many bits are unknown and thus many pages need to be examined, even though only a few of the pages are relevant. This problem can be reduced by using additional indexing. If, for example, the first attribute has high selectivity one could maintain an inverted list on this attribute [15] and any query which has the first attribute specified would use the inverted list to retrieve the matching records. Another approach is to use a descriptor file which contains a signature for each page. These signatures are derived using the attribute values of all records in the page. In this method, a page is accessed only when the associated signature indicates that it potentially contains matching records [11].

Even if we use additional indexing methods, such as superimposed codewords or inverted files, in conjunction with multi-attribute hashing, we cannot entirely eliminate this problem as the matching records might be scattered among many pages. One way in which this problem *can* be solved is to maintain multiple copies of the data and to organise each copy using a different clustering scheme. In a single file system, the number of pages which need to be searched to answer a particular query is 2^k, where k is the total number of bits contributed by the unspecified attributes. If we maintain multiple copies of the data, we can find a copy whose clustering is such that we need to search only 2^j pages, where $j \leq k$. For example, in a file containing four attributes A_1, A_2, A_3, A_4, we may cluster the first copy on attributes A_1 and A_4 and cluster the second copy using attributes A_2 and A_3. Thus the problem now becomes how to choose the best bit-allocation among these files so that the average query cost is minimised.

Good clustering improves several aspects of query evaluation performance: it reduces the cost of input/output, by reducing the number of disk accesses and the amount of data transmission; it reduces processing time as fewer records need to be scanned to determine the true matches; the amount of space required to keep a *working set* of matching pages in main memory is less (this is particularly important in applications where operations such as *join* are frequently performed).

Another benefit of multiple clusterings is that in relational database systems one can to a large extent avoid pre-partitioning the files in performing efficient joins. For example, consider two relations: p with attributes A_1, A_2 and q with attributes A_3, A_4, A_5. Assume two file copies for relation p: p_1 clustered on attribute A_1 and p_2 clustered on attribute A_2. Similarly we have two copies for relation q: q_1 clustered on attributes A_3 and A_4, and q_2 clustered on attribute A_5. If we want to perform an equijoin on the relations p and q with A_2 equal to A_3, we only need to partition the q relation on attribute A_3. This can be performed very efficiently using the relation copy q_1 as it is already partially partitioned on attribute A_3. For a detailed description of such a method, see [16].

Let us assume that the file contains 2^d pages. Each record in the file has attributes $\{A_1, A_2, ..., A_n\}$. The number of copies of the file is k. P_Q is the probability of specifying a query of type $Q \subset \{A_1, A_2, ..., A_n\}$. Let h_i^j be a hashing function which maps the values specified for the ith attribute to the set of all strings of d_i^j for the jth copy of the file, where $d_i^j \geq 0$, and $d_1^j + d_2^j + ... + d_n^j = d$ for $j = 1, 2, ...k$.

When a record is added to a relation, we insert it into all of the k copies of the data. The address for the jth copy is computed using the d_i^j's in an analogous manner to the single copy version. In such a scheme, the average query cost is given by:

$$C_{multi} = \sum_Q p_Q \left\{ \text{MIN}_{j=1..k} \left(\prod_{A_i \notin Q} 2^{d_i^j} \right) \right\} \quad (3)$$

where the summation is over all subsets $Q \subseteq \{A_1, A_2, ...A_n\}$, and where

$$\text{MIN}_{j=1..k}(a_j) = minimum(a_1,\ a_2,\ ...a_k)$$

In other words, when we answer a query in a multi-file organisation, we choose the copy which has the minimum cost for queries of that type. In an implementation of this scheme, one could maintain a table of size 2^n (where n is the number of attributes) that maps the query type to the file copy to be used to process the query.

We pay a price in the cost of updates to obtain this query performance, since each record has to be inserted into each copy of the file. If the average insertion cost for a single file is given by in (see [6]) then the average insertion cost for a system with k copies of the data is given by:

$$I_a v = in.k \quad (4)$$

In the above discussion, we implicitly assumed that each attribute has an infinite domain (and thus can be allocated any number of bits). However, in practice attributes may have constraints on the size of their domains. For example, an attribute denoting **sex** can have at most two values, thus requiring only one bit to be allocated; an attribute to denote **age** in years would range from 0 to (say) 150, thus requiring a maximum of eight bits. Let 2^{dmax_i} be the smallest power of two which is larger than the size of the domain of attribute A_i (that is, $dmax_i$ is the minimum number of bits required to represent all elements in the domain). Then the optimisation problem becomes to minimise C_{multi} (Equation (3)) such that $d_1^j + d_2^j + ... + d_n^j = d$ for $j = 1, 2, ...k$ and $0 <= d_i^j <= dmax_i$ for $i = 1, 2, ...n$ and $j = 1, 2, ...k$.

3 Heuristic Algorithms for Generating Bit-allocations

In this section, we describe four heuristic algorithms to generate bit-allocations for the multi-file organisation. We first review a method for generating optimal bit-allocations for a single file copy when attributes are known to be independently specified.

3.1 Aho/Ullman Method for Independently Specified Attributes

In [1] Aho and Ullman derived a formula to determine optimal solutions to the bit-allocation problem when the attributes are independently specified. When a file is size 2^d and each record has n attributes, then the number of bits allocated to the ith attribute, d_i is given by:

$$d_i = \frac{d}{n} + log\frac{p_i}{1-p_i} + \frac{1}{k}\sum_{j=1}^{n} log\frac{p_j}{1-p_j} \qquad (5)$$

This method is applicable only when there is a single copy of the data; it is not extendible in any simple manner to the situation where there are multiple copies. As well, the method does not handle general query probability distributions, since it is applicable only when the probability of specifying attributes is independent. For these reasons, the method is not suitable for our purpose: determining optimal bit-allocations for multiple data copies. However, we use it as a reference for one of our sample distributions which does have independently specified attributes.

3.2 Minimal Marginal Increase

The *minimal marginal increase* (*mmi*) algorithm presented here is a generalisation of the algorithm for the single file case in [6]. Informally, for the *mmi* algorithm on a single file, we initially allocate zero bits to all the d_i's. We then tentatively allocate the first bit to attribute A_1 and compute the cost using Equation (3). We then compute the cost giving the bit instead to attribute A_2, and then to A_3, and so on, until we have tried all of the attributes. We note which attribute gives the lowest cost and then permanently allocate that bit to the selected attribute. This process is repeated until all of the d bits are allocated. The *mmi* method has been shown [6] to yield the optimal bit-allocation when the attribute specification is independent. For the multi-file organisation, the *mmi* algorithm builds up bit-allocations for each file one bit at a time, optimising the total cost at each step. In the *mmi* method as described so far, the cost function is computed $d \times n^k$ times in order to find the best allocation when the file contains 2^d pages. Observation of the results of this algorithm on many different probability distributions showed that it produced minima when each attribute was allocated bits in only one file. Thus the algorithm was

```
minimal_marginal_increase:
    start with 0 bits for each copy
    for each successive bit up to maximum file size do
        add an extra bit to one attribute in each copy
            such that it gives the minimum cost
    endfor
```

Figure 1: Simple Minimal Marginal Increase (*smmi*) Algorithm for generating bit allocations

```
minimal_marginal_increase:
    start with 0 bits for each copy
    for each successive bit up to maximum file size do
        add an extra bit to one attribute in each copy
            such that no attribute is allocated bits
                in two or more copies
            and such that it gives the minimum cost
    endfor
```

Figure 2: Minimal Marginal Increase (*mmi*) Algorithm

augmented to reduce the search space by ensuring that if bits were allocated to a given attribute in one file, they would not be allocated to that attribute in any other files. This corresponds to adding a test to the above algorithm such that the bit-allocations are mutually exclusive between any two copies. This reduces the number of times the cost function is computed to $d \times m_1 \times m_2 \times \ldots \times m_k$, where m_i is the number of attributes chosen for the ith copy and $m_1 + m_2 + \ldots + m_k = n$. The *mmi* algorithm is important because it increases bit-allocations *incrementally* rather than recomputing a (possibly) different bit-allocation each time the file is expanded. This allows us to incrementally expand the indexing as the database grows, without needing to reorganise the file when a new indexing bit added. This is important when optimal bit-allocation is required for dynamic files; this point is discussed further in section 8.

When we use the *mmi* algorithm to generate an optimal bit-allocation for a relation where there are constraints on some of the d_i values, it handles the problem of *saturation* (allocating as many bits to an attribute as are needed to represent its distinct values) as follows: the mutual exclusion condition is maintained for a given copy until all of the constrained attributes in that copy are saturated (that is, for copy j, $\forall i: d_i^j = dmax_i$ if $dmax_i < \infty$). After that, bits may be allocated to any unsaturated attribute, provided that they satisfy the conditions: $d_1^j + d_2^j + ... + d_n^j = d$ for $j = 1, 2, ...k$ and $0 \leq d_i^j \leq dmax_i$ for $i = 1, 2, ...n$ and $j = 1, 2, ...k$.

3.3 Exhaustive *mmi*

The *mmi* algorithm described above is quite efficient and generates reasonable solutions. However, it ignores large areas of the search space by committing to a particular partitioning of attributes to files in the very early stages (when the file size is small). This makes the allocation algorithm more efficient to run but means that different arrangements of attributes, possibly with much better performance at query time, are ignored.

We denote a partitioning of attributes to file copies by, for example, $A - BCD$ which indicates that we have two copies of the data, where one copy has indexing bits only for attribute A and the other copy has indexing bits for attributes B, C, and D. Note that the partitioning does not specify how many bits are allocated to the attributes in a file; it simply indicates which attributes are indexed in which files.

Consider a database with four attributes and a multi-file organisation where there are two copies of the data. There are seven possible ways of partitioning the bit-allocations for the attributes over the files, where each attribute has bits allocated in only one file:

$$A - BCD \quad B - ACD \quad C - ABD$$

$$D - ABC \quad AB - CD \quad AC - BD \quad BC - AD$$

The *mmi* algorithm described above will, after allocating at least one bit to every attribute, have selected one of these arrangements, and will consider only that arrangement as the file size grows larger. A modified version of the algorithm was developed where all possible (non-overlapping) arrangements of attributes was considered. The algorithm iterates over the arrangements of attributes, applying the basic *mmi* method to each arrangement. It then selects the arrangement with the minimum cost. An important question with this method is: how many possible arrangements are there for a given number of attributes and a given number of file copies? For example, with an eight-attribute relation with four

```
exhaustive_mmi:
    for each arrangement of attributes and files do
        fix attributes available for bit allocations
        apply minimal_marginal_increase method
        measure cost
        if best cost so far then
            remember it
        endif
    endfor
```

Figure 3: Exhaustive Minimal Marginal Increase (*xmmi*) Algorithm

m_1	m_2	m_3	m_4	C
1	1	1	5	56
1	1	2	4	420
1	1	3	3	280
1	2	2	3	840
2	2	2	2	105
			Total	1701

Table 1: Arrangements for 8-attribute/4-copy problem

copies the number of possible arrangements can be calculated as follows: Let m_i be the number of attributes given to the ith copy. If we choose $m_1 = 1$, $m_2 = 2$, $m_3 = 2$ and $m_4 = 3$, then the attribute for the first copy can be selected in $\binom{8}{1}$ ways, the two attributes for the second file can be selected in $\binom{7}{2}$ ways, the attributes for the third copy in $\binom{5}{2}$ ways and the remaining attributes are given to the last file in $\binom{3}{3}$ (i.e. 1) way. The number of arrangements C for the m_i values chosen above is given by $\binom{8}{1} \times \binom{7}{2} \times \binom{5}{2} \times \binom{3}{3}$. However, since we do not distinguish permutations of the copies (for example, arrangement $A - BC - DE - FGH$ is considered to be the same $FGH - DE - BC - A$), the possible permutations are $\frac{C}{1!2!1!}$ for the above chosen m_i values. Table 1 gives the numbers of all possible arrangements (C is the number of combinations). This kind of searching is not feasible for large problems; for example, a twenty-attribute relation with three copies has in excess of 5×10^8 arrangements.

When the exhaustive *mmi* method is applied to problems with constraints on the size of attribute domains, we may choose attributes for bit-allocations which are not specified by the arrangement only when all of the specified attributes reach their maximum allocation.

3.4 Simulated Annealing

A different approach was adopted in an algorithm using the methods of *simulated annealing* [9] to generate bit-allocations. This algorithm begins by selecting a random bit-allocation; in each iteration, the algorithm perturbs the bit-allocation, maintaining $d_1+d_2+...+d_n = d$ and $\forall i : d_i \leq dmax_i$. The new allocation is accepted as the basis for further perturbations if it improves the cost function or when the *cooling function* determines that it be accepted. The cooling function is a monotonically decreasing function which specifies the probability of accepting a solution which does not improve the cost function. In the early iterations, the probability of accepting a solution that does not improve the cost function is high, but approaches zero in the later stages. There are a number of parameters which can be used to control the amount of computational resources used by the algorithm: it can be run for S iterations (steps), or can terminate when the cost has not improved after L steps since the last accepted allocation. In our implementation, we use T random starting allocations (trials) and iterate over each of these, finally selecting the best over all trials.

When *simulated annealing* is applied to problems with constraints, the only change to the algorithm is to include, in the test for a valid allocation, the condition that no d_i value ever exceeds its corresponding $dmax_i$.

```
simulated_annealing:
  global_best := ∞
  for specified number of trials (T) do
    trial_best := ∞
    generate random bit allocation for each file
    for specified number of steps (S) do
      repeat
        randomly select a file
        randomly select an attribute (A)
        randomly select another attribute (B)
        subtract one bit from attribute A
          in selected file
        add one bit to attribute B in selected file
        if not valid allocation then
          undo changes
        endif
      until have a valid allocation
      calculate cost
      if cost < trial_best or
        cooling function determines then
        accept new allocation
      else
        undo the changes
      endif
      if cost < trial_best then
        trial_best := cost
        remember new bit-allocation
      endif
      if cost not improved for last L steps then
        terminate this trial
      endif
    endfor
    if trial_best < global_best then
      global_best := trial_best
      remember bit-allocation
        associated with trial_best
    endif
  endfor
```

Figure 4: Simulated Annealing (*sann*) Algorithm

3.5 Exhaustive Query-type Distribution

The previous methods have all generated bit-allocations directly, using various means to indicate that specific attributes are to be indexed by specific file copies. In this method, we generate the bit-allocations indirectly by considering all possible arrangements of query types over the copies of the files. In fact, the program which generates mutually exclusive bit patterns for *xmmi* can be used to generate query type allocations, since they are required to be mutually exclusive. For each arrangement of query types, we determine the attributes which must be allocated to each file to handle the query types, and then apply the *mmi* method with these allocation masks. This gives a larger set of possibilities than either the *mmi* or the *xmmi* methods, and will find a better solution than either of these if one exists. However, because of its high combinatorial complexity, it is even less feasible for large problems than the other algorithms and so we do not consider it further in our analysis.

4 Performance of Bit-allocation Algorithms

We chose three sets of query probability distributions and applied the three algorithms described in the previous section to each of them. Each algorithm was applied twice. In the first application there were no constraints on the number of bits which could be allocated to any attribute. In the second application, we constrained the number of bits d_i for some attributes A_i to be less than a certain value $dmax_i$, corresponding to the situation where the attributes have few distinct values.

We have produced a series of graphs from this analysis (see Appendix) which show the average query cost C_{multi} (in terms of disk accesses) plotted against file size (in numbers of pages). Logarithmic scales are used as a wide range of values is covered (from two pages to over one million pages); the reader should keep this in mind when noting the improvements in average query cost from storing multiple copies.

4.1 Aho & Ullman's Independent attribute Distribution

The first probability distribution is taken from [1]. In this distribution the probability of an attribute occurring in a query is independent of the probability of other attributes occurring. The probabilities of the individual attributes are: $p_{A_1} = 0.8$, $p_{A_2} = 0.1$, $p_{A_3} = 0.9$, $p_{A_4} = 0.2$, and $p_{A_5} = 0.5$. The complete query probability distribution is given in the Appendix. For the constrained case of this distribution we set $dmax_1 = 1$, $dmax_2 = 5$ and $dmax_4 = 10$ (indicating that attribute A_1 has only two distinct values, A_2 has 32 distinct values, and A_4 has 1024 distinct values).

4.2 Six-attribute Distribution

The next experiment used a random probability distribution for query types for a relation with six attributes taken from [11]. The complete query probability distribution is given in the Appendix. The constraints applied to the attributes in this case were $dmax_4 = 6$, $dmax_5 = 4$ and $dmax_6 = 2$.

4.3 Eight-attribute Distribution

The next experiment used a random probability distribution for query types for a relation with eight attributes. There are 2^8 query types for such a relation; in our random query distribution, there is little variation in the probabilities for various query types. The complete query probability distribution is given in the Appendix. The constraints applied to the attributes in this case were $dmax_2 = 1$ and $dmax_4 = 4$.

4.4 Comparison of Methods

In all of the experiments, we used the algorithms to compute bit-allocations for one to four copies of the data, considering file sizes ranging from two pages ($d = 1$) to over one million pages ($d = 20$). In the analysis below, we have ignored the cost of the query in which no fields are specified. No bit-allocation can hope to improve the cost of answering such open queries, since they consider no indexing bits. We assume that the likelihood of being asked an open query is very close to zero for a database of any reasonable size. Note also that the cost function does not take account of overflow chain lengths; if required, this can be approximated by multiplying the cost function by a constant that depends on the load factor (for more details see [6]).

Table 2 indicates how the algorithms and query distributions are denoted in the analysis. For the case of the simulated annealing algorithm, T represents the number of trials used, S represents the maximum number of iterations used in each trial, and L represents the number of iterations to wait before terminating the trial if no further improvement is observed. The graphs in figures 5 to 10 plot the average query cost against file size for various numbers of copies of the data for the *mmi* bit-allocation algorithm. The graphs show clearly that the average query cost is lower when multiple copies are used. Note that the best performance is obtained when the number of

Algorithms used in the analysis	
mmi	standard *mmi* with disjoint bit-allocations
xmmi	exhaustive *mmi* with disjoint bit-allocations
sa1	simulated annealing ($T = 10, S = 1000, L = 100$)
sa2	simulated annealing ($T = 100, S = 100, L = 100$)
sa3	simulated annealing ($T = 500, S = 100, L = 100$)
Query probability distributions (D)	
5a	Aho & Ullman's five-attribute distribution
6a	random six-attribute distribution
8a	random eight-attribute distribution

Table 2: Naming conventions

k	D	Average query cost ($d = 20$)				
		mmi	*xmmi*	*sa1*	*sa2*	*sa3*
1	5a	2681.1	2681.1	2681.1	2681.1	2681.1
2	5a	303.4	266.3	266.3	266.3	266.3
3	5a	71.6	24.0	24.0	24.0	24.0
4	5a	3.6	3.6	6.1	3.6	2.6
1	6a	11631.1	11631.1	11631.1	11631.1	11631.1
2	6a	5503.8	1524.9	1594.8	1570.1	1524.9
3	6a	259.4	259.4	271.9	268.9	259.4
4	6a	191.9	66.3	69.4	66.3	66.2
1	8a	6359.7	6359.7	6359.7	6359.7	6359.7
2	8a	2006.6	876.5	958.7	969.6	876.5
3	8a	677.5	218.2	234.7	225.0	221.4
4	8a	165.6	58.5	55.8	55.6	55.5

Table 3: Average query costs for bit-allocations produced by various algorithms

copies equals the number of attributes, and every non-open query requires only one page to be read. The graphs also show that the query cost rises at a slower rate for multiple copies. As far as the relative performance of the algorithms is concerned, the bit-allocations produced by the *xmmi* and *simulated annealing* algorithms are equally good. In general, *mmi* produces bit-allocations which are nearly as good as those produced by *xmmi*, but shows a tendency to sometimes stray away from good solutions at larger file sizes.

Table 3 shows the average query costs for the bit-allocations produced by the algorithms for a file size of 2^{20} pages for various numbers of file copies (k). We note that the results for the single file copy for distribution 5a under all methods are the same as the results obtained using Aho and Ullman's analytical method (see section 3.1).

Table 4 shows the CPU time required to determine bit-allocation for file sizes from 2^1 to 2^{20} and for one to four copies of the data. The algorithms were implemented in C and executed on a Sun 4/260 with a hardware floating-point unit. The times were measured using the Unix *time(1)* program and are in units of CPU-seconds, including both user time and system time.

D	*mmi*	*xmmi*	*sa1*	*sa2*	*sa3*
5a	2.9	6.7	234.2	2179.9	10881.4
6a	9.3	75.2	470.4	4196.1	21032.7
8a	149.1	11012.3	1872.1	17442.6	86234.1

Table 4: CPU time required to determine bit-allocations

The amount of time required by the simulated annealing algorithm can be controlled (by varying the number of trials and the number of iterations in each trial), but it is still very much more expensive to execute than the *mmi* algorithm. The other interesting feature of the above table is the rapid growth in the cost of executing the *xmmi* algorithm due to the rapid increase in the number of combinations as the number of attributes increases. Of course, one should remember that this is a one-time cost that determines the efficiency of all queries in the database.

The experiments with the algorithms demonstrate that there are a considerable number of local minima in the search space. Nevertheless, all of the algorithms described above provide results which, even if not optimal, demonstrate that significant performance improvement is always obtained using multiple copies. As one would expect, *xmmi* gave results which were always at least as good as *mmi*; simulated annealing gave results at least as good as *xmmi* if enough trials were made.

For relations with a small number of attributes (less than twelve) we can apply the *mmi*, *xmmi* and simulated annealing algorithms. In these cases, one should try both *xmmi* and simulated annealing and choose the best allocation of bits. For relations with a large number of attributes, the *mmi* and simulated annealing methods can be applied to design optimal bit-allocations. For such relations, the *xmmi* algorithm is not feasible as there is a very large number of arrangements. In these cases, we can use the *mmi* method instead to check that the solution found by the simulated annealing method is reasonable.

4.5 Effect of Constraints

The graphs in figures 5, 7 and 9 (and the values in Table 3) show that when there are no constraints on the number of bits which are allocated to each attribute, considerable improvement in the average query cost can be obtained by maintaining multiple copies of the data. For example, the average query cost in the five-attribute case for a file of size 2^{20} pages, falls from 2681 disk accesses for a single file to 266 for two copies, to 24 for three copies, and to 2.6 for four copies.

The graphs in figures 6, 8, and 10 show that when there are constraints on the numbers of bits allocated, improvements in average query cost are observed for small file sizes. However, when the files grow beyond a certain size, little benefit accrues from multiple copies because the constrained attributes have been "saturated" and the file size for *optimal clustering* has been achieved. For example, in a database with two attributes with $dmax_1 = 4$ and $dmax_2 = 8$, optimal clustering is achieved at a file size of 2^{12}. In such a system multiple copies do not improve the performance once the file size reaches 2^{12} pages. When constraints are present in a system, the number of copies beyond which no performance improvement is observed depends on the constraints themselves and on the file size.

Table 5 gives the bit-allocations for various numbers of copies for Aho and Ullman's distribution as determined by the *mmi* algorithm for file-size 2^{20} pages when there are no constraints. Note that the *mmi* algorithm produces the same results for the single copy case as Aho and Ullman's analytical method (section 3.1). Table 6 shows the bit-allocations for the same problem with the constraints $dmax_1 = 1$, $dmax_2 = 5$ and $dmax_4 = 10$. Note that the cost function is considerably higher for the problem with constraints. This high cost is inherent in the problem, and no algorithm can achieve low costs once the bit-allocations are saturated and records with the same values for the attributes with small domains become spread over a large number of pages in the file.

k	Bit-allocations ($d = 20$)					cost
	d_1	d_2	d_3	d_4	d_5	
1	6	1	7	2	4	2681.1
2	9	0	0	4	7	303.4
	0	6	14	0	0	
	20	0	0	0	9	
3	0	0	20	0	0	71.7
	0	5	0	7	8	
	20	0	0	0	0	
4	0	0	20	0	0	3.6
	0	9	0	11	0	
	0	0	0	0	20	

Table 5: Bit-allocations for query distribution 5a (no constraints)

k	Bit-allocations ($d = 20$)					cost
	d_1	d_2	d_3	d_4	d_5	
1	1	2	9	3	5	17641.4
2	1	5	0	6	8	15356.9
	0	0	20	0	0	
	1	5	4	10	0	
3	0	0	20	0	0	15184.6
	0	0	0	0	20	
	0	0	20	0	0	
4	0	0	0	10	10	15189.3
	0	0	0	0	20	
	1	5	14	0	0	

Table 6: Bit-allocations for query distribution 5a (with constraints)

4.6 Distributions with Known Optimal Attribute Partitions

Another set of experiments was also conducted to assess the effectiveness of the heuristic algorithms in determining the optimal partitioning of attributes over the copies of the file. This was accomplished using probability distributions with known optimal attribute partitioning generated by the method described below.

The basic idea behind our method of generating query distributions is to start from a partitioning of the attributes over the copies and then determine, for each query type, which partition should be used to answer it. If we cannot determine this in an "obvious" manner, we simply remove that query type (by setting its probability to zero). The exact method for generating query probability distributions for a system with n attributes and k copies is as follows:

1. partition the n attributes arbitrarily over the k copies such that no partition contains less than two attributes
2. for each query type Q, where the set of attributes specified in Q is denoted by $spec(Q)$, test the following conditions:
   (a) $\nexists k$ s.t. $P_k \in spec(Q)$
   (b) $\exists i,j$ s.t. $i \in Q$ and $j \in Q$ and $i \neq j$ and $i \in P_m$ and $j \in P_n$ and $m \neq n$
3. for a given Q, if conditions (a) and (b) hold, then set p_Q to zero; otherwise, set it to a non-zero value ensuring that $\sum_Q p_Q = 1$.

Condition (b) tests whether a query type contains attributes belonging to different partitions. Condition (a) tests whether a query type is already answered optimally under a given partition; if the attributes specified in the query are a superset of the attributes in the partition, then queries of this type can be answered in one disk access in that partition, regardless of whether the query type also contains attributes from other partitions.

For a system with four attributes (A,B,C,D) and two copies of the data file, and partitioned so that $P_1 = \{A,C\}$ and $P_2 = \{B,D\}$, we obtain the query probability distribution shown in Table 7. For this example, the optimal bit-allocation uses bits for the first and third attributes in one copy and bits for the second and fourth attributes in the other. The actual numbers of bits allocated to each attribute will depend on the values of the query probabilities.

Using the above algorithm, we generated a large number of distributions and found that, in all cases, the *mmi*, *xmmi*, and simulated annealing schemes found the known optimal attribute partitions.

Query Type	p_Q	Query Type	p_Q
$\_,\_,\_,\_$	>0	$\_,\_,\_,D$	>0
$A,\_,\_,\_$	>0	$A,\_,\_,D$	0
$\_,B,\_,\_$	>0	$\_,B,\_,D$	>0
$A,B,\_,\_$	0	$A,B,\_,D$	>0
$\_,\_,C,\_$	>0	$\_,\_,C,D$	0
$A,\_,C,\_$	>0	$A,\_,C,D$	>0
$\_,B,C,\_$	0	$\_,B,C,D$	>0
$A,B,C,\_$	>0	A,B,C,D	>0

Table 7: Query probability distribution with known optimal attribute partitioning

5 Optimal Bit-allocations for Multiple File Copies

As noted in Section 1, we conjecture that the problem of selecting bit-allocations so as to minimise the query cost over multiple file copies is NP-hard even when the attributes are independently specified. Our conjecture is based on the fact that we can devise a query distribution where the attributes are independently specified for the case of one copy, but when we partition them up among multiple copies in any known optimal manner, they are no longer independent within each copy (partition). We demonstrate this by showing that the assumption that they are independent within a partition leads to a contradiction.

Consider a query distribution in which the probability of specifying any of the four attributes (A,B,C,D) is independent of the probability of specifying any of the others. Assume the additional properties hold: $p(A) = p(C)$, $p(B) = p(D)$ and $p(A) \gg p(D)$. For two copies, the best allocation would involve partitioning the attributes so that one highly probable attribute is paired with a less probable attribute, as in, for example: $P_1 = \{A,B\}$ and $P_2 = \{C,D\}$. The partitioning of attributes allows us to partition the set of query types. Most query types can be allocated to partitions in a straightforward manner. For example, the query types:

$$(A,\_,\_,\_) \quad (\_,B,\_,\_) \quad (A,B,\_,\_)$$

should obviously be answered using partition P_1. Some other query types (such as (A,B,C,D)) may be allocated to either partition. We allocate the fol-

Query Type	p_Q	Query Type	p_Q
$A,\_,\_,\_$	>0	$A,\_,\_,D$	>0
$\_,B,\_,\_$	>0	$\_,B,\_,D$	>0
$A,B,\_,\_$	>0	$A,B,\_,D$	>0
$\_,\_,C,\_$	0	$\_,\_,C,D$	0
$A,\_,C,\_$	>0	$A,\_,C,D$	0
$\_,B,C,\_$	0	$\_,B,C,D$	0
$A,B,C,\_$	>0	A,B,C,D	>0

Table 8: Query probability distribution associated with partition P_1

lowing query types to partition P_1:

$$(A,\_,\_,\_)\ (\_,B,\_,\_)\ (A,\_,\_,D)$$

$$(A,B,\_,\_)\ (A,B,C,\_)\ (A,B,\_,D)$$

and allocate these query types to partition P_2:

$$(\_,\_,C,\_)\ (\_,\_,\_,D)\ (\_,B,C,\_)$$

$$(\_,\_,C,D)\ (A,\_,C,D)\ (\_,B,C,D)$$

The following query types can be placed under either partition:

$$(\_,\_,\_,\_)\ (A,\_,C,\_)\ (\_,B,\_,D)\ (A,B,C,D)$$

and so we arbitrarily place them under P_1.

Once we have determined an optimal allocation of query-types to partitions, the problem then becomes to find optimal bit-allocations for each partition. In order to determine optimal bit-allocations in each partition, the query-types that are not included in that partition are given zero probability. For example, in determining optimal bit-allocations for P_1, we are not interested in query types which will be answered using partition P_2, and so we consider their probabilities to be zero. For the sake of argument, we restrict our attention to partition P_1. This does not affect the validity of our conclusion since, because of the symmetry of the problem, similar types of reasoning could be used with respect to partition P_2. Partition P_1 has query probability distribution shown in Table 8. We know from this distribution that, if the attributes are independent, then they must all have a non-zero probability in partition P_1; that is:

(a) $p(A) > 0$ **and** $p(B) > 0$ **and** $p(C) > 0$ **and** $p(D) > 0$

Given the set of query types that have zero probability in the above distribution, we can state some relationships which must hold among the individual attribute probabilities. Since the probability of query type $(\_,\_,C,\_)$ is zero, then, if the probabilities of attributes are independent, we know that either $p(A) = 0$ or $p(B) = 0$ or $1 - p(C) = 0$ (or, alternatively, $p(C) = 1$) or $p(D) = 0$. If we perform this analysis on each of the above query types that have a probability of zero, we obtain the following set of formulae which must all be true:

(b) $p(A) = 0$ **or** $p(B) = 0$ **or** $p(C) = 1$ **or** $p(D) = 0$
(c) $p(A) = 0$ **or** $p(B) = 0$ **or** $p(C) = 0$ **or** $p(D) = 1$
(d) $p(A) = 0$ **or** $p(B) = 1$ **or** $p(C) = 1$ **or** $p(D) = 0$
(e) $p(A) = 0$ **or** $p(B) = 0$ **or** $p(C) = 1$ **or** $p(D) = 1$
(f) $p(A) = 1$ **or** $p(B) = 0$ **or** $p(C) = 1$ **or** $p(D) = 1$
(g) $p(A) = 0$ **or** $p(B) = 1$ **or** $p(C) = 1$ **or** $p(D) = 1$

Since it is not possible for (b)-(g) to hold at the same time as (a) holds, we conclude that our assumption that the attributes are independent must be false with respect to partition P_1. Note that we used the smallest possible set of zero-valued query probabilities to reach this conclusion; if we add some of the other query types which we arbitrarily allocated to partition P_1, we will not eliminate the contradiction. Thus, we cannot devise a partitioning which maintains the independence of attributes. The problem of finding an optimal bit-allocation for a single file is is known to be NP-hard for the non-independent case. This example suggests that, in general, the problem of bit-allocation over multiple copies is NP-hard, even when attribute probabilities are independently specified.

6 Comparison with other Indexing Methods

Most of the currently available software for efficient partial-match retrieval is based on some form of inverted file organisation. However, inverted files can be quite expensive for multi-term queries or for queries which are not very selective. For example, when the query has several key values we are required to perform several list intersection operations; if the queries are not selective the lists can be quite long. Another property of inverted file schemes is that the more attributes specified in a query, the more work is needed to answer the query, while the number of matching records becomes smaller. In these schemes, inverted lists are usually maintained as ordered lists to make the intersection operation efficient. Because of the cost of maintaining the inverted lists in order, this organisation can be expensive in situations where the database is highly dynamic. Assuming that it requires m disk accesses to insert an entry into the ordered list, then it requires $m \times n$ disk accesses for an n attribute file. In addition, the amount of space required to store the inverted lists is similar to the amount of space required to store the data itself [3].

As we have already seen, superimposed codeword indexing is an efficient method for partial-match retrieval. Its major disadvantage compared to multi-attribute hashing is that update operations are considerably more expensive. Assuming each attribute value sets p bits in the signature file, inserting a record in an n attribute file requires $p \times n$ disk accesses. Superimposed codeword schemes also require a significant amount of storage for descriptors for efficient retrieval.

Unlike the above schemes, multi-attribute hashing with multiple file copies is effective for dynamic files as the insertion cost is proportional to the number of copies and does not depend on the number of attributes. Multi-attribute hashing methods have one disadvantage relative to inverted files and superimposed coding schemes: because they use a single value from each of a fixed number of attributes to compute the address of a record, they cannot be used in situations where the records have a variable number of attribute values.

It should be noted that clustering improves the retrieval performance of all indexing schemes. However, using multiple copies of the data for improving clustering for inverted files and superimposed codeword files also requires multiple copies of the indices as the record locations are different in each copy. When multiple file copies are used for these methods, it is also required that records have a fixed number of attributes and that only a single value can be specified for each attribute.

7 Comparison with other File Organisations Employing Redundancy

Rivest [13] and Burkhard [2] have proposed file organisations which are similar to ours. In Rivest's scheme, the m-bit multi-attribute hash value for a record is split into n parts, and each part is used as a hash value (index) into a table of size $2^{m/n}$. For a query with k unspecified bits, at least one of the parts of the hash will have k/n or less bits specified. If we use that part to search the corresponding hash table, we will need to examine at most $2^{k/n}$ entries in the hash table. Burkhard's scheme is quite similar to Rivest's, and neither scheme takes into account the query distribution. We take account of the probability distribution of query types and the size of the attribute domains in determining the bit-allocation.

The method of *compound files* described in [7] also uses redundant storage to maintain multiple inverted index files, each of which is "specialised" to a given set of query types. This method aims to eliminate the n-way intersection of index lists required in inverted files to answer a query which has n attributes specified. For example, if we wish to eliminate all 2-way to k-way intersections in answering queries on a file with of m attributes, we require $\binom{m}{k}$ index lists. In this scheme it is possible to cluster index values according to query type. However, it does not attempt to cluster data to optimise retrieval performance over all query types. If we assume that, rather than duplicating indices, we apply this method directly to the data then we require considerably more storage. For example, an eight-attribute relation in this scheme requires seventy copies. To achieve optimal clustering in our scheme requires a maximum of eight copies and, if there are constraints on the size of the domains of attributes, may require even fewer.

Note that the multi-file organisation can be used without any other indexing schemes. However, it could be combined with complementary indexing schemes such as *compound files* or *superimposed codeword indexing* to achieve further improvements in performance.

8 Dynamic Files

Multi-attribute hashing is particularly suited to partial-match retrieval in dynamic files. Work in [6, 11] shows how random reorganisation of records in dynamic files can be avoided by ensuring that the number of bits allocated to each attribute does not decrease as the file grows. Therefore it is important that any algorithm used to generate bit-allocations for dynamic files should preserve this property. Although the *simulated annealing* algorithm can be tuned to produce, on average, better results than the *mmi* algorithm, it does not preserve the above property.

The best strategy for allocating index bits for dynamic files incorporates *simulated annealing*, *mmi* and a *maximal marginal decrease* (*mmd*) algorithm. The *mmd* algorithm selects one bit to be de-allocated from each file in such a way that the average cost is minimised (that is, the cost is decreased by the maximum amount). Under this strategy, we generate choice vectors based on the optimal bit-allocations for each file before the database is constructed, and use these choice vectors to allocate and de-allocate indexing bits as the file size changes. We use *simulated annealing* to generate the initial bit-allocation for the file at a certain size, since this generally gives us the best solution. We then use the *mmi* method to determine which attribute will be allocated each extra bit when the file grows above this initial size. We use the *mmd* method to determine the order in which bits are to be de-allocated when the file shrinks below the initial size. Provided that the file does not change in size by more than a few orders of magnitude, these bit-allocations will be close to optimal. If the file size does vary by a considerable amount, it may be best to re-compute the choice vector using the above strategy, starting from the current size of the file (assuming that to be the new mean size). This may involve a complete reorganisation of the data.

We have implemented the above composite algorithm (*simulated annealing* + *mmi* + *mmd*) and obtained the results shown in Table 9 for Aho and Ullman's five-attribute, independent query probability distribution. In our analysis, we generated the initial bit-allocation using simulated annealing for a file size of 2^{16} pages. These preliminary results are very encouraging as we observe no substantial degradation in performance, even when the file size varies by several orders of magnitude. In the table, k is the number of copies of the data, d is the number of bits allocated (thus, the file size is 2^d), and *dyn* is the name given to the composite algorithm described above. Note that for the case of five copies all of the methods yielded the known optimal solution where each copy indexes one attribute and the average query cost is always one page access.

9 Conclusion

Good clustering of the records stored in a database file improves query evaluation performance by reducing the I/O time, processing time, and the amount of space required to keep a cluster in main memory. Maintaining multiple copies of data in a database system allows us to provide excellent clustering in systems which use multi-attribute hashing. Experimental results in this paper show that maintaining two copies of the database can improve the average query cost by a factor of ten. This chapter has described several methods for generating optimal bit allocations for the attributes of the records in each copy, and shown several ways that these methods can be improved in practice. With the decreasing cost of mass storage devices, these methods could become attractive for large database systems where response time is of paramount importance.

Acknowledgements

Thanks to Alan Kent for *graph+*, which made it so much easier to perform the analyses reported in this paper. Zoltan Somogyi stood like a brick wall between us and the completion of this paper but by the time it made it over the wall it was in considerably better shape than it would otherwise have been. This work was supported by funding from the Australian Research Council.

References

[1] Aho, A.V. and Ullman, J.D., "Optimal partial-match retrieval when fields are independently specified", ACM Transactions on Database Systems, v.4, no.2, June 1979, pp.168-179.

[2] Burkhard, W.A., "Partial-match hash coding: benefits of redundancy", ACM Transactions on

k	d	Average query cost using algorithms			
		mmi	*xmmi*	*sann*	*dyn*
1	10	17.2	17.2	17.2	17.2
	12	43.5	43.5	43.5	43.5
	14	118.6	118.6	118.6	118.6
	16	327.1	327.1	327.1	327.1
	18	963.3	963.3	963.3	963.3
	20	2681.1	2681.1	2681.1	2681.1
	22	8216.1	8216.1	8216.1	8216.1
2	10	4.6	4.6	4.5	4.5
	12	9.9	9.9	9.9	9.9
	14	23.3	23.3	21.7	21.7
	16	54.5	54.5	48.6	48.6
	18	124.6	124.6	115.1	115.1
	20	303.4	281.2	266.3	266.3
	22	736.7	619.9	596.8	632.5
3	10	1.7	1.6	1.6	1.6
	12	2.8	2.4	2.4	2.4
	14	5.4	3.8	3.8	3.8
	16	11.7	6.7	6.7	6.7
	18	29.0	12.4	12.4	12.4
	20	71.7	24.0	24.0	24.0
	22	171.7	47.0	47.0	47.0
4	10	1.1	1.1	1.1	1.1
	12	1.2	1.2	1.2	1.2
	14	1.3	1.3	1.3	1.3
	16	1.6	1.6	1.6	1.6
	18	2.3	2.3	2.3	2.3
	20	3.6	3.6	3.6	3.6
	22	6.1	6.1	6.1	6.1

Table 9: Average query cost using various bit allocation algorithms

Database Systems, v.4, no.3, September 1979, pp.228-239.

[3] Cardenas, A.F., "Analysis and performance of inverted database structures", Communications of the ACM, v.18, no.5, 1975, pp.253-263.

[4] Knuth, D.E., "The art of computer programming. vol.3: searching and sorting", Addison-Wesley, Reading Mass., 1973.

[5] Lloyd, J.W., "Optimal partial-match retrieval", Bit, v.20, 1980, pp.406-413.

[6] Lloyd, J.W. and Ramamohanarao, K., "Partial-match retrieval for dynamic files", Bit, v.22, 1982, pp.150-168.

[7] Lum, V.Y., "Multi-attribute retrieval with combined indexes", Communications of the ACM, v.13, no.11, 1970, pp.660-665.

[8] Moran, S., "On the complexity of designing optimal partial-match retrieval systems", Proceedings of the 22nd Design Automation Conference, 1985, pp.748-752.

[9] Nahar, S., Sahni S., and Shragowitz, E., "Experiments with simulated annealing", Proceedings of the 22nd ACM/IEEE Design Automation Conference, Las Vegas, Nevada, June 1985, pp.748-752.

[10] Nievergelt, J., Hinterberger, H., and Sevcik, K., "The grid file: an adaptable symmetric multikey file structure", ACM Transactions on Database Systems, v.9, no.1, March 1984, pp.38-71.

[11] Ramamohanarao, K., Lloyd, J.W., and Thom, J.A., "Partial-match retrieval using hashing and descriptors", ACM Transactions on Database Systems, v.8, no.4, December 1983, pp.552-576.

[12] Ramamohanarao, K., and Sacks-Davis, R., "Recursive linear hashing", ACM Transactions on Database Systems, v.9, no.3, September 1984, pp.369-391.

[13] Rivest, R.L., "Partial match retrieval algorithms", SIAM Journal of Computing, v.5, no.1, pp.19-50.

[14] Roberts, C.S., "Partial match retreival via the method of superimposed codes", Proceedings of the IEEE, v.67, no.2, 1979, pp.522-528.

[15] Rothnie, J.B., and Lozano, T., "Attribute based file organization in a paged memory environment", Communications of the ACM, v.17, no.2, 1974, pp.63-69.

[16] Thom, J.A., Naish, L., and Ramamohanarao, K., "A superjoin algorithm for deductive databases", Foundations of Deductive Databases and Logic Programming, Morgan Kaufmann Publishers, Los Altos California, 1988, pp.519-544.

A Experimental Results

A.1 Aho & Ullman's Independent-attribute Distribution

Query type	p_Q	Query type	p_Q	Query type	p_Q
_,_,_,_,_	0.0072	A,B,_,D,_	0.0008	_,B,C,_,E	0.0072
A,_,_,_,_	0.0288	_,_,C,D,_	0.0162	A,B,C,_,E	0.0288
_,B,_,_,_	0.0008	A,_,C,D,_	0.0648	_,_,_,D,E	0.0018
A,B,_,_,_	0.0032	_,B,C,D,_	0.0018	A,_,_,D,E	0.0072
_,_,C,_,_	0.0648	A,B,C,D,_	0.0072	_,B,_,D,E	0.0002
A,_,C,_,_	0.2592	_,_,_,_,E	0.0072	A,B,_,D,E	0.0008
_,B,C,_,_	0.0072	A,_,_,_,E	0.0288	_,_,C,D,E	0.0162
A,B,C,_,_	0.0288	_,B,_,_,E	0.0008	A,_,C,D,E	0.0648
_,_,_,D,_	0.0018	A,B,_,_,E	0.0032	_,B,C,D,E	0.0018
A,_,_,D,_	0.0072	_,_,C,_,E	0.0648	A,B,C,D,E	0.0072
_,B,_,D,_	0.0002	A,_,C,_,E	0.2592		

Table 10: Five-attribute Independent Query Probability Distribution

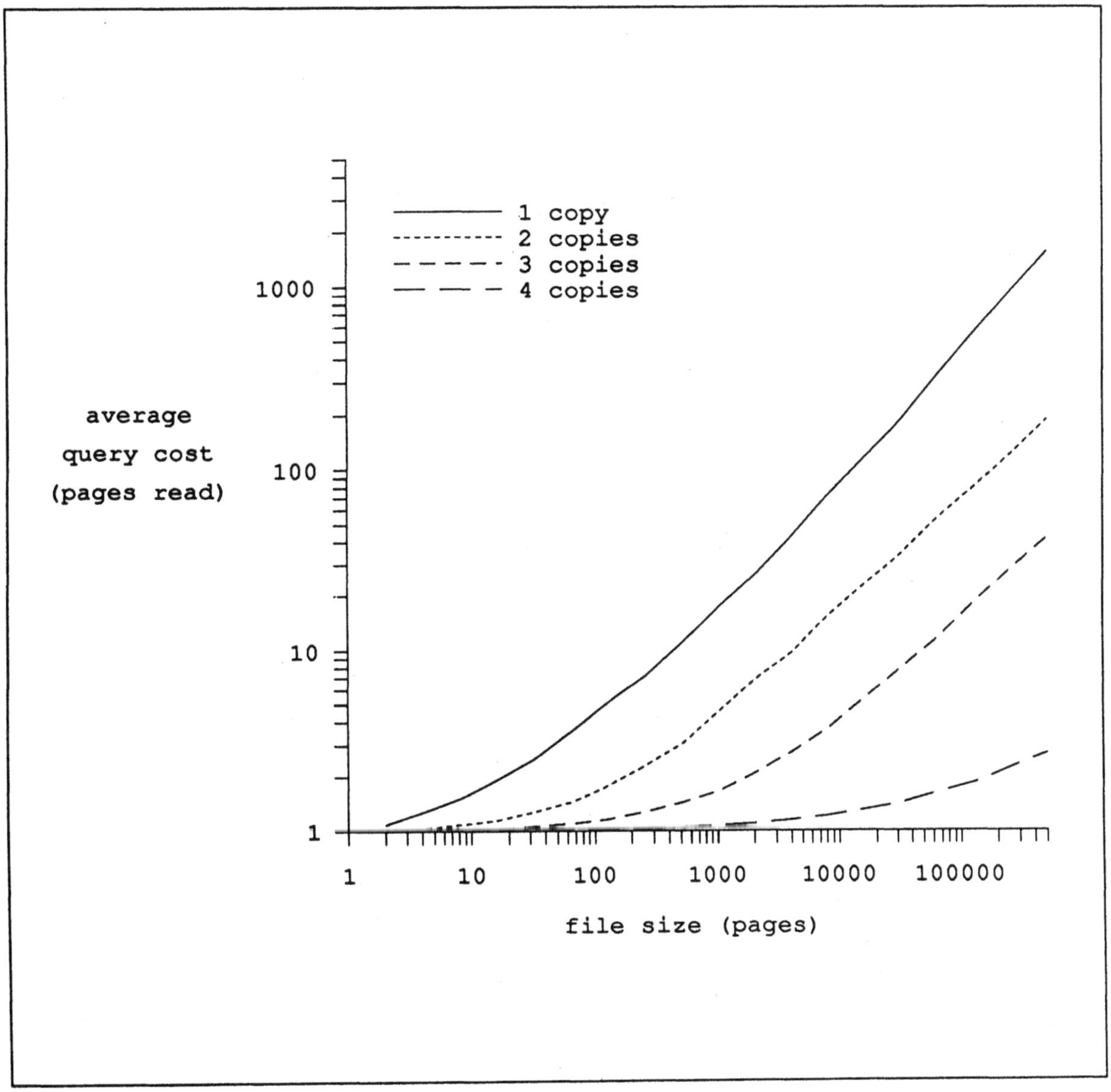

Figure 5: Average Query Cost vs. File Size (five-attribute independent query distribution, *mmi* bit-allocation)

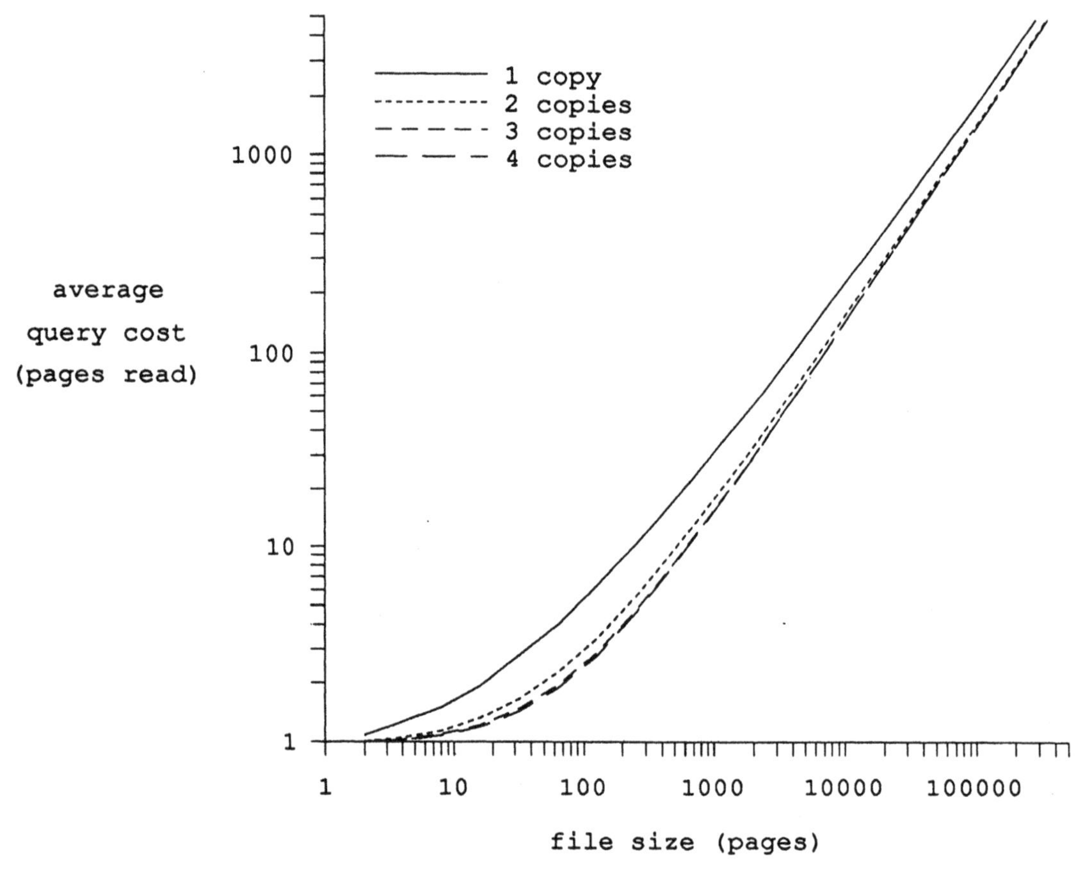

Figure 6: Average Query Cost vs. File Size (five-attribute independent query distribution with constraints, *mmi* bit-allocation)

A.2 Six-attribute Distribution

Query type	p_Q	Query type	p_Q	Query type	p_Q
_,_,_,_,_	0.0000	A,B,_,D,_	0.0008	_,B,C,_,E	0.0072
A,_,_,_,_	0.0288	_,_,C,D,_	0.0162	A,B,C,_,E	0.0288
_,B,_,_,_	0.0008	A,_,C,D,_	0.0648	_,_,_,D,E	0.0018
A,B,_,_,_	0.0032	_,B,C,D,_	0.0018	A,_,_,D,E	0.0072
_,_,C,_,_	0.0648	A,B,C,D,_	0.0072	_,B,_,D,E	0.0002
_,_,_,_,_,_	0.0000	_,B,C,_,E,_	0.0196	_,_,C,D,_,F	0.0197
A,_,_,_,_,_	0.0027	A,B,C,_,E,_	0.0192	A,_,C,D,_,F	0.0179
_,B,_,_,_,_	0.0085	_,_,_,D,E,_	0.0128	_,B,C,D,_,F	0.0158
A,B,_,_,_,_	0.0197	A,_,_,D,E,_	0.0207	A,B,C,D,_,F	0.0280
_,_,C,_,_,_	0.0235	_,B,_,D,E,_	0.0068	_,_,_,_,E,F	0.0035
A,_,C,_,_,_	0.0226	A,B,_,D,E,_	0.0079	A,_,_,_,E,F	0.0186
_,B,C,_,_,_	0.0202	_,_,C,D,E,_	0.0242	_,B,_,_,E,F	0.0073
A,B,C,_,_,_	0.0023	A,_,C,D,E,_	0.0116	A,B,_,_,E,F	0.0009
_,_,_,D,_,_	0.0088	_,B,C,D,E,_	0.0312	_,_,C,_,E,F	0.0206
A,_,_,D,_,_	0.0035	A,B,C,D,E,_	0.0147	A,_,C,_,E,F	0.0252
_,B,_,D,_,_	0.0315	_,_,_,_,_,F	0.0194	_,B,C,_,E,F	0.0136
A,B,_,D,_,_	0.0239	A,_,_,_,_,F	0.0136	A,B,C,_,E,F	0.0232
_,_,C,D,_,_	0.0268	_,B,_,_,_,F	0.0199	_,_,_,D,E,F	0.0036
A,_,C,D,_,_	0.0106	A,B,_,_,_,F	0.0077	A,_,_,D,E,F	0.0310
_,B,C,D,_,_	0.0254	_,_,C,_,_,F	0.0176	_,B,_,D,E,F	0.0140
A,B,C,D,_,_	0.0051	A,_,C,_,_,F	0.0225	A,B,_,D,E,F	0.0127
_,_,_,_,E,_	0.0312	_,B,C,_,_,F	0.0044	_,_,C,D,E,F	0.0029
A,_,_,_,E,_	0.0216	A,B,C,_,_,F	0.0182	A,_,C,D,E,F	0.0190
_,B,_,_,E,_	0.0255	_,_,_,D,_,F	0.0248	_,B,C,D,E,F	0.0266
A,B,_,_,E,_	0.0029	A,_,_,D,_,F	0.0087	A,B,C,D,E,F	0.0011
_,_,C,_,E,_	0.0116	_,B,_,D,_,F	0.0220		
A,_,C,_,E,_	0.0009	A,B,_,D,_,F	0.0186		

Table 11: Six-attribute Random Query Probability Distribution

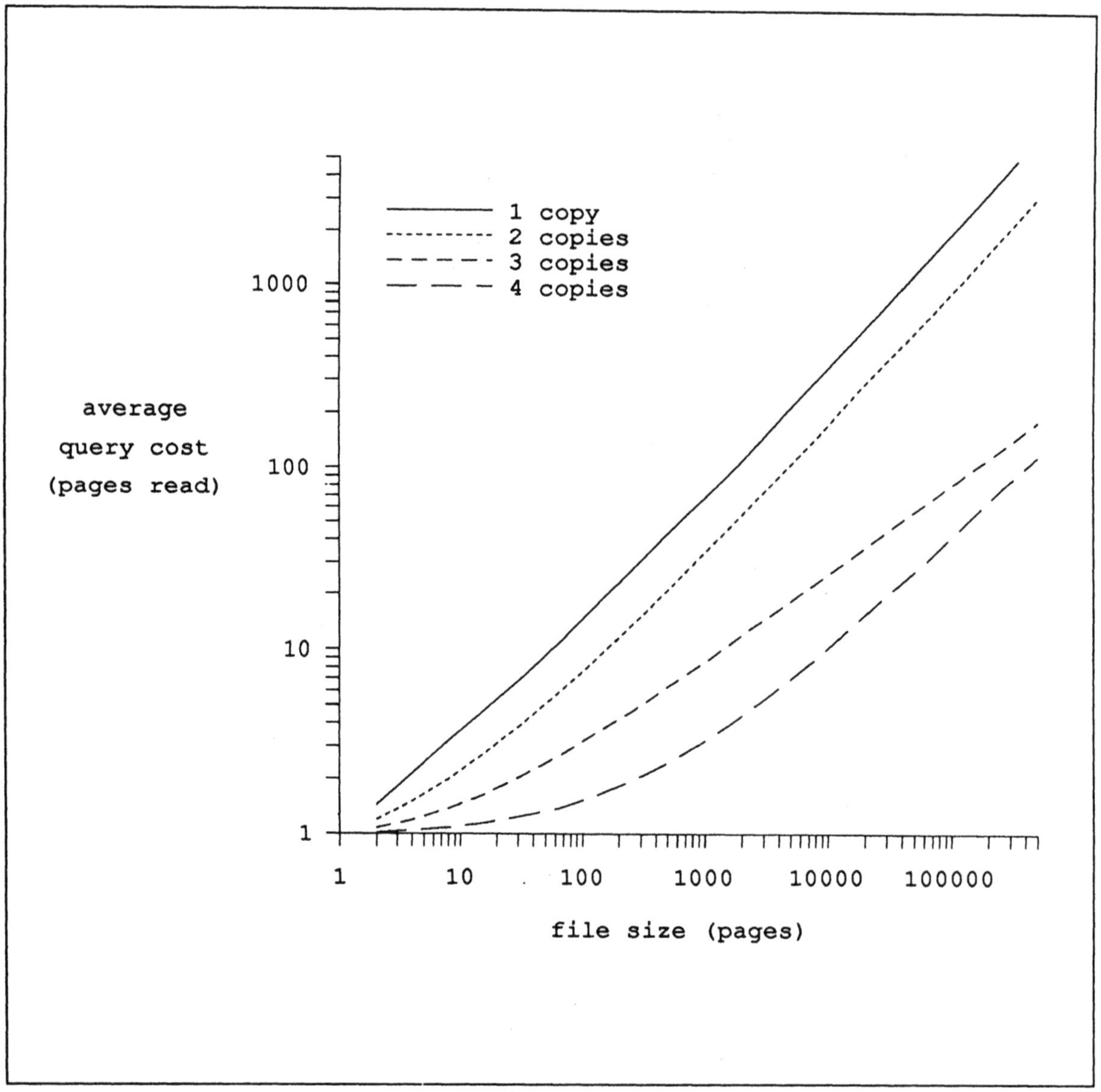

Figure 7: Average Query Cost vs. File Size (six-attribute random query distribution, *mmi* bit-allocation)

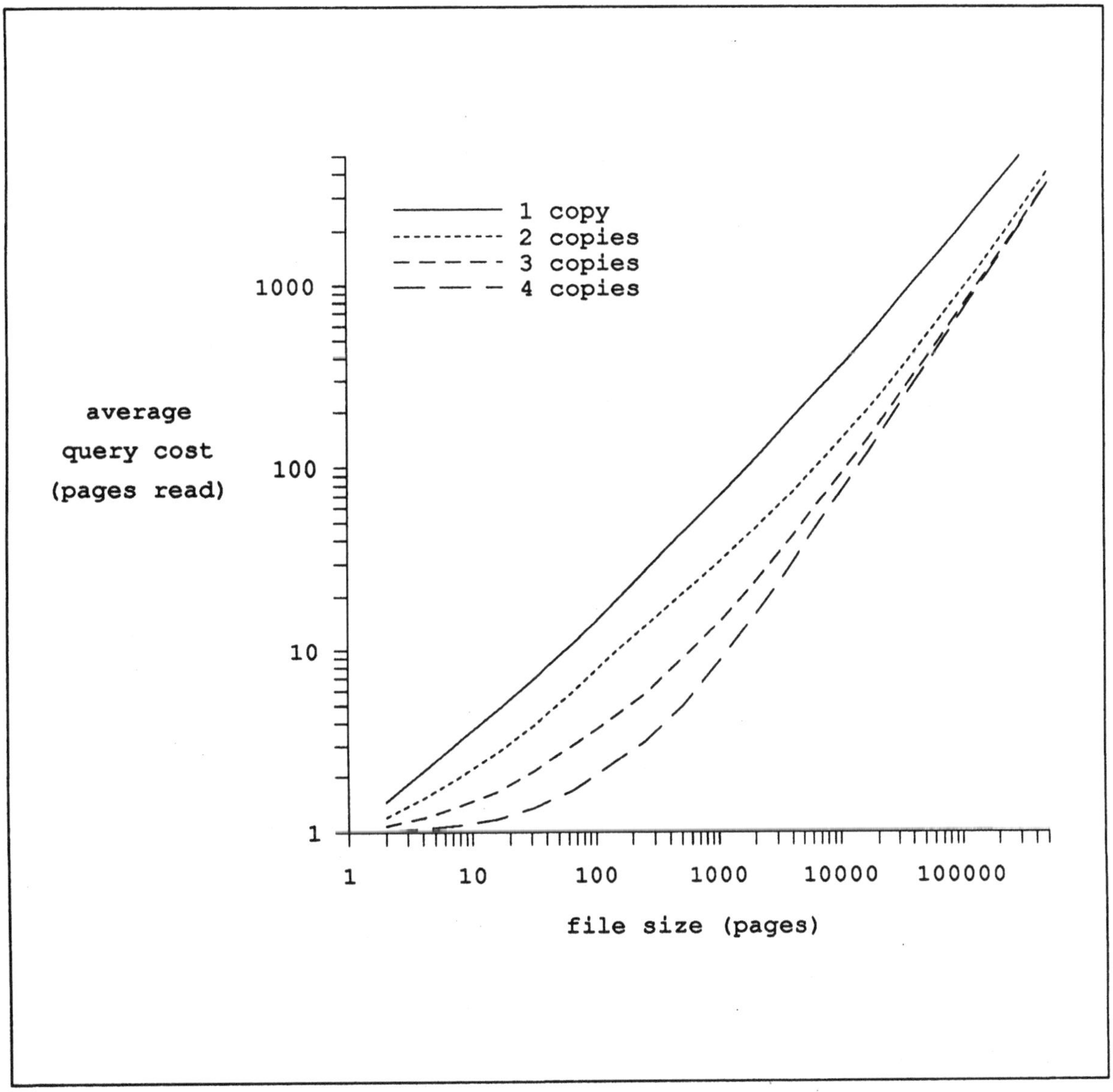

Figure 8: Average Query Cost vs. File Size (six-attribute random query distribution with constraints, *mmi* bit-allocation)

A.3 Eight-attribute Distribution

Query type	p_Q	Query type	p_Q	Query type	p_Q
_,_,_,_,_,_,_,_,	0.0000	_,B,C,_,E,_,G,_,	0.0004	_,_,C,D,_,F,_,H,	0.0007
A,_,_,_,_,_,_,_,	0.0010	A,B,C,_,E,_,G,_,	0.0058	A,_,C,D,_,F,_,H,	0.0021
_,B,_,_,_,_,_,_,	0.0046	_,_,_,D,E,_,G,_,	0.0021	_,B,C,D,_,F,_,H,	0.0069
A,B,_,_,_,_,_,_,	0.0008	A,_,_,D,E,_,G,_,	0.0056	A,B,C,D,_,F,_,H,	0.0074
_,_,C,_,_,_,_,_,	0.0069	_,B,_,D,E,_,G,_,	0.0072	_,_,_,_,E,F,_,H,	0.0079
A,_,C,_,_,_,_,_,	0.0004	A,B,_,D,E,_,G,_,	0.0063	A,_,_,_,E,F,_,H,	0.0031
_,B,C,_,_,_,_,_,	0.0042	_,_,C,D,E,_,G,_,	0.0015	_,B,_,_,E,F,_,H,	0.0065
A,B,C,_,_,_,_,_,	0.0000	A,_,C,D,E,_,G,_,	0.0021	A,B,_,_,E,F,_,H,	0.0072
_,_,_,D,_,_,_,_,	0.0057	_,B,C,D,E,_,G,_,	0.0068	_,_,C,_,E,F,_,H,	0.0022
A,_,_,D,_,_,_,_,	0.0029	A,B,C,D,E,_,G,_,	0.0014	A,_,C,_,E,F,_,H,	0.0053
_,B,_,D,_,_,_,_,	0.0008	_,_,_,_,_,F,G,_,	0.0044	_,B,C,_,E,F,_,H,	0.0008
A,B,_,D,_,_,_,_,	0.0038	A,_,_,_,_,F,G,_,	0.0024	A,B,C,_,E,F,_,H,	0.0068
_,_,C,D,_,_,_,_,	0.0015	_,B,_,_,_,F,G,_,	0.0057	_,_,_,D,E,F,_,H,	0.0003
A,_,C,D,_,_,_,_,	0.0000	A,B,_,_,_,F,G,_,	0.0007	A,_,_,D,E,F,_,H,	0.0053
_,B,C,D,_,_,_,_,	0.0081	_,_,C,_,_,F,G,_,	0.0044	_,B,_,D,E,F,_,H,	0.0076
A,B,C,D,_,_,_,_,	0.0071	A,_,C,_,_,F,G,_,	0.0021	A,B,_,D,E,F,_,H,	0.0078
_,_,_,_,E,_,_,_,	0.0014	_,B,C,_,_,F,G,_,	0.0021	_,_,C,D,E,F,_,H,	0.0069
A,_,_,_,E,_,_,_,	0.0075	A,B,C,_,_,F,G,_,	0.0010	A,_,C,D,E,F,_,H,	0.0026
_,B,_,_,E,_,_,_,	0.0061	_,_,_,D,_,F,G,_,	0.0043	_,B,C,D,E,F,_,H,	0.0078
A,B,_,_,E,_,_,_,	0.0069	A,_,_,D,_,F,G,_,	0.0050	A,B,C,D,E,F,_,H,	0.0054
_,_,C,_,E,_,_,_,	0.0011	_,B,_,D,_,F,G,_,	0.0001	_,_,_,_,_,_,G,H,	0.0058
A,_,C,_,E,_,_,_,	0.0064	A,B,_,D,_,F,G,_,	0.0058	A,_,_,_,_,_,G,H,	0.0014
_,B,C,_,E,_,_,_,	0.0022	_,_,C,D,_,F,G,_,	0.0006	_,B,_,_,_,_,G,H,	0.0029
A,B,C,_,E,_,_,_,	0.0044	A,_,C,D,_,F,G,_,	0.0068	A,B,_,_,_,_,G,H,	0.0064
_,_,_,D,E,_,_,_,	0.0054	_,B,C,D,_,F,G,_,	0.0026	_,_,C,_,_,_,G,H,	0.0044
A,_,_,D,E,_,_,_,	0.0003	A,B,C,D,_,F,G,_,	0.0031	A,_,C,_,_,_,G,H,	0.0006
_,B,_,D,E,_,_,_,	0.0047	_,_,_,_,E,F,G,_,	0.0067	_,B,C,_,_,_,G,H,	0.0008
A,B,_,D,E,_,_,_,	0.0074	A,_,_,_,E,F,G,_,	0.0076	A,B,C,_,_,_,G,H,	0.0008
_,_,C,D,E,_,_,_,	0.0022	_,B,_,_,E,F,G,_,	0.0011	_,_,_,D,_,_,G,H,	0.0057
A,_,C,D,E,_,_,_,	0.0000	A,B,_,_,E,F,G,_,	0.0019	A,_,_,D,_,_,G,H,	0.0018
_,B,C,D,E,_,_,_,	0.0040	_,_,C,_,E,F,G,_,	0.0056	_,B,_,D,_,_,G,H,	0.0008
A,B,C,D,E,_,_,_,	0.0032	A,_,C,_,E,F,G,_,	0.0017	A,B,_,D,_,_,G,H,	0.0065
_,_,_,_,_,F,_,_,	0.0043	_,B,C,_,E,F,G,_,	0.0079	_,_,C,D,_,_,G,H,	0.0072
A,_,_,_,_,F,_,_,	0.0038	A,B,C,_,E,F,G,_,	0.0076	A,_,C,D,_,_,G,H,	0.0078
_,B,_,_,_,F,_,_,	0.0074	_,_,_,D,E,F,G,_,	0.0024	_,B,C,D,_,_,G,H,	0.0057
A,B,_,_,_,F,_,_,	0.0032	A,_,_,D,E,F,G,_,	0.0021	A,B,C,D,_,_,G,H,	0.0071
_,_,C,_,_,F,_,_,	0.0043	_,B,_,D,E,F,G,_,	0.0058	_,_,_,_,E,_,G,H,	0.0028
A,_,C,_,_,F,_,_,	0.0068	A,B,_,D,E,F,G,_,	0.0040	A,_,_,_,E,_,G,H,	0.0042
_,B,C,_,_,F,_,_,	0.0032	_,_,C,D,E,F,G,_,	0.0076	_,B,_,_,E,_,G,H,	0.0063
A,B,C,_,_,F,_,_,	0.0018	A,_,C,D,E,F,G,_,	0.0078	A,B,_,_,E,_,G,H,	0.0001

Table 12: Eight-attribute Random Query Probability Distribution (part1)

Query type	p_Q	Query type	p_Q	Query type	p_Q
_,_,_,D,_,F,_,_,	0.0050	_,B,C,D,E,F,G,_,	0.0007	_,_,C,_,E,_,G,H,	0.0047
A,_,_,D,_,F,_,_,	0.0074	A,B,C,D,E,F,G,_,	0.0039	A,_,C,_,E,_,G,H,	0.0024
_,B,_,D,_,F,_,_,	0.0008	_,_,_,_,_,_,_,H,	0.0021	_,B,C,_,E,_,G,H,	0.0071
A,B,_,D,_,F,_,_,	0.0065	A,_,_,_,_,_,_,H,	0.0015	A,B,C,_,E,_,G,H,	0.0050
_,_,C,D,_,F,_,_,	0.0026	_,B,_,_,_,_,_,H,	0.0081	_,_,_,D,E,_,G,H,	0.0076
A,_,C,D,_,F,_,_,	0.0008	A,B,_,_,_,_,_,H,	0.0017	A,_,_,D,E,_,G,H,	0.0018
_,B,C,D,_,F,_,_,	0.0007	_,_,C,_,_,_,_,H,	0.0038	_,B,_,D,E,_,G,H,	0.0081
A,B,C,D,_,F,_,_,	0.0040	A,_,C,_,_,_,_,H,	0.0053	A,B,_,D,E,_,G,H,	0.0015
_,_,_,_,E,F,_,_,	0.0035	_,B,C,_,_,_,_,H,	0.0061	_,_,C,D,E,_,G,H,	0.0044
A,_,_,_,E,F,_,_,	0.0069	A,B,C,_,_,_,_,H,	0.0033	A,_,C,D,E,_,G,H,	0.0029
_,B,_,_,E,F,_,_,	0.0061	_,_,_,D,_,_,_,H,	0.0022	_,B,C,D,E,_,G,H,	0.0022
A,B,_,_,E,F,_,_,	0.0047	A,_,_,D,_,_,_,H,	0.0064	A,B,C,D,E,_,G,H,	0.0022
_,_,C,_,E,F,_,_,	0.0051	_,B,_,D,_,_,_,H,	0.0010	_,_,_,_,_,F,G,H,	0.0044
A,_,C,_,E,F,_,_,	0.0036	A,B,_,D,_,_,_,H,	0.0029	A,_,_,_,_,F,G,H,	0.0053
_,B,C,_,E,F,_,_,	0.0043	_,_,C,D,_,_,_,H,	0.0003	_,B,_,_,_,F,G,H,	0.0004
A,B,C,_,E,F,_,_,	0.0057	A,_,C,D,_,_,_,H,	0.0071	A,B,_,_,_,F,G,H,	0.0040
_,_,_,D,E,F,_,_,	0.0072	_,B,C,D,_,_,_,H,	0.0013	_,_,C,_,_,F,G,H,	0.0010
A,_,_,D,E,F,_,_,	0.0008	A,B,C,D,_,_,_,H,	0.0069	A,_,C,_,_,F,G,H,	0.0047
_,B,_,D,E,F,_,_,	0.0050	_,_,_,_,E,_,_,H,	0.0065	_,B,C,_,_,F,G,H,	0.0000
A,B,_,D,E,F,_,_,	0.0013	A,_,_,_,E,_,_,H,	0.0025	A,B,C,_,_,F,G,H,	0.0068
_,_,C,D,E,F,_,_,	0.0042	_,B,_,_,E,_,_,H,	0.0042	_,_,_,D,_,F,G,H,	0.0017
A,_,C,D,E,F,_,_,	0.0008	A,B,_,_,E,_,_,H,	0.0040	A,_,_,D,_,F,G,H,	0.0042
_,B,C,D,E,F,_,_,	0.0079	_,_,C,_,E,_,_,H,	0.0075	_,B,_,D,_,F,G,H,	0.0003
A,B,C,D,E,F,_,_,	0.0004	A,_,C,_,E,_,_,H,	0.0072	A,B,_,D,_,F,G,H,	0.0008
_,_,_,_,_,_,G,_,	0.0047	_,B,C,_,E,_,_,H,	0.0068	_,_,C,D,_,F,G,H,	0.0039
A,_,_,_,_,_,G,_,	0.0024	A,B,C,_,E,_,_,H,	0.0017	A,_,C,D,_,F,G,H,	0.0061
_,B,_,_,_,_,G,_,	0.0036	_,_,_,D,E,_,_,H,	0.0013	_,B,C,D,_,F,G,H,	0.0079
A,B,_,_,_,_,G,_,	0.0042	A,_,_,D,E,_,_,H,	0.0079	A,B,C,D,_,F,G,H,	0.0018
_,_,C,_,_,_,G,_,	0.0010	_,B,_,D,E,_,_,H,	0.0010	_,_,_,_,E,F,G,H,	0.0054
A,_,C,_,_,_,G,_,	0.0021	A,B,_,D,E,_,_,H,	0.0007	A,_,_,_,E,F,G,H,	0.0011
_,B,C,_,_,_,G,_,	0.0013	_,_,C,D,E,_,_,H,	0.0075	_,B,_,_,E,F,G,H,	0.0021
A,B,C,_,_,_,G,_,	0.0013	A,_,C,D,E,_,_,H,	0.0017	A,B,_,_,E,F,G,H,	0.0054
_,_,_,D,_,_,G,_,	0.0013	_,B,C,D,E,_,_,H,	0.0081	_,_,C,_,E,F,G,H,	0.0035
A,_,_,D,_,_,G,_,	0.0021	A,B,C,D,E,_,_,H,	0.0047	A,_,C,_,E,F,G,H,	0.0011
_,B,_,D,_,_,G,_,	0.0078	_,_,_,_,_,F,_,H,	0.0067	_,B,C,_,E,F,G,H,	0.0024
A,B,_,D,_,_,G,_,	0.0040	A,_,_,_,_,F,_,H,	0.0081	A,B,C,_,E,F,G,H,	0.0064
_,_,C,D,_,_,G,_,	0.0063	_,B,_,_,_,F,_,H,	0.0017	_,_,_,D,E,F,G,H,	0.0029
A,_,C,D,_,_,G,_,	0.0038	A,B,_,_,_,F,_,H,	0.0024	A,_,_,D,E,F,G,H,	0.0056
_,B,C,D,_,_,G,_,	0.0032	_,_,C,_,_,F,_,H,	0.0004	_,B,_,D,E,F,G,H,	0.0079
A,B,C,D,_,_,G,_,	0.0017	A,_,C,_,_,F,_,H,	0.0078	A,B,_,D,E,F,G,H,	0.0075
_,_,_,_,E,_,G,_,	0.0025	_,B,C,_,_,F,_,H,	0.0057	_,_,C,D,E,F,G,H,	0.0004
A,_,_,_,E,_,G,_,	0.0046	A,B,C,_,_,F,_,H,	0.0026	A,_,C,D,E,F,G,H,	0.0054
_,B,_,_,E,_,G,_,	0.0017	_,_,_,D,_,F,_,H,	0.0011	_,B,C,D,E,F,G,H,	0.0049
A,B,_,_,E,_,G,_,	0.0028	A,_,_,D,_,F,_,H,	0.0018	A,B,C,D,E,F,G,H,	0.0000
_,_,C,_,E,_,G,_,	0.0033	_,B,_,D,_,F,_,H,	0.0008		
A,_,C,_,E,_,G,_,	0.0060	A,B,_,D,_,F,_,H,	0.0047		

Table 13: Eight-attribute Random Query Probability Distribution (part2)

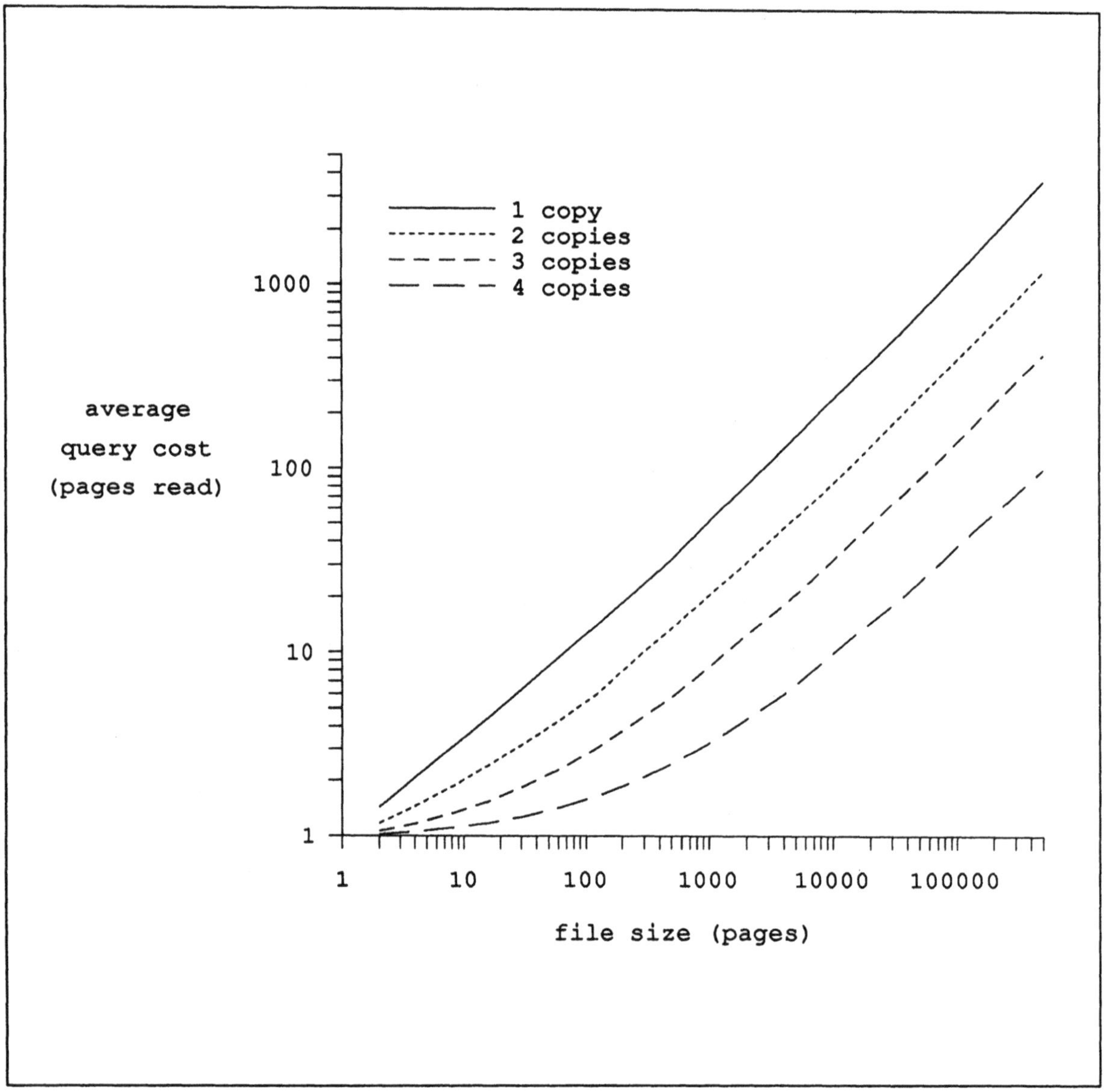

Figure 9: Average Query Cost vs. File Size (eight-attribute random query distribution, *mmi* bit-allocation)

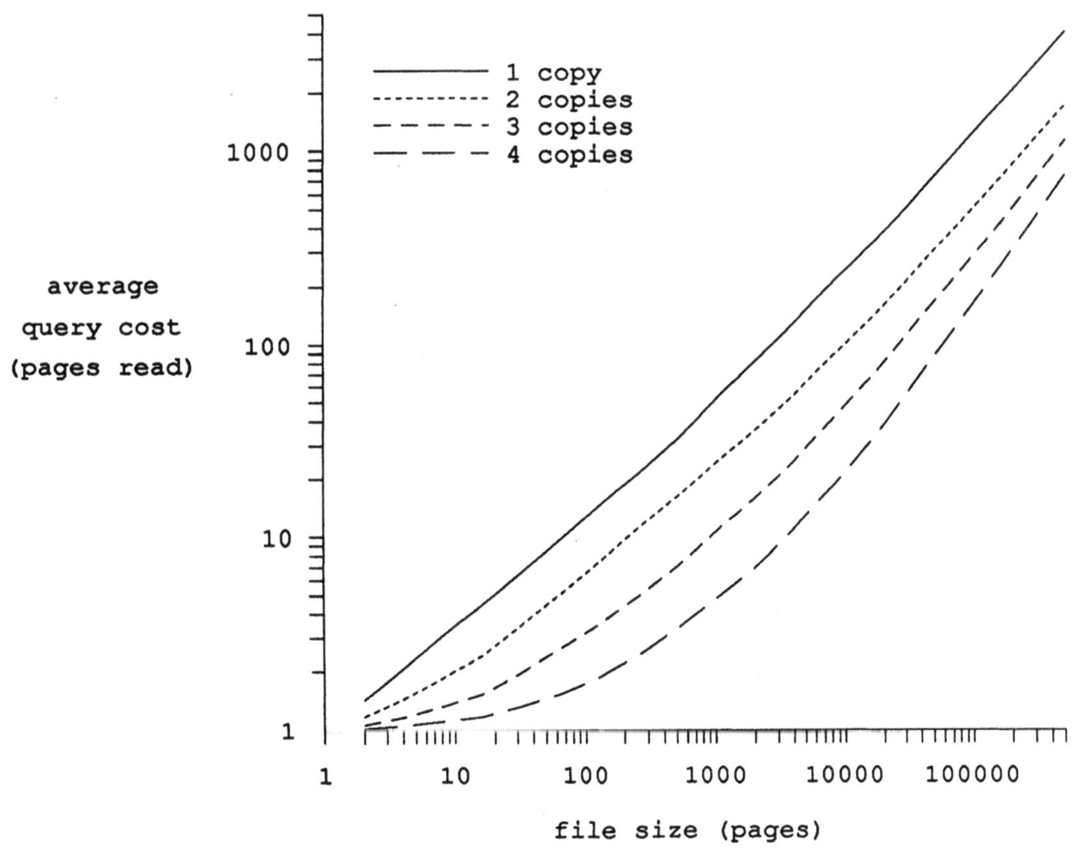

Figure 10: Average Query Cost vs. File Size (eight-attribute random query distribution with constraints, *mmi* bit-allocation)

Multikey Access Scheme Based on Term Discrimination and Signature Clustering

Jae W. Chang and Yoon J. Lee

Department of computer Science, KAIST
P.O. Box 150, Chongryang, Seoul, Korea 131

ABSTRACT

In order to improve the two-level signature file scheme proposed by Sacks-Davis et al. [19], we propose a new multikey access scheme based on term discrimination, we create a separate, efficient access method for the terms frequently used in user queries. We in addition cluster similar signatures by means of these terms so that we may achieve good performance on retrieval. Meanwhile we provide the gross space-time analysis of our scheme and compare it with that of the two-level signature file scheme. We show that our scheme can achieve 20-30% savings in retrieval time. Finally we propose a family of access methods constructed using our scheme.

1. INTRODUCTION

Traditional database management systems are well suited for a variety of applications in the commercial world such as air line reservation, banking, etc. These applications typically use formatted data. Recently, there have been many attempts to extend conventional systems so that they can handle documents (or records) containing both formatted fields and free texts [3,4,11,14]. Among such applications, there are library systems, medical records systems, and office information systems [12].

Because it is essential to efficiently store and retrieve both formatted data and free text, efficient access methods are required in such systems. An approach widely advocated for both data bases uses the signature file method [13]. Signature file methods, in fact, have been proposed for various applications, such as multikey retrieval [16,17,18], text retrieval [5,10], office systems [3,9], and prolog systems [1,2,15,21].

A signature (descriptor) in the signature file method is associated with each record, the signature being an encoding of the index terms used to retrieve the record. When a query is processed, the file of signatures, rather than the data file, is examined for potential matches. This method provides good retrieval performance and efficient storage usage [5]. As well as forming record signatures for individual records, it is possible to maintain block signatures for blocks of records, thus forming the two-level signature file scheme [17,19]. In this scheme, the file of block signatures is viewed as a bit slice representation whereas the file of record signatures is built using a bit string one.

In this paper, we propose a new multikey access scheme which improve the above two-level scheme using term discrimination and record signature clustering. Faloutsos & Christodoulakis [8] considered it unrealistic to assume both the uniform query and the uniform occurrence frequencies. They proposed an encoding scheme to allow special treatment to terms with high discriminatory power, so as to improve the performance of the signature file method. The terms with high discriminatory power are the ones which are frequently used in user queries but are infrequently occurring in data file. In our scheme, we also distinguish terms with high discriminatory power from ones with low discriminatory power and specially treat the former terms to acquire good retrieval performance. However, instead of using a special encoding scheme, we construct an additional, efficient access method such as the inverted file, for the terms with high discriminatory power.

Meanwhile we cluster similar record signatures so that we can achieve better performance on retrieval to records (documents). To make the clustering easy and effective, it is possible to combine term discrimination and record signature clustering. That is, we can form clusters by means of the similarity between terms with high discriminatory power, rather than all the terms. This still keeps clustering benefits to a high degree.

The remainder of the paper is organized as follows. First we present a brief overview of the signature file method. In section 3, we propose a new, efficient multikey access scheme based on term discrimination and record signature clustering. In section 4, we provide the gross space-time analysis of our scheme. In section 5, we compare our scheme with the two-level signature file scheme, We, in section 6, propose a family of access methods constructed based on our scheme. The conclusions and further works are presented in section 7.

2. SIGNATURE FILES

In a recent review of text retrieval methods, Faloutsos [5] has presented the signature file method as an access method applicable to both formatted and unformatted data. In fact, the signature file is an abstraction which contains the signatures of the records (documents) in data file. A signature is a bit string formed from terms that are used to index a record. Indexing to use signature files assigns a signature to every record in the data file. To answer a query, the signature file, rather than the data file, is examined first for immediately discarding many non-qualifying records.

Signature files typically use superimposed coding [13] to create the signature of a record. When a record consists of n terms, each term is converted into a bit string (term descriptor) using a hash function. A record descriptor is formed by superimposing (inclusive ORing) the n term descriptors. For example, we assume that a record consists of 2 terms, say Database and Data. The record signature of this record using superimposed coding is given bellow.

Database	0010 0100
Data	1000 1000
Record Signature	1010 1100

This method naturally supports variable numbers of terms per record since the number of terms does not affect the signature length. Thus records with multi-valued fields (fields in a record which can contain more than one value) and free text are handled easily because there is no distinction made between terms (values) belonging to the same field.

To check if a signature matches a query, the query terms are also hashed to form a query descriptor using exactly the same way used to generate the record signatures. If every bit set in the query descriptor is also set in the record signature, then the record signature is potential match. Superimposed coding can result in cases where the query descriptor qualifies the record signature, but the record does not actually contain the query terms. This is called a false match. The probability of a false match occurred is a function of the number of bits in the query descriptor and the record signature. False matches plays a practical restriction on the number of terms that a record may contain for a given signature size. Detailed formulas for calculating false match probability and values for k and b are presented in [3], where b is the signature size and k is the number of bits set to 1.

Meanwhile many works have focused on the search time of signature files. To efficiently access signature files, four strategies have been adopted as follows [12]:

(i) The use of bit slice representations
(ii) The use of multilevel indexes
(iii) The use of special encoding methods based on term discrimination
(iv) The use of compression techniques

Roberts [16] proposed a bit sliced representation to improve a bit string one. A bit slice approach reduced the amount of signature file that must be retrieved on query. Instead of viewing the signature file as consisting of N strings of b bits in length (where N is the number of records and b is the signature size), the bit slice approach stores the signature file as b strings, each of length N. For example, we assume that a data file contains 5 records and their signatures are 001, 101, 110, 001, and 111 respectively. Both representation of this example are seen as below.

Bit string Representation	Bit slice Representation
001	01101
101	00111
011	11011
111	

If a signature have b bits in size and a query contains w 1's, then with the bit slice representation, relevant w bits of every record signature without fetching any of the other bits. Thus only w *N rather than b*N bits of the signature file need be examined on a query. This approach can contribute considerable savings, since typically w << b.

The second strategies for reducing the amount of signature file accessed is based on a multilevel signature file, rather than a single-level file. For very large data files, queries using the bit slice approach can still be expensive. For example, we suppose there is k=4 slices, each containing n = 500,000 bits and each page in the secondary store has a capacity of p=8192 bits. As many as 248 disk access are required to determine the matching records, since the number of disk access is at least k*[n/p]. This show that one-level scheme is somewhat expensive even if using a bit slice representation. By Sacks-Davis et al. [19], a two-level scheme is proposed for which a data file of N records is viewed as consisting of Ns blocks, each containing Nr records where N = Ns*Nr. Thus both block signatures and record signatures are stored in this scheme. A block signature is formed analogously to a record signature using all the records contained in that block. The block signature is first examined on a query to identify which blocks of records match, and then the record signature of records from the matching blocks are examined to identify the individual matching records. The block signature file is stored as the bit slice representation to facilitate efficient query processing, whereas the record signatures are stored as the bit string one.

The third strategy uses special encoding techniques based on term discrimination. In general, many works [3,16,17] assume that the occurrence probability of any term in a user query is uniform (uniform query frequency assumption), as well as that the terms appear with equal frequency in the text (uniform occurrency frequency assumption). But Faloutsos & Christodoulakis [8] argued that both these assumptions were unrealistic. They improved the performance of the signature file method by allowing special treatment to terms with high discriminatory power (high query frequency and low occurrency frequency). And they demonstrated the 50% savings in false drops in case the 80-20 rule holds. If the number of false drops is kept constant, the savings in false drops result in the decrease in signature length. This after all reduces the search time of signature files.

The fourth strategy use compression techniques on signatures. Although the bit slice representation is much faster than the bit string one, there may be room for improvement. On searching, each search term requires the retrieval of k bit slices, where k is the number of bits set to 1. The retrieval time can be improved if k is forced to be one. In that case, the signature size has to be increased in order to maintain the same false drop probability. But the corresponding bit slices will be sparse and they can be compressed. As a result, the small amount of signature file can still maintain the same false match. We finally classify the works concerning signature files from the viewpoint of above four strategies as shown in Table 1.

(N/A : Not Applicable)

		Bit String		Bit Slice	
		No Special Encording	Special Encording	No Special Encording	Special Encording
One-level	No Com.	File & Huskey [10]	Faloutsos & Christodoulakis [8]	Roberts [16]	N/A
	Com.	Faloutsos [6]	N/A	Faloutsos & Chan [7]	N/A
Multi-level	No Com.	Sack-Davis & Ramamohanarao [17]	Sack-Davis & et al. [19]	Sack-Davis & Ramamohanarao [17]	Sack-Davis & et al. [19]
	Com.	N/A	N/A	Faloutsos & Chan [7]	N/A

Table 1. Classification of Related Works

3. NEW MULTIKEY ACCESS SCHEME

As described in the previous section, the two-level signature file scheme is an encouraging one to combine two strategies for efficiently accessing signature files. But there can be rooms for improvement. Faloutsos & Christodoulakis [8] distinguished terms with high discriminatory power from terms with low discriminatory power, which is called term discrimination, and made use of a special encoding scheme for the former terms to improve the performance of the signature file method. Here the terms with high discriminatory power are the ones which are frequently used in user queries but are infrequently occurring in data file, while the terms with low discriminatory power are opposite. Besides Sacks-Davis et al. [19] improved the two-level signature file scheme by identifying the terms in the database which occur most frequently (referred to as common terms) and by using a special encoding scheme for these terms in creating the block signature file. Therefore we take term discrimination into account to improve the two-level signature file scheme. However instead of using a special encoding scheme (i.e. the third strategy in section 2), we construct a separate, efficient access method, such as the inverted file, for terms with high discriminatory power.

In addition to four strategies described in section 2, the use of clustering method is another promising strategy to efficiently access signature files. In fact the clustering method is the dominating access method in library science [20]. Similar documents in the method are grouped together to form clusters. Usually they are stored physically together. However it seems that the clustering method can not handle insertion easily, and moreover may fail to retrieve some documents even though they qualify. We use the clustering method to cluster similar record signatures rather than similar records (documents), and therefore avoid above two problems caused by the clustering method. To make the clustering easy and effective, it is required to integrate term discrimination with signature clustering. That is, we construct clusters by means of the similarity between only terms with high discriminatory power, rather than all the terms. This leads to fast retrieval to the records required by a user query.

Based on term discrimination and signature clustering, we present the framework of a new multikey access scheme as shown in Fig. 1. In the following, we will call primary terms with high discriminatory power and secondary terms ones with low discriminatory power. Also we will call primary block descriptors block descriptors for primary terms and secondary block descriptors ones for secondary terms. In our scheme there are two block descriptor files, primary and secondary block descriptor files. For a query with a primary term, we must access the primary block descriptor file following path 1, while for secondary term, we must following path 2. Since there exist two paths to retrieve records in data file, it is necessary to select paths effectively in cases of queries with multiple terms. However for simplicity, queries with a single term are considered in this paper. On the other hand, we adopt the signature file method to construct the secondary block descriptor file. Record signatures are stored as a bit string representation, while the secondary block descriptor file is viewed as a bit slice one. Thus the path 2 is exactly the same as the two-level signature file scheme. When we use the compression technique for the primary block descriptor file, we can combine four strategies in section 2 as well as the signature clustering strategy into our scheme. As a result, it becomes a very efficient scheme for retrieving both formatted data and free texts.

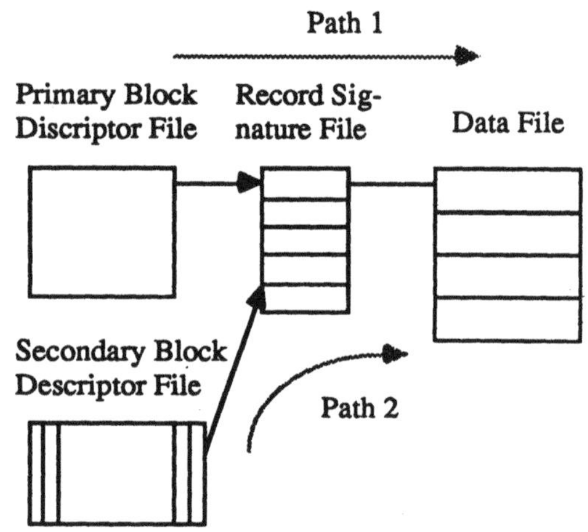

Figure 1. New Multikey Access Scheme

4. ANALYSIS

Here we will provide the gross space-time analysis of our scheme. Since we don't determine a specific access method for the primary block descriptor file, we provide three variables for the analysis: $r(w,N_s)$, $o(w,N_s)$ and $i(w,N_s)$. Here N_s is the size of the record signature file in blocks (or pages) and w is a variable dependent on an access method. These variables respectively mean disk accesses for retrieval, storage overhead, and disk accesses for insertion when we access the primary block descriptor file. In the following, we will re quire an estimate of the expected number of blocks containing r randomly chosen tokens, given that m is the number of tokens per block and n is the number of blocks. We define e(r,m,n) as the expected number of blocks containing the r tokens. Similarly, we define c(r,m,n) as the expected number of blocks containing the r tokens when m*n tokens are clustered in n blocks, according to their similarity. The input and design parameters for the analysis are given in Table 2.

Sy.	Definition
N	Total number of records
P	Page size in bits
A	Number of records that satisfy query
N_s	Size of record signature file in blocks
Nr	Number of record signatures in a block (where N = Ns * Nr)
bs	Size of secondary block signature in bits
ks	Number of bits set to '1' by a term in a secondary block signature
F_{s1}	False block match through Path 1
F_{s2}	False block match through Path 2
F_{r1}	False record match through Path 1
F_{r2}	False record match through Path 2
a	Probability that primary terms are used in user queries on the average
s	Number of all the terms in a record
r	Number of primary terms in a record

Table 2. Input and Design Parameters

Now we will examine the performance measure for given input and design parameters. The measures we are interested in are listed below:

- R_c : number of disk accesses on retrieval. They include the disk accesses to search the descriptors, as well as to retrieve the qualifying records.
- R_1 : number of disk accesses through path 1
- R_2 : number of disk accesses through path 2
- O_v : disk storage overhead in pages
- I_c : number of disk accesses on insertion
- I_a : number of additional disk accesses in splitting blocks for clustering

Retrieval

$$R_c = a * R_1 + (1 - a) * R_2 \text{ disk accesses}$$

$$R_1 = r(w,N_s) + c(A,N_r,N_s) + F_{s1} + A + F_{r1}$$

$$R_2 = k_s * \left\lceil \frac{N_s}{P} \right\rceil + e(A,N_r,N_s) + F_{s1} + A + F_{r1}$$

Storage overhead

$$O_v = c(W,N_s) + \left\lceil \frac{b_s * N_s}{P} \right\rceil + N_s \text{ pages}$$

Insertion

$$I_c = r * i(w,N_s) + (s - r) * k_s + 2 + I_a / N_r$$

disk accesses

$$I_c = 2 + N_r * (r * i(w,N_s) + (s - r) * k_s)$$

5. COMPARISON

In order to show the efficiency of our scheme, we will compare our scheme with the two-level signature file scheme. In the following, k_s', N_s', N_r', F_s', F_r' correspond to k_s, N_s, N_r, F_{s2}, F_{r2} respectively in section 4 and f is an average filing factor in a block. We, for comparison, will make use of the following measures.

- R_{c1}, R_{c2} : number of disk accesses on retrieval, in our scheme and in the two-level signature file scheme, respectively
- G_r : ratio of R_{c1} to R_{c2}
- O_{v1}, O_{v2} : disk storage overhead in both schemes
- G_o : ratio of O_{v1} to O_{v2}
- I_{c1}, I_{c2} : number of disk accesses on insertion in both schemes
- G_i : ratio of I_{c1} to I_{c2}

5.1 Retrieval

$$R_{c1} = \alpha * (r(w, N_s) + c(A,N_r,N_s) + F_{s1} + A + F_{r1}) +$$

$$(1 - \alpha) * (k_s * \left\lceil \frac{N_s}{P} \right\rceil + e(A,N_r,N_s) + F_{s1} + A + F_{r1})$$

$$R_{c1} = k_s' * \left\lceil \frac{N_s'}{P} \right\rceil + e(A,N_r',N_s') + F_s' + A + F_r', \text{ where}$$

$$N_s' * N_r' = N, \; N_s' = N_s * f, \text{ and } N_r' = N_r / f.$$

For simplicity, we assume that F_{s1}, F_{r1}, F_s', F_r', F_{s2}, F_{r2} << A. If the disk accesses for searching the block descriptors are very small compared to those for retrieving the qualifying records, that is

$$r(w, N_s), \; k_s * \left\lceil \frac{N_s}{P} \right\rceil, \; k_s' * \left\lceil \frac{N_s'}{P} \right\rceil << A, \text{ then}$$

$$R_{c1} \approx \alpha * (c(A,N_r,N_s) + A) + (1 - \alpha) * (e(A,N_r,N_s) + A)$$

$$R_{c1} \approx e(A,\frac{N_r}{f},N_s) + A$$

Meanwhile,

$e(r,m,n) = r/g$ and
$c(r,m,n) = r/b$ where g, b are some constants.
Here $g \approx 1$ when r << n.

Therefore if we assume that A << N_s, $N_s * f$, then

$$R_{c1} \approx \alpha * (\frac{A}{\beta} + A) + (1 - \alpha) * 2 * A = (\frac{\alpha}{\beta} - \alpha + 2) * A$$

$$R_{c1} \approx 2 * A$$

In order to acquire the ratio of R_{c1} to R_{c2},

$$G_r = \frac{R_{c1}}{R_{c1}} \approx \frac{\frac{\alpha}{\beta} - \alpha + 2}{2} = \frac{2 - \alpha * (1 - \frac{1}{\beta})}{2}$$

In the expression, $\frac{\alpha * (1 - \frac{1}{\beta})}{2}$ is the ratio of the reduced disk accesses over the two-level signature file scheme. Here it is shown that as a and b increase, we can acquire better performance. Table 3 presents the ratio of the decreased disk accesses with respect to a and b. In addition, Figure 2.1 and 2.2 describe the disk accesses on retrieval with respect to A when b = 2 and 3 respectively, given a = 0.7, 0.8 and 0.9.

(Unit : %)

α \ β	1.5	2	2.5	3	3.5	4
0.5	8.3	12.5	15.0	16.7	17.9	18.9
0.6	10.0	15.0	18.0	20.0	21.4	22.5
0.7	11.7	17.5	21.0	23.3	5.0	26.2
0.8	13.3	20.0	24.0	26.7	28.6	30.0
0.9	15.0	22.5	27.0	30.0	32.1	33.8
1.0	16.7	25.0	30.0	33.3	35.7	37.5

Table 3. Ratio of Decreased Disk Accesses

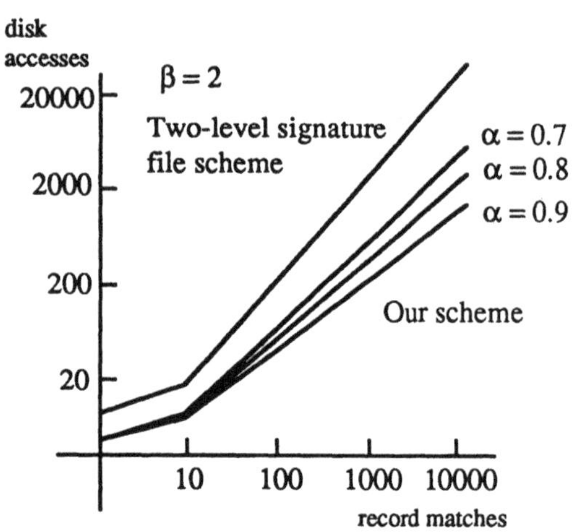

Figure 2(1). Disk Accesses on Retrieval when b = 2

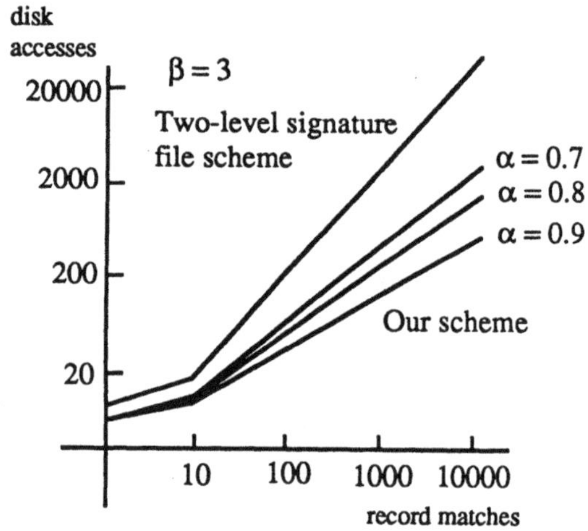

Figure 2(2). Disk Accesses on Retrieval when b = 3

5.2 Storage Overhead

$$O_{v1} = \alpha(W,N_s) + \left\lceil \frac{b_s * N_s}{P} \right\rceil + N_s$$

$$O_{v2} = \left\lceil \frac{b_s' * N_s'}{P} \right\rceil + N_s', \text{ where } N_s' = N_s * f.$$

If the storage overhead for the block descriptors in our scheme approximates those in the tow-level signature file scheme, then $\alpha(W,N_s) + \left\lceil \frac{b_s * N_s}{P} \right\rceil \approx \left\lceil \frac{b_s' * N_s'}{P} \right\rceil$. We let $\frac{b_s'}{P} = \Theta$, where Q is the size of a bit slice in pages. Then,

$$G_s = \frac{O_{v1}}{O_{v2}} \approx \frac{N_s + \Theta * N_s * f}{N_s * f + \Theta * N_s * f} = \frac{f * (1+\Theta) + (1-f)}{f * (1+\Theta)}$$

In the expression, $\frac{1-f}{f * (1+\Theta)}$ is the ratio of the increased storage overhead over the two-level signature file scheme. In an environment where records are only inserted without any deletion, it is known that f = 0.75. As our scheme is used for library records (or documents), there are little deletion of records in data file. So we can set f = 0.75 approximately. When the size of a bit slice in pages are 1,2,3 and 4, the additional storage overhead in our scheme are 16.7, 11.1, 8.3 and 6.7% respectively. Through this result, it is shown that the additional overhead is small.

5.3 Insertion

$$I_{c1} = 2 * (r * i(w,N_s) + (s - r) * k_s) + 2$$
$$I_{c2} = s * k_s' + 2$$

We assume that $k_s \approx k_s'$. If the disk accesses for the primary block descriptor file approximate those for the secondary block descriptor file, $i(w,N_s) \approx k_s$. Then,

$$I_{c1} \approx 2 * s * k_s + 1$$
$$I_{c2} \approx s * k_s + 1$$

To acquire the ratio of I_{e1} to I_{e2}, we will find G_i:

$$G_i = \frac{I_{e1}}{I_{e2}} \approx \frac{2 * s * k_s + 1}{s * k_s + 1} \approx 2$$

This means that we acquire twice disk accesses than the two-level signature file scheme.

6. MULTIKEY ACCESS METHODS

Depending on a way to construct the primary block descriptor file, we propose three different access methods, Primary-signature-based Two-level Signature file Method (PTSM), Inversion-based Two-level Signature file Method (ITSM) and Hash-table-based Two-level Signature file Method (HTSM).

6.1 PTSM

PTSM is an access method which is directly constructed using our scheme. As a primary block descriptor file, PTSM creates a separate signature file called primary block signature file and store it in a bit slice representation, like the secondary block signature file. Thus there exists primary and secondary block signature files. Fig. 3 illustrates this methods. By two separate block signature files, the method can allows as few false drops as the special encoding technique described in section 2. That is, since primary terms yield their own block signature in their separate signature file, there is no false drop occurring when primary terms and secondary terms are mixed to create a block signature. In addition, as primary terms are frequently used in user queries, it is necessary to increase the size of primary block descriptors. This results in smaller false drops, thus providing good retrieval performance.

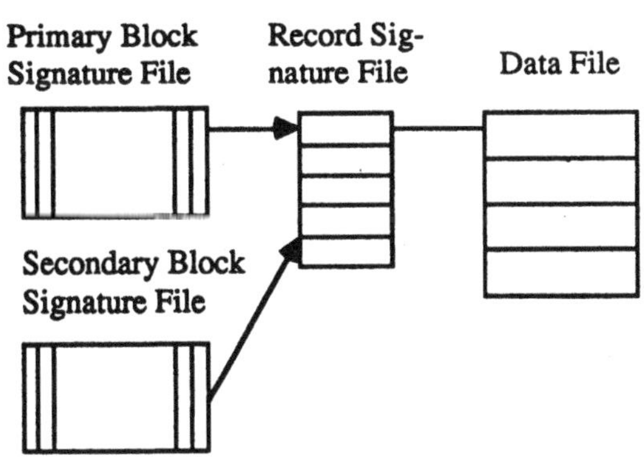

Figure 3. Illustration of PTSM

6.2 ITSM

Analogously to PTSM, ITSM also creates a separate block descriptor file for primary terms. But it adopts the inversion method, instead of the signature file method. The motivation behind this methods to avoid false drops completely by storing actual terms in the primary block descriptor file, thus achieving fast retrieval on user queries. However this method also suffers from two problems of the inversion method: slow insertion and much storage overhead. But this is not critical since we construct the inverted file for only primary terms. Another different point from a conventional inversion method is that a posting file points a block containing record signatures, rather than actual records. This method is illustrated in Fig. 4.

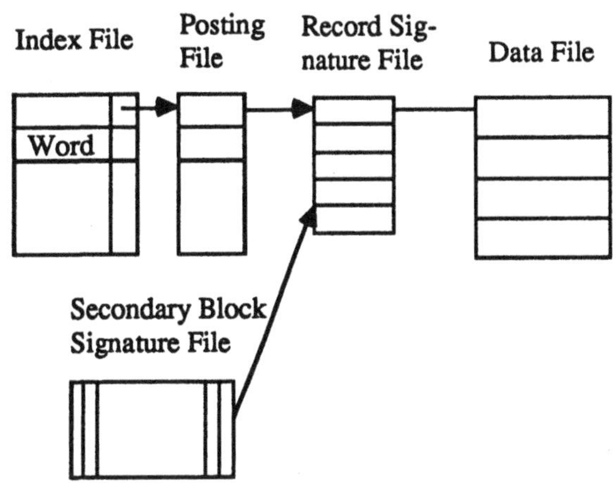

Figure 4. Illustration of ITSM

6.3 HTSM

PTSM is one extreme which allows false drops but provides good performance on insertion and storage overhead. On contrary, ITSM is the other extreme which concentrates on fast retrieval by suppressing false drops completely but gives rise to much storage overhead and slow insertion. HTSM can be regarded as a bridge between above two extreme. This method makes use of hash table to suppress false drops to a small degree. But it contains only pointers without storing actual terms, thus leading to small storage overhead and easy insertion. As a result, this method is considered very suitable because it provides good performance in both sides: retrieval side and insertion, storage overhead side. Fig. 5 illustrates the method.

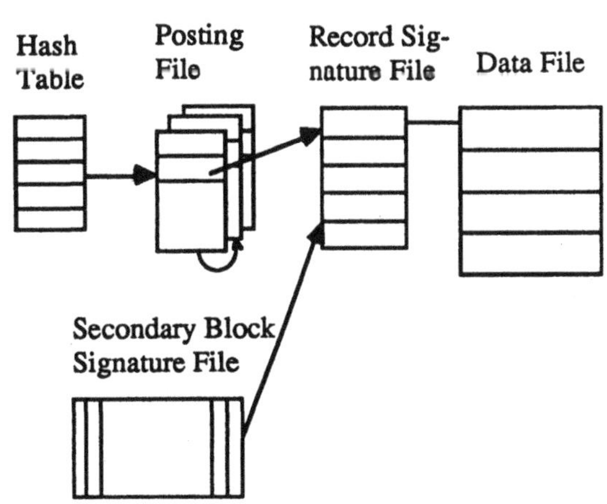

Figure 5. Illustration of HTSM

7. CONCLUSIONS AND FURTHER WORKS

In order to improve the two-level signature file scheme, we proposed a new multikey access scheme using term discrimination and signature clustering. By term discrimination, we can separate primary terms from all the terms used for indexing records. Thus it is possible to create a new, efficient access method for primary terms, so that we may achieve good performance on retrieval. In addition, we can cluster similar record signatures to provide better performance. To make the clustering easy and effective, we construct clusters by means of the similarity between primary terms, rather than all the terms.

Using above two concepts, our scheme can achieve 20-30% savings in retrieval time when the clustering factor is 2-3 and the probability that primary terms are used in user queries is 0.7-0.9. Moreover our scheme causes only a small, additional storage overhead. Based on our scheme, we also proposed three different access methods depending on a way to construct the primary block descriptor file: PTSM, ITSM and HTSM. PTSM gives small storage overhead and good insertion performance, while ITSM concentrates on fast retrieval. HTSM is a bridge between both extremes which can be considered as a promising method to provide good performance in both sides: retrieval side and insertion, storage overhead side.

Now we are under evaluating the detailed performance of three different access methods. In addition, in order to validate the gross space-time analysis of our scheme, we are implementing the PTSM, ITSM and HTSM methods. Further works can deal with the following issues:

- Performance analysis on multi-term queries
- Efficient path selection for multi-term queries
- Performance comparison with the conventional inversion method

ACKNOWLEDGMENT

We would like thank Joon H. Lee for his helpful comments on the preliminary versions of this paper. We are also grateful to the referees for their valuable suggestions.

REFERENCE

[1] P.B. Berra et al., "Computer Architecture for a Surrogate File to a Very Large Data/Knowledge Base," IEEE Computer, Vol. 20, No. 3, Mar. 1987, 25-32.

[2] R.M. Colomb and J. Jayasooriah, "A Clause Indexing System for Prolog Based on Superimposed Coding," The Australian Computer J., Vol. 18, No. 1, Feb. 1986, 18-25.

[3] S. Cristodoulakis and C. Faloutsos, "Design Considerations for a Message File Server," IEEE Trans. Soft. Eng., SE-10, No. 2, 1984, 201-210.

[4] B.C. Desai, T. Goyal and F. Sdri, "A Data Model for Use with Formatted and Textual Data," J. Am. Soc. Inf. Sci.(JASIS), Vol. 37, No. 3, May 1986, 158-165.

[5] C. Faloutsos, "Access Methods for Text," Computing Survey, Vol. 17, No. 1, Mar. 1985, 49-74.

[6] C. Faloutsos, "Signature Files: Design and Performance Comparison of Some Signature Extraction Methods," ACM SIGMOD, May 1985.

[7] C. Faloutsos and R. Chan, "Fast Text Access Methods for Optical and Large Magnetic Disks: Design and Performance Comparison," VLDB, Aug. 1988, 280-293.

[8] C. Faloutsos and S. Christodoulakis, "Design of a Signature File Method That Accounts for Non-Uniform Occurrence and Query Frequencies," VLDB, Aug. 1985, 165-170.

[9] C. Faloutsos and S. Christodoulakis, "Description and Performance Analysis of Signature File Methods," ACM TOOIS, vol. 5, no. 3, pp. 237-257, 1987.

[10] J.R. Files and H.D. Huskey, "An Information Retrieval System Based on Superimposed Coding," Proceedings of the Fall Joint Computer Conference, vol. 35, AFIPS Press, 423-432.

[11] R.L. Haskin and R.A. Lorie, "On Extending the Functions of a Relational Database System," ACM SIGMOD, Jun. 1982, 207-212.

[12] A. Kent, R. Sacks-Davis, and K. Ramamohanarao, "A Superimposed Coding Scheme Based on Multiple Block Descriptor Files for Indexing Very Large Data Bases," VLDB, Aug. 1988, 351-359.

[13] D.E. Knuth, "The Art of Computer Programming, vol 3: Sorting and Searching," Addison-Wesley, 1973.

[14] I.A. Macleod and A.R. Reuber, "The Array Model: A Conceptual Modeling Approach to Document Retrieval," J. Am. Soc. Inf. Sci.(JASIS), Vol. 38, N0. 3, May 1987, 162-170.

[15] K. Ramamohanarao, and J. Shepherd, "A Superimposed Codeword Indexing Scheme for Very Large Prolog Databases," Proceedings of the Third International Conference on Logic Programming, 1986, 569-576.

[16] C.S. Roberts, "Partial-Match Retrieval via the Method of Superimposed Codes," Proc. IEEE 67, Dec. 1979, 1624-1642.

[17] R. Sacks-Davis and K. Ramamohanarao, "A Two Level Superimposed Coding Scheme for Partial Match Retrieval," Information System, Vol. 8, No. 4, 1983, 273-280.

[18] R. Sacks-Davis and K. Ramamohanarao, "Performance of a Multi-Key Access Method Based on Descriptors and Superimposed Coding Techniques," Information System, Vol. 10, No. 4, 1985, 391-403.

[19] R. Sacks-Davis et al., "Multikey Access Methods Based on Superimposed Coding Techniques," ACM Tran. Database Systems, Vol. 12, No. 4, Dec. 1987, 655-696.

[20] G. Salton and M.J. McGill, "Introduction to Modern Information Retrieval," McGraw-Hill, 1983.

[21] M.J. Wise, and D.M.W. Powers, "Indexing Prolog Clauses via Superimposed Code Words and Field Encoded Words," Proceedings of International Symposium on Logic Programming, 1984, 203-210.

Overview of Functional Disk System

Masaru KITSUREGAWA, Miyuki NAKANO, Mikio TAKAGI

Institute of Industrial Science
University of Tokyo
22-1,Roppongi 7, Minato-ku, Tokyo
Japan

ABSTRACT

Functional Disk System with Relational database engine(FDS-R) is a relational storage system designed to accelerate relational algebraic operations. FDS-R employs a filtering and dynamic clustering mechanism as a special hardware function and provides an intelligent data management and an efficient data processing. The relation size which could be handled on the first prototype, however, was limited to the size of a staging buffer. Then we built up the second version of FDS-R, FDS-RII, which is designed to handle large relations efficiently. We have presented the processing strategy: the "Extended Task Cycle" for relational algebraic operations on FDS-RII, where the strategy is selected at run time form two algorithms(Nested Loop and Grace Hash Algorithms) by comparing the estimated I/O costs of them.

In this paper, we present the overview of Hardware configuration and Software system of FDS-RII. First we show the basic Task Cycle and give the performance evaluation results using the original Wisconsin Benchmark for small relations, where filtered relation can be staged on the staging buffer. FDS attains higher performance than the current database systems such as INGRES, Oracle and IDM. Next we explain the "Extended Task Cycle" which was introduce to handle the relations larger than the staging buffer size. With the expanded version of Wisconsin Benchmark, we measured the FDS-RII performance. FDS-RII attained a high performance for processing large relations as compared to other large database systems such as Gamma and Teradata. While FDS-RII uses just one disk and three MC68020, Teradata uses 40 disks and 20 AMP's and Gamma requires 8 disks and 17 VAX 11/750's.

1. INTRODUCTION

Recently the demands for large database processing have been increasing more and more. While the CPU performance has very much improved during the past decade, the same cannot be stated about the secondary storage, whose performance has been a very serious problem on large data processing. Aiming at the dissolution of this "I/O bottleneck" between CPU and the secondary storage, we have proposed the idea of "Functional Disk System(FDS)" in [1]. FDS is not a simple storage system but introduces some semantics of data processing in the storage system itself, incorporating a large staging buffer and a parallel processing mechanism. FDS can reduce the large overhead of the I/O drivers of conventional computer systems and provide a high-level data interface with the host.

In order to clarify the effectiveness of FDS, we have developed FDS-R which we called "Functional Disk System with Relational database engine". FDS-R employs a filtering and dynamic clustering mechanisms as a special hardware function to accelerate database operations, provides an intelligent data management and performs efficient data processing using multiple processors. The first version of the FDS-R prototype (FDS-RI) has been constructed and the preliminary performance evaluation of the system with the Wisconsin Benchmark has already been reported in [1]. It attained a very high performance in comparison with other database systems. In order to improve the performance, we have developed a revised system, FDS-RII. We have presented the processing algorithm employed in FDS-RII to handle large relations in [12]. On FDS-RII, we select the processing algorithm at run time from two algorithms, the Nested Loop and the Grace Hash Algorithms, by comparing their estimated I/O costs. The performance of basic relational operations was analyzed extensively by measuring the execution time. The I/O cost function used for algorithm selection was shown to be very effective.

In this paper, we describe the overview of Functional Disk System and report the basic query processing on FDS-R, which is called "Task Cycle". We evaluate the basic performance of FDS-RII for small relations with the Wisconsin Benchmark. FDS-RII attains a high performance in comparison with the other database systems such as INGRES, ORACLE, IDM and DIRECT. Then, we briefly introduce the "Extended Task Cycle" for large data processing. With the expanded version of Wisconsin Benchmark, we evaluate the performance of FDS-RII for large relations. FDS-RII attained a very high performance in comparison with Gamma and Teradata. While FDS-RII uses just one disk and 3 MC68020 CPU's, Teradata uses 40 disks and 20 AMP's and Gamma requires 8 disks and 17 VAX11/750's.

Section 2 briefly introduces the hardware and software configurations of FDS-RII. In section 3, we present the data flow of FDS-R and the query processing cycle when the size of the filtered relation is less than that of the staging buffer. In section 4 the basic performance of FDS-RII is measured using selection, projection, aggregation and join queries with Wisconsin Benchmark. Then we introduce the query processing method for large relations whose size far exceeds that of the staging buffer in section 5. The cost formula to choose the run time algorithm is also presented. In section 6, the performance evaluation of FDS-RII with the expanded version of Wisconsin Benchmark is presented. At the time of rewriting this paper in 1992 which was published in 1989, we completed the evaluation of Functional Disk System and finally obtained very promising results as we had expected. More elaborate evaluation details can be found in [13,14]. The concept of "Functional Disk System" is deeply discussioned in [15]. As a next step, we are now researching the multiple-functional disk system, which is to be an ultimate powerful relational storage system, FDS's are interconnected each other with enhanced omega network. We name this system SDC(Super Database Computer) [16]. This paper summerizes the architecture and performance of original FDS. More recent articles also would contain interesting hot information to readers.

2. HARDWARE AND SOFTWARE CONFIGURATION OF FDS-RII

2.1. Hardware Configuration of FDS-RII

Fig.1 shows the hardware configuration of the revised version of FDS-R. FDS-RII consists of three parts : the processing part, the staging buffer and the disk part.

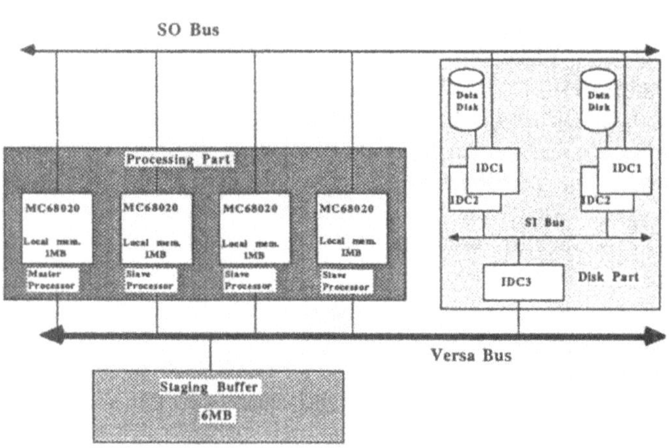

Fig.1 The Hardware Configuration of FDS-RII

The processing part consists of four processors, and the staging buffer is shared by these four processors, one of them being the master and the other three the slave processors. Each processor board is a commercial one which contains the MC68020 CPU(16MHz) and 1 MB of local memory. The staging buffer consists of 6MB dynamic memory. The processing part, the staging buffer and the disk part are connected by Versa Bus, the standard MOTOROLA bus. Also, in order to increase the I/O bandwidth, another special bus which we call "SO Bus" is added to the system. It connects the processor boards to the disk part and is used only to store the result relations into the disk.

The disk part is composed of 8 inch disks(NEC D2257) and the "Intelligent Disk Controller(IDC)". The IDC is the heart of this disk part and is responsible for the control of the disks and for the filtering and dynamic clustering of the data read from them.

2.2. Software Configuration

Fig.2 shows the configuration of the FDS-R system software.

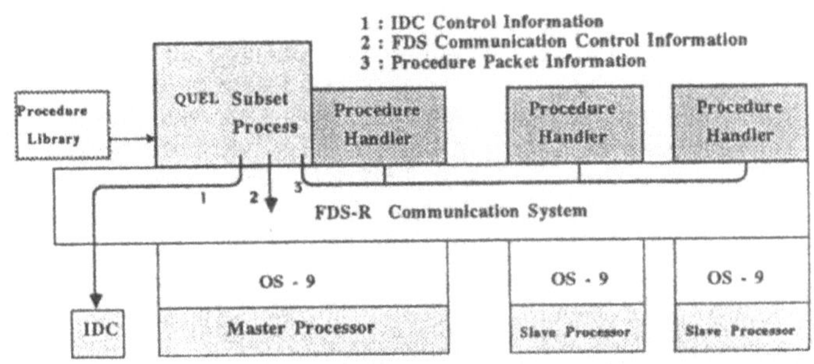

Fig.2 The Software Configuration of FDS-RII

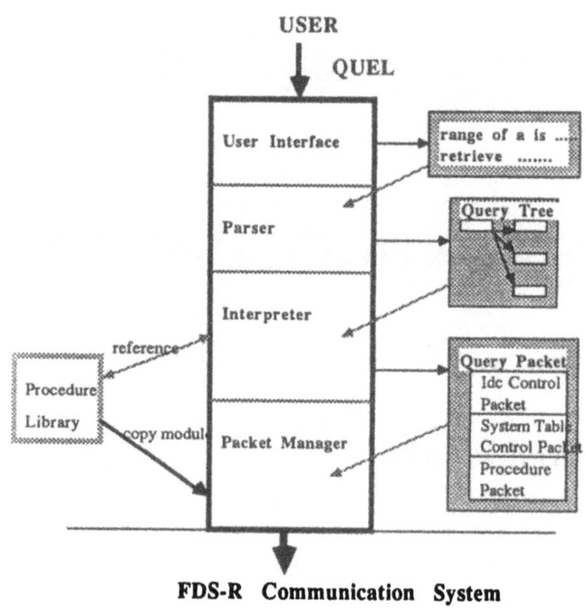

Fig.3 QUEL Subset Process

A ROM based MICROWARE OS-9 is used as the kernel on each processor. Since OS-9 is an operating system for a single processor, we developed the FDS-R communication system(FDS-R CS). FDS-R CS supports the message passing among processes on multiple processors.

The QUEL Subset System(QSS) is constructed on top of FDS-R CS. It consists of two processes : the QUEL subset process(Q-PS) on the master processor and the procedure handler process(PH-PS) on each of the four processors.

QUEL Subset Process runs on the master processor and is composed of the four elements shown in Fig.3. Q-PS provides the user interface, parses the queries, interprets the query tree and controls both IDC and PH-PS on each processor via FDS-R CS. Q-PS generates a query packet corresponding to one relational algebraic operation after interpreting the query. A query packet consists of an IDC packet, a procedure packet and a system packet. The IDC packet contains informations about the source relations and the filtering and clustering of their tuples. The procedure packet contains informations about the relational operation to be executed. The system packet contains the information necessary to the multiple processors and the staging buffer management. According to a query packet, Q-PS drives the IDC, controls the synchronization of the multiple processors and manages the space of the staging buffer. Each of the PH-PS invokes a procedure packet sent by Q-PS in parallel.

3. TASK CYCLE

In FDS-R a query is decomposed into a combination of simple relational operations such as selection, projection, join, aggregation. The hash-based algorithm is applied for each of the simple relational algebraic operations. As described in [3], [4], [5], [6], [11] and [12], hash-based algorithms are efficient for large data processing. One of the properties of the hash-based algorithms is the load reduction of the operations, and the other is the natural opportunity of parallel processing provided by them.

In the following, we consider the execution of a simple relational operation and present the processing cycle for a query execution on FDS-R, in detail.

The execution of a relational operation consists of 2 phases : the Staging Phase and the Processing Phase.

(1) Staging Phase

IDC reads relations from the disk and clusters them into the staging buffer. When reading a relation from the disk and transferring it to the staging buffer, IDC examines each tuple; according to some specified parameters, it filters some attribute fields and applies a hash function to a target attribute field, and then clusters the relation on the fly. At the same time, IDC also builds a hash table.

(2) Processing Phase

After the Staging Phase, each processor gets a cluster from the hash table of IDC and transfers it into its own local memory. The clusters are processed in parallel and the result tuples are written back to the disks via the SO Bus.

Since one query is composed of several relational operations, the query execution on FDS-R implies that the data repeatedly streams out the disk, and then back to the disk. This one cycle of dataflow out disk to disk is the unit of a query execution on FDS-R and here we call it "Task Cycle". In FDS-RI, we only considered the case in which the data could be processed in one Task Cycle, that is, the source data could fit into the staging buffer. The Task Cycle of FDS-RI is shown in Fig.4 and explained in detail as follows.

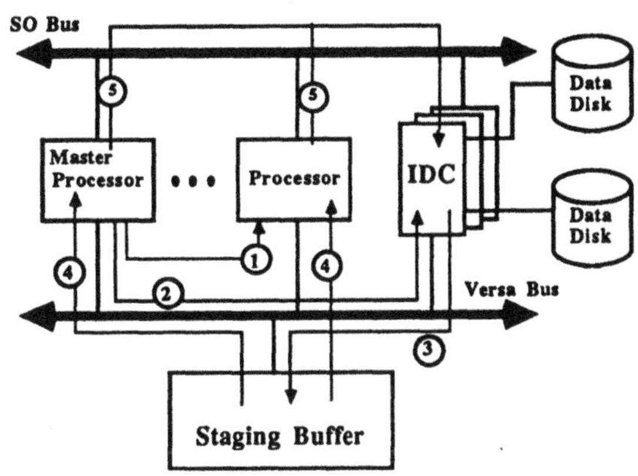

Fig.4 Task Cycle

1) Q-PS parses and compiles the user query and generates three query packets(procedure, IDC, system). Each query packet contains all the information for the execution of the Task Cycle. Q-PS on the master processor sends the procedure packet to all PH-PSs. Each PH-PS waits for a start signal from Q-PS.

2)Q-PS sets up the IDC according to the IDC packet.

Staging Phase:

3)When Q-PS drives the IDC, the data is retrieved from the disks and staged into the buffer after being filtered and clustered. After the IDC reads out all the data, it issues an interruption to Q-PS, signing that the Staging Phase of the data stream is finished.

Processing Phase:

4)The Processing Phase starts. As soon as it gets the interrupt signal from IDC, Q-PS invokes all PH-PSs. The clustered data are transferred from the staging buffer to the local memory of each processor and the processing specified in the procedure packet is performed. This is done by all the processors in parallel.

5)Each PH-PS writes back the results into the disks via SO Bus when the local buffer is full.

4. PERFORMANCE EVALUATION Of FDS-RII WITH THE ORIGINAL WISCONSIN BENCHMARK

In this section we show some results of the performance measurement of simple relational operations on FDS-RII for small relations. FDS-RII is compared with current relational database systems with the original Wisconsin Benchmark[8].

Table 1. The execution time of selection queries with the Wisconsin Benchmark

range of e is tenKtuple
retrieve into tmp (e.all) where e.a0 < 1000

Selection Query(10% selectivity)	
U-INGRES	64.4 sec
C-INGRES	53.9 sec
ORACLE	230.6 sec
IDM noDAC	33.4 sec
IDM DAC	23.6 sec
DIRECT	46.0 sec
FDS-R	3.4 sec

Table 2. The execution time of projection query with the Wisconsin Benchmark

range of e is oneKtuple
retrieve unique into tmp (e.all)

Projection Query(Duplicate Elimination)	
U-INGRES	236.8 sec
C-INGRES	132.0 sec
ORACLE	199.8 sec
IDM noDAC	122.2 sec
IDM DAC	68.1 sec
DIRECT	58.0 sec
FDS-R	1.5 sec

Table 3. The execution time of join query with the Wisconsin Benchmark

range of e is tenKtuple
range of f is tenKtuple
retrieve into tmp (e.all,f.all) where e.a1 = f.a1 and e.a1 < 1000

Join Query(10% Join selectivity)	
U-INGRES	10.2 min
C-INGRES	1.8 min
ORACLE	300 min
IDM noDAC	300 min
IDM DAC	300 min
DIRECT	10.2 min
FDS-R	6.5 sec

Table 4. The execution time of aggregation query with the Wisconsin Benchmark

range of e is tenKtuple
retrieve (e.a2, sum=sum(e.a1 by e.a2))

Aggregation Query(Partitions = 100)	
U-INGRES	174.2 sec
C-INGRES	484.8 sec
ORACLE	1487.5 sec
IDM noDAC	67.5 sec
IDM DAC	38.2 sec
DIRECT	229.5 sec
FDS-R	2.5 sec

One disk drive, 6 MB of staging buffer memory and 3 processors are activated under the measurement. According to the Wisconsin Benchmark[8], we use 1,000, 10,000 tuples as benchmark relations and each tuple is 182 bytes long. The attribute a0, a1 and a2 are 2-byte integers. The attribute a0 is unique and randomly ordered integer between 0 and 9999. The attribute a2 is randomly ordered integer between 0 and 99.

We use the following four queries for the performance measurement.

Table 1 shows the result of selection query. In this query, the benchmark relation is 10,000 tuples and the selectivity is 10 %. Therefore, we get the result relation whose size is 1,000 tuples. The result relation is written back to the disk. On FDS-RII, the predicate e.a0 < 1000 is evaluated by IDC.

Table 2 shows the results of the projection query. This query is the duplicate elimination. In this query, the benchmark relation is 1,000 tuples and each tuple has an unique value so that the result relation is equal to the source relation. The result relation is written back into the disk.

Table 3 shows the results of the join query. In this query, both of the two relation have 10,000 tuples. The predicate e.a0 < 1000 is executed by IDC and the selected tuples are clustered with the value of attribute a0. Dynamically clustered tuples are processed in parallel by activated three processors. We have the result relation whose size is 1,000 tuples. The result relation is written back into the disk.

Table 4 shows the results of the aggregation query. In this query, the attribute a2 is randomly ordered 2 byte integer between 0 to 99 so that the source relation whose size is 10,000 tuples is partitioned into 100 clusters with the value of the attribute a2. On FDS_RII, only the two attribute fields are extracted and staged on the staging buffer. At the same time, tuples are clustered with the value of the attribute a2 by IDC and each cluster is processed in parallel.

All results shows that FDS-R attains a high performance in comparison with the other database systems. Especially, the result of join query is very fast. This is because Functional Disk System can reduce the large overhead of the I/O driver and IDC can provide the efficient data management.

5. QUERY EXECUTION FOR LARGE RELATION ON FDS-R

5.1. Extended Task Cycle[12]

For processing relations larger than the size of the staging buffer, it is important to divide the source relation into the size of a staging buffer and to manage the staging buffer for processing divided data. On FDS-RII, we employ two algorithms for large data processing in order to get high performance. FDS-RII selects the processing method from two algorithms: the Nested Loop and the Grace Hash Algorithms[3,4].

(1) Nested Loop Algorithm

It may not be necessary to explain this algorithm. This is the most simple iterative method. Usually this method is considered to be inefficient, since the outer pages of the relation are read many times. Later it is shown, however, that it outperforms the next partitioning algorithm for relations under a certain size.

```
ExtendedTaskCycle(data ,operation)

  StagingPhase(data ,operation)
  Begin
    select the processing method
        from Nested Loop Algorithm and Data Partitioning Algorithm
    if Data Partitioning Algorithm is selected
      Begin
        determine the number of I/O clusters
         make I/O clusters of source data
         for each overflowed I/O cluster
            StagingPhase(the overflowed I/O cluster, operation)
      End
     else Nested Loop Algorithm is selected
      Begin
         determine the number of outerloops and innerloops
      End
  End

  ProcessingPhase(data ,operation)
  Begin
    for each I/O cluster of outer relation
      for each I/O cluster of inner relation
        load the specified data into the staging buffer
        process data on the staging buffer according to the
        operation
  End

Begin
  StagingPhase(data ,operation);
  for each I/O cluster
    ProcessingPhase(I/O cluster, operation)
End
```

Fig.5 The Extended Task Cycle

(2) Grace Hash Algorithm

In this method, the source data is partitioned into clusters which do not exceed the size of the staging buffer by applying an appropriate hash function, and the generated clusters are stored back into the disk. Then the clusters are read one by one from the disk. The tuples of the cluster on the staging buffer are processed as described above.

FDS-RII supports large data processing by extending the Task Cycle. Here we introduce the extended Task Cycle where the processing algorithm is chosen at run time from two algorithms and the staging buffer is managed properly. Fig.5 shows this Extended Task Cycle. In the Staging Phase of the Extended Task Cycle, a run time method is selected from two algorithms with using the estimated I/O cost and the source relations are divided into small data partitions which are termed "I/O clusters". The Processing Phase is invoked as many times as the number of I/O clusters generated at the Staging Phase.

5.2. Selection Criteria for the Run Time Algorithm

On FDS-RII, the run time algorithm is determined with using the I/O cost formula, which are described in [12] in detail. In this paragraph, we show only conditions for choosing the run time routine from the two algorithms. The following parameters is used to express the selection criteria for the run time algorithm on FDS-RII.

R : size of relation R in bytes

M : size of staging buffer in bytes

f_r , f_s : filtering factor of relation R,S

(1) Join Operation

The number n of outerloops for the smaller relation R is given by $n = \left\lceil \frac{f_r R}{M-\alpha} \right\rceil$ (α = 1 page). The condition under which the I/O cost of the Nested Loop Algorithm is better than that of the Grace Hash Algorithm is given as follows.

$$n < 1 + 2f_s + 2f_r < 5 \qquad \text{cond(1)}$$

The condition under which the I/O cost of the Nested Loop Algorithm with the filtered inner relation is better than that of the GRACE Hash Algorithm is given as follows.

$$n < 2 + 2\frac{f_r |R|}{f_s |S|} < 4 \qquad \text{cond(2)}$$

The following condition determines whether the inner relation S is written back at the Nested Loop Algorithm.

$$f_s < 1 - \frac{1}{n} \quad (n \geq 2) \qquad \text{cond(3)}$$

(2) Projection and Aggregation Operations

As well as the join operation, the number n of outerloops is given by $n = \left\lceil \frac{f_r R}{M-\alpha} \right\rceil$ (α = 1 page). The condition under which the I/O cost of the Nested Loop Algorithm is better than that of the Grace Algorithm is given as follows.

$$n < 1 + 4f_r \qquad \text{cond(4)}$$

6. PERFORMANCE EVALUATION OF FDS-RII WITH THE EXPANDED VERSION OF WISCONSIN BENCHMARK

In this section we show some results of the performance measurement of the prototype machine of FDS-RII for large relations. For the evaluation of results, we compare them with the result of the expanded version of Wisconsin Benchmark[7].

One disk drive, 6 MB of staging buffer memory and 3 processors are activated under the measurement. According to the Wisconsin Benchmark[7,8], we use 10,000, 100,000, 1,000,000 tuples as benchmark relations and each tuple is 208 bytes long. In this evaluation, we do not support an index structure in the database, that is, our results are measured by using no indexed relations only.

6.1. Selection Query

We measured the performance of the following selection query. The result relation is written back into the disk.

range of e is relation R
retrieve into tmp (e.all) where e.a1 < X

Table 5. The execution time of selection queries with the expanded version of Wisconsin Benchmark

Selection Query(1% selectivity)			
Tuple	10,000	100,000	1,000,000
Gamma	1.6 sec	13.8 sec	134 sec
Teradata	6.9 sec	28.2 sec	213 sec
FDS-R	2.9 sec	24.8 sec	244 sec

Selection Query(10% selectivity)			
Tuple	10,000	100,000	1,000,000
Gamma	2.1 sec	17.4 sec	182 sec
Teradata	16.0 sec	111.0 sec	1107 sec
FDS-R	3.8 sec	34.9 sec	355 sec

The selection query is the basic query which characterizes the performance of the system. On FDS-RII, the predicate e.a1 < X is executed by IDC on the fly. So we expect that the execution costs of a selection query will be almost equal to the I/O costs and that the execution time will increase as a linear function of the reading and writing data sizes. Our measurement used two sets of selection queries; first with 1% selectivity and then with 10% selectivity. Table 5 shows the results of FDS-RII and the other systems, Gamma and Teradata whose performance is shown in [7]. The execution time of FDS-RII is 2.5 times as large as that of Gamma. Although FDS-RII activates just one disk, while Gamma and Teradata activate 8 disks and 20 disks respectively, FDS-RII attains a high performance.

6.2. Join Query

We execute the following join query for the performance measurement. The result relation is written back into disk.

range of e is relation R
range of f is relation S
retrieve into tmp (e.all,f.all) where e.a1 = f.a1 and e.a1 < X

On FDS-RII, the predicate e.a1 < X is executed by the filtering function of IDC and selected tuples are clustered by the value of attribute a1. Then the clustered data are staged on the staging buffer and are joined by processors. The relation R and S have the same number of tuples.

Table 6. The execution time of join query with the expanded version of Wisconsin Benchmark

Join Query(10% join selectivity)			
Tuple	10,000	100,000	1,000,000
FDS-R	7.4 sec	69.7 sec	994 sec
Teradata	35.6 sec	331.7 sec	3535 sec
Gamma	5.1 sec	36.3 sec	703 sec

Table 6 shows the measurement results of join query. From the results of measurement in Table 6, the execution time of join query increases as a linear function of the input and output data sizes as discussed in section 4. As shown in Table 6, the execution time of FDS-RII is three times as large as that of Gamma. However, while the measurement environment of Gamma consists of 8 disk nodes(the processors with disks), 8 nondisk processors and 1 scheduler[7], that of FDS-RII consists of only one disk and 3 CPU's. Since the cost of join query on FDS-RII is almost the same as the I/O cost, we expect that the disk-reading cost will be easily decreased by using multiple disks.

6.3. Projection Query

We execute the following projection query for the performance measurement. This query is the duplicate elimination. All tuples have an unique value, which means that the source relation is no duplicate data. The result relation is written back into disk.

range of e is relation R
retrieve unique into tmp (e.all)

On FDS-RII, tuples are clustered by the value of attribute a1. Then the clustered data are staged on the staging buffer and are searched by processors in parallel.

Table 7 The execution time of projection queries with the expanded version of Wisconsin Benchmark

Projection Query(Duplicate Elimination)			
Tuples	1,000	10,000	100,000
FDS-R	1.7 sec	13.9 sec	286 sec

Table 7 shows the measurement results of projection query. From the results of measurement in Table 7, the execution time of 100,000 tuples is 20 times larger than that of 10,000 tuples. This is because Grace Hash Algorithm is used for 100,000 tuple source relation. In Grace Hash, the source relation is at first read and partitioned with hash function. Then each partition is written back to the disk. The partitions are read one by one to be processed by the processors. Finally the result tuples are written into the disk. Thus two disk reads and two disk writes are required. In this case, the result relation has the same number of tuples as the source relation. Therefore the I/O cost for the Grace Hash Algorithm is two times larger than that of one Task Cycle, which means the time for 100,000 tuple processing, 286 sec is almost 20 times as large as 10,000 tuple processing, 13.9 sec.

6.4. Aggregation Query

We execute the following aggregation query for the performance measurement.

range of e is relation R
retrieve (e.a2, sum=sum(e.a1 by e.a2))

On FDS-RII, tuples are clustered by the value of attribute a2. Then the clustered data are staged on the staging buffer and are processed by processors in parallel.

Table 8 The execution time of aggregation queries with the expanded version of Wisconsin Benchmark

Aggregation Query(Partitions = 100)			
Tuples	10,000	100,000	1,000,000
Partitions	100	1,000	10,000
FDS-R	2.9 sec	24.9 sec	307 sec

Table 8 shows the measurement results of aggregation query. In case of 1,000,000 relation, the Grace Hash Algorithm is applied. From Table 8, we can find that the execution time increases as a linear function of the relation sizes contrary to the projection query. The execution time of 1,000,000 relation is almost ten times larger than that of 100,000 relation. On FDS-RII, only two aggregation fields are extracted from original tuples and the I/O clusters are very small. Therefore the reading cost of source relation dominate the total processing time , while the cost of making I/O clusters and reading these clusters are very small.

7. CONCLUSIONS

We present the performance of FDS-RII, which is designed to handle large relations efficiently. At first, we present the Task Cycle which is the unit of the query execution on FDS-R. We measure the basic performance of FDS-RII with simple relational operations. With the Wisconsin Benchmark, we evaluate the performance of FDS-RII and find that FDS-RII attains a high performance in comparison with the other database systems such as INGRES, ORACLE, IDM and DIRECT. We introduce the Extended Task Cycle to handle large relations on FDS-RII. On FDS-RII, the processing algorithm is selected at run time from two algorithms (Nested Loop Algorithm, Grace Hash Algorithm), by comparing their estimated I/O costs. With the expanded version of Wisconsin Benchmark, we measured the performance of FDS-RII for large relations. FDS-RII attained a high performance for very large relations as compared to other large database systems such as Gamma and Teradata. While FDS uses just one disk and three MC68020, Teradata uses 40 disk(20 AMP's) and Gamma requires 8 disks and 17 VAX750's.

In this paper, we measured the performance of FDS-RII by using the uniformly distributed data. We are planning to implement the Dynamic Hybrid Grace Hash Algorithm[9] and to measure the performance for large relations which are not uniformly distributed and to analyze results when the I/O cluster overflows.

Acknowledgement

This research is partially supported by Casio Foundation, Denki-Tsushin-Fukyu Foundation, Inamori Foundation and the Murata Science Foundation.

[References]

[1] M.Kitsuregawa, M.Nakano, L.Harada, M.Takagi,"Functional Disk System for Relational Database," Proc. of the 3rd Int. Conf. on Data Engineering, pp.88-95, 1987

[2] M. Stonebraker et al.,"The Design and Implementation of INGRES," ACM Transaction on Database Systems, Vol.1, No.3, September, 1976.

[3] M.Kitsuregawa, H.Tanaka, T.Motooka, "Application of Hash to Data Base Machine and Its Architecture," New Generation Computing, Vol.1, No.1, 1983.

[4] D.J.DeWitt et al.,"Implementation Techniques for Main Memory Database Systems," Proceedings of the 1984 SIGMOD Conference, 1984

[5] L.D.Shapiro, "Join Processing in Database Systems with Large Main Memory", ACM Transaction on Database Systems, pp.239-264, Vol.11, No.3, September, 1986

[6] R.Gerber, "Dataflow Query Processing using Multiprocessor Hash-Partitioned Algorithms," PhD Thesis and Computer Science Technical Report #672, University of Wisconsin-Madison, October, 1986

[7] D.J.DeWitt et al.,"A Single User Evaluation of the GAMMA Machine," Proceedings of the 5th Int. Workshops on Database Machine, pp.43-59, October, 1987

[8] D.Bitton et al.,"Benchmarking Database Systems," Computer Science Technical Report #526, University of Wisconsin-Madison, 1983

[9] M.Nakayama, M.Kitsuregawa, M.Takagi, "Hash-Partitioned Join Method Using Dynamic Destaging Strategy," Proc. of the 14th Int. Conf. on Very Large Data Bases, pp.468-478, 1988

[10] Y.Yamane,"A Hash Join Technique for Relational Database Systems," Proceedings of the Int. Conf. on Foundations of Data Organization, pp.388-398, May, 1985

[11] K.Bratbergsengen,"Hashing Method and Relational Algebra Operations," Proc. of the 10th Int. Conf. on Very Large Data Bases, pp.323-332, August, 1984

[12] M.Kitsuregawa, M.Nakano, M.Takagi,"Query Execution for Large Relations on Functional Disk System," Proc. of the 5th Int. Conf. on Data Engineering, pp.159-167, February, 1989

[13] M.Kitsuregawa, M.Nakano, M.Takagi,"Performance Evaluation of Functional Disk System with Nonuniform Data Distribution", Proc. of the second Int. Symp. on Databases in Parallel and Distributed Systems, 1990, pp.80-89

[14] M.Kitsuregawa, M.Nakano, M.Takagi,"Performance Evaluation of Functional Disk System(FDS-R2)", Proc. of the 7th Conf. on Data Engineering, 1991, pp.416-425

[15] M.Kitsuregawa, M.Nakano,"Functional Disk System: Relational Database Processing and Its Performance Evaluation", The Transaction of the Institute of Electronics, Information and Communication Engineers, Vol.J74-D-I, No.8, 1991, pp.496-507

[16] M.Kitsuregawa, et al.,"The Super Database Computer(SDC): System Architecture, Algorithm and Preliminary Evaluation", Proc. of the 25th Hawaii Int. Conf. on System Architecture, 1992, pp.308-319

AUTOMATIC TUNING OF DATA PLACEMENT AND LOAD BALANCING IN DISK ARRAYS

Peter Scheuermann
Department of Elec. Eng.
and Computer Science
Northwestern University
Evanston, IL 60208

Gerhard Weikum and Peter Zabback
Department of Computer Science
ETH - Zentrum
CH-8092 Zurich, Switzerland

ABSTRACT

Large arrays of small disks are providing an attractive approach for high performance I/O systems. They allow for low-cost, reliable storage and can achieve higher throughput compared to large disks. However, in order to make effective use of the commercially available architectures, it is necessary to develop intelligent software tools that allow automatic tuning of the disk arrays to varying workloads. In this paper we describe an integrated set of algorithms and the implementation of a file manager for automatic file partitioning and allocation and for load balancing on disk arrays. Our approach consists of modular building blocks that can be invoked independently of each other; thus, algorithms for file allocation and disk load balancing can be used regardless of whether striping is employed or not. Our heuristic method for file partitioning aims to determine the optimal striping unit of a file, depending on the access characteristics of the file and the overall workload. Our heuristic method for file allocation and load balancing deals with dynamically changing access frequencies of files by reallocating file extents, thus "cooling down" hot disks. In addition, the method takes into account the fact that some files exhibit periodical access patterns, and considers explicitly the cost of performing the cooling operations.

1 INTRODUCTION

Large arrays of small disks (also known as RAIDs) provide an attractive alternative over large disks in terms of cost, volume and power [8,12,19]. In addition, disk arrays provide the potential for high performance I/O by exploiting the bandwidth of several disks to service a single logical request or multiple independent requests in parallel. High data reliability can be achieved through techniques that introduce data redundancy by using error-correcting codes or variations of mirroring [7,10,16]. Disk array technology is rapidly evolving in the commercial market as indicated by a number of products and product plans of startup companies (e.g., Maximum Strategy, Array Technology), as well as those of major computer vendors [11,15].

1.1 Disk Array Architectures

In principle, we can distinguish three types of disk array architectures [11,12]. In a *synchronous* disk array [21], all disks are synchronized with respect to spindle rotation and arm movement. Thus, the disk array appears as a single logical disk with increased bandwidth (i.e., data transfer rate), since all disks can transfer data in parallel. The increased hardware complexity of this architecture pays off only for requests that are large enough to benefit from the increased transfer rate. Thus, typical applications for synchronous disk arrays are in the supercomputing area.

An *asynchronous* disk array is very similar to a synchronized one, except that there is no hardware support for spindle synchronization. Here again the disk array is used as a single logical disk, and all disks are involved in servicing an I/O request.

In a *loosely coupled* disk array, each disk can be accessed individually by the operating system. Thus, a loosely coupled disk array can service many independent I/O requests in parallel, in order to improve the throughput of the I/O requests; alternatively a subset of the disks can service a single request in parallel, in order to decrease the transfer time of a request. This architecture is similar to conventional multi-disk systems (also known as disk farms). However, loosely coupled disk arrays are based on inexpensive small disks and standardized channel architectures (e.g., SCSI-2, HIPPI) rather than high-end technology and proprietary interconnections.

In our work, we assume that the operating system can access disks individually; hence our algorithms for automatic tuning of data placement are applicable to both disk arrays with loosely coupled disks and to disk farms.

1.2 I/O Parallelism

In order to effectively exploit the potential for I/O parallelism in a disk array, files must be partitioned and distributed across disks. File striping or declustering [13,14,19,20] is a technique for file organization which divides a file into runs of logically consecutive blocks (called "stripes") which are then spread across a number of disks in order to reduce the transfer time of a single request or to improve the throughput for multiple requests. The striping unit denotes the number of logically consecutive data blocks stored per disk, and the degree of declustering of a file denotes the number of disks over which a file is spread.

The degree to which the potential I/O parallelism of a disk array can be effectively exploited in an application depends on the placement of the application's data. The partitioning of a file determines the degree of parallelism in servicing a single request to the file, and the allocation of the file partitions onto disks determines the load balance in the array. Finally, the degree of intra-request parallelism and the load balancing together determine the throughput and the effective speed-up of requests.

1.3 Outline of the Paper

The paper presents our approach to automatic tuning of data placement for loosely coupled disk arrays. Section 2 discusses the heuristic methods that we have developed for partitioning files so as to exploit I/O parallelism and for allocating file partitions so as to balance the load across all disks of the array. Section 3 generalizes the load balancing method by considering predictable as well as unpredictable dynamic changes of access characteristics. Finally, Section 4 briefly discusses extensions of our work to include global file reorganizations and application-based data partitioning.

2 AUTOMATIC TUNING OF DATA PLACEMENT

The goal of our research on I/O parallelism is to develop algorithms and to build system software (i.e., a file manager and a low-level storage manager for advanced database systems) that can effectively exploit loosely coupled disks. Since the performance of a disk array depends critically on the placement of data, we have especially investigated algorithms for tuning the placement of files towards the workload characteristics of an application.

In principle, the data placement problem can be viewed as a file assignment problem, which has been intensively studied in many variants and is known to be NP-hard. Hence, viable solutions must be based on a heuristic approach. In the ample work reported on the file assignment problem [5,25] such heuristics have been investigated only for the static case, that is, when all files are to be allocated at the same time and the access characteristics of the files are completely known in advance. Also, the issue of I/O parallelism in servicing a single request has been disregarded so far. In advanced data-intensive applications such as object-oriented database systems or multimedia storage servers, data placement methods must take into account the potential performance gains of intra request parallelism as well as its overhead and deal with dynamic file allocations and deletions, with expansions or shrinkage of files, and with unpredictable changes in the access characteristics of existing files. Moreover, since the tuning of data placement should be automated and incorporated into the file manager or database system, practically viable algorithms for file partitioning and allocation must be invoked dynamically at low execution costs.

We have developed such a low-overhead heuristic method for tuning the placement of files on a disk array or conventional multi-disk system [23,24]. This method consists of a file partitioning algorithm based on striping and a file allocation algorithm which aims to ensure good load balancing. The main properties of these two components are outlined in Subsections 2.1 and 2.2; the benefits and potential applications of our approach as well as a brief discussion of a performance evaluation are summarized in Subsection 2.3.

2.1 Data Partitioning based on File Striping

Our approach to file partitioning is based on striping. In a striped file system, the striping unit must be chosen carefully, as it determines both the degree of intra-request parallelism and the parallelism of independent requests. A large striping unit tends to cluster a file on one disk, so that no intra-request parallelism would be exploited. A small striping unit, on the other hand, increases the total amount of device-busy time that is consumed for servicing a request, because a single request of relatively small size utilizes multiple disk arms [1]. In this case, striping severely limits the maximum achievable throughput of requests.

In virtually all disk array architectures or disk-array-based file systems that have been developed or proposed so far, the striping unit is chosen globally, that is, uniformly for all files. In [2] a heuristic method is proposed to determine the striping unit of a disk array, based on the application's throughput requirements, i.e., knowledge of the average request size and the expected multiprogramming level (in a closed queueing model). This method seems to be suitable for applications such as scientific data repositories or pure on-line transaction processing (OLTP), in which all files have approximately the same sort of access characteristics (i.e., only large requests or only single-block requests). However, it seems that a global striping unit is inappropriate if the access characteristics of files are highly diverse within a single application, for example, in a combined OLTP/batch environment, in an object-oriented or extended relational database system, or in a multimedia storage manager (e.g., for office document filing).

We have designed and built a multi-disk file system prototype, called FIVE[1] [23], in which the striping unit can be chosen individually for each file or even portions of a file, so that files with different average request sizes can be treated differently. An example of such file-specific striping units is shown in Figure 1. Our system allows relatively small striping units for files with very large request sizes and/or critical response time constraints, while using very coarse striping units for other files or even not striping other files at all because of throughput considerations [8]. Moreover, the capability to deal with file-specific striping units is of great advantage if the workload characteristics of the application change over time. In this case, some files (e.g., the most frequently accessed files or the files with the most critical response time) can be individually restriped without having to unload and reload the entire file system.

We have developed a simple analytic model for heuristically determining the optimal striping unit and degree of declustering of a new file, based on an estimate of the file's average request size. The algorithm chooses a degree of parallelism that minimizes the response time of requests subject to the constraint that the achievable throughput of the array is at least as high as the application's arrival rate of requests. The striping unit and the degree of declustering of the file are then derived from this optimal

[1]FIVE stands for FIle system with adaptiVe Enhancements.

number of related statistics: the heat of extents and disks, where the heat is defined as the sum of the number of block accesses of an extent or disk over a certain period of time, and the temperature of extents, which is defined as the ratio between heat and size.

A simple but effective heuristic algorithm for the static allocation problem, where all files are to be allocated at the same time and the heat of each extent is known or can be estimated in advance, is discussed in [3]. The algorithm first sorts all extents by descending heat, and extents are allocated in this sort order. For each extent allocation, the algorithm selects the disk with the lowest accumulated heat among the disks that have not yet been assigned another extent of the degree of parallelism. This heuristic method for tuning the striping units of files is illustrated in Figure 2. An experimental study [24] indicates that file-specific striping units as determined by our method can significantly improve performance compared to the best possible global striping unit.

2.2 Data Allocation and Load Balancing

Having decided to decluster a file over a particular number of disks, all striping units of the file that would be mapped to the same disk are combined into a single allocation unit called an extent. We then have to select the disks on which the file extents are actually placed. When the various files have different access patterns, an intelligent decision is crucial for disk load balancing. Our system keeps track of a same file.

We have extended this greedy algorithm so as to deal with dynamic allocations. In [23] we have developed a class of disk selection algorithms which provide a good compromise between access time minimization, load balancing and extra I/Os due to partial reorganization. Partial disk reorganization may have to be performed if due to file additions and deletions there is room to store a file on a disk, but the space is not contiguous. At one end of our spectrum of disk selection algorithms, we have the option to select the

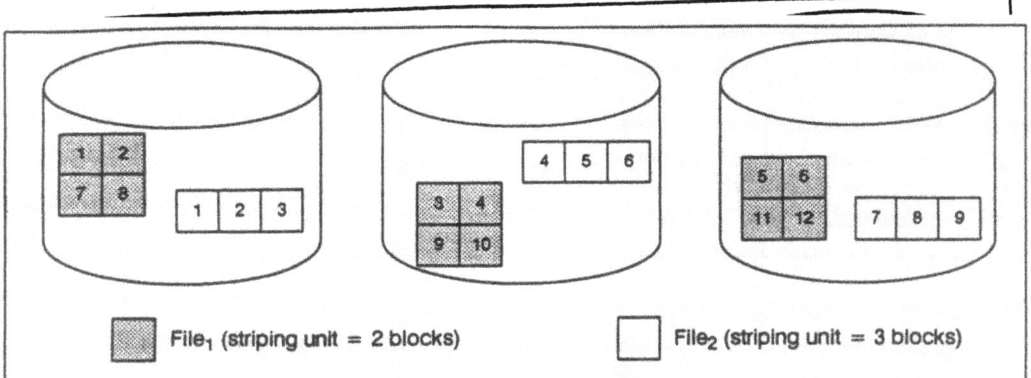

Figure 1: File-specific striping units

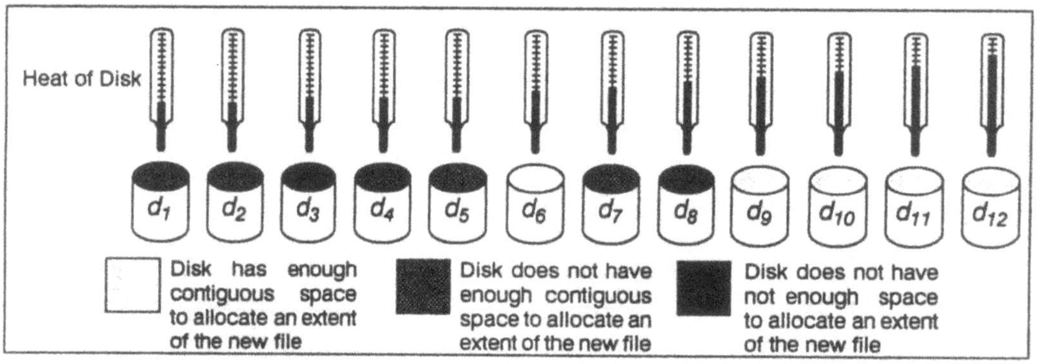

Figure 2: Example of heat and free-space distribution of a disk array

Figure 2: Example of heat and free-space distribution of a disk array

disks in increasing heat order without regard to reorganization costs. At the other end of the spectrum, we may select the disks in multiple passes, where in the first pass we choose only disks which have enough contiguous space. Our algorithms are geared towards a dynamic environment where not only entire files can be added or deleted on request, but also existing files may expand or shrink.

As an example, consider the disk array and the heat distribution shown in Figure 3, and assume that a new file with a degree of declustering of 8 is to be allocated; the file consists of 8 extents that are to be placed on 8 different disks. If on-line reorganizations are acceptable, then our algorithm would select the disks d_1 through d_8, i.e., the 8 coolest disks. This would incur partial disk compactions on disks d_1, d_2, d_4, d_5, and d_7; in order to allocate the extents on disks d_3 and d_8, sufficient free space would have to be reclaimed on these two disks by reallocating one or more of their coolest extents onto another disk or by migrating them to tertiary storage (e.g., optical disks or automatic cassette archives). If, on the other hand, on-line reorganizations are to be avoided at any cost, then our algorithm would select the disks $d_6, d_9, d_{10}, d_{11}, d_{12}, d_1, d_2, d_4$ (in this order). In this case, the load (im)balance in the array would become worse if the newly allocated file turned out to be frequently accessed; however, the allocation of the new file would incur relatively low reorganization costs.

If a certain disk is selected for allocation in a given strategy due to space or access time constraints, our algorithms also allow the invocation of a dynamic load balancing step, called disk cooling. This is basically a greedy algorithm which removes from the disk a number of extents in decreasing order of temperature and places them on the coolest disks which do not yet hold extents of the corresponding files. The temperature metric is used as the criterion for selecting the extents that are to be reallocated, because temperature reflects the benefit/cost ratio of a reallocation since benefit is proportional to heat (i.e., reduction of heat) and cost is proportional to size (of the reallocated extents). In our current file system prototype, disk cooling is automatically invoked whenever significant load imbalances are detected in the disk array at allocation or deallocation time.

2.3 Application and Evaluation of the Method

The developed heuristic method for file partitioning, file allocation, and dynamic load balancing has the following salient properties:

- It consists of modular building blocks that can be invoked independently; in particular, the algorithm for file allocation and disk load balancing can be used regardless of whether striping is employed or not.
- It can take into account explicitly specified constraints on data placement for recovery, security and other administrative purposes.
- It uses simple but effective heuristics that incur only little overhead.
- Its constituent algorithms can be invoked on-line, i.e., concurrently with regular requests to existing files.
- It is beneficial for a variety of application classes, including on-line transaction processing (OLTP), relational database systems, object oriented database systems, network file servers, multimedia applications, and scientific applications.
- It is mostly motivated by the evolving disk array technology; however, it is applicable to all sorts of multi-disk architectures.

2.3.1 Performance evaluation

The algorithms for file partitioning, file allocation, and dynamic load balancing are implemented in an experimental file system prototype [23]. After a successful performance evaluation based on synthetic workloads [23,24], we performed a comprehensive evaluation, based on I/O traces from the OLTP system of a large Swiss bank (Union Bank of Switzerland).

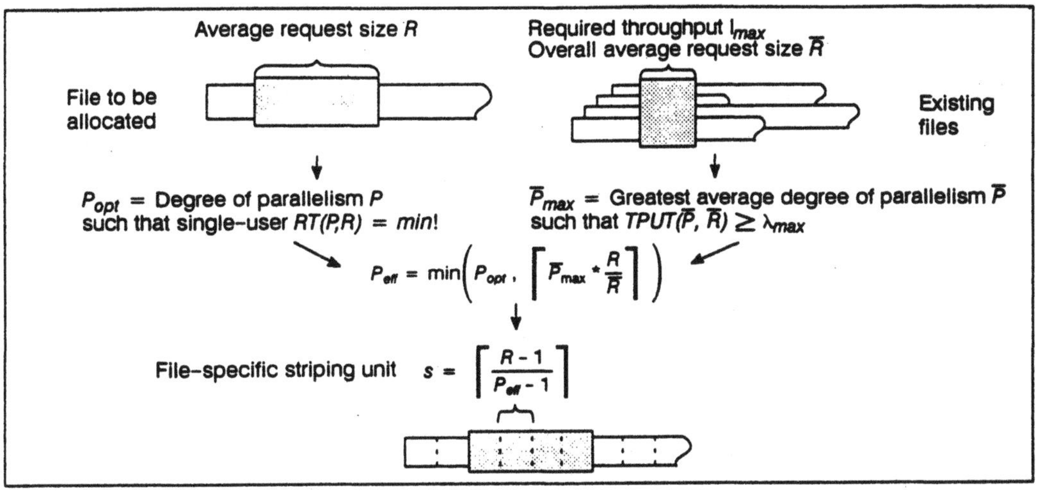

Figure 3: Method to determine the striping unit of a file

Due to the static nature of this application (new files are allocated only twice a year) and the homogeneous workload with respect to the size of the I/O requests (almost all requests were one block in size), the most important issue in this study was that of load balancing.

The on-line database of the bank consists of more than 150 files with a total size of about 23 GBytes. The I/O trace recorded more than 550000 I/O requests to these files. In our performance study, we assumed a priori knowledge of the heat and the average request size of the files. This information, which is relatively stable in the underlying OLTP system, was obtained by pre-analyzing the trace.

We compared three different allocation heuristics using a simulated disk array with 48 disks of capacity 0.5 GBytes each. *Space-balancing* is a heuristic that selects the disk with the largest available space for allocating a file partition. *Round-robin* allocates the file partitions in a circular manner, and thus balances the number of disk partitions per disk. *Heat-balancing* selects the disk with the lowest accumulated heat.

We combined these allocation strategies with four different striping methods. The first two striping methods were global ones, i.e., the striping unit was chosen to be the same for all files: one block (8KB) or one cylinder (55 blocks of 8 KB each), given that the average request size in our environment was a block. The third method employed file-specific striping units that were chosen using the heuristic method of Section 2.1. Finally, the last method did not use striping at all, i.e., each file was allocated to one disk.

Table 1 shows the average response time of an I/O request (in milliseconds) at an average arrival rate of 1100 requests per second. The heat-balancing approach is the clear winner, regardless of the striping method. Heat-balancing outperformed the other two allocation methods by more than 30 %. This shows that striping alone (i.e., combined with a very simple allocation heuristic like Round-robin) does not guarantee good load balancing.

Without striping, however, we observed a disastrous response time degradation. In the case with no striping, we had to reduce the arrival rate of the requests by a factor of 5; with the original arrival rate, the system was not able to handle the load. In this case, the disks with the hottest files became a premature bottleneck and limited the performance of the disk array. So file partitioning seems to be necessary to obtain a sufficient number of allocation units to be distributed by the heat-balancing heuristic.

With a striping unit of one block, the system performed slightly better compared to a striping unit of one cylinder. This effect was due to the fact that the distribution of block access frequencies was heavily skewed within files. Block striping did a better job on distributing the hot partitions of files across multiple disks, and thus achieved much better load balancing than the cylinder striping method. The file-specific striping method performed only slightly better than a global striping unit of one block, since most requests were single-block requests. However, for particular files with few but large requests, file-specific striping achieved significant performance gains.

The load balancing achieved by the various allocation heuristics is directly reflected in the disk utilization of the array, as summarized in Table 2 (with a striping unit of one block).

3 GENERALIZED LOAD BALANCING

Our original framework[23] allowed for the various files to have different access patterns, but the access pattern of a given file was considered fixed in time. In practice, however, this is not the case, rather we encounter many environments in which the heat of the files changes over time, and, further, some files exhibit a periodical pattern of heat changes. Under these con-

Table 1: Average response time [msec] for different allocation and striping methods

	Allocation Method		
Striping Method	Space-balancing	Round-Robin	Heat-balancing
Cylinder (440 KB)	63	61	41
Block (8 KB)	45	44	31
File-specific	41	42	30
No Striping	(408)	(110)	(70)

Table 2: Disk utilization for different allocation methods

	Disk utilization [%]			
Allocation Method	Min	Avg	Max	Standard deviation
Space-balancing	44.8	50.2	62.6	0.04
Round-robin	43.2	50.1	61.2	0.03
Heat-balancing	43.1	44.1	44.8	0.004

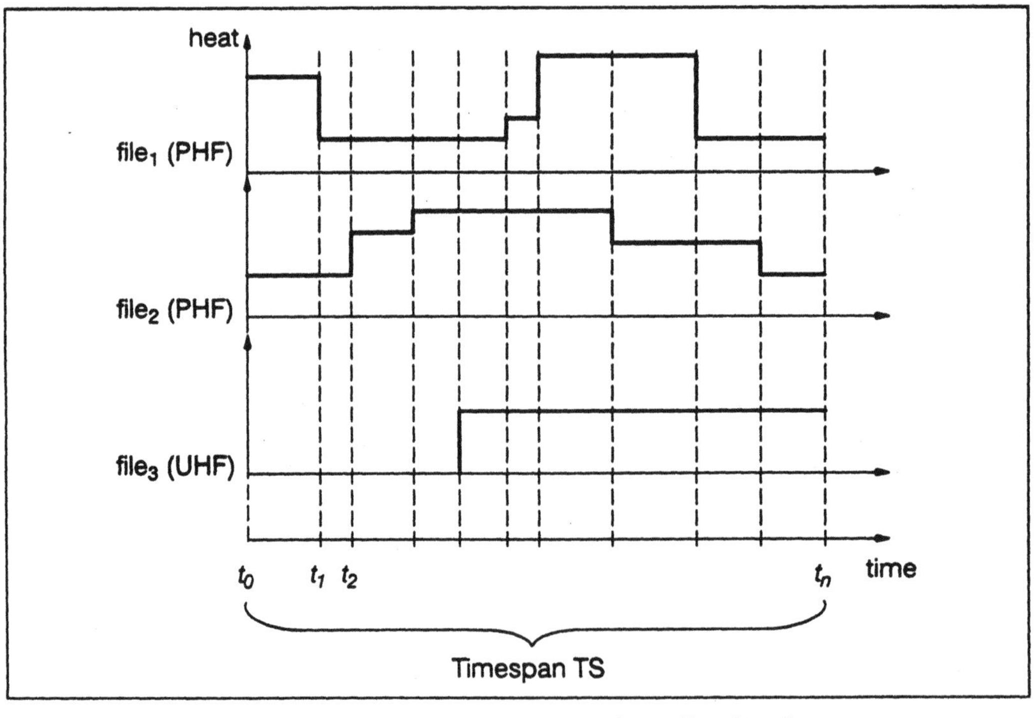

Figure 4: Temporal heat changes of predictable-heat and unpredictable-heat files

ditions, load balancing needs to be performed even if no striping is used, i.e., the files are allocated in their entirety to a single disk. Thus, it becomes necessary to invoke a generalized disk cooling procedure periodically, not only at file allocation time. We also need to consider explicitly the cost of performing the cooling, which was not included in our earlier model, as well as use a generalized objective function which represents the variance of the disk array heat over a certain interval of time.

We distinguish between Predictable Heat Files (PHF), which exhibit a periodical heat pattern over a given cycle, and Unpredictable Heat Files (UHF), for which we can observe only the current heat. The optimization time span, TS, of the load balancing procedure can be chosen, as shown in Figure 4, as the maximum cycle of all the cycles of the PHFs. The union of the points in time where the individual PHFs change heat patterns induces a partition of TS into n time intervals. Thus, more formally we can define TS as the vector : $TS = [(t_1 - t_0), (t_2 - t_1), ...(t_n - t_{n-1})]$ and denote by interval j the interval of length $(t_j - t_{j-1})$. Let us also denote by $H(i,j)$ the heat of disk i in interval j. Correspondingly, the weighted disk heat of disk i over the time span TS is defined as:

$$WDH(i,TS) = \sum_{j=1}^{n} H(i,j) * (t_j - t_{j-1}).$$

The objective cost function to be minimized by our generalized load balancing procedure is the Weighted Disk Heat Variance (WDHV) over the time span TS:

$$WDHV(H,TS) = \sum_{j=1}^{n}\sum_{i=1}^{D} (\bar{H}(j) - H(i,j))^2 * (t_j - t_{j-1})$$

where H is a matrix whose element in position (i,j) is $H(i,j)$

D = number of disks in the array

$\bar{H}(j) = \sum_{i=1}^{D} H(i,j)/D$

We will consider a number of heuristic strategies for generalized disk cooling. In a serial strategy, we will determine a sequence of beneficial actions to be executed immediately. Let us define an action as a record type with the following components:

```
type action = Record
        extent: Record
                no: extent-id;
                size : no-of-blocks;
                heat: access-frequency;
               End;
        origin : disk-no;
        target : disk-no;
        read:    Record
                begin: point-of-time;
                duration: time-interval
               End;
        write:   Record
                begin: point-of-time;
                duration: time-interval
               End;
      End;
```

Our algorithm is basically a greedy procedure that for each consecutive action determines the extent to be removed (action.extent), by picking the disk with the highest weighted heat (action.origin) and then choosing the extent with the highest weighted temperature. We then determine to which disk the extent should be moved (action.target), by choosing the disk with the lowest weighted heat subject to some constraint. Let us denote by $WDHV'$ the weighted disk heat variance over the time span TS after a given action is executed:

$$WDHV'(H,T,action) = \sum_{j=1}^{n}\sum_{i=1}^{D} (\bar{H}^*(j) - H^*(i,j))^2 * (t_j - t_{j-1})$$

where $H^*(i,j) = H(i,j)$ if i $\neq$ action.target or action.origin

$H^*(i,j) = H(i,j)$ + action.extent.heat if i = action.target

$H^*(i,j) = H(i,j)$ - action.extent.heat if i = action.origin

A high level version of the Generalized Disk Cooling algorithm (GDC) is given in Figure 5. In order to determine whether a given action is beneficial or not we have to consider not only the reduction in heat on the origin disk and the addition in heat on the target disk, but also the additional heat caused by the reorganization process itself as shown in Figure 6a. The cooling process is executed during two intervals of time, the first corresponding to the read phase of the action and the second corresponding to the write phase of the action. The read and write phases introduce an amount of additional of heat on the origin and target disks which is computed by dividing the size of the extent to be moved by the corresponding duration of the phase.

The duration times of the read and write phases of an action can be calculated by making use of an M/G/1 queueing model with a non-preemptive prioritized server. We consider that our system consists of requests with two priorities: regular user requests have high priority, while the cooling requests have low priority. Cooling requests represent the read/write phases of the cooling actions. Let L_c denote the proportion of disk utilization due to cooling requests and L_r the proportion of disk utilization due to regular requests. Then, RT_c, the response time of a cooling request with a non-preemptive server is given by [9]:

Generalized Disk Cooling Algorithm (GDC)
Input : D – number of disks
Matrix H – $H(i,j)$ is heat of disk D_i in interval j;
Matrix T – $T(k,j)$ is the temperature of extent e_k in interval j
Vector TS – intervals of time span;
t_{cur} – current point in life cycle;
Output : actions-to-do–list of cooling actions;
benefit = true;
actions-to-do = empty;
start-next-action= t_{cur};
While benefit =true do
Step 0 : If trigger-condition = true then execute remaining steps;
Step 1 : Choose new extent and origin disk:
action.origin = the disk with the highest weighted heat;
action.extent.no = the extent on action.origin with the highest weighted temperature;
Step 2 : Choose new target disk:
action.target = the disk with the lowest weighted heat such that this disk does not hold already an extent of the file to which action.extent belongs;
Step 3: Estimate the cooling time:
action.read.begin = the point in time at which the read phase of the cooling action will start = start-next-action;
action.read.duration = the time it takes to read action.extent from action.origin into memory
action.write.begin = start-next-action + action.read.duration
action.write.duration = the time it takes to write action.extent onto action.target
Step 4 : Determine the intervals m and n when action.read.begin and action.write.begin occur;
Step 5: Calculate E, the Extra-Weighted Disk Heat Variance due to action:

$$E = \sum_{i=1}^{D} (\bar{H}'(m) - H'(i,m))^2 * \text{action.read.duration} + \sum_{i=1}^{D} (\bar{H}''(n) - H''(i,n))^2 * \text{action.write.duration};$$

Step 6: Compute $WDHV$, the current weighted disk heat variance, and $WDHV'$, the weighted disk heat variance if action is to be executed ;
Step 7: If $WDHV$ - $(WDHV' + E) >$ Epsilon
then
add action to actions-to-do
start-next-action = start-next-action + action.read.duration + action.write.duration
else benefit = false;
endwhile

Figure 5: GDC algorithm

$$RT_c = \frac{kLT}{(1-L)(1-L_r)} + T_c$$

where L is the total disk utilization ($L = L_c + L_r$), T is the average service time for requests of both priorities, T_c is the average service time for cooling requests and k denotes the time to finish the current request when a new one arrives. The distribution coefficient of the service time, k, is given by the Khintchine and Pollaczek equation as $k = \frac{1}{2} * \frac{E(T^2)}{T^2}$.

In an open queueing model, L_r, the disk utilization due to regular requests, can be calculated as : $L_r = T_r * \lambda_r$, where T_r is the average service time for regular requests and λ_r is the corresponding arrival rate. If we assume that the cooling request is currently performed on disk i and that it occurs during time interval m, then λ_r can be computed by using the formula:

$$\lambda_r = \frac{H(i,m)}{\bar{R}}$$ where $\bar{R}$ is the average request size.

Since cooling requests do not have an observable arrival rate, we shall estimate λ_c by the following upper bound :

$$\lambda_c \leq \frac{1}{(optimal\ service\ time\ for\ avg\ cooling\ request)}$$

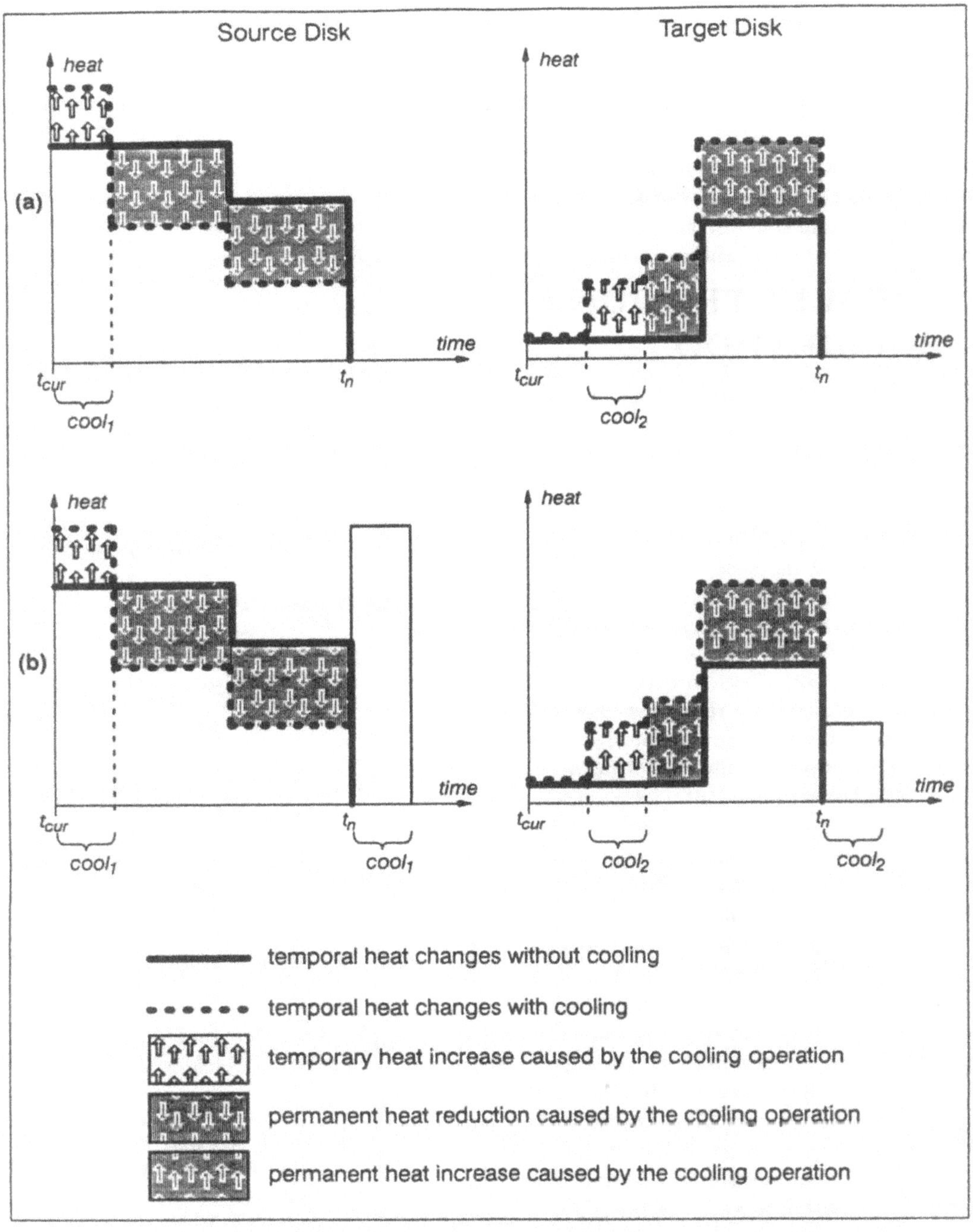

Figure 6: (a) Cost and benefit of cooling
(b) adjustment of weighted heat variance

In step 4 of the GDC algorithm we compute E, the Extra-Weighted Disk Heat Variance, by making use of the following approximation technique. In order to avoid splitting the current time interval, and possibly the next one (see Figure 6a), and thus incurring expensive recalculations of $WDHV$, we add two "dummy" intervals to the load balancing cycle to account for the two cooling phases of the action, as shown in Figure 6b. During such a dummy interval the heat of each disk, except for the disk which is the subject of the cooling operation, is taken to be the same as the heat of the disk during the time interval when the corresponding cooling process started. Thus, the extra contributions to the $WDHV$ are computed as given below:

$H'(i,j)= H(i,j)$+action.extent.size/action.read.duration
for i = action.origin
$H'(i,j) = H(i,j)$ otherwise
$H''(i,j)=H(i,j)$+action.extent.size/action.write.duration
for i = action.target
$H''(i,j) = H(i,j)$ otherwise.

We are currently implementing the GDC algorithm in our FIVE system [23] and we will perform comprehensive experiments with various synthetic and real workloads. We plan to investigate when to trigger this cooling procedure and whether the time span TS for the optimization should be equal to the maximum life cycle of the PHFs or shorter. We also will develop and experiment with a parallel disk cooling algorithm where extents can be removed or allocated in parallel, subject to certain constraints with regard to the amount of buffer space available in memory.

4 FURTHER EXTENSIONS OF OUR METHOD

4.1 Global File Reorganization and Restriping

Due to dynamic growth and shrinkage, some files may end up having multiple extents on the same disk. A global file reorganization procedure could then be invoked in order to improve the seek time by reallocating the multiple extents of the file(s) that reside on the same disk such as to achieve physical proximity, similar to the procedure used for record clustering in [18]. However, a more cost effective reason for a reorganization may be dictated by restriping needs. If it is determined that the average request size of a file changes over time, then the file should be reallocated with a different striping unit and/or different degree of declustering in order to improve the response time or to meet the application's throughput requirements. Since our file allocation strategy assigns different striping units and degrees of declustering to individual files, the restriping can be done on a file basis, thus allowing the reorganization process to run concurrently with user transactions [17]. When dealing with large disks, the reorganization often is performed in place due to space restrictions [22]. As opposed to this approach, we are investigating a restriping algorithm that always attempts to choose new disks for the reallocation in order to achieve the maximum degree of parallelism between the read and write phases of the reorganization and to maintain a good load balancing. We plan to study how the original file allocation algorithm proposed in [23] can be incorporated in the restriping procedure in order to account for the various free-space states of a disk.

4.2 Application-based Declustering

So far, our work has concentrated on partitioning at the block level. This is generally a feasible approach since all data types are ultimately mapped into block-structured files. However, further performance gains may be obtained by employing partitioning schemes that are directly based on the application's data types. For example, in a relational database system, tables can be partitioned into fragments based on attribute values by applying a hash function or by range-partitioning the domain of the corresponding attribute [4,6,14]. In applications that deal with complex objects (e.g., CAD or office information systems), a variety of partitioning schemes need to be considered based on the various access patterns. In addition, in some of these applications the partitioning is subject to real-time constraints dictated by visualization requirements (e.g, multimedia applications, scientific data repositories).

We plan to investigate such application-based partitioning schemes and to develop heuristics for optimal partitioning of complex objects and sets of complex objects. Furthermore, we intend to develop appropriate mapping strategies from application-based partitioning schemes to our block-level partitioning scheme. We note here that our method for data allocation and disk load balancing consists of flexible generic procedures that can be used with any application-based partitioning scheme.

References

[1] Bitton, D. and Gray,J.N.,"Disk shadowing," Proc 14th International Conference on Very Large Databases, 1988, pp. 331-338.

[2] Chen, P.M., and Patterson, D.A.," Maximizing Performance in a Striped Disk-Array," Proceedings of the 17th International Symposium on Computer Architecture, 1990, pp. 322-331.

[3] Copeland, G., Alexander, W., Boughter E., and Keller, T., "Data Placement in Bubba," Proc. ACM International Conference on Management of Data, 1988, pp. 99-108.

[4] DeWitt, D.J., and Gray, J.N., "Parallel Database Systems," ACM SIGMOD Record, Vol. 19, No. 4, 1990.

[5] Dowdy, L.W., and Foster, D.V.," Comparative Models of the File Assignment Problem," ACM Computing Surveys, Vol. 14, No. 2, June 1982, pp. 95-121.

[6] Ghandeharizadeh, S., and DeWitt, D.J., "Hybrid-Range Partitioning Strategy: A New Declustering Strategy for Multiprocessor Database Machines," Proc. 16th International Conference on Very Large Data Bases, 1990, pp. 481-492.

[7] Gibson, G.A., Hellerstein, L., Karp, R.M., Katz, R.H. and Patterson, D.A., "Failure Correction Techniques for Large Disk Arrays", Proc. Third ACM Intern. Conf., on Architectural Support for Programming Languages and Operating Systems, 1989, pp. 123-132.

[8] Gray, J.N., Horst B., and Walker, M., "Parity Striping of Disc Arrays: Low-Cost Reliable

Storage with Acceptable Throughput," Proc. 16th International Conference on Very Large Data Bases, 1990, pp. 148-161.

[9] Highleyman, W., Performance Analysis of Transaction Processing Systems, Prentice Hall, 1989.

[10] Hsiao, H. and DeWitt, D.J., "Chained Declustering: A New Availability Strategy for Multiprocessor Database Machines," Proc. Sixth IEEE International Conference on Data Engineering, 1990, pp. 456-465.

[11] Katz, R.H.," High Performance Network and Channel-based Storage," Sequoia 2000 Technical Report #91/2, University of California at Berkeley, 1991.

[12] Katz, R.H., Gibson, G.A., and Patterson, D.A., "Disk System Architectures for High Performance Computing", Proc. of the IEEE, Vol. 77, No. 12, 1989, pp. 1842-1858.

[13] Kim, M.Y.,"Synchronized Disk Interleaving," IEEE Transactions on Computers, Vol. C-35, No. 11, 1986, pp. 978-988.

[14] Livny, M., Khoshafian, S., and Boral, H., "Multi-Disk Management Algorithms," ACM SIGMETRICS Conference, 1987, pp. 69-77.

[15] Moad, J.,"Relief for Slow Storage Systems," Datamation, September 1, 1990.

[16] Muntz, R.R. and Lui, J.C.,"Performance Analysis of Disk Arrays Under Failure," Proc. 16th International Conference on Very large Databases, 1990, pp. 162-173.

[17] Omiecinski, E., Lei, L. and Scheuermann, P.," Concurrent File Reorganization for Record Clustering: A Performance Study," Proc. Eight International Conference on Data Engineering, 1992, pp. 265-272.

[18] Omiecinski, E. and Scheuermann, P.,"A Parallel Algorithm for Record Clustering," ACM Transactions on Database Systems, Vol. 15, No, 9, December 1990, pp. 569-624.

[19] Patterson, D.A., Gibson, G., and Katz, R.H., "A Case for Redundant Arrays of Inexpensive Disks (RAID)," Proc. ACM SIGMOD International Conference on Management of Data, 1988, pp. 109-116.

[20] Salem, K., and Garcia-Molina, H.,"Disk Striping," Proc. Second International Conference on Data Engineering, 1986, pp. 336-342.

[21] Sierra, H.M., An Introduction to Direct Access Storage Devices, Academic Press, San Diego, CA, 1990

[22] Scheuermann, P., Park, Y.C. and Omiecinski, E., "A Heuristic File Reorganization Algorithm based on Record Clustering," BIT, Vol.29, 1989, pp. 428-437.

[23] Weikum, G., Zabback, P., and Scheuermann, P., "Dynamic File Allocation in Disk Arrays," Proc. ACM SIGMOD International Conference on Management of Data, 1991, pp. 406-415 (extended version available as: Technical Report No. 147, Computer Science Dept., ETH Zurich, 1990).

[24] Weikum, G., and Zabback, P., "Tuning of Striping Units in Disk-Array-Based File Systems," Proc. Second International Workshop on Research Issues on Data Engineering: Transaction and Query Processing (RIDE-TQP), 1992, pp. 80-87

[25] Wolf, J., "The Placement Optimization Program: A Practical Solution to the Disk File Assignment Problem," Proc. ACM SIGMETRICS and Performance'89 International Conference on Measurement and Modeling of Computer Systems, Berkeley, 1989, pp. 1-10.

IMPLEMENTATION OF A PARALLEL QUERY PROCESSING SYSTEM SUPPORTING APPLICATION-SPECIFIC DATABASE OPERATIONS

Yasushi KIYOKI, Takahiro KUROSAWA, Peng LIU
Institute of Information Sciences and Electronics
University of Tsukuba, Tsukuba, Ibaraki 305, JAPAN
E-MAIL: kiyoki@is.tsukuba.junet

Kazuhiko KATO, Takashi MASUDA
Department of Information Science, Faculty of Science
University of Tokyo, 7-3-1 Hongo, Bunkyo-ku 113, Tokyo, JAPAN

Abstract

This paper presents an implementation method of a parallel query processing system using our proposed stream-oriented parallel processing scheme. This scheme is based on demand-driven evaluation incorporating stream processing and used to manipulate application-specific and/or user-defined database operations in parallel.

A primitive set has been designed as basic operators for implementing this scheme. Specific database operations for each database application can be described and executed in parallel by using these primitives. An implementation method of these primitives in the environments where message passing is used for interprocessor communication is presented. This method is used to realize stream-oriented parallel processing by message passing. This paper also shows several experimental results of actual query processing in a parallel processing environment where multiple conventional processors are loosely connected to a conventional high-speed network.

1 Introduction

Relational database systems usually support a fixed set of basic operations called relational database operations. For supporting database applications, such as knowledge bases and engineering applications, it is necessary to allow the database designers to specify new basic operations and data types, and to integrate them into the system. The key issue is to provide database designers with facilities to implement specific operations and data types and to enable them to be integrated into the system.

Furthermore, those operations should be executed efficiently. To enhance the processing performance of relational database operations, many algorithms and database machine architectures have been proposed (see e.g.,[2, 3]). In general, these algorithms and architectures have been designed to execute relational database operations efficiently. That is, these algorithms and architectures have been oriented for a fixed set of operations.

For supporting advanced database applications, database systems should have facilities to execute arbitrary database operations efficiently. We have proposed a stream-oriented parallel processing scheme(stream-oriented scheme) for basic operations of relational databases [4] and inference operations for deductive databases[5]. This scheme is based on the demand-driven evaluation[11, 12] incorporating stream processing. We have designed primitives as a set of basic facilities for implementing the stream-oriented scheme[4]. By using these primitives, database operations for a wide variety of database applications can be described and executed in parallel.

Two parallel processing environments are considered for implementing the stream-oriented parallel processing scheme as follows:

(1) Multiple conventional processors are connected to a conventional high-speed network. In this environment, message passing is performed to communicate stream elements and demands among multiple processors.

(2) Multiple processors are tightly connected through shared memory. In this environment, stream elements and demands are sent and received through shared memory that is allocated among multiple processors.

In this paper, we present an implementation method of the primitives in the environment (1). In this method, the communication between processors is performed by using the message passing mechanism. Furthermore, we show several experimental results and discuss the efficiency of our implementation method.

2 Stream-oriented parallel processing

2.1 The Stream-oriented scheme

In this section, the stream-oriented scheme described in [4] is briefly reviewed. In this scheme, demand-driven evaluation is used to exploit parallelism in processing queries for databases. Independent function nodes, which are allocated to different processors, are executed in parallel. Furthermore, the *stream-oriented parallelism* is also exploited between function nodes (e.g. relational operation nodes) which are served as producers and consumers of intermediate streams. A function node, which consumes intermediate stream, is referred to as a "consumer node", and a function node, which produces intermediate stream, is referred to as a "producer node".

When a consumer node completes the processing of a grain (or a page) of stream elements which corresponds to its input buffer size, the node issues a demand to the producer node in order to have the input buffer refilled with the next grain of stream elements.

When a producer node receives a demand from the consumer node, the consumer node accesses a grain of stream elements from its input buffer and it executes the computation until the node has completed the production of one grain of resulting stream elements in the output buffer. The output buffer is then useed as the input buffer for the consumer node. Once a grain is accessed by a consumer node, the grain can be removed from the buffer.

Not every function node creates a whole intermediate stream for a single demand. Each node creates only a single grain of stream elements for a single demand. Therefore, each buffer does not need to have a capacity for storing the whole intermediate stream, that is, the buffer size is not related to the size of the intermediate stream. The size of the buffer corresponds to grain size. The grain size differs among function nodes, that means, each grain size is fixed according to the size of the each buffer allocated to each function nodes.

If both the producer node and the consumer node of an intermediate stream are allocated to different processors, the double buffering mechanism is supported in a buffer between them, in order to exploit the stream-oriented parallelism.

In terms of references to the same stream, two reference methods named "re-computation method" and "caching method" are supported and used alternatively. In the re-computation method, if a stream is referenced more than once, the corresponding stream is reproduced each time it is referenced. In this case, each stream element can be deleted just after a reference to it is completed. If this method is employed, the computation to the stream can be performed within limited memory resources. However, when the same stream is referenced more than once, it must be reproduced, that is, the computation which produces the stream must be re-executed. On the other hand, in the caching method, a stream is produced only once when the first reference to it is performed. The produced stream is then used in the other references to the stream. In this method, the stream must be retained until every reference to it is completed. If the stream is huge, like a stream of tuples in a relation, it seems that the memory could be swamped. However, reproduction of the same stream is unnecessary.

2.2 Primitives

We have designed the primitives, as basic facilities to implement the stream-oriented scheme. A set of our primitives has been exploit parallelism inherent in arbitrary basic operations by incorporating the demand-driven evaluation with stream processing. In our system, an arbitrary basic operation is defined as a function, and the function is transformed into the procedural object codes which include primitives. A function activated at execution time is referred to as a function instance. Each function instance is allocated to one of the multiple processors, and parallel processing is then performed among function instances which are allocated to different processors.

Primitives are classified as follows:

(1) The creation of a function instance and a channel. (primitives: new , channel)

The primitive "new" creates a specified function instance on the specified processor. The primitive "channel" creates a channel, which connects to function instances to facilitate the passing and receiving of stream elements and demands between function instances. Every channel includes a buffer to store a grain of stream elements whose size is specified as "granularity".

(2) The sending and receiving of stream elements and demands. (primitives: get, put, send, receive, pre-demand)

There are two cases for transferring a stream between function instances ("f" and "g").

The first case is that the output stream of a function instance ("g" or "h") becomes the input stream of another function instance ("f") as an actual argument.

In this case, the primitive "get" is used in the consumer function ("f") to fetch a stream element from the buffer of the channel allocated between two function instances ("f" and "g"). When the buffer is vacant, this primitive issues a demand to the producer function ("g"). Then, it waits until the buffer is refilled with the next grain of stream elements. At this time, if the double-buffering mechanism is supported in the buffer, as discussed in section 2.1, and the next grain has already been produced due to the pre-issued demand, this primitive begins to fetch a stream element from the other area of the buffer. In this case, stream-oriented parallelism is exploited. When the producer function ("g") receives a demand, it stores a stream element in the buffer by using the primitive "put". Until the buffer is filled this primitive stores stream elements. Then, the primitive waits for its next demand.

The other case is that a function instance ("f") invokes another function instance ("g") in the function body by using the primitives "new" and "channel".

In this case, primitives "send" and "receive" are used in the function instance "f". In the function instance "f", to pass a stream element to the child function instance "g", the primitive "send" stores the stream element in the buffer. This primitive does not wait for the next demand when the buffer is filled with stream elements. Until the next demand arrives, this primitive does not store a stream element, that is, this primitive is ignored at the execution of the function instance "f". In the function instance "f", the primitive "receive" receives a stream element from the buffer as a part of a return value of the child function instance "g". When the buffer becomes vacant, this primitive issues a demand to the child function instance "g". However, at this time, this primitive does not wait for the next grain of stream elements. This primitive is ignored at the execution of function instance "f", until the next grain of stream elements is stored into the buffer by the child function instance.

The primitive "pre-demand" is used when the double buffering mechanism is supported in the buffer of a channel. In this case, stream-oriented parallelism is exploited between function instances which are allocated to different processors. For the producer function instance of a stream, this primitive is issued only once at the beginning of execution of the consumer function so as to have the producer function create the first grain of stream elements eagerly.

(3) The implementation of "re-computation method" and "caching method". (primitive: rewind)

As reference methods to the same stream, "re-computation method" and "caching method" are alternatively used in our system. In supporting the re-computation method, the primitive "rewind" is used to request the re-production of the stream to the producer function instance. This primitive initializes the producer function instance and the channel allocated between these function instances. If the caching method is specified, the re-computation of the stream is not necessary, but the intermediate stream elements must be stored in the caching directory to cope with the next references to the same stream.

(4) Nondeterministic selection of a single stream element from multiple streams. (primitives: select, disable, enable)

By using the concept of "nondeterminism", when a function instance sends and receives several streams and demands through channels, higher parallelism is exploited. That is, when the function instance sends and receives several streams and demands, a higher degree of parallelism can be exploited by choosing one of the demands or one of the streams in the nondeterministic way.

The primitive "select" chooses one of channels, which are connected to the function instance. In the case of this primitive not being supported, some primitives in the function instance may wait for the arrival of stream elements or a demand at a channel, which is not activated due to the delay of the arrival of stream elements. In this case, the execution of the function instance is suspended and, as a result, the parallelism may decrease.

The primitive "select" is used incorporating with the primitives "disable" and "enable". The primitive "disable" removes the specified channel from candidates for the nondeterministic selection. The primitive "enable" adds the specified channel to candidates for the nondeterministic selection.

3 An implementation method

In this section, we present an implementation method of the primitive operators. This method is thought of as being novel, for implementing parallel processing environments for databases by using multiple conventional processors connected to a general-purpose network. Using only conventional processors and networks, arbitrary basic operations for a wide variety of database applications can be executed in parallel.

In this method, communication of stream elements and demands is performed by using message-passing between function instances allocated to different sites. On the other hand, stream elements and demands are sent or received through the shared segment of a memory, between function instances which are allocated to the same site.

When several function instances are allocated to the same site, the stream-oriented scheme enables those function instances to be executed in pseudo parallel within limited buffer resources. Two approaches to implementation of a single site have been considered. First approach is based on the method that the function instances allocated to a single processor are activated and executed within a single process. In this approach, stream elements and demands are transferred within the single process. The kernel in the process manages the transition of control to one of executable function instances. We adopt this approach to the implementation of a single site. The other approach is based on the method that a single process is assigned to each function instance. In general, communication and switching among processes may cause overhead, because the transition of control is managed by the operating system. In this case, since stream elements and demands are transferred by communication and switching among processes, the overhead of communication and switching becomes unacceptable. Therefore, we do not employ this approach.

Each site consists of *a communication process (CP)* and *a functional computation process (FCP)* as shown in Fig. 1. At each site, only two processes are required to execute the basic operations and to communicate the stream elements and demands among the sites. Function instances and channels are created within the FCP. The message passing mechanism is implemented at CP to transfer stream elements and demands between the sites.

3.1 Kernel

A kernel is implemented at each site in order to manage communication among function instances, and to schedule the execution order of function instances that are allocated to a site. One kernel is provided for each site, and its facilities are separately implemented in FCP and CP as follows:

(1) creation of function instances.(FCP)

(2) creation of channels.(FCP)

(3) scheduling for pseudo parallel execution of function instances allocated to the single site.(FCP)

(4) control of interprocessor communication.(CP)

The interpretation of primitives, "new" and "channel", corresponds to (1) and (2), respectively. As (3), the kernel controls the execution of function instances which are allocated to the same site. In our implementation method, several function instances can be allocated to the same site. This allocation enables a query to be executed within the limited processor-resources, allowing the function instances in the same site to be executed in pseudo parallel as coroutines. The kernel obtains control when a producer function instance, which has completed producing a grain of stream elements, has suspended and is waiting for a next demand, or when a consumer function instance has suspended and is waiting for the next grain of stream elements. When the scheduler is activated by the kernel, it selects one of the executable function instances, and transfers control to it.

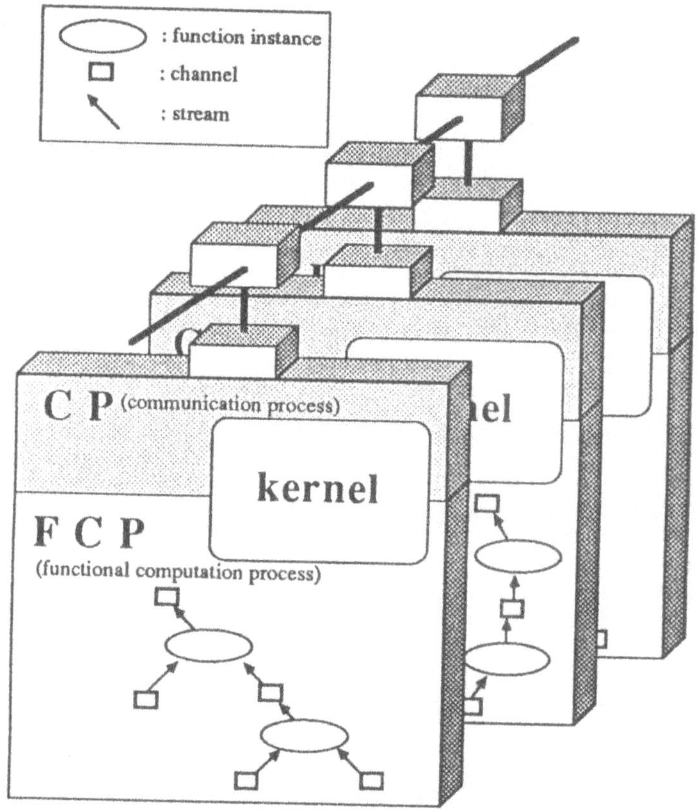

Figure 1: An overview of the system

In terms of (4), when function instances are allocated to different sites, the interprocessor communication is required to transfer demands and stream elements. At each site, for each interprocessor communication request, the kernel facility in the CP sends a grain of stream elements or a demand to the destination site through the network.

3.2 Function instance

Each function instance is sequentially executed, but parallelisms can be exploited among function instances. Each function instance receives one or several streams, and creates a stream as a return value. Stream elements and demands are transferred through a "channel" which is allocated between function instances.

Each function instance transits states as follows:

1. Executing State:
   This is the state that the function instance is executing. From this state, it transits to the waiting state when one of the following conditions occurs.
   (1) When the function instance completes producing a

grain of stream elements, it transits to the waiting state to wait for the next demand. In this case, the waiting state is called "Waiting for the next demand".

(2) When it completes consuming a grain of stream elements, it transits to the waiting state to wait for the next grain of stream elements. In this case, the waiting state is called "Waiting for the next grain of stream elements".

2. Waiting for the next demand:
When the function instance transits to the waiting state due to the condition (1), it waits for the next demand issued by its consumer function instance. When this function instance receives a demand, it transits to the Ready state.

3. Waiting for the next grain of stream elements:
When the function instance transits to the waiting state due to the condition (2), it waits for a grain of stream elements which has been produced by the producer function instance, after issuing the demand. In this state, when the function instance receives the grain, it transits to the Ready state.

4. Ready state:
If several function instances are allocated to the same site, the function instance transited from the waiting state cannot be always executed immediately. First, the function instance transits to the Ready state, but not to the Executing state. From the Ready state, the function instance, which has obtained control from the scheduler, transits to the Executing state. Each kernel includes a scheduler. Then, the scheduler searches for the function instances which are ready to be activated, and gives control to one of these function instances. Currently, round-robin scheduling is employed.

3.3 Channel

Function instances use a "channel" to transfer demands and stream elements between them, as shown in Fig. 2. The channel has a communication buffer for transferring grains of stream elements and demands. By using the channel, communication between function instances can be performed *transparently*. A channel has two main roles; one is to be the interface to a function instance as a "channel port", the other is to perform communication between channel ports in a single channel.

(1) channel port:
A channel port is the interface to a function instance. We call the channel port connected to the producer function instance *the producer channel port*. We call the channel port connected to the consumer function instance *the consumer channel port*. Each channel port is allocated to the site where the function instance, which is connected to it, is allocated. Communication between function instances is performed through the producer and consumer channel ports in a single channel according to requests of demand or data transfers.

(2) communication between channel ports:
When function instances connected to a channel are allocated to single site, or to different sites, they are executed in pseudo-parallel, or in parallel, respectively. The communication between producer and consumer channel ports is performed as follows:

(a) channel port communication within a single site:
When the producer and consumer channel ports are allocated to the same site, a shared segment of memory is used to communicate stream elements and demands as shown in Fig. 2-(a). In our method, since the function instances allocated to the same site behave as coroutines,

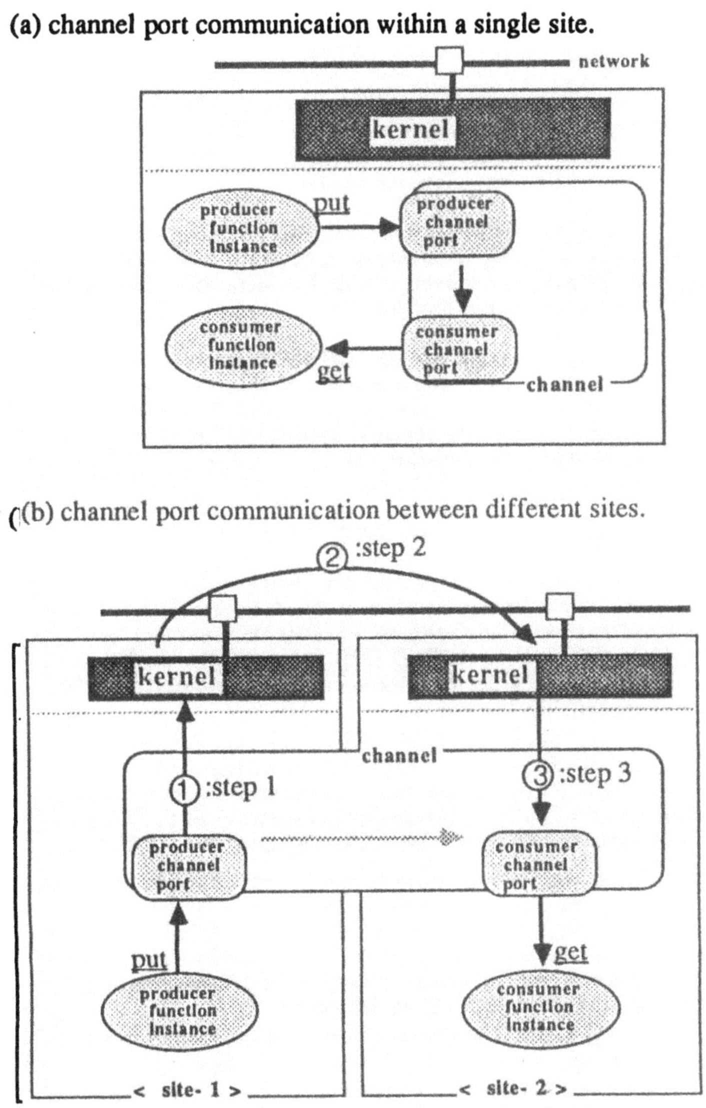

Figure 2: Communication between function instances

the execution and suspension of each function instance is managed under the control of a scheduler, thus the mutual exclusion can be performed. Accordingly, the accesses to the shared segment of memory by producer and consumer function instances are serialized and performed without conflict.

(b) channel port communication between different sites:
When the producer and consumer channel ports are allocated to different sites, message-passing is performed to communicate stream elements and demands. Stream elements and demands are transferred as message packets. The interprocessor communication is performed as shown in Fig. 2-(b).
step 1:
By the function instance in the FCP, stream elements and demands are stored in the shared segment of memory that has been allocated between the FCP and the CP. A large amount of data may be transferred between the FCP and the CP. Therefore, we use communication with shared segments. Because the FCP and the CP are in the same site, they can communicate with shared segments. This method does not need to call the operating system for each communication request, so the overhead of commu-

nication is relatively small. (Currently, we are also implementing the parallel processing environment with the tightly-coupled multiprocessors with shared memory. In this environment, we utilize the communication method using shared segments for transferring stream elements and demands among processors.) Accesses to shared segments are serialized by ordering the access requests incorporating a semaphore mechanism.

step 2:
The kernel facility in the CP creates a packet including a grain of stream elements or a demand, which are stored in the shared segment, it then transfers the packet to the CP of the destination site.

step 3:
In the destination site, the CP stores the received stream elements or a received demand into the shared segment of memory which is allocated between the FCP and the CP. Then, the function instance receives the grain of stream elements or the demand.

3.4 Interprocessor communication

We have implemented a parallel processing system SMASH on the basis of the implementation method discussed above. The current hardware environment consists of a number of Sun-3 workstations(Unix 4.2BSD [10]) connected to the Ethernet [10]. We use facilities of interprocessor communication which are supported in Unix.

We have chosen the UDP [10] as the communication protocol among the sites. In the communicating model of UDP, interprocessor communication is performed through a shared bus. In comparing to the communication protocol TCP [10], we explain the reasons why we have adopted the UDP.

1. Since the UDP is a lower level communication protocol than the TCP, its communication can be performed more efficiently than that of the TCP. That is, since the UDP is simple protocol, its overhead for network communication is small, and it is advantageous for transferring a large amount of data, such as databases.
2. In the UDP, a processor can dynamically select the communication partner when it receives a request for communication. That is , unlike the TCP, it is not necessary to statically fix a one-to-one virtual circuit between the processors. On the other hand, the TCP is based on the communication model of *Client and Server*. This forces the processors to communicate with each other as a master and a servant. However, in our implementation method, there is no special processor such as a supervisor, and parallel processing is performed by communicating with processors of the same ability. Therefore, the UDP is suited to our method.
3. Communication in the UDP is less reliable than that in the TCP. Therefore, the reliability of communication must be assured within the framework of our implementation. In our system, the CP supports reliable communication. On the other hand, the TCP has a higher reliability than the UDP. However, this higher reliability in the TCP often causes heavy overhead, especially, for applications of database processing which are required to manipulate large amounts of data. In comparing the TCP with the UDP, we found the UDP to be more efficient.

4 Experiments and results

We have performed several experiments on the experimental system for examining the effectiveness of our implementation method presented in this paper. In addition, we have measured the execution time of several queries. The execution time includes the actual CPU time, system call time for disk I/O processing, and communication time among sites.

4.1 Queries for experiments

Our system can support a wide variety of database operations. Here, queries consisting of relational database operations are used, for examples. We utilize four simple queries, with the same structure, consisting of three join and three selection operations, as shown in Fig. 3. Selection and join nodes are allocated to different sites, and executed in parallel by the stream-oriented scheme. In each join node, the tuples of the grain stored in the outer-relation buffer are sorted on joining attribute(s), and each tuple in the inner-relation buffer is compared with the sorted tuples by using the *binary-search* algorithm. The operand base-relation of each selection node is stored in the site where the node is allocated.

Table 1 shows the parameter settings of relation sizes and selectivity factors [7, 9, 13] for each query.

In *Query 1*, the size of the intermediate relation produced by each join node is the same as the size of the operand inner-relation. In *Query 2*, *Join-3* produces an intermediate relation with twice the size of the operand inner-relation. *Join-2* and *Join-1* produce relations of the same size as that of the intermediate relation produced by *Join-3*. In *Query 3*, each node (*Join-1, Join-2, Join-3*) produces a relation with twice the size of the operand inner-relation. In *Query 4*, each node produces a relation with half the size of the operand inner-relation.

In the stream-oriented scheme, if the selectivity factors and the buffer sizes are kept constant, the frequency of communications, the amount of transfer data and the comparison times between pages will remain constant. Although the total execution time becomes longer with the increase of base-relation size, neither parallelism nor effect on communication traffic changes. Therefore, we did not perform experiments on various settings of base-relation sizes.

We considered the queries with the same base-relation sizes and different join selectivity factors. Tuples in all the relations are 64 bytes long, each including 4 byte integer attributes as selection and joining attributes. All of the integer attributes have uniformly distributed values, but the range of their distributions varies to generate different join selectivity factors.

4.2 Experimental results

In these experiments, the re-computation method has been used as the parameter passing method in the stream-oriented scheme. In employing re-computation method, the total number of computations is dependent only on the size of the outer-relation buffer which has been allocated to each operation node. The outer-relation buffer size has an effect not only on the number of computations, but on the parallelism between the operations which are being executed at different sites. Therefore, it is very important to allocate available buffer resources optimally to each outer-relation buffer. In parallel processing cases, the size of the grain being transferred between sites also affects parallelism. In the experiments, this grain size corresponds to the inner-relation buffer size. Furthermore, buffer sizes for base relations affect the number of disk I/O operations. Therefore, it is important to optimally allocate buffer resources to inner-relation buffers and buffers for base relations. That is, the limited buffer resources must optimally be allocated to each buffer for each operation node. In [6, 7, 8], for implementing the stream-oriented scheme in sequential, parallel and distributed processing environments, we have presented several algorithms to optimally allocate the buffer resources to each buffer. These algorithms are used to minimize the number of computations and disk I/O operations, and to exploit parallelism in query processing. The experiments discussed in this

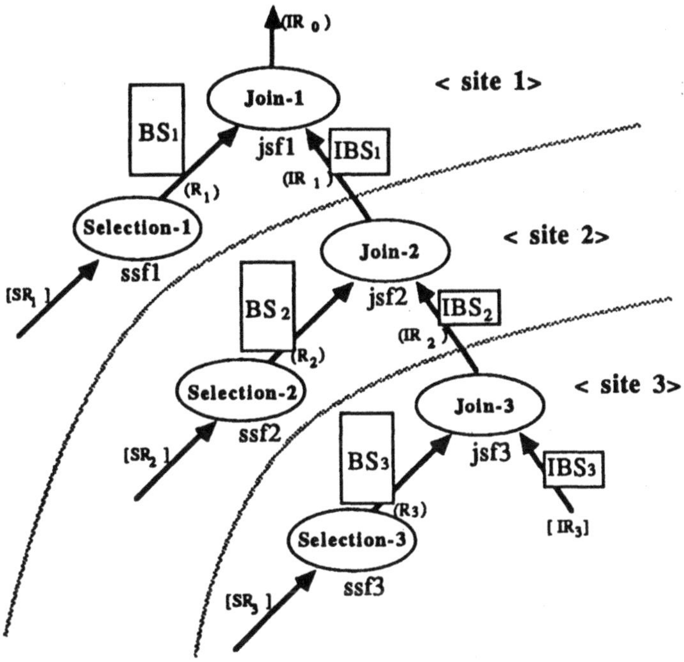

BS_1, BS_2, BS_3	:	*outer−relation buffer size (tuples)*
IBS_1, IBS_2, IBS_3	:	*inner−relation buffer size (tuples)*
SR_1, SR_2, SR_3, IR_3	:	*base−relation size (tuples)*
R_1, R_2, R_3	:	*outer−relation size (tuples)*
IR_1, IR_2, IR_3	:	*inner−relation size (tuples)*
IR_0	:	*result relation size (tuples)*
jsf_1, jsf_2, jsf_3	:	*join selectivity factor*
ssf_1, ssf_2, ssf_3	:	*selection selectivity factor*

(intermediate relation size =
jsf * (inner-relation size * outer-relation size))
(intermediate relation size = ssf * base-relation size)

Figure 3: The type of query for experiments

Table 1: Base-relation sizes and selectivity factors in the evaluated queries

		Query1	*Query2*	*Query3*	*Query4*
Selection−3	ssf_3	1/10	1/10	1/10	1/10
	SR_3	10240	10240	10240	10240
Join−3	jsf_3	1/1024	1/512	1/512	1/2048
	R_3	1024	1024	1024	1024
	IR_3	1024	1024	1024	1024
Selection−2	ssf_2	1/10	1/10	1/10	1/10
	SR_2	10240	10240	10240	10240
Join−2	jsf_2	1/1024	1/1024	1/512	1/2048
	R_2	1024	1024	1024	1024
	IR_2	1024	2048	2048	512
Selection−1	ssf_1	1/10	1/10	1/10	1/10
	SR_1	10240	10240	10240	10240
Join−1	jsf_1	1/1024	1/1024	1/512	1/2048
	R_1	1024	1024	1024	1024
	IR_1	1024	2048	4096	256
output	IR_0	1024	2048	8192	128

section have been focused on the investigation of the effects of the outer-relation buffer size and the inner-relation buffer size on the number of computations and parallelisms.

4.2.1 Effects of buffer resources

Three processors(sites) were used to execute each query. To store outer-relation tuples of each join operation, the same amount of buffer resources was allocated to each site, that is, $BS_1 = BS_2 = BS_3$. Fig. 4 shows the execution time in parallel processing of *Query 1, 2, 3* and *4* in varying the outer-relation buffer size.

The execution time is shortened with the increase of the outer-relation buffer size (BS_1, BS_2, BS_3). This is because, the increase of the outer-relation buffer size decreases the number of computations in query processing. Execution time is shortened discontinuously with the increase of the buffer size. The number of re-computations of the join operation does not continuously change with the increase of the buffer size. In the range of the buffer sizes with which the number of re-computations does not change, the execution time of a query is not always shortened with the increase of the buffer size.

4.2.2 Effects of the outer-relation buffer size on parallelism

Resource allocation to the outer-relation buffer of each join node gives a significant effect on parallelism inherent in a query. In [6], we have introduced a criterion for resource allocation to exploit the stream-oriented parallelism inherent in the operation nodes. Here, we briefly review the criterion. We consider parallelism inherent between two nodes (*Join-2,Join-3*) in Fig. 3. It is assumed that two operation nodes are being executed by different sites.

If *Join-2* performs the comparisons between two operand grains currently stored in the input buffers (BS_2, IBS_2), and *Join-3* completes producing the next inner-relation grain during the comparisons in *Join-2*, the pipeline delay is eliminated. (That is, the stream-oriented parallelism is exploited.) In other words, a suspension of operation execution causes a pipeline delay, which occurs in the absence of the next inner-relation grain.

The number of comparisons between an inner-relation grain IBS_2 and a sorted outer-relation grain BS_2 in *Join-2* is

$$IBS_2 * (\log_2 BS_2 + jsf_2 * BS_2). \quad (1)$$

The number of comparisons in *Join-3*, to produce an inner-relation grain (IBS_2) of *Join-2* by using the *binary-search* algorithm ($1/jsf_2$ is the average number of comparisons required to generate one output tuple by the *nested-loop*) is

$$IBS_2 * (\log_2 BS_3 + jsf_3 * BS_3)/(jsf_3 * BS_3). \quad (2)$$

The criterion to execute *Join-2* continuously without pipeline delay is as follows:

(1) $\geq$ (2).

If this criterion is satisfied in any adjacent nodes served as producer and consumer nodes at different sites, the root-node of a query tree (e.g. *Join-1*) can be executed without the suspension.

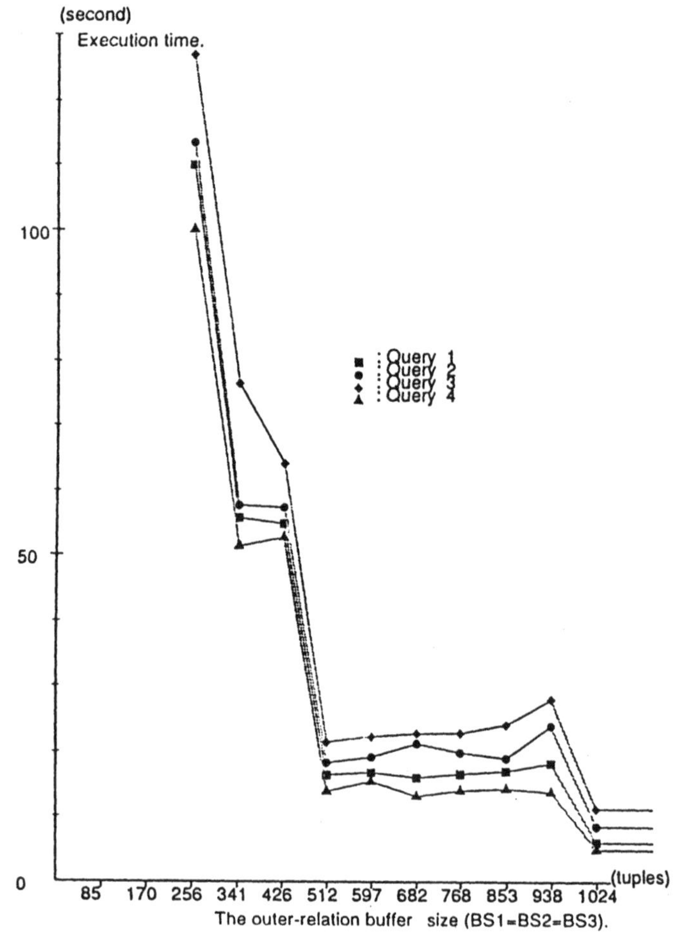

Figure 4: Relationship between the outer-relation buffer size and execution time.

Fig. 4 shows the execution time of the queries *Query 1, 2, 3* and *4*. In Fig. 4, with the size (1024 tuples) of outer-relation buffer resources available at each site, the criterion for exploiting parallelism mentioned above is satisfactory in executing *Query 1,2,* and *3*. In this size, there is no need to perform the re-computation for the inner-relations in executing *Query 1,2,3* and *4* because the buffer size is large enough to contain all the tuples of the outer-relations. As a result, the best execution efficiency is shown.

The increase of the outer-relation buffer size contributes both to reducing the number of computations and to satisfying the criterion for exploiting parallelism.

4.2.3 Effects of communication granularity on parallelism

The size of the inner-relation buffer does not influence the number of computations in query processing. However, it influences the number of times it takes to transfer stream elements and the number of times it takes to issue demands. We varied the size $IBS_i (i = 1,2,3)$ of the inner-relation buffer in *Query 1, 2, 3,* and *4* to examine its effects on the number of times it takes to transfer packets of stream elements, and the number of times it takes to issue demands. The change of IBS_i corresponds to that of granularity for message-passing. Fig. 5 shows the relationship between the execution time and the alternation of the inner-relation buffer size, when all the tuples of the outer-relations are contained in the outer-relation buffers. As shown in this figure, with the smaller size of the inner-relation buffer, the execution time becomes longer, because the overhead has become heavier due to the increase of the number of times it takes to transfer packets of stream elements or demands. With the larger size of the inner-relation buffer, the execution time also becomes longer because the increase of the buffer size decreases the parallelism in stream-oriented processing. In particular, the setting of granularity is important in the small granularity range.

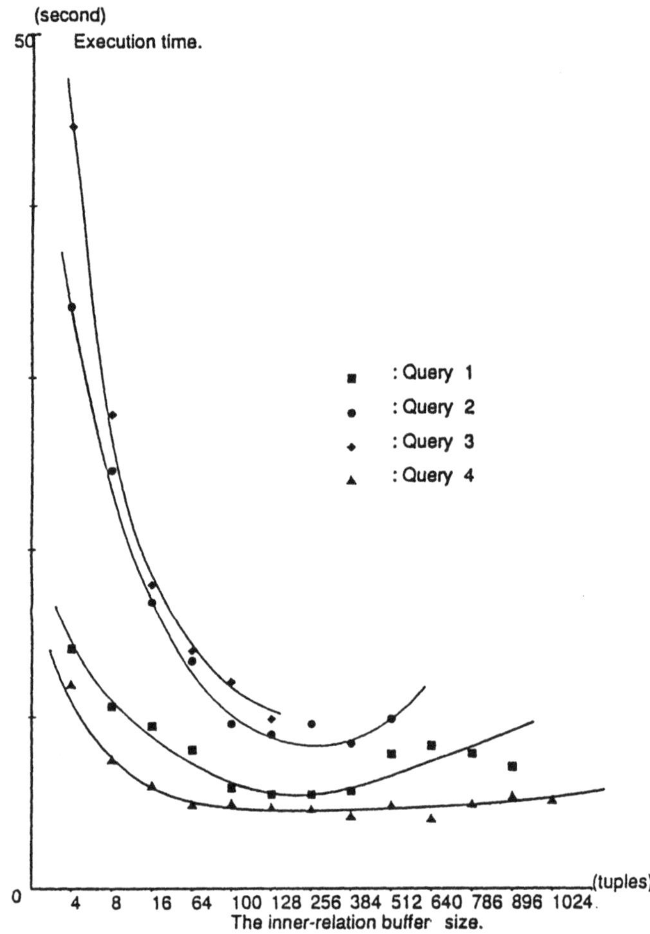

Figure 5: Execution time in various settings of communication granularity.

5 Conclusion

In this paper, we have presented an implementation method of a parallel query processing system supporting a wide variety of database operations. Our experimental results have shown that this implementation method is effective in performing parallel processing of actual queries. This implementation method can be applied to a wide variety of parallel processing environments in which the message passing mechanism is used for the interprocessor communication. Currently, we are designing another implementation method of the primitives for implementing the stream-oriented parallel processing scheme on tightly-coupled multiple processors with shared memory. In utilizing this method, the communication schemes between function instances are different from those presented in this paper. Furthermore, resource allocation strategies are also different.

We are extending our primitives so as to support a wide variety of advanced database applications. In particular, in extending our primitives, the flexibility and extensibility for descriptions and manipulations of complex objects[1] are very important.

References

[1] M. P. Atkinson and O. P. Buneman, "Types and persistence in database programming languages," *ACM Comput. Surv.*, Vol. 19, No. 2, pp. 105-190, 1987.

[2] P. B. Hawthoron and D. J. DeWitt, "Performance analysis of alternative database machine architectures," *IEEE Trans. Softw. Eng.*, Vol. SE-8 No. 1, pp. 61-76, 1982.

[3] Y. Kiyoki, K. Tanaka, N. Kamibayashi and H. Aiso, "Design and evaluation of a relational database machine employing advanced data structures and algorithms," *in Proc. 8th Int. Symp. on Computer Architecture*, pp. 407-423, 1981.

[4] Y. Kiyoki, K. Kato and T. Masuda,"A relational database machine based on functional programming concepts," *in Proc. 1986 ACM-IEEE Computer Society Fall Joint Computer Conf.*, pp. 969-978, Nov. 1986.

[5] Y. Kiyoki, K. Kato, N. Yamaguchi and T. Masuda, "A stream-oriented approach to parallel processing for deductive databases," *in Proc. 5th Int. Workshop on Database Machines*, pp. 102-115, 1987.

[6] Y. Kiyoki, P. Liu and T. Masuda, "A resource allocation strategy in the stream-oriented parallel processing scheme for relational database operations," *Transactions of Information Processing Society of Japan(in Japanese)*, Vol. 28, No.11, pp.1177-1192, 1987.

[7] P. Liu, Y. Kiyoki and T. Masuda, "A computation method for buffer resource allocation in the stream-oriented processing scheme for relational database operations," *Transactions of Information Processing Society of Japan(in Japanese)*, Vol. 29, No. 8, pp.770-781, 1988.

[8] P. Liu, Y. Kiyoki and T. Masuda, "Efficient algorithms for resource allocation in parallel and distributed query processing environments," *Proceeding of the IEEE Distributed Computing Systems*, pp.316-323, 1989

[9] P.G. Selinger, M. M. Astrahan, D. D. Chamberlin, R. A. Lorie and T. G. Price, "Access path selection in a relational database system," *Proc. of the ACM-SIGMOD Conf.*, pp.23-34, 1979 .

[10] "Programming reference manual for the Sun workstation," *Sun Micro Systems, Inc.*, 1986.

[11] P. C. Treleaven, D. R. Brownbridge and R. P. Hopkins, "Data-driven and demand-driven computer architecture, " *ACM Comput. Surv.*, Vol. 14, No. 1, Mar. 1982.

[12] S. R. Vegdahl, "A survey of proposed architectures for the execution of functional languages," *IEEE Trans. Comput.*, Vol. C-33, No. 12, pp. 1050-1071, Dec. 1984.

[13] C. T. Yu and C. C. Chang, "Distributed query processing," *ACM Computing Surveys*, Vol. 16, No.4, pp. 399-433, Dec. 1984.

AUTHOR INDEX

www.ingramcontent.com/pod-product-compliance
Lightning Source LLC
LaVergne TN
LVHW071222011026
849280LV00009B/47
* 9 7 8 9 8 1 0 2 1 3 1 5 2 *